Adjudicatory Authority in Private International Law

THE HAGUE ACADEMY OF INTERNATIONAL LAW MONOGRAPHS

Volume 5

The titles in this series are listed at the end of this volume.

THE HAGUE ACADEMY OF INTERNATIONAL LAW

Adjudicatory Authority in Private International Law
A Comparative Study

by

Arthur T. von Mehren

Late Story Professor of Law, Emeritus, Harvard Law School

Completed with the assistance of Dr. Eckart Gottschalk

MARTINUS NIJHOFF PUBLISHERS
LEIDEN • BOSTON

A c.i.p. record for this book is available from the Library of Congress.

Printed on acid-free paper.

ISBN: 978 9004 15881 8

Copyright 2007 The Hague Academy of International Law, The Netherlands.
Koninklijke Brill NV incorporates the imprints Brill, Hotei Publishers, IDC Publishers, Martinus Nijhoff Publishers and VSP.

http://www.brill.nl

Typeset by jules guldenmund layout & text, The Hague.

Printed and bound in The Netherlands.

Table of Contents

Preface

In January 2006 Professor Arthur T. von Mehren passed away as he was in the final stages of preparing this second edition. This book is a revised and expanded version of Professor von Mehren's 1996 General Course on Private International Law, published by the Hague Academy in 2002 under the title "Theory and Practice of Adjudicatory Authority in Private International Law: A Comparative Study of the Doctrine, Policies and Practices of Common- and Civil-Law Systems", Vol. 295 Collected Courses.

Since the publication of the General Course there have been important developments. In June 2005 the Hague Conference of Private International Law adopted a Convention on Choice of Court Agreements that has been called "Arthur's baby" concluding a project Professor von Mehren has been involved in from the very beginning. On the European level the European Court of Justice rendered fundamental decisions elaborating on judicial fine tuning instruments such as antisuit injunctions and *forum non conveniens*. In addition, a new regulation concerning jurisdiction and the recognition and enforcement of judgments in matrimonial matters and the matters of parental responsibility was promulgated ("Brussels IIa").

In producing this second edition of Adjudicatory Authority in Private International Law three Joseph Story Research Fellows collaborated with Professor von Mehren at Harvard Law School: Felix Blobel (2003-2004), Giesela Rühl (2004-2005) and Eckart Gottschalk (2005-2006) all coming from the Max Planck Institute for Comparative and International Private Law in Hamburg, Germany. The family of Professor von Mehren assigned to me, as the last Joseph Story Research Fellow, the honorable task to prepare the updated manuscript for publication. It was a pleasure for me to accept this.

Cambridge, Massachusetts
Eckart Gottschalk

Acknowledgements to the First Edition

This volume is the fruit of half a century of scholarship and teaching. During that period I have learned much from friends, colleagues, and students. Without the pleasure and stimulation of such company, the scholarly life would be lonely indeed. Thanks is owed to so many that it must be silently given, with one exception.

This book as conceived and executed could not have been written had not a colleague and dear friend, Dr. Kurt H. Nadelmann, who died in 1984, established the Joseph Story Fund by a bequest to the Harvard Law School. By 1993, the fund was producing an annual income sufficient to fund one Story Fellow each year.

Beginning in 1993, when I started work on a general course on private international law for the Hague Academy, I have been assisted by a Story Fellow. My Hague lectures dealt in some detail with German theory and practice; accordingly, the Joseph Story Research Fellows in Private International Law have been drawn from either the Max-Planck-Institut für Ausländisches und Internationales Privat- und Verfahrensrecht in Hamburg or the Institut für Ausländisches und Internationales Privat- und Wirtschaftsrecht in Heidelberg.

Over the last decade nine Fellows collaborated with me in producing this comparative study of the Theory and Practice of Adjudicatory Authority in Private International Law: Oliver Furtak (1993-1995), Martin Gebauer (1995-1996), Dietmar Baetge (1996-1997), Jan von Hein (1997-1998), Mathias Weller (1998-1999), Ralf Michaels (1999-2000), Michael von Hinden (2000-2001), Christian Thiele (2001-2002) and Moritz Bälz (2002-2003).

In accuracy, scope, and depth the book owes much to each of them; to all of them I am profoundly grateful. Special thanks are due to Christian Thiele, who discharged brilliantly the difficult task of coordinating the book's seven chapters and preparing the manuscript for publication, and Moritz Bälz, who showed equal skill in handling the many problems that attend a manuscript's transformation into a printed volume.

Over the years, Stephen B. Burbank, David Berger Professor for the Administration of Justice, University of Pennsylvania, has been a dear friend and has taught me much. He generously read the manuscript and corrected and deepened my analysis and insight on many points.

Reflecting on the changes in the manuscript that had to be made in light of the European Union's increasing importance after 1995 and other post-1995 developments, I realize the great skill and patients that Bradford Conner, my assistant, showed in making the many revisions that were necessary. Master of the computer, knowledgeable in German and French, and dedicated to his work, he contributed far more than mechanical skill to the enterprise.

One last acknowledgment remains to be made. The book is dedicated to my wife Joan: to whom so much is due.

Table of Cases

Australia

CSR Ltd. v. *Cigna Insurance Australia Ltd.*, 189 CLR 345 (HCA 1997).
Voth v. *Manildra Flour Mills Pty. Ltd.* (1990) 97 ALR 124.

Canada

Amchem Products Ltd. v. *British Columbia (Worker's Compensation Board)*
[1993] 1 Can. SCR 897.

European Union Courts

Andrew Owusu v. *N.B. Jackson* – Case C-281/02 [2005] ECR I-1383.
Danværn Production A/S v. *Schuhfabriken Otterbeck GmbH & Co* – Case C-341/93 [1995] ECR I-2053.
DFDS Torline A/S v. *SEKO* – Case C-18/02 [2004] ECR I-1417.
Drouot assurances SA v. *Consolidated metallurgical industries (CMI industrial sites), Protea assurance and Groupement d'intérêt économique (GIE) Réunion européenne* – Case 351/96 [1998] ECR I-3075.
Dumez France SA and Tracoba SARL v. *Hessische Landesbank and others* – Case C-220/88 [1990] ECR I-49.
Elefanten Schuh GmbH v. *Jacqmain* – Case C 150/80 [1981] ECR 1671.
Erich Gasser GmbH v. *MISAT s.r.l.* – Case C-116/02 [2003] ECR I-14693.
Estasis Salotti v. *Rüwa* – Case C-24/76 [1976] ECR 1831.
Gantner Electronic GmbH v. *Basch Exploitatie Maatschappij BV* – Case C-111/01 [2003] ECR I-4207.
G.I.E. Groupe Concorde and Others v. *The Master of the vessel "Suhadiwarno Panjan" and Others* – Case C-440/97 [1999] ECR I-6307.
Gubisch Maschinenfabrik KG v. *Giulio Palumbo* – C-144/86 [1987] ECR 4861.
Handelskwekerij GJ Bier BV v. *Mines de potasse dAlsace SA* – Case 21/76 [1976] ECR 1735.
Group Josi Reinsurance Company SA v. *Universal General Insurance Company (UGIC)* – Case C-412/98 [2000] ECR I-5925.

France

Germany

United Kingdom

United States

Federal Courts

Prologue

A. Introductory

Private international law and conflict of laws address the three topics that arise when controversies are significantly connected with more than one legal order: (1) Which legal orders have a legitimate claim to adjudicate the controversies (jurisdiction to adjudicate in the international sense); (2) Which legal orders' law should determine the existence *vel non* of the substantive rights and duties that are contested (choice of the applicable law); (3) When and to what extent will determinations of rights and duties by one legal order be recognized by other legal orders (recognition and enforcement of foreign judgments).

In what order are these topics best addressed? Chronologically, one would address adjudicatory authority first and recognition and enforcement last. Where the relevant substantive issues are governed by hard rules and principles of international law – either customary or conventional – a strong argument can be made for addressing choice-of-law first. Where such rules and principles are in question, subject to certain qualifications and exceptions, where "substantive" rules and principles are in issue, the same result should be reached in all forums seised of the matter. On the other hand, if choice of law is ultimately a matter for each sovereign state to decide, the rules and principles applicable in adjudicating controversies are intrinsically state law and thus, in the final analysis, will turn on the forum seised of the matter. Where such is the case, jurisdictional rules are crucial and can conveniently be discussed before turning to choice-of-law issues. This book addresses adjudicatory authority. It is the author's intention to discuss choice of law in a second volume.

B. The Province of Private International Law and of Conflict of Laws

Where social, governmental, and economic relations concern but a single legal-political unit the disciplines of private international law and conflict of laws have no role to play. These matters lack practical interest as well for a closed island realm without intercourse with other politically organized societies as for a regime exercising exclusive, centralized authority over the planet's entire range of social, governmental, and economic relations. Jurists of hermit kingdoms and of world governments would look upon private international law and conflict of laws as the province of philosophers and historians.

Hermit kingdoms are known to history as is the aspiration – though not the reality – of a true world government. The gradations on the spectrum that runs from localism to universality have varied greatly over history. In the West, due to the Roman Empire's commercial and governmental achievements, the first centuries of the first millennium AD were, socially, economically, and governmentally speaking, much less localized than were its closing centuries. By the beginning of the second millennium, a trend away from localism was under way. In the course of the next thousand years the dimensions and complexity of social, economic, and governmental activity and relations increased greatly. Dealing wisely and justly with activities and situations significantly related to and interesting more than one society or legal order has become increasingly important – and difficult – as our world becomes ever more complex and internationalized.

Were the spheres of economic and social intercourse, on the one hand, and of governmental and legal authority, on the other, so intertwined as to expand and contract together and in a manner such that the former never escaped the confines of the latter, there would be no private international law or conflict of laws. But the forces that determine the boundaries of economic and social activities and of legal and governmental authority are not the same. Even where these activities are largely localized, the merchant's quest for goods and markets, the traveler's *Wanderlust*, and the intellectual's search for knowledge inevitably spill across governmental and legal frontiers. In time, cross-boundary activities – especially those economic in nature and encouraged by the development of global communication systems of which the internet is a contemporary example – draw existing legal systems into larger, more comprehensive legal-political units. Typically, increases in the reach of governments and legal systems are fully realized only long after the relevant cross-boundary economic or social activities first assumed importance. In all events, private international law and conflict of laws are increasingly called on as the activities – economic and social in nature – that give rise to controversy are not, in all significant respects, linked to a single, unified political-legal order.

In western Europe, with first the schism in the Church and the rise of secular authorities and, many centuries later, the defeat of Napoleon, the two forces were lost that might have enabled that Continent's governmental and legal units to grow at the same pace as – or more rapidly than – their related social and economic units.[1] Early in the second millennium, the medieval fairs called forth a delocalized law, the *lex mercatoria*. As the millennium's final century drew to

---

1   One can generalize that, historically speaking, the size of effective governmental units is – depending upon the epoch in question – determined by religion, moral teaching, political ambition, and the existence – due to social, economic, and political circumstances – of broadly based and widely shared interests and concerns that need, for reasons of social cohesion, efficiency, and effectiveness, a co-extensive legal and governmental order. It can also be remarked that religion, moral teaching, and political ambition can establish – and maintain, at least for a time – legal and gov-

a close, the reality of interregional and international trade was a major force behind federation movements, of which the most successful is the European Union.
Yet, despite the emergence of these more inclusive social, economic, and political
units, a true world government is far in the future and may well never be a reality.
For a long time to come, it will be the task of private international law and conflict
of laws to ensure appropriate and wise handling, legally speaking, of situations that
can, depending upon one's preferences, be denominated as multisystem, multistate, or transnational (international).[2]

C.   The Contemporary Scene

1.   Introductory

In the contemporary world, ordinary citizens in many societies have a general
understanding not only of how law is made and administered in their country
but as well of the basic values that inform its norms and institutions. Knowledge
and understanding of the many other co-existing legal and political systems vary
greatly, of course. In recent decades, the study of foreign substantive law has increased as economic and social activities have increasingly flowed across national
boundaries. As a result, comparative study of fields of law such as domestic relations, contract, delict, and civil procedure have dramatically increased.

Study of comparative law presents difficulties that are not encountered in
the study of one's native law. Comparative study is best begun by ascertaining
the policies and purposes that are served by the rules and principles of one's own
laws. These having been established, the jurist can identify the foreign-law rules
and principles that address these issues, the extent to which the legal systems in
question agree at the level of policy, and, finally, where the systems under consideration hold different policies or purposes, how and why this comes about. The
comparative study of law thus raises issues a jurist studying a single legal system's
handling of intramural controversies can ignore. A principal merit of comparative study is that it leads the jurist to a deeper and richer understanding of how
contemporary societies make and administer law.

When jurists turn from the study of how a legal system addresses law making
and administration in intramural situations to the handling of these matters in
extramural situations, new issues are raised and extramural purposes and values
should be taken into account.

---

ernmental orders that are more inclusive than contemporary economic and social
activities require.

2   Arguably the expression "multisystem" is to be preferred. In some societies, the relevant unit for legal purposes is defined not in political or territorial – but rather
religious or tribal – terms. Since in the contemporary world such situations are quite
rare, the expression multistate – which covers as well States in the international-law
sense as sister states in a federal system – is more easily grasped. One can also speak
of transnational or international situations.

2.   The Juridical Character of Rules and Principles of Law Applicable to Extramural Controversies and Situations

The legal rules and principles that apply to *intramural* controversies and situations are those of the legal-political unit that alone is significantly interested in or connected with the matters in issue. Where, on the other hand, the controversy or situation in question is extramural, issues of jurisdiction to adjudicate, applicable substantive law, and recognition and enforcement of foreign judgments arise that have no parallels in *intramural* situations.

What is the juridical character of the rules and principles applicable to such matters? Are the rules and principles in question controlled by the state seised of the controversy or are the rules and principles in question sanctioned internationally? In sum, to what extent, if any, do "hard" rules and principles of international law apply?

For international rules and principles to apply in a strong sense an international authority – *e.g.*, the International Court of Justice – must assure their uniform interpretation and application. A significant and growing body of truly international public law now exists. In private-law matters, on the other hand, examples of hard international rules and principles remain sparse.

The conventions prepared and sponsored by the Hague Conference on Private International Law constitute "soft" international law. States that ratify Hague Conventions assume an international obligation, moral or political in its nature, to harmonize certain areas of law by recognizing and applying certain rules and principles where *extramural* situations or controversies are in issue, but the conventional law in question is independently interpreted and applied by national authorities.

To pass from the imperfect harmonization that Hague Conference Conventions provide to "hard" international law is extremely difficult. Regional unifications, such as the European Union, may in time develop the institutional structures and the political consensus that the creation of a regional international order requires. A comparable development on a world-wide scale is, to say the least, highly unlikely. For the most part, one can not hope to achieve more than a significant degree of harmonization in the approach of national court systems to the handling of *extramural* controversies. In the 18th and 19th centuries the jurisprudence of conceptions provided jurists with a basis for claiming that certain propositions – *e.g.*, the territorial principle – were, in the nature of things, true. This manner of thinking is seen in Joseph Story's 1842 decision in *Swift* v. *Tyson*,[3] Joseph Beale's 1934 Restatement of the Conflict of Laws,[4] and Friedrich Carl von Savigny's (1779 – 1861) seat (*Sitz*) theory which

---

3   41 US (16 Pet.) 1 (1842).
4   American Law Institute, *Restatement of the Law of Conflict of Laws* (St. Paul, American Law Institute Publishers, 1934).

assigned each legal relationship to one particular state regardless of whether that state had expressed, through statute or otherwise, a wish to apply its law, and regardless of the content of that law.[5]

In the contemporary world it is fair to say that theory and analysis are far too empirical and realistic to accept the assumptions on which these jurists – and their times – sought to ground hard international-law rules and principles. Speaking realistically, such rules and principles can only be achieved by entrusting their interpretation and application to international authorities.

3. The European Union

In 1980, the supranational political and economic structure now known as the European Union, began the process of establishing for its member States private international law rules and principles to govern situations that involve a choice between the laws of different countries. The 1980 Rome Convention on the law applicable to contractual obligations,[6] which entered into force on 1 April 1991, was concluded between the then member States of the EEC as a conventional multilateral treaty. The Convention originates in a more integrated context than, for example, the Hague Conventions, since the participating States aspired to a measure of economic and political unification. The Rome Convention sought to achieve greater legal certainty and to eliminate disruptions caused by the diversity of national choice-of-law rules in the emerging internal market.[7] The Convention did not, however, constitute "hard" private international law in the sense in which this term is used here. The European Court of Justice (ECJ) lacked supervisory jurisdiction to control and assure the uniform application of the Convention. Such control had been long proposed but not achieved until 2004.[8] Prior thereto, although the desire for a harmonious interpretation was expressed in the Conven-

---

5   E. Scoles, P. Hay, P. Borchers and S. Symeonides, *Conflict of Laws* §2.6, p. 17 (St. Paul, West, 4th ed., 2004).

6   [1980] OJ L 266, 1.

7   See the Report on the Convention on the law applicable to contractual obligations by Mario Giuliano and Paul Lagarde (Giuliano/Lagarde-Report), [1980] OJ C 282, 1-50.

8   The First and the Second Protocol on the Interpretation of the 1980 Convention were inoperative for well over a decade after the entry into force of the Convention itself. The First Protocol deals with the reference procedure to be observed by the national courts, the Second Protocol confers jurisdiction on the ECJ. The First Protocol required ratification by only seven member States, but was not to enter into force until the Second Protocol did; the Second Protocol did not enter into force until ratified by all member States (Art. 3). Belgium did not ratify the Second (and the First) Protocol until 2004. Both Protocols thereupon entered into force on 1 August 2004 (except for Ireland, which still has not ratified the First Protocol). See Communication from the Council, [2004] OJ C 277, 1.

tion,[9] supranational means of enforcement were not provided and its provisions were, on occasion, given divergent interpretations by the national courts of different member States.[10]

In the fields of jurisdiction to adjudicate and recognition and enforcement of foreign judgments, the Brussels Convention[11] (and its successor, the Brussels Regulation[12]) had contained since 1971 rules and principles less soft than those then found in the Rome Convention. Under the 1971 Protocol,[13] the ECJ was, at the request of designated national courts, to give authoritative interpretations of the Brussels Convention. In its decision in the *Turner* case (2004), the Court went beyond giving mere interpretations of terms or provisions in the Convention to hold that these interpretations bound national courts regardless of conflicts with national procedural law.[14]

Turner involved an antisuit injunction, a procedural device frequently employed by English courts, by which a party is enjoined from initiating or continuing court proceedings in another state. The Brussels instruments being arguably silent on the permissibility of antisuit injunctions, English courts had continued to issue them. The courts in the other member States were, of course, free to

---

9   Art. 18 of the Rome Convention provides that "[i]n the interpretation and application of the preceding uniform rules, regard shall be had to their international character and to the desirability of achieving uniformity in their interpretation and application." Comparable language is contained in some of the more recent conventions adopted by the Hague Conference; see, *e.g.*, Art. 13 of the Convention on the Law Applicable to Certain Rights in Respect of Securities Held With an Intermediary of 13 December 2002.

10   A prominent example for the non-harmonious interpretation of the Rome Convention is the variety of views on the relationship between the general presumption of Art. 4 (2) in the absence of a choice of law by the parties and the escape clause in Art. 4 (5). See Max Planck Institute for Foreign Private and Private International Law, "Comments on the European Commission's Green Paper on the conversion of the Rome Convention of 1980 on the law applicable to contractual obligations into a Community instrument and its modernization", 68 *RabelsZ* 1, at 39-45 (2004).

11   Convention of 27 September 1968 on jurisdiction and the enforcement of judgments in civil and commercial matters, [1972] OJ L 299, 32.

12   Council Regulation (EC) No 44/2001 of 22 December 2000 on jurisdiction and the recognition and enforcement of judgments in civil and commercial matters, [2001] OJ L 12, 1. The Brussels Regulation is binding for all EU states except Denmark. However, at the time of this writing a new Convention with Denmark, which would reflect the provisions of the Regulation, is under way. See the Council Decision of 27 April 2006 concerning the conclusion of the Agreement between the European Community and the Kingdom of Denmark on jurisdiction and the recognition and enforcement of judgments in civil and commercial matters, [2006] OJ L 120, 22.

13   Protocol of 3 June 1971 on the interpretation by the Court of Justice of the Convention of 27 September 1968 on jurisdiction and the enforcement of judgments in civil and commercial matters, [1975] OJ L 204, 28.

14   *Turner v. Grovit and Others*, Case C-159/02, [2004] ECR I-3565.

disagree with the English position but could not prevent sister states from issuing injunctions. In *Turner*, the ECJ held such injunctions inconsistent with the Brussels Convention where the injunction is directed against proceedings in another Convention State. The ECJ's assertion in *Turner* of supranational authority imposes a common European standard on the use of antisuit injunctions by the courts of member States. It has to be borne in mind, however, that intervention by the ECJ depends on a reference duly made to it by the national courts of member States. Individual litigants cannot bring issues of interpretation of Brussels instruments to the ECJ,[15] nor can the Court intervene in national proceedings of its own right.[16]

Amendments to the EC Treaty by the Treaty of Amsterdam took a further step towards creating an EU system of "hard" private international law and conflict of laws by establishing the proposition that the Community had ultimate authority in these fields. As of 1 March 2002, the Brussels Convention was replaced by the Brussels Regulation ("Brussels I"). Relying on the powers granted the Community by the Treaty of Amsterdam, the Union adopted "Brussels II", a Regulation setting out rules and principles respecting jurisdiction in actions for divorce and parental responsibility, with binding force comparable to that of the jurisdictional rules and principles contained in Brussels I.[17] In 2003 agreement was reached on a "Brussels IIa" Regulation, which significantly extended the scope of application of Brussels II in the field of parental responsibility.[18] In the same year the European Council adopted a "Draft Programme" of measures for implementation of the principle of mutual recognition of decisions in civil and commercial matters.[19]

---

15   Kropholler considers this rule an inherent weakness of the preliminary-reference procedure. See *Europäisches Zivilprozeßrecht*, Einl. No. 36 (Frankfurt am Main, Verlag Recht und Wirtschaft, 8th ed., 2005).

16   Under the 'abstract' reference procedure of Art. 68 (3) of the EC Treaty, the Council, the Commission or a member State can request a ruling from the Court on a question of interpretation of an instrument adopted under the new powers conferred to the EU in the field of private international law. No such request has been filed yet, however, and the procedure appears unlikely to gain practical importance.

17   Council Regulation (EC) No 1347/2000 of 29 May 2000 on jurisdiction and the recognition and enforcement of judgments in matrimonial matters and in matters of parental responsibility for children of both spouses, [2000] OJ L 160, 19.

18   Council Regulation (EC) No 2201/2003 ([2003] OJ L 338, 1-29) of 27 November 2003. As of 1 March 2005 the Brussels IIa Regulation has replaced the Brussels II Regulation. However, the Commission has issued a proposal for amending Regulation (EC) No 2201/2003. See the Proposal for a Council Regulation amending Regulation (EC) No 2201/2003 as regards jurisdiction and introducing rules concerning applicable law in matrimonial matters, COM (2006) 399 final. The proposal introduces, *inter alia*, a limited possibility for the spouses to designate by common agreement the competent court ("prorogation") in a proceeding relating to divorce and legal separation.

19   [2001] OJ C 12, 1-9.

The Treaty of Amsterdam also proposed the possibility, for the first time, of hard rules dealing with choice of law. The newly introduced Art. 65 (b) of the EC Treaty grants to the Community the power, *inter alia*, to promote "the compatibility of the rules applicable in the Member States concerning the conflict of laws", insofar as is necessary for the proper functioning of the internal market. Accordingly, the Community now has authority to enact hard rules and principles not only for jurisdiction and enforcement of judgments but also for choice of law. Since the entry into force of the Treaty of Nice, hard rules and principles in the field of private international law can be adopted by a qualified majority of the EC Council in co-operation with the European Parliament (so called co-decision procedure).[20] No member State has a veto to block legislation in this area and full consensus is no longer required to enact private-international-law or conflict-of-laws instruments.[21]

The first instrument adopted under the co-decision procedure is the Regulation creating a European Enforcement Order for uncontested claims.[22] Although the member States strove to achieve consensus, the Netherlands voted against the final proposal; it was then adopted by a qualified majority. These changes in the authority of the Union make hard rules and principles of private international law and conflict of laws possible for a vast area of law.[23]

---

20   See Art. 67 (5) of the EC Treaty, as amended by the Treaty of Nice, which makes an exception for "aspects relating to family law". Family law matters can, however, also be subjected to the co-decision procedure by a (unanimous) decision of the EC Council. The various steps of the co-decision procedure, which confers real legislative authority on the European Parliament, are set out in Art. 251 of the EC Treaty.

21   For some time it seemed as if the EC Treaty was soon to be replaced by the Treaty Establishing a Constitution for Europe, [2004] OJ C 310, 1. However, after the French and the Dutch did not approve of the Constitution in the referendums of 29 May 2005 and 1 June 2005, the chances that the Constitution will ever become effective are very low.

22   Regulation (EC) No 805/2004 of the European Parliament and of the Council of 21 April 2004 creating a European Enforcement Order for uncontested claims, [2004] OJ L 143, 15.

23   Currently, the Commission has proposed the "communitarization" of the Rome Convention, i.e. its transformation into a genuine Community instrument, most likely a Regulation ("Rome I"). See the Commission's Proposal for a Regulation of the European Parliament and the Council on the law applicable to contractual obligations ("Rome I"), COM (2005) 650 final. The Commission has also issued an amended proposal for a "Rome II" Regulation, laying down choice-of-law rules for non-contractual obligations. See the amended Proposal for a Regulation on the law applicable to non-contractual obligations ("Rome II"), COM (2006) 83 final. In addition, the Commission has proposed rules concerning applicable law in family affairs ("Rome III"). See the Proposal for a Council Regulation amending Regulation (EC) No 2201/2003 as regards jurisdiction and introducing rules concerning applicable law in matrimonial matters, COM (2006) 399 final. See also the proposal for a Council Regulation on jurisdiction, applicable law, recognition and enforcement of decisions and cooperation in matters relating to maintenance obligations, COM (2005) 649 final. See also the Commission's

It remains to be seen to what extent the EU and its members are prepared to exercise their new power. Doubtless the degree to which unification and hard rules are accepted will vary from area to area. Moreover, no-one fully understands what would be involved in creating a legal system appropriate for an EU that wished to communitarize large areas or even the entire field of private international law and conflict of laws. Presumably, the instruments adopted in the future will normally provide for *hard* rather than soft private international law rules and principles. Enacted by a supranational authority, their uniform application and interpretation would, at least initially, be the responsibility of the European Court of Justice under the preliminary-reference procedure provided in Art. 234 of the EC Treaty.[24] The process of "Communitarization"[25] will doubtless encounter, over time, many problems; it may well be that the Commission lacks the expertness necessary to develop wise solutions for the many issues that will arise in devising hard rules and principles of private international law and conflict of laws.[26]

Furthermore, it is by no means clear whether the Commission's view that diverging choice-of-law rules within the Community present an obstacle to the

---

Green paper on conflicts of laws in matters concerning matrimonial property regimes, including the question of jurisdiction and mutual recognition, COM (2006) 400 final. A possible further instrument could include community legislation on intestate and testate succession where there is an international dimension ("Rome IV"). See the Commission's Green Paper on succession and wills, COM (2005) 65 final.

24   Art. 68 of the EC Treaty, however, contains a substantial qualification. While under Art. 234, any court or tribunal of a member State may request a ruling from the European Court, Art. 68 provides that where the interpretation of instruments adopted under Art. 65 is in issue only those courts or tribunals of a member State "against whose decisions there is no judicial remedy under national law" shall refer the case to the ECJ. This qualification was intended to limit the increase in the European Court's caseload. According to Art. 67 (2) second indent, however, the EC Council shall, after 1 May 2004, and after consulting the European Parliament, take a decision with a view to adapting the provisions relating to the powers of the Court. At the time of writing, no such decision has been taken.

25   Communitarization will, of course, have broad consequences outside the EU. It will, *inter alia*, diminish the role of the Hague Conference: C. von Bar/P. Mankowski, *Internationales Privatrecht, Band I, Allgemeine Lehren* (2nd ed., Munich, C. H. Beck, 2003) § 3 No. 61 states that the Hague Conference will have to "fight for survival". Communitarization will also affect scholarship in the form of a growing body of academic literature on "European Private International Law". See, *e.g.*, the works of T. Kadner Graziano, *Gemeineuropäisches internationales Privatrecht* (Tübingen, Mohr Siebeck, 2002); P.-E. Partsch, *Le droit international privé européen* (Brussels, De Boeck & Larcier, 2003); see also J. Basedow, "European Conflict of Laws under the Treaty of Amsterdam", in P.J. Borchers and J. Zekoll (eds.), *International Conflict of Laws for the Third Millenium, Essays in Honor of Friedrich K. Juenger* 175-192 (Ardsley, New York, Transnational Publishers, 2001); K. Boele-Woelki/R.H. van Ooik, "The Comunitarization of Private International Law", 4 Yearbook of Private International Law 1-36 (2002).

26   See E. Jayme, "Zum Jahrtausendwechsel: Das Kollisionsrecht zwischen Postmoderne und Futurismus", 20 *IPRax* 165, at 167 (2000).

creation of a genuine internal market[27] will be found convincing. The argument is already advanced that the impediments to the free circulation of goods, services and persons due to differing rules and principles of private international law or conflict of laws are more apparent than real and of negligible importance.

Perhaps the most crucial and deep-seated questions respect, however, the institutional consequences that would follow from such a vast increase in community powers and whether the member States would accept them. The preliminary-reference system could well prove to be too inefficient, slow, and burdensome to handle the volume of litigation that such an increase would entail. Is the European Court institutionally capable of giving rulings on the whole range of private international law and conflict of laws (as well as all other fields of Community law)? Or would a successful policy of communitarization require the establishment of a complete system of EU courts vested with jurisdiction over private-law disputes involving community law? Efforts to create such a system would raise complex questions touching on the organizational structure of the European Union and the demarcation line between member State sovereignty and community powers. Finally, creating a consistent and coherent set of common private-international-law and conflict-of-law rules is in itself not only a complex task but one that raises as well difficult problems with respect to the relationship of the new Regulations with other Community instruments and with existing international conventions to which member States are parties.[28] Whether, how, and to what extent such "Communitarization" is desirable and – if so – whether and how it should be accomplished, are questions that may well require generations to answer.

---

27   See, *e.g.* the Commission's Green Paper on the conversion of the Rome Convention of 1980 on the law applicable to contractual obligations into a Community instrument and its modernization", COM (2002) 654 final, p. 8.

28   This concerns, in particular, the Hague Conventions on traffic accidents and product liability. See A. Struycken, "Das Internationale Privatrecht der Europäischen Gemeinschaft im Verhältnis zu Drittstaaten und zur Haager Konferenz", 12 *ZEuP* 276-295 (2004).

PART 1

The Foundations and Emergence of Jurisdictional Theory

Chapter I   Adjudicatory Authority: Reasons for Its Existence and Its Principal Types

A.   General Introduction

Even within close-knit units such as family or kinship groups, human relations are not always harmonious and co-operative. Human nature and the eternal competition for scarce resources make effective dispute-resolution mechanisms essential if society is to be ordered and peaceful. Furthermore, as economies and societies become more complex and interrelated, institutions, principles, procedures, and rules are needed to facilitate co-ordination and co-operation for common purposes. The legal order seeks not only to prevent one person interfering with another's private sphere, but also assists and guides private ordering by individuals. Identifying the adjudicators from whom relief may be sought – and establishing the premises for their work – can be relatively complex tasks where only one society is in the picture; complexities and difficulties multiply as controversies implicate more than one group or society, especially where the groups or societies differ in their values and institutions.

The importance of theory ultimately rests on a trait of human nature, one stronger in some societies than in others, namely, "an extraordinary, seemingly innate preference for action that is consistent, and at a more sophisticated state, can be *seen and expressed* to be consistent with what has gone before".[1] Theories respecting the nature and exercise of adjudicatory authority are, however, not the only force by far that shapes a legal order's jurisdictional practices; many other considerations, including administrability, regulatory concerns, and economic and social circumstances, are factored, with varying weights, into a legal order's law respecting jurisdiction to adjudicate.

Mankind's innate need to explain – and justify – the conditions of human existence extends to the exercise of adjudicatory authority. Justification and explanation have taken such varied forms as myth, religious teaching, and economic, political, and social theory. Modes and styles of explanatory justification are shaped, here as elsewhere, by the insights and understandings of ordinary mem-

---

1   T. M. Franck, *The Structure of Impartiality: Examining the Riddle of One Law in a Fragmented World*, at 18 (New York, NY, Macmillan, 1968).

bers of society, of the society's elites, and of scholars and philosophers.[2] The views and theories offered may – or may not – overlap or coincide in whole or in part. As the frequency and range of inter-societal relations increase, views and understandings respecting these matters tend to become less parochial.

The elaboration of general theories of adjudicatory authority is a relatively modern phenomenon. Theory's significance for practice turns on various considerations. In 19th century Germany, the legislature provided relatively simple and clear-cut jurisdictional rules that, for the most part, were perceived as reasonable and balanced.[3] The impetus for theoretical discussion was not as great as in the United States, where the theory and practice of adjudicatory authority were shaped and tested by courts that could invoke constitutional requirements.[4] The American federal system provides for greater opportunities than does the German for experimentation with – and theoretical analysis of – adjudicatory authority. Not only was the German law of jurisdiction to adjudicate regulated on a national basis, but constitutional requirements were of little importance until the closing decades of the 20th century.[5]

1.   *The Structural Differences of the German and American Federal Systems*

As already remarked, the design and structure of the German federal system differ fundamentally from the American. The latter has separate, co-existing state and federal systems; the former combines in one system state and federal elements. The American approach gives states a much greater role in the development of rules and principles of adjudicatory authority than the German states (*Länder*) enjoy.

German courts of first instance and of appeal are state courts in the sense that their costs are paid and their judges appointed by the state (*Land*) in which the court sits. At the same time, they are federal courts in that their adjudicatory authority and procedural law, as well as the qualifications and advancements of their judges, rest almost exclusively on national law.

In American federalism, each state has its own judicial system staffed by judges selected and appointed by the state in question. The methods of selection and appointment vary considerably. Some states elect their judges; others appoint them. The qualification required, the compensation paid, and retirement policies vary from state to state.

The constitutionalization of the law respecting adjudicatory authority, especially in light of the Fifth and Fourteenth Amendments to the Constitution of the

---

2   Scholars and philosophers as a class claim the capacity to give insights into societies – even those remote in space or time – that differ fundamentally from their own.

3   See Chap. III. B., pp. 117 *et seq.*, *infra*.

4   See Chap. II. D. 1., pp. 57 *et seq.* and Chap. III. A. 1., pp. 79 *et seq.*, *infra*.

5   See Chap. III. B. 4., pp. 131 *et seq.*, *infra*.

United States,[6] has resulted in a substantial and complex body of federal law that binds federal and state courts alike. Subject to constraints based on constitutional commands or on exercises by the federal government of authority bestowed on it by the Constitution, states are largely free to develop their own law of jurisdiction to adjudicate.[7]

2. *The Early History of Private International Law and Conflict of Laws*[8]

(a) Introduction

The earliest recognition of the problematic of private international law and conflict of laws occurred in controversies involving testamentary or delictual claims. Greek and Egyptian adjudicators appear to have applied, in such matters, either the law of the testator's "fatherland" – akin to later-day domicile or nationality – or the law of the forum. Another solution is found in a decree, applicable in Hellenistic Egypt, which provided that the language (Greek or Egyptian) in which a contract was written determined both adjudicatory authority and applicable law.

The Roman approach differed; only the jurisdictional issue was addressed. The resolution of controversies with foreign (non-Roman) elements fell to the *praetor peregrinus*. Instead of making a choice among the laws of concerned legal orders, the *praetor* crafted an *ad hoc* substantive rule for the case at hand. Over time, out of this practice new substantive-law rules or principles arose; they eventually formed the *ius gentium*.

In 533 A.D. the Emperor Justinian's *Corpus iuris civilis* "codified" the *ius civile* (the law that governed relations between Roman citizens) and the *ius gentium*. No part of the Corpus, not even the vast compilation of Roman law contained in the *Digest*, addresses private international-law and conflict-of-laws rules and principles.

(b) The decline and fall of the Roman Empire in the West

In 476 Odovaker deposed Romulus Augustulus, the son of a Roman mercenary and last of the line of imperial rulers in the West.[9] Paradoxically, the most important single event for the subsequent history of law on the European Continent occurred less than a century later. The Eastern Empire, with its seat at Constantinople, continued after the Western Roman Empire's fall. [There,] [i]In 528, Justinian (527-565) ordered the great compilation, systematization and consolidation of Roman law that later came to be known as the *Corpus juris civilis*. The *Corpus* com-

---

6   See Chap. III. A. 1., pp. 79 *et seq., infra.*

7   See Chap. III. A1., pp. 79 *et seq., infra.*

8   This discussion draws heavily on the discussion in Symeonides et al, *Conflict of Laws: American, Comparative, International, Cases and Materials,* at 6-13 (St. Paul, Minn., West, 2nd ed., 2003).

9   For a brief discussion of the decline and fall of the Western Empire see A. von Mehren and J. Gordley, *The Civil Law System,* at 4-15 (Boston and Toronto, Little, Brown and Company, 2nd ed., 1977).

prises the Institutes, the Digest, the Code (a collection of imperial enactments) and the Novels (a collection of post 534 imperial enactments). The Institutes, the Digest and the Code were promulgated between 533 and 534.[10]

The Digest, also known as the Pandects, is important for the study of Roman law. It compiles the writings of the great Roman jurists, especially those of the classical period. As the Digest was intended to state current law, the original texts were altered ("interpolations") to reflect the 6th century Roman law of the Eastern Empire. The Digest's great importance for the development of law in Continental Europe was not the light it cast on the history of Roman law but the rules and principles that it set out. These could claim authority as received from the Roman Empire; most important of all, they provided a vision of law as a body of rules and principles that could form the basis for the legal rules of the societies and economies that were emerging in what was once the Western Empire. Because of the approach taken by Roman law to the resolution of controversies with non-Roman elements, the *Corpus iuris civilis* had, however, very little to offer where private international law and conflict of laws were concerned; indeed, the Digest was silent on these matters.

The study of law as a coherent, systematic body of rules and principles began in Western Europe with the lectures of Irnerius at Bologna in the early 12th century. The importance and the influence of the revived Roman law spread rapidly. By the end of the 12th century there were at Bologna alone 10,000 students in law. Study of the *Corpus iuris* was first undertaken by the so-called Glossators; in the 13th century they were succeeded by the Commentators, the greatest of whom was Bartolus (1313-1357). Prior to Bartolus, private international law and conflict-of-laws issues had been recognized in the study of law, but, as they were not grounded on the *Corpus iuris,* they lacked authority. Although nothing was said about these subjects in the Digest, Bartolus found a way to bring them within the *Corpus iuris* scope.

The first sentence of the Code states that

> All peoples who are subject to our [the emperor Justinian's] merciful sway, we desire them to live under that religion which the divine apostle Peter has delivered to the Romans.

Bartolus saw that the Emperor claimed authority only over his subjects and thus implicitly recognized the claim of other sovereigns to govern their subjects.[11] Private-international law and conflict-of-laws thus found a niche in the *Corpus iuris*, and the study of choice of law began.

Bartolus and his fellow statutists began by exposing a

> [s]implistic classification of local laws (*statuta*) into two categories: real or personal. Real statutes were those that operated only within the territory of the enacting state,

---

10   The imperial legislation contained in the Novels was never officially collected.

11   See Symeonides et al, *supra* footnote 8, at 8.

but not beyond. In contrast, personal statutes operated beyond the territory of the enacting state and bound all persons that owed allegiance to it.[12]

The implicit assumption that legal rules and principles are never meaningfully connected with more than one legal order is, of course, plainly wrong. Moreover, the statutists' classifying criterion was ridiculous: The sequence of the statute's wording was decisive. If the first reference was to a person – the first-born child shall succeed to the property – the statute is personal; contrariwise, if the property is mentioned first – the propriety shall devolve to the first-born child – the statute is real. The early statutists clearly had little understanding of choice-of-law purposes and problems. Their early effort to understand and deal effectively with methodological and policy issues nevertheless initiated discussions that still continue today.[13]

The statutists developed a unilateral choice-of-law methodology that replaced the special substantive-rule methodology used by the Roman *praetor peregrinus*. The statutists focused on the extent to, and manner in, which the controversy involves conflicts between forum law and the potentially applicable foreign law. In time the unilateral method was challenged by bilateral choice-of-law methods; these evaluate objectively the policies and concerns of the legal orders concerned without giving particular weight to the forum's policies. The struggle between unilateralists and bilateralists continues to the present day.

Our understanding of the problematic of private international law and conflict of laws has become far deeper and broader since Bartolus' day. Yet many of the issues that he and his fellow statutists addressed still remain controversial.

3.   *General Theories Regarding Governmental Authority*

Political philosophy undertakes, *inter alia*, to explain in general terms the existence, organization, and exercise of governmental authority, including the prescribing of conduct, imposing civil and criminal sanctions, and collecting taxes. Explanations typically rest on the ties of individuals – whether independently or as a collectivity – to a single, politically organized society; the relationship is analysed with a view to establishing the legitimacy of society's exercise of governmental authority.

The form and reach of the explanations and justifications for the exercise of authority and the existence of society vary from age to age and culture to culture. At the dawn of history, if explanations were offered at all, they were presumably supernatural in nature. A god or deity invested the chief or ruler with authority; rule was by divine right or immemorial custom. Such propositions satisfied societies in which tradition was the principal instrument of social control and each member's place and status were relatively fixed.

---

12   Symeonides et al, *supra* footnote 8, at 8.

13   See *idem*, 9-16.

(a)   The principal theoretical accounts

Over time, the circumstances that sustained explanations and justifications supernatural or traditional in nature eroded and were replaced by more rational and secular explanations. Growing social mobility and the increasing scope and tempo of commercial activity were among the forces that called into question the traditional order of society. Inevitably, supernatural and traditional explanations of the sources of governmental authority encountered increasing resistance; older views were challenged by more worldly and, ultimately, instrumental political philosophies. These took three paradigmatic forms: relational, power, and instrumental.

The feudal systems of medieval Europe saw governmental authority as resting on a complex of rights and duties existing between lord and tenant. Tenants owed loyalty and services to their lord; in return, he protected them and rendered them justice. The existence and legitimacy of governmental authority flow from this personal bond. As lords and kings increasingly gathered governmental power into their hands, the relational theory lost some, but not all, of its explanatory power. Subjects still owed a duty of loyalty to the lord or king – and, later, the State – as the source of authority and the fountain of justice.

As the modern State emerged, the relational theory was largely replaced by other explanations of, and justifications for, governmental authority. One view, associated with such figures as Bodin, Hobbes, and Austin, emphasized the reality of power and its hierarchical organization; power became in a sense its own justification. Another perspective, found in the works of Locke and Bentham among many others, views society and government in more instrumental and utilitarian terms.

Thomas Hobbes (1588-1679) saw ordered civil society as the alternative to a cruel and hazardous state of nature. The primordial need for security – which, in his view, ultimately could be provided only by conferring absolute power on the ruler – explained and justified the individual's acceptance of governmental authority. John Locke (1632-1704) invoked, as had Hobbes, the metaphor of contract, but the compact was not between ruler and ruled but between free men each of whom voluntarily consented either explicitly or implicitly.

> Since the compact is made between members of the community, sovereignty ultimately remains with the people. The sovereign, in the form of a legislative body, and executive, or both, is the agent and executor of the sovereignty of the people.[14]

To the central question of political philosophy – "Why should one obey the state and respect its institutions?" – the Hobbesian answered that authority – effective power – was indispensable to ordered civil society.[15] For Lockeans, on the other

---

14   J. Clapp, John Locke, in *The Encyclopedia of Philosophy* III (ed. P. Edwards) 487, at 499-500 (New York, NY, Macmillan, 1967).

15   For Hobbes "[t]he subject is released from his obligation only if the sovereign fails to do what he is there to do, namely, to guarantee security. This marks the extent of the

hand, consent – real or implied – rather than brute necessity and efficacy was the source of authority.

Both philosophies are instrumental in the sense that each sees society as existing to secure certain goals. Yet both interpose between an instrumental evaluation of law and legal institutions a dogmatic proposition. For thinkers in the Hobbesian tradition the necessity and reality of governmental power dominates discourse. Thus John Austin (1790-1850) felt

> the grip of a certain idea, the idea that law is simply the impressing of the will of the stronger upon the weaker. Austin's chief virtue was that he systematically developed, defended, and refined this idea, stripping it of excess philosophical baggage.[16]

If Hobbesian dogma puts too great store on power, Lockeans over-emphasize consent; in real life, governments often act in the absence of anything resembling consent on the part of at least some of those affected and in resolving disputes apply rules and principles to which the individual can hardly be taken to have agreed.

As already remarked, instrumental themes, implicit in the dogmatic propositions advanced by Hobbes and Locke, have become a fundamental concern of contemporary political philosophy. Instrumentalism takes many forms; perhaps the most pervasive and influential is utilitarianism, associated with the name of Jeremy Bentham (1748-1832). For the utilitarian, the answer to the question when one should obey the State is "just as far as obedience will contribute more to the general happiness than disobedience". For utilitarian instrumentalism, "the state is not a super-entity with purposes and a will of its own, but a human contrivance to enable men to realize so many of their desires as possible".[17] Contemporary theorists often disagree profoundly with Bentham's hedonic calculus – the sum of pleasures and pains of individuals – but accept the proposition that, in many ways, an instrumental view of political authority and of governmental activity comes closer to the mark than Hobbes's power or Locke's consent metaphor.

(b)   The relevance of these accounts for claims of adjudicatory authority over multistate transactions and controversies

Disputes always involve more than one person; in adjudicating a controversy the adjudicator inevitably pronounces on the rights and duties of two or more persons. No theory can, therefore, completely explain or justify the existence or exercise of adjudicatory authority unless the theory's rationale reaches to all those that the adjudication is to bind. Such is, of course, the case where the matter is entirely intramural with respect to the legal order whose adjudicatory authority

---

subjects' ... 'right to resist'." R. Peters, Thomas Hobbes, in *idem* 30, at 43.

16   H. Morris, John Austin, in *idem* I, 209, at 210.

17   D. Monro, Jeremy Bentham, in *idem* 280, at 284.

is at issue; so far as our present concerns go, nothing turns on whether one is a disciple of Hobbes, of Locke, or of yet another political philosopher.

In the case of multisystem or multistate controversies, the situation is different in at least two crucial respects. Firstly, controversies that are, in the light of a given general theory, indubitably within one legal order's adjudicatory authority may well be connected in a jurisdictionally significant fashion to other legal orders as well. These connections may – or may not – be of the same nature as those that relate the controversy to the first legal order. For example, where both parties are nationals of one State their dispute may be over real property situated in another State. A relational theory can unhesitatingly assign adjudicatory authority to the first State; a power theory, to the second. Moreover, where the legal orders concerned accept the same general theory, that theory may justify the exercise of adjudicatory authority by more than one of them. A power theory, for example, justifies jurisdiction as well in the State in which all the parties live as in the State where the real property, whose ownership is in dispute, is located. Likewise, an instrumental theory may well recognize in more than one legal order a plausible claim to exercise adjudicatory authority over a given dispute.

Accordingly, even if all contemporary claims of adjudicatory authority rested on but one of these three theories, in many – if not most – multistate controversies more than one legal order would have a basis for claiming jurisdiction. The question arises of how to treat situations in which two or more legal orders claim adjudicatory authority on bases that are supportable under the general theory or theories considered relevant.

If they adhere strictly to their theoretical premise, relational theories face difficulties that are avoided by instrumental and strict power theories. Where one party has a social, political, or economic relationship to the forum but the other party has none, can it be said that the forum has adjudicatory authority over both? Strictly conceived, adjudicatory authority resting on a relationship reaches only to the party or parties that stand in the relevant relationship to the adjudicator. In pure logic, therefore, a lord is only entitled to give judgment against – but not *for* – his tenant.[18] Adherence to this dryly logical proposition would greatly reduce the theory's usefulness in multistate situations where all parties were not the adjudicator's tenants, subjects, or citizens. The French Civil Code removes the difficulty in a way that cannot be fully explained or justified in strict relational terms; *either* party's relationship to France can establish French adjudicatory authority over both parties.[19]

---

18   Recognition and enforcement abroad of judgments against non-tenants or non-subjects of the adjudicator were indeed refused under the relational theory:

> Only the sovereign, thus only the natural judge, can condemn the subject, and, as each sovereign wishes to see that his authority is respected, a sovereign whose subject has been condemned by a foreign judge will refuse to recognize the judgment.

D. Holleaux, *Compétence du juge étranger et reconnaissance des jugements*, p. 204 (Paris, Dalloz, 1970).

19   See Chap. IV. B. 1. *(a)*, pp. 159-161, *infra*.

A strict version of the Lockean justification of governmental authority in terms of consent as applied to multistate situations encounters a somewhat similar difficulty. Locke never contemplated citizens entering into social contracts with more than one society; unless both parties belong to the same society, the consent of each runs to a different adjudicatory authority. To escape the dilemma, consent must be understood not – as Locke did – embracively as a social contract but as given for specific situations and successively to many societies:

> [I]n theory, the power exercised by a court over a party flows from the consent of the party itself. This consent could at times be actual, but more frequently is implied through benefits obtained or risk created by the party while inside the political forum in which the court sits.[20]

Instrumental theories may well face the problem *not* of setting too narrow limits to a society's exercise of adjudicatory authority *but of* tending to open the door too wide. The nature of these theories is such that in multisystem or multistate controversies the presence of instrumental justifications for the assumption of jurisdiction by a number of legal orders can only rarely be excluded *a priori*; each legal order with which either a party or the underlying situation or transaction can be said to be significantly connected arguably has a claim of some weight to exercise adjudicatory authority.

A power theory raises rather different problems than those faced by relational and instrumental theories. Analysis under a pure power theory is in a sense simpler since, unlike relational and instrumental theories, the exercise of adjudicatory authority requires explanation and justification only with respect to the defendant's position. A power theory's criterion for asserting adjudicatory authority is automatically satisfied with respect to the plaintiff because, by initiating proceedings, he submits to jurisdiction. The theory can accordingly simplify analysis and achieve predictable results by concentrating on the defendant's position. A high price is paid, however; both unduly expansive and unduly restrictive exercises of adjudicatory authority are – so long as one remains true to the power principle – inescapable.[21]

B.   Appropriate Terminology for Comparative Analysis: Basic Categories of Adjudicatory Authority

1.   The Insularity of Traditional Terminologies

The terms utilized in contemporary discussions of adjudicatory jurisdiction vary considerably from one legal order to another. French jurists distinguish between

---

20   R. Cappalli, "Locke as the Key: A Unifying and Coherent Theory of In Personam Jurisdiction", 43 *Case W. Res. L. Rev.* 97, at 102 (1992).

21   See the description of the American experience, Chap. III. A. 2., pp. 86 *et seq.*, *infra*.

ordinary *(ordinaires)* and supplementary *(supplementaires)*[22] bases of jurisdiction *(compétence).* Anglo-Americans have long spoken of jurisdiction over "persons" and over "things": jurisdiction *in personam, in rem,* and *quasi in rem.* German law recognizes one general jurisdiction *(allgemeiner Gerichtsstand)* and a number of special jurisdictions *(besondere Gerichtsstände).*[23]

Each of these vocabularies have been shaped by contingent historical and systemic considerations and implies different conceptual frameworks. The French usage reflects the declining importance in contemporary thinking and decisional law of jurisdiction based on the plaintiff's – or the defendant's – nationality. Having once enjoyed pride of place in French practice, these two bases are now seen as "supplementing" various "ordinary jurisdictional bases".

The traditional common-law terminology tells us more about adjudicatory authority. Two distinctions are taken: the first – between persons and things – relates to the objects over which, in a formal sense, adjudicatory authority is exercised; the second concerns the judgment's effect, does it seek to bind the whole world or only the parties and their privies?

> A judgment *in personam* imposes a personal liability or obligation on one person in favor of another. A judgment *in rem* affects the interests of all persons in designated property. A judgment *quasi in rem* affects the interests of particular persons in designated property. The latter is of two types. In one the plaintiff is seeking to secure a pre-existing claim in the subject property and to extinguish or establish the non-existence of similar interests of particular persons. In the other the plaintiff seeks to apply what he concedes to be the property of the defendant to the satisfaction of a claim against him. ... For convenience of terminology this opinion will use *'in rem'* in lieu of *'in rem* and *quasi in rem'.*[24]

The expressions used in the German literature – general and special jurisdiction – adopt a third perspective. For German jurists a general jurisdictional basis is one that establishes, in principle, adjudicatory authority irrespective of the type of claim or controversy involved; a special basis is one available either only for certain types of claims or only where the claim or the controversy out of which the litigation arose has a significant connection with the forum. The sole characteristic common to all special jurisdictions in the German sense is that none constitutes a basis of general jurisdiction as defined by §12 of the German Code of Civil Procedure (ZPO):

---

22   The latter term is applied to jurisdiction based on the plaintiff's or the defendant's French nationality.

23   *Gerichtsstand* comprehends both venue and jurisdiction to adjudicate in the international sense. See Chap. II. D. 2. *(b)* (i), p. 65, *infra.* For purposes of the present discussion only the second sense of the word is relevant.

24   Chief Justice Warren, writing for the Court, in *Hanson* v. *Denkla,* 357 US 235, at 246, note 12 (1958).

The court, where a person has his *allgemeinen Gerichtsstand*, is competent *(zuständig)* for all actions *(Klagen)* brought against him, except where an exclusive *Gerichtsstand* is provided for the action.

German law recognizes only two important bases of general jurisdiction: jurisdiction over a natural person at his permanent residence *(Wohnsitz);*[25] jurisdiction over a juristic person at its seat *(Sitz).*[26] Despite quite different characteristics *inter se,* all other important jurisdictional bases can be denominated "special" in the sense of not being a general basis as defined by §12.[27]

ZPO §23 establishes adjudicatory authority for "pecuniary *(vermögensrechtliche)* claims"[28] "against a person who has no domestic *Wohnsitz*" at the place where "his property *(Vermögen)* is".[29] The claim to be litigated can result from a contractual, delictual, or other obligation; no linkage is required between the claim and the assets that form the basis for jurisdiction. §23 jurisdiction is "special" because it is limited to actions for "pecuniary claims".

ZPO §29 provides a special jurisdiction with very different characteristics: adjudicatory authority over "controversies arising out of a contractual relation-

---

25   ZPO §13. §7 of the German Civil Code (BGB) defines *Wohnsitz* as "the place where one is permanently settled *(sich ständig niederläßt)*". With respect to those lacking a permanent residence, ZPO §16 provides for general jurisdiction at their place of residence *(Aufenthaltsort)* in Germany or, where the place of residence is not known, at their last permanent residence in Germany. See P. Murray and R. Stürner, *German Civil Justice,* at 138 (Durham, N.C., Carolina Academic Press, 2004).

26   ZPO §17.

27   Commentators characterize as "special" the jurisdictional bases that the ZPO terms *dingliche (in rem) –* §§24-26 *–* and exclusive *–* §§24, 29a, and 621. See R. Zöller (-Vollkommer), *Kommentar zur ZPO* (Cologne, Dr. Otto Schmidt, 25th ed., 2005), §12, No. 7; H. Thomas and H. Putzo (-Hüßtege), *Zivilprozeßordnung* (Munich, C. H. Beck, 27th ed., 2005), Introduction §12, No. 3. See for a detailed account of "special" jurisdictions under German law Murray and Stürner, *supra* footnote 25, at 138-143. *Dingliche* jurisdiction exists where immovable property is located in the court's territory. Adjudicatory authority is established *–* under ZPO §§24 and 25 *–* for actions for damage done to such property or arising from its expropriation *(Enteignung)* and *–* under ZPO §26 *–* for claims against the owner or possessor arising from his ownership or possession. The term "exclusive jurisdiction" is self-explanatory. ZPO §24 recognizes such jurisdiction for actions to remove or to enforce a real encumbrance *(dingliche Belastung)* on an immovable, to draw boundaries, to partition, and to resolve possessory claims.

28   "Pecuniary claims" comprise claims grounded on a legal relationship intended to allocate money or rights that can be valued in monetary terms. A claim not so grounded is likewise pecuniary if the action seeks relief that can be given an economic value. See F. Stein and M. Jonas (-Roth), *Kommentar zur Zivilprozeßordnung,* Vol. 1 (Tübingen, Mohr Siebeck, 22nd ed., 2003), §1, Nos. 49-51.

29   Where the jurisdictional claim rests on the presence of intangible assets *(Forderungen)*, §23 provides that the asset "is located at the debtor's *(Schuldners) Wohnsitz*".

ship or over its existence *(Bestehen)*" lies with the courts of the place "where the disputed duty *(Verpflichtung)* was to be performed".

2.   The Inadequacies of Traditional Terminologies for Comparative and Theoretical Discourses

None of these nomenclatures is satisfactory for comparative and theoretical work. The French terminology has very little explanatory power and rests on developments particular to French law. Common-law usages have greater explanatory potential but are closely tied to historical developments and to a specific jurisdictional theory, that of power. Furthermore, the dichotomy on which the terminology rests is fatally flawed; it fails to recognize that adjudication always involves a determination of the rights and duties of persons; things have no rights or duties but are the subjects and objects of rights and duties.[30] A final difficulty is that the terms tend to obscure the policy considerations that are relevant in evaluating the appropriateness of exercising adjudicatory authority. For example, so-called jurisdiction *"quasi in rem"* suggests that a close relationship at the level of theory exists with jurisdiction *"in rem"*. These relationships may be considered strong by systems that accept the power theory but are weak in the light of other rationales. For systems that basically reject the power theory, markedly different reasons must be advanced to justify exercise of *in rem* and *quasi in rem* jurisdiction.[31]

3.   Terminology and Concepts for Comparative and Theoretical Purposes: Herein of General Jurisdiction, Category-Specific Jurisdiction, and Specific Jurisdiction

In the early 1960s my late colleague Professor Donald Trautman and I proposed a lingua franca[32] designed not only for the discussion of jurisdictional bases used in the United States but for comparative analysis as well. We took a basic distinction

---

30   Restatement Second of Conflict of Laws would overcome the difficulty by explaining the phrase "jurisdiction over a thing" as "a customary elliptical way of referring to jurisdiction over the interests of persons in a thing". *Idem*, Introductory Note to Chap. 3, Top. 2, Tit. A, Vol. I, p. 192 (1969).

31   See, e.g., the development in the United States after *International Shoe*, Chap. III. A. 4., pp. 97 *et seq.*, *infra*.

32   This now widely used terminology first employed by the Supreme Court of the United States in *Helicopteros Nacionales de Columbia, S.A. v. Hall*, 466 US 408 (1984), and the analysis on which it rests were advanced in A. von Mehren and D. Trautman, *The Law of Multistate Problems*, espc. at 653-656 (Boston, MA, Little Brown, 1965). See also von A. Mehren and D. Trautman, "Jurisdiction to Adjudicate: A Suggested Analysis", 79 *Harv. L. Rev.* 1121-1179, espc. at 1135-1137, 1164-1166 (1966); A. von Mehren, "Adjudicatory Jurisdiction: General Theories Compared and Evaluated", 63 *Boston U. L. Rev.* 279, at 282-290 (1983).

between *general* and *specific* jurisdiction.[33] The former can be asserted by individuals or juristic persons considered to be connected either directly – through, for example, his physical presence, the doing of business, incorporation, habitual residence, or domicile – or indirectly – in particular, through the ownership of local property – with a legal order in a manner that establishes, subject to relatively limited exceptions, a legal order's power to adjudicate essentially any kind of controversy involving that person regardless whether the matters in issue derive from, or are related to, the circumstances relied upon to establish adjudicatory authority. *Specific* jurisdiction, on the other hand, exists where the adjudicatory authority claimed extends *only* to controversies deriving from, or closely related to, the very circumstances relied upon to justify the forum's claim of adjudicatory authority.

Claims of adjudicatory authority can be either *unlimited* or *limited*. *Unlimited* claims exists where judgments run, in principle, against the judgment debtor's global assets, existing or future; claims are *limited* where, in principle, judgments may not be given for an amount that exceeds the value of the defendant's specific funds or assets located – at the time the action was entertained – on the forum's territory. In the contemporary world, a widely accepted basis for unlimited general jurisdiction is the defendant's domicile or habitual residence. The claim of jurisdiction is *general* – the matters to be litigated need not have any special connection or affiliation with the forum's community – and *unlimited* – judgments may be given for the full value of the claim regardless of the value of the judgment debtor's assets present on the forum's territory. Traditional common law *quasi in rem* jurisdiction, on the other hand, is a claim of *limited general* jurisdiction: *general* because the presence in the state of assets belonging to the defendant establishes the forum's adjudicatory jurisdiction over claims that give rise to a money judgment, including claims having no connection with the asset, or the fact of its presence in the forum; but *limited* because the judgment given may not exceed the value of the defendant's assets on which the forum's adjudicatory authority rested.

Analysis of adjudicatory authority in terms of general and specific jurisdiction leaves out of account a third form of jurisdiction that can be denominated category-specific. The claim of adjudicatory authority asserted is *general* in the sense that, unlike specific jurisdiction, the particular claims to be litigated need not be linked to the forum, but the adjudicatory authority claimed, extends only to controversies of a particular juridical character, for example, contractual or tortious (delictual) claims.

The appropriateness of claims of general jurisdiction and of category-specific jurisdiction are assessed *ex ante*. The jurisdictional claim must satisfy a "group norm" requirement; that is to say the appropriateness of jurisdiction must be established for the generality – but not for all – of the situations over which adju-

---

33   This terminology encounters the *faux amis* problem; as will appear, the terms general and special are used in a sense that differs greatly from the German terms *allgemeiner* and *besonderer Gerichtsstand*. See p. 22, *supra*.

dicatory authority is claimed. As Justice Holmes wrote in *Blinn* v. *Nelson*,[34] "constitutional law, like other mortal contrivances, has to take some chances, and [it is enough that] in the great majority of instances ... justice will be done".[35] Claims of specific jurisdiction, on the other hand, rest directly on the proposition that, *in light of the circumstances of the particular case*, litigational justice permits the exercise of adjudicatory authority. There, the appropriateness is assessed *ex post* and in controversy specific terms.

In certain areas of law, the limitation of the claim of adjudicatory authority to controversies of a particular juridical character increases significantly the probability that the indicated forum will be appropriate under a group-norm standard. The basic instrumental rationale is the same as that underlying claims of general jurisdiction: in light of considerations of convenience and predictability, the forum identified is, in the case of general jurisdiction, likely to be appropriate for adjudicating essentially any type of claim – or, in the case of category-specific jurisdiction, any claim of a specific juridical character – against the defendant.

§29 of the German Code of Civil Procedure recognizes adjudicatory authority "over controversies arising out of a contractual relationship or respecting its existence in the courts of the place where the disputed obligation is to be performed". This claim of category-specific jurisdiction by the place of performance can cover not only disputes respecting the fact or quality of the contract's performance but also disputes respecting the contract's creation, such as fraud in the inducement and formal validity.[36]

---

34   222 US 1 (1911).

35   *Idem* 7.

36   Article 5 of the Brussels Regulation and Article 6, alternative B, of the Hague Interim Text of June 2001, both provide category-specific forums. The Regulation's Article 5 (1) recognizes adjudicatory authority:

    (a)   in matters relating to a contract, in the courts for the place of performance of the obligation in question;

    (b)   for the purpose of this provision and unless otherwise agreed, the place of performance of the obligation in question shall be:
       — in the case of the sale of goods, the place in a Member State where, under the contract, the goods were delivered or should have been delivered,
       — in the case of the provision of services, the place in a Member State where, under the contract, the services were provided or should have been provided,

    (c)   if subparagraph *(b)* does not apply then subparagraph *(a)* applies.

Draft Article 6, Alternative B, of the Hague Interim Text, which constituted Article 6 in the October 1999 draft, provides that

[a] plaintiff may bring an action in contract in the courts of a State in which –

    (a)   in matters relating to the supply of goods, the goods were supplied in whole or in part;

    (b)   in matters relating to the provisions of services, the services were provided in whole or in part;

    (c)   in matters relating both to the supply of goods and the provision of services, performance of the principal obligation took place whole or in part.

The arguments for recognition of category-specific jurisdiction thus parallel those advanced for general jurisdiction; a forum is provided that can be easily and clearly identified in advance of litigation and that does not depend upon the controversy-specific enquiries required where specific jurisdiction is in question.[37] Category-specific jurisdiction for contractual obligations is thought by some to enjoy a further advantage: the forum indicated is unlikely to change between the time the parties enter into the relevant legal relationship and the time that their dispute arises.[38]

Family law provides category-specific adjudicatory authority when it takes jurisdiction to divorce on the basis of the moving party's domicile, habitual residence, or nationality. The jurisdictional claim can reach all controversies that fall within the specified juridical category or be framed more modestly, extending, for example, not to all family-law matters but only to divorce and support.

At first blush, the general, category-specific, and specific trinity may seem "quite similar" to the German general-special duality.[39] When these terminologies are applied to particular jurisdictional bases, however, the differences are clear. For German jurists, ZPO §§23 and 29 are both special jurisdictions.[40] Under the terminology proposed above, §23 is a *general* jurisdiction; it recognizes claims of adjudicatory authority over controversies that are entirely unrelated to the prop-

---

37   In practice, this advantage may be illusive because of disagreement respecting the location of the connecting factor. "Place of performance", utilized by Article 5 (1) of the Brussels Convention leaves, in practice, a great deal to be desired so far as administrability and predictability are concerned. See G. Droz, "Delendum est forum contractus?", *Recueil Dalloz*, [1997] *Chronique* 351, at 351. The difficulty does not arise, however, from a flaw in the concept but from the difficulties of implementing it in a clear-cut and easily administrated manner.

38   This argument is not available for other forms of category-specific jurisdiction such as jurisdiction to divorce based on the moving party's domicile or habitual residence at the time the action is begun.

39   Professor Haimo Schack is one of the few German jurists who argues on substantive grounds that special and specific jurisdiction are comparable because both are usually related to the controversy. See H. Schack, *Internationales Zivilverfahrensrecht*, at 73, No. 191 (Munich, C. H. Beck, 4th ed., 2006). However, ZPO §23, a special jurisdiction in the German terminology, relies on the presence of property and that property ordinarily has no connection with the controversy for which its presence establishes adjudicatory authority. Likewise, special jurisdiction under ZPO §29 will frequently result in the exercise of adjudicatory authority by a forum that has no litigational or substantive connection with the controversy.

40   A recent dissertation sees in §23 an example of general jurisdiction as the author of this book uses the term. See T. Kleinstück, *Due Process-Beschränkungen des Vermögensgerichtsstandes durch hinreichenden Inlandsbezug und Minimum Contacts*, at 92 (Munich, C. H. Beck, 1994). See also P. Schlosser, "Jurisdiction in International Litigation – The Issue of Human Rights in Relation to National Law and to the Brussels Convention", 74 *Rivista di diritto internazionale* 5, at 26 (1991).

erty whose presence establishes adjudicatory authority.[41] On the other hand, §29 is a *category-specific* jurisdiction; the place "where the disputed [contractual] duty was to be performed" can claim adjudicatory authority only over "controversies arising out of ... [the] contractual relationship and over its existence *(Bestehen)*".

C.   The Appropriate Link of Jurisdiction and Choice-of-Law

1.   *Introductory*

In multi-state litigations, to what extent should rules and principles on choice of law and authority to adjudicate be linked? Generally speaking, contemporary law and practice are reluctant to link in principle jurisdictional and the substantive issues. Relatively few legal systems insist on the application of their own substantive law if the proceedings are to continue before their courts. Likewise, few contemporary legal orders refuse to accept jurisdiction when their domestic laws do not apply to the merits of the case. There are, however, situations in which special considerations support linking the issue of adjudicatory authority and applicable law. After dealing with the question in general terms, several of these special situations are discussed.

(a)   In general

Jurisdiction and choice of law can be linked in various ways. First, legal orders could always apply their domestic law, thereby making choice of law dependent on the jurisdiction seised.[42] Alternatively, jurisdiction could be assumed only if, under the forum's choice of law rules, its domestic law applied to the merits of the case.[43]

---

41   The German terminology does not distinguish between *limited* and *unlimited* jurisdiction. In our scheme, §23 is an example of unlimited jurisdiction because the amount for which judgment can be given is – unlike the common law's *quasi in rem* jurisdiction – not subject to a ceiling established by the value of the assets whose presence on the forum's territory grounds adjudicatory authority. However, there are proposals to read §23 as providing jurisdiction only to the extent that the value of the assets present in Germany actually cover the amount sued for. See R. Geimer, *Internationales Zivilprozessrecht*, at 435-436, Nos. 1363-1365 (Cologne, Dr. Otto Schmidt, 5th ed., 2005); Schack, *supra* footnote 39, at 120-122, Nos. 327-330. See also Chap. III. B. 5. (a) (ii), pp. 145-147, *infra*.

42   This was the ideal for von Wächter. See C. von Wächter, "über die Collision der Privatrechtsgesetze verschiedener Staaten", 24 *AcP* 230-311 (1841) and 25 *AcP* 361-419 (1842). It is also, at least in principle, claimed in the United States by Currie and Ehrenzweig. See B. Currie, *Selected Essays on the Conflict of Laws*, at 46-58 (Durham, NC, Duke University Press, 1963); A. Ehrenzweig, *A Treatise on the Conflict of Laws*, at 309-326, §§102-108 (St. Paul, Minn., West, 1962).

43   By domestic law is understood the rules and principles that the legal order would apply to the controversy if it were intramural.

Adopting either approach in principle would be most problematic in the contemporary world. It would merge the issue of applicable law and exercise of adjudicatory authority with potentially great costs to both. In particular, automatic application of the forum's internal-law rules to controversies where general jurisdiction is taken on the basis of the defendant's domicile or habitual residence or upon service upon him within the jurisdiction would produce randomly unacceptable results.[44]

Where specific jurisdiction is claimed, linking jurisdiction and applicable law is less likely to produce objectionable results. Nevertheless, in many situations, either litigational convenience or choice-of-law values would be compromised. Choice-of-law solutions would turn in significant measure on whether procedural conflicts justice would be well served by the forum asserting adjudicatory authority; jurisdictional solutions appropriate in terms of procedural justice would be modified to take substantive conflicts justice into account. The resulting rules and principles would be significantly less just overall than those available to legal orders that consider jurisdiction and choice-of-law to be, in principle, separate provinces.

Allowing jurisdiction to adjudicate to turn on the applicability to the underlying controversy of domestic rules and principles would also present severe administrative problems. Especially in systems that approach choice of law through rule – rather than jurisdiction – selecting methods,[45] the applicability *vel non* of the forum's domestic law often would not be established until the controversy had been fully presented to the court. Were the local law then held inapplicable, time and effort would be wasted. Arbitrary choice-of-law solutions would be encouraged for, once litigation had progressed to this point, the temptation would be great to apply local law and dispose of the controversy on the merits.

No modern legal order seriously considers having its adjudicators entertain only litigation subject in all respects to local rules and principles. This position does entail costs, however. Unless forum law is automatically applied, litigation involving significant non-domestic elements inevitably presents choice-of-law issues and often raises comparative-law problems as well. Both may be of considerable intellectual difficulty and the latter can also involve real dangers of misunder-

---

44　The *forum non conveniens* doctrine – see Chap. VI. B., pp. 269 *et seq.*, *infra* – could hardly remove the difficulty; the doctrine would have to be applied with such frequency that, in effect, all exercises of jurisdiction would be highly particularized and the advantages that generalized jurisdictional standards provide would be lost.

45　The rule-selecting approach to choice of law, particularly favored by American jurists, has influenced many legal systems' approach to choice-of-law problems. On the impact of the U.S. conflicts of laws "revolution" on the European approach to choice of law see F. Vischer, "New Tendencies in European Conflict of Laws and the Influence of the U.S. Doctrine – A Short Survey", in J. Nafziger and S. Symeonides (eds.), *Law and Justice in a Multistate World, Essays in Honor of Arthur T. von Mehren*, at 459-471 (Ardsley, New York, Transnational Publishers, 2002).

standing and misapplication of the relevant non-domestic rules and principles.[46] With variations in emphasis and details two premises thus underlie contemporary handling of multi-state litigation: (1) adjudicatory jurisdiction in the international sense will be assumed when justified, in the putative forum's view, by concerns for the persons involved or for the underlying situation even though rules and principles applicable in comparable domestic matters will not ultimately regulate the matter, and (2), in principle, choice of law does not follow jurisdiction – nor jurisdiction choice of law – but each depends upon a separate analysis with significantly different considerations determining the appropriateness of asserting adjudicatory authority and the law to be applied.

(b) Qualifications of the separateness principle

Many legal systems express by the categories and classifications they employ the proposition that adjudicatory authority and applicable law are, in principle, not intertwined; thus the former is characterized as civil procedure, the latter, as substantive law. German law, for example, considers jurisdiction to adjudicate an aspect of international civil procedure while choice of law falls to private international law. Assignment to different doctrinal categories does not indicate, however, that the legal system never links the assertion of adjudicatory authority with the application of the forum's domestic law. Whether – and to what extent – such linkage occurs varies with the subject matter and the legal order in question. Two areas in which linkage occurs with some frequency are divorce and compensation of workers for injuries suffered in the course of employment. In other areas of law, a court may exceptionally encounter a situation where the choice-of-law process cannot function effectively; in such cases it may on occasion be appropriate to relax the separateness principle.

(i)   Divorce

Our discussion of exceptions to the separateness principle begins with divorce proceedings. For divorce – and, indeed, for family-law matters generally – most legal orders today take jurisdiction on the basis of either party domicile (or habitual residence) or nationality. Jurisdiction based on consent is recognized by some legal orders, especially those providing "divorces of convenience".

The marked tendency to limit assumption of jurisdiction in divorce to legal orders with which at least one spouse is closely affiliated through either domi-

---

46   Since the plaintiff's substantive rights arose in France, it becomes necessary to consider the French law. We undertake this with diffidence, especially as we have not had the benefit of the considered opinion of any French lawyer upon the particular facts of this case but have been obliged to come to our conclusions solely by taking judicial notice of the provisions of the French code, of statements by French legal writers, and of the decisions of French courts which have been submitted by the parties under G.L. (Ter. Ed.) c. 233, §70. In dealing in this manner with foreign law with which we are unfamiliar there is always the possibility that something that might affect the result has not come to our attention or that we have failed properly to correlate the material supplied.

Lenn v. Riché, 331 Mass. 104, at 109, 117 NE 2d 129, at 132 (1954).

cile (habitual residence) or nationality results, at least in part, from sovereignty concerns: the view that the divorce laws of these communities should regulate the marital conduct and status of persons closely linked to them by social, sociological, or political ties. At the same time, legitimate party and court litigational concerns are normally as well or better served by these bases than by other possible ones.[47]

If this analysis is correct, it serves to explain why, in principle, the links of domicile (habitual residence) and nationality are widely accepted for divorce as justifying not only the assertion of adjudicatory authority but also the application of forum law. Would it also be appropriate for a legal order to take jurisdiction on other jurisdictional bases – consent, service, or the place where the events occurred on which the divorce action is predicated – on the condition that the divorce law of one spouse's – or, more restrictively, both spouses' – domicile, habitual residence, or nationality would regulate the controversy?

In the United States, this question was addressed in *Alton* v. *Alton*.[48] The court of first instance had taken jurisdiction on the basis of consent by both spouses; a divorce was granted under the forum's divorce law. Upon appeal, the divorce was set aside; the Virgin Islands was not the domicile of either spouse and, accordingly, its courts lacked adjudicatory authority.[49]

Judge Hastie, in dissent, argued that the due process clause of the United State Constitution "does not prevent the entertaining and adjudication of a divorce action in any American state or territory which has personal jurisdiction over both spouses". However, he qualified his position by observing

> that if a state proceeds upon ... [his proposed] new basis of divorce jurisdiction another conflict of laws difficulty must be faced before the merits of the claim can be decided. That difficulty is the proper choice of law to govern the controversy.[50]

> [I]t may well be that under correct application of conflict of laws doctrine, even under the due process clause, it is incumbent upon the Virgin Islands, lacking connection with the subject matter, to apply the divorce law of some state that has such connection, here Connecticut [the domicile of both spouses].[51]

---

47   Consent would doubtless serve better the spouses' litigational convenience; however, most contemporary legal orders do not consider appropriate selection of a forum in order to obtain the benefit of its domestic divorce law.

48   207 F. 2d 667, 678, at 682-685 (3rd Cir. 1953), *cert. granted*, 347 US 911 (1954), *vacated as moot*, 347 US 610 (1954).

49   See *idem* 676-677. The majority relied on the jurisdictional theory established by *Williams* v. *North Carolina [I]*, 317 US 287 (1942), and applied in *idem [II]*, 325 US 226 (1945).

50   207 F. 2d at 684.

51   *Idem* 685.

Judge Hastie's suggestion, which contemplates essentially the same separation of jurisdiction and choice of law in divorce matters as in litigation generally, evoked no response in the United States.[52] So long as jurisdiction and choice of law remain intertwined for divorce, the observation of the majority in *Alton* is compelling: "if our states are really to have control over the domestic relations of their citizens",[53] a jurisdiction, such as the Virgin Islands, lacking a legitimate claim to regulate the marriage, should not exercise adjudicatory authority. The parties' litigational concerns must yield to sovereignty concerns until divorce is seen as an entirely private matter.[54]

Nor was Judge Hastie's suggestion attractive to the spouses or to the forum in question. The spouses had agreed to litigate in the Virgin Islands because its divorce law – not that of their domicile – would be applied. Their aim – to divorce under a law that suited their purposes – and that of the forum – to gain economic benefits by facilitating divorce of parties without significant affiliation with the Islands – could be accomplished only by linking jurisdiction with the application of domestic law. By accepting Judge Hastie's approach, the Virgin Islands of this world would lose their attraction for divorce and thus defeat their own purpose – to derive financial gain by providing "divorces of convenience".

Even a legal order acting from purely altruistic motives might well, however, hesitate to take jurisdiction to divorce and apply the law of the parties' domicile or nationality. Application of another jurisdiction's divorce laws often presents special difficulties. These laws employ general standards – incompatibility of temperament or irreparable breakdown of the marriage, for example; a foreign court may encounter difficulties in determining how such rules are to be understood and applied. Such concerns may, however, not be so serious as to recommend the American position that, when jurisdiction to divorce is taken, local divorce law

---

52   The concept of domicile is still central to divorce-jurisdiction theory in the Unites States. See E. Scoles, P. Hay, P. Borchers and S. Symeonides, *Conflict of Laws*, §§15.1-15.11 (St. Paul, Minn., West Group, 4th ed., 2004). In light of the rise of "no fault" divorce by mutual consent – now far more common in the United States than either contested or *ex parte* divorce – the domicile requirement has lost much of its importance and is seen by some as "out of step with the way people live today and with the way law has developed in related areas". H. Garfield, "The Transitory Divorce Action: Jurisdiction in the No-Fault Era", 58 *Tex. L. Rev.* 501, at 546 (1980).

53   207 F. 2d at 676.

54   It is worth noting that an effort to incorporate in Louisiana's codification of private international law a provision somewhat along the lines proposed by Judge Hastie was emphatically rejected. The Reporter to the Council of the Louisiana Law Institute, Dean Symeon Symeonides, proposed that where Louisiana had adjudicatory authority to divorce, a "court of this state [Louisiana] *may* grant a divorce ... for grounds provided by the law of this state". The clear implication was that the court could also grant a divorce under the law of another state. See S. Symeonides, "Louisiana PIL Codification", 57 *RabelsZ* 460, at 484 (1993). "[T]he Council did not like this implication ... [and] replaced the permissive with negative language so as to prohibit the application of foreign law to this issue." *Idem* at 484-485.

must be applied.[55] They help to explain, however, the tendency, strongest in common-law systems, to intertwine jurisdiction and choice of law so that jurisdiction is exercised only by a legal order that is the domicile, habitual residence, or national State of at least one spouse, and the forum applies its law of divorce.

Ernst Rabel's summary of the situation, still substantially accurate although written nearly a half century ago and before the rise of no-fault divorce, points out that many legal systems do not link jurisdiction and applicable law as firmly and completely as does American practice: "A divorce suit is considered to belong to a court either, by virtue of some domiciliary connection or of the nationality of both, or possibly one, of the parties."[56] For choice of law in the United States,

> [t]he principle ... is that a divorce court applies the law of the forum to determine whether divorce is admissible, as well as whether the party's conduct or other event complained of constitutes a ground for divorce.[57]

> In most civil law countries, the two questions of jurisdiction and applicable law are distinguished as a matter of course, and, with respect to the latter, consideration is given to the *lex fori* in conjunction with the *lex patriae*.[58]

Contemporary German law exemplifies the position of a highly developed civil-law system respecting jurisdiction to divorce and the law applicable in divorce

---

55   For military personnel whose community attachments are often of relatively brief duration due to the requirements of military service, the domicile requirement for jurisdiction has been relaxed but the forum continues to apply its local divorce law. *Crownover* v. *Crownover*, 58 NM 597, 274 P. 2d 127 (1954), upheld a New Mexico statute providing that military personnel "continuously stationed in any military base or installation in the state for one year shall be deemed residents in good faith" on the ground that a presumption of domiciliary intent is created and is reasonable. The court also pointed to the practical problem faced by military personnel in marital difficulty. This latter line of reasoning was emphasized by the Chief Justice in a special concurrence, 58 NM at 609-612, 274 P. 2d at 134-143. Similar statutes, under all of which the domestic divorce law would be applied, have been upheld by the courts of Kansas and Texas. *Craig* v. *Craig*, 143 Kan. 624, 56 P. 2d 464 (1936); *Wood* v. *Wood*, 159 Tex. 350, 320 SW 2d 807 (1959).

56   E. Rabel, *The Conflict of Laws: A Comparative Study*, Vol. I at 425 (Ann Arbor, Mich., University of Michigan, 2nd ed., 1958). Rabel remarks that

> [o]ther grounds for assuming divorce jurisdiction have sometimes been deemed to include the place where the marriage has been celebrated or the place where an offense against the marriage has been committed. The first conception is derived from regarding marriage as a contract and dissolutions of marriage as a rescission thereof; the second reflects the idea that divorce is of a penal nature and therefore governed by the law of the place of the wrong. These conceptions no longer retain roots in the present legislation ... .

> *Ibid.*

57   *Idem* 453-454.

58   *Idem* 459.

actions. Jurisdiction is addressed in the Code of Civil Procedure; ZPO §606a (1)[59] provides that German courts have jurisdiction:

1. if one spouse is a German national or was one at the time of marriage,
2. if both spouses have their habitual residence *(gewöhnlichen Aufenthalt)* in Germany,
3. if one spouse is stateless with a habitual residence in Germany or
4. when one spouse has his habitual residence in Germany, unless it appears the judgment to be given clearly *(offensichtlich)* would not be recognized under the law of any State of which one of the spouses is a national *(angehört)*.

These jurisdictions are not exclusive.[60]

The Introductory Law to the Civil Code *(Einführungsgesetz zum Bürgerlichen Gesetzbuch)* deals with choice of law in actions for divorce.[61] The general principle, set out in EGBGB Article 17 (1), is that divorce is regulated under the law applicable to the marriage relationship in general *(die allgemeinen Wirkungen der Ehe)*. Article 14 provides that

[I]   The general effects of the marriage are governed by
1. the law of the State of which both spouses are nationals, or were nationals at one time during the marriage, if one of them is still a national of this State; if not
2. the law of the State in which both spouses have their habitual residence *(gewöhnlichen Aufenthalt)*, or had their habitual residence, at one time

---

59   Venue is separately regulated by §606. In 1986, changes of some significance were made in the legislation respecting as well jurisdiction to adjudicate as choice of law in family matters. See generally U. Spellenberg, "Die Neuregelung der internationalen Zuständigkeit in Ehesachen", 8 *IPRax* 1-7 (1988); Stein and Jonas (-Schlosser), *Kommentar zur Zivilprozeßordnung*, Vol. 5/2 (Tübingen, Mohr Siebeck, 21st ed., 1993), §606a, No. 1; *Münchener Kommentar zur Zivilprozessordnung* (-Bernreuther), Vol. 2 (Munich, C. H. Beck, 2nd ed., 2000), §606a, Nos. 1-2; H. Schack, *Internationales Zivilverfahrensrecht*, at 165-167, Nos. 369-374 (Munich, C. H. Beck, 3rd ed., 2002). The revision of §606a continued and altered in some respects provisions previously found in §§606a and 606b. (The Code no longer contains a §606b.) These changes did not affect significantly the matters under discussion.

60   ZPO §606a (2) goes on to provide that the rule of §606a (1), No. 4 never prevents German recognition of a foreign divorce decree nor do Nos. 1-3 prevent recognition when the decree "is recognized by the State of which the spouses are nationals *(angehören)*". The relevance, in practical terms, of ZPO §606a has been drastically diminished by the coming into force of the "Brussels II" and "Brussels IIa" Regulations, discussed at pp. 36-37, *infra*. See H. Schack, "Das neue Internationale Eheverfahrensrecht in Europa", 65 *RabelsZ* 615, at 631 (2001); Schack, *supra* footnote 39, at 134-135, No. 368-371.

61   See for a detailed description of Article 17 EGBGB J. Kropholler, *Internationales Privatrecht*, at 364-377 (Tübingen, Mohr Siebeck, 6th ed., 2006).

during the marriage, if one of them still has his habitual residence in that State; or, where neither of the above applies *(hilfsweise)*,

3. the law of the State with which the two spouses together are in other ways most closely connected *(auf andere Weise gemeinsam am engsten verbunden sind)*.

[II] If one spouse is a national of several States, the spouses ... can choose the law of one of these States, if the other spouse is also a national of that State.

[III] Spouses can choose the law of a State of which [only] one of them is a national, when paragraph I, no. 1, does not apply and

1. neither spouse is a national of the State in which both spouses have their habitual residence, or

2. the spouses do not have their habitual residence in the same State.

The effects of such a selection end when the spouses acquire a common nationality.

The intertwining of adjudicatory authority and choice of law in divorce matters is thus less pronounced in German than in United States law. The German system is, however, very far from accepting the complete separation that Judge Hastie espoused in *Alton v. Alton.*[62] In the course of the 1986 revision of §606a,[63] a proposal, first made in 1962, that accepted Hastie's approach but only for a very limited situation, was revived – and rejected.[64] It called for German courts to take jurisdiction to divorce on the basis of a spouse's mere sojourn in Germany *(bei schlichtem Inlandsaufenthalt)* in the exceptional case where one of the spouses had no habitual residence whatsoever. A prudential concern stood in the way of accepting the proposal; "in view of the unusually great danger of jurisdictional underhandedness *(Zuständigkeitserschleichungen)*" presented, "[s]uch a jurisdiction would go too far ...".[65]

Contemporary German law thus is not prepared to accept even a minor qualification to the proposition that jurisdiction to divorce cannot properly be assumed by a forum whose interest in the marriage is minimal. A proposal to base jurisdiction to divorce on the spouse's consent would clearly encounter the same objection.[66] Although contemporary German law does not link jurisdiction and

---

62   207 F. 2d 667 (3rd Cir. 1953).

63   See *supra* footnote 59.

64   See J. Pirrung, *Internationales Privat- und Verfahrensrecht nach dem Inkrafttreten der Neuregelung des IPR,* at 200 (Cologne, Bundesanzeiger, 1987).

65   Report of the Legal Committee *(Rechtsausschuß)* of the Bundestag, quoted *ibid.*

66   The drafters of the ZPO explicitly rejected forum-selection agreements even for domestic divorces. See C. Hahn (continued by B. Mugdan), *Die gesammten Materialien zu den Reichs-Justizgesetzen,* Vol. II/1, at 398 (Berlin, R. v. Decker's Verlag, 2nd ed., 1881). (Under EGBGB Article 14 (2)-(3), the spouses enjoy in some circumstances a limited power to stipulate the applicable law.) Unsurprisingly, very little discussion of the possibility of basing jurisdiction to divorce on consent is found in the German literature. Cf. J. von Staudinger (-Spellenberg), *Kommentar zum Bürgerlichen Gesetzbuch: EGBGB/Internationales Verfahrensrecht in Ehesachen,* (Berlin & New York, NY, Sellier & de Gruyter,

choice of law for divorce to the extent of requiring application of the forum's domestic law, the legal order avoids – by using as well for jurisdiction as for choice of law connecting factors that reflect sovereignty concerns – regulating a marriage under the law of a society that has no legitimate interest in it.

Since the coming into force of the EU "Brussels II" Regulation[67] on 1 March 2001, replaced by the "Brussels IIa" Regulation[68] as of 1 March 2005, jurisdiction for divorce proceedings is governed by a uniform set of rules for all Member States of the European Union except Denmark. Article 3 of the Brussels IIa Regulation[69] sets out seven grounds of jurisdiction based on the habitual residence of one or both of the spouses (Article 3 (1)(a)) or their common nationality (Article 3 (1)(b)).[70] The Regulation thus accepts the principle favored in domestic German law that jurisdiction over divorce actions shall only be assumed by a forum with a legitimate interest in the case.[71] However, it breaks the linkage between juris-

---

Neubearbeitung, 2005), §606a ZPO, No. 316-317; Zöller (-Geimer), *supra* footnote 27, §606a, Nos. 86-87; Stein and Jonas (-Schlosser), *supra* footnote 59, §606a, No. 7.

67   Council Regulation (EC) No 1347/2000 ([2000] OJ L 160, 19-29) of 29 May 2000 on jurisdiction and the recognition and enforcement of judgments in matrimonial matters and in matters of parental responsibility for children of both spouses, [2000] OJ L 160/19. On the jurisdictional regime established by Brussels II see I. Niklas, *Die europäische Zuständigkeitsordnung in Ehe- und Kindschaftsverfahren* (Tübingen, Mohr Siebeck, 2003).

68   Council Regulation (EC) No 2201/2003 ([2003] OJ L 338, 1-29) of 27 November 2003 concerning jurisdiction and the recognition and enforcement of judgments in matrimonial matters and the matters of parental responsibility, repealing Regulation (EC) No 1347/2000. The rules on jurisdiction in divorce proceedings were not changed. See on the Brussels IIa Regulation in general P. McEleavy, "Brussels II bis: Matrimonial Matters, Parental Responsibility, Child Abduction and Mutual Recognition", 53 *Int'l & Comp. L. Quart.* 503-512 (2004); P. McEleavy "The Communitarization of Divorce Rules: What Impact for English and Scottish Law?", 53 *Int'l & Comp. L. Quart.* 605-642 (2004); Schack, *supra* footnote 39, at 134-135, Nos. 368-371. See also Chap. II. D. 3. *(c)*, pp. 76-77, *infra*.
      In the meantime the Commission has issued a proposal for amending Regulation (EC) No 2201/2003. See the Proposal for a Council Regulation amending Regulation (EC) No 2201/2003 as regards jurisdiction and introducing rules concerning applicable law in matrimonial matters, COM (2006) 399 final. The proposal introduces, *inter alia*, a limited possibility for the spouses to designate by common agreement the competent court ("prorogation") in a proceeding relating to divorce and legal separation.

69   Article 2 of the Brussels II Regulation.

70   This proliferation of forums for divorce actions has been criticized by some writers as unduly facilitating divorce. See Schack, *supra* footnote 60, at 617; Schack, *supra* footnote 39, at 134, No. 370; E. Jayme, "Zum Jahrtausendwechsel: Das Kollisionsrecht zwischen Postmoderne und Futurismus", 20 *IPRax* 165, at 168 (2000).

71   See also the 12th recital of the Brussels II Regulation according to which "[t]he grounds of jurisdiction accepted in this Regulation are based on the rule that there must be a real link between the party concerned and the Member State exercising jurisdiction ...".

diction and choice of law found in the American and German national systems previously discussed. As the Brussels IIa Regulation has, as yet,[72] no counterpart in the field of choice of law, courts in EU Member States exercising jurisdiction under the Regulation will determine the substantive law applicable in divorce proceedings under their own national choice of law rules. This may well result in the application of a law other than that of the forum.[73] Moreover, unlike ZPO §606a, jurisdiction under the Regulation is in no way linked to the prospect of recognition of the resulting judgment.

(ii) Workers' compensation

Workers' compensation acts, largely a post-nineteenth century phenomenon, supplement the law of delict or tort; they subject the employer and, on occasion, other persons as well, to liability without regard to fault for injuries suffered by employees in the course of their employment. Many acts further provide that the employer is, except in special circumstances, relieved of normal delictual or tortious liability to the employee.

A peculiarity of contemporary workers' compensation law is that normally relief can only be given under the forum's statute. This state of affairs, at least in the main, does not flow from sovereignty concerns. It is rather the sheer difficulty or impracticability of applying another legal order's compensation statute that stands in the way of recourse to choice of law. As a result, jurisdiction to adjudicate a compensation claim is, for many legal orders, inexorably inter-twined with application of domestic law. It follows that forms of general jurisdiction accepted by some legal orders for actions sounding in contract or in delict or tort – service of process upon an employer transiently present in the legal order's territory or presence of his assets on the territory, for example – are not available for workers' compensation actions; to assert jurisdiction, "the State … [must have] some … reasonable relationship to the occurrence, the parties and the employment".[74]

To the extent that a legal order accepts the proposition that choice-of-law is not available for workers' compensation claims, the system is under pressure to assert category-specific jurisdiction in a variety of situations where adjudicatory

---

72 Following the EU's "Action Plan" of December 1998 on how best to implement the provisions of the Treaty of Amsterdam on an area of freedom, security and justice ([1999] OJ C 19, 1), the Commission has proposed harmonized conflict-of-law rules in matters of divorce. See the Proposal for a Council Regulation amending Regulation (EC) No 2201/2003 as regards jurisdiction and introducing rules concerning applicable law in matrimonial matters, COM (2006) 399 final.

73 Several commentators point out that the multiplicity of available forums coupled with diverging national choice of law rules may lead to undesired forum shopping in divorce matters. See Schack, *supra* footnote 60, at 633; W. Hau, "Internationales Eheverfahrensrecht in der Europäischen Union", *FamRZ* 1999, 484, at 488.

74 Restatement Second of Conflict of Laws §181 (f) (St. Paul, Minn., American Law Institute Publishers, 1971). The Restatement restates, of course, only rules and practices followed in the United States. However, for purpose of the present discussion, §181 (f) illustrates a proposition that follows where the adjudicator is required to apply local law.

authority might well not be claimed were a choice of law permitted. Jurisdiction to adjudicate thus tends to follow, and become a reflex of, choice of law; where the legal order sees sufficient reason to make relief available under its statute, there, and there only, it claims adjudicatory authority.

The intertwining of adjudicatory authority and choice of law in workers' compensation matters results in a much greater proliferation of jurisdictional claims than in the case of divorce.[75] The larger the number of jurisdictional bases available, the greater is the risk of inconsistent adjudications. Inconsistency is much more serious where marital status is at issue than where compensation for work-related injuries is at stake. A generally accepted policy against "limping marriages" operates to deter claims of adjudicatory authority in marginal situations. No comparable deterrent concern is present in the case of compensation claims since local enforcement of the award is all that is normally required[76] while purely local enforcement of a divorce decree is typically undesirable.

The great scope and variety of the bases for assertion of adjudicatory authority that are appropriate in workers' compensation matters are suggested by §181 of the Restatement Second of Conflict of Laws; category-specific or specific jurisdiction can appropriately be claimed in a compensation action where:

(a)   the person is injured in the State, or
(b)   the employment is principally located in the State, or
(c)   the employer supervised the employee's activities from a place of business in the State, or
(d)   the State is that of most significant relationship to the contract of employment with respect to the issue of workmen's compensation under the rules of §§187-188 and 196,[77] or

---

75   The proliferation of category-specific jurisdiction bases in compensation cases is due as well to a policy of assisting the worker who is considered, economically and socially speaking, the weaker party. For further discussion of jurisdictional bases that are justified by protective concerns, see Chap IV. C. 2., pp. 167-173, *infra.*

76   Problems do arise regarding the effect of an award where an employee brings a second action in another legal order under its more generous statute. In such cases, if further recovery is permitted, the second award is reduced by the value of the first. For the handling of this problem in United States' law, see *Thomas* v. *Washington Gas Light Co.*, 448 US 261 (1980).

77   §187 deals with party stipulation for the governing law. §188 (1) provides for the application, in the absence of an effective party stipulation, of "the local law of the state which, with respect to that issue, has the most significant relationship to the transaction and the parties under the principles stated in §6". §196 provides for application of

the local law of the state where the contract requires that the services, or a major portion of the services, be rendered unless, with respect to the particular issue, some other state has a more significant relationship under the principles stated in § 6 to the transaction and the parties … .

(e)   the parties have agreed in the contract of employment or otherwise that their
rights should be determined under the workmen's compensation act of the
State, or

(f)   the State has some other reasonable relationship to the occurrence, the parties
and the employment.

The view that choice of law is not available in workers' compensation actions is
closely connected with the fact that most compensation statutes are administered
by commissions rather than courts. Although the United States case law is sparse,
relief may be available under foreign compensation acts that provide for *court*
– rather than commission – enforcement.[78] On the other hand, numerous cases
have refused court enforcement to foreign commission-administered acts.[79] A
few states permit by statute enforcement of such acts by the state's compensation
commission. The Vermont law provides:

> If a worker who has been hired outside of this state is injured while engaged in his
> employer's business and is entitled to compensation for such injury under the law of
> the state where he was hired, he shall be entitled to enforce against his employer his
> rights in this state, if his rights are such that they can be reasonably determined and
> dealt with by the commissioner and the court in this state.[80]

Almost identical provisions are found in Arizona[81] and Hawaii.[82]

In *Johnson* v. *Falen,*[83] the Idaho court applied in form a foreign statute, but,
as it had not been proved, presumed that the statute was identical with the local statute. The Vermont court refused, in *Grenier* v. *Alta Crest Farms, Inc.,*[84] to
enforce a compensation claim arising under a Massachusetts statute that made a
proceeding before the Massachusetts commission a condition precedent to the
right of recovery. The theory on which the court relied – that the employee, having agreed with his employer to come under the Massachusetts statute, waived
whatever other rights he would have had – did not, however, preclude in principle
the local enforcement of foreign acts.

What can be said in general terms respecting the desirability of providing
local enforcement for foreign compensation acts? Is local-court enforcement of

---

78   E.g., *Floyd* v. *Vicksburg Cooperage Co.,* 156 Miss. 567, 126 So. 395 (1930); *Texas Pipe
Line Co.* v. *Ware,* 15 F. 2d 171 (8th Cir. 1926). *Contra: Johnson* v. *Employers Liability
Assurance Corp.,* 99 SW 2d 979 (Tex. Civ. App. 1936).

79   E.g., *Green* v. *J. A. Jones Const. Co.,* 161 F. 2d 359 (5th Cir. 1947); *Davis* v. *Swift & Co.,*
175 Tenn. 210, 133 SW 2d 483 (1939); *Logan* v. *Missouri Valley Bridge & Iron Co.,* 157
Ark. 528, 249 SW 21 (1923).

80   Vt. Stats. Ann., tit. 21, §620 (2001).

81   Ariz. Rev. Stats. §23-904(B) (2000).

82   Hawaii Rev. Stats. Ann. §386-6 (2001).

83   65 Idaho 542, 149 P. 2d 228 (1944).

84   115 Vt. 324, 58 A.2d 884 (1948).

a foreign court-administered act easier to justify than enforcement of a foreign commission-administered act? And is local-commission enforcement of a foreign commission-administered act or of a foreign court-administered act feasible? Do the objections to enforcement derive from forum concerns or from concerns of the jurisdiction whose act would be enforced? Finally, are the forum's objections primarily related to *court* enforcement of a commission-administered act? If so, should not the forum *commission* in appropriate cases grant recovery based, to the extent feasible, on the foreign act?

In this connection, the following differences between the workers' compensation law, particularly under commission-administered statutes, and such areas as tort and contract are relevant. In the first place, not only in common-law jurisdictions but to a large extent in all legal systems within the Western legal tradition, areas of law such as tort and contract today have their centers of growth and adjustment in courts that share a central conception of the judicial process – the reasoned application and development of rules and principles on the basis of authoritative materials contained for the most part in statutes and prior judicial decisions. Each judicial system provides some public record of its processes of analysis and reasoning, and in every system these materials are the subject of critical discussion. These various elements enable a court of one jurisdiction to model its handling of a controversy on the treatment that the controversy would receive in the courts of another jurisdiction.[85]

In an area of law whose administration and development are committed to a commission, the accessibility and similarity that render feasible the modeling of one jurisdiction's solution upon that of another are diminished. A central, shared conception of the administrative process has not yet clearly emerged within the Western legal tradition. The process often relies on data and policies that are not fully matters of public record and frequently does not produce full and reasoned statements of the administrator's grounds for decision. Commissions also differ from courts in that they typically assume a substantially greater burden of investigation.[86] Finally, commissions do not benefit as fully from the support of an ancient tradition and of an active and critical profession; and the quality of their work and personnel are typically perhaps not as high as that of courts.

A further difficulty in the way of commission enforcement of a foreign compensation act is rooted in a difference between the constitutional positions of administrative agencies and of courts. Most legal orders see courts as an independent, co-ordinate branch of government deriving inherent authority from tradition, general conceptions of the judicial power and function, and constitutional conventions or provisions. On the other hand, the powers exercised by administrative agencies are more derivative. As units of the executive branch of government,

---

85   Of course, identical results are rarely, if ever, achievable. Procedural arrangements are seldom fully comparable. Attitudes of judges and of jurors, where the system uses jurors, are conditioned by different societies and different legal traditions.

86   However, this difference need not be significant if a commission is prepared to proceed under a foreign act in the same way that it would under the domestic act.

agencies enjoy certain inherent powers, but their authority is, for the most part, defined by statute. Unless a commission finds in its statutory charter an authorization to apply an out-of-State compensation law, the preparing of proceeding under a foreign act is problematic.[87] Understandably, legislatures rarely address the question whether the local commission should be authorized to apply foreign acts.

To sum up, the reluctance of one legal order to apply another system's compensation act is explainable, for the reasons set out above, by the difficulty of accurately establishing how the foreign act is administered in practice. This task, though inappropriate for the forum's courts, could be discharged by the forum's compensation commission. Commission adjudicatory authority is, however, typically exercised only in actions under the local statute.

(iii) Where serious choice-of-law difficulties, not normally encountered, arise

For the most part, contemporary legal orders assume adjudicatory authority on the premise that, where appropriate, non-domestic rules and principles can be applied. The risk exists that, in particular instances, the foreign system will provide for a remedy – for example, commission or administrative determination under general standards applied in unreported decisions – that the local forum can not effectively administer.

For example, an action to recover for injuries suffered in a two-car accident may be brought against the driver of the other car not only at the place where the accident occurred but also at his domicile or habitual residence in another State, or – where the circumstances are such as to render his employer directly or vicariously liable – against the latter at its place of incorporation in a third State. If all three forums apply the *lex loci delicti*, what are the courts of the two latter States to do when it turns out that the State in which the accident occurred regulates liability on a strictly *ad hoc* basis? Or, to take a less extreme possibility, what is to be done if under the law of the State of the accident the issue of liability is handled by a commission whose decisions are not published?[88]

In such cases, there is no decisive, *a priori* ground for giving priority to the forum's law.[89] The forum could, in light of the unforeseen choice-of-law difficulties that have arisen, dismiss the action without prejudice. The disappointed plaintiff would then be without a remedy except at the place of the accident unless another

---

87   Restatement Second of Conflict of Laws explains the non-use of choice of law in compensation matters on this ground:

> [T]he statutes normally provide for their enforcement by special administrative tribunals and such tribunals do not consider themselves competent to give relief under any statute but their own.

Introductory Note to Topic 3 of Chap. 7, Vol. I, p. 536 (1969).

88   A case that suggests these issues – which were not, however, discussed by the court – is *Walton* v. *Arabian American Oil Co.*, 233 F. 2d 541 (2d Cir. 1956).

89   See H. Neuhaus, "Internationales Zivilprozeßrecht und Internationales Privatrecht", 20 *RabelsZ* 201, at 258 (1955).

jurisdiction was prepared to adjudicate the controversy despite the practical impossibility of applying the law of the place of the accident.

Alternatively, for these exceptional cases a forum could provide a special, supplementary choice-of-law rule or principle and apply, for example, the forum's domestic law[90]. The California Code of Civil Procedure was amended in 1957 to allow, where it cannot be

> determine[d] what the law of a foreign country or of a political subdivision of a foreign country is, the court ..., as the ends of justice require, either [to] apply the law of ... [California] if it can do so consistently with the Constitutions of this State and of the United States or [to] dismiss the action without prejudice.[91]

A more nuanced approach would admit an additional choice-of-law possibility: application of the law of the legal order whose claim to regulate the issue was – once the possibility of applying the normally applicable law is excluded – the strongest in the circumstances.

Where a choice between dismissal without prejudice and application of a special choice of law rule is open, a forum might well proceed to decision under the special rule unless the legal order whose law would normally apply provided facilities – for example, authorizing its consular offices to handle claims – through which the plaintiff could obtain relief relatively conveniently and expeditiously.

2. Recognition of Judgments Abroad

A legal order that accepts the doctrine of *forum non conveniens* may on occasion take into account the prospects for recognition and enforcement of its judgments abroad in deciding whether to exercise adjudicatory authority that its courts enjoy in principle.[92] The problem to be addressed below is different; to what extent is recourse to certain jurisdictional bases conditioned in principle upon the certainty

---

90   See *idem* 259.

91   Calif. Stats. c. 249 (1957); see California Law Revision Commission, Recommendation and Study Relating to the Judicial Notice of the Law of Foreign Countries I-8, I-20 (1957).

The California provision was considered in 1963 in connection with the revision of the New York Civil Practice Law and Rules. The Advisory Committee concluded that the proposal had "merit, but the problem seems at this time best left for solution through case law development". Advisory Committee Notes to Rule 4511, 11 *NY Stan. Civ. Prac. Ser.* 172, at 174 (1963). In 1967, Section 249 became Section 311 of the Calif. Evidence Law. Stat. 1965, c. 299, operative 1 January 1967. Section 311 contains technical changes that do not affect substance.

92   On *forum non conveniens* generally, see Chap. VI. B., pp. 269 *et seq.*, *infra.*

– or at least the probability – of recognition or enforcement abroad of the resulting judgment?[93]

A requirement that, for jurisdiction to be taken, judgments had to be assured of recognition abroad would be virtually impossible to administer even if only the views of a limited number of States, easily identifiable when the litigation began, were to be taken into account. Accordingly, assertions of adjudicatory authority are only rarely subject to a recognition test.

Indeed, jurisdiction is taken even where the resulting judgment is likely to be unenforceable abroad and has, in the circumstances, no present prospects of local enforcement. §23 of the German ZPO provides that

> [f]or complaints asserting pecuniary claims[94] against a person who has no *Wohnsitz* within the country, the court of the district within which this person has property *(Vermögen)* ... has jurisdiction ... .

The value of the property need not bear any significant relationship to the amount in controversy. A commercial account book, "of 300 pages, of which 180 contain entries" relating "to commercial transactions, not yet completed, of a branch business" belonging to the defendant suffices to establish adjudicatory authority over claims no matter how large.[95] That the prospects for enforcement are nil at home and the jurisdictional claim's "exorbitant" character precludes recognition and enforcement abroad,[96] do not stand in the way of exercising §23 jurisdiction.[97]

---

93   Some American states have refused, perhaps as a matter of principle rather than discretion, to exercise *Harris* v. *Balk* jurisdiction in cases in which foreign States, being free of the full-faith-and-credit command, could refuse to recognize the judgment and might well require the garnishee to pay twice. See Chap. III. A. 2. *(a)*, pp. 88-89, *infra*.

94   See *supra* footnote 28.

95   RG, 7 April 1902, 51 *RGZ* 163.

96   §23 jurisdiction cannot be invoked, however, against defendants domiciled in the European Union or EFTA countries. Article 3 of the Brussels Regulation – similar language is contained in Article 3 of the Brussels and Lugano Conventions – provides that

    (1)   Persons domiciled in a Member State may be sued in the courts of another Member State only by virtue of the rules set out in Sections 2 to 6 of this Title.

    (2)   In particular the rules of national jurisdiction set out in Annex I [, which include §23 of the German Code of Civil Procedure,] shall not be applicable as against them.

Protection against §23 jurisdiction is not extended, however, to defendants that are not domiciliaries of the European Union or one of the EFTA countries. The Regulation's Article 4 – language to the same effect is contained in Article 4 of the two Conventions – provides that:

    (1)   If the defendant is not domiciled in a Member State, the jurisdiction of the courts of each Member State shall ... be determined by the law of that Member State.

97   See, e.g., BGH, 28 October 1996, 50 NJW 325, at 326 (1997). At the drafting stage of the ZPO, a proposal to limit the exercise of §23 adjudicatory authority to the value of the defendant's local assets was rejected. See Hahn, *supra* footnote 66, at 532 and

Indeed, arguably the policy that informs §23 is advanced by completely separating the issues of jurisdiction and enforceability:

> Usually, the plaintiff will not utilize this basis for jurisdiction when he cannot expect any satisfaction out of the property that the defendant has in the district. Nevertheless plaintiffs are not precluded from using this basis for jurisdiction in cases in which such satisfaction cannot be expected. And in some situations this makes considerable sense. The creditor, who is inconvenienced by his debtor's lack of a *Wohnsitz* [in Germany], may be interested, for the time being, only in a judgment which he can, at some later opportunity, use at once in pursuing his rights.[98]

The argument for closely linking exercise of jurisdiction and recognizability abroad is strongest where, as in divorce and some other family-law matters, decisional harmony is especially valued. In the United States, to ensure that a couple would not be considered married by some States and divorced by others, jurisdiction over divorce actions was, at one time, essentially exercised only by the "marital domicile".[99] Ultimately, however, the matrimonial-domicile rule was abandoned, in large measure because the divorce laws of many States were thought to be too restrictive and to give insufficient weight to the concerns of the spouse seeking divorce and of that spouse's community.[100]

So far as the United States is concerned, abandoning the matrimonial domicile test does not produce "limping marriages"; the full-faith and credit clause requires that a divorce decree given by a state with adjudicatory authority be recognized by all sister states. Of course, the full-faith command does not apply to recognition by foreign-country courts.[101]

Treaty arrangements can establish a full-faith command for international divorces. In the absence of such arrangements, a legal order may seek to ensure decisional harmony by linking the assumption of jurisdiction with the prospects

---

537-538. Had the limitation been accepted, §23 would, as a practical matter, have been useful only where meaningful local enforcement was available.

In the United States, general jurisdiction based on the local presence of assets belonging to the defendant – held unconstitutional in *Shaffer* v. *Heitner* (see Chap. III. A. 4. *(b)*, pp. 102-104, *infra*) – was limited to the value of such assets when the action began. This position rested, for the most part, on doctrinal considerations. However, the Supreme Court noted an administrability concern that is served by linking jurisdiction in this type of case with foreseeable enforceability; to hold otherwise "would introduce a new element of uncertainty in judicial proceedings". *Pennoyer* v. *Neff*, 95 US 714, at 728 (1877).

98   RG, 29 April 1881, 4 *RGZ* 408, at 410.

99   *Haddock* v. *Haddock*, 201 US 562 (1906).

100   The watershed decision is *Williams* v. *North Carolina [I]*, 317 US 287 (1942).

101   In certain international situations, the prospects for recognition are improved because the court addressed decides the jurisdictional issue under the law of a third State. See, e.g., *Travers* v. *Holley*, [1953] P. 246 (C.A. 1953).

for recognition of the judgment abroad. Otherwise, the risk of creating a limping marriage exists whenever two or more concerned legal orders disagree as to the circumstances in which a foreign judgment dissolving a marriage is entitled to recognition. No legal order conditions its exercise of adjudicatory authority in matrimonial causes on the certainty – or near certainty – that recognition will be forthcoming everywhere. The domicile of the spouses will take jurisdiction regardless whether the State of their common nationality will recognize the divorce if one is granted; conversely, the State of their common nationality does not condition its exercise of adjudicatory authority on whether recognition will be given by the spouses' domicile.

Where the spouses have different domiciles or nationalities, the likelihood of non-recognition increases significantly; nevertheless, legal orders are likely to assert adjudicatory authority on the basis of either the domicile or the nationality of one spouse without establishing that recognition will be given abroad. Introducing a recognition requirement into all jurisdictional bases that turn on the existence of a significant connection between one spouse – rather than both spouses – and the putative forum would ignore, *inter alia*, the social and sociological considerations that led to the abandonment of the matrimonial-domicile rule.

In all events, in the contemporary world most legal orders will not introduce a recognition qualification into their jurisdictional equations until at least one – unqualified – jurisdictional basis has been provided that rests squarely on *one* spouse's connections with the forum. Accordingly, typically only weaker forms of unilateral connection between spouse and putative forum are likely to be subjected to such a requirement.

The German system incorporates a limited recognition requirement into its jurisdictional rules for matrimonial causes, in particular, divorce. ZPO §606a (1) No. 4[102] does not recognize jurisdiction based on one party's habitual residence where "the decision that is to be made clearly *(offensichtlich)* would not be recognized by the law of any State of which one of the spouses is a national".[103]

As submitted to parliament, the draft of §606a (1) No. 4 had required a finding that the German decision *would be recognized*. The Legal Committee of the Bundestag substituted the less rigorous standard of *clear* non-recognition.[104] The Bundesrat went still further; it sought without success to delink completely jurisdiction and putative recognition.[105] Conditioning the exercise of jurisdiction on

---

102 For the text of §606a, see p. 34, *supra*.

103 ZPO §606a (4) replaced a provision, found before the 1986 revisions in §606b, that had linked jurisdiction and recognition more broadly and more closely:

If neither spouse is a German national, a German court has jurisdiction ...

3.   when the habitual residence of the husband or of the wife is in Germany and, under the national law *(Heimatrecht)* of the husband, the decision to be given by the German court would be recognized ...

104 See Pirrung, *supra* footnote 64.

105 Printed Matter of the Lower House of Parliament *(Bundestagsdrucksache)* 10/504, pp. 101-102, printed in *idem* 201.

a recognition requirement imposed on courts a difficult task, particularly since the contemporary law and practice of many legal orders respecting recognition of divorce decrees are unclear. Moreover, due to the possibility of mistakes, linkage – no matter how qualified – of adjudicatory authority with putative recognition cannot exclude the possibility of limping marriages. German jurists tend to sympathize with the Bundesrat's arguments. Schlosser, for example, regrets that the "disproportionally irksome" recognition requirement was retained in §606a (1) No. 4.[106]

D.   Further Considerations Affecting the Assertion of Adjudicatory Authority

The rationales for asserting adjudicatory authority that inform relational and power theories obviously leave out of account considerations that could well significantly affect a legal order's jurisdictional practices. On the other hand, the open-ended nature of instrumental theories permits their jurisdictional equations to encompass a wide range of considerations. In the practical application of all these theories, on occasion, considerations of a general, albeit often unacknowledged, and, at times, perhaps inappropriate, nature can play a role. Some examples of this phenomenon are briefly considered below.

1.   An Inherent Right and Duty to Dispense Justice

To what extent, if at all, do – and should – civilized societies have an inherent obligation to dispense justice? A State can claim adjudicatory authority "to enforce its criminal laws that punish universal crimes or other non-territorial offenses within the state's jurisdiction to prescribe";[107]

> [a] state has jurisdiction to define and prescribe punishment for certain offenses recognized by the community of nations as of universal concern, such as piracy, slave trade, attacks on or hijacking of aircraft, genocide, war crimes, and perhaps certain acts of terrorism ... .[108]

---

106   See Stein and Jonas (-Schlosser), *supra* footnote 59, §606a No. 16. Pfeiffer goes further; he considers the provision unconstitutional as applied to certain situations. See T. Pfeiffer, *Internationale Zuständigkeit und prozessuale Gerechtigkeit*, at 496-502 (Frankfurt am Main, Klostermann, 1995).
    In order to facilitate application of the requirement, the leading commentaries provide information respecting the recognition *vel non* by various States of §606a (4) divorces granted to their nationals.

107   Restatement Third of Foreign Relations Law of the United States, Vol. 1, §423 (St. Paul, Minn., American Law Institute Publishers, 1987).

108   *Idem* §404.

Exercises of adjudicatory authority so justified typically concern alleged criminal offences; however, arguably adjudicatory jurisdiction also exists, in principle, in these matters over claims sounding in tort or restitution[109]. For these special situations, our common humanity and shared civilized values may permit national legal orders to act as surrogates for an – as yet unrealized – international legal order.

2.   A Legal Order's Interest in Development of Certain Areas of Law

Assertions of adjudicatory authority can rest on the interest that a legal order has in developing the legal rules and principles that regulate certain areas of international intercourse such as insurance, shipping, and commerce. A State for which international commerce is of great importance may have a strong interest in contributing through adjudication in its courts to the development of a *lex mercatoria* and, accordingly, is likely to be more willing and desirous than are States in general to adjudicate controversies whose only connection is a party stipulation for the forum.

A concern to ensure that courts have available the raw materials – namely, disputes – through which law can be developed and refined is doubtless less strongly held by civil- than by common-law systems; the latter rely in private-law matters more heavily than the former on creative judicial activity. The concern that the common-law courts have available the materials needed to discharge this responsibility affects not only their willingness to exercise adjudicatory authority but has led as well to restrictions upon the scope allowed to private dispute-resolution mechanisms such as arbitration. Until 1997, English law on arbitration reflected a concern that the courts continue to play a central role in the development of the law respecting international commerce, especially in such areas as commodities, insurance, and shipping.[110]

---

109   *Idem* comment *b* to §404:

In general, jurisdiction on the basis of universal interests has been exercised in the form of criminal law, but international law does not preclude the application of non-criminal law on this basis, for example, by providing a remedy in tort or restitution for victims of piracy.

110   Section 4 of the Arbitration Act of 1979, which permitted a degree of judicial intrusion into commercial arbitration in these areas, was repealed by §107 (2), Sch. 4, of the Arbitration Act of 1996. Parties may by agreement now exclude court determination of questions "of law arising in the course of the [arbitral] proceedings"— §45 (1) – as well as appeals to the courts on questions "of law arising out of an award made in the proceedings" – §69 (1).

3.   *Economic Considerations*

Other considerations that can affect a legal order's willingness to make its adjudicatory agencies available are economic in nature. Economics doubtless influences to a degree the willingness of various legal systems to take jurisdiction over commercial disputes even though justification runs in terms of ensuring that the courts will have the material they need to develop and refine the law applicable to commercial activities.

At times, the significance of economic considerations for jurisdictional practices is painfully clear.[111] The forum's economy derives a net benefit from the provision of official adjudicatory agencies if the costs of maintaining the judicial establishment allocable to the type of litigation in question are more than offset by the income earned, *inter alia*, from court costs assessed on parties,[112] fees earned by local lawyers, and income to hotels and restaurants.[113]

The effect of such considerations on the availability of local courts is not always benign. The so-called "migratory divorce" furnishes crass examples of economic considerations leading legal orders to make their courts available despite the absence of any generally accepted ground for asserting adjudicatory authority over the matter in question. A number of court systems – those of Haiti, certain Mexican states and the Virgin Islands, for example – have been prepared to assume jurisdiction in divorce actions on the basis of party consent. Legislation authorizing this practice was urged upon the Virgin Islands Legislative Assembly in the following terms:

---

111   The same can be said of certain choice-of-law practices. For example, Section 3-5.1 *(h)* of New York's Estate, Powers and Trusts Law (N.Y. Stat. ch. 952) contains a unilateral choice-of-law rule that requires – where the testator has so stipulated – New York courts to apply New York law regardless of the testator's or the estate's contacts with New York.

112   In some systems, for example, those of continental Europe, these can be quite substantial. In the United States, on the other hand, court costs – as distinguished from attorneys' fees – are nominal.

113   In this connection, it is worth noting that economic considerations have in recent decades engendered among many national legal orders considerable competition to attract an unofficial form of dispute resolution: international commercial arbitration. Among the competitors are Brussels, Cairo, Geneva, Hong Kong, London, New York, Paris, Singapore, Stockholm, and Zurich. This competition has rendered many arbitration venues more user-friendly than would otherwise have been the case. For example, to improve London's competitive position, the English Arbitration Act of 1979 relaxed considerably the control traditionally exercised by English courts over the arbitration process. The purpose of the 1979 Act has been characterized as "to attract more international arbitration to London". T. Sanders, "International Commercial Arbitration – How to Improve Its Functioning?", 46 *Arbitration* 9, 12 (1980). The Arbitration Act of 1996 restricts judicial control even further and precludes (see §1 *(c)*) intervention by the courts unless the Act expressly provides otherwise. See Chap. V. E. 3. *(a)*, pp. 237-239, *infra*.

The divorce business in the Virgin Islands is quite a thriving business. I understand that this business provides quite an income for the municipalities since it is estimated that over $300,000 a year is spent within the Virgin Islands by persons who have been using the facilities of our divorce law to put homes in order.... I consider this [legislation providing for jurisdiction to divorce spouses domiciled elsewhere] ... a means of enhancing the economy of our islands ...[114]

114   Proceeding and Debates, 17th Legislative Assembly of the Virgin Islands of the United States, 3d Sess., 1955, at 46-47 (Rohlsen). It was observed by another speaker (Heywood) that he had "heard that there is anticipated a half million dollars-business [due to divorce] in this current year which will be distributed among lawyers, hotel bills, taxi cabs and other business ventures in this community". *Idem*, 2d Sess., 1953, at 10. The legislation passed the Virgin Islands legislature but was struck down on a variety of grounds, some constitutional in nature, in *Granville-Smith* v. *Granville-Smith*, 349 US 1 (1955); see also *Alton* v. *Alton*, 207 F. 2d 667 (3rd Cir. 1953).

Chapter II   The Design of Jurisdictional Provisions

A.   Basic Policies and Tensions

Speaking very generally, two sets of policies control the design of jurisdictional provisions applicable to multistate litigation: ease of administration and predictability, on the one hand; litigational fairness, on the other. Notionally, these need not necessarily conflict: ease of administration and predictability are formal policies; litigational fairness focuses on normative issues. Yet the means through which one set of policies is given effect can be, to a degree, incompatible with the other set of policies' goals.[1] Ease of administration and predictability will usually depend on clear-cut and clearly defined abstract rules. Litigational fairness, on the other hand (and irrespective of a particular legal order's concept of fairness), often has to take into account particularities of individual cases; it is, therefore, often best served by rules that are either tailored for the 'specific/ cases or formulated so as to allow fact-sensitive application.

Along with these policies, the design of jurisdictional provisions takes into account two further concerns: proportionality and vindication of important State regulatory policies. The first seeks to ensure not only that the forums in which claims can be pursued are appropriate and sufficient in number but also no more numerous than is required to give the plaintiff, absent exceptional circumstances, a fair opportunity to litigate his cause. The second concern arises from the forum State's interest in making its courts available for litigation that touches significantly important governmental policies.

Issues arising from the tension between predictability and ease of administration, on the one hand, and ensuring litigational justice, on the other, dominate contemporary jurisdictional theory and practice. The manner in which this tension is resolved turns on the interaction of several considerations: (1) the general theory – relational, power, or convenience, fairness and justice – that informs the legal system's approach to jurisdiction;[2] (2) the type of adjudicatory authority

---

[1]   Certain forms of general and category-specific jurisdiction escape this dilemma. See pp. 53-54 *infra*. Such bases are, jurisdictionally speaking, of higher quality than are bases that must subordinate one set of policies to the other.

[2]   See Chap. I. B. 2., pp. 24 *et seq.*, *supra*.

claimed – general, category-specific, or specific;[3] (3) the design of the jurisdictional rules or principles in question, and (4) the authorities responsible for its application.

B.   Connecting Factors: Their Design and Systemic Importance

1.   *The Paradigms: Administrability and Predictability; Litigational Convenience, Fairness, and Justice*

Drafting connecting factors to reflect the balance struck by one's legal order between the two paradigms is often a task both difficult and delicate. The characteristics of the connecting factors typically appropriate for use in light of each paradigm's value preferences differ greatly. The first paradigm requires the use of factors whose elements are few – ideally, singular – in number, objective in nature, and not controversy-specific. Connecting factors that satisfy the second paradigm must, on the other hand, often employ multi-factor criteria that include subjective as well as objective elements and are controversy-specific.

Illustrative first-paradigm connecting factors are bases of general jurisdiction such as service of process upon a natural person within the forum State, the defendant's domicile or habitual residence in that State or, in the case of legal persons, their incorporation or principal place of business there, and the presence of assets belonging to the defendant in the forum State.[4] Each of these connecting factors uses a single, largely objective, element that is not controversy-specific. Only two – domicile and habitual residence – have a subjective dimension and in recent decades there has been a movement from "domicile" to "habitual residence"[5] based largely on the argument that the latter is a less complex and more objective concept.[6]

Second-paradigm connecting factors, on the other hand, are at times controversy-specific, comprised of many elements, and include subjective as well as

---

3   See Chap. I. B. 3., pp. 24 *et seq.*, *supra*.

4   The claim of general adjudicatory authority made may be limited to the asset's value, as in *quasi in rem* jurisdiction (no longer constitutional in the United States, see Chap. III. A. 4. (b) pp. 102-104, *infra*) or unlimited, as under §23 of the German Code of Civil Procedure (see Chap. III. B.1. p. 118, *infra*).

5   The Hague Conference now employs "habitual residence", as does Article 3 of the Brussels IIa Regulation (Article 2 of the Brussels II Regulation) see p. 36, *supra*. The 1968 Brussels Convention and the Brussels I Regulation, on the other hand, have retained "domicile". Neither system provides a uniform definition of the concept it employs. For the European Union, see R. Fentiman, *Foreign Law in English Courts: Pleading, Proof, and Choice of Law,* at 126-129 (Oxford, Oxford University Press, 1998).

6   See E. Clive, "The Concept of Habitual Residence", [1997] *The Juridical Review* 137-147.
    A further argument advanced in favor of habitual residence is that it will, in a significant number of cases, be more accessible for the defendant than his domicile.

objective criteria. The courts work with directive formulas such as "minimum contacts", "purposeful availment" of the relevant legal order's economic and legal structures, and the appropriateness, in light of "traditional conception[s] of fair play and substantial justice, ... [of] permit[ting] the state to enforce the obligations ... [the defendant] has incurred there".[7]

The design of connecting factors thus reflects, *inter alia*, the legal order's policy choices respecting the weight to be given to administrability and litigational justice, respectively.

2.   The Tensions between the Paradigms

Ideally, of course, all the connecting factors used by a legal order would be both easily administered and ensure litigational justice. Regrettably, usually these policy goals are in tension. To carry out the first, connecting factors that are singular and objective are needed; implementing the second, typically requires plural factors that include subjective elements and take into account the characteristics of the specific controversy to be adjudicated. It follows that normally a connecting factor cannot systematically advance equally both administrability and litigational justice.

General jurisdiction based on in-State service of process ranks, for example, very high in terms of administrability and very low in terms of litigational justice. Contrariwise, specific jurisdiction based on such intrinsically unpredictable and difficult to administer connecting factors as "minimum contacts" or "purposeful availment", is far more sensitive to litigational justice than to administrability and predictability concerns.

The clearest example of a connecting factor that scores well on both counts is general jurisdiction based on either the defendant's domicile or habitual residence. The moving party's decision to proceed alleviates concern that the forum is litigationally unjust from the plaintiff's perspective. The cultural, social, and political ties that normally attach as well to domicile as to habitual residence establish that, in principle, it is litigationally just for the action to proceed. In particular instances, the matter may be one in which the ties between the parties, the controversy, and the forum are so attenuated as to render the exercise of adjudicatory authority unfair[8]. This objection is for many overcome, however, by the predictability and administrative convenience gained overall by exercising adjudicatory authority despite the occasional litigational injustice that may result. A legal order might, of course, adopt the view that every exercise of adjudicatory

---

7   *International Shoe* v. *State of Washington*, 326 US 310, at 320 (1945) (Chief Justice Stone's opinion for the Court). For discussion of *International Shoe* and its progeny, see Chap. III. A. 4., pp. 97 *et seq.*, *infra*.

8   In some legal orders courts can deal with such cases by invoking the *forum non conveniens* doctrine which, however, reduces predictability. See Chap. VI. B., pp. 269 *et seq.*, *infra*.

authority must be tested in controversy-specific terms.[9] Doing so would give decisive weight to claims of litigational justice at the expense of predictability and administrability.

There are also connecting factors that rank low both with respect to administrability and predictability, on the one hand, and litigational justice, on the other. This phenomenon – one to be avoided – is encountered when a connecting factor comprises elements that are multiple, complex, and involve subjective evaluation but that are not – or at least not consistently – category-specific.[10]

The Brussels Convention and Regulation provide category-specific jurisdiction for certain claims sounding in tort or contract. Article 5 (3) of the Regulation accepts that, "in matters relating to tort, *delict* or *quasi-delict*", adjudicatory authority lies in "the courts for the place where the harmful event occurred or may occur". For "matters relating to individual contracts of employment", Article 5 (1) of the Convention – Article 19 (2) *(a)* of the Regulation – contains a grant of category-specific jurisdiction to the "place ... where the employee habitually carries out his work".

These connecting factors identify in a reasonably clear and stable fashion the legal order or orders to which adjudicatory authority is granted. On the other hand, the connecting factor utilized by Article 5 (1) for category-specific jurisdiction over contracts in general – "the place of performance of the obligation in question" – has given rise to many difficulties.[11] The basic problem is that the legal order or orders upon which adjudicatory authority is conferred are all too often uncertain because the connecting factor itself is susceptible of multiple interpretations and can be manipulated by parties to their advantage. These qualities, highly undesirable in connecting factors, have caused some jurists to call for deletion of the category-specific jurisdiction established by Article 5 (1) of the Brussels Convention.[12]

---

9   Some American jurists accept this view. See Chap. III. A. 5., pp. 106 *et seq., infra*.

10   See ZPO §29 and Article 5 (1) of the Brussels Convention and Regulation, discussed Chap. I. B. 3, pp. 26-27, *supra*.

11   See also ZPO §29. The various obstacles to a harmonious and even-handed application of Article 5 (1) are thoroughly analysed by J. Newton, *The Uniform Interpretation of the Brussels and Lugano Conventions* at 47-161 (Oxford and Portland, Oregon, Hart Publishing, 2002). The problems are alleviated to a considerable extent by the autonomous definition of the place of performance for contracts for the sale of goods or the provision of services now provided in Article 5 (1) (b) of the Brussels Regulation. These definitions, however, also raise new questions of interpretation. See J. Kropholler and M. von Hinden, "Die Reform des europäischen Gerichtsstands am Erfüllungsort (Article 5 Nr. 1 EuGVÜ)", in H. Schack (ed.), *Gedächtnisschrift für Alexander Lüderitz*, at 408-411 (Munich, C. H. Beck, 2000).

12   See G. Droz, "Delendum est forum contractus?", *Recueil Dalloz*, [1997] *Chronique* 351-356. Reasons for retaining a jurisdictional base for contractual disputes are offered by Kropholler and von Hinden, *supra* footnote 11, at 413-414.

C.   The Designers of Jurisdictional Provisions

1.   *In General*

The several branches of government, as well as private persons from many walks of life, contribute to the fashioning of a legal order's law respecting jurisdiction to adjudicate in the international sense. In the contemporary world, except in those states of the United States that have authorized their courts to exercise jurisdiction on any basis not inconsistent with the constitution of the state or of the United States,[13] design is initially the responsibility of the executive and legislative branches,[14] often in collaboration.[15] Yet in every system, courts have an opportunity in the course of interpreting and applying regulations and laws to influence their legal order's jurisdictional practices and standards; the judiciary's role increases, of course, in legal orders that practice judicial review under constitutional standards.

Judicial design of jurisdictional norms and of the connecting factors that implement them takes place in three contexts: (1) interpreting authoritative starting points for legal reasoning, for example, treaties, laws and regulations; (2) declaring rules and principles to fill gaps in the existing law respecting the exercise of adjudicatory authority; (3) reviewing under constitutional standards the norms and connecting factors that (1) and (2) provide.

Because the principal task of courts is to decide concrete controversies while the executive and legislative branches are charged with laying down general rules and principles, judicial design, especially where constitutional standards are applied, tends to reflect – and to be formulated – in more controversy specific terms than are provisions designed by the legislative and executive branches to deal with the same general subject matter. The degree to which connecting factors are controversy specific varies, moreover, from one legal order to another. The common law has traditionally recognized a more creative role for judges than has the civil law. Judges accustomed to such a role will tend, as interpreters and designers of jurisdictional norms, to give greater weight to litigational justice than do judges whose legal order views the judicial function as limited to applying, in a rather strict sense, the norms designed by another branch of government.

2.   *In the United States*

Over time, the role and influence of the branches of government can change in fundamental respects. A dramatic example is the change in the role of the Ameri-

---

13   See p. 55, *infra*.

14   The relationship between the executive and legislative branches varies with, *inter alia*, the State's constitutional arrangements, its party system, and whether the design of domestic or international instruments is in question.

15   The degree and form of collaboration vary greatly from country to country as do the extent and manner of governmental consultation with the private sector.

can courts that resulted from the constitutionalization of the law of adjudicatory jurisdiction that followed the United States Supreme Court's decision in *Pennoyer v. Neff*.[16] By the end of the twentieth century judicial review under federal constitutional standards dominated the designing of jurisdictional norms. The executive and legislative branches of government, by claiming adjudicatory authority to the extent constitutionally permitted, abdicated their designing role in any save the most general sense.

3.   In Germany

The German development has been quite different. Prior to World War II, judicial review was not practised in Germany. The judicial influence on design increased modestly in the last half of the twentieth century as the Bundesgerichtshof showed a greater readiness than had the Reichsgericht, its predecessor, to develop new jurisdictional norms and connecting factors in the course of interpreting the relevant provisions of the Code of Civil Procedure.[17] The availability of judicial review under the Basic Law of 1949 gave the Constitutional Court (*Bundesverfassungsgericht*)[18] authority – fairly modest in its nature – to redesign norms and connecting factors in light of constitutional requirements.

The Basic Law obliges German courts to interpret, if at all possible, statutory provisions so that they are compatible with constitutional standards *(verfassungskonforme Auslegung)*. Where such an interpretation cannot be given, the court is to refer the matter to the Constitutional Court, which alone has the power to declare legislation void or inapplicable.[19]

At the same time, the emergence of the European Union, the entrance into force in 1973 of the Brussels Convention, and the creation of the European Court of Justice, whose responsibilities include providing authoritative interpretations of the Convention and its successor Regulation, shifted authority over the design and interpretation of large and very important areas of the law of jurisdiction from national governmental authorities to European Union authorities. Courts – national and international – now play, for Germany and many other European countries, an ever more important role in the design and interpretation of jurisdictional norms and connecting factors. Moreover, the European Union's executive branch takes an increasingly active and important role in shaping jurisdictional policy and practice for the Union's member States.[20]

---

16   See Chap. III. A. 1. *(b)* (ii), pp. 85 *et seq.*, *infra*.

17   See Chap. III. B. 5. *(a)* (i) and (ii), pp. 142 *et seq.*, *infra*.

18   The power of judicial review is also exercised in various situations by the Bundesgerichtshof and other regular courts. See *ibid*.

19   Article 100 para. 1 of the Basic Law. For the jurisprudence of the Constitutional Court, see Chap. III. B. 5. *(a)* (iii) and (iv), pp. 147-149, *infra*.

20   See pp. 74-78, *infra*.

D.   Designing Jurisdictional Rules and Norms

1.   The United States

(a)   Introductory: the influence of federalism

In litigation with international dimensions, the federal government, under its constitutional power over foreign relations[21] and foreign commerce,[22] as supplemented by necessary and proper clause[23] powers, could no doubt limit, or even displace, state authority. For interstate matters, limitation or displacement could occur under the commerce clause.[24] The federal government has, however, left legislation respecting the design of adjudicatory authority essentially to the states; as a result the exercise by state courts of adjudicatory authority is regulated by state legislation so long as the statutory norms pass muster under the Constitution of the United States.

State statutes were early enacted to give guidance to parties and courts respecting the situations in which the forum was to exercise adjudicatory authority. Indeed, a statutory basis is, in principle, required for a court to take jurisdiction.[25] States traditionally based jurisdiction, *inter alia*, on service of process within the state, doing of business there, and attachment of locally present property. Later statutes established non-traditional jurisdictional bases to handle, for example, claims against non-resident motorists involved in local traffic accidents.[26]

(b)   Legislative reactions to the International Shoe decision

(i)   State legislation

Most states did not react legislatively to the revolutionary implications of the *International Shoe* decision,[27] which was to increase dramatically the practical importance of national constitutional standards for the law of jurisdiction in both interstate and international litigation; existing legislation was for the most part left in place. Some states did pass new statutes but these did no more than recycle pre-*International Shoe* concepts such as "doing business" and "implied consent".[28]

---

21   Constitution of the United States, Article I, §8, para. 3, (Congress's power to regulate commerce with foreign nations), Article II, §2, para. 2 (President's power to make treaties with advice and consent of the Senate).

22   *Idem*, Article I, §8, para. 3.

23   *Idem*, Article I, §8, para. 18.

24   *Idem*, Article I, §8, para. 3.

25   Except to the extent that the state's constitution directly confers adjudicatory authority on the courts, their authority is regulated by legislation.

26   See *Hess* v. *Pawloski*, 274 US 352 (1927); discussed Chap. III. A. 3., pp. 95-97, *infra*.

27   See *supra* footnote 7; discussed at length Chap. III. A. 4., pp. 97 *et seq.*, *infra*.

28   See F. Juenger, "American Jurisdiction: A Story of Comparative Neglect", 65 *U. Colo. L. Rev.* 1, at 10 (1993).

The use of old concepts in a new and significantly different intellectual setting did nothing to clarify jurisdictional theory and practice.[29]

A few states supplemented their existing statutory regimes by passing general long-arm statutes specifically designed to assert the new jurisdictional claims that *International Shoe* permitted.[30] The most common form of these statutes sets out acts or categories of acts upon which jurisdiction could be based.[31] In 1955, Illinois enacted the first such statute; it was widely copied.[32] In 1962, the Uniform Interstate and International Procedure Act, patterned largely upon the Illinois statute, was proposed by the National Conference of Commissioners on Uniform State Laws.[33] Nine states now have adopted a form of this statute.[34]

---

29   Consider, for example, the 1959 Texas statute, repealed in 1985, which read in part as follows:

> [With respect to] [a]ny foreign corporation ... that engages in business in this State ... and does not maintain a place of regular business in this State

> ... the act or acts of engaging in such business within this State shall be deemed equivalent to an appointment by such foreign corporation ... of the Secretary of State of Texas as agent upon whom service of process may be made in any action, suit or proceedings arising out of such business done in this State, wherein such corporation ... is a party or is to be made a party.

> For the purpose of this Act ... any foreign corporation ... shall be deemed doing business in this State by entering into a contract ... with a resident of Texas to be performed in whole or in part by either party in this State, or the committing of any tort in whole or in part in this State. The act of recruiting Texas residents, directly or through an intermediary located in Texas, for employment inside or outside of Texas shall be deemed doing business in this State.

Act of 1 April 1959, 1959 Tex. Gen. Laws ch. 43, amended by 1979 Tex. Gen. Laws, ch. 245, §1, repealed by Acts of 1985, ch. 959, §9 (1).

30   An excellent discussion and critique of this legislation is D. Welkowitz, "Going to the Limits of Due Process: Myth, Mystery and Meaning", 28 *Duquesne L. Rev.* 233-270 (1990).

31   See *idem* 237.

32   See *ibid*.

33   See 13 ULA 361 (1986). In 1977, the Act was withdrawn from recommendation for enactment by the National Conference due to it being obsolete. See 13 Pt. II ULA 127 (2002). It is currently in force, occasionally with variant provisions, in Arkansas, Massachusetts, Michigan, Pennsylvania, the District of Columbia, and the Virgin Islands. See 13 ULA (1986), 2002 Cumulative Annual Pocket Part, at 145. For a brief discussion of the history and work of the National Conference, see A. von Mehren, *Law in the United States: A General and Comparative View*, 45-46 (Deventer & Boston, MA, Kluwer, 1988).

34   Welkowitz, *supra* footnote 30, at 240. The statutes are discussed *idem* 240-269. The nine states referred to at 240, in footnote 40 have enacted what the author terms a "type 3 statute", i.e. a combination of "jurisdiction to the limits permitted by the Constitution" and the specific-acts approach. The type of statute modelled on the 1962 Uniform Act ("type 2") is discussed by Welkowitz at 247-249, without, however, a specific reference to the states that follow this approach.

Six states – California, Oklahoma, New Jersey, Rhode Island, Vermont, and Wyoming – took a different approach and simply claimed jurisdiction to the constitutionally permissible extent.[35] California provided, for example, that its courts "may exercise jurisdiction on any basis not inconsistent with the Constitution of this State or of the United States".[36] A third group of states has combined Illinois's categorical-act and California's general-clause approaches.[37]

In almost every state whose statute adopts the categorical-act approach, "court decisions have determined that the statute was intended to extend jurisdiction to the extent permitted by the due process clause";[38] however, under these statutes jurisdiction is on occasion refused where the claim of adjudicatory authority could pass due-process muster but the matter in litigation does not fit within any of the statutory categories.[39]

(ii) Treaties and federal legislation

a.   In general

Traditionally, Congress has not sought to legislate with regard to state-court jurisdiction in either interstate or international litigation.

Nor has the United States had recourse to the treaty-making power. Indeed, in light of the federal nature of the American legal system and the traditional sensibilities of states regarding interference with the administration of justice in their courts, obtaining the Senate's consent to treaties dealing with jurisdiction was, until quite recently, considered next to impossible.

In the closing decades of the twentieth century a notable change occurred in views respecting the propriety and usefulness of federal action with respect to various aspects of litigation with international dimensions. On 15 October 1964, the United States joined the Hague Conference on Private International Law. Since then, the United States has become a party to a number of important conventions adopted by the Conference.[40] In 1970, the significant and unprecedented step was taken of ratifying a major multilateral international recognition convention, the 1958 United Nations Convention on the Recognition and Enforcement of Foreign Arbitral Awards.[41] A few years later, the United States and the United Kingdom entered into bilateral negotiations for a Convention on the Recipro-

---

35   See *idem* 237. These statutes are discussed *idem* 237-240.

36   Cal. Civ. Proc. Code §410.10 (2001).

37   See Welkowitz, *supra* footnote 30, at 237.

38   *Idem* 248.

39   See *idem* 249-251, 267.

40   E.g., the Convention on the Service Abroad of Judicial and Extrajudicial Documents in Civil and Commercial Matters of 1965, the Convention on the Taking of Evidence Abroad in Civil and Commercial Matters of 1970, and the Convention on the Civil Aspects of International Child Abduction of 1980.

41   Convention on the Recognition and Enforcement of Foreign Arbitral Awards, *opened for signature* 10 June 1958, *entered into force* 7 June 1959, 21 UST 2517, *TIAS* No. 6997, 330 *UNTS* 38 (1959).

cal Recognition and Enforcement of Judgments in Civil Matters.[42] Although the negotiations were ultimately unsuccessful, they evidenced a willingness on the part of the federal government to utilize the treaty-making power to deal with problems arising in international litigation. In 1996, the Hague Conference began work on a convention to address not only the recognition and enforcement of foreign judgments but also the adjudicatory authority of courts in international litigation.[43] After several years of negotiations, however, the project failed in 2003, when it became evident that fundamental differences between the participating States could not be overcome.[44] Instead, a convention much more limited in scope, dealing only with exclusive choice of court agreements was adopted.[45] Had the far-reaching and ambitious project of a comprehensive jurisdiction and enforcement convention succeeded and the United States become a party to the resulting convention, the effects on the exercise of adjudicatory authority in international litigation would have been both significant and salutary.[46] However, as the twenty-first century progresses neither treaties nor legislation – federal or state – has so far made a significant contribution to simplifying, rationalizing and harmonizing jurisdictional theory and practice in litigation with international dimensions.

b.   The role of international conventions and federal legislation

So far as predictability and administrability are concerned, state legislation has only made the situation worse. The nature of the jurisdictional problem may well be such that reliance on state legislation to improve matters is misplaced. Some jurists argue that, were jurisdictional law to be deconstitutionalized by overruling *Pennoyer*, *International Shoe*, and their respective progeny, the "states ... [would] draft sensible and clear long-arm statutes".[47] State legislatures already have power

---

42   See A. von Mehren, "Recognition and Enforcement of Foreign Judgments: A New Approach for the Hague Conference", 57 *Law & Contemp. Probs.* 271, at 273-274 (1994); P. North, "The Draft U.K./U.S. Judgments Convention: A British Viewpoint", 1 *Northwestern J. Int'l. Law & Business* 219-239 (1979).

43   See Chap. VII. B. 3., pp. 358 *et seq., infra.*

44   See H. Buxbaum, "Forum Selection in International Contract Litigation: The Role of Judicial Discretion", 12 *Willamette J. Int'l L. & Disp. Resol.* 185, at 206 (2004); K. Miller, "Playground Politics: Assessing the Wisdom of Writing a Reciprocity Requirement into U.S. International Recognition and Enforcement", 85 *Geo. J. Int'l. L.* 239, at 257-261 (2004); E. Teitz, "Both Sides of the Coin: A Decade of Parallel Proceedings and Enforcement of Foreign Judgments in Transnational Litigation", 10 *Roger Williams U. L. Rev.* 1, at 59-62 (2004).

45   Convention on Choice of Court Agreements of June 2005 available at http://www.hcch.net. See also Chapter VII. C. 2. *(c)*, pp. 370 *et seq., infra.*

46   Some had hoped that the Hague Convention work would inspire a federal jurisdictional statute. See K. Clermont, "Jurisdictional Salvation and the Hague Treaty", 85 *Cornell L. Rev.* 89, at 121-123 (1999). See also pp. 62-64, *infra.*

47   P. Borchers, "The Death of the Constitutional Law of Personal Jurisdiction: From *Pennoyer* to *Burnham* and Back Again", 24 *U. C. Davis L. Rev.* 19, at 104 (1990).

to enact such statutes, subject only to due-process constraints that set outer limits to claims of adjudicatory authority. With those constraints removed, no doubt greater simplicity and predictability could be achieved by opening ever wider the courthouse door. Whether solutions along these lines would be "sensible" is, however, debatable.

A basic obstacle to the enactment of "sensible" state legislation is the understandable reluctance of states to give up assertive jurisdictional practices unless, by and large, others are prepared to show similar self-restraint. Plaintiffs' attorneys constitute a pressure group that favors taking jurisdiction to the fullest extent constitutionally permitted because the plaintiffs' forum-selecting opportunities increase – as does the potential for a successful outcome on the merits and generous recoveries – as a function of the number of legal orders among which the plaintiff can choose in deciding where to bring his case. Individual states acting independently are functionally incapable of doing what is ultimately needed: deciding for all putative forums the jurisdictional bases that should be recognized in view of the respective litigational situation of various categories of plaintiffs and defendants, of the adjudicator's task, and of the legitimate concerns of the legal orders with which the parties and the controversy are connected. Individual states may conclude that certain jurisdictional claims are exorbitant and forego them; a state is not likely to abstain, however, from the use of marginal bases even though more appropriate – or "sensible" – bases are available which, in a global assessment of both parties' situation, fairly accommodate the plaintiff's litigational needs and set appropriate limits to his forum-selecting advantage.

For international controversies, the executive, legislative, and judicial branches of the federal government are in a better position than their state counterparts to make and implement appropriate choices regarding these matters. What is needed could best be accomplished through conventions implemented by federal legislation. The question remains, of course, whether and when the wisdom, will, energy, and determination will be found to address these difficult and particularly sensitive tasks.

The federal structure of the legal system of the United States has, since *Erie R.R. Co.* v. *Tompkins*,[48] resulted in non-procedural[49] state law applying in diversity cases to recognition and enforcement of internationally foreign judgments regardless whether the matter is litigated in a federal or a state court. A considerable effort has been made to harmonize the states' laws respecting such matters. Over half of the states have adopted the Uniform Foreign Money Judgments Rec-

---

48   304 US 64 (1938). Under *Swift* v. *Tyson*, 41 US 1 (1842), recognition and enforcement of foreign judgments was for federal – but not state – courts a matter of federal common law. For a discussion of *Swift* and *Erie*, see Chap. V. E. 3. *(b)* (ii) *b*, pp. 249 *et seq.*, *infra*.

49   "Non-procedural law" for *Erie* purposes comprises rules that are not "outcome determinative". See Chap. V. E. 3. *(b)* (ii) *b*, pp. 250-251, *infra*.

ognition Act;[50] others apply the Act's principles as their common law. Significant differences remain, however, in state recognition law; for example, some states impose a reciprocity requirement while others do not, and the jurisdictional requirements for recognition and enforcement vary considerably. In the last half of the twentieth century, American awareness of the complexities of the problems presented has deepened. Federal rules and principles now seem destined to play a far more significant role in the new century than they did in the past.

Perhaps the best example of what an international instrument implemented by a federal statute can accomplish in federalizing the law of jurisdiction and recognition is the United Nations Convention on the Recognition and Enforcement of Foreign Arbitral Awards of 1958 and its implementing legislation contained in Chapter 2, §§201-208, of the Federal Arbitration Act. The federalizing treaty *cum* federal-implementing-legislation approach has been effectively used as well for the 1980 Hague Convention on the Civil Aspects of International Child Abduction[51] and the 1993 Hague Convention on Protection of Children and Co-Operation in Respect of Country Adoption.[52]

The work that began in 1996 at The Hague on a draft jurisdiction and enforcement convention has served to concentrate the minds of American jurists on the complexities and shortcomings of the traditional American approach to the handling of jurisdictional and enforcement issues in international litigation. In mid-1999 the American Law Institute resolved to explore how a Hague Convention dealing with such matters might best be implemented[53] and, should The Hague fail to produce an acceptable convention, what federal action might accomplish on its own by a statute that federalized various aspects of American law regarding recognition and enforcement of foreign judgments. In the course of the discussions and in light of the diminishing prospect of a successful outcome of The Hague negotiations, support for proposing a federal statute on the recognition and enforcement of internationally foreign judgments, which would replace the Uniform Foreign Country Money-Judgments Act, has grown. A Discussion

---

50   13 Pt. II ULA 39 (2002). As of 2006 in force in Alaska, California, Colorado, Connecticut, Delaware, District of Columbia, Florida, Georgia, Hawaii, Idaho, Illinois, Iowa, Maine, Maryland, Massachusetts, Michigan, Minnesota, Missouri, Montana, New Jersey, New Mexico, New York, North Carolina, North Dakota, Ohio, Oklahoma, Oregon, Pennsylvania, Texas, Virgin Islands, Virginia, and Washington. See *idem*, 2006 Cumulative Annual Pocket Part, at 20. Meanwhile, a revision of the Uniform Foreign Money-Judgments Recognition Act is under way. See *idem* 2006 Cumulative Annual Pocket Part, at 5.

51   Ch. 121 of the Public Health and Welfare Code, 42 USC §§11601-11610.

52   Ch. 143 of the Public Health and Welfare Code, 42 USC §§14901-14954.

53   The Jurisdiction and Judgments Project was approved in May 1999. See The American Law Institute, International Jurisdiction and Judgments Project, Report (14 April 2000), *passim* (American Law Institute, Philadelphia, 2000); L. Silberman and A. Lowenfeld, "A Different Challenge for the ALI: Herein of Foreign Country Judgments, an International Treaty, and an American Statute", 75 *Indiana L . J.* 635-647 (2000).

Draft of such federal legislation was published in 2002,[54] followed by revised Drafts, presented to the ALI Annual Meetings in 2003,[55] 2004[56] and 2005,[57] which, *inter alia*, introduced a reciprocity requirement.[58] The Uniform Foreign Money-Judgments Recognition Act does not contain a reciprocity clause, although some states have added one to their respective adoption of the Uniform Act.[59] By making the recognition and enforcement of foreign judgments dependant upon reciprocity, the Drafters are hoping to create a genuine incentive to foreign countries to commit to recognition and enforcement of comparable judgments rendered by United States courts.[60] In order to simplify the handling of the reciprocity requirement, the proposed Act authorizes the Secretary of State to negotiate agreements with foreign states or groups of states, setting forth reciprocal practices concerning recognition and enforcement of judgments rendered in the United States.[61] With a view to the practice in various foreign countries of denying enforcement to judgments for punitive, exemplary or multiple damages, while enforcing the compensatory portion of such judgment,[62] the proposed legislation makes clear

---

54   The American Law Institute, International Jurisdiction and Judgments Project, Discussion Draft (29 March 2002) (American Law Institute, Philadelphia, 2002).

55   The American Law Institute, International Jurisdiction and Judgments Project, Tentative Draft (14 April 2003) (American Law Institute, Philadelphia, 2003).

56   The American Law Institute, International Jurisdiction and Judgments Project, Tentative Draft No. 2 (13 April 2004) (American Law Institute, Philadelphia, 2004). For an outline of the 2004 Draft see Miller, *supra* footnote 44, at 270-287; L. Silberman, "The Impact of Jurisdictional Rules and Recognition Practice on International Business Transactions: The U.S. Regime", 29 *Hous. J. Int'l L.* 327, at 359-361 (2004).

57   The American Law Institute, Recognition and Enforcement of Foreign Judgments: Analysis and Proposed Federal Statute, Proposed Final Draft (11 April 2005) (American Law Institute, Philadelphia, 2005).

58   The American Law Institute, *supra* footnote 57, §7 (1), at 91 and Comment on §7, at 93-97. See for a critical assessment of the reciprocity requirement Miller, *supra* footnote 44, at 287-318.

59   See The American Law Institute, *supra* footnote 57, Reporters' Notes on §7, at 99.

60   See The American Law Institute, *supra* footnote 57, Comment on §7, at 94.

61   See The American Law Institute, *supra* footnote 57, §7 (e), at 92-93.

62   For Germany see BGH, 4 June 1992, 118 *BGHZ* 312; for England *Lewis* v. *Eliades*, [2004] 1 WLR 692 (Court of Appeal). The Court of Appeal's case, decided under the UK Protection of Trading Interests Act 1980, differs slightly from the German case in that it concerned a composite US judgment, consisting of a treble damages award under the RICO Act, and a purely compensatory award of damages for breach of fiduciary duty and fraud. The Court of Appeal held that the non-enforceability of the RICO claim did not infect the enforcement of the basic compensatory award under common law rules, pointing out, however, (per Lord Jacob, at para. 62 of the judgment) that it did not deal with the enforceability of the compensatory part of a multiplied award.

that partial non-recognition of United States judgments of this kind shall not be regarded as denial of reciprocal enforcement as required by the Act.[63]

The federal structure of procedural and substantive law in the United States resulted in a complex allocation of enforcement jurisdiction over foreign judgments.

If the recognizability and enforceability of internationally foreign judgments were to be regulated by treaty or by federal legislation, the federal courts could be given by statute jurisdiction over actions that raise these issues.

Presently, such actions can be brought in federal courts only where there is diversity of citizenship and the amount-in-controversy requirement is satisfied. (Of course, litigation predicated on federal question jurisdiction can recognize – and thus in the broad sense enforce – internationally foreign judgments.) Federal-court jurisdiction, provided for actions brought to enforce internationally foreign judgments, could either be shared with state courts or limited to federal courts.[64] Where jurisdiction is shared, the ALI Reporters recommend that removal to federal courts of actions brought in state courts should be provided for where the plaintiff seeks to enforce a foreign judgment or the defendant seeks recognition for a foreign judgment offered as a defense by way of preclusion to the plaintiff's action.[65]

2. Germany

(a) Introductory

The United States remains a federal union whose states have large authority to determine, among other important issues, when their courts may exercise adjudicatory authority. The substantial degree of autonomy enjoyed by the American states over matters as well of private law as of administration of justice, combined with the systemic effects of judicial review under the Constitution of the United States, lead to claims of adjudicatory authority to the constitutionally permissible extent. As a result, the principles that shape contemporary American jurisdictional practices, especially those regarding adjudicatory authority in the international sense, are largely a product of federal and state case-law applying federal constitutional standards.

The German situation is fundamentally different. Modern Germany achieved political unity in 1871; with respect to adjudicatory authority, the Reich was – and the Bundesrepublik remains – a centralized rather than a federal State. Until the

---

63   The American Law Institute, *supra* footnote 57, §7 (d), at 92.

64   In view of the heavy work-load of the federal courts, it is clear that their jurisdiction over foreign judgments would – just as is jurisdiction over non-domestic arbitration covered by the New York Convention (see Chap. V. E. 3. *(b)* (ii), p. 246 *passim* and Chap. V. E. 4., pp. 256 *et seq. passim, infra*) – be shared with state courts.

65   See The American Law Institute, *supra* footnote 53, xvii-xviii; at 21-23. §8 of the 2005 Draft now incorporates the general removal procedures and time limits of 28 U.S.C. §1446(b).

1970s, German jurisdictional rules and principles were essentially designed by the national executive and legislature.

So far as matters involving the European Union – but not the rest of the world – are concerned, the Brussels Convention and Regulation have largely replaced the Code of Civil Procedure's jurisdictional norms; in the foreseeable future, within the Union, the German and other national governments are likely, so far as design is concerned, to be increasingly displaced by European Union authorities, especially the Commission.

(b) The German Code of Civil Procedure (1877): Executive and legislative design

(i) The original design

The brief survey that follows discusses features of the Code of Civil Procedure's jurisdictional norms crafted through a process in which representatives of the Reich's constituent *Länder* controlled the drafting and their product was then approved, with relatively few changes, by the national legislature.[66]

Drafting in the 1870s at a time when German economic and social life was relatively localized, jurists saw little need to provide theoretical explanations or justifications for the exercise of adjudicatory authority in non-local matters.

Moreover, the German judges of the period were comfortable in their role as expounders and appliers of the relevant statutory provisions.

The Constitution of the Reich (1871) had given the federal government broad powers in various fields, including civil procedure, the organization of courts, bankruptcy, criminal law, and criminal procedure.[67] In 1877, the Code of Civil Procedure (*Zivilprozeßordnung*, originally spelled *Civilprocessordnung*) was enacted.[68] This national legislation, administered by a judicial system headed, where private-law matters were in question, by a national supreme court (the *Reichsgeri-*

---

66   For general discussion in English of the ZPO's procedural system see B. Kaplan, A. von Mehren and R. Schaefer, "Phases of German Civil Procedure I & II", 71 *Harv. L. Rev.* 1193-1268, 1443-1472 (1958); A. von Mehren and J. Gordley, *The Civil Law System* 148-208 (Boston, MA & Toronto, Little Brown, 2nd ed., 1977); A. von Mehren, "Some Comparative Reflections on First Instance Civil Procedure: Recent Reforms in German Civil Procedure and in the Federal Rules", 63 *Notre Dame L. Rev.* 609-627 (1988); J. Langbein, "The German Advantage in Civil Procedure", 52 *U. Chi. L. Rev.* 823-866 (1985); R. Allen, S. Köck, K. Reichenberg and D. Rosen, "The German Advantage in Civil Procedure: A Plea for More Details and Fewer Generalities in Comparative Scholarship", 82 *Northwestern U. L. Rev.* 705-762 (1988); J. Langbein, "Trashing the German Advantage", *idem* 763-784; R. Allen, "Idealization and Caricature in Comparative Scholarship", *idem* 785-807; P. Murray and R. Stürner, *German Civil Justice* (Durham, N.C., Carolina Academic Press, 2004).

67   Under the Constitution, the federal power extended to commercial law, bills of exchange, and obligations. In 1873, the Constitution was amended to give the federal Government power over virtually the entire field of private law.

68   The same year also saw the enactment of the Law Governing the Organization of the Courts *(Gerichtsverfassungsgesetz)*, the Code of Criminal Procedure *(Strafprozeßord-*

cht, later the *Bundesgerichtshof*), and supplemented since 1973 first by the Brussels Convention and, since 2002, by the Brussels Regulation,[69] contains the basic provisions on which rest contemporary German thinking and practice respecting jurisdiction to adjudicate in the international sense. Although in some areas the Code has undergone significant changes, relatively few have touched jurisdiction to adjudicate.[70] When the Code was drafted, only a limited body of German theory and practice specifically addressed jurisdiction to adjudicate in the international sense;[71] neither reflection nor experience had made clear the role and significance of adjudicatory jurisdiction in the international sense[72] and a sharp distinction was yet to be made between it and venue – the territorial allocation of litigation among domestic courts.

Under the inclusive term *"allgemeiner Gerichtsstand"*, the Code treats venue and jurisdiction together and, for the most part, in the same way. This unitary approach was so self evident for the drafters that neither through explicit statement nor terminology does the ZPO make clear to the uninitiated that provisions such as §12 apply, at one and the same time, to venue *(örtliche Zuständigkeit)* and to adjudicatory authority in the international sense *(internationale Zuständigkeit)*. ZPO §12 reads as follows:

> *Concept of allgemeiner Gerichtsstand (general jurisdiction).* The court, where a person has his *allgemeiner Gerichtsstand*, is competent *(zuständig)* for all actions brought against him except where an exclusive *Gerichtsstand* is provided for the action.

ZPO §13 continues: "General jurisdiction over a person is at his *Wohnsitz* (dwelling place)." As a purely textual matter, §§12 and 13 could be read as applicable to venue alone, or to international jurisdiction alone, or to both. The same ambiguity is displayed by the great majority of the *Gerichtsstand* provisions that came into force in 1879. Except for §606a, which explicitly applies exclusively to interna-

---

nung), and the Bankruptcy Law *(Konkursordnung*, as of 1 January 1999 replaced by the Insolvency Law, *Insolvenzordnung).*

The ZPO was revised – mostly in technical respects – in 1898 to harmonize it with the German Civil Code *(Bürgerliches Gesetzbuch)* that entered into force on 1 January 1900.

69   See D. 3. *(b)* (ii), pp. 72 *et seq., infra.*

70   On the most significant of these changes see Chap. V. D. 2. *(c)* (ii) *c*, pp. 222 *et seq.*, on the reform of §§38–40, and Chap. III. B. 4. *(d)*, pp. 139 *et seq.*, on §32a, *infra.*

71   Pfeiffer speaks of "the lack of a developed doctrine of international procedural law". T. Pfeiffer, *Internationale Zuständigkeit und prozessuale Gerechtigkeit*, at 74 (Frankfurt am Main, Klostermann, 1995).

72   J. Kropholler, "Internationale Zuständigkeit", in *Handbuch des Internationalen Zivilverfahrensrechts*, Vol. I, Chap. 3, No. 31, at 211, (Tübingen, Mohr Siebeck, 1982).

tional jurisdiction,[73] the ZPO regulates the two matters together and in the same manner.[74]

(ii) The gradual increase in the importance of the courts

In 1965, the Bundesgerichtshof first specifically addressed the difference between venue and jurisdiction:[75]

> [V]enue and jurisdiction in the international sense remain different things: Venue entails allocation of litigation between German courts of first instance; jurisdiction in

---

73 See *infra* footnote 74.

74 Pfeiffer speaks of the "original complete linking of venue with international jurisdiction." See Pfeiffer, *supra* footnote 71, at 74.
Provisions such as §§15, 16, 23, and 27, para. 2, make clear the legislator's intention to regulate jurisdiction and venue together. The ZPO's conflation of these matters is not limited to §§12-37. The issues are not distinguished in the provisions – §606 (old and new version alike) – regulating the *Gerichtsstand* for actions respecting marriage *(Ehesachen)*, including divorce, nor in the provision – §642 – applicable to actions to establish the legal relation between parents and children.
Jurists first began in the 1950s to distinguish between the venue and the jurisdictional effects of Code provisions respecting *Gerichtsstand*. ZPO §606b, enacted in 1957 – (BGBl. I 1957, 609) – appears to have been the first ZPO provision that standard commentaries explicitly characterized as jurisdictional in nature. It addressed *Ehesachen*-actions in which neither spouse was a German national. As printed in successive editions of the well-known Baumbach and Lauterbach Commentary, beginning with the 25th edition in 1958, §606b carried the unofficial heading: *Internationale Zuständigkeit* (jurisdiction in the international sense).
Prior to the enactment of §606b, the term "Internationale Zuständigkeit", though not used as a heading, had occasionally appeared in commentaries upon the earlier – but identical – provisions of ZPO §606, para. 3. See, e.g., R. Zöller, *Zivilprozeßordnung* 416 (Munich, W. Stutz, 8th ed., 1957). After the enactment of §606b, commentators were slow to follow the lead of Baumbach and Lauterbach and adopt "Internationale Zuständigkeit" as the heading for the new section. For example, Zöller preferred "Zuständigkeit für Ausländer" (jurisdiction for foreigners). See Zöller, *supra*, at 435 (Munich, W. Stutz, 9th ed., 1958). Thomas and Putzo used "Grenzen der deutschen Zuständigkeit" (limits to German jurisdiction). See H. Thomas and H. Putzo (Munich, C. H. Beck, 2nd ed., 1965). Perhaps the first commentary to follow Baumbach and Lauterbach was Thomas and Putzo in 1968. See H. Thomas and H. Putzo, *supra* (3rd ed., 1968). The Zöller commentary followed suit in its 11th edition of 1974.
In 1986, after having been held unconstitutional by the Constitutional Court, §606b was repealed. Its operative language, in an amended version, formed part of a revised §606a, which regulated comprehensively the jurisdiction of German courts in actions involving matrimonial matters *(Ehesachen)*. The revised section now bears the heading "Jurisdiction in the International Sense" *(Internationale Zuständigkeit)*, which – since the Reform of Civil Procedure Law of 27 July 2001, BGBl. 1887 – is 'official' *(amtlich)*.

75 BGH, *Großer Senat für Zivilsachen*, 14 June 1965, 44 *BGHZ* 46. See for a more detailed discussion of this decision Chap. III. B. 5. *(a)* (i), pp. 142 *et seq.*, *infra*.

the international sense, on the other hand, determines whether a litigation with connections abroad should be decided by German or by foreign courts.[76]

The court went on to analyze the differing interests and policies underlying provisions respecting venue and jurisdiction[77] and, in general, reaffirmed the traditional position of German law: "Insofar as a German court has venue according to [ZPO §§12 *et seq.*], under German law it has also jurisdiction."[78]

Conflation of venue and jurisdiction to adjudicate in the international sense suggests to judges and lawyers that each presents the same level of difficulty and involves comparable policies. The relatively late emergence in Germany, as compared with the United States, of theory specifically respecting jurisdiction is attributable, at least in part, to a failure to realize that venue and adjudicatory authority in the international sense are quite different problems. Courts and jurists might well have been more inclined to critique the Code's jurisdictional rules had they stood alone.

On the other hand, linking venue and international jurisdiction closely ensured that the German system would, for purposes of jurisdiction in the international sense, in principle treat foreign and German parties alike. The Code of Civil Procedure proceeded on the "basic proposition of non-discrimination between locals and foreigners with respect to *Gerichtsstand* ...".[79] Only in rare special cases – e.g., those involving a deserted German wife seeking a divorce or declaration of incapacity *(Entmündigungsklagen)* – did "the Draft ... [make] a few exceptions from the general rule [of equal treatment of locals and of foreigners] in favor of the former".[80]

3.   *The Brussels and Lugano Conventions and the Brussels Regulation*

(a)   Introductory: The influence of European integration

Over the past three decades, Western European theory and practice respecting jurisdiction to adjudicate in the international sense have been shaped increasingly by the process of European integration. Today, no court of a Member State of the

---

76   *Idem* 47. In a recent decision the Bundesgerichtshof affirmed the difference between jurisdiction in the international sense and venue: "Jurisdiction in the international sense is of far greater importance [than venue]. It concerns the delineation (*Abgrenzung*) to the sovereignty rights of other States. The issue is to what extent German courts can, in controversies with an international element, claim for themselves adjudicatory authority." See BGH, 28 November 2002, 56 *NJW* 426, at 427 (2003) and Chapter III. B. 5. *(a)* (i), pp. 144 *et seq., infra.*

77   *Idem* 48-52. See also BGH, 28 November 2002, 56 *NJW* 426, at 427 (2003) and Chap. III. B. 5. *(a)* (i), pp. 144 *et seq., infra.*

78   *Idem* 47.

79   C. Hahn (continued by B. Mugdan), *Die gesammten Materialien zu den Reichs-Justizgesetzen*, Vol. II/1, at 149 (Berlin, R. v. Decker's Verlag, 1881).

80   *Idem* 150.

European Union or of the European Free Trade Association can decide jurisdictional issues in civil or commercial disputes involving parties domiciled in different Western or Central European States solely on the basis of its national rules of jurisdiction. Judges, many with little training in international law, must apply the Brussels Convention and Regulation and the Lugano Convention and, on occasion, engage in comparative-law analysis in interpreting these instruments' provisions. Their importance for international civil litigation is well understood. A considerable literature discusses them and substantial commentaries serve practitioners and scholars.[81]

The Brussels Convention is without doubt one of the most successful treaties ever concluded dealing with private international law. It has, for better or worse, led to a major shift of power over the design of jurisdictional rules from national legislatures to Union executive and judicial authorities, in particular, the European Court of Justice and the Council and Commission of the European Union. A growing number of Member States of the Union have, moreover, revised their national rules of civil procedure to conform with the Brussels Convention and Regulation, thereby creating an increasingly harmonized body of law respecting both jurisdiction to adju-dicate in the international sense and recognition and enforcement of foreign judgments.[82]

The success of the Brussels instruments rests in large part on their character as a convention or, respectively, a Regulation, that provides rules respecting both jurisdiction to adjudicate in the international sense and recognition and enforcement,[83] their supremacy over conflicting national laws of civil procedure, including those respecting bases of jurisdiction regarded as exorbitant, and its autonomous interpretation by a supranational body, the European Court of Justice. These qualities serve the instruments' overarching goal, "to facilitate as far as possible the free movement of judgments".[84] The broader philosophy behind this goal and the adoption and subsequent revision of the Brussels and Lugano Conventions are considered below.

---

81 For a comparative review of leading commentaries, see H. Schack, "Die Gerichts-stands- und Vollstreckungsübereinkommen von Brüssel und Lugano: Eine Übersicht über aktuelle monographische Werke", 7 *ZEuP* 783-796 (1999).

82 For a discussion of the Brussels Convention's influence on national codes of civil procedure, see J. Kropholler, *Europäisches Zivilprozeßrecht* (Frankfurt am Main, Verlag Recht und Wirtschaft, 8th ed., 2005), Einl. No. 18.

83 The characteristics of single, double, and mixed conventions are discussed in Chap. VII. B. 1., pp. 355 *et seq., infra.*

84 For the Brussels Convention see Report by P. Jenard on the Convention of 27 September 1968 on jurisdiction and the enforcement of judgments in civil and commercial matters (Jenard Report), [1979] OJ C 59, 1, at 42. The original version of the Report in French was disseminated in 1967 as an unpublished mimeograph.

(b)   The emergence of a European legal regime for jurisdiction and the recognition and enforcement of foreign judgments

(i)   The Brussels and Lugano Conventions

On 22 October 1959, the European Economic Community's Commission sent a note to the Community's six Member States (Belgium, France, the Federal Republic of Germany, Italy, Luxembourg, and the Netherlands), inviting them to negotiate a convention on jurisdiction and the recognition and enforcement of foreign judgments. The Commission stated that

> a true internal market between the six [Member] States will be achieved only if adequate legal protection can be secured. The economic life of the Community may be subject to disturbances and difficulties unless it is possible, where necessary by judicial means, to ensure the recognition and enforcement of the various rights arising from the existence of a multiplicity of legal relationships. As jurisdiction in both civil and commercial matters is derived from the sovereignty of Member States, and since the effect of judicial acts is confined to each territory, legal protection and, hence, legal certainty in the common market are essentially dependent on the adoption by the Member States of a satisfactory solution to the problem of recognition and enforcement of judgments.[85]

A committee, consisting of delegates from the six Member States and observers from, among others, the Hague Conference on Private International Law, was promptly established and charged with drafting an intergovernmental Convention based on Article 220 of the Treaty establishing the European Community (EC Treaty) (now Article 293).[86] Paul Jenard, Director in the Belgian Ministry of Foreign Affairs and External Trade, was appointed *rapporteur* and entrusted with the task of providing an explanatory report in the form of a commentary on the draft Convention.[87]

The Convention was signed in Brussels on 27 September 1968 by Belgium, France, the Federal Republic of Germany, Italy, Luxembourg and the Netherlands and entered into force on 1 February 1973.[88] To ensure its uniform interpretation,

---

85   See *idem* 3.

86   Pursuant to Article 293 of the EC Treaty, "Member States shall, so far as is necessary, enter into negotiations with each other with a view to securing for the benefit of their nationals: ... the simplification of formalities governing the reciprocal recognition and enforcement of judgments of courts or tribunals and of arbitral awards."

87   The report was first published in French for the purposes of the committee of experts. Its official publication in the OJ, including an English version of the text, did not take place until 1979, see *supra* footnote 84.

88   In 1968, no country for which English was an official language was party to the Treaty of Rome; accordingly, an official English text of the Convention was not prepared at the time. An unofficial English text was published in the EC Bulletin, [1969] *EC Bulletin*, Supp. No. 2, at 17. In 1978, an official English version of the 1968 Convention was published in the Official Journal of the European Communities, [1978] OJ L 304, 36.

the Contracting States conferred jurisdiction to interpret the Convention on the European Court of Justice by a Protocol to the Convention that entered into force on 1 September 1975.

The 1968 text of the Convention has been amended four times, each triggered by an enlargement of the European Community: 9 October 1978, on the accession of Denmark, Ireland, and the United Kingdom; 25 October 1982, on the accession of Greece; 26 May 1989, on the accession of Spain and Portugal; and 29 November 1996, on the accession of Austria, Finland, and Sweden.[89] The new Member States, in particular the United Kingdom, accepted the Brussels Convention and its sometimes unfamiliar or alien structure as part of a package deal in order to obtain the advantage of membership in an emerging economic and political union. There is no doubt that the Convention would be different in many respects had the United Kingdom, with its distinct legal tradition, been at the negotiating table from the outset.

Official reports cover each stage of the Convention's evolution except the last. Two reports are of particular interest and significance: the already mentioned Jenard Report[90] (covering the 1968 Convention and the Protocol on Interpretation by the EC Court of Justice) and the Schlosser Report[91] (on the accession of Denmark, Ireland, and the United Kingdom).[92] The former contains important general discussions respecting the purpose and nature of the Convention as well as detailed guidelines with regard to the interpretation of the original text; the latter treats the substantial amendments made necessary, in considerable measure, by the accession of common-law countries.

In the early 1980s, seeing the continuing economic success of European integration, other European countries that, for various reasons, had not aspired to an "ever closer union among the peoples of Europe"[93] but preferred to preserve their political independence, felt the need to facilitate trade both with the European Community and among themselves. As part of a series of measures abolishing restrictions on trade, the then Member States of the European Free Trade Association (Finland, Iceland, Norway, Austria, Sweden, and Switzerland) and the Member States of the European Community concluded the Lugano Convention on 16 September 1988.[94] This Convention, complemented by an explanatory report prepared by Jenard and Möller,[95] is almost identical with the contemporaneous text of the Brussels Convention. The principal difference between the two Con-

---

89   A consolidated version of the text was published in [1998] OJ C 27, 1.

90   See *supra* footnote 84.

91   [1979] OJ C 59, 71-151.

92   The other two reports are the Evrigenis and Kerameus Report (on the Greek accession), [1986] OJ C 298, 1-27, and the Almeida Cruz, Desantes Real and Jenard Report (on the Spanish-Portuguese accession), [1990] OJ C 189, 35-56.

93   See the Preamble of the EC Treaty.

94   [1988] OJ L 319, 9.

95   [1990] OJ C 189, 57.

ventions concerns their interpretation: while the European Court of Justice gives, as a final arbiter, binding rulings on the interpretation of the Brussels Convention and the Regulation, no comparable supranational institution is available under the Lugano Convention. Lugano, "[c]onsidering the substantial link between [it] ... and the Brussels Convention", refers in the Preamble of a Protocol to the jurisprudence of the European Court of Justice and expresses the desire to "arrive at as uniform an interpretation as possible of the provisions of the [Lugano] Convention ... and of the Brussels Convention".[96] In practice, the national courts of the Lugano countries have followed closely the jurisprudence of the European Court of Justice.[97]

Following the accession in 1995 to the European Union of former EFTA members Finland, Sweden, and Austria, the Lugano Convention lost some of its significance in Western Europe. For a brief period, Lugano appeared to gain new ground as States of Central and Eastern Europe were preparing for the enlargement of the European Union in 2004.[98] Accession to the Lugano Convention represented, for these States, an interim step on their way to becoming Member States of the European Union. The renewed importance of the Lugano Convention proved, however, to be short-lived and rather limited in scope. Of the ten Central and Eastern European States that acquired the full Membership of the EU on May 1, 2004, only Poland acceded to the Lugano Convention prior to joining the Union and thereby becoming a Member State of the Brussels Regulation.[99]

(ii)   "Communitarization" of the conflict of laws: The Brussels Regulation

Beginning in 1973, the basis for judicial co-operation in Europe became an international convention – concluded in Brussels – based on Article 220 of the EC

---

96   See the Preamble of Protocol No. 2 on the Uniform Interpretation of the Convention, [1988] OJ L 319, 29.

97   See Kropholler, *supra* footnote 82, Einl. Nos. 59-66; H. Bull, G. Musger and F. Pocar, "Second Report on National Case Law on the Lugano Convention", 22 *IPRax* 315-326 (2002); E. Jayme and Ch. Kohler, "Europäisches Kollisionsrecht 2005: Hegemonialgesten auf dem Weg zu einer Gesamtvereinheitlichung", 25 *IPRax* 481, at 492 (2005).

98   For a discussion of the Polish accession to the Lugano Convention see D. Martiny and U. Ernst, "Der Beitritt Polens zum Luganer Übereinkommen", 21 *IPRax* 29-31 (2001).

99   The reluctance of the majority of the candidate States – and a corresponding hesitance of their EU counterparts – to join the Lugano Convention can, at least in part, be explained by the complicated accession process that such a step would entail and by the fact that Lugano was not designed for accession by non-EFTA-States. See H. Heiss and A. Suprón-Heidel, "EU Enlargement: Aspects of (International) Procedural Law", 4 *European Journal of Law Reform* 147 (2002), at 150-154. The (technical) changes to the Brussels Regulation necessitated by the accession of the ten new Member States were implemented by Annex II to the Act concerning the accession of the new Member States and the adjustments to the Treaties on which the European Union is founded, Chapter 18. A. 3, [2003] OJ L 236, 33, at 715-718.

Treaty[100] (now Article 293). The Maastricht Treaty, as ratified in 1993, brought judicial co-operation within the competence of the Justice and Home Affairs Pillar of the European Union (the so-called third pillar). Relying on this pillar, the European Commission began preparatory work in 1996 on a substantial revision of the Brussels Convention. At first, only amendment was contemplated. After the Treaty of Amsterdam entered into force in 1997, the Commission became more ambitious. Amsterdam amended Article 65 of the EC Treaty[101] to give the Community, *inter alia*, competence for "improving and simplifying: ... the recognition and enforcement of decisions in civil and commercial cases, including decisions in extrajudicial cases". Whether this language was intended to provide a broad basis for regulating jurisdiction to adjudicate in the international sense is arguable.[102] The Commission has, however, repeatedly shown its determination to read the Justice and Home Affairs Pillar as establishing Union authority over large areas of private international law. In the Commission's view, the Community now has competence to adopt regulations pursuant to Article 65 and thus "communitarize" private international law.[103]

In the spring of 1999, the European Commission proposed that the Brussels Convention be replaced by a Council Regulation on the basis of Article 65 of the EC Treaty.[104] After various amendments were agreed, the Council of the European Union adopted the Brussels Regulation on 22 December 2000;[105] it entered into force on 1 March 2002. The Regulation supersedes, as its Article 68 provides, the Brussels Convention, except as regards those territories of the Member States

---

100   For some time it seemed as if the EC Treaty was soon to be replaced by the Treaty Establishing a Constitution for Europe, [2004] OJ C 310, 1. However, after the French and the Dutch did not approve of the Constitution in the referendums of 29 May 2005 and 1 June 2005, the chances that the Constitution will ever become effective are very low.

101   Article III-269 of the European Constitution. See for the chances of the Constitution to enter into force *supra*, note 100.

102   See Ch. Kohler, "Interrogations sur les sources du droit international privé européen après le traité d'Amsterdam", 88 *Rev. crit. dr. int. priv.* 1 (1998).

103   See J. Basedow, "The Communitarization of the Conflict of Laws under the Treaty of Amsterdam", 37 *Common Market L. Rev.* 687-708 (2000). Article III-269 of the European Constitution, while, for the most part, closely following the wording of Article 65 of the EC Treaty, appears to grant even broader powers to the Union since it is no longer a requirement that the measures taken are necessary for the proper functioning of the internal market. However, for the reasons given *supra* note 100, it is unlikely that the Constitution will ever enter into force.

104   See Proposal for a Council Regulation (EC) on jurisdiction and the recognition and enforcement of judgments in civil and commercial matters, COM (1999) 348 final.

105   Council Regulation (EC) No 44/2001 of 22 December 2000 on jurisdiction and the recognition and enforcement of judgments in civil and commercial matters, [2001] OJ L 12, 1-23.

that are excluded pursuant to Article 299 of the EC Treaty,[106] and, more importantly, as regards the relations between Denmark and the other Member States
(Article 1, para. 3). The latter exception, which could give rise to serious complications, follows from a Protocol to the Treaty on the European Union, which
exempts Denmark from certain measures taken by the Union.[107]

At least for the time being, the Convention thus remains in force as regards
the relations between Denmark and the other Member States; however, a new
Convention with Denmark, which would reflect the provisions of the Regulation,
is under way.[108] Similarly, in order to ensure parallelism and conformity of judgments in the EFTA countries, the Lugano Convention will have to be revised.[109]

Rules on jurisdiction and the recognition and enforcement of judgments
in civil and commercial matters governed by a Community legal instrument are
part of the *"acquis communautaire"*, which largely ensures their adoption by new
Member States. It should be noted that the jurisdiction of the European Court of
Justice to give rulings interpreting the Brussels Regulation now follows directly
from Article 234 of the EC Treaty[110] (formerly Article 177) rather than from a
separate Protocol conferring jurisdiction.

(c)   The philosophy of European integration

The Brussels Convention and Regulation should be considered and understood
in the broader context of European integration. They are part of an historic attempt to transcend national borders and create an economic – and, increasingly,
political – union. The basic assumption is that the Member States, at least for the
purposes of trade, are to be treated as a single entity. As Jenard put it in his report
on the 1968 Brussels Convention:

---

106   Article IV-440 of the European Constitution. See for the chances of the Constitution
to enter into force *supra* note 100.

107   A public referendum held in Denmark on 2 June 1992 had rejected the Treaty. It was
only after the other Member States accepted the Danish opt-outs specified in the
Protocol that Denmark eventually approved the Treaty by public referendum on 18
May 1993.

108   See the Council Decision of 27 April 2006 concerning the conclusion of the Agreement between the European Community and the Kingdom of Denmark on jurisdiction and the recognition and enforcement of judgments in civil and commercial
matters, [2006] OJ L 120, 22.

109   The revision process has been delayed due to a controversy as to whether it is for the
EC alone to sign the revised convention or whether it is the subject of a "mixed" competence of both the EC and the Member States. The question has been referred to the
European Court of Justice by the EC Council on 5 March 2003 under the procedure
devised in Article 300 (6) of the EC Treaty, [2003] OJ C 101, 1. On 7 February 2006
the Court gave the opinion that "[t]he conclusion of the new Lugano Convention ...
falls entirely within the sphere of exclusive competence of the European Community"
(Opinion 1/03).

110   Article III-365 of the European Constitution. See for the chances of the Constitution
to enter into force *supra*, note 100.

Underlying the Convention is the idea that the Member States of the European Economic Community wanted to set up a common market with characteristics similar to those of a vast internal market. Everything possible must therefore be done not only to eliminate any obstacles to the functioning of this market, but also to promote its development. From this point of view, the territory of the Contracting States may be regarded as forming a single entity ...[111]

Seeking "to facilitate as far as possible the free movement of judgments"[112] within this entity, the Brussels Convention reduced the number of grounds that could preclude the recognition and enforcement of judgments and, at the same time, simplified the enforcement procedure in the Member States. Where jurisdiction to adjudicate is concerned, the philosophy of economic integration and judicial co-operation has led to the adoption of rules intended to be easily administered and highly predictable. An examination of the case law of the European Court of Justice suggests that these goals have, on occasion, proved difficult to achieve.[113] The drafters sought to provide "a genuine legal systematization which will ensure the greatest possible degree of legal certainty".[114] They were not interested in maintaining distinct legal traditions nor, for the most part, in securing the national interests of the Contracting Parties; such preoccupations were inconsistent with the philosophy of the common market as a single entity.

Mutual trust and reliance on the capacity of each other's courts are more easily achieved among States that share values and traditions, aspire to an ever closer union, and undertake to harmonize not only jurisdiction and the recognition and enforcement of foreign judgments but many other areas of the law as well. In this respect, one should note the important link between the unification of rules respecting jurisdiction, on the one hand, and choice-of-law, on the other. Where choice-of-law rules are truly harmonized or unified, "decisional harmony" in the sense of Savigny's teachings (international uniformity of decisions) perhaps is a goal not beyond attainment so that jurisdictional rules can be considered essentially outcome-neutral. The Brussels Convention's faith that the bases of adjudicatory authority it provides can, in practice, be administrable and predictable, has been strengthened by the unification in recent decades of choice-of-law rules in Europe, both through multilateral conventions (such as the Rome Convention

---

111   Jenard Report, *supra* footnote 84, at 13.

112   *Idem* 42.

113   See e.g. the discussion of Article 5 (1), 54, *supra*. For an analysis of divergences in the case-law of the national courts on the interpretation of a number of provisions of the Brussels Regulation see J. Newton, *The Uniform Interpretation of the Brussels and Lugano Convention* (Oxford and Portland, Oregon, Hart Publishing, 2002).

114   Jenard Report, *supra* footnote 84, at 15.

on the Law Applicable to Contractual Obligations[115]) and by Community legislation.[116]

The Treaty of Amsterdam inserted into the EC Treaty a new Title IV conferring, as mentioned above, competence for the harmonization of conflict-of-law rules (Article 65 of the EC Treaty). Significant activity designed to implement what the European Council meeting in Tampere (Finland) in October 1999 called the general "principle of mutual recognition of judgments" is now under way.[117] The Brussels Regulation ("Brussels I) is today but one of a variety of Community instruments promoting greater convergence in the civil procedure laws of the Union's Member States: in 2000 the European Council adopted a Regulation on insolvency proceedings[118] and a Regulation on jurisdiction and the recognition and enforcement of judgments in matrimonial matters and in matters of parental responsibility for children of both spouses ("Brussels II").[119] In 2001 agreement was reached on a "Brussels IIa" Regulation, which significantly extended the scope of application of Brussels II in the field of parental responsibility.[120] In the same year the European

---

115   Plans are currently under way to transform the Rome Convention into a Regulation. See the Proposal for a Regulation of the European Parliament and the Council on the law applicable to contractual obligations ("Rome I"), COM (2005) 650 final.

116   So far, choice-of-law rules have only been enacted by means of secondary legislation as part of certain sector-specific instruments; e.g. Article 6 (2) of the Council Directive 93/13/EEC of 5 April 1993 on unfair terms in consumer contracts, [1993] OJ L 95, 29; for further examples see Max Planck Institute for Foreign Private and Private International Law, "Comments on the European's Green Paper on the conversion of the Rome Convention of 1980 on the law applicable to contractual obligations into a Community instrument and its modernization", 68 *RabelsZ* 1, at 12 (2004). In a more comprehensive effort, the Commission has presented an amended Proposal for a Regulation on the law applicable to non-contractual obligations ("Rome II"), COM (2006) 83 final. In addition, the Commission has proposed rules concerning applicable law in family afairs ("Rome III"). See the Proposal for a Council Regulation amending Regulation (EC) No 2201/2003 as regards jurisdiction and introducing rules concerning applicable law in matrimonial matters, COM (2006) 399 final. See also the proposal for a Council Regulation on jurisdiction, applicable law, recognition and enforcement of decisions and cooperation in matters relating to maintenance obligations, COM (2005) 649 final. See also the Commission's Green paper on conflict of laws in matters concerning matrimonial property regimes, including the question of jurisdiction and mutual recognition, COM (2006) 400 final. A possible further instrument could include community legislation on intestate and testate succession where there is an international dimension ("Rome IV"). See the Commission's Green Paper on succession and wills, COM (2005) 65 final.

117   For a discussion of this principle see W. Kennett, *Enforcement of Judgments in Europe* (Oxford, Oxford University Press, 2000), pp 3-58.

118   Council Regulation (EC) No 1346/2000 ([2000] OJ L 160, 1-13) of 29 May 2000.

119   Council Regulation (EC) No 1347/2000 ([2000] OJ L 160, 19-29) 29 May 2000. Brussels II was originally signed as a Convention ([1998] OJ C 221, 2). See W. Kennett, "The Brussels II Convention", 48 *Int'l & Comp. L. Quart.* 467-473 (1999).

120   Council Regulation (EC) No 2201/2003 ([2003] OJ L 338, 1-29) of 27 November 2003. As of 1 March 2005 the Brussels IIa Regulation has replaced the Brussels II Regula-

Council adopted a "Draft Programme" of measures for implementation of the principle of mutual recognition of decisions in civil and commercial matters.[121]

Another significant milestone on the path towards an ever more swift judicial cooperation is the Regulation on the Creation of a European enforcement order for uncontested claims agreed upon in 2004.[122] The Regulation that has entered into force on 21 October 2005 abolishes the exequatur proceedings for certain categories of "uncontested" claims, including, but not limited to default judgments.[123] Once a decision has been declared a European enforcement order by the originating court, the debtor has no further means of recourse in the State of enforcement.[124] Thus, the task of safe-guarding the defendant's right to a fair trial is entirely left to the court of origin,[125] which is a marked difference to the system of the Brussels Convention and Regulation that retains a minimum of judicial control for the courts in the enforcement state.[126] Other far-reaching measures to be taken in the near future respecting could include community legislation on the

---

tion. See for a detailed discussion of the new regime P. McEleavy, "Brussels II bis: Matrimonial Matters, Parental Responsibility, Child Abduction and Mutual Recognition", 53 *Int'l & Comp. L. Quart.* 503-512 (2004); P. McEleavy "The Communitarization of Divorce Rules: What Impact for English and Scottish Law?", 53 *Int'l & Comp. L. Quart.* 605-642 (2004). See also Chap. I. C. 1. *(b)* (i), pp. 36-37, *supra.*

In the meantime the Commission has issued a proposal for amending Regulation (EC) No 2201/2003. See the Proposal for a Council Regulation amending Regulation (EC) No 2201/2003 as regards jurisdiction and introducing rules concerning applicable law in matrimonial matters, COM (2006) 399 final. The proposal introduces, *inter alia*, a limited possibility for the spouses to designate by common agreement the competent court ("prorogation") in a proceeding relating to divorce and legal separation.

121   [2001] OJ C 12, 1-9.

122   Council Regulation (EC) No 805/2004 of 21 April, 2004 ([2004] OJ L 143, 15-39). Like the other instruments adopted under Article 65 of the EC Treaty, the Regulation does not apply in relation to Denmark, Article 2 para. 3.

123   A definition of uncontested claims is given in Article 3 of the Regulation. According to some estimates, about 90% of all decisions that are the subject of cross-border enforcement within the European Union will henceforth qualify as European enforcement orders; *cf.* A. Stadler, "Das Europäische Zivilprozessrecht – Wie viel Beschleunigung verträgt Europa? Kritisches zur Verordnung über den Europäischen Vollstreckungstitel und ihrer Grundidee", 24 *IPRax* 2, at 6 (2004) with further references.

124   Article 5 of Regulation 805/2004.

125   Due to the fact that the European enforcement order severely curtails the defendant's rights in the enforcement state it has stirred both scholarly debate and criticism. See e.g. P. Mankowski, Entwicklungen im Internationalen Privat- und Prozessrecht 2003/2004 (Teil 2), 50 *RIW* 587, at 587-588 (2004); A. Stadler, "Kritische Anmerkungen zum Europäischen Vollstreckungstitel", 50 *RIW* 801-808 (2004); Stadler, *supra* footnote 123, 24 *IPRax* 2-11 (2004).

126   Even if the judgment in question would qualify for declaration as an enforcement order, it is still open to the creditor to proceed under the Brussels Convention or, as the case may be, the Brussels I Regulation instead. See Article 27 of Regulation 805/2004.

law applicable to divorce and on intestate and testate succession.[127] Various ancillary measures have already been enacted, including inter alia a Regulation on the service in the Member States of judicial and extrajudicial documents in civil or commercial matters[128] and on the taking of evidence.[129] In the light of these comprehensive efforts, the Brussels Regulation can be seen as the core of an emerging European law of civil procedure.[130]

---

127 See the Commission's Green Paper on applicable law and jurisdiction in divorce matters (COM [2005] 82 final, "Rome III") and the Commission's Green Paper on succession and wills (COM [2005] 65 final, "Rome IV").

128 Council Regulation (EC) No 1348/2000 ([2000] OJ L 160, 37-52) of 29 May 2000. The Regulation entered into force on 31 May 2001. See generally B. Heiderhoff, in T. Rauscher (ed.), *Europäisches Zivilprozeßrecht, Vol. 2* (Munich, Sellier, 2nd ed. 2006), EG-ZustellVO; S. Rahlf and E. Gottschalk, "Das Europäische Zustellungsrecht", 15 *EWS* 303-310 (2004); A. Stadler, "Neues europäisches Zustellungsrecht", 21 *IPRax* 514-521 (2001).

129 Council Regulation (EC) No 1206/2001 ([2001] OJ L 174, 1-24) of 28 May 2001. The Regulation entered into force on 1 January 2004. By virtue of its Article 21 (1), it takes precedence over the 1954 Hague Convention relating to civil procedure and the 1970 Hague Evidence Convention as among the EU Member States. See generally P. Beaumont and H. Raulus, Update on Private International Law in the European Union – 2001, 96 *Am. Soc'y Int'l L. Proc.* 109, at 112-113 (2002); C. Berger, "Die EG-Verordnung über die Zusammenarbeit der Gerichte auf dem Gebiet der Beweisaufnahme in Zivil- und Handelssachen (EuBVO)", 21 *IPRax* 522-527 (2001); J. von Hein, in T. Rauscher (ed.), *Europäisches Zivilprozeßrecht*, Vol. 2 (Munich, Sellier, 2nd ed. 2006), EG-BewVO.

130 See Kropholler, *supra* footnote 82, Einl. No. 1.

Chapter III   The Emergence of Jurisdictional Theory in the United States and Germany

A.   The United States

The United States is perhaps unique even among common-law jurisdictions in the degree that, in the course of the nineteenth and twentieth centuries, theories and practices of adjudicatory authority in the international sense have been shaped and controlled by judges. The causes are at least three: (1) the central role that courts have traditionally played in the development of legal rules and principles in common-law systems; (2) the federal character of the American polity established by the Constitution of the United States in 1789; (3) the potential for far-reaching judicial control over executive and legislative power contained in certain provisions of the Constitution, in the first ten Amendments – in particular the Fifth – and in the Fourteenth Amendment of 1868.

Our discussion begins with a brief survey of the constitutional bases for judicial control of the exercise of adjudicatory authority in the international sense prior to the 1877 decision of the Supreme Court of the United States in *Pennoyer* v. *Neff*.

1.   The Constitutional Bases for Judicial Control over Exercises of Adjudicatory Authority

American thinking and practice respecting adjudicatory authority evolved in a rich and complex historical setting. The story is long, convoluted, and not lacking in ambiguity. For the most part, the growing point of American jurisdictional theory and practice has been in the courts. Early judicial practice and thinking are obscure; not only do we lack a full understanding of the contemporary practices and institutions but we are accustomed to viewing law in positivist terms while earlier periods saw

> the common law ... not ... as the peculiar province of any sovereign's will, though, of course, it was possible for a government to supplant or modify customary rules operating within its territory by legislation.[1]

---

1   R. Whitten, "The Constitutional Limitations on State-Court Jurisdiction: A Historical-Interpretative Reexamination of the Full Faith and Credit and Due Process Clauses", Part I, 14 *Creighton L. Rev.* 499, at 590 (1981).

Furthermore, from the nineteenth century onwards, federal constitutional provisions – in particular the full faith and credit and due process clauses – have provided the basic propositions upon which American thinking respecting adjudicatory authority has in large measure rested.

(a)   The full faith and credit clause

The antecedents of the full faith and credit clause of Article IV, section 1, of the Constitution of the United States were prior English practice, efforts by the colonies to deal with the effects of judgments rendered in sister colonies, and the full faith and credit clause of the Articles of Confederation (1781). The historical evidence "tends toward a limited meaning" of the clause contained in the Articles. The colonies were primarily concerned with the "reception per se of sister-colony judgments as evidence. More importantly, it seems unlikely that the draftsmen of the Articles would have been willing to prescribe a conclusive effect on the merits, given their general desire to preserve state autonomy".[2]

In light of the historical background and the debates in the Constitutional Convention,

> [t]he most sensible reading of the language [of the full faith and credit clause of Article IV, section 1] ... is ... that sister-state statutes, records and judgments must be admitted into evidence as full proof of their existence and contents, but that no more particular effect is commanded for them, the latter being left to Congress to prescribe when and if it so chose ... Until Congress acted, the states would apply sister-state statutes and enforce their judgments in accordance with the rules they had theretofore followed, international conflict of laws rules; but there is no evidence that such rules were *incorporated* into the clause by the language used ...[3]

Congress promptly exercised its authority under Article IV, section 1, by enacting on 26 May 1790 "An Act to prescribe the mode in which the public Acts, Records, and judicial Proceedings in each State, shall be authenticated so as to take effect in every other State."[4] The Act's title suggests that its provisions deal only with authentication; however, language was added in the course of the Act's consideration to the effect that properly authenticated records and judicial proceedings "shall have such faith and credit given to them in every court within the United States, as they have by law or usage in the courts of the state from whence the records are or shall be taken".

On its face, the addition seems to require "that a res judicata effect be given sister-state judgments when they would receive this effect in the rendering state".[5] However, it is strongly argued that "the intent of the last sentence of the statute

---

2   *Idem* 541.

3   *Idem* 553-554 (emphasis in original). For a brief discussion of the differing views advanced by Professors Nadelmann and Crosskey, see *idem* 554-555.

4   Act of 26 May 1790, ch. 11, 1 Stat. 122.

5   Whitten, *supra* footnote 1, at 556.

was only to require that state judgments be *admitted into evidence* to the same extent only, and no further, that they would be admitted in the rendering state".[6] In *Mills* v. *Duryee*[7] the Supreme Court accepted the broader reading of the Act. Justice Story wrote that "no rational interpretation of the act of congress [can be perceived], unless it declares a judgment conclusive, when a court of the particular state where it is rendered would pronounce the same decision".[8] The Constitution's command – as distinguished from that of the Act of 1790 – remained, however, "a limited 'evidentiary' one; the question [decided in *Mills* v. *Duryee*] was whether the words 'faith' and 'credit' were being used by Congress in a sense *different* than they had been used in the Constitution".[9] So far as adjudicatory authority was concerned, there was general agreement that

> international conflict of law rules, including their jurisdictional components, were not incorporated into the constitutional command through the use of the language, 'full faith and credit', although Congress was given plenary authority to legislate on this topic.[10]

In *D'Arcy* v. *Ketchum* (1850)[11] the Supreme Court observed that the state courts had uniformly held judgments rendered by a tribunal without jurisdiction as judged under common-law rules of "international" jurisdiction void.[12] The Court's opinion stated that

> the international law as it existed among the States in 1790 was, that a judgment rendered in one State, assuming to bind the person of a citizen of another, was void within the foreign State, when the defendant had not been served with process or voluntarily made defense, because neither the legislative jurisdiction, nor that of the courts of justice, had binding force.[13]

The Court then held that Congress had not intended to overthrow the old rule by passing the Act of 26 May 1790.

---

6   *Idem* 557. The arguments are discussed *idem* 557-570.

7   11 US (7 Cranch) 481 (1813).

8   *Idem* 485.

9   Whitten, *supra* footnote 1, at 569.

10   *Idem* 570.

11   52 US (11 How.) 165 (1850).

12   See Whitten, *supra* footnote 1, at 582.

13   52 US (11 How.) at 176. Prior to *Pennoyer* v. *Neff*, 95 US 714 (1877), there was no federal constitutional or legislative control over jurisdictional requirements in sister-state recognition practice; accordingly, presumably the state in which recognition was sought in the *D'Arcy* case – Louisiana – could have required its courts through legislation to recognize and enforce judgments rendered on the jurisdictional basis asserted by New York. See pp. 84-86, *infra*.

In *D'Arcy* the Court's sole concern was with whether the full faith and credit clause and statute of 1790 had altered the principles of international law respecting jurisdiction;[14] the decision affirmed the position taken by the state courts that neither the Constitution nor the Act of 1790 dealt with jurisdictional rules.[15] *Swift* v. *Tyson* (1842) had already made clear that federal courts were free to apply, according to their own lights, rules – including those respecting jurisdiction – of the general common law.[16] Accordingly, "the Court had, in cases within its jurisdiction, the authority to enforce the international rules against the states to preserve their sovereign authority vis-à-vis each other".[17]

Although the historical record is by no means entirely clear, at this juncture American theory and practice respecting adjudicatory authority in matters with significant non-domestic elements is plausibly summarized by Whitten as follows:

> [N]either the Constitution nor the [implementing] Act of 1790 were designed to ... affect the international, territorial, common-law rules of legislative or judicial jurisdiction operating between the states in 1787, although Congress was given the authority ... to alter these rules as they pertained to [sister-state] statutes, records, and judgments.[18]

Moreover, insofar as requirements for recognition and enforcement of sister-state judgments were concerned, only the Congress had "authority to modify the fundamental rules of jurisdiction, as those rules existed between the states as independent sovereigns in 1787".[19] Individual states lacked "power unilaterally to expand their jurisdiction [for full faith and credit purposes] from what it would have been under the international rules ...";[20] sister states remained free to deny effects to judgments rendered on expanded bases. So far as *intrastate* recognition of judgments given on such bases was concerned, however, "the sole question was whether the court rendering the judgment followed the applicable state statutes".[21]

In short, on the one hand, neither the United States Constitution nor the Act of 1790 were thought to impose limits upon state claims of adjudicatory author-

---

14   P. Borchers, "The Death of the Constitutional Law of Personal Jurisdiction: From *Pennoyer* to *Burnham* and Back Again", 24 *U. C. Davis L. Rev.* 19, at 29 (1990).

15   Whitten, *supra* footnote 1, at 583.

16   41 US (16 Pet.) 1 (1842). *Swift* was overruled in 1938 by *Erie R. R. Co.* v. *Tompkins*, 304 US 64 (1938). For a discussion of *Swift* and *Erie*, see Chap. V. E. 3. *(b)* (ii) *b*, pp. 249 *et seq.*, *infra*.

17   Whitten, *supra* footnote 1, at 583.

18   *Idem* 599-600.

19   *Idem* 600. In cases within their jurisdiction, the federal courts could, of course, enforce *traditional* rules against the states. *Ibid.*

20   *Ibid.*

21   Borchers, *supra* footnote 14, at 32.

ity; on the other, under the Constitution as well as the Act, a state could deny effect to a sister-state judgment that did not rest on the essentially territorial rules of jurisdiction in effect between the states in 1787. With respect to the assertion of adjudicatory authority for its own purposes and to the jurisdictional test that sister-state judgments had to satisfy for recognition and enforcement purposes, each state was sovereign. Congress had authority to change the situation with respect to recognition and enforcement of sister-state judgments; it had not done so in the Act of 1790.

(b) The due process clause
(i) The background

The ratification in 1868 of Amendment XIV to the Constitution of the United States added new material for, and ultimately great complexity to, American thinking and practice respecting adjudicatory authority; the Amendment's relevant passage provides as follows: "nor shall any State deprive any person of life, liberty, or property, without due process of law ...". The Amendment is directed to the several states of the United States; very similar language, applicable to the federal government rather than to the states, is contained in the Fifth Amendment (1791): "nor shall any person ... be deprived of life, liberty, or property, without due process of law ...". These provisions are susceptible of very broad and varied applications.[22] Of crucial importance is the fact that the Fourteenth Amendment – unlike the full faith and credit clause, whose applicability is limited to situations involving recognition of public acts, records, or judicial proceedings of sister states – provided the Supreme Court with a plausible basis for exercising direct control over state claims of adjudicatory authority where the resulting judgment's intrastate effects are in question.

The due process formula, which traces back to Magna Carta,[23] had found expression in English law, in the laws of the American colonies,[24] and, after the Declaration of Independence of 1776, in the constitutions of the newly sovereign American States. Although the record is not unambiguous, the colonial understanding of due process of law was probably "a requirement of a regular judicial proceeding, with an opportunity to be heard in defense".[25] After the Constitution of the United States came into force in 1789, "a substantial body of case law grew up dealing with due process of law",[26] including decisions of the Supreme Court of the United States under the Fifth Amendment.[27] "[T]he states took different views

---

22   There are situations in which the commands of the two clauses may differ. See generally D. Welkowitz, "Going to the Limits of Due Process: Myth, Mystery and Meaning", 28 *Duquesne L. Rev.* 233-270 (1990).

23   See Whitten, *supra* footnote 1, Part II, 14 *Creighton L. Rev.* 735, at 738 (1981).

24   See *idem* 738-755.

25   *Idem* 754.

26   *Idem* 755.

27   Several important Supreme Court decisions under the Fifth Amendment, which applies only to the federal Government, are discussed by Whitten. See *idem* 772-774, 796-798.

of the meaning of the phrase ... as it was applied to particular issues, including jurisdiction over nonresident defendants."[28]

It seems that, "*in general*, ... the expression due process of law required an opportunity to be heard in a 'regular' judicial proceeding prior to any deprivation of life, liberty, or property".[29] "However, the cases never defined precisely what was necessary to constitute a 'judicial' proceeding ...". Clearly, however, "wide latitude [was left] to the legislature to dispense with 'ordinary' judicial proceedings".[30]

Moreover, although

> one consistent thread running through due process of law from the English context up to and including the pre-fourteenth amendment decisions is the opportunity to be heard in defense before life, liberty, or property might be taken by the government[], ... the ... decisions reveal a very broad power in the legislature to provide [not only the best form of notice that is practical but] ... constructive notice by publication, rather than personal service of process or some other form of personal notice to a defendant.[31]

Prior to the Fourteenth Amendment, due process was seen as controlling the notice given to defendants of pending litigation but not as affecting the power of the legislature to enact jurisdictional rules, binding on its own courts, inconsistent with the then accepted international rules of *territorial* jurisdiction.[32]

The exercise of adjudicatory authority by a state's courts was con-sequently controlled by the common-law territorial rules unless state legislation provided for the assertion of "extraterritorial" jurisdiction.[33] Such extensions of a state's adjudicatory authority did not, however, qualify the resulting judgments for recognition and enforcement in sister states; "the [common-law] territorial rules ... govern[ed] the authority of other sovereigns' proceedings on collateral attack".[34]

To sum up, "the predominant pre-fourteenth amendment view would have rejected due process as limiting the legislature's power to exceed the *territorial* rules of jurisdiction[] and only slightly limiting its power to modify pure notice rules".[35] The question remains whether the history of the Amendment's framing reveals a different understanding of due process. After examining the historical

---

28   *Idem* 756. Important state decisions are discussed by Whitten. See *idem* 774-795.

29   *Idem* 795.

30   *Idem* 796.

31   *Idem* 798.

32   See *idem* 799-800.

33   See *idem* 801.

34   *Ibid.*

35   *Idem* 803-804. In view of the fundamental importance of opportunity to be heard, due process has the potential to generate new applications of notice rules. When the mail is expensive and unreliable, notice by publication may be acceptable; once the mail is inexpensive and reliable, its use may be required in place of notice by publication. A similar argument can be made respecting the imposition of due-process

record, "[i]t does not seem plausible ... to reason that the fourteenth amendment originally imposed the traditional rules of international jurisdiction on the states directly through the due process clause".[36]

(ii)   The first steps towards constitutional control of state-court exercises of adjudicatory authority: Pennoyer v. Neff (1877)

Despite the lack of support in the historical record, *Pennoyer* v. *Neff*[37] brought "the traditional, sovereignty-based, international territorial rules of jurisdiction into the due process clause of the fourteenth amendment ...".[38] *Pennoyer* involved an effort by the one-time owner of a tract of land in Oregon to recover the property, which had been executed upon and sold at a sheriff's sale to satisfy a state-court judgment against him. He argued that the sale was invalid because the judgment, having been rendered by a court without jurisdiction, was void. The lower federal court found that, under Oregon law, the service used to establish jurisdiction over the non-resident defendant in the original proceedings was defective in two respects: the affidavit of publication was from the newspaper's "editor" rather than its "printer" and the plaintiff's affidavit to establish that, "after due diligence", the defendant could not be found within the state, was too cursory to be sufficient.[39]

---

limits where a jurisdictional basis is one that arguably tends to deny defendants an opportunity to be heard.

36   *Idem* 821. In all events, even if the contemporary rules of international territorial jurisdiction were thought of as a component of the due process clause, the "minimum contacts" theory announced in 1945 by *International Shoe* v. *Washington* clearly was not. See *ibid*.

37   95 US 714 (1877).

38   Whitten, Part II, *supra* footnote 23, at 835. Whitten believes that the *Pennoyer* Court saw the due process clause not only as providing a *mechanism* for challenging, in the state of rendition as well as elsewhere, state-court assertions of adjudicatory authority but also as setting limits to the contents of the jurisdictional rules upon which the courts could act. See Borchers, *supra* footnote 14, at 38-39. Borchers, on the other hand, argues that Justice Field in *Pennoyer* saw the due process clause as serving only the first function. See *idem* 40-43; Borchers, "Pennoyer's Limited Legacy: A Reply to Professor Oakley", 29 *U.C. Davis L. Rev.* 115-165 (1995). A similar view is taken by Perdue.
"The basic premise of the opinion is that there are limitations on state power that are simply inherent in the nature of government. Having described these limitations, Field then goes on to invoke the due process clause as a mechanism to which the federal courts may turn to ensure that states do not exceed the inherent limitations on their power...." W. Perdue, "Sin, Scandal and Substantive Due Process: Personal Jurisdiction and *Pennoyer* Revisited", 62 *Wash. L. Rev.* 479, at 502 (1987); see also *idem* 505 ("Field treats the 14th Amendment not as a *source* of the rights in question but as a device for recognizing and enforcing preexisting and inalienable rights"). In all events, in the long run the view expressed by Whitten prevailed in the courts.

39   See Borchers, *supra* footnote 14, at 32-34.

The Supreme Court, rejecting the lower court's interpretation and application of the Oregon statute, proceeded to take the momentous step of invoking the Fourteenth Amendment. Justice Field wrote:

> Since the adoption [in 1868] of the Fourteenth Amendment to the Federal Constitution, the validity of ... judgments may be directly questioned, and their enforcement in the State resisted, on the ground that proceedings in a court of justice to determine the personal rights and obligations of parties over whom that court has no jurisdiction do not constitute due process of law .... [As applied to judicial proceedings, these terms] mean a course of legal proceedings according to those rules and principles which have been established in our systems of jurisprudence for the protection and enforcement of private rights. To give such proceedings any validity, there must be a tribunal competent by its constitution – that is, by the law of its creation – to pass upon the subject-matter of the suit; and, if that involves merely a determination of the personal liability of the defendant, he must be brought within its jurisdiction by service of process within the State, or his voluntary appearance.[40]

The full implications of *Pennoyer* did not become entirely clear until *Riverside & Dan River Cotton Mills* v. *Menefee* was decided in 1915.[41] *Menefee* firmly established that the Fourteenth Amendment provided not only a mechanism, but also a standard, for limiting state-court claims of adjudicatory authority.[42] State courts and legislatures could still – and on occasion do – impose more rigorous requirements than the Supreme Court mandates, but that Court has long established for all American courts and many legislatures the basic elements of American thinking and practice respecting the legitimacy of exercises of adjudicatory authority. What the Supreme Court has wrought can be divided into two epochs: the period that began with the decision in *Pennoyer* and the post-1945 period.

2.   The Reign of the Power Theory: 1877-1945

(a)   The theory in operation

Pennoyer v. *Neff* and its progeny gave constitutional standing to territorial approaches to the allocation of adjudicatory authority and the power theory of jurisdiction. In 1917, Justice Holmes expressed the essence of early twentieth-century American thinking respecting adjudicatory authority: "The foundation of jurisdiction is physical power ..."[43] His aphorism embodies the then-accepted explanation and justification for paradigmatic cases such as the 1870 decision of the Supreme Judicial Court of Massachusetts in *Peabody* v. *Hamilton*.[44]

---

40   95 US at 733.

41   237 US 189 (1915).

42   See Borchers, *supra* footnote 14, at 51.

43   *McDonald* v. *Mabee*, 243 US 90, at 91 (1917).

44   106 Mass. 217 (1870).

An action was brought in Massachusetts for breach of a contract that had no connection with Massachusetts. The plaintiffs were English citizens resident in London; the defendant, a citizen of the United States who lived in New York, owned no property in Massachusetts. A passenger on an English steamer, boarded in Halifax, Nova Scotia and en route to New York, the defendant was served with process while the vessel was docked in East Boston. He sought to quash service on the ground that "the circumstances set forth are not sufficient to give jurisdiction" to the court.[45] The Supreme Judicial Court, reasoning in power terms, gave the objection short shrift. "When the party is in the state, however transiently, and the summons is actually served upon him there, the jurisdiction of the court is complete, as to the person of the defendant."[46] The court's rationale for assuming jurisdiction in *Peabody* could only rest on considerations of power.[47]

A mid-twentieth-century version of the *Peabody* case is *Grace* v. *MacArthur*.[48] Arkansas's adjudicatory authority was there established by service made aboard a "non-stop flight from Memphis, Tenn. to Dallas, Texas", when the "airplane was in the Eastern District of Arkansas and directly above Pine Bluff, Arkansas ...".[49] The argument that the court lacked jurisdiction because the defendant had "not been properly served with process in this action *within the State of Arkansas*"[50] was rejected. To the extent that the court looked behind the ritual of service of process, it discussed the propriety of asserting jurisdiction in terms of power:

> It may be conceded, perhaps, that a time may come, and may not be far distant, when commercial aircraft will fly at altitudes so high that it would be unrealistic to consider them as being within the territorial limits of the United States or of any particular State while flying at such altitudes.[51]

---

45   *Idem* 218.

46   *Idem* 220. The history of the jurisdictional rule applied in *Peabody* is discussed from an American perspective in J. Weinstein, "The Early American Origins of Territoriality in Judicial Jurisdiction", 37 *St. Louis Univ. LJ* 1-61 (1992), and T. Kogan, "A Neo-Federalist Tale of Personal Jurisdiction", 63 *Southern California L. Rev.* 257-372 (1990). See also J. Weinstein, "The Dutch Influence on the Conception of Judicial Jurisdiction in 19th Century America", 38 *Am. J. Comp. L.* 73-101 (1990), and N. Hatzimihail, "Pre-Classical Conflict of Laws: An Essay on the Writing of the History of Private International Law", Chap. 1. I. C. 2. and Chap 5. V. C. 1. (S.J.D. thesis, Harvard, 2002, on file with the Harvard Law Library) for respectively the use of history in modern American conflict of laws and for a criticism of Weinstein's interpretation of Huber.

47   But see the opinions in *Burnham*, discussed on pp. 108 *et seq.*, *infra*.

48   170 F. Supp. 442 (ED Ark. 1959).

49   *Idem* 443.

50   *Ibid.* (emphasis in original).

51   *Idem* 447.
       The result reached in *Grace* is problematic under a strict power analysis because the forum never had power to hold the defendant. Accordingly, unless the possibility of power at some future date is to be considered sufficient, Arkansas lacked jurisdiction under a power theory. The mere possibility that a legal order might establish,

Peabody and *Grace* exercised the form of *in personam* adjudicatory authority that can be denominated unlimited general jurisdiction.[52] The power rationale equally served to establish limited general jurisdiction, traditionally referred to as jurisdiction *quasi in rem*. A legal order where one's property is located or where one could sue a debtor has power, and accordingly adjudicatory authority – measured by the asset's value – over one.

The logic and practice of this form of jurisdiction are exemplified by the decision of the Supreme Court of the United States in *Harris v. Balk*.[53] In this landmark case, Justice Peckham rationalized Maryland's exercise of adjudicatory authority as follows:

> Power over the person of the garnishee confers jurisdiction on the courts of the State where the writ issues …. If, while temporarily there, his creditor might sue him there and recover the debt, then he is liable to process of garnishment, no matter where the *situs* of the debt was originally.[54]

Some sixty years later an interesting variation of the type of power-based jurisdiction exemplified by *Harris v. Balk* was asserted in *Seider v. Roth*.[55] The plaintiffs, New York residents, were injured in an automobile accident in Vermont. The allegedly negligent driver of the other car, a Quebec resident, was insured under a policy issued in Quebec by an insurance company that was incorporated in Connecticut and did business in many jurisdictions, including New York. Adjudicatory authority was asserted by the New York courts on the basis of an attachment of the insurer's contractual obligation to defend and indemnify the driver. The insurer did business in New York and the Quebec driver could have sued the company there to enforce the defense and indemnity obligation; the plaintiffs urged that they could attach this "debt" and apply its value to satisfy their personal injury claims against the Quebec driver.

A majority of the Court of Appeals accepted the argument: "Jurisdiction is properly acquired by this attachment since the policy obligation is a debt owed to the defendant by the insurer, the latter being regarded as a resident of this State ..."[56] Three members of the seven-judge court dissented. They, like the majority, reasoned in terms of power but reached a different result: because the

---

at a later date, power over the defendant or his property did not, however, suffice in American law to establish jurisdiction. See *Pennoyer v. Neff, supra* footnote 13. In the final analysis *Grace* illustrates how personal service, originally an assertion of power and a condition for its exercise, had declined by the 1950s into a mechanical ritual.

52   See Chap. I. B. 3., p. 24, *supra*.

53   198 US 215 (1905).

54   *Idem* 222.

55   17 NY 2d 111, 216 NE 2d 312 (1966). *Seider v. Roth* jurisdiction was held unconstitutional in *Rush v. Savchuk*. See *infra* footnote 63.

56   *Idem* 114, 216 NE 2d at 315.

insurer's promise to indemnify was contingent on an award of damages against the insured, "there was [when the suit was initiated,] nothing in this State to which the levy could apply".[57]

Just as *Grace*,[58] *Seider* illustrates the extent to which by the 1950s the power theory had come to be relied upon to justify assumptions of adjudicatory authority that were, at the best, highly dubious when so rationalized. Such cases clearly use the traditional power rationale to reach results that, though arguably reasonable, can hardly be justified in terms of power.

When the power theory was at its high-water mark, American courts, relying expressly on fairness considerations, occasionally refused to exercise *quasi in rem* jurisdiction in *Harris* v. *Balk*-type situations. Since a sovereign's power is rarely, if ever, complete and exclusive, what one sovereign does, another may be able to undo in whole or in part. Had *Harris* v. *Balk* arisen in an international setting lacking the full-faith-and-credit compulsion available in the federal system of the United States, North Carolina could have compelled Harris to pay Balk even though another sovereign had already required payment by Harris to Epstein.

Although never held to be constitutionally required, the potential unfairness to garnishees, who bear no responsibility for the dispute between the real parties in interest, caused many states to forgo jurisdiction when the garnishee would be exposed to a substantial risk of having to pay twice. Thus, the Supreme Court of Arizona concluded that where

> the [defendant's] services were all rendered in the Republic of Mexico for a [garnishee] corporation whose plant is entirely in that country, and ... the debt was made and payable therein, the [garnishee] ought not to be compelled to pay such debt to an Arizona creditor when it is not only possible but probable it would have to pay it again.[59]

Courts drew back as well from other possible implications of the power principle where persons not parties to the underlying dispute were directly affected. Many courts refused to base jurisdiction on the sovereign's power over persons controlling property belonging to another when the property was situated abroad;

> in the absence of any fraud or connivance on the part of the garnishee to aid the debtor in defrauding his creditors, personal property or real estate which is lawfully

---

57   *Idem* 115, 216 NE 2d at 315.

58   See *supra* footnote 48.

59   *Weitzel* v. *Weitzel*, 29 Ariz. 117, at 125, 230 P. 1106, at 1108 (1924); see also *Parker, Peebles & Knox, Inc.* v. *National Fire Ins. Co.*, 111 Conn. 383, 150 A. 313 (1930) (unlikelihood of Haiti's recognizing Connecticut judgment led to court's refusal to order garnishee to pay insurance proceeds to plaintiff).

in the possession or under the control of the garnishee outside of this state is not the subject of garnishment ....[60]

Likewise, a common carrier was usually not required to stop and hold in the state property in transit when it was sought to establish *quasi in rem* jurisdiction over the property's owner.[61]

> The nature of the possession and control which the railroad company has of and over personal property in actual transit, the interruption of business, and the general inconvenience which must necessarily result from holding such property the subject of the garnishee process ... are amply sufficient to justify us in making such property an exception to the general rule, in the absence of any positive declaration of the legislature subjecting such property to the process ....[62]

These concessions were not thought to be constitutionally required; in other contexts, jurisdiction fully justified in power terms was usually not relinquished because of considerations of fairness. The converse was also true: when jurisdiction was not justified in power terms, fairness considerations were normally not invoked – at least explicitly – to overcome the difficulty. A comparison of *Harris* v. *Balk* with *Seider* v. *Roth* is instructive in this connection. For a power theory, the contingent nature and value of the insurance company's obligation makes *Seider* jurisdiction far more problematical than *Harris* jurisdiction. Indeed, the latter was widespread in the United States while the former was most exceptional. Yet, viewed in terms not of power but of fairness, *Seider* jurisdiction seems clearly the more acceptable.[63] An insurance company is better able than an ordinary gar-

---

60   *Bates* v. *Chicago, Milwaukee & St. Paul Ry.*, 60 Wis. 296, at 302, 19 NW 72, at 75 (1884). The court further remarked:

> It is unnecessary to intimate the difficulties and hardships which would result from the enforcement of a rule against garnishees compelling them to deliver up to the processes of the courts of this state any property they may have under their control, belonging to the principal debtor, situated in another state.

Idem 304, 19 NW at 76. But cf. *United States* v. *First Nat'l City Bank*, 379 US 378 (1965) (US district court has jurisdiction to grant, in aid of the enforcement of internal revenue laws, a temporary injunction "freezing" a foreign corporation's account in respondent bank's foreign branch pending establishment of jurisdiction over the corporation).

61   See, e.g., *idem* 305-310, 19 NW at 76-78 (1884).

62   *Idem* 306, 19 NW at 77; see Annotation, 46 ALR 933 (1927). An early Massachusetts case, *Adams* v. *Scott*, 104 Mass. 164 (1870), reached the opposite result: "There is no reason why a common carrier should not be liable to the trustee process, in the same manner as other bailees are ..." *Idem* 165.

63   This is not to say, of course, that either jurisdictional claim is acceptable when assessed in terms of litigational justice. Indeed, the Supreme Court has rejected both as unconstitutional. See *Rush* v. *Savchuk*, 444 US 320 (1980) and *Shaffer* v. *Heitner*, 433 US 186 (1977). See for a detailed discussion of *Shaffer* v. *Heitner* pp. 102 *et seq., infra*.

nishee to bear the burden of litigating in the forum selected by the plaintiff; the principal debtor's position vis-à-vis the plaintiff is much less prejudiced since, even if the plaintiff could not prevail in another forum, the insured is not out of pocket; and, finally, the garnishee runs no risk of having to pay twice as any payments under the policy redound to the insured's benefit and reduce the insurer's obligations. (The action brought by the third party against the insurance company can, however, adversely affect the insured to some extent – for example, under collateral estoppel principles or by exhaustion of the policy if there are other claimants.)

The Supreme Court, applying the territorially based power theory, refused on many occasions to recognize considerations of fairness as a basis for asserting adjudicatory authority. *New York Life Insurance Co.* v. *Dunlevy* furnishes an instructive example.[64] In 1907, Boggs & Buhl recovered a valid judgment in the Pennsylvania courts against Mrs. Dunlevy, at the time a resident of Pennsylvania. In 1909, some $2,500 became due under a life insurance policy that New York Life, an insurance company doing business in Pennsylvania, had issued to Gould, a resident of Pennsylvania. Boggs & Buhl, asserting that Gould had assigned the policy in 1893 to his daughter, Mrs. Dunlevy, sought to enforce their 1907 judgment against her out of the proceeds that had fallen due. Gould, protesting that no assignment had been made, also claimed the proceeds. New York Life, faced by two claims to the same fund, asked the Pennsylvania court to decide which claimant was entitled to it. The court took jurisdiction. Dunlevy, by now a California resident, was notified of the proceedings but did not enter an appearance. The issue whether Gould had assigned the policy to his daughter was litigated and judgment given for Gould. New York Life thereupon paid him the amount due under the policy.

Subsequently, Dunlevy sued New York Life in California to recover the amount that had been paid her father. The company defended on the ground that she was bound by the judicial proceedings in Pennsylvania which had held the policy to be Gould's property. The California judgment for Dunlevy was affirmed by the United States Supreme Court.[65] Had the Pennsylvania courts found New York Life indebted to Dunlevy, the insurer could have been compelled to pay the policy proceeds to Boggs & Buhl in satisfaction of their claim against her. But the logic of the power theory led the Court to conclude without hesitation that, since the Pennsylvania courts had found that New York Life was not her debtor, she had no assets in Pennsylvania. It followed that, as – in the view of the Pennsylvania courts – no asset of hers was present, the state improperly claimed *quasi in rem* jurisdiction.[66]

A strict power theory finds no room for the argument that justice requires that at least one forum have jurisdiction to adjudicate conflicting claims in cases

---

64   241 US 518 (1916).

65   *Idem* 523.

66   See *idem* 522-523.

where otherwise the debtor, through no fault of his own, would be exposed to the risk of having to pay twice. The forums that might, were this argument accepted, reasonably be seized on the *Dunlevy* facts are Pennsylvania, California, and the state in which the insurance company was incorporated or had its head office. Among these, litigational fairness and overall convenience probably favor Pennsylvania. If so, a strong argument in terms of convenience and fairness can be made for Pennsylvanian jurisdiction to determine which claimant was entitled to the proceeds of the insurance policy.[67]

(b)   Power-theory "metaphysics"

The results and reasoning in *Harris* v. *Balk* and *Dunlevy* illustrate the "metaphysical" side of American power theories. Concepts such as "power" and "presence" are reasonably manageable both practically and theoretically when natural persons and tangible objects are in question. Difficulties arise, however, when these notions are applied to legal persons or to intangibles. Where are legal persons or intangibles present? In what circumstances and in what sense do sovereigns have power over them? Somewhat comparable ambiguities arise when adjudicatory authority is to be exercised over complex relations involving two or more natural persons, for example, the marriage relation.

(i)   The "presence" of intangibles

Whether intangibles can be said to have a situs was considered in *Harris* v. *Balk*.[68] Balk argued that the situs of the debt Harris owed him was in North Carolina; accordingly, the Maryland court's hold over Harris due to his temporary presence in that state did not give control over the debt he owed Balk. This argument was rejected. In the United States Supreme Court's view, Balk could have sued Harris in Maryland for payment; "[t]he obligation of the debtor to pay his debt clings to and accompanies him wherever he goes".[69]

The proposition that intangibles do not have a situs explains for power theories the result in *Dunlevy*. If the insurance company's obligation had a location in space – a situs – then the Court, using a power theory and drawing an analogy to tangible property, would have held that the situs had jurisdiction to decide to whom the property belonged. The company's obligation having in the court's view no situs, the Pennsylvania court's decision could bind both claimants only if both were subject on another ground or grounds to its adjudicatory authority. Such authority existed with respect to the father; he was a resident of Pennsylvania. Dunlevy, however, had not been served with process in Pennsylvania, was

---

67   Cf. *Atkinson* v. *Superior Court*, 49 Cal. 2d 338, 316 P. 2d 960 (1957) (upholding, on the basis of fairness, the assertion of state-court jurisdiction to adjudicate claims of resident plaintiffs against a resident defendant for certain royalty payments also claimed by a third party who, were there no need to protect the resident defendant against the possibility of having to pay twice, would not have been subject to jurisdiction).

68   198 US 215 (1905).

69   *Idem* 222.

no longer resident there, and – since her father was ultimately held to be entitled to the insurance proceeds – neither an asset nor a debtor of hers was present in Pennsylvania to establish its adjudicatory authority. All this is metaphysical and mysterious, but a power theory cannot logically take the view that debts both cling to the debtor and have a fixed location in space.

Another issue with metaphysical overtones is the significance that a power theory attaches to the "embodiment" of an intangible in a document:

> A debt or mere right of action with nothing more is wholly incorporeal, with no evidence or representative which can give it habitation anywhere. As to such property, whether it seeks to tax or adjudicate, sovereign power must proceed in personam simply because there is nothing to take hold on for proceeding in rem or quasi in rem. Hence there can be no jurisdiction to adjudge ownership save as there is jurisdiction in personam over the persons who must be bound in order to settle that issue …. But, when debtor and creditor create such a corporeal thing as bearer bonds, they have created something upon which jurisdiction of any kind may act. They have made more than mere symbol. They have fabricated a matrix-like container for the property, wherein it is to be carried from place to place, jurisdiction to jurisdiction, at the will of the possessor.[70]

(ii)   The "presence" of legal persons

The notional apparatus required by a power theory also encounters metaphysical problems with respect to jurisdiction over legal persons, in particular corporations. An initial issue is whether a corporation can be "present" outside its state of incorporation. At one time, American courts took the view that a sovereign's power to create legal persons ran to its boundaries but not beyond; accordingly, a corporation "can have no legal existence out of the boundaries of the sovereignty by which it is created".[71] As a consequence, in the early decades of the nineteenth century a corporate defendant could ordinarily be sued only in its state of incorporation unless it had property in another state.[72] The resulting situation, however satisfactory from a purely doctrinal perspective, was unacceptable as a practical matter; the power theory could hardly be totally blind to considerations of fairness and justice and give corporate defendants overall greater protection than natural persons with respect to the assumption of adjudicatory authority over them.

The first efforts to find a solution that could be squared with the reigning power theory utilized the idea of consent.[73] Legislation was passed which, resting upon a state's power to exclude a foreign corporation from doing business within

---

70   *First Trust Co.* v. *Matheson*, 187 Minn. 468, at 474, 246 NW 1, at 3 (1932).

71   *Bank of Augusta* v. *Earle*, 38 US (13 Pet.) 519, at 588 (1839).

72   See G. Henderson, *The Position of Foreign Corporations in American Constitutional Law* 77 (Cambridge, MA, Harvard University Press, 1918).

73   For discussion of what can be called "metaphorical consent" see Chap. V. A. 1., pp. 175-176, *infra*.

the state, required as a condition for the doing of business that the corporation submit to jurisdiction by consenting to being sued in the state's courts on causes of action arising from business done in the state.[74]

Because personal service is basic for power theories, the problem of where a legal person is present remained insistent. As a practical matter, a corporation clearly has

> existence, vitality, efficiency, beyond the jurisdiction of the sovereign which created it, provided it be voluntarily exercised. If it be said that all these acts are performed by its agents, as they may be in the case of a private individual, and that the corporation itself is not present, the answer is, that a corporation [unlike a natural person] acts nowhere, except by its officers and agents. It has no tangible existence, except through its officers .... Its existence anywhere and everywhere is but ideal.[75]

The view that a corporation was present wherever its offices or agents performed certain acts on its behalf and request did not resolve all the difficulties raised by the power theory. In particular, adjudicatory authority could not be exercised over a corporation for acts done on its behalf that had effects within a state unless an office or agent were physically present in the state when service of process was attempted. Yet another tack was therefore taken, one that foreshadowed an instrumental theory of jurisdiction based on litigational fairness. Courts began to ask whether, in the particular circumstances, "the service of process ... is so unreasonable, so contrary to natural justice and the principles of natural law, that it ought not to be sanctioned".[76] The corporation

> having voluntarily entered th[e] jurisdiction, and transacting business there; having invoked the comity and the protection of the laws of that sovereign for their own benefit, can[not] ... complain that the contracts there made are enforced within that sovereignty and in accordance with its laws ....[77]

If analysis along these lines had been generally accepted in the latter half of the nineteenth century, an instrumental jurisdictional theory based on litigational fairness might well have challenged the power theory, at least where corporate defendants were concerned, much earlier than in fact occurred. But, instead of advancing a competing theory, jurists, faced with the proposition that a legal person's presence – even in its state of incorporation – is only "ideal", overcame the difficulties raised for the power theory by equating "presence" with activity.

---

74   Cf. *Warren Mfg. Co.* v. *Etna Ins. Co.*, 29 F. Cas. 294 (CCD Conn. 1837) (No. 17,206) (Maryland default judgment against Connecticut corporation doing business there not entitled to full faith and credit only because Maryland's consent statute, enacted after the cause of action arose, was without retroactive effect).

75   *Moulin* v. *Trenton Mut. Life & Fire Ins. Co.*, 25 NJL 57, at 60-61 (1855).

76   *Idem* 62.

77   *Idem* 62-63.

By the latter decades of the nineteenth century, American courts asserted adjudicatory authority over legal persons on the basis of either "consent" or "presence". Because of various complications and difficulties inherent in the consent approach, by the end of the second decade of the twentieth century, presence had for most practical purposes supplanted consent. Justice Brandeis formulated the proposition succinctly:

> A foreign corporation is amenable to process to enforce a personal liability, in the absence of consent, only if it is doing business within the State in such manner and to such extent as to warrant the inference that it is present there.[78]

Difficulties remained for the power theory even after the metaphysical proposition that a legal person is present where activities are done on its behalf was accepted. Does any activity whatsoever in the state constitute presence? Moreover, must the activities be going on when the litigation is initiated? In the final analysis, adjudicatory authority over legal persons was never fully nor comfortably explained in strict power terms. When Justice Brandeis spoke of a legal person "doing business within the State in such manner and to such extent as to warrant the inference that it is present there", he raised considerations that cannot be analysed or evaluated in terms of a general theory of jurisdiction based on power. It is thus understandable that Chief Justice Stone's opinion in *International Shoe Co.* v. *Washington*[79] – the decisive step in the emergence in the United States of an alternative theory of jurisdiction instrumental in nature and based on litigational fairness – addressed adjudicatory authority over legal rather than natural persons.

3.   The Passage from a Power to a Litigational-Justice Theory of Adjudicatory Authority

The emergence in the United States of a jurisdictional theory based on litigational justice was due more to the constraints that the power theory imposed than to the excesses that it permitted. In order to allow assertions of adjudicatory authority when intuitively held standards of convenience and fairness required, the strict logic of power was, in the manner just described, first subtly undermined in the case of legal persons. Their activity was eventually equated with a natural person's physical presence. By the second decade of the twentieth century a somewhat comparable development with respect to adjudicatory jurisdiction over natural persons could be discerned.

In *Hess* v. *Pawloski*[80] the Supreme Court considered whether Massachusetts could assert jurisdiction over a Pennsylvania resident who, while driving his car in Massachusetts, struck and injured the plaintiff. The Massachusetts jurisdictional

---

78   *Philadephia & Reading Ry. Co.* v. *McKibbin*, 243 US 264, at 265 (1917).

79   326 US 310 (1945), see pp. 97 *et seq., infra.*

80   274 US 352 (1927).

statute invoked in *Hess* sought to justify the adjudicatory authority claimed in power-theory terms. The statute provided that:

> The acceptance by a nonresident of the rights and privileges conferred by section three or four, as evidenced by his operating a motor vehicle thereunder ... shall be deemed equivalent to an appointment by such nonresident of the registrar or his successor in office, to be his true and lawful attorney upon whom may be served all lawful processes in any action or proceeding against him, growing out of any accident or collision in which said nonresident may be involved while operating a motor vehicle on ... a [public] way, and said acceptance or operation shall be a signification of his agreement that any such process against him which is so served shall be of the same legal force and validity as if served on him personally.[81]

In essence, Massachusetts sought to apply to natural persons a version of the consent-based-on-activity theory that had been developed to justify assertions of adjudicatory jurisdiction over legal persons. However, as Justice Butler pointed out in his opinion for a unanimous Supreme Court,

> [a] personal judgment rendered against a non-resident, who has neither been served with process [within the State] nor appeared in the suit is without validity .... The mere transaction of business in a State by non-resident natural persons does not imply consent to be bound by the process of its courts .... The power of a State to exclude foreign corporations, although not absolute but qualified, is the ground on which such an implication is supported as to them .... But a State may not [in view of the privileges and immunities clause of the Constitution] withhold from non-resident individuals the right of doing business therein.[82]

Butler's opinion then entered into a discussion that was, under strict power-theory logic, irrelevant:

> Motor vehicles are dangerous machines; and, even when skillfully and carefully operated, their use is attended by serious dangers to persons and property. In the public interest the State may make and enforce regulations reasonably calculated to promote care on the part of all, residents and non-residents alike, who use its highways. The measure in question operates to require a non-resident to answer for his conduct in the state where arise causes of action alleged against him, as well as to provide for a claimant a convenient method by which he may sue to enforce his rights. Under the statute the implied consent is limited to proceedings growing out of accidents or collisions on a highway in which the non-resident may be involved.[83]

---

81   *Idem* 353-354.
82   *Idem* 355.
83   *Idem* 356.

An argument having thus been made in terms of convenience and fairness, the opinion sought to bring the situation within the ambit of a power theory of jurisdiction:

> [I]n advance of the operation of a motor vehicle on its highway by a non-resident, the State may require him to appoint one of its officials as his agent on whom process may be served in proceedings growing out of such use .... [T]he state [has the power] to exclude a non-resident until the formal appointment is made. And, having the power so to exclude, the State may declare that the use of the highway by the nonresident is the equivalent of the appointment of the registrar as agent on whom process may be served .... The difference between the formal and implied appointment is not substantial, so far as concerns the application of the due process clause of the Fourteenth Amendment.[84]

Thus, the Massachusetts statute was sustained under an analysis that sorely strained – but still professed – the power theory of jurisdiction.[85]

4.   *The Litigational-Justice Theory: International Shoe (1945) and Beyond*

In the United States, an alternative to a theory of jurisdiction based on power first decisively emerged in *International Shoe Co. v. Washington*.[86] Speaking for the Court, Chief Justice Stone took the view that the mechanical or quantitative tests of presence – congenial to an approach to adjudicatory authority in terms of power – were no longer appropriate.

> Whether due process is satisfied must depend rather upon the quality and nature of the activity in relation to the fair and orderly administration of the laws which it was the purpose of the due process clause to insure.[87]

International Shoe itself suggests that, historically, the emergence in the United States of a jurisdictional theory based on convenience and fairness was due more to the constraints that the power theory imposed upon plaintiffs seeking to establish jurisdiction than to the excesses that the approach permitted. The State of Washington brought an action in its courts to recover from the International Shoe Company – a Delaware corporation, whose principal place of business was

---

84   *Idem* 356-357 (citing *Kane* v. *New Jersey*, 242 US 160, at 167 (1916)).

85   For a discussion of how the jurisdictional basis asserted in *Hess* is justified under a fairness theory, see pp. 109-111, *infra*.

86   See *supra* footnote 79; the case is also discussed in Chap. VI. B. 2. *(a)*, pp. 272, *infra*. An interesting discussion of the facts of this case and of the drafting history of Stone's opinion is C. Cameron and K. Johnson, "Death of a Salesman? Forum Shopping and Outcome Determination under International Shoe", 28 *U.C. Davis L. Rev.* 769-862 (1995).

87   326 US at 319.

in St. Louis, Missouri – unpaid contributions to the state unemployed compensation fund. Because a tax claim was involved, the suit might well not have been entertained by the courts of Missouri or Delaware, which clearly had, under a power theory, adjudicatory authority over the corporation.[88]

The corporation had arranged its activities – the manufacture and sale of footwear – in such a fashion as to reduce to a minimum – and, if possible, entirely avoid – what the power theory at the time would have considered doing of business in Washington. It had neither an office nor a stock of merchandise in the state and made there no contracts for either the sale or the purchase of merchandise. All orders were filled by f.o.b. shipments from points outside Washington to purchasers within the state. During the years for which unemployment contributions were claimed, the corporation employed about a dozen salesmen who were under the direct supervision and control of sales managers located in St. Louis. The salesmen resided in Washington and their principal activities were in that state. The corporation supplied them with samples and reimbursed them for the rent of inventory display rooms. They exhibited samples and solicited orders but had no authority to enter into contracts or make collections. All orders were accepted or rejected in St. Louis.

The Washington courts found the corporation's activities, in particular the regular and systematic solicitation of orders within the state by its salesmen, which resulted in a continuous flow of the corporation's products into the state, sufficient to constitute doing business there. The corporation brought the matter to the Supreme Court, arguing "that its activities within the state were not sufficient to manifest its 'presence' there" so that the assertion of jurisdiction violated due process.[89]

Chief Justice Stone's opinion for the Court, after stating the facts and the arguments, which had been couched in terms of the power theory, approached the jurisdiction issue in new terms:

> Historically the jurisdiction of courts to render judgment *in personam* is grounded on their de facto power over the defendant's person. Hence his presence within the territorial jurisdiction of a court was prerequisite to its rendition of a judgment personally binding him .... But now that the *capias ad respondendum* has given way to personal service of summons or other form of notice, due process requires only that in order to subject a defendant to a judgment *in personam*, if he be not present within the territory of the forum, he have certain minimum contacts with it such that the maintenance of the suit does not offend 'traditional notions of fair play and substantial justice'. ... Since the corporate personality is a fiction, ... it is clear that unlike an indi-

---

88   See *Moore v. Mitchell*, 30 F. 2d 600 (2d Cir. 1929), *aff'd on other grounds*, 281 US 18 (1930). But cf. *State ex rel. Oklahoma Tax Comm'n v. Rodgers*, 238 Mo. App. 1115, 193 SW 2d 919 (1946) (revenue law of foreign state enforced against former resident of that state). See generally E. Scoles, "Interstate and International Distinctions in Conflict of Laws in the United States", 54 *Calif. L. Rev.* 1599, at 1607-1608 (1966).

89   326 US at 315.

vidual its 'presence' without, as well as within, the state of its origin can be manifested only by activities carried on in its behalf by those who are authorized to act for it. To say that the corporation is so far 'present' there as to satisfy due process requirements … is to beg the question to be decided. For the terms 'present' or 'presence' are used merely to symbolize those activities of the corporation's agent within the state which courts will deem to be sufficient to satisfy the demands of due process …. Those demands may be met by such contacts of the corporation with the state of the forum as make it reasonable, in the context of our federal system of government, to require the corporation to defend the particular suit which is brought there. An 'estimate of the inconveniences' which would result to the corporation from a trial away from its 'home' or principal place of business is relevant in this connection.[90]

The Chief Justice then explained certain solutions reached under the aegis of the power theory in terms of convenience, fairness, and justice:

[I]t has been generally recognized that the casual presence of the corporate agent or even his conduct of single or isolated items of activities in a state in the corporation's behalf are not enough to subject it to suits on causes of action unconnected with the activities there …. To require the corporation in such circumstances to defend the suit away from its home or other jurisdiction where it carries on more substantial activities has been thought to lay too great and unreasonable a burden on the corporation to comport with due process.[91]

In Stone's view, a mechanical or quantitative test of presence in terms of power was not decisive.

Whether due process is satisfied must depend rather upon the quality and nature of the activity in relation to the fair and orderly administration of the laws which it was the purpose of the due process clause to insure.[92]

Stone continued:

Applying these standards, the activities carried on in behalf of appellant in the State of Washington were neither irregular nor casual. They were systematic and continuous throughout the years in question. They resulted in a large volume of interstate business, in the course of which … [the corporation] received the benefits and protection of the laws of the state, including the right to resort to the courts for the enforcement of its rights. The obligation which is here sued upon arose out of those very activities. It is evident that these operations establish sufficient contacts or ties with the state of the forum to make it reasonable and just, according to our traditional conception of

---

90   *Idem* 316-317.
91   *Idem* 317.
92   *Idem* 319.

fair play and substantial justice, to permit the state to enforce the obligations which appellant has incurred there.[93]

In principle, Stone's reasoning in *International Shoe* is applicable to claims of general, category-specific, and – most importantly – specific jurisdiction. To survive Stone's test, claims of general and category-specific jurisdiction have to establish that, viewed *ex ante* and in group-norm terms, the claim was convenient, fair, and just. General jurisdiction based on the defendant's domicile satisfies that standard; general jurisdiction based on the defendant's engaging in relatively limited activities in the jurisdiction does not. In order to recognize the adjudicatory authority of the State of Washington over International Shoe, the jurisdictional claim must rest either on a power theory – which Stone rejects – or on an *ex post*, controversy-specific application of the convenience, fairness, and justice standard that Stone had proposed.

International Shoe thus proposed not only a new standard on which claims of adjudicatory authority could be validated but also proposed that it be applied not only in *ex ante*, group-norm but also *ex post*, case-specific terms. The debates and difficulties that *International Shoe* has engendered relate essentially to Stone's second proposition.

(a)   The tension between power and litigational-justice theories

International Shoe did not declare the power theory unacceptable but announced an alternative theory based on convenience, fairness, and justice. Some jurists argue that, although the decision "undoubtedly ... ushered in an era of expanded jurisdictional reach for state courts", it merely "fit[ted] the assertion of jurisdiction [by the State of Washington] into one of the traditional territorial bases, in this case in personam jurisdiction based on 'presence' ...".[94] In the final analysis, the Court "justif[ied] its exercise of jurisdiction in terms of the metaphor of corporate 'presence' ...".[95]

Chief Justice Stone's "minimum contacts" language and his use of the "presence" metaphor do have territorial undertones and these are heightened by his essentially exclusive focus on the defendant's activities and convenience. Nevertheless Stone's emphasis on "the fair and orderly administration of the law which it was the purpose of the due process clause to insure"[96] and on "fair play and substantial justice"[97] clearly seems designed to loosen the hold over jurisdictional theory and practice of territorial metaphors such as "presence" and of territorially based thinking generally.

---

93   *Idem* 320.

94   Borchers, *supra* footnote 14, at 54-55.

95   *Idem* 56.

96   326 US at 319.

97   *Idem* 320.

In all events, at the time the view was widely held that *International Shoe* announced a new jurisdictional theory without excluding the older, territorially based, power theory. The unesasy co-existence of *Pennoyer* and *International Shoe* is seen in the Restatement Second of Conflict of Laws, promulgated in 1969.[98] Its section 24 (1) speaks in fairness terms: "A state has power to exercise judicial jurisdiction over a person if the person's relationship to the state is such as to make the exercise of such jurisdiction reasonable." Section 56 (1)[99] announces the same standard: there is "judicial jurisdiction to determine interests in a thing if the relationship of the thing to the state is such as to make the exercise of such jurisdiction reasonable". On the other hand, section 28 recognizes that "[a] state has power to exercise judicial jurisdiction over an individual who is present within its territory, whether permanently or temporarily".[100] And section 68 restates the rule of *Harris* v. *Balk*:

> A state has power to exercise judicial jurisdiction to apply to the satisfaction of a claim an obligation owed to the person against whom the claim is asserted if the obligor is subject to the judicial jurisdiction of the state ... .[101]

The authors of the Restatement were fully aware, of course, of the tension between the jurisdictional theory set out in sections 24 (1) and 56 (1) and the jurisdictional bases recognized by sections 28 and 68. As the courts were now using both the

---

98   In the 1980s, Restatement Second was revised in several respects in order to take into account changes – due in large measure to the US Supreme Court's jurisprudence – in the practice and theory of jurisdiction to adjudicate. Unless otherwise indicated, all quotations from the Restatement Second of Conflict of Laws are of the 1969 text.

99   In 1988, "determine" was substituted for "affect" in Section 56 (1) and the Comments to this section were rewritten "to reflect the decision of the Supreme Court in *Shaffer* v. *Heitner*, 433 US 186 (1977)" (discussed on pp. 102 *et seq.*, *infra*). See Restatement Second of Conflict of Laws, Revisions, at 60-62 (1988).

100 In 1988, Section 28 was revised in light of the *Shaffer* decision by striking "whether permanently or temporarily" and adding "unless the individual's relationship to the state is so attenuated as to make the exercise of such jurisdiction unreasonable". See *idem* 28.

101 Section 68, though revised in 1988, still bears the same title as before; its meaning is entirely different, however. The original Section 68 stated the rule in *Harris* v. *Balk*, 198 US 215 (1905), see pp. 88, *supra*. The revisions rest on *Shaffer* v. *Heitner*, 433 US 186, which overruled *Harris*. Under *Harris*, a plaintiff could establish adjudicatory authority over his debtor by serving the latter's debtor within the state. As revised, in order to establish jurisdiction in such situations the plaintiff must not only establish jurisdiction over the ultimate defendant's debtor but also demonstrate, under Section 66 (1), that "[t]he court could properly exercise jurisdiction to adjudicate the claim under the rules stated in §§27-65; or ... [that] [t]he exercise of such jurisdiction is otherwise reasonable". (Section 27 of the Restatement Second of Conflict of Laws lists the principal bases for establishing adjudicatory authority, including, *inter alia*, domicile, consent, doing business in the state, and "other relationships to the state which make the exercise of judicial jurisdiction reasonable".)

older and the newer jurisdictional rationales, the Restaters felt compelled to accept both. The ambivalence that resulted is recognized in Comment *a* to section 28:

> The rule that physical presence is a basis of judicial jurisdiction may result at times in a defendant being compelled to stand suit in a state to which he has no relationship other than the fact that he was served with process while passing through that state's territory. It can also be contended that the rule is inconsistent with the basic principle of reasonableness which underlies the field of judicial jurisdiction (see §24).

Likewise, Comment *c* to section 68 notes that

> [t]he rule that the temporary presence of the garnishee in the state provides an adequate basis of garnishment jurisdiction might be thought inconsistent with the basic principle of reasonableness which underlies the field of judicial jurisdiction (see §§24, 56).

(b) Confrontation?: *Shaffer* v. *Heitner* (1977)

Not until 1977 did the Supreme Court face the significance for American jurisdictional theory and practice of the co-existence of *Pennoyer* and *International Shoe* and their respective progeny. The two lines of authority were distinguishable. In *International Shoe*, the Court evaluated for due process purposes in *ex post*, controversy-specific terms an assertion of adjudicatory authority. Such claims can, in their very nature, only be evaluated in controversy-specific terms. *International Shoe* establishes the admissibility of such claims and the due-process standard they must satisfy, namely, litigational convenience, fairness, and justice.

Pennoyer and its progeny dealt, on the other hand, with jurisdictional claims that rested not on the manifold and particular characteristics of the specific controversy that was to be adjudicated but on general characteristics – for example, the defendants' domicile in the forum, service of process on the defendant in the forum, or the presence there of assets belonging to the defendant – that were taken to justify the assertion of adjudicatory authority regardless of the quality of the particular controversy's relationship to the forum.

Some jurists saw the Supreme Court's decision in *Shaffer* v. *Heitner*[102] as the full and final rejection of *Pennoyer* and its progeny. Heitner, a non-resident of

---

102   See *supra* footnote 101. Acceptance of an instrumental theory in principle would not extirpate all power elements from the jurisprudence of adjudicatory authority. In the first place, effectiveness, which is linked to power, is relevant for non-power theories of jurisdiction. Secondly, certain jurisdictional bases – for example, jurisdiction based on physical presence – that can be seen as resting on a power-based analysis remained – and still remain – in general use in the United States. See pp. 107 *et seq.*, *infra*. Finally, the language and analysis used by the courts in approaching jurisdictional issues continue to exhibit not insignificant elements that can be said to derive from power theory. See, e.g., *World-Wide Volkswagen Corp.* v. *Woodson*, 444 US 286 (1980).

Delaware, brought suit in Delaware against Greyhound Corporation, Greyhound Lines, a wholly owned subsidiary, and various present and former officers and directors of one or both of the foregoing. Greyhound was incorporated in Delaware, Greyhound Lines in California; the principal place of business of both was Phoenix, Arizona. Heitner

> alleged that the individual defendants had violated their duties to Greyhound by causing it and its subsidiary to engage in actions that resulted in the corporations being held liable for substantial damages in a private antitrust suit and a large fine in a criminal contempt action.[103]

The conduct in question took place in Oregon. Jurisdiction was sought to be established over the individual defendants by sequestering, as Delaware law permitted, stock and stock options belonging to them. The certificates representing the stock were not physically present in Delaware but, under Delaware law, the "situs of ownership of all stock in Delaware corporations" is Delaware.[104] The individual defendants challenged this assertion of jurisdiction on several grounds, including "that under the rule of *International Shoe Co.* v. *Washington* ... they did not have sufficient contacts with Delaware to sustain the jurisdiction of that State's courts".[105] The Delaware Supreme Court gave this argument short shrift. In a brief, two paragraph decision, the court took the position that jurisdiction can be based either on considerations of fairness or on power, and that the jurisdiction asserted plainly rested on the latter and satisfied traditional constitutional standards.[106]

As Justice Marshall noted in his opinion for the US Supreme Court, this "analysis assumes the continued soundness of the conceptual structure founded on the century-old case of *Pennoyer* v. *Neff* ...".[107] After a thoughtful discussion, he concluded that

> [t]he fiction that an assertion of jurisdiction over property is anything but an assertion of jurisdiction over the owner of the property supports an ancient form without substantial modern justification. Its continued acceptance would only serve to allow state-court jurisdiction that is fundamentally unfair to the defendant.
> We therefore conclude that all assertions of state-court jurisdiction must be evaluated according to the standards set forth in *International Shoe* and its progeny.[108]

---

103   433 US at 190.

104   *Idem* 192 (citing Del. Code Ann. tit. 8, §169 (1975)).

105   *Idem* 193.

106   See *idem* 195 (quoting *Greyhound Corp.* v. *Heitner*, 361 A. 2d 225, at 229 (Del. 1976)).

107   *Idem* 196.

108   *Idem* 212.

Justice Rehnquist took no part in the consideration or decision of *Shaffer* v. *Heit-ner*. All the other justices – except Justice Powell on a limited issue[109] and Justice Stevens on a broader basis[110] – agreed with the proposition that, in the *Shaffer* setting, exercises of adjudicatory jurisdiction can no longer be based on a conceptual structure derived from a power theory.[111]

---

109 Justice Powell's possible qualification respected whether

> the ownership of some forms of property whose situs is indisputably and permanently located within a State may, without more, provide the contacts necessary to subject the defendant to jurisdiction within the State to the extent of the value of the property. In the case of real property, in particular, preservation of the common-law concept of *quasi in rem* jurisdiction arguably would avoid the uncertainty of the general *International Shoe* standard without significant cost to 'traditional notions of fair play and substantial justice'.

Idem 217 (Powell, J., concurring).

110 Justice Stevens's basic position was that an exercise of jurisdiction is constitutionally acceptable so long as the "requirement of fair notice" is met. For him, fair notice "includes fair warning that a particular activity may subject a person to the jurisdiction of a foreign sovereign". *Idem* 218 (Stevens, J., concurring). Accordingly, he would uphold jurisdiction in the following circumstances:

> If I visit another State, or acquire real estate or open a bank account in it, I knowingly assume some risk that the State will exercise its power over my property or my person while there. My contact with the State, though minimal, gives rise to predictable risks.

Ibid.

It follows that Stevens would not "invalidate *quasi in rem* jurisdiction where real estate is involved" nor "other long-accepted methods of acquiring jurisdiction over persons with adequate notice of both the particular controversy and the fact that their local activities might subject them to suit". *Idem* 219.
Stevens went on to say, regarding the case at hand, that

> [p]erhaps the same consequences should flow from the purchase of stock of a corporation organized under the laws of a foreign nation, because to some limited extent one's property and affairs then become subject to the laws of the nation of domicile of the corporation.

He then argues the counter-intuitive proposition that this conclusion does not follow when one purchases shares of stock of a corporation organized under the laws of a state of the United States as one "can hardly be expected to know that he has thereby become subject to suit in a forum remote from his residence and unrelated to the transaction". *Ibid.* The risk and burden are, he notes, especially great in the case of Delaware because it, "[u]nlike the 49 other States … treats the place of incorporation as the situs of the stock, even though both the owner and the custodian of the shares are elsewhere". *Ibid.*

111 Justice Brennan "fully agree[d]" with the portion of the Court's opinion discussed above but dissented from the Court's conclusion that Delaware's assertion of jurisdiction did not satisfy the *International Shoe* standard. *Idem* 219-220 (Brennan J., concurring in part and dissenting in part).
For present purposes, the contrasting views of Marshall and Brennan on this issue need not be discussed; Delaware not having asserted adjudicatory authority on a

5. Can Claims of General and Category-Specific Jurisdiction Pass Constitutional Muster in Terms of Their Typical Effects?

Chief Justice Stone in *International Shoe* did not discuss whether claims of general and category-specific jurisdiction had to satisfy the due-process standard – namely, litigational justice rather than power – applicable to claims of specific jurisdiction nor, if so, how the convenience, fairness, and justice standard was to be applied to such claims.

Justice Holmes's rationale for determining constitutionality *vel non* in *ex ante*, group-norm – rather than controversy-specific – terms is ample enough to cover jurisdictional issues:

> Now and then an extraordinary case may turn up, but constitutional law like other mortal contrivances has to take some chances, and in the great majority of instances no doubt justice will be done.[112]

Objectively evaluated, a high quality basis of general jurisdiction, such as the defendant's domicile or habitual residence, withstands constitutional challenge; these relationships typically identify forums in which one can, in principle, appropriately be required to defend against claims not otherwise specifically connected with the forum. On the other hand, lower quality bases such as service within the forum upon the defendant (tag jurisdiction) or on the defendant's debtor (*quasi in rem* jurisdiction) so evaluated are unconstitutional; they do not identify what are, in principle, appropriate forums in which to litigate any type of claim brought against the defendant.[113]

Group-norm evaluation is used in American law in applying due-process requirements respecting the giving of notice to defendants. In *Mullane* v. *Central Hannover Bank & Trust Co.*,[114] Justice Jackson wrote as follows:

> [T]his Court has not hesitated to approve of resort to publication as a customary substitute [for actual notice] ... where it is not reasonably possible or practicable to give more adequate warning. Thus it has been recognized that, in the case of persons missing or unknown, employment of an indirect and even a probably futile means of

---

minimum-contacts basis, Part IV of Marshall's opinion – and Brennan's response – are, technically speaking, lengthy dictums.

112   *Blinn* v. *Nelson*, 222 US 1, at 7 (1911).

113   Some types of "*quasi in rem* jurisdiction" could perhaps qualify as constitutional under a general-effects test. Justice Powell, concurring in *Shaffer*, so argued with respect to jurisdiction based upon seizure of the defendant's immovable property in the forum state. See *supra* footnote 109.

114   339 US 306 (1950). It is worth remarking that *Mullane* was decided five years after *International Shoe*.

notification is all that the situation permits and creates no constitutional bar to a final decree foreclosing their rights.[115]

Some American jurists today reject, however, the proposition that a jurisdictional norm's constitutionality can be established on the basis of its group-norm effects; for them, jurisdictional norms are of a special character such that their constitutionality *vel non* must be evaluated in controversy-specific terms. Professor Twitchell writes that, although the "group norm test" is acceptable for resolving constitutional issues in many areas of law, claims of adjudicatory authority are unique in that

> an individual is claiming that the state has absolutely no power over him to decide the claim submitted. Group norm tests presuppose such authority and the only question is the scope of that power ... .
>
> The ultimate issue here is whether the injury suffered by a single individual unconstitutionally subjected to state authority can be traded off for the advantages to be gained by preserving a rule that produces fair results in most cases. I think not ... .[116]

For those who agree with Professor Twitchell, every claim of adjudicatory authority must be fair and reasonable when evaluated in controversy-specific terms. But do theoretical or practical considerations justify this position? Ease of administration and predictability of results are important values that support an *ex ante* group-norm test in which the jurisdictional claim does not depend on the manifold and particular characteristics of the controversy. An *ex ante*, group-norm evaluation is plainly feasible, and seems appropriate, where claims of general[117] or category-specific jurisdiction are in issue.[118]

Concurring in *Burnham* v. *Superior Court of California*,[119] Justice White took a position diametrically opposed to Professor Twitchell's. To establish that a basis of general or category-specific jurisdiction violated due process, it was not enough to establish that the elements of the connecting factor in question – for

---

115   *Idem* 317. Justice Jackson's discussion was directed to the question of what constitutes adequate notice of the pending proceedings. The approach should be acceptable as well when the constitutionality of a given jurisdictional basis is in question unless there is a fundamental difference for due process purposes between notice and assertions of adjudicating authority.

116   M. Twitchell, "*Burnham* and Constitutionally Permissible Levels of Harm", 22 *Rutgers LJ* 659, at 672 (1991). It is worth noting that a somewhat similar argument with respect to the special character of jurisdictional claims is made when the adjudicatory authority *vel non* of an arbitral tribunal is in question.

117   Compare *Milliken* v. *Meyer*, 311 US 457 (1940) (upholding jurisdiction at the defendant's domicile).

118   Compare *Williams* v. *North Carolina [I]*, 317 US 287 (1947) (upholding jurisdiction to divorce at the petitioner's domicile).

119   495 US 604 (1990); for a full discussion of *Burnham*, see pp. 107 *et seq.*, *infra*.

example, service of process on the defendant while he was present within the jurisdiction – did not establish a rational and litigationally fair basis for the state's claim of adjudicatory authority. Through a controversy-specific analysis of actual cases in which the state's courts had asserted adjudicatory authority in light of the jurisdictional rule in question, it must be established

> that as a general proposition the rule is so arbitrary and lacking in common sense in so many instances that it should be held violative of due process in every case. Furthermore, until such a showing is made, which would be difficult indeed, claims in individual cases that the rule would operate unfairly as applied to the particular nonresident involved need not be entertained .... Otherwise, there would be endless, fact-specific litigation in the trial and appellate courts, including this one.[120]

The novelty in White's suggestion is not his use of both group-norm and specific-effect tests – Justice Marshall had used a cumulative approach in *Shaffer* – but rather the very heavy burden that he places on defendants to establish that the jurisdictional claim is "arbitrary and lacking in common sense" in order to avoid "endless, fact specific litigation in the trial and appellate courts, including this one".[121] Professor Twitchell had this aspect of White's opinion in mind when she wrote in 1991 that she had

> never seen an approach like his in any personal jurisdiction decision: he affirms an assertion of jurisdiction based upon service in the forum because defendant has not shown that a significant number of people are hurt by this practice.[122]

In effect, Justice White's approach would end constitutional control of state claims of adjudicatory authority, a step that some jurists have advocated.[123] Only if the practices of individual states were controlled by international conventions or federal legislation would such a step merit serious consideration.[124]

6.   *Co-existence:* Burnham v. Superior Court of California *(1990)*

After *Shaffer*, the argument could be made with considerable force that litigational fairness had vanquished power in American jurisdictional thinking and practice. Indeed, section 28 of the Restatement Second of Conflict of Laws, which originally recognized that a state had adjudicatory authority "over a defendant who is present within the territory", was qualified by adding "unless the individu-

---

120   495 US at 628. White intimates, however, that the general-effects test might be decisive "when presence in the forum State is [not] intentional ...". *Ibid.*

121   *Ibid.*

122   Twitchell, *supra* footnote 116, at 659.

123   See Borchers, *supra* footnote 14, at 104.

124   See Chap. II. D. 1. *(b)* (ii), pp. 59 *et seq., supra.*

al's relationship to the state is so attenuated as to make the exercise of such jurisdiction unreasonable".[125] In a comment, it is remarked that *Shaffer* had "made clear that the principles of *International Shoe* ... apply generally to questions of jurisdiction, whether over persons or things".[126] However, in less than a decade, the decision in *Helicopteros Nacionales de Colombia, S.A.* v. *Hall* raised doubts.[127] Justice Blackmun's majority opinion relied in substantial measure upon a 1923 decision[128] in which Justice Brandeis, speaking for a unanimous court, had made "clear that purchases and related trips, standing alone, are not a sufficient basis for a State's assertion of [general] jurisdiction".[129] In deciding that the contacts of the defendant

> foreign corporation with the State of Texas were [not] sufficient to allow a Texas state court to assert jurisdiction over the [defendant] corporation in a cause of action not arising out of or related to the corporation's activities within the State,[130]

Blackmun relied on authority before as well as after *International Shoe*.[131] The fact that his analysis does not rest principally and explicitly on litigational justice considerations suggests that for him the power theory was still viable. In dissent, Justice Brennan remarked that

> [t]he Court ... looks for guidance to our 1923 decision in *Rosenberg* ... which until today was of dubious validity given the subsequent expansion of personal jurisdiction that began with *International Shoe* ... in 1945 ...[132]

The Supreme Court's 1990 decision in *Burnham* v. *Superior Court of California*,[133] removed all doubt that American jurisdictional thinking and practice still had two strands: one resting on power, the other on convenience, fairness and justice.

---

125   The original text of Section 28 expressly provides that temporary presence suffices.

126   Restatement Second of Conflict of Laws (1988 Revision), Comment *b*, *The requirement of reasonabless.*

127   466 US 408 (1984).

128   *Rosenberg Bros. & Co.* v. *Curtis Brown Co.*, 260 US 516 (1923).

129   466 US at 417. Brandeis's opinion used, of course, power-theory language: "The sole question for decision is whether ... defendant was doing business within the State of New York in such manner and to such extent as to warrant the inference that it was present there." 260 US at 517.

130   466 US at 409.

131   See *idem* 418-419 where he gives essentially equal weight to *Rosenberg*, which involved claims of general jurisdiction, and to *Kulko* v. *California Superior Court*, 436 US 84 (1978), where specific jurisdiction was claimed.

132   *Idem* 419, at 421. Brennan considers the "view of *in personam* jurisdiction adopted by the Court in Rosenberg" to be "narrow" and not to "comport[] with 'the fundamental transformation of our national economy' that has occurred since 1923". *Idem* 422.

133   495 US 604 (1990).

In *Burnham* the issue was whether service of process upon a person, transiently present in the state, sufficed to establish general jurisdiction over him. The Court unanimously sustained the jurisdictional claim; however, no single theoretical justification of the result commanded a majority.

The dispute was matrimonial in nature; Mrs. Burnham sought legal separation, spousal and child support, determination of matrimonial property rights, and custody. The parties seemed to have disagreed principally about economic benefits – "support and property distributions and the enforceability of an agreement about those rights signed by the parties". Under *Williams* v. *North Carolina [I]*,[134] the domicile of either spouse had jurisdiction to divorce; under *Estin* v. *Estin*,[135] however, the petitioner's domicile lacked authority to regulate the financial consequences of the divorce. The Supreme Court does not discuss whether *Estin* should be overruled so that California could assert category-specific jurisdiction over the support clause and related claims. The proposition that "the tail must go with the hide ..."[136] having been rejected in *Estin*, Mrs. Burnham could obtain in California the relief that she sought only by establishing general jurisdiction over Mr. Burnham.

Justice Scalia announced the court's judgment and authored an opinion, joined in by Chief Justice Rehnquist, Justice Kennedy, and – except as to Parts II-D and III – Justice White, which takes the position that

> jurisdiction based on physical presence alone constitutes due process because it is one of the continuing traditions of our legal system that define the due process standard 'traditional notions of fair play and substantial justice' ... .[137]

Part II-D of the opinion continues:

> The logic of *Shaffer*'s holding – which places all suits against absent nonresidents on the same constitutional footing ... – does not compel the conclusion that physically present defendants must be treated identically to absent ones. As we have demonstrated at length, our tradition has treated the two classes of defendants quite differently, and it is unreasonable to read *Shaffer* as casually obliterating that distinction ...[138]

---

134   317 US 787 (1942). For a discussion of the applicability of *Williams* to the issues in *Burnham*, see L. Silberman, "Reflections on *Burnham* v. *Superior Court*: Towards Presumptive Rules of Jurisdiction and Implications for Choice of Law", 22 *Rut. L. J.* 569, at 590-595 (1991).

135   334 US 541 (1948). The defendant's – as distinct from the plaintiff's – domicile is, of course, an accepted base for general jurisdiction under power and litigational justice theories alike.

136   *Idem* 544 (Douglas J.).

137   495 US at 619 (Part II-C).

138   *Idem* 621.

Although in Justice Scalia's view, the Court's holding "does not contradict *Shaffer*", he freely admits that

> our basic approach to the due process question is different. We have conducted no independent inquiry into the desirability or fairness of the prevailing in-state service rule, leaving that judgment to the legislatures that are free to amend it; for our purposes, its validation is its pedigree, as the phrase '*traditional notions* of fair play and substantial justice' makes clear ....[139]

This position is, with nuances, supported by Justice White and Stevens in their respective concurring opinions. White wrote that

> [t]he rule allowing jurisdiction to be obtained over a nonresident by personal service in the forum State, without more, has been and is so widely accepted throughout this country that I could not possibly strike it down, either on its face or as applied in this case, on the ground that it denies due process of law guaranteed by the Fourteenth Amendment ....[140]

Justice Stevens accepts, without indicating the weight of each, a medley of arguments – "the historical evidence and consensus identified by Justice Scalia, the considerations of fairness identified by Justice Brennan, and the common sense displayed by Justice White ..." – and finds that the case is "a very easy" one.[141]

In the final analysis, four justices thus take the view that the acceptability of general jurisdiction based on personal service can turn either on long accepted practice or on considerations of litigational justice. At least for them, power and litigational justice theories of jurisdiction continue to co-exist in the United States. On the other hand, Justice Brennan's concurring opinion, in which Justices Blackmun, Marshall, and O'Connor joined,[142] takes the position that today

> all rules of jurisdiction, even ancient ones, must satisfy contemporary notions of due process .... [The] *holding* in *Shaffer* may have been limited to *quasi in rem* jurisdiction, ... [the Court's] mode of analysis was not .... [W]e were willing in *Shaffer* to examine anew the appropriateness of the *quasi in rem* rule ....[143]

In support of his view that California could constitutionally exercise general jurisdiction over the defendant spouse, Justice Brennan relied not on tag jurisdiction's pedigree but on considerations of litigational justice. He advanced three

---

139   *Ibid.* (emphasis in original).

140   *Idem* 628. He took the view that jurisdictional claims are acceptable unless they are "so arbitrary ... in so many instances that ... [they] should be held violative of due process *in every case*" (emphasis added). *Ibid.*

141   *Idem* 640.

142   *Idem* 628-640.

143   *Idem* 630.

propositions: (1) a visitor to a state knowingly assumes the risks that adjudicatory jurisdiction can there be established over him with respect to any controversy regardless whether the controversy was connected with the visit; (2) during a visit, one avails himself – as needed – of, *inter alia*, police, fire, and emergency medical services and uses local roads and waterways; (3) out-of-staters will not find defending local actions unduly burdensome in light of modern transportation and communication facilities and, since Mr. Burnham had recently visited the state, the forum should not be unduly inconvenient for him. In light of these considerations, Brennan concludes that "as a rule the exercise of personal jurisdiction over a defendant based on his voluntary presence in the forum will satisfy the requirements of due process".[144]

Taken to its logical conclusion, this line of argument allows a state, subject to the giving of some form of adequate notice, for example, by registered mail or local service of process, to exercise adjudicatory authority over any person who, knowingly and voluntarily, had recently sojourned in the state. Brennan's arguments justifying the assertion of jurisdiction in these circumstances are neither strengthened nor weakened by the service *vel non* of process upon the defendant while he is physically present in the forum.

The additional, entirely formal, requirement of service has, it is true, the salutary effect of limiting the scope of an exorbitant jurisdictional claim. But this ameliorating effect does not transmute a substantively exorbitant claim into a proper one. The basic objections to California's exercise of adjudicatory authority remain; the only significant difference is the claim's greater modesty. Service adds nothing, however, that goes to the claim's intrinsic propriety. Only in exceptional circumstances should cumulation of jurisdictional bases with the same intrinsic defect result in an acceptable basis. *Ex nihilo nihil fit.*

Justice Scalia's argument for the pedigree principle is less persuasive than his demonstration of the emptiness of Justice Brennan's analysis:

> Justice Brennan lists the 'benefits' Mr. Burnham derived from the State of California – the fact that, during the few days he was there, '[h]is health and safety [were] guaranteed by the State's police, fire, and emergency medical services; he [was] free to travel on the State's roads and waterways; he likely enjoy[ed] the fruits of the State's economy....' Three days worth of these benefits strike us as powerfully inadequate to establish, as an abstract matter, that it is 'fair' for California to decree the ownership of all Mr. Burnham's worldly goods acquired during the ten years of his marriage, and the custody over his children .... Even less persuasive are the other 'fairness' factors alluded to by Justice Brennan. It would create 'an asymmetry', we are told, if Burnham were *permitted* (as he is) to appear in California courts as a plaintiff, but were not *compelled* to appear in California courts as defendant;[145] and travel being as easy

---

144   *Idem* 639.

145   Brennan's asymmetry argument may have some superficial plausibility, but it cannot survive analysis. He reasons that, because the defendant in a given controversy could – were he the plaintiff – sue in the same court the person now suing him, symmetry

as it is nowadays, and modern procedural devices being so convenient, it is no great hardship to appear in California courts …. The problem with the[] [foregoing] assertions is that they justify the exercise of jurisdiction over *everyone, whether or not he ever* comes to California. The only 'fairness' elements setting Mr. Burnham aside from the rest of the world are the three days' 'benefits' referred to above – and even those, do not set him apart from many other people who have enjoyed three days in the Golden State (savoring the fruits of its economy, the availability of its roads and police services) but who were fortunate enough not be served with process while they were there and thus are not (simply by reason of that savoring) subject to the general jurisdiction of California's courts …. In other words, even if one agreed with Justice Brennan's conception of an equitable bargain, the 'benefits' we have been discussing would explain why it is fair to assert general jurisdiction over Burnham-returned-to-New-Jersey-after-service only at the expense of proving that it is also 'fair' to assert general jurisdiction over Burnham-returned-to-New-Jersey-*without*-service – which we *know* does not conform with 'contemporary notions of due process'.[146]

7.   Ambiguities and Uncertainties in American Jurisdictional Theory and Practice as the Twenty-First Century Begins

Three fundamental and troubling issues challenge American jurists as a new century has dawned: (1) what should be the role and scope of power and of litigational fairness for the theory and practice of adjudicatory authority; (2) to what extent should theory and practice take into account state – as distinct from party – concerns in dealing with claims of adjudicatory authority; and (3) can connecting factors be devised that are theoretically appropriate but less complex, diverse, and elusive in nature than those that have emerged in recent decades?

(a)   The contemporary role and scope of power and litigational-fairness theories

Does the *Burnham* decision[147] apply to the bases of unlimited general jurisdiction – or even of limited general jurisdiction – whose "pedigrees" were less clearly and

---

requires that the court have jurisdiction over him in the present action. This jurisdictional theory is nonsensical: It is true – and can be seen as a requirement of symmetry – that, when an action is brought against a party, the court seized has jurisdiction over related *counterclaims* that the defendant may choose to bring, although this court would have had no jurisdiction to entertain the claims had the counterclaimant appeared before it as a plaintiff. See Chap. V. C. 3., pp. 194 *et seq., infra*. This is, however, entirely different from the propositions advanced by Brennan. How can the fact that one who *could* have – but *did not* – seize a forum, confer on that forum adjudicatory authority over him that it would not otherwise have? The theory is absurd on its face.

146   *Idem* 623-624 (emphasis in original).

147   The consequences of applying the pedigree principle to international litigation are also not entirely clear. The fairness objections to tag jurisdiction are usually stronger in international than in interstate litigation; some argue that fairness considerations

firmly established than was tag jurisdiction when *International Shoe* was decided? For example, does the availability of unlimited general jurisdiction over legal persons based on the doing-of-business within the legal order turn on pre-1945 standards and practices – the pedigree – or on an analysis in fairness terms?

In view as well of the eclectic quality of Justice Blackmun's opinion in the *Helicopteros* case,[148] as of the analogy – drawn long before *International Shoe* – between the presence of natural persons and the doing of business by legal persons, Scalia's analysis in *Burnham* could well apply to claims of general jurisdiction over legal persons. If so, the constitutionality of general jurisdiction on the basis of activities wholly or largely unconnected with the controversy to be adjudicated could turn today either on historical pedigree or litigational justice.

Litigational-justice theories raise – just as do power theories – indubitable difficulties. In a very real sense, the *Burnham* decision perpetuates – for the contexts to which it applies – the worst of both worlds: the adverse effects that fairness theories have upon administrability and predictability remain, as does the potential for unfairness that lurks in power theories.

Furthermore, with two strings to his bow of theory, a plaintiff is free to derive advantage from both of two ultimately incompatible theories.

(b)   The respective importance of state and party concerns

Pennoyer v. *Neff* approached the constitutionality of state claims of adjudicatory authority from the perspective of its allocation among sovereign States; *International Shoe Co.* v. *Washington* added another dimension to the jurisdictional inquiry, is the claim appropriate from the parties' perspective? The Supreme Court has vacillated in recent decades on whether the latter position should be adopted to the exclusion of the former or jurisdictional theory should give weight to both.

In 1958, Chief Justice Burger remarked in *Hanson* v. *Denkla* that

> the requirements for personal jurisdiction over nonresidents have evolved from the
> rigid rule of *Pennoyer* v. *Neff* ... to the flexible standard of *International Shoe Co.* v.
> *Washington* .... But it is a mistake to assume that this trend heralds the eventual de-
> mise of all restrictions [under the Due Process Clause] on the personal jurisdiction
> of state courts .... Those restrictions are more than a guarantee of immunity from

---

could here displace pedigree. See P. Hay, "Transient Jurisdiction, Especially over International Defendants: Critical Comments on *Burnham* v. *Superior Court of California*", [1990] *U. Ill. L. Rev.* 593, at 602-603; cf. also *Asahi Metal Industry Co., Ltd.* v.
Superior Court of California, 480 US 102 (1987). The principle could, by weighing fairness considerations comparatively, be limited to interstate litigation. Such a limitation is, of course, inconsistent with the pedigree test as formulated by Justice Scalia.
It is also discussed whether, in light of *Burnham*, *Shaffer* can – and perhaps must – be
read restrictively. R. Weintraub, "An Objective Basis for Rejecting Transient Jurisdiction", 22 *Rut. L. J.* 611, at 625 (1991).

148   466 US 408 (1984).

inconvenient or distant litigation. They are a consequence of territorial limitations on the power of the respective States.[149]

Some years later, Justice Marshall wrote for the Court in the *Shaffer* case that, after *International Shoe*,

> the relationship among the defendant, the forum, and the litigation, rather than the mutually exclusive sovereignty on which the rules of *Pennoyer* rest, became the central concern of the inquiry into personal jurisdiction.[150]

Only three years passed before Justice White reiterated in *World-Wide Volkswagen Corp.* v. *Woodson*[151] the jurisdictional significance of sovereignty:

> The concept of minimum contacts ... perform[s] two related, but distinguishable, functions. It protects the defendant against the burdens of litigating in a distant or inconvenient forum. And it acts to ensure that the States, through their courts, do not reach out beyond the limits imposed on them by their status as coequal sovereigns in a federal system.[152]

Two years later, in *Insurance Corp. of Ireland* v. *Compagnie des Bauxites de Guinée*,[153] Justice White recanted;

> [t]he requirement that a court have personal jurisdiction flows ... from the Due Process Clause. The personal jurisdiction requirement recognizes and protects an individual liberty interest. It represents a restriction on judicial power not as a matter of sovereignty, but as a matter of individual liberty.[154]

Within five years, Justice O'Connor returned to the sovereignty theme in *Asahi Metal Industry Co.* v. *Superior Court of California*:[155]

> *World-Wide Volkswagen* ... admonishe[s] courts to take into consideration the interests of the 'several States', in addition to the forum state, in the efficient judicial

---

149   357 US 235, at 250-251 (1958).

150   *Shaffer* v. *Heitner*, 433 US 186, at 204 (1977).

151   444 US 286 (1980).

152   *Idem* 291-292.

153   456 US 694 (1982).

154   *Idem* 702. *Bauxites* upheld on a waiver theory the propriety of sanctioning the defendant's refusal to obey discovery orders, which sought evidence bearing on jurisdiction, by assuming that jurisdiction was properly claimed. But, "if the federalism concept operated as an independent restriction on the sovereign power of the court, it would not be possible [for a party] to waive the personal jurisdiction requirement ...". *Idem* 702.

155   480 US 102 (1987).

resolution of the dispute and the advancement of substantive policies. In the present case, this advice calls for a court to consider the procedural and substantive policies of other *nations* whose interests are affected by the assertion of jurisdiction by the California court. The procedural and substantive interests of other nations in a state court's asserting of jurisdiction over an alien defendant will differ from case to case. In every case, however, those interests, as well as the Federal Government's interest in its foreign relations policies, will be best served by a careful inquiry into the reasonableness of the assertion of jurisdiction in the particular case, and an unwillingness to find the serious burdens on an alien defendant outweighed by minimal interests on the part of the plaintiff or the forum State ....[156]

Thus, "[i]n the space of twenty-nine years [1958 to 1987] the Court . . accepted, then rejected, then accepted, then rejected, and then accepted the 'federalism' or 'sovereignty' factor in the jurisdictional calculus ...".[157] It is not clear what one should make of this history. A plausible view is that, although the Court has remained sensitive to sovereignty concerns, it has, for one reason or another, on occasion preferred to give them expression by linking them to individual liberty concerns through the rhetoric of "minimum contacts". Moreover, as *Hanson* v. *Denkla* illustrates, on various occasions, jurisdictional requirements have been used to affect indirectly state choice-of-law practices that the Court hesitated to control directly.[158] In *Hanson*, from a sheerly litigational point of view, Florida was at least as convenient a forum as Delaware; however, on the issue presented – the validity of a trust – Florida's view was egregious. The Court, by striking down Florida's assertion of adjudicatory authority over the Delaware trustee, was spared the task of deciding upon the constitutionality of Florida's choice-of-law rule.[159] One jurist goes so far as to suggest that "the Court since *Hanson* v. *Denkla* has used jurisdiction primarily as a method of policing and forestalling state court choices of law ...".[160]

(c)   The complex, diverse, elusive, and changing nature of connecting factors resting on convenience, fairness, and justice

The law of jurisdiction is in trouble when, as under the "minimum contacts" analysis of *International Shoe* and its progeny, "the threshold determination of per-

---

156   *Idem* 115.

157   Borchers, *supra* footnote 14, at 78.

158   See A. von Mehren and D. Trautman, "Constitutional Control of Choice of Law: Some Reflections on *Hague*", 10 *Hofstra L. Rev.* 35-57 (1981).

159   See A. von Mehren and D. Trautman, "Jurisdiction to Adjudicate: A Suggested Analysis", 79 *Harv. L. Rev.* 1121, at 1174-1175 (1966).

160   H. Reynolds, "The Concept of Jurisdiction: Conflicting Legal Ideologies and Persistent Formalist Subversion", 18 *Hastings Const. LQ* 819, at 822 (1991). For a discussion of *Kulko, Volkswagen, Rush* v. *Savchuk, Helicopteros*, and *Asahi* from this perspective, see *idem* 862-874.

sonal jurisdiction ... become[s] one of the most litigated issues in state and federal courts ...".[161] Since *International Shoe*,

> [t]he Supreme Court has formulated and reformulated the minimum contacts test many times ..., often in ways that have appeared inconsistent with prior formulations. A tremendous amount of scholarship has been devoted to attempting to untangle this case law, and each new case brings a flood of commentary.[162]

Justice Brennan begins the substantive portion of his opinion for the Court in *Burger King Corp.* v. *Rudzewicz* (1985)[163] "with a seven-page laundry list of the various formulations of the minimum contacts test ... since [1945]".[164] Among the factors mentioned are "fair warning" that jurisdiction may attach, purposeful direction of activities towards forum residents, purposeful availment by the defendant of the privilege of conducting activities within the forum state, the burden on the defendant, the forum's interest in adjudicating the dispute, the plaintiff's interest in obtaining convenient relief, the interest of the interstate judicial system in obtaining the most efficient resolution of controversies, and the shared interests of the several states in furthering fundamental substantive social policies. Not only is the list long, the weight to be assigned to each factor and the way in which the factors interact are less than clear.

The various considerations that the Supreme Court has taken into account in applying *International Shoe* and its progeny where specific jurisdiction is claimed can be distilled into a three-pronged test:

(1)   the defendant must purposefully avail itself of the privilege of conducting activities in the forum;

(2)   the cause of action must arise out of these activities; and

(3)   the exercise of jurisdiction must also be reasonable under the [five] *Asahi* factors.[165]

---

161   R. Weintraub, "A Map out of the Personal Jurisdiction Labyrinth", 28 *U.C. Davis L. Rev.* 531, at 531 (1995).

162   Borchers, *supra* footnote 14, at 56-57.

163   471 US 462 (1985).

164   Borchers, *supra* footnote 14, at 73. The relevant pages of *Burger King* are 471 US at 471-478.

165   Weintraub, *supra* footnote 161, at 540. The five *Asahi* factors are:

> the burden on the defendant, the interest of the forum State, ... the plaintiff's interest in obtaining relief, ... the 'interstate judicial system's interest in obtaining the most efficient resolution of controversies[,] and the shared interest of the several states in furthering fundamental substantive social policies'. *Asahi Metal Industry Co., Ltd.* v. *Superior Court of California*, 480 US 102, at 113 (1987).

The Court of Appeals for the First Circuit has treated these considerations as "Gestalt factors". See *Ticketmaster-New York, Inc.* v. *Alioto*, 26 F. 3d 201, at 209 (1st Cir. 1994).

These general propositions must inevitably be applied in a highly controversy-specific manner. As Justice Marshall remarked in *Kulko* v. *Superior Court of California*,

> [l]ike any standard that requires a determination of 'reasonableness', the 'minimum contacts' test of *International Shoe* is not susceptible of mechanical application; rather, the facts of each case must be weighed to determine whether the requisite 'affiliating circumstances' are present. *Hanson* v. *Denkla*, 357 U.S. 235, 246 (1958). We recognize that this determination is one in which few answers will be written 'in black and white. The greys are dominant and even among them the shades are innumerable.' *Estin* v. *Estin*, 334 U.S. 541, at 545 (1948) ...[166]

Winston Churchill's characterization of the Soviet Union as "a riddle wrapped in a mystery inside an enigma" has been said "aptly [to] describe the doctrinal vagaries of the concept of personal jurisdiction".[167] "Determining personal jurisdiction ... [remains] more an art than a science."[168] Understandably, "the case law [is] in a muddle ...".[169] "Worse than the strange results, ... [are] the lack of predictability and the resources consumed in litigating" jurisdictional questions.[170]

B.   Germany

The modern history of adjudicatory authority in the international sense, both as a matter of theory and practice, can be seen as beginning in 1877 for the United States and the then newly established German Reich. *Pennoyer* v. *Neff*, decided in

---

> This aspect of the jurisdictional inquiry remains something of an unknown quantity. The gestalt factors have been applied by the [Supreme] Court only once (in *Asahi*); beyond mere mention, they have been discussed on rare occasions by the courts of appeals ... and they have been used regularly to defeat jurisdiction only in the Ninth Circuit ... .

Ibid.

> [T]he machinery of jurisdictional analysis is designed to refine judges' intuitions about the relevant equities, not to eliminate those equities from the decisional process. Relatedness and purposeful availment are cogs in this analytic machinery. The gestalt factors comprise the machinery's fail-safe device; they are not a necessary part of the machinery's day-to-day operation, but if, in the course of a particularized analysis, the gears mesh imperfectly because a given set of facts does not fit into any of the standard molds, the gestalt factors take hold [as in the instant case].

Idem 212.

166   436 US, at 92.

167   *Donatelli* v. *National Hockey League*, 893 F. 2d 459, at 462 (1st Cir. 1990).

168   *Idem* 468, footnote 7.

169   *Ticketmaster-New York, Inc.* v. *Alioto*, 26 F. 3d at 208; see also F. Juenger, "A *Shoe* Unfit for Globetrotting", 28 *U.C. Davis L. Rev.* 1027, at 1027 (1995): "There is no longer any doubt: American jurisdictional law is a mess." Professor Weintraub speaks of "the chaotic state of adjudicating personal jurisdiction ...." Weintraub, *supra* footnote 161, at 540; see *idem* 540-545 for illustrations.

170   Borchers, *supra* footnote 14, at 102.

that year, dominated American jurisdictional theory and practice until the *International Shoe* decision (1945) and still retains considerable importance. Contemporary German theory and practice respecting the exercise of adjudicatory authority go back as well to 1877. In that year, the Reichstag and Bundesrat enacted the Code of Civil Procedure. Except where displaced in matters that implicate the European Union by the Brussels Convention or Regulation,[171] *Book I, First Section, Title 2 (Gerichtsstand)* still provides the foundation on which German theory and practice respecting adjudicatory authority in the international sense rests.

The growing point of German jurisdictional theory and practice, unlike the American, has traditionally been not in the courts but in the executive and the legislative branches of government and, more recently, in juristic writing as well. After World War II, the role of the courts became more important with the provision of limited judicial review of jurisdictional practices and norms.[172] German practice and thinking about adjudicatory jurisdiction in the international sense has been significantly affected as well by its membership in what is today the European Union. Fundamental aspects of German theory and practice respecting jurisdiction to adjudicate in the international sense are considered below.

1.   *The Code of Civil Procedure* (Zivilprozeßordnung) *(1877)*

In the Germany of the 1870s, international jurisdiction problems were neither numerous nor pressing. Furthermore, by the end of the century the dominant concern of German jurists had become an on-going effort to establish legal unity while refining and adapting to contemporary circumstances a continental European legal science whose origins trace back to Irnerius's lectures at Bologna at the close of the eleventh century. Problems of adjudicatory authority were either not discussed at all or were considered, without differentiation, along with venue.

A general theory of adjudicatory jurisdiction can perhaps be teased out of *Book I, First Section, Title 2* of the ZPO; however, neither the Code's drafters nor the jurists of the period strove to provide such a theory; nor were they disturbed by the discordant note introduced by §24 – now §23 (unlimited general jurisdiction based on presence of property, whose value can be insignificant, in the forum). Nor was the question explored as to whether venue and jurisdictional rules should, for the most part, be the same.

To the extent that a general theory of jurisdiction to adjudicate is implied by the provisions of *Book I, First Section, Title 2* of the ZPO, that theory can be seen as largely resting on – though it did not derive directly from – considerations of convenience, administrability, and predictability. Relational and power considerations are not, subject to some exceptions,[173] assigned fundamental and independent significance.

---

171   See Chap. II. D. 3., pp. 68 *et seq., supra.*

172   See Chap. II. D. 2. *(b)* (ii), pp. 67-68, *supra.*

173   For example, jurisdiction in family matters is largely based on nationality. See Chap. I. C. 1. *(b)* (i), pp. 32-37, *supra.* The theoretical justification of §23 ZPO, on the other

With the promulgation of the German Civil Code (BGB) in 1900, the basic institutional, procedural, and substantive elements of the new, unified law were in place, but the effort to understand, explicate, and refine the BGB and the other national codes had just begun. From World War I to the early 1950s a variety of circumstances hampered the work of jurists; war, inflation, political turmoil, the rise of the Third Reich in the 1930s, the outbreak of World War II, defeat, and the Occupation that followed explain in considerable measure why general theoretical discussion of international adjudicatory authority remained exceedingly sparse. A further contributing reason, of course not specific to Germany, is that until after World War II international economic and social intercourse was far less pervasive, varied, and intense than it has since become.

Explorations of the theoretical foundations of the German rules respecting jurisdiction to adjudicate in the international sense are, in all events, until the late 1960s relatively few in number and, with rare exceptions, limited in scope.

2. The Emergence of General Theory

Theoretical discussions of adjudicatory authority by scholars in the German tradition first appeared in the late nineteenth and early twentieth centuries. These approached the topic in general terms and gave much less attention to statutory provisions and judicial decisions than is found in American work from the same period; however, essentially the same basic themes are encountered: the relevance for the exercise of adjudicatory authority of public international law, of territorial sovereignty, and of power.

German writing in the field is still today more abstract and general than American; it lacks the focus and continuity that the latter gains from its task of explaining and guiding judicial practice. In both legal orders instrumental considerations significantly affect – albeit in different ways – contemporary views respecting the propriety *vel non* of exercising adjudicatory authority. Overall, German theories give considerably more weight than do American to predictability and accordingly eschew controversy-specific bases of jurisdiction.

(a) The first efforts

German discussions of adjudicatory authority in the nineteenth and early twentieth centuries do not entirely ignore theoretical issues. Writing near the turn of the century, like his American contemporaries Ludwig von Bar embraced a power theory; "the source of jurisdiction really rests at bottom on subjection either of a person, or of property belonging to him, to the sovereignty of the State".[174] Joseph Story is quoted to the effect that

---

hand, must rest largely on a power theory combined with considerations of administrative convenience.

174 L. von Bar, *The Theory and Practice of Private International Law*, at 886 (Hannover, Hahn, 2nd ed., 1889) (English translation by G. Gillespie of Theorie und Praxis des Internationalen Privatrechts Edinburgh, W. Green & Sons, 1892).

no sovereignty can extend its process beyond its own territorial limits, to subject either persons or property to its judicial decisions. Every exertion of authority of this sort beyond this limit is a mere nullity, and incapable of binding such person or property in any other tribunals.[175]

A 1915 discussion of ZPO §23, which establishes unlimited general jurisdiction that rests on the presence on the State's territory of property belonging to the defendant, continued the emphasis on power;[176] "[t]he adjudicatory authority of a State is an emanation *(Ausfluß)* of its sovereignty *(Staatsautorität)*"[177] and "the principle [is] that the adjudicatory authority of States extends in general over all such persons and things, as find themselves on the State's territory".[178]

Neither von Bar nor Waizenegger attempted to develop systematically the implications in various circumstances of a power theory of adjudicatory authority. Both emphasize historical practices and consider whether domestic-law provisions respecting venue deserve analogical application where jurisdiction in the international sense is in issue. Waizenegger concludes that §23 as applied by the courts is unacceptable;[179] however, he argues not in terms of power or fairness but of historically accepted practices. His ultimate view – that §23 should be retained with the concept of wealth *(Vermögen)* restricted to objects *(Sachen)* and claims *(Ansprüche)* upon which execution could be levied – reflects not a principled

---

175   *Idem* 886, footnote 22, quoting J. Story, *Commentaries on the Conflict of Laws*, §539 (Boston, MA, Charles C. Little & James Brown, 2nd ed., 1841).

176   §23 is less consistent than were its pre-1871 precursors with a power theory. The latter established only *limited* general jurisdiction and required, in some form, prior seizure of the defendant's property. In 1809, a provision supplementing the Prussian *Allgemeine Gerichtsordnung* introduced a modest change that began a progressive relaxation of the power criterion, which ultimately culminated in §23; the seizure requirement was removed for the benefit of Prussian subjects *(Untertanen)* seeking to enforce claims against foreigners who had movable or immovable property in Prussia. See M. Grävell, *Praktischer Kommentar zur Allgemeinen Gerichtsordnung für die preußischen Staaten*, Vol. I, at 259-260 (Erfurt, 1825). ZPO §23 later removed all citizenship requirements and, far more importantly, provided for unlimited general jurisdiction. See R. Waizenegger, *Der Gerichtsstand des §23 ZPO und seine geschichtliche Entwicklung*, at 43-44 (Göttingen, Dieterich'sche Universitätsbuchdruckerei, 1915); J. Schröder, *Internationale Zuständigkeit: Entwurf eines Systems von Zuständigkeitsinteressen im zwischenstaatlichen Privatverfahrensrecht aufgrund rechtshistorischer, rechtsvergleichender und rechtspolitischer Betrachtungen*, at 388-389 (Opladen, Westdeutscher Verlag, 1971). Schröder remarks that "[a]fter the jurisdictional anchor of seizing the property *(Arrestschlag)* had been lifted, obviously there was no stopping place on the road to an unlimited and generally available international jurisdiction based on property". *Idem* 390.

177   Waizenegger, *supra* footnote 176, at 2.

178   *Idem* 100-101.

179   *Idem* 103.

evaluation of the claim of adjudicatory authority, but a minimal concession to fairness; his proposed revision would prevent the improper utilization of "insignificant trifles" to establish unlimited general jurisdiction.[180]

Von Bar's treatment of various generally accepted bases of jurisdiction exhibits traits similar to those seen in Waizenegger's discussion of §23; in particular, he gives great weight to history, fails to develop a general theory, and justifies the results reached at times in power, at times, in fairness terms. His summary of the "various kinds of jurisdiction to be recognized in international relations"[181] discusses "[for] status and family law, the *judex domicilii* ... ; ... [for] questions as to things, the *judex rei sitae*; [and for] questions as to obligatory relations .... the *judex domicilii* ... [and] the court of the place of contract or delict".[182] So far as the *judex domicilii* is concerned

> [t]he acquisition of an actual domicile must count as a voluntary submission of all legal relations that are subject to a free power of disposal to the courts of that country, excepting only ... such moveables as are permanently attached to any particular place.[[183]] The foreigner who sets the centre of his affairs and of his life as a citizen in another place, thereby recognizes the protection which is afforded to him by the law of that place, and the courts that are established there ....
>
> In dealing with persons who cannot point to any domicile, a residence of a certain duration ... must be allowed to constitute a subsidiary *forum* in place of the *forum domicilii*. Otherwise there would be many actions which could never be raised against such persons.[184]

Where obligations *ex delicto* are concerned, von Bar strikes a convenience, fairness, and justice chord:

> the person who has received damage must be allowed some more efficient protection than the creditor enjoys in other obligations which rest upon free will .... In ... [the] case [of obligations *ex delicto*] the creditor is absolutely entitled to choose between the *forum delicti commissi* and the *forum domicilii*.[185]

For von Bar, jurisdictional bases explainable in fairness terms not only ground jurisdiction but also entitle judgments to recognition abroad. Where, as in the

---

180   *Idem* 111.

181   Von Bar, *supra* footnote 175, at 908.

182   *Idem* 908-909.

183   Von Bar argues that, in the case of immovables, exclusive jurisdiction lies with the forum *rei sitae* inasmuch as the *materia subjecta* is such that the owner does not control its location. See *idem* 911. The explanation rests, at least in part, on a power consideration, but the point is not developed.

184   *Idem* 909-910.

185   *Idem* 910.

case of "residence" and "arrestment", jurisdiction to adjudicate rests essentially on power, international recognition should be refused:

> Every one, then, so long as he is personally present in any State, is subject to the sovereignty of that State in so far as relates to his person, and so long as he possesses property there or makes claim to property there, in so far as concerns that property and these claims. It is, then, not repugnant to principles of international law, that the debtor himself, if he happens to be in the country, should be seized,[186] or his property arrested; and in consequence a judgment be pronounced without the necessity of establishing any other right of jurisdiction, giving decree – in the former case to the amount of caution required for liberation, in the latter to the amount of value of the goods arrested. Such a jurisdiction, however, rests upon an actual exercise of power at the moment of detention, and ultimately therefore must be referred to a complete distrust of the judicial system of other States, and to an endeavour to claim for our own jurisdiction, in a one-sided and partial fashion, as many suits as possible in which subjects of this country are concerned, and to wrest them from the courts which ought naturally, according to the leading principles which we have already laid down, to have the right of decision. It seems right, therefore, to refuse international recognition to such a jurisdiction ....[187]

Somewhat similar characteristics are observable in the early twentieth-century writings on jurisdiction of the Swiss jurist, Friedrich Meili. He states broadly that "the exercise of jurisdiction must rest on principles of justice *(Gerechtigkeit)*" and that neither "arbitrary power *(Willkür)* nor the one-sided advantage of the local citizen should be decisive".[188] He approves of

> the forum of the domicile [of the defendant] for contractual and delictual *(obligationenrechtlich)* claims, the forum where the object is located for claims respecting immovables ..., the forum of the inheritance *(Erbschaft)*, and the stipulated forum.[189]

In addition, he is prepared to recognize the *forum delicti commissi* and, in order to facilitate international commerce, the place of performance for obligations resting on commercial instruments *(Wechselverpflichtungen)* and obligations incurred at markets and fairs.[190]

---

186   "The 'mesne arrest' *('Arresto medio')* ... was a practice widely used in ... [the 17th century in Europe], and still commonly used in the 18th and early 19th century in England and America ..." Weinstein, *supra* footnote 46, at 81.

187   Von Bar, *supra* footnote 174, at 912.

188   F. Meili, *Das internationale Civilprozessrecht auf Grunde der Theorie, Gesetzgebung und Praxis*, at 199 (Zurich, O. Füssli, 1906).

189   *Idem* 201.

190   *Idem* 201-202.

Meili advances no sustained analysis in either power or fairness terms, however, to explain why these jurisdictional claims are appropriate and others are not. A general theory of jurisdiction is not put forward.

(b) Pioneering works

Neuner's pioneering 1929 work, *Internationale Zuständigkeit*, takes into account not only considerations of power but also of fairness. He sees adjudicatory authority as ultimately based on a power – or dominion – relation between the State and individual persons or things.[191] This principle establishes the basis and ultimate limits of jurisdiction but does not suffice to allocate adjudicatory authority among the members of the international community; the needed allocation is to be made through a comity-like accommodation of the claims of the various legal orders that have an interest in the matter.[192]

Neuner discusses three bases for general jurisdiction: the defendant's nationality, domicile *(Wohnsitz)*, and presence (or residence). Although all three of these can be justified under a power theory, in principle, he accepts only the second, domicile, which is, in his opinion, the most predictable and most likely to be at the centre of the defendant's life so that access to proof is usually facilitated as are recognition and enforcement of the judgment abroad. In his view, nationality suffers, *inter alia*, from often being difficult to ascertain; presence may be fortuitous as well as transitory and is, in itself, unlikely to have a connection with the matter to be litigated.[193]

For status matters *(Familienstandsklagen)*, Neuner proposes bases for category-specific jurisdiction; he accepts not only domicile but also nationality, the latter because many legal orders now regulate status under national law.[194] Where the controversy relates to rights in immovables, he justifies jurisdiction at the situs under a variety of rationales: convenience, effective control, enforcement considerations, and the likelihood that the local law will apply to substantive issues.[195]

In effect, Neuner limits the exercise of adjudicatory authority grounded on power in light of convenience, fairness, and justice considerations.

Pagenstecher's long article, published in 1937,[196] does not attempt a general theory. However, a proposition of fundamental theoretical importance – one not

---

191   R. Neuner, *Internationale Zuständigkeit* (Mannheim, Bensheimer, 1929).

192   *Idem* 21.

193   *Idem* 23-24.

194   *Idem* 25.

195   *Idem* 26.

196   M. Pagenstecher, "Gerichtsbarkeit und internationale Zuständigkeit als selbständige Prozeßvoraussetzungen", 11 *RabelsZ* 337-483 (1937).
       Fritz Reu's *Die staatliche Zuständigkeit im internationalen Privatrecht* (Marburg, N.G. Elwert & G. Braun, 1938), another work of interest, is marred by an acceptance of national-socialist legal thinking. Like Neuner and Pagenstecher, Reu does not propose a general theory.

accepted at the time by the highest German civil court[197] – is advanced: venue and adjudicatory jurisdiction are not two sides of a single coin but are governed by different considerations.[198]

Understandably, between the late 1930s and the end of the 1940s, no important German legal writing dealing with aspects of jurisdictional theory appeared. In 1949, Riezler published the first important post-war discussion of jurisdiction to adjudicate.[199] His book was followed in 1955 by Matthies's monograph,[200] and articles by Neuhaus,[201] Kralik,[202] and, in 1967, Walchshöfer's article.[203] For present purposes, only the Neuhaus article requires more than summary discussion.

(c)   Neuhaus

In a 1955 article, characterized by him as "A Sketch", Neuhaus discussed various efforts to regulate wisely practices respecting jurisdiction to adjudicate in the international sense and offered a variety of thoughtful and useful insights. Many ingredients are provided for a general theory, although an overall synthesis is not attempted.

The proposition is advanced that, under the accepted principle of territoriality, adjudicatory authority *(Gerichtsbarkeit)* represents an exercise of sovereignty *(staatliche Hoheitsfunktion)*. Seen in this perspective, the authority is exercisable only within the State's boundaries and is, in principle (i.e. subject to extraterrito-

---

197   Cf. Pagenstecher, *supra* footnote 196, at 346-348, esp. footnote 2; further references at 371, footnote 202.

198   *Idem* 348-350.

199   E. Riezler, *Internationales Zivilprozeßrecht und prozessuales Fremdenrecht* (Berlin, de Gruyter & Tübingen, Mohr Siebeck, 1949). Riezler provides a helpful comparative survey of Austrian, English, French, Italian, and Swiss law respecting international adjudicatory authority and discusses at length party agreement as a basis for jurisdiction. *Idem* 253-295, 293-317.

200   H. Matthies, *Die deutsche internationale Zuständigkeit* (Frankfurt a.M., Klostermann, 1955). Matthies does not propose general solutions nor a theoretical system; his purpose is to explain the various respects in which international jurisdiction and venue differ.

201   P. Neuhaus, "Internationales Zivilprozeßrecht und internationales Privatrecht", 20 *RabelsZ* 201-269 (1955). The discussion is summarized and brought up to date in several respects in P. Neuhaus, *Die Grundbegriffe des internationalen Privatrechts*, at 415-432 (Tübingen, Mohr Siebeck, 2nd ed., 1976).

202   W. Kralik, "Die internationale Zuständigkeit", 74 *ZZP* 2-48 (1961).

203   A. Walchshöfer, "Die deutsche internationale Zuständigkeit in der streitigen Gerichtsbarkeit", 80 *ZZP* 165-229 (1967). Walchshöfer examines the relationship between venue and international jurisdiction and concludes that differences in the nature of the two subject matters require the development of several new rules for the latter. He proposes that jurisdiction by necessity be extended and that jurisdiction based on expediency or public interest be limited to situations in which the judgment would be susceptible of *effective* enforcement either in the forum State (see *idem* 203) or abroad (see *idem* 207).

rial qualifications),[204] unlimited and exclusive.[205] Each State has authority to set aside foreign judgments and foreign arbitral awards without regard to the persons or subject matter of the proceedings.[206] A State may not adjudicate a controversy *(Sachverhalt)* that has no relationship to it.[207] International law gives, however, little or no guidance on how national legal systems should approach the problems of adjudicatory authority in situations that have significant non-domestic aspects; within very broad limits, each national legal order is free to establish its own rules and principles.

Historically speaking, the German law respecting adjudicatory authority rests on the idea of submission *(Gerichtsunterworfenheit)* and of power. A general submission for jurisdictional purposes is assumed at one's domicile *(Wohnsitz)* and at the location of one's property *(Lageort)*; more particularized submissions result from the selection of the place for performance of an obligation, stipulation of a forum, and doing of juridical acts (place of contracting, place of acting).[208]

Neuhaus's analysis represents, theoretically speaking, an advance over prior discussion in that it gives weight explicitly to considerations of convenience, fairness, and justice. Accordingly, he discusses the significance for jurisdictional purposes of various elements: (1) the parties; (2) the situation *(Sachverhalt)*; (3) the law (procedural, choice-of-law, and substantive) that would apply in a local adjudication; (4) the independence, qualifications, and integrity of the local judicial establishment; and (5) the enforceability of a local judgment.[209]

On the ground of convenience, he would exclude from the jurisdictional equation considerations respecting the independence, qualifications, and integrity of the judicial establishment. For international purposes, jurisdictional theory must assume that the administration of justice in national courts is essentially equal on such scores as impartiality, conscientiousness, and adjudicatorial capacity; *Gleichwertigkeit der Rechtspflege* is assumed, subject, however, to corrective action in individual cases.[210] On the other hand, the relationship of the situation *(Sachverhalt)* to various national legal orders assumes great importance because of its significance for litigation of the case and enforcement of the judgment.

---

204 E.g., procedural immunity of foreign States and of their diplomatic representatives.

205 Neuhaus, *supra* footnote 201, at 209.

206 *Idem* 210.

207 *Idem* 214. Conversely, another State's adjudicatory authority must be recognized when the controversy's only connections are with that State. Rules of customary international law have arisen for a few situations – e.g., immovable property – that seem to fall into this category. *Ibid.*

208 *Idem* 230.

209 *Idem* 229.

210 *Ibid.* Neuhaus would, in principle, also exclude what he calls unnecessary public-law (political) arguments from the jurisdictional equation. For example, adjudicatory authority should not turn on the nationality of one (or both) of the parties. *Idem* 230-231.

Neuhaus takes these litigational realities into account by recognizing jurisdiction in the legal system or systems to which the controversy is spatially closest – the *nächstgelegene* court.[211] Three localities qualify as connecting factors:[212] Influenced doubtless by venue provisions, the spatial connections of domicile *(Wohnsitz)* and residence *(Aufenthalt)* are emphasized. In this context, the question whether one party's domicile or residence should be decisive and – if so – which party's, is raised but not resolved.[213] A forum in which property in dispute – or other property belonging to the defendant that is susceptible of execution *(pfändbares Vermögen)* – is located offers litigational and enforcement advantages[214] as does the forum on whose territory the controverted event or events *(umstrittenes Geschehen)* occurred and where the means of proof are typically concentrated.[215]

Neuhaus next considers the significance of differences in language for jurisdiction.[216] Since it is impossible, at least as a practical matter, to provide every litigant with a proceeding conducted in his mother tongue, the choice of forum often imposes differential linguistic burdens on parties and their lawyers. Nevertheless, linguistic considerations cannot provide a principled basis for resolving issues respecting adjudicatory authority in the international sense.

Diversity in the legal rules and principles accepted by different legal orders often leads to great difficulty and uncertainty where foreign law is applicable. Procedural provisions – for example, those respecting proof – can result in distorted application of non-domestic substantive rules. Local judges are not trained in foreign law or the comparative method. Furthermore,

> the judge does *not feel* himself *called* to an independent, law-creating development of foreign law and will, accordingly, hesitate to accept, for example, a new scholarly thesis or to hand down a fundamental, ground-breaking decision even when he is convinced that it is 'due' in view of the development of the law in the other country and that there a judge in his position would so decide.[[217]] It is also problematical how to handle foreign-law norms that have to be filled out and discretionary provisions that are based, for example, on 'good morals' or envisage a 'fair' monetary compensation for harm that is not financial in nature *(nichtvermögensrechtlicher Schaden)*.[218]

---

211 See *idem* 232.

212 See *idem* 232-233, footnote 54.

213 For discussion of this fundamental issue, see Chap. IV., pp. 153 *et seq. infra*.

214 Reference is made, *inter alia*, to ZPO §§23, 24, 27, 31, and 919.

215 Reference is made to ZPO §30 (fair or market) – now abolished – and ZPO §32 (place of acting *(Handlung)* for delicts). See Chap. IV., pp. 153 *et seq., passim, infra*.

216 See *idem* 233-234.

217 For a comparable reflection on the problem United States federal courts face with respect to state law under the *Erie* doctrine by a distinguished common-law jurist, see C. Wyzanski, "A Trial Judge's Freedom and Responsibility", 65 *Harv. L. Rev.* 1281, at 1300-1301 (1952).

218 Neuhaus, *supra* footnote 201, at 245-246 (emphasis in original).

Does the non-fungibility of national legal systems mean that jurisdiction should follow applicable law? Neuhaus considers this question from two perspectives: the spatial relationship of the forum to the situation *(Sachverhalt)*, understood in the broadest sense to include parties and enforcement, and the relative difficulty and complexity faced by the adjudicators in each system in determining and applying the applicable substantive-law rules.[219] The spatial relationship between forum and controversy identifies the *forum causae*; the relative difficulty in determining and applying the substantive law determines the *forum legis*. The *forum causae* can be established under general and objective standards. The *forum legis* cannot be identified in a like manner; reason teaches, and experience confirms, that a universally acceptable choice-of-law system is unattainable.[220] Accordingly, identifying the forum on the basis of choice-of-law considerations would amount to abandoning general and objective jurisdictional standards. The advantages gained by forums applying their own law are far too small to justify so drastic a step.[221] In practice, a *forum legis* will usually amount to either a concealed *forum causae* or a *forum legis causae*. That is to say, the assertion of jurisdiction will rest in some measure, but by no means entirely, on choice-of-law considerations.

For Neuhaus, the only way to enjoy without incurring unacceptable costs the advantages that result from a coincidence between the exercise of adjudicatory authority and the application of domestic substantive law, is to use similar factors to determine both jurisdiction and choice-of-law. Such parallelism can result from chance or from a conscious policy of co-ordination.[222] At least since the latter part of the nineteenth century, due in good measure to Savigny's influence on choice-of-law and the decoupling of the notions of domicile and citizenship *(Bürgerrecht)*, parallelism has become less frequent. With the rise in the nineteenth century of the new concept of *Staatsangehörigkeit* (national citizenship), for many legal orders nationality replaced domicile as the connecting factor determining the applicable law for personal, family, and inheritance matters; no comparable displacement occurred with respect to jurisdiction although, for certain matters, additional bases grounded on nationality were introduced.[223] More recently, this lack of parallelism has been increased by the emergence of jurisdictional rules designed to hold down litigation expenses by ensuring the availability

---

219 See *idem* 247-256 ("IV. Einklang von Zuständigkeits- und Rechtsanwendungsnormen?").

220 See *idem* 248-249.

221 Neuhaus does not discuss the situation specifically, but the inappropriateness of allowing the applicable law to turn automatically on forum selection where general jurisdiction based on domicile or presence is asserted can serve to illustrate the difficulty.

222 See *idem* 250-251. Historically, the considerable parallelism found in German law seems to have come about by chance rather than calculation. See *idem* 251, footnote 85.

223 See *idem* 251-252.

of forums that are convenient for the gathering and presentation of evidence or by permitting the consideration of related matters in one proceeding.[224]

Neuhaus poses – or suggests – a variety of questions, issues, and notions that a general theory of jurisdiction should – and properly can – take into account.

For the most part, however, he does not assign relative weights to the various considerations discussed nor does he develop a comprehensive and integrated theory.

3.   The Contemporary Scene

By the late 1960s the German scene was ready for comprehensive theoretical discussions of adjudicatory jurisdiction. The reshaping of American jurisdictional theory and practice stemming from the *International Shoe* decision in 1945,[225] was by then well known in Europe. Furthermore, negotiations – begun in 1959 among the Member States of the European Economic Community – on what was to become known as the Brussels Convention[226] had been successfully completed in 1968. In addition, after four years of work,[227] the Hague Conference on Private International Law had approved in 1966 a Convention on the Recognition and Enforcement of Foreign Judgments in Civil and Commercial Matters.[228] Preparation of these two Conventions not only stimulated interest in jurisdictional theory and practice,[229] but deepened knowledge and understanding of many legal systems' views respecting these matters.

(a)   Heldrich

In 1969, the first major German work focused on jurisdiction to adjudicate – Andreas Heldrich's Internationale Zuständigkeit und anwendbares Recht – appeared.[230] The book's main themes are the interaction and interconnection of choice-of-law and jurisdiction to adjudicate.

The analysis is functional or instrumental; Heldrich explores the purposes served by a forum's exercise of adjudicatory authority over controversies with sig-

---

224 See *idem* 255.

225 See Chap. III. A. 4., pp. 97 *et seq.*, *supra*.

226 See Chap. II. D. 3., pp. 68 *et seq.*, *supra*.

227 See Conférence de La Haye de droit internationale privé, Actes et documents de la session extraordinaire 13 au 26 avril 1966: Exécution des jugements (La Haye, 1969).

228 1 February 1971, 1144 *UNTS* 249. Having been signed by Cyprus, the Netherlands, and Portugal – as well as by the non-member State Kuwait –, the Convention has technically entered into force. However, it is not in effect because the aforesaid States have not concluded the required bilateral agreements, nor are they likely to do so.

229 The Hague Convention – unlike the Brussels Convention – does not deal directly with jurisdiction to adjudicate. However, foreign judgments must normally satisfy jurisdictional standards in order to obtain recognition and enforcement.

230 A. Heldrich, *International Zuständigkeit und anwendbares Recht* (Berlin and Tübingen, De Gruyter and Mohr Siebeck, 1969).

nificant non-domestic aspects and considers why, in such matters, a forum on occasion applies non-domestic legal rules or principles. His jurisdictional equation takes into account such factors as decisional harmony, litigational convenience of parties and witnesses, judicial economy, and protection of the parties.

> The development of self-sufficient *(eigenständiger)* rules of international jurisdiction began relatively late in the legal orders of continental Europe. The consequences are everywhere gaps and uncertainty as to the governing *(maßgeblichen)* principles. Agreement is lacking even as to the general principles grounding jurisdiction to adjudicate.[231]

In this state of affairs, the jurisprudence of conceptions *(Begriffsjurisprudenz)* that dominated German legal thinking until the early years of the twentieth century had no role to play; analysis along the lines proposed by the jurisprudence of interests *(Interessenjurisprudenz)* for private law generally was required.[232]

Using a Heckian interest analysis, Heldrich concludes that the purposes and policies that properly control, on the one hand, jurisdiction to adjudicate and, on the other, choice of law, are so different that a general theory of jurisdiction cannot be based on their close linkage.[233] The book offers many interesting and useful suggestions respecting how various interests and policies can shape jurisdictional theory and practice. Heldrich finds a large number of such interests, often in conflict with each other.[234] However, he does not undertake a systematization; a full-blown general theory is not attempted.

(b) Schröder

In 1971 Schröder's voluminous – 852 pages – contribution appeared.[235] The author's ambitious programme was

> to sketch out a system of interests, based on comparative-law research and guided by considerations of legal policy *(rechtspolitisch ausgerichtet)*, capable of justifying *(zu tragen)* – perhaps even influencing – international adjudicatory jurisdiction.[236]

---

231 *Idem* 102.

232 Writings of such leading proponents during the 1920s and 1930s of *Interessenjurisprudenz* as Philipp Heck are translated in M. Schoch (ed.), *Jurisprudence of Interests: Selected Writings* (Cambridge, MA, Harvard University Press, 1948).

233 See Heldrich, *supra* footnote 230, at 130-131.

234 See also A. Heldrich, "Die Interessen bei der Regelung der internationalen Zuständigkeit", in Murad Ferid (ed.), *Festschrift für Hans G. Ficker*, at 205-224 (Frankfurt/Main and Berlin, Alfred Metzner, 1967).

235 See *supra* footnote 176.

236 *Idem* 100. The method is clearly influenced by Schröder's teacher, Kegel. See G. Kegel, "Begriffs- und Interessenjurisprudenz im internationalen Privatrecht", in *Festschrift für Hans Lewald*, at 259-288 (Basle, Helbing & Lichtenhahn, 1953).

The work is rich in comparative and historical materials and provides many thoughtful and important insights.

Whether plaintiffs should, in principle, seek out defendants is discussed at length under the heading of *actor sequitur forum rei*.[237] The catalogue of interests discussed includes those analysed by Heldrich but is more encyclopedic and is viewed in a broader historical and comparative perspective. Schröder distinguishes three classes of interests: party interests, court interests, and system interests *(Ordnungsinteressen)* and discusses various aspects of all three.

The work differs from Heldrich's in its broader focus — the interaction and interconnection of choice-of-law and jurisdiction is only one theme among many[238] — and its greater comparative and historical depth. Schröder's catalogue of interests and policies is generally similar to Heldrich's, though more detailed and elaborate. The two books are comparable as well in that no general theory emerges. Schröder does not carry out his programme of creating a true "system of interests ... capable of justifying ... international adjudicatory jurisdiction".[239]

(c) Kropholler

In 1982, Kropholler's important contribution to the German literature on jurisdiction to adjudicate appeared.[240] His analysis takes into account a variety of interests, public as well as private. In general, the State's approach to jurisdiction has come to be

> more influenced by the parties' interests in obtaining judicial protection *(Gerichtsschutz)* than by the supposed *(vermeintlich)* interests of the State itself. Today, the task of the legal order is above all to find a just balance *(Ausgleich)* of the competing interests of the parties.[241]

Objective criteria are needed in terms of which the determination can be made whether the plaintiff's interest in judicial protection *(Gerichtsschutzinteresse)* prevails over the defendant's concerns.[242] Kropholler, following Neuhaus, proposes an analysis involving four criteria of procedural fairness, all of which reflect the matter's proximity — in various senses and from several perspectives — to the forum: (1) the parties' economic and sociological connections; (2) the litigational

---

237 *Idem* 229-351. For a general discussion of this principle, see Chap. IV., pp. 153 *et seq.*, *infra*.

238 See *idem* 504-556.

239 Cf. P. Neuhaus, Book Review, 37 *RabelsZ* 814-816 (1973).

240 J. Kropholler, "Internationale Zuständigkeit", in *Handbuch des Internationalen Zivilverfahrensrechts*, Vol. I, (Tübingen, Mohr Siebeck, 1982), Ch. 3, at 183-533, Nos. 1-901.

241 Kropholler, *supra* footnote 240, at 205-206, No. 18. Kropholler's dichotomy can be compared with the United States Supreme Court's distinction between liberty and sovereignty concerns. See pp. 113 *et seq.*, *supra*.

242 *Idem* 206, No. 19.

connections of the situation's factual elements *(Sachverhalt)*, including the availability of evidence and witnesses and the concentration of proceedings in complex situations; (3) the accessibility of the applicable law; (4) the effectiveness of any resulting judgment, in particular, its potential for enforcement.

In applying these criteria, the defendant should be given the jurisdictional benefit of the *actor sequitur forum rei* principle subject to an exception in favor of socially weaker plaintiffs;[243] in principle, adjudicatory authority should thus rest on connections – direct or indirect – between the forum and the defendant rather than the plaintiff. These connecting criteria can be ranked in various areas of the law but not overall.[244] Generally speaking, in German law the first two are decisive; considerations of international procedural justice should ordinarily prevail even where another forum could better apply the applicable law.[245]

Kropholler goes on to discuss in a detailed and thoughtful fashion the contemporary German approach to jurisdiction to adjudicate in the international sense. The connecting factors utilized are considered in general terms[246] and the jurisdictional bases accepted in German law are discussed at length.[247] The relation between applicable law and assumption of jurisdiction,[248] claims to exclusive jurisdiction,[249] forum-shopping,[250] *forum non conveniens*,[251] and the procedural handling of issues respecting adjudicative authority[252] are explored.

Kropholler's approach is persuasive in many respects; he identifies the obstacles to the protection of rights that must be faced where the situation is not localized in a single legal order and addresses the tasks of jurisdictional law. Many ingredients for a general theory of adjudicatory jurisdiction are discussed; a fully developed and integrated approach is not presented, however.

(d) Geimer

The most comprehensive of the current treatises on German international civil procedure is perhaps Geimer's;[253] he treats jurisdiction to adjudicate at length.[254]

---

243   *Idem* 206, No. 20.

244   *Idem* 207, No. 22.

245   *Ibid.*

246   *Idem* 220-227, Nos. 61-78.

247   *Idem* 299-533, Nos. 251-901.

248   *Idem* 239-250, Nos. 105-132.

249   *Idem* 255-259, Nos. 148-156.

250   *Idem* 260-268, Nos. 157-181.

251   *Idem* 277-283, Nos. 204-212.

252   *Idem* 284-296, Nos. 215-245.

253   R. Geimer, *Internationales Zivilprozessrecht* (Cologne, Dr. Otto Schmidt, 5th ed., 2005). Schack's *Internationales Zivilverfahrensrecht* (Munich, C. H. Beck, 4th ed., 2006), focuses less on general jurisdictional theory and more on specific aspects; but see *idem*, 86-102, Nos. 185-231.

254   Geimer, *supra* footnote 253, at 294-594, Nos. 844-1905.

For jurisdictional purposes, the only relevant principle of international law is that no State may restrict access to its courts where a denial of justice *(déni de justice)* would result.[255] Adjudicatory jurisdiction should not be seen as primarily an exercise of sovereignty but rather as the striking of a reasonable balance between the interests of the parties.[256] Where jurisdiction to adjudicate is in issue, Geimer emphasizes the plaintiff's claim to access to justice.[257] In this he agrees with Kropholler that the law of jurisdiction should give primary weight to party rather than state interests; on the other hand, unlike Kropholler, he rejects the *actor sequitur* principle.[258]

Geimer begins his discussion of how jurisdictional interests *(Zuständigkeitsinteressen)* should be evaluated as follows:

> In establishing jurisdiction to adjudicate in the international sense, fundamental questions of procedural justice are in issue. The jurisdictional interests of the parties are to be balanced. The defendant is concerned with the delimitation of his duty to appear in court; he is to be protected from unreasonable *(unzumutbaren)* forums. For the plaintiff the claim to obtain justice *(Justizgewährungsanspruch)* is at stake. This claim must not be unreasonably limited *(unzumutbar beschnitten)* by giving exaggerated protection to the defendant.[259]

To these considerations of procedural fairness, Geimer adds his "golden rule" of administrability and predictability: Jurisdictional law must be – and remain – clear and simple.[260] At the end of the day, he takes the position that jurisdiction is, *inter alia*, appropriately claimed as well by the plaintiff's domicile as by a forum with an especially close connection with the subject *(Gegenstand)* of the complaint.[261]

The degree to which Geimer emphasizes the plaintiff's right of access to justice is seen in his enthusiasm for ZPO §23. For him, the "affinity" that the owner of property in a State has with that State is sufficient to establish the owner's duty

---

255   *Idem* at 296, No. 849.

256   *Idem* at 298, No. 856.

257   *Idem* at 298, Nos. 855-856.

258   In his view, the principle "neglects the plaintiff's legitimate jurisdictional interests". *Idem* at 383-384, No. 1131.

259   *Idem* at 382, No. 1126. Geimer points out that advocates of the proposition – which he rejects – that jurisdiction lies when the forum's domestic law applies *(forum legis)* add to the jurisdictional equation the forum's interest in applying its law.

260   See R. Geimer, Note to KG, 25 July 1979, and to OLG Köln, 13 February 1980, 27 *FamRZ* 790 (1980).

261   Geimer, *supra* footnote 253, at 382-383, Nos. 1128-1129. In the case of related litigations, the judicial system's interest in concentrating proceedings in one forum justifies assertion of adjudicatory authority on the ground of *fora connexitatis. Idem* at 383, No. 1130.

to appear before the local courts.[262] The jurisdictional claim is justified by "practical necessity"; litigation in the defendant's domicile *(Wohnsitzstaat)* may either be unreasonably difficult for the plaintiff or the resulting judgment may not be enforceable in Germany because reciprocity is required when enforcement of a foreign judgment is sought.[263]

4. Constitutional Control and the Emergence of Comprehensive Theory: Pfeiffer's Contribution (1995)

Pfeiffer's book published in 1995[264] is the most sustained German theoretical effort so far not only to identify the policies and principles relevant for jurisdiction to adjudicate and to understand their significance for jurisdictional practices, but also to address priorities in the event of countervailing considerations and thus to establish a comprehensive approach to – or theory of – jurisdiction to adjudicate in the international sense. The views and solutions presented are related to values implicitly contained in – and sanctioned by – the German Constitution (the Basic Law of 1949). Pfeiffer's analysis invites the Constitutional Court to assume a more active role than heretofore in this branch of German Law. Regardless whether the invitation is ultimately accepted, the book is a significant contribution to jurisdictional thinking.

(a) Pfeiffer's system

Pfeiffer's theoretical developments proceed against the background provided by Kropholler and Geimer. He finds Kropholler's approach persuasive in many respects; it addresses the obstacles to the protection of rights that exist in international legal intercourse and appropriately identifies the tasks of jurisdictional law.[265] Geimer, on the other hand, does not provide a comparable criterion-oriented approach; largely disregarding the defendant's position, he reasons too exclusively from the plaintiff's constitutionally guaranteed right of access to the court *(Justizanspruch, Justizgewährungsanspruch*[266]*)*.

Pfeiffer's enterprise is to articulate for contemporary German jurisdictional thinking a value system, grounded in the principle of jurisdictional justice

---

262   *Idem* at 431, No. 1347 and at 433, No. 1356. This view is shared by Schack. See Schack, *supra* footnote 253, at 121-122, No. 330; see also H. Schack, "Vermögensbelegenheit als Zuständigkeitsgrund – exorbitant oder sinnvoll? §23 ZPO in rechtsvergleichender Perspektive", 97 *ZZP* 46-68 (1984).

263   Geimer, *supra* footnote 253, at 431, No. 1349. See also R. Geimer, "Rechtsschutz in Deutschland nur bei Inlandsbezug?", 44 *NJW* 3072-3074 (1991).

264   T. Pfeiffer, *Internationale Zuständigkeit und prozessuale Gerechtigkeit* (Frankfurt am Main, Klostermann, 1995). See also the review, from a US standpoint, by F. Juenger, 44 *Am. J. Comp. L.* 521-529 (1996).

265   *Idem* 190.

266   Pfeiffer prefers the former (*idem* 335), and Geimer (*supra* footnote 253, at 382, No. 1126) the latter, term.

(Zuständigkeitsgerechtigkeit). To give content to the concept, Pfeiffer analyses three sets of contrasting paradigms: (1) the authoritarian and the freedom models *(hoheitliches Modell versus Freiheitsmodell)*; (2) the categorical and fact-specific models *(Typisierung versus individuelle Abwägung)*; (3) an autonomous concept of jurisdictional justice as contrasted with a concept that takes into account concern for substantively just results *(autonome Zuständigkeitsgerechtigkeit versus materiale Ergebnisethik)*.

The first of these sets of contrasting paradigms is the most complex and the most important for jurisdictional theory and practice. The authoritarian model sees the administration of justice as an expression of State sovereignty.[267] State authority can be thought of as ultimately territorially or, as in feudal systems, relationally based. The common denominator is that in all authoritarian models the administration of justice is seen as the State's prerogative and as serving its purposes.

The contrasting paradigm is the freedom model found in legal orders committed to the proposition that the fundamental task of courts is to guarantee for individuals spheres of freedom and of rights. For such a legal order, individual rights must be protected so that they can be enjoyed. In addition, to prevent State subordination of individual rights by giving unreasonable emphasis to jurisdictional considerations of a political nature *(staatliche Zuständigkeitspolitik)*, the parties must be ensured a *status negativus* (a sphere of liberty).[268]

---

267   Pfeiffer, *supra* footnote 264, at 201.

268   *Ibid*.
   Pfeiffer's conception of the individual's claim to a *status negativus* (a sphere of liberty) has an interesting and suggestive analogy in Professor Margaret Stewart's right to "unconnectedness". This right rests on "two premises, each inherent in the United States structure of government. One is the continuing constitutional relevance of state lines, ... which ... still define the entity [or entities] with which a party may choose to remain unconnected .... The ability of each state to create and control its own judiciary, one inherent attribute of sovereignty, was perhaps the attribute least affected by the adoption of the [US] Constitution; the independence of those judiciaries has not been radically altered in the intervening two hundred years .... The second premise underlying an individual's right to remain unconnected with, and to be treated as unconnected to, a sovereign is equally basic to ... [the American] governmental structure. That the legitimacy of all governmental authority derives from the 'consent' of those governed is a political truism .... 'Consent' in this sense cannot imply the right to refuse to accept regulation or regulated consequences; there is no freedom to 'opt out'. Rather, consent is derived from the right to participate in the decision-making process, so that the authority, which is exercised over those governed is exercised by them. Those not within the polity, those without the right to participate in the creation and control of its authority, those who are 'unconnected', cannot be subject to its authority, whether regulatory or judicial." M. Stewart, "New Litany of Personal Jurisdiction", 60 *Colo. L. Rev.* 5, at 18-20 (1989).

For Anglo-American jurists the authoritarian-freedom distinction calls to mind the contrasting views of Hobbes and Locke;[269] like the latter's social contract, the freedom model requires that organized society provide a sphere of irreducible autonomy for the individual. Conversely, legal orders whose jurisdictional practices are but mirror images of the State's ability to give effect to the decisions of its adjudicators are authoritarian in the full sense of the term.[270]

Against this background, Pfeiffer develops his conception of international procedural justice. Taking a cosmopolitan and internationalist perspective, he sees as the informing principle of jurisdiction to adjudicate in the international sense the protection of the exercise of individual rights, without regard to the legal order in which the rights have their source. To establish the outer limits of what constitutes a procedurally just exercise of adjudicatory authority, Pfeiffer reasons from the individual's right – developed by the German Constitutional Court – to an efficient judicial process under rule-of-law principles (the *Justizanspruch*).[271] Applied as well to domestic as to multistate situations, the principle requires a judicial system that functions efficiently, impartially, and independently.[272]

(b) The appropriate treatment for jurisdictional purposes of plaintiffs and defendants

Having developed the related propositions that procedural justice is a free-standing concept whose aim is to secure individual rights and that individuals are, as a matter of principle, entitled to access to an effective adjudicatory system to protect their rights under the rule of law, Pfeiffer explores the implications of these positions for the treatment of both plaintiffs and defendants.

In matters significantly connected with only one legal order, one's claim to adjudicatory process is absolute only with respect to that legal order. Where the matter is significantly connected to several legal orders, one may have an absolute claim to adjudication in each of these forums. This claim is not universal, howev-

---

269 See Chap. I. A. 3. *(a)*, pp. 18 *et seq.*, *supra*.

270 Pfeiffer claims that the distinction between the authoritarian and freedom models is essentially the same as the contrast between power and fairness approaches (see *idem* 201, note 6); he considers jurisdictional theories that rest on power – whether territorial or relational in nature – as authoritarian. See *idem* 201-202. However, a pure relational theory declines to exercise jurisdiction in many situations in which the legal order could give effect to its decisions. The same observation can be made with respect to those power theories that conceive of power in strictly territorial terms. The jurisdictional prototype of the authoritarian State would, in principle, exercise jurisdiction wherever it could effectively do so. Because jurisdictional practice always to some extent factors in elements of the parties' positions and needs, in practice the authoritarian model is not encountered in a pure form. However, a power model, *simpliciter*, has a stronger authoritarian tendency than a relational model.

271 See *idem* 356.

272 Pfeiffer considers the *forum non conveniens* doctrine incompatible with a person's *Justizanspruch*; the doctrine denies fundamental rights by making access to the courts depend upon judicial discretion rather than the rule of law. See *idem* 381-432.

er; local adjudication requires a significant connection between the controversy and the forum. On the other hand, no principled exclusion of local adjudicatory authority can be based on the foreign nationality of parties, the applicability of foreign law, or the localization of the underlying controversy in another legal order.[273] Whether such connections are present can be evaluated either *ex ante* in group-norm terms or *ex post* in controversy-specific terms. Pfeiffer's approach thus accommodates the three basic forms of adjudicatory authority: general jurisdiction, category-specific jurisdiction, and specific jurisdiction.[274]

The exercise of adjudicatory authority must, however, not be unreasonably burdensome on the defendant. The defendant's fundamental right, as an individual, to be free from undue interference by the state, requires that interventions be limited to situations connected with the society that asserts adjudicatory authority. The connection to the legal order in question can take various forms: (1) a party is domiciled or habitually resident there (general jurisdiction); (2) a party engaged there in a specific type of juristic activity (category-specific jurisdiction); (3) or a party engaged in conduct that occurred or had effects there (specific jurisdiction).

Where such a connection exists, the question still remains whether the interference is "undue". An interference that is undue when the plaintiff could clearly obtain legal protection in another forum, may be acceptable when denying local adjudication would create a real danger that the plaintiff would be deprived of legal protection. Accordingly, a normally undue exercise of adjudicatory authority is acceptable where required to ensure legal protection for a class of plaintiffs – consumers, for example – that would otherwise typically find it difficult to assert their claims.[275] The determination of undueness thus requires weighing both parties' claim to legal protection.

Against this background, Pfeiffer addresses the issue posed by the *actor sequitur forum rei* principle.[276] Where the plaintiff and defendant each can claim the same ground of adjudicatory authority – for example, when general jurisdiction based on domicile or habitual residence is in question – should the plaintiff be denied the right to establish adjudicatory authority at his domicile or habitual residence? Pfeiffer concludes that the plaintiff should not to be able to claim general jurisdiction in these circumstances. Plaintiffs normally enjoy the advantage of

---

273 *Idem* 434-439.

274 Pfeiffer's analysis does not explicitly use these categories; in the writer's view it implies them, however.

275 Pfeiffer considers the minimum contacts theory, as developed and practised in the United States, too fact-specific; considerations of administrability and predictability require the development of general standards. See *idem* 594-596. It is not clear how this can be accomplished, however, where specific jurisdiction is in question.

276 See *idem* 596-603. Pfeiffer's discussion of the *actor sequitur* principle neither distinguishes between notional and substantive defendants' forums nor explores in depth the implications for the principle of the plaintiff's range of choice among available forums. For a discussion of these matters, see Chap. IV., pp. 153 *et seq.*, *passim*, *infra*.

choice between, or among, forums.[277] Invoking the *actor sequitur* principle serves as a counterbalance to the plaintiff's advantage of choice. Moreover, litigation in the defendant's community usually simplifies enforcement of judgments. The *actor sequitur forum rei* principle should, therefore, limit the exercise of adjudicatory authority where the parties have, in principle, identical claims to general jurisdiction.

Adjudicatory authority can be claimed not only to vindicate the plaintiff's claim to justice *(Justizanspruch)* but to advance government regulatory policies *(Regelungsziele)*. To be legitimate, a jurisdictional claim must serve at least one of these purposes, be needed *(erforderlich)*, and meet the proportionality requirement. Pfeiffer explores the proportionality *(Verhältnismäßigkeit)* problem largely in terms of connecting factors that can, *a priori*, appropriately establish jurisdiction; he does not discuss whether the doctrine of proportionality should operate as well to limit the number of claims to jurisdiction that a given situation can engender. His basic thesis is that, to the extent that persons enter into relations – be they contractual, delictual, or of another nature – each reciprocally relinquishes a part of the independence that, in principle, he enjoys from the other. Likewise, when a person engages in activity – for example, delivers goods – that brings him into a relationship with a person abroad, he gives up a part of the independence he in principle enjoyed from that state's legal order.

These conclusions do not rest on a fictitious or implicit submission but on objective participation in the civil society *(bürgerlicher Zustand)* served by the legal order in question.[278] Conduct such as taking up permanent residence accepts fully the local order as guarantor of one's rights; on the other hand, many forms of conduct accept the local order only with respect to certain aspects of one's life. Claims of adjudicatory authority that relate to matters for which the legal order's authority has, in either of these senses, been accepted, satisfy the proportionality requirement.

(c)   The relevance of (minimum) contacts

Pfeiffer's analysis has some similarities with – and a fundamental difference from – American "minimum contacts" theory.[279] In his view, the American approach in assessing appropriateness counts any kind of minimum connection between the controversy and the forum. For Pfeiffer a connection serves to establish adjudica-

---

277   Theoretically, this argument could be blunted by giving the defendant the right to select the forum to adjudicate from among those open to the plaintiff through, for example, transfer from the forum initially selected by the plaintiff to another available forum. Even if such an approach were theoretically attractive, it would be costly, cumbersome, result in substantial delay, and spawn additional litigation. See *idem* 601-602.

278   *Idem* 612-619.

279   An important point in common is that the defendant has a *Freiheitsanspruch*, that is to say, is not obligated to litigate locally unless he is, in some fashion and degree, connected with the legal order in question. See *idem* 614.

tory authority only where, functionally considered, the contact is of a kind that, in view of the role and function of courts, justifies assertion of adjudicatory authority. Factoring teleological concerns in this way into the jurisdictional equation has, according to him, the advantage not only of establishing criteria of relevance but of allowing jurisdictional practice to adjust to developments of a technical, social, or economic nature. Pfeiffer believes that his approach can, for example, accommodate more easily than can a mechanical "minimum contacts" theory a new legal phenomenon such as mass torts.[280]

In discussing the "minimum contacts" theory, some American jurists have argued that for facts to count they must both occur within the relevant legal order and be required to establish the claim.[281] Pfeiffer is attracted by this criterion's relative clarity and by its recognition that the contact must touch the civil society, that is to say, be within the *"Außengrenzen der Gesellschaft."*[282] Nevertheless, he finds it ultimately unacceptable. The limits it sets to claims of adjudicatory authority are, he believes, illusory; a legal order can, by changing its substantive law, extend its jurisdictional claims almost without limit.[283] The outer limits of civil society turn, in part, on decisions political in nature that are reflected in legislation; the significance of such extensions for jurisdictional purposes should, however, be limited by the requirement of proportionality. Proportionality also requires that the plaintiff's claim to justice be balanced against the defendant's claim to be left alone (his *status negativus*). The strongest case for rejecting claims of adjudicatory authority for violation of the proportionality principle arises when a legal order claims jurisdiction to advance a regulatory or protectionist policy and the connecting factor invoked is not the central element *(Schwerpunkt)* of the basic legal relationship. Here the realization of the regulatory or protectionist goal through jurisdictional means is likely to impose a disproportionate burden on defendants.

Pfeiffer considers the factual-component-of-claim test to be under-inclusive in certain situations. In contractual matters, the place of performance is an acceptable basis for category-specific jurisdiction even though that geographical fact does not ground a claim. In Pfeiffer's view, connection must be understood procedurally: a relation must exist between the underlying sociological situation

---

280 See *ibid.*

281 See *idem* 616 (citing L. Brilmayer, "How Contacts Count: Due Process Limitations on State Court Jurisdiction", [1980] *Supreme Court Review* 77, at 88; L. Brilmayer and K. Paisley, "Personal Jurisdiction and Substantive Legal Relations: Corporations, Conspiracies, and Agency", 74 *U. Calif. L. Rev.* 1, at 25 (1986); M. Murphy, "Personal Jurisdiction and the Stream of Commerce Theory: A Reappraisal and a Revised Approach", 77 *U. Ky. LJ* 243, at 297 (1989).

282 Pfeiffer quotes in this connection, Brilmayer's observation that "when substantively relevant activities occur within the forum, the forum has an interest in adjudicating their consequences". *Idem* 617 (citing L. Brilmayer, "Related Contacts and Personal Jurisdiction", 101 *Harv. L. Rev.* 1444, at 1457 (1988)).

283 *Idem* 618.

(the *Lebenssachverhalt)* and the forum's sphere of adjudicatory authority either through local presence of a factual component of the claim (e.g., place of tortious conduct: specific jurisdiction) or through a factual element related to the content of the claim (e.g., place of performance of a contract: category-specific jurisdiction).[284]

(d) Application of Pfeiffer's theory

Having formulated as a matter of general theory the limits upon a State's adjudicatory authority, Pfeiffer applies his analysis to various provisions of the German Code of Civil Procedure. Of particular interest is his conclusion that ZPO §23 is unconstitutional because one's ownership of local property does not constitute sufficient participation in the civil society to extinguish one's general right to a *status negativus*; accordingly, the provision violates the individual's constitutionally guaranteed sphere of freedom because the requirements of domestic connection and of proportionality are not satisfied.[285] All arguments for and against the provision having been considered, he concludes that §23's methods are disproportionate to its legitimate goals,[286] which can be reached in other ways.

Two other Code provisions do not pass muster for Pfeiffer: §32a's exclusive jurisdiction for claims based on environmental damage caused by emissions from certain installations and some applications of §606a which sets out the adjudicatory authority of German courts over marriages.[287]

Pfeiffer offers ZPO §32a as another example of a provision that does not satisfy his proportionality requirement. The section's practical importance is limited; it does not apply to litigation within the scope of the Brussels instruments or the Lugano Convention. Nevertheless, a brief discussion of Pfeiffer's critique of the provision can serve to illustrate his understanding of proportionality.

The legislative history of §32a is unusual. In the course of deliberations on the Environmental Liability Law *(Umwelthaftungsgesetz)*,[288] the Bundestag proposed adding to the ZPO a new provision – now the first sentence of §32a – providing for exclusive jurisdiction over claims for environmental damage against owners of installations – to be specified in an annex to the Environmental Liability Law – in the court of the district in which the emitting installation is situated. Sub-

---

284 *Idem* 619.

285 *Idem* 620-650. Pfeiffer addresses specifically – and finds unacceptable – various arguments advanced by supporters of §23. He points out, *inter alia*, that §23 in a random and one-sided fashion advantages plaintiffs in general without the justification that, in the majority of cases, otherwise a *déni de justice* would occur. *Idem* 633.

286 *Idem* 641-642. In light of the language of the statute and clear legislative intent, Pfeiffer considers restrictive interpretation by the courts improper and corrective action by the parliament unlikely. He concludes, therefore, that only action by the Federal Constitutional Court – in which the power of judicial review is concentrated – can bring about legislative change. *Idem* 647.

287 See Chap. I. C. 1. *(b)* (i), pp. 33-34, *supra.*

288 10 December 1990, BGBl. I 2634 (1990).

sequently, the Bundesrat added the language that is now the second sentence of §32a and thus made explicit what was already implied: the new provision applied only to installations situated in Germany.

Section 32a, while not standing in the way of German courts exercising jurisdiction under §32 over foreign installations whose emissions cause harmful effects in Germany, precludes, by claiming exclusive jurisdiction, recognition by German courts of judgments rendered by foreign courts against owners of German installations whose emissions have caused harm abroad.

Pfeiffer begins his proportionality analysis by considering whether §32a is capable of advancing one or more rational policies.[289] Two such policies are identified: (1) defending German standards of delictual liability against lower standards held by other legal orders; (2) protecting owners of German installations against excessive foreign judgments. (A third policy, procedural in nature – mentioned, but not considered in connection with proportionality, by Pfeiffer in his 1993 Article[290] – is suggested by the legislative history of §32a:[291] the courts of the place of emission can best gather and evaluate evidence respecting the cause of the polluting emissions.)

None of these policies is facially irrational and §32a is able to serve each. Accordingly, a second question must be put: could these policies be effectively pursued by other means at a smaller cost to constitutionally protected values? Discussing the first two policies, Pfeiffer concludes that the answer is, in both cases, yes.[292] Where the application of higher German standards is in question, the plaintiff's ability to pursue his claim in the German courts will ordinarily result in the litigation being brought in Germany. From the perspective of this policy, §32a is thus superfluous.[293]

Is the provision then needed to protect German owners against foreign judgments that are, by German standards, excessive? Pfeiffer concludes that other provisions of German law provide protection against excessive judgments. He relies in the first instance on ZPO §328 (1), No. 4, foreign judgments are to be denied recognition when they produce results that are clearly incompatible with a fundamental principle of German law. Accordingly, *non-compensatory* damages – punitive or treble damages, for example – should be denied enforcement under ZPO §328. It is far from clear, however, that the *amount* of *compensatory* damages can constitute under ZPO §328 (1), No. 4, a violation of the *ordre public*. Some jurists take the position that a foreign judgment awarding an excessive amount, one that exceeds by far what would be awarded under German law, will not be

---

289 See Pfeiffer, *supra* footnote 264, at 619; T. Pfeiffer, "Der Umweltgerichtsstand als zuständigkeitsrechtlicher Störfall", 106 *ZZP* 159-179 (1993).

290 *Idem* 160.

291 See Report of the Legal Committee *(Rechtsausschuß)*, BT-Drs. 11/7881, at 38.

292 See Pfeiffer, *supra* footnote 289, at 175-179.

293 Of course, problems could arise if the German owner were to bring an action abroad for a negative declaratory judgment; this problem could be handled, however. See Chap. VI. D. 5. *(a)* (ii), p. 306-307, *infra*.

enforced. But they do not distinguish between non-compensatory and compensatory damages.[294] One commentary does state flatly that, under §328, any "excessively high damage award is contrary to the *ordre public*".[295] Other commentaries are more cautious; they point out that foreign judgments are generally enforced even though higher damages than would be available under German law have been awarded.[296] Nor has the Bundesgerichtshof refused recognition to foreign judgments on the ground that the amount awarded is considerably larger than would have been given had the matter been litigated in Germany.[297]

It seems, therefore, that a policy of protecting German owners of installations against foreign judgments that would be excessive under German law is today more effectively and completely vindicated by §32a than would be possible under other provisions of existing German law.

The third possible policy – that of concentrating, for procedural reasons, environmental litigation at the place of wrongful conduct – would be fully served by a more moderate provision than §32a. Deleting the section's second sentence would concentrate litigation at the place of emission and remove the discrimination against foreign defendants.

If Pfeiffer's reading of ZPO §328 (1), No. 4, is correct, the policies on which §32a could rationally rest can be effectively pursued under §328 (1) at a cost to the constitutionally protected value of access to justice less than that exacted by §32a. To the extent, however, that one does not accept Pfeiffer's reading of §328, a third inquiry is necessary: does the purpose served by §32a advance constitutional values that outweigh the values that the section affects adversely? This question is not explored by Pfeiffer in either his treatise or 1993 article. His answer could well be, however, that the rational policy or policies served by §32a are of less value than is the plaintiff's constitutionally protected right of access to justice which the section limits.

For the rest, Pfeiffer finds acceptable the Code's jurisdictional bases as well as their derivation from venue provisions.[298] Aside from the exceptions already noted, the Code's bases for general as well as for specific jurisdiction satisfy his proportionality and domestic-connection standards.[299]

---

294 See, e.g., R. Zöller (-Geimer), *Kommentar zur ZPO* (Cologne, Dr. Otto Schmidt, 25th ed., 2005), §328, No. 169; Geimer, *supra* footnote 253, at 937-938, No. 2974.

295 F. Stein and M. Jonas (-Roth), *Kommentar zur Zivilprozeßordnung*, Vol. 4/1 (Tübingen, Mohr Siebeck, 21st ed., 1998), §328, No. 134.

296 See, e.g., *Münchener Kommentar zur Zivilprozeßordnung* (-Gottwald), Vol. 1 (Munich, C. H. Beck, 2nd ed. 2000), §328, No. 96; A. Baumbach, W. Lauterbach, J. Albers and P. Hartmann (-Hartmann), *Kommentar zur Zivilprozeßordnung* (Munich, C. H. Beck, 64th ed., 2006), §328, Nos. 43-44.

297 Cf. BGH, 4 June 1992, 118 *BGHZ* 312.

298 Pfeiffer, *supra* footnote 264, at 482-483.

299 Note that in 2005 a new ZPO §32b has been introduced. See Article 2 No. 2 of the Gesetz zur Einführung von Kapitalanleger-Musterverfahren of 16.8.2005, BGBl. I 2437 (2005). The provision is modeled on ZPO §32a and provides for an exclusive basis of

5. The Contribution of the German Courts

German courts have played but a small role in the development and refinement of general theory respecting jurisdiction to adjudicate in the international sense.[300] Only rarely has the task of interpreting and applying the relevant provisions of the ZPO and of international conventions been thought to require theoretical discussion. With few exceptions, the applicable code and convention provisions are couched in fairly specific and straightforward terms; furthermore, until after World War II, judicial review of legislation on constitutional grounds was not practised in Germany. Only with the coming into force of the Basic Law in 1949 did challenges on constitutional grounds to an exorbitant jurisdictional basis – ZPO §23, for example – become a realistic possibility.[301]

(a)   The principal decisions

For a variety of reasons – in particular, the legislator's essentially moderate approach to international jurisdiction and the lack of an explicit natural justice or due process clause in the Basic Law – the contributions of German courts to jurisdiction theory still are, and are likely to remain, far less important than those of American courts. Indeed, since 1950, only four decisions – two of the *Bundesgerichtshof* and two of the *Bundesverfassungsgericht* – warrant discussion.

(i)   Uncoupling adjudicatory jurisdiction and venue: BGH 14 June 1965

A 1965 decision of the Großer Senat of the Bundesgerichtshof[302] (the highest civil court) is arguably the first judicial decision to make a significant contribution to general jurisdictional theory. At issue was the application of ZPO §549 (2) and of

---

jurisdiction for investors' claims based on insufficient or false information. It is assumed that the new provision would not satisfy *Pfeiffer's* proportionality test. See for a discussion of the proposed ZPO §32b J. von Hein, "Der ausschließliche Gerichtsstand für Kapitalanleger-Musterverfahren – eine Lex Anti-Americana?" 50 *RIW* 602 (2004). See for a discussion of the Kapitalanleger-Musterverfahrensgesetz (Act on Model Proceedings in Capital Market Disputes) in general V. Vorwerk and C. Wolf, *KapMuG - Kapitalanleger-Musterverfahrensgesetz* (Munich, C. H. Beck, 2006); B. Hess and C. Michailidou, "Das Gesetz über Musterverfahren zu Schadensersatzklagen von Kapitalanlegern", 25 *ZIP* 1381 (2004); F. Reuschle, "Musterverfahren als neuer Weg zur prozessualen Bewältigung von Massenschäden", *ZBB* 518 (2004).

300   See R. Schütze, "Die Bedeutung der Rechtsprechung als Rechtsquelle im deutschen internationalen Zivilprozeßrecht", 92 *ZvglRWiss* 29, at 33-34 (1993).

301   See pp. 139 *et seq.*, *supra*, for Pfeiffer's views respecting the unconstitutionality of ZPO §§23, 32a, and 606a. For a brief discussion of the introduction of judicial review in Germany after World War II, see A. von Mehren, "Constitutionalism in Germany – The First Decision of the New Constitutional Court", 1 *Am. J. Comp. L.* 70, at 72-74 (1952).

302   BGH, *Großer Senat für Zivilsachen*, 14 June 1965, 44 *BGHZ* 46. Cases in the Bundesgerichtshof are ordinarily decided by a senate. However, where a civil senate proposes to depart from the past decision of another civil senate or of the Great Civil Senate

§512a, enacted, respectively, in 1905 and 1924.[303] Under §549 (2) (now § 545 [2]), *Revision* (review limited to questions of law) was not available in the highest civil court[304] on the ground that the court of first instance had incorrectly found that it had venue *(örtliche Zuständigkeit)*; essentially identical language in §512a (now § 513 [2]) excluded challenges before intermediate courts by way of appeal *(Berufung)*[305] to determinations by courts of first instance that they had venue. These limitations were introduced to reduce the workload of the highest civil court and the intermediate civil courts, respectively.[306]

In 1915, the Reichsgericht held that §549 (2) applied to determinations of jurisdiction in the international sense.[307] Although the High Court had by then recognized the distinction between venue and adjudicatory authority,[308] it saw no "intrinsic reason *(innerer Grund)*" to distinguish the two issues for purposes of §549 (2).[309] In view of its very similar language, §512a was in due course also applied to the issue of jurisdiction in the international sense.[310] When, after 1949, the Bundesgerichtshof first faced these issues, it accepted the Reichgericht's position.

The 1965 decision was a new departure both in result and reasoning. The Bundesgerichtshof begins by discussing the sense and purposes of §§512a and 549 (2). It points out that venue decisions do not affect the applicable procedural and substantive law; what is principally at stake in venue cases is which party will enjoy the convenience of litigating in his local court. Furthermore, it is a matter of indifference to the State – so far as the particular controversy is concerned – where the litigation proceeds.[311] When jurisdiction in the international sense is at issue, however, "[t]he pattern of interests *(Interessenlage)* is fundamentally dif-

---

(Großer Senat für Zivilsachen), it must refer the matter to the Great Senate for decision.

For the structure of the German court system and the role of the *Bundesgerichtshof*, see A. von Mehren and J. Gordley, *The Civil Law System*, at 128-141 (Boston, MA & Toronto, Little Brown, 2nd ed., 1977).

303   In 1976, ZPO §549 (2) was made applicable as well to decisions respecting subject-matter jurisdiction *(sachliche Zuständigkeit)*.

304   Originally, the Reichsgericht; since 1950, the Bundesgerichtshof. See von Mehren and Gordley, *supra* footnote 302, at 130-133.

305   See for a detailed account of German appellate remedies including *Revision* and *Berufung* P. Murray and R. Stürner, *German Civil Justice*, at 369-417 (Durham, N.C., Carolina Academic Press, 2004).

306   See BGH, 14 June 1965, 44 *BGHZ* 46, at 48.

307   See P. Neuhaus, Note, 21 *JZ* 239, at 239 (1966).

308   *Ibid.*

309   RG, 25 June 1915, [1915] Warneyer, *Rechtsprechung des Reichsgerichts in Zivilsachen* 376, No. 274.

310   See RG, 6 February 1930, 24 *Leipziger Zeitschrift für Handels-, Konkurs- und Versicherungsrecht* 1502 (1930).

311   See BGH, 14 June 1965, 44 *BGHZ*, 46 at 49.

ferent".[312] The jurisdictional decision determines which party will be more familiar with, and trusting of, the court that is to decide the controversy. Procedural and substantive law can be affected in fundamental ways by jurisdiction; indeed, the choice of court may well be outcome-determinative.[313]

The Bundesgerichtshof concludes that the significance and consequences of decisions respecting adjudicatory jurisdiction in the international sense and venue are fundamentally different. The purpose of the amendments to the ZPO in question being to exclude from appellate review "only points of dispute of minor importance", it cannot be assumed that the provisions, which speak of venue *(örtliche Zuständigkeit)*, cover as well international jurisdiction *(internationale Zuständigkeit)*.[314] Furthermore, to interpret §§512a and 549 (2) as the Reichsgericht did is inconsistent with the exclusion from the scope of the provisions in question of issues respecting subject-matter jurisdiction *(sachliche Zuständigkeit)*.

The importance of the 1965 decision – and its contribution to general jurisdictional theory – lies both in the decoupling of adjudicatory jurisdiction and venue, issues that had been closely linked by the courts and by many jurists in previous theory and practice under the ZPO, and in the instrumental analysis advanced to explain the holding.[315]

In its judgment of 28 November 2002, after §549 (2) had been transformed into §545 (2) by the ZPO Reform Act of 2001,[316] the BGH confirmed its holding in the 1965 decision as to the distinction between venue and jurisdiction in the international sense.[317] In light of the more inclusive language of the new provision in §545 (2), which only speaks of jurisdiction *(Zuständigkeit)* of the court of first instance – as opposed to the former §549 (2) which specifically mentioned subject-matter jurisdiction and venue *(sachliche und örtliche Zuständigkeit)* as being beyond the scope of an appeal on a point of law – some scholars had argued that henceforth venue and jurisdiction in the international sense would have to be

---

312   *Ibid.*

313   *Idem* 50-51.

314   *Idem* 51.

315   Neuhaus considers "[t]he [Senate's] reasoning *(Begründung)* ... a classic example *(Musterstück)* of jurisprudence of interests *(Interessenjurisprudenz)*". Neuhaus, *supra* footnote 307, at 240.

       In certain situations, practical considerations result in a "recoupling" of the two issues. Where venue and adjudicatory jurisdiction are regulated in common, and the latter issue is brought before the Bundesgerichtshof in *Revision*, the High Court will decide the venue issue as well in order to avoid the possibility of "jurisdiction without courts". BGH, 21 November 1996, 134 *BGHZ* 127, at 130.

316   BGBl. I 1887 (2001).

317   BGH, 28 November 2002, 56 *NJW* 426 (2003). See for a detailed account P. Mankowski, "Entwicklungen im Internationalen Privat- und Prozessrecht 2003/2004 (Teil 2)", 50 *RIW* 587, at 591-592 (2004).

treated alike for the purposes of appellate review.[318] The BGH held that, despite of its wide wording, the provision did not prevent the appeal court from re-examining of the German courts' jurisdiction in the international sense.[319] In its opinion, the court reiterated the fundamental differences between venue on the one hand and jurisdiction in the international sense on the other, and made abundant reference to its 1965 decision.[320]

(ii)   Restricting the scope of ZPO §23: BGH 2 July 1991

In 1991, the Eleventh Senate of the Bundesgerichtshof handed down another decision of importance for general jurisdictional theory.[321] The case, which turned on the reach of ZPO §23, arose out of a contract between a Cypriot construction firm and a Libyan entity to build a harbor (*Hafenanlage*) in Libya for US$ 221,000,000. The owner, who was obligated under the contract to pay the construction firm an advance of 37 million dollars, provided an Advance Payment Guarantee; in connection therewith, the contractor arranged for the defendant, a Turkish bank with an office (*Niederlassung*) and representation in Germany, to guarantee that any advances made that were not ultimately earned by the contractor would be returned to the owner. As security for this obligation, the contractor deposited 20 million dollars with the bank.

Difficulties subsequently developed, the construction contract was terminated, and the Turkish bank refunded to the owner the 20 million dollars advance payment made on the owner's behalf to the contractor. The latter took the position that no refunds were due. Accordingly, it sued the Turkish bank in England for 20 million dollars. The English court stayed the suit on *forum non conveniens* grounds.

The contractor thereupon assigned its restitution claim to its managing director and her husband. They, basing jurisdiction on ZPO §23, sued the Turkish bank in the German courts for 3 million dollars, plus interest. The court of first instance took jurisdiction; upon appeal, the judgment was reversed for lack of

---

318   See, e.g. *Münchener Kommentar zur Zivilprozessordnung* (-Wenzel), Aktualisierungsband (Munich, C. H. Beck, 2nd ed., 2002), §545 No. 16; H. Thomas and H. Putzo (-Reichold), *Zivilprozessordnung* (Munich, C. H. Beck, 24th ed., 2002), §545, No. 11. In the 2005 edition, Reichold has abandoned this view in the light of the 2003 decision of the BGH. See H. Thomas and H. Putzo (-Reichold), *Zivilprozessordnung* (Munich, C. H. Beck, 27th ed., 2005), §545, No. 11.

319   *Ibid.*

320   *Idem* 427. The court also draw heavily on another argument: If the question of jurisdiction in the international sense was beyond the scope of a *Revision* – and consequently, with a view to the parallel wording in §513 (2), also of a *Berufung* – German courts would, in effect, be prevented from making a preliminary reference on the interpretation of the Brussels Regulation to the ECJ. Such a result, the BGH found, clearly could not have been intended by the legislature. See *idem* 427.

321   BGH, 2 July 1991, 115 *BGHZ* 90.

jurisdiction.[322] The plaintiff's challenge to the court of appeal's decision was unsuccessful.[323]

The Stuttgart court of appeals took the position that, for §23 jurisdiction to exist, a more substantial domestic connection *(Inlandsbezug)* than the mere presence of assets was required. Such a connection – for example, the "proximity of the controversy *(Sachverhalt)* to German law or to elements of proof located in Germany",[324] the plaintiffs' domicile *(Wohnsitz)* in Germany, or a domestic interest of the plaintiffs that deserved protection – did not exist, however.

Exercising its review on issues of law, the Eleventh Senate recognized that the prior case law, in view of the explicit language of §23, had refused to condition adjudicatory jurisdiction on the value of the property or on the controversy's domestic connection with Germany.[325] The Senate pointed out, however, that unqualified application of §23 had been adversely criticized in the literature. In particular, limiting §23 jurisdiction by requiring that the property *(Vermögen)* establishing jurisdiction have – value-wise – a reasonable relationship to the amount in controversy had been urged.[326] The Senate took no position on that issue; in the instant case, the value relationship between property and claim was clearly sufficient.[327]

The Senate held, however, that the controversy lacked a domestic relationship sufficient to establish jurisdiction. In its view the sense and purpose of §23, as revealed by the drafting history, required this interpretation.[328] The provision's primary purpose was to give locals *(Inländer)*, without regard to their nationality, the possibility of suing a foreigner having local property; there was no intention to provide a forum for controversies between foreigners who lack any domestic connection with Germany. The Senate concluded that, at the minimum, this history justifies requiring a stronger domestic connection than the mere presence of property.[329]

An interpretation of §23 along these lines also finds support in international conventions, which increasingly exclude or restrict jurisdiction based on the

---

322 OLG Stuttgart, 6 August 1990, [1991] *IPRspr.*, No. 166.

323 See BGH, 115 *BGHZ* 90, at 90-99.

324 The relevant German text is "Rechts- oder Beweisnähe des Sachverhalts". See *idem* 91.

325 *Idem* 92.

326 This is the position taken by Austrian law; see Jurisdiktionsnorm, Sec. 99 (1), second sentence.

327 BGH, 115 *BGHZ* at 93.

328 *Idem* 94.

329 *Idem* 95. The Court goes on (*idem* 98) to reject explicitly the view expressed by some jurists that "the mere acquisition or possession of property in Germany, indicates an 'affinity to the Federal Republic of Germany', that justifies the owner's or possessor's duty to appear *(Gerichtspflichtigkeit)* before German courts".

presence of property.³³⁰ The Senate concluded that §23 must be interpreted, where jurisdiction in the international sense is in issue, in a way that reflects its true sense and purpose;³³¹ "to read §23 literally, ... promotes 'forum shopping', ... the calculated selection of forums".³³² The decision of the Bundesgerichtshof's Eleventh Senate thus rests not on a constitutional ground but on statutory interpretation.

Professor Schlosser, commenting on the 1991 decision, opined that the Eleventh Senate had taken the "more cautious path *(vorsichtiger Weg)*" in restricting the provision's scope to situations in which "a sufficient local connection of the controversy *(hinreichender Inlandsbezug des Rechtsstreits)*"³³³ could be established. He considered this solution unfortunate because it interjected – in his view for the first time – into the German law of jurisdiction a concept with the indefinite character of a general clause.³³⁴ In order to avoid unfortunate consequences,³³⁵ he believed the courts would have to mark out well defined factual categories so that the existence *vel non* of §23 jurisdiction can be determined for most situations without recourse to litigation.³³⁶

(iii) Dictum of the Constitutional Court respecting ZPO §23: BVerfG 12 April 1983

Constitutional requirements play, as the twenty-first century begins, but a minor role in German thinking respecting jurisdiction in the international sense.³³⁷

---

330 BGH, 115 *BGHZ*, at 95. Relevant provisions of international conventions are discussed *idem* 95-97.

331 *Idem* 97.

332 *Idem* 98.

333 P. Schlosser, "Einschränkung des Vermögensgerichtsstandes", 12 *IPRax* 140, at 142 (1992).

334 *Ibid.*

335 Schlosser's concern here does not seem to be for the predictability and administrability in general of jurisdictional requirements. He fears that litigating §23's applicability will be unduly expensive for parties until clear-cut norms have been developed because of the way in which the German system reimburses lawyers for litigation. The fee to be paid is not calculated on the basis of the time expended at an agreed hourly rate but rather on the basis of the amount in controversy and the stages reached in the litigation process. When a court dismisses an action for lack of jurisdiction, all three procedural stages are considered completed with the consequence that the parties must pay the same fee as would have been owed had the decision been on the merits. See *ibid.* For a discussion of the German fee system, see B. Kaplan, A. von Mehren and R. Schaefer, "Phases of German Civil Procedure", Part II, 71 *Harv. L. Rev.* 1443, at 1461-1467 (1958); Murray and Stürner, *supra* footnote 305, at 112-115 and 341-354.

336 Schlosser, *supra* footnote 333, at 142.

337 But see generally, R. Geimer, "Verfassung, Völkerrecht und Internationales Zivilverfahrensrecht", 33 *ZfRV* 321, at 321-335 (1992); Geimer, *supra* footnote 253, at 104-110, Nos. 249-254.

Indeed, only two decisions of the Constitutional Court address the constitutionality of provisions of law respecting jurisdiction. A 1983 decision involved the use of ZPO §23 jurisdiction to create a preliminary attachment of funds *(dinglicher Arrest)* pending the outcome of litigation.[338] The Court held that assertion of jurisdiction to order attachment of locally present property *(Anordnung der Pfändung)* did not violate general rules of international law, treaty obligations, or constitutional provisions.[339] Whether the property's presence would also suffice to establish jurisdiction over the underlying controversy was not in issue; however, the Court went on to state that, had the issue been before it, "significant *(erhebliche)* questions of international law and of a legal-political *(rechtspolitisch)* nature would have arisen".[340]

(iv) Unconstitutionality of ZPO §606b, No. 1: BVerfG 3 December 1985

In 1985, the Constitutional Court struck down on constitutional grounds §606b, No. 1[341] of the Code of Civil Procedure.[342] This provision regulated the adjudicatory authority of German courts over divorce actions where neither spouse was a German national.[343] In such cases, German courts were given adjudicatory authority only when "either the habitual residence of the husband or the wife is in

---

The Basic Law has so far been of greater importance for choice of law and recognition and enforcement of foreign judgments. See generally, *Münchener Kommentar zum Bürgerlichen Gesetzbuch* (-Sonnenberger), Vol. X (Munich, C. H. Beck, 4rd ed., 2006), Nos. 336-343; Geimer, *supra* footnote 253, at 110-111, Nos. 255-256a (recognition and enforcement).

338   BVerfG, 12 April 1983, 61 BVerfGE 1. A similar issue arises in the United States in connection with the *Shaffer* case. See pp. 102 *et seq.*, *supra*. In American law the presence of property clearly establishes jurisdiction to order its temporary sequestration.

339   BVerfG, 61 BVerfGE at 20.

340   *Idem* 18.

341   BVerfG, 3 December 1985, 41 *JZ* 336 (1986). The provision was repealed in 1986 by the IPR-Gesetz, BGBl. I 1142 (1986).

342   The provision traced back to ZPO §606 (4) – enacted in 1898. See RGBl. 525 (1898). The 1898 provision gave German courts adjudicatory authority in divorce proceedings between two foreigners living in Germany, where the courts of the husband's national State would have jurisdiction to adjudicate. The additional requirement of recognition of the German courts' decision by the courts of the husband's national State was introduced in 1941 by amending §606 (3), No. 1. See DurchfVO zum Ehegesetz of 25.10.1941, RGBl. I 654 (1941). In 1957, §606 (3), No. 1 and No. 2 became, without substantive change, §606b, No. 1. See Article 2, No. 2 of the Gesetz über die Gleichberechtigung von Mann und Frau auf dem Gebiet des bürgerlichen Rechts of 18. 6. 1957, BGBl. I 609 (1957).

343   Adjudicatory authority over annulment *(Aufhebung)*, declarations of nullity *(Nichtigkeitserklärung)*, and declarations that the marriage did – or did not – exist was broader; it could rest either on §606b No. 1 or No. 2. The latter provision provided for German jurisdiction when the woman was a German national at the time the marriage was contracted *(Eheschließung)*.

Germany and the husband's national law would recognize the German decision or one of the spouses is stateless ...". The Constitutional Court, relying in part on a series of cases respecting the constitutionality of certain choice-of-law provisions applicable in marriage and divorce actions,[344] held §606b unconstitutional under Article 3 (2) of the Basic Law which provides that "men and women have equal rights".

(b)   The significance of the case law

This paucity of decisions strongly suggests that – so far as jurisdiction in the international sense is concerned – the German courts are unlikely to play a leading role in the development of either theory or practice. The Eleventh Senate in its 1991 decision did not bind the Bundesgerichthof as a whole; it remains to be seen whether ultimately even the Eleventh Senate's modest restriction of §23 through statutory interpretation will prevail.

In any event, a literal application of §23 is not, in the Eleventh Senate's view, a violation of either constitutional law or international law.[345] The only obvious constitutional restraints on exercises of adjudicatory authority rest on Article 25 of the Basic Law, which provides that "generally accepted principles of international law are part of federal law", on Article 3 (2) – "men and woman have equal rights" – and on Article 6 (1) – "marriage and the family are under the special protection of the state". Constitutional standards regulating jurisdictional practices may also eventually emerge drawing on the values implicit in the Basic Law.

---

344   See BVerfG, 4 May 1971, 31 BVerfGE 58; BVerfG, 22 February 1983, 63 BVerfGE 181; BVerfG, 8 January 1985, 68 BVerfGE 384.

345   BGH, 115 *BGHZ*, at 92.

PART 2

Basic Themes and Pervasive Issues

Chapter IV   The *Actor Sequitur Forum Rei* Principle: Are Defendants Jurisdictionally Preferred? Should They Be?*

A.   Introductory

Formulated by Roman jurists near the end of the third century ad,[1] the maxim *actor sequitur forum rei* is of ancient lineage. *"Rei"* being the genitive form as well of *res*, a thing, as of *reus*, a defendant, the phrase signifies that the moving party must seize, as the case may be, the forum of the defendant or of the property in suit. The formula stands today – in the words of a German jurist – "for a legal principle *(Rechtssatz)* that is known everywhere, widely recognized, and universally approved ... [, namely,] that the plaintiff must go to the defendant's forum *(Gerichtsstand)*".[2]

In localized matters, those involving only local parties, transactions, and situations that will normally be adjudicated by a singular legal order,[3] one rarely speaks of defendants' and plaintiffs' forums. In these cases, regardless of the venue selected, the same conflictual, procedural, and substantive rules and principles will apply.[4] One party may, of course, prefer a particular venue for reasons of familiarity, convenience, and expense;[5] where such is the case, the notion of a

---

* This Chapter draws in part on the author's Graveson Memorial Lecture (1997) delivered on 8 May 1997 in memory of Professor R. H. Graveson. The lecture, entitled "Must Plaintiffs Seek Out Defendants? The Contemporary Standing of Actor Sequitur Forum Rei", appears in 8 *King's College L. J.* 23-42 (1997).

1 For the history of the maxim, see J. Schröder, *Internationale Zuständigkeit*, at 229-232 (Opladen, Westdeutscher Verlag, 1971).

2 *Idem* 229.

3 In some situations, inherently local matters may be litigated in a non-local forum because of their connection with a multi-state controversy or because the parties have so agreed.

4 For a brief discussion of the relative importance of venue and jurisdictional rules for litigation, see Chap. III. B. 5. *(a)* (i), pp. 142-145, *supra*.

5 Where venue is in issue, the plaintiff is often required to go to the defendant's domicile or residence. "In most instances, the purpose of statutorily specified venue is to protect the *defendant* against the risk that a plaintiff will select an unfair or inconvenient place of trial. For that reason, Congress has generally not made the residence

party's forum is meaningful. Where the litigation involves a non-localized matter, alternative forums are likely to be available some of which will be more attractive to one party than to the other in terms of litigational convenience, expense, procedural arrangements (for example, the availability of discovery or of jury trial), and the applicable law.

What criteria govern the determination whether a given forum is a defendants', a plaintiffs' or a neutral forum? And is this characterization to be made concretely, in light of the facts of the particular case and the procedural and substantive laws of the forum in question, or abstractly, without regard to the facts of the case or the laws of the forum?

An abstract characterization implies a subjective standard that emphasizes social and cultural ties between party and forum. Does the party think of himself as a member of the community and share its culture and values? Broadly speaking, does the party feel "at home" there? A concrete characterization on the other hand, rests on pragmatic and utilitarian considerations. Do the rules and practices of the forum favor – not abstractly but in light of the controversy to be adjudicated – the plaintiff's or the defendant's position? If abstract and concrete characterization are used concurrently and each points to different forums how – if at all – does the *actor sequitur* principle apply?

That these issues are rarely – if at all – addressed in practice or in the literature suggests that the *actor sequitur* principle is "widely recognized" and "universally approved" only in a formulaic sense.

B.   The Principle's Standing in Practice

In assessing the contemporary standing of the *actor sequitur* principle, two issues are addressed: (1) Do contemporary legal systems claim to practice the principle? (2) Does the principle in reality affect thinking and practice respecting the exercise of adjudicatory authority?

1.   Do Contemporary Legal Systems Claim to Practise the Principle?

At least rhetorically, contemporary legal systems claim to accept in principle the proposition that the plaintiff must go to the defendant's forum. The argument traditionally advanced is that the former are the aggressors; it is they who disturb the *status quo*. As Martin Wolff explained:

---

of the plaintiff a basis for venue in nondiversity cases." *Leroy* v. *Great Western United Corp.*, 443 US 173, at 183-184 (1979) (emphasis in original); see also *Stafford* v. *Briggs*, 444 US 527, at 543-544 (1980) (construing venue statute, 28 USC §1391 *(e)* (1976), providing that suits against federal officers may be brought in the district in which the plaintiff resides, as not covering suits in which the individual officer may be held personally liable). See generally E. Sunderland, "The Provisions Relating to Trial Practice in the New Illinois Civil Practice Act", 1 *U. Chi. L. Rev.* 188, at 192 (1933).

[the] *plaintiff's* interest is to bring his action in the courts of that country in which he can expect to be able to enforce the judgment he hopes to attain .... This ... interest, however, will not be protected where it conflicts with the *defendant's interest* [] ... to be sued in a court which is easily accessible to him and his witnesses ...; this follows from the general maxim that a defendant can claim greater protection than his aggressor .... The principle *actor forum rei sequitur* is rightly recognized everywhere. The defendant's, not the plaintiff's, domicile, residence, or presence is the test for the competence of a court to entertain an action.[6]

"[T]he maxim *actor sequitur forum rei*" "is an expression of the law's conservative spirit which gives priority to him who defends the *status quo* and not to him who seeks to change it".[7]

Almost all contemporary German jurists consider *actor sequitur forum rei*, in light of ZPO §§12 and 13,[8] a jurisdictional principle that underlies German law and informs as well the Brussels and Lugano Conventions and the Brussels Regulation. The various "special" bases of jurisdiction *("besondere Gerichtsstände")* recognized by these instruments are exceptions to the basic principle and are, accordingly, to be interpreted restrictively.[9]

The legislative history of §§12 and 13 lends support to the proposition that the ZPO's jurisdictional provisions were designed to prefer, in general, defendants. The drafters saw §§12 and 13 – which have remained virtually unchanged since their enactment – as embodying a "general principle of law" *(allgemeines Rechtsprinzip);*[10] the draft, which was hardly discussed in this respect, survived the legislative process without amendment.[11]

---

6   M. Wolff, *Private International Law*, at 62-63 (Oxford, Clarendon Press, 2nd ed., 1950).

7   Ch. Fragistas, "La compétence internationale en droit privé", 104 *Recueil des cours* 199 (1962); see also H. Schack, *Internationales Zivilverfahrensrecht*, at 74, No. 192 (Munich, C. H. Beck, 4th ed., 2006) (the *actor sequitur* principle places the burden on the plaintiff because "he attacks the *status quo*"). See also L. De Winter, "Excessive Jurisdiction in Private International Law", 17 *Int'l and Com. L. Q.* 706, at 717 (1968) *("in dubio pro reo")*; P. Neuhaus, "Internationales Zivilprozeßrecht und internationales Privatrecht", 20 RabelsZ 201, at 232 footnote 54 (1955) *("melior est causa possidentis")*.

8   For a discussion of these provisions see Chap. II. D. 2. *(b)* (i), p. 66, *supra*.

9   The contrary argument has, however, been made that the purpose of "general" bases of jurisdiction is to ensure that the plaintiff has available a jurisdictional basis of last resort. See B. Buchner, *Kläger- und Beklagtenschutz im Recht der internationalen Zuständigkeit*, at 5 (Tübingen, Mohr Siebeck, 1998).

10   See C. Hahn (continued by B. Mugdan), *Die gesammten Materialien zu den Reichs-Justizgesetzen*, at 149-150 (Berlin, R. v. Decker's Verlag, 2nd ed., 1881). See also G. von Wilmowski and M. Levy, *Kommentar zur Civilprozeßordnung*, vor §12, No. 1 (Berlin, Verlag Franz Vahlen, 1895) (stating that the venue provisions of the ZPO "are, in general, dominated by the rule *actor sequitur forum rei*").

11   See Hahn, *supra* footnote 10, at 530 and 938.

The *Hannoversche Prozesskommission*, which had prepared a draft in 1863, was somewhat more explicit. The *Kommission* saw the provision of a forum at the plaintiff's domicile as a "great anomaly"; the notion that the defendant had to litigate in the plaintiff's forum somehow violated one's "legal feeling" *(juristisches Gefühl)*.[12] Although its draft was eventually not adopted, the system of jurisdictional bases proposed by the *Prozesskommission* strongly influenced the 1870 draft of the *Norddeutsche Bund*,[13] which served as a model for the ZPO.[14]

The German courts still consistently state that the *actor sequitur* principle underlies the ZPO. Sections 12 and 13 constitute the rule; the "special" bases are exceptions. The Bundesgerichtshof, for example, has written that

> the bases of jurisdiction provided by ZPO §§12 and 13, which grant the party, who is, usually against his will, subjected to a lawsuit, the advantage of litigating ... at the place of his domicile, are to be observed as far as possible in the interest of a fair distribution of procedural burdens. Deviations from this rule can only be justified for objectively compelling reasons [in the German original: *aus sachlich vorrangigen Gründen*].[15]

In this context, German courts today unanimously agree that the provisions of the ZPO are not based on incidental considerations of convenience *(nebensächliche Zweckmäßigkeitserwägungen)*, but on principled legal considerations *(prinzipielle rechtliche Erwägungen)*.[16]

Reasoning that plaintiffs, procedurally speaking, generally have an advantage and that the *favor defensoris* principle underlying the provisions of the ZPO was intended to counter-balance this advantage, one court explained that

> [t]he law puts the burden of litigating abroad ..., in general, on the plaintiff. This allocation is based on the fundamental principle of law *(grundlegendes Rechtsprinzip)* that, wherever one party is to be preferred ... the defendant, not the plaintiff, should be; as long as it is uncertain who is right, it is more acceptable to deprive the plaintiff – as the one trying to change the *status quo* – of his rights rather than, *visa versa*,

---

12   See Schröder, *supra* footnote 1, at 232-233 (citing Protokolle der Kommission zur Beratung einer allgemeinen Zivilprozeßordnung für die deutschen Bundesstaaten II [1863] 427-431).

13   *Entwurf einer Civilprozeßordnung für den Norddeutschen Bund* (Berlin, Verlag der Königlichen Geheimen Ober-Hofbuchdruckerei (R. v. Decker), 1870).

14   See M. Fricke, *Anerkennungszuständigkeit zwischen Spiegelbildgrundsatz und Generalklausel* 79 (Bielefeld, Gieseking, 1990).

15   BGH, 16 April 1986, 39 *NJW* 3209, at 3209 (1986); see also BGH, 2 July 1991, 115 *BGHZ* 90, at 92 (stating that ZPO §23 is "an exception to the principle that an action must be brought before the defendant's court"); OLG Hamm, 15 May 1986, 40 *NJW* 138, at 138 (1987) (stating that special bases of jurisdiction are "exceptions" to the maxim of *actor sequitur forum rei*).

16   See, e.g., LG Karlsruhe, 3 April 1989, 44 *JZ* 690, at 693 (1989).

burdening somebody who, owing nothing, is unjustly sued and has a judgment rendered against him.[17]

The virtually unanimous view among legal commentators is that the Brussels and Lugano Conventions take a position similar to that of the ZPO: the principle of *actor sequitur forum rei*, laid down in Article 2 of the Conventions, provides the rule; the special bases of jurisdiction are exceptions to that rule.[18] Again, however, neither the language nor the systematics of the Conventions are entirely conclusive on the issue. What is "special" about the "special" bases of jurisdiction in the Conventions is that they generally confer authority to adjudicate only for claims of a specific juridical nature, while under Article 2 the defendant may be sued in his forum regardless of the juridical nature of the claim; this fact in itself, however, does not compel the conclusion that these bases of jurisdiction are to be treated as mere exceptions to Article 2.[19] Indeed, the *Rapporteur* for the original Brussels Convention has explained that Articles 5-15 are considered special bases of jurisdiction because they, unlike Article 2, typically deal not only with authority to adjudicate in the international sense, *but also with venue.*[20]

The drafting history of the Brussels Convention clearly indicates that Articles 5-15 were considered special in another – and more profound – sense, as well. For the drafters, Article 2 sets out one of the main principles on which the Convention's rules of jurisdiction are based: "the rule that a defendant domiciled in a Contracting State is in general to be sued in the courts of that state".[21] The drafters proceeded from the assumption that the rationale underlying the Convention was that

> [t]he maxim *'actor sequitur forum rei'* which expresses the fact that law leans in favor of the defendant, is even more relevant in the international sphere than it is in national law. It is more difficult ... to defend oneself in the courts of a foreign country than in those of another town in the country where one is domiciled.[22]

Taking into account this rationale, the European Court of Justice has on various occasions held that the general principle underlying the Brussels Convention is that jurisdiction is generally vested in the courts of the State of the defendant's domicile; only by way of exception to this general rule is jurisdiction attributed

---

17   *Ibid.*
18   See, e.g., B. von Hoffmann, "Gegenwartsprobleme internationaler Zuständigkeit", 2 *IPRax* 217, at 219 (1982); H. Stoll, "Gerichtsstand des Erfüllungsortes nach Artikel 5 Nr. 1 EuGVÜ bei strittigem Vertragsschluß, 3 *IPRax* 52, at 54 (1983); I. Schwenzer, "Internationaler Gerichtsstand für die Kaufpreisklage", 9 *IPRax* 274, at 275 (1989).
19   See Buchner, *supra* footnote 9, at 6.
20   See Report by Mr. P. Jenard on the Convention of 27 September 1968 on jurisdiction and the enforcement of judgments in civil and commercial matters, [1979] OJ C 59, 1, at 22.
21   *Idem* 18.
22   *Ibid.*

to the courts of the plaintiff's domicile.[23] Consequently, the Court has taken the view that the special bases of jurisdiction must be interpreted in such a manner as to exclude the possibility of the jurisdiction of the defendants' domicile being called into question.[24] In *Shearson v. TVB-GmbH*, for example, the court had to consider various issues in connection with Article 14 of the Convention, which in consumer litigation provides for jurisdiction at the consumer's domicile. The Court construed this provision narrowly holding that

> under the system of the Convention the general principle, stated in the first paragraph of Article 2, is that the national courts of the Contracting State in which the defendant is domiciled are to have jurisdiction …. It is only by way of derogation from that general principle that the Convention provides for cases, … in which a defendant domiciled or established in a Contracting State may, where the situation comes under a rule of special jurisdiction, … be sued in the courts of another Contracting State…. Consequently, rules of jurisdiction which derogate from that general principle cannot give rise to an interpretation going beyond the situations envisaged by the Convention …. Apart from the cases expressly provided for, the Convention appears clearly hostile towards the attribution of jurisdiction to the courts of the plaintiff's domicile …[25]

The Preamble of the Brussels Regulation, successor to the Convention, explicitly addresses the *actor sequitur* issue in its No. 11:

> [R]ules of jurisdiction must be highly predictable and founded on the principle that jurisdiction is generally based on the defendant's domicile …

2. Is the Actor Sequitur *Principle Consistent with the Principal Theories of Adjudicatory Authority?*

Three theories of adjudicatory authority have, during the last two centuries, dominated Western thinking respecting jurisdiction to adjudicate: relational; power; and convenience, fairness, and justice. Insight into the contemporary standing of the *actor sequitur forum rei* principle can be gleaned by considering whether these theories tend systematically to ground bases of adjudicatory authority that are consistent with the principle.

(a) Relational theories

Contemporary relational theories ground adjudicatory authority over *both* parties on a relationship – for example, domicile or nationality – between *one* of the

---

23   See, e.g., *Kalfelis* v. *Bankhaus Schröder* – Case 189/97 – [1988] ECR 5565, at 5583; *Dumez France* v. *Hessische Landesbank* – Case C 220/88 – [1990] ECR I-49, at 79; *Six Constructions Ltd* v. *Paul Humbert* – Case 32/88 – [1989] ECR 341, at 364; *Group Josi Reinsurance Company SA* v. *Universal General Insurance Companny (UGIC)* – Case 412/98 – [2000] ECR I-5925, at 5952 et seq.

24   See the *Kalfelis* case, *ibid.*

25   *Shearson* v. *TVB* – Case 89/91 – [1993] ECR I-139, at 167.

parties and the forum.[26] The Civil Code of France (1804) takes jurisdiction where either party is a French national; the Code of Civil Procedure of the Netherlands makes a comparable claim on the basis of either party's domicile in the Netherlands.[27]

Articles 14 and 15 of the Civil Code of France furnish the classic example of a relational theory of adjudicatory authority in the international sense. Article 14, which provides that

> [a]n alien, even one not residing in France, may be summoned *(cité)* before the French courts for the fulfilment of obligations contracted by him in France with a French person; he may be brought *(traduit)* before the French courts for obligations contracted by him in a foreign country towards French people,[28]

---

26   Originally, relational theories established adjudicatory authority only over the party related to the forum. See Chap. I. A. 3. *(b)*, pp. 19-21, *supra*.

27   See Article 99 (1) and 109 of the Wetboek van Burgerlijke Rechtsvordering.
Article 99 (1) provides:
> If not provided otherwise, the judge at the defendant's domicile has jurisdiction to adjudicate.

Article 109 states:
> If Articles 99 to 108 do not provide for jurisdiction to adjudicate, the judge at the plaintiff's domicile has jurisdiction .... .

28   The French courts have consistently refused to limit the scope of Article 14. In an early decision – *Ingelheim* v. *Friedberg*, [1808] *Sirey Recueil General* I. 453 (Cass. req., 7 September 1808) – it was argued that, in the case of obligations contracted abroad, the defendant had to be brought *(traduit)* before the French courts. Consequently, jurisdiction would exist only if the foreign defendant were found in France. This argument was countered by the contention that the omission of the phrase "if he is found in France", contained in the first draft of Article 14 after *"traduit"*, indicated that the legislator had not desired to maintain the suggested distinction. The high Court accepted the broad reading of Article 14.
Among the issues that next arose respecting the Article's scope was whether it applied to non-contractual obligations, in particular, delicts. In *Compagnie du Britannia* v. *Compagnie du Phénix* – [1843] *Sirey* I.14 (Cass. req., 13 December 1842) – the court was urged to distinguish the two situations: unlike the foreigner who commits a delict,
> [t]he foreigner who contracts knows to what he obligates himself by his contract. He will submit himself, by his full and free will to the French jurisdiction. The jurisdiction is not imposed on him; he adopts it. *It is a jurisdiction based on consent. Idem* 15.

The proposed distinction was rejected.
During the same period in *Bertin* v. *de Bagration* – [1836] *Sirey* I.217 (Cass. civ., 26 January 1836); see also *Morris* v. *Perrinot-Morris*, [1931] *Dalloz Heb.* 313, [1931] *Sirey* I. 247 (note) (Cass. req., 29 April 1931) – it was held that Article 14 was available to a French national even though he was not domiciled in France. *Bertin* quashed a court of appeal's decision which took the position that
> the reasons that justify this article of the Code do not exist when the obligation was contracted with a stranger having a business established in the stranger's own country,

gives no weight whatsoever to the *actor sequitur forum rei* principle. Article 15 is to the effect that "[a] Frenchman may be called before a French court for obligations contracted by him in a foreign country, even towards an alien". Jurisdiction does not depend upon the defendant being domiciled or resident in France.[29] Although perhaps consistent with a "subjective" conception of a defendants' forum, in practice, it is unlikely that Article 15 will be invoked unless it is, for practical, objective reasons, the plaintiff's preferred forum.

Both Articles 14 and 15 operate to protect French parties against the risks of litigating abroad.[30] French courts are considered the natural judges in litigation involving a French party – whether plaintiff or defendant and living abroad or in France. French persons were not to be subjected to process in foreign courts except with their consent.

Relational theories, as exemplified by Articles 14 and 15, do not approach adjudicatory authority in terms of the plaintiff-defendant dichotomy that underlies the *actor sequitur forum rei* principle; the basic distinction is instead between parties, whether plaintiff or defendant, who stand – and who do not stand – in the relevant relation to the forum. The forum seeks to advantage its *ressortis-*

---

under the protection of [that country's] laws, by Frenchmen without a domicile or an establishment in France. In this case, the Frenchman cannot argue the difficulty of leaving his domicile and the inconvenience of pursuing the debtor; he has no ground for objecting to his subjection to foreign laws, under which he placed himself. Finally, in such situations, this article of the Code deceives, as it were, foreigners who, having dealt with individuals established in their country, had no reason to expect that they would be called before foreign courts. Such deception would be more harmful than useful to Frenchmen." *Bertin* v. *de Bagration*, [1834] *Sirey* II.159-160 (Cour royale de Paris, 3d Chamber, 20 March 1834).

Article 14 jurisdiction still attaches today when the French plaintiff has neither a domicile nor a residence in France.

Finally it can be noted that the rule has long been established that the French plaintiff need not have been a party to the original transaction out of which the litigation arises. In *Inglée* v. *Detape* – [1833] *Sirey* I.100 (Cass. req., 26 January 1833) – a New York merchant drew bills of exchange in favor of an American firm. The bills were then endorsed to another New York merchant, who protested their non-payment when due. After the non-payment and protest the instruments were endorsed to a Paris banker. When the maker subsequently visited Paris, the holder obtained his provisional arrest in order to assure payment of the bills. The case came to the highest French court ; its decision turned on the existence of Article 14 jurisdiction since the French system does not recognize the defendant's presence as a basis for asserting adjudicatory authority. The court held that, as the holder had a direct right against the maker, Article 14 jurisdiction attached.

29   See H. Batiffol and Ph. Francescakis, "Compétence Internationale, Nos. 36-37", in 1 *Répertoire de Procédure Civile et Commerciale*, at 620 (Paris, Dalloz, 1955). It can be noted that Article 15 jurisdiction exists as well when both parties are French. *Idem*, No. 37 (Mise à jour (1964) 68).

30   See L. Rigaud, "La conception nationaliste de la compétence judiciaire en droit international privé; sa persistance et ses origines", 33 *Rev. crit. dr. int.* 604, at 609 (1938).

sants to the extent that it can. In practice, *ressortissant* plaintiffs can be more effectively advantaged than *ressortissant* defendants; the former obtain judgments
from "their" forum, the latter usually receive its protection only when successful
foreign plaintiffs seek to enforce in France the foreign judgment.

(b) Power theories

Unlike relational theories, power theories require that plaintiffs go to defendants
in the sense of seizing a forum in a position to exercise power over the defendant
or his property. A natural person could be sued at his domicile,[31] at any place where
he was present and process was served on him,[32] as well as where his tangible property could be attached or where a debtor of his could be served with process.[33]

It is readily apparent that, except when a natural person's domicile or a legal
person's place of incorporation or principal place of business is in question, no
ground exists for assuming that any of these forums will, as a rule, be either litigationally or substantively more attractive to defendants than to plaintiffs. Instead,
when the plaintiff's power to select from among the available forums is taken
into account, the odds are great that the controversy will be litigated in the available forum most favorable for the plaintiff's cause. As Lord Simon of Glaisdale
remarked in *The Atlantic Star*, "if you offer a plaintiff a choice of jurisdiction, he
will naturally choose the one in which he thinks his case can be most favorably
presented ..."[34]

Consider the common law's tag-jurisdiction. Notionally, the plaintiff is required to go to the defendant; however, as a practical matter, jurisdiction based
on service of process upon a "present" defendant often results in defendants being
forced to litigate in what is, in terms of procedural and choice-of-law considerations, a plaintiff's forum. Persons journeying by steamer from Halifax, Nova Scotia, to their home in New York and served *en route* with process while their ship
is docked in Boston, are most unlikely to consider Massachusetts their forum.[35]
Contrariwise, the forum chosen will, at least under an objective, pragmatic definition, always be a plaintiffs' forum.

An even more egregious and prolific source of notional defendants' forums that
often amount – in practical terms – to plaintiffs' forums is *quasi in rem* jurisdiction
of the type upheld by the United States Supreme Court in *Harris v. Balk*.[36] *Harris*

---

31 In the case of a legal person, jurisdiction could be established at its place of incorpo-
    ration and at its principal place of business.

32 A legal person was considered present wherever it "did business".

33 These two jurisdictional bases were available as well where the defendant was a legal
    person.

34 [1974] AC 436, at 471 (HL 1973).

35 Compare *Peabody* v. *Hamilton*, 106 Mass. 217 (1870), discussed Chap. III. A. 2. *(a)*,
    pp. 86-87, *supra*. Nor would a legal person (that is to say its owner) consider that any
    place where it "did business" was its forum.

36 198 US 215 (1905); *Harris* was held unconstitutional in *Shaffer* v. *Heitner*, 433 US 186
    (1977), discussed at length Chap. III. A. 4. *(b)*, pp. 102 *et seq.*, *supra*.

and its progeny enabled plaintiffs to establish limited general jurisdiction over their debtors in any state in which a debtor of their debtor was physically present.

Clearly, a power theory of adjudicatory authority does not systemically produce what are, realistically speaking, defendants' forums. Quite the contrary is true. Moreover, the theory justifies the exercise of adjudicatory authority on grounds that can often be satisfied by multiple legal orders; accordingly, plaintiffs typically have a choice among a relatively large number of possible forums. The forum chosen will, of course, normally be the one most favorable – litigationally and substantively speaking – for the plaintiff's cause.

(c)   Convenience, fairness, and justice theories

For the last half century, in many legal orders thinking respecting jurisdiction to adjudicate has increasingly emphasized convenience, fairness, and justice rather than relationship or power. Since Chief Justice Stone's decision in the *International Shoe* case.[37] the American approach to jurisdiction to adjudicate has come to turn in considerable measure, though by no means exclusively, on fairness rather than power considerations; similar tendencies can be observed in other legal orders.

Does a convenience, fairness, and justice approach to the problem of adjudicatory authority in the international sense tend systematically to vindicate the *actor sequitur forum rei* principle? In his opinion for the court in *International Shoe*, Justice Stone wrote that the demands of due process

> may be met by such contacts of the corporation with the state of the forum as make it reasonable, in the context of our federal system of government, to require the corporation to defend the particular suit which is brought there. An 'estimate of the inconveniences' which would result to the corporation from a trial away from its 'home' or principal place of business is relevant in this connection.[38]

The Chief Justice then explained certain solutions reached under the aegis of the power theory in terms of convenience, fairness, and justice:

> [I]t has been generally recognized that the casual presence of the corporate agent or even his conduct of single or isolated items of activities in a state in the corporation's behalf are not enough to subject it to suits on causes of action unconnected with the activities there …. To require the corporation in such circumstances to defend the suit away from its home or other jurisdiction where it carries on more substantial activities has been thought to lay too great and unreasonable a burden on the corporation to comport with due process.[39]

---

37   *International Shoe* v. *Washington*, 326 US 310 (1945); for discussion at length of the decision and its progeny, see Chap. III. A. 4., pp. 97 *et seq.*, *supra*.

38   *Idem* 317.

39   *Ibid.*

In Stone's view, a mechanical or quantitative test of presence in terms of power was not decisive.

> "Whether due process is satisfied must depend rather upon the quality and nature of the activity in relation to the fair and orderly administration of the laws which it was the purpose of the due process clause to insure.[40]

Stone continued:

> Applying these standards, the activities carried on in behalf of appellant in the State of Washington were neither irregular nor casual. They were systematic and continuous throughout the years in question. They resulted in a large volume of interstate business, in the course of which ... [the corporation] received the benefits and protection of the laws of the state, including the right to resort to the courts for the enforcement of its rights. The obligation which is here sued upon arose out of those very activities. It is evident that these operations establish sufficient contacts or ties with the state of the forum to make it reasonable and just, according to our traditional conception of fair play and substantial justice, to permit the state to enforce the obligations which appellant has incurred there.[41]

Stone's analysis in *International Shoe* does not, systematically speaking, favor either party. It may, or may not, bring the plaintiff to the defendant's forum. (In *International Shoe*, the forum was, of course, that of the plaintiff.) The analysis employed increases the number of available forums, with the result that ordinarily a plaintiff's forum is produced. Moreover, *International Shoe* left tag-jurisdiction and *quasi in rem* jurisdiction *à la mode* of *Harris* v. *Balk* undisturbed; its immediate effect accordingly was to provide an additional string for the plaintiff's jurisdictional bow – and thus further undermine the *actor sequitur forum rei* principle. The overruling in 1977 of *Harris* v. *Balk* was to improve the jurisdictional position of defendants; plaintiffs continue, however, to enjoy a range of jurisdictional opportunity such that contemporary American practice can hardly be seen as embracing even a weak version of the *actor sequitur* principle.

3.   Do Plaintiffs' or Defendants' Forums Predominate in Contemporary Practice?

The *actor sequitur forum rei* principle ultimately rests on a premise that is not tenable today, namely, that defendants' forums exist as Platonic concepts. One can imagine simpler worlds in which non-local controversies could be litigated in two – but only two – forums, one in the plaintiffs', the other in the defendants', home State. In such a setting, the notion of a plaintiffs' and a defendants' forum has a meaning that does not turn on the particular circumstances of disparate

---

40   *Idem* 319.
41   *Idem* 320.

controversies. In the modern world, ordinarily a number of forums will be available and the choice of the forum for litigation will be made by the moving party in light of a variety of circumstances of which being a member of the forum community will frequently not be decisive. Parties normally seek to seize the forum that, all things considered, is the most advantageous for their cause. Today, in order for the *actor sequitur forum rei* principle to have real significance, the choice of forum would have to be made by the defendant. Proposals along these lines have been advanced from time to time. They raise, however, very difficult issues, both normative and practical in character, and have attracted very little support.

Realistically speaking, the likelihood that controversies will be litigated in a forum that the defendant would not have chosen had the choice been his, increases as the range of choice among forums increases. The Brussels Convention and Regulation, despite the latter's Preambulary assertion "that jurisdiction is generally based on the defendants' domicile" and that "special" jurisdictional bases are exceptional and should be restrictively interpreted, have increased the plaintiffs' range of forum choice by providing broad bases of "special" jurisdiction.

Consider, for example, jurisdictional bases accepted by the Brussels I Regulation:[42] Article 5 [3], recognizes adjudicatory authority, "in matters relating to tort, delict or quasi delict, in the courts for the place where the harmful event occurred or may occur". This language has been held by the European Court of Justice to permit the assertion of jurisdiction as well where the wrongful conduct took place as where it had its effects.[43] Article 6 (1) recognizes, in case of multiple defendants, adjudicatory authority

> where any one of them is domiciled, provided the claims are so closely connected that it is expedient to hear and determine them together to avoid the risk of irreconcilable judgments resulting from separate proceedings.[44]

Nor are all – or at least most – contemporary legal systems committed to the minimalist proposition that the *actor sequitur forum rei* principle expresses; namely, that between categories of parties that enjoy essentially equal litigational capacity, the forums that, objectively considered, systematically favor defendants are

---

42   For discussion of the Brussels I Regulation, see Chap. II. D. 3. *(b)* (ii), pp. 72-74, *supra*.

43   *Handelskwekerij G.J. Bier B.V.* v. *Mines de Potasse d'Alsace S.A.* – Case 21/76, [1976] ECR 1735; recently confirmed in *DFDS Torline A/S* v. *SEKO* – Case C-18/02, [2004] ECR I-1417, at para. 40.

44   In a recent judgment the European Court of Justice held that Article 6 (1) does not apply in European patent infringement proceedings involving a number of companies established in various Member States in respect of acts committed in one or more of those States even where those companies, which belong to the same group, may have acted in an identical or similar manner in accordance with a common policy elaborated by one of them. See *Roche Nederland BV and Others* v. *Frederick Primus, Milton Goldenberg* – Case 539/03, [2006] ECR I-0000, at para. 41.

to be preferred. Does not the observable tendency to proliferate forums suggest that contemporary legal orders are quite prepared to give plaintiffs considerable choice among forums even though the inevitable effect is to reduce – or eliminate – the significance of the *actor sequitur* principle?

At the end of the day, many – indeed most – legal systems prefer, jurisdictionally speaking, plaintiffs that are members of the forum community over foreign defendants. The Swiss Act on Private International Law[45] disregards the *actor sequitur* principle where necessary to ensure that certain categories of plaintiffs will have available a jurisdictionally convenient forum in which to pursue defendants that are of *equal* litigational capacity. Under Article 3, when the Act does not provide for jurisdiction in the Swiss courts, yet it would be unreasonable to require that the action be brought in a foreign country, the Swiss judicial or administrative authorities at the place with which the case has a sufficient connection have – exceptionally – jurisdiction. This provision covers, *inter alia*, situations involving parties of equal litigational capacity in which a defendant without – and a plaintiff with – Swiss connections live in countries that are geographically remote from each other and the plaintiff cannot establish, in the courts of his domicile, jurisdiction over the defendant.[46] In such cases, either the plaintiff or the defendant must litigate in a forum that is not, jurisdictionally speaking, reasonably accessible to his adversary. One party must be favored; the Swiss system prefers the plaintiff with Swiss connections, although they do not suffice in principle to establish Swiss jurisdiction, over a defendant that lacks Swiss connections. Were the *actor sequitur* principle applied to such cases, the plaintiff would go to the defendant's jurisdiction.

Assessed in realistic rather than formal terms, contemporary jurisdictional practice can hardly be said to recognize widely or to approve universally the proposition that "the plaintiff must go [at least in principle] to the defendant's forum".[47] A broader question remains, however: what is the appropriate allocation between plaintiffs and defendants of litigational risks and opportunities?

C.   The Allocation of Litigational Risks and Opportunities between Plaintiffs and Defendants

The rise of convenience, fairness, and justice approaches has encouraged a more perceptive analysis of jurisdictional theory and practice than was undertaken during the reign of the power approach. The meaning, efficiency, and merit of the *actor sequitur* principle can be assessed more realistically today than in the past. In deciding how jurisdictional risks and opportunities can and should be

---

45   Bundesgesetz über das internationale Privatrecht (IPR-Gesetz) of 18 December 1987; in force since 1 January 1989.

46   See Schlußbericht der Expertenkommission zum Gesetzentwurf, Bundesgesetz über das internationale Privatrecht (IPR-Gesetz), 13 *Schweizer Studien zum Internationalen Recht* 44 (Zurich, Schulthess, 1979).

47   Cf. Schröder, *supra* footnote 1, at 229.

allocated between plaintiffs and defendants, one must first identify the factors that make a forum more attractive to one party than to the other. Thereafter, several related issues can be faced: should plaintiffs or defendants be preferred where each category's litigational capacity is relatively equal? What consequences should follow for the allocation of adjudicatory authority from a determination that a given plaintiffs' or defendants' category has distinctly superior – or inferior – litigational capacity? If litigational equality between plaintiffs and defendants is the goal, how – and in what measure – can it be achieved?

1.   What Makes a Forum More Attractive to One Party than to the Other?

A party will, other things being equal, prefer to litigate in a forum that is, geographically speaking, readily accessible, impartial (or even inclined to favor him), and whose administration of justice is within his cultural and legal tradition. Certain jurisdictional bases make available forums that systemically favor, in these – though not necessarily in other – respects, plaintiffs rather than defendants, and *vice versa*. A forum based on the party's domicile (or habitual residence) will, for example, normally advantage that party on these scores.

Few, if any, jurisdictional bases are, on the other hand, systemically linked with pro-plaintiff or pro-defendant procedural and substantive rules and principles. In a particular case, the defendant's domicile may well turn out to favor – except with regard to accessibility and familiarity – the plaintiff while the plaintiff's domicile favors the defendant.[48] Typically, the jurisdictional bases that a legal order provides tell us little about its procedural and substantive laws.[49] Their content turns largely on legal, economic, and social history. As a result, plaintiffs may well fare much better under a developed – and defendants under a developing – country's law. In the well-known litigation initiated by those harmed by the explosion of Union Carbide Company's chemical plant in Bhopal, India, the Indian plaintiffs were understandably anxious to litigate at the defendant's place of incorporation in the United States, while Union Carbide placed great store on proceeding in the Indian courts.[50]

Whether plaintiffs or defendants will typically prefer a given forum on the basis of procedural or substantive law considerations is unpredictable where bases such as the following are in question: one or both parties acted – or the effects of party conduct were felt – in the forum, the controversy or one or both parties

---

48   See Buchner, *supra* footnote 9, at 80.

49   In certain subject matters a connection may exist. For example, divorce mills supply substantive rules that make divorce easy to obtain and provide as well jurisdictional bases such as the moving party's residence or both parties' consent that make its courts easy to enter.

50   See *In re Union Carbide Corporation Gas Plant Disaster at Bhopal, India in December, 1984*, 634 F. Supp. 842 (SDNY 1986); 809 F. 2d 195 (2nd Cir. 1987), *cert. denied sub nom. Executive Comm. Members v. Union of India*, 484 US 871 (1987).

had "minimum contacts" with the forum or one or both parties "purposefully availed" themselves of the forum's laws and protection.

Forums that satisfy these jurisdictional criteria may – or may not – permit contingent fee arrangements, require the unsuccessful party to pay the other party's litigational expenses, provide jury trial, award damages for pain and suffering and punitive damages, apply substantive rules favorable to the plaintiff's cause, or make available such robust techniques for gathering and taking evidence as discovery and direct and cross-examination. Moreover, not all plaintiffs favor – nor all defendants disfavor – discovery, direct and cross-examination, or jury trial. The relative attractiveness of the forum or forums whose doors a given jurisdictional criterion opens accordingly cannot be known in the abstract. The party that a given forum advantages depends upon the interaction of the facts of the case with that forum's conflictual, procedural, and substantive law.

The great majority of jurisdictional bases, standing alone and considered in the abstract, accordingly cannot be characterized as providing either a plaintiff's or a defendant's forum. A few bases – for example, the plaintiff's or the defendant's domicile – do have a pro-plaintiff or pro-defendant tendency but largely only with respect to such matters as accessibility and familiarity with cultural, legal, and social traditions. Basically, therefore, there is no necessary systemic linkage between a forum's use of a given jurisdictional basis and whether the forum is, generally speaking, pro-plaintiff or pro-defendant. The demonstration that, in the abstract, neither plaintiffs' nor defendants' forums exist – that a forum's party-favoring tendencies depend on particular circumstances – does not lead to the conclusion that litigation typically proceeds in a neutral forum. Considered concretely, probably no forum is equally attractive – or unattractive – to all the contending parties.

Whether jurisdictional theory and practice are plaintiff or defendant oriented thus depends on the interaction of two factors: (1) the number and variety of the jurisdictional bases available and (2) which party ultimately controls forum selection. Analysis is complicated by the fact that, except where regulated by an international convention, the elements that collectively constitute the first factor will vary from one legal order to another. In all events, the party that selects the forum is, in practice, the party that is jurisdictionally preferred and the degree of preference enjoyed increases as a function of the number of forums among which the choice is to be made.

2.   *Should Plaintiffs or Defendants Be Preferred for Jurisdictional Purposes?*

The highest ideal of procedural justice in civil matters is that, insofar as possible, each party should be treated equally. Of course, here as elsewhere, what is meant by equality is not a simple matter. In all events, where the parties are considered essentially equal in litigational capacity and neither's claim to corrective justice is thought to be stronger than the other's neither should be accorded a jurisdictional preference. Unfortunately, in practice normally giving a preference cannot be avoided and a dilemma arises that has no solution. A possibility might be – were it practicable – to proceed on a purely random basis, for example, by tossing a coin. As we see,[51] a more likely solution is for each legal order to prefer the jurisdictional claim of the party that is more – or most – closely connected to it. Firstly, however, we consider whether it is appropriate to prefer plaintiffs on grounds of corrective justice and in order to ensure procedural economy and simplicity. After considering the jurisdictional treatment of categories of litigationally disadvantaged plaintiffs, the dilemma that is presented where the parties' litigational capacities and claims to corrective justice are essentially equal is discussed.

(a) Preferring plaintiffs on grounds of corrective justice and to ensure procedural economy and simplicity

In support of a jurisdictional preference for defendants, at least where their litigational capacity is not markedly greater than that of the relevant category of plaintiffs, the argument has traditionally been advanced that the latter are the aggressors; it is they who disturb the status quo.[52] In recent decades, some jurists have reversed the argument; they assert, as a matter of corrective justice, that plaintiffs are significantly more likely than defendants to be in the right.[53] Accordingly, realistically considered, the latter are responsible for provoking the controversy and should be required to litigate in plaintiffs' forums.

This argument is usually implicit. It is said, for example, that the right to raise jurisdictional challenges should be reserved

> primarily for individuals or mom and pop operations that do not customarily engage in interstate transactions and are the real parties in interest, not nominal parties defended and indemnified by an interstate insurer.

"[T]he burden on the defendant [attacking jurisdiction on fairness grounds] will ['with the exception of individuals and small enterprises'] be heavy."[54] Accordingly,

> in suits by United States plaintiffs against United States defendants ... due process [must be regarded] as requiring only that the forum have some rational basis for wishing to decide the case – either because the plaintiff resides in the forum state or because the defendant acted or caused consequences there, or both.[55]

---

51   See p. 165, *supra*.

52   See pp. 153-157, *supra*.

53   It would be more accurate to speak here of "natural" plaintiffs and "natural" defendants, since in litigation seeking a *declaratory* judgment, the moving party may well be a natural defendant seeking to preserve the status quo. See Chap. VI. D. 5. *(a)* (ii), p. 305, *infra*.

54   R. Weintraub, "A Map out of the Personal Jurisdiction Labyrinth", 28 *U.C. Davis L. Rev.* 531, at 547 (1995).

55   *Idem* 545. In the case of "defendants residing or headquartered abroad", Professor Weintraub proposes a standard that would, in practice, be somewhat less plaintiff-

Another American jurist framed the argument as follows:

> Perhaps there are some cases in which a defendant is put to the test of defending or
> defaulting, and it is economically rational for the defendant to make a motion to dis-
> miss for lack of personal jurisdiction. This much, however, should be clear: if there are
> such cases, they are few and far between. Such a motion should require a defendant
> to show a practical inability to defend.[56]

In 1968, the Supreme Court of Oregon expressed a similar point of view:

> [A] defendant has no greater claim to preferred treatment than has a plaintiff. So
> long as the defendant is not compelled to defend himself in a distant state with which
> he has had no relevant connection, he cannot be said to have been denied either fair
> treatment or substantial justice.[57]

The proposition that, generally speaking, plaintiffs should be preferred over defendants for jurisdictional purposes underlies as well the argument that Justice
Brennan made in his dissent to *World-Wide Volkswagen Corp.* v. *Woodson.*[58]

---

oriented:

> that the defendant have some contact with the United States, *not with any individual
> state*, that makes it reasonable under the circumstances to order the foreigner to appear
> and defend …. [in the United States].

Ibid. (emphasis added).

The argument that greater weight should be given to the litigational problems of foreign than domestic defendants was made by Justice O'Connor in *Asahi Metal Industry Co., Ltd.* v. *Superior Court of California*, 480 US 102, at 115 (1987):

> [The forum] court [is] to consider the procedural and substantive policies of other *na-
> tions* whose interests are affected by the assertion of jurisdiction …. The procedural and
> substantive interest of other nations in a state court's assertion of jurisdiction over an
> alien defendant will differ from case to case. In every case, however, those interests, as
> well as the Federal Government's interest in its foreign relations policies, will be best
> served by a careful inquiry into the reasonableness of the assertion of jurisdiction in the
> particular case, and an unwillingness to find the serious burdens on an alien defendant
> outweighed by minimal interests on the part of the plaintiff or the forum State ….

56   P. Borchers, "The Death of the Constitutional Law of Personal Jurisdiction: From *Pennoyer* to *Burnham* and Back Again", 24 *U.C. Davis L. Rev.* 19, at 99 (1990). In order to
obtain a dismissal the defendant should also be required to show the "availability of
some other forum in which the plaintiff can meaningfully pursue the claim". *Ibid.*

57   *State of Oregon, ex rel. White Lumber Sales, Inc.* v. *Sulmonetti*, 252 Ore. 121, at 127,
448 P. 2d 571, at 574 (1968). The court does not say how the jurisdictional issue would
be resolved where either the plaintiff or the defendant must go to a distant state with
which he has no relevant connection.

58   444 US 286, at 299 (1980).

The model of society on which the [jurisdictional preference for defendants is based] is no longer accurate. Business people, no matter how local their businesses, cannot assume that the goods remain in the business' locality. Customers and goods can be anywhere else in the country usually in a matter of hours and always in a matter of a very few days.[59]

Brennan's thesis, as he states it, is a two-edged sword; greater mobility of goods and services and greater ease of communication and travel affect comparable categories of plaintiffs and defendants in equal measure. Not only today, but in the past as well, the relative inconvenience of litigating in the other party's forum is, in the abstract, no greater for the corporate plaintiff that buys goods on interstate markets than for the corporate defendant that sells on those markets. Ultimately Brennan's position can only rest on an unarticulated premise that, on one ground or another, plaintiffs should, in principle, be preferred for jurisdictional purposes over defendants. Of the arguments so far considered, the only one that furnishes across-the-board support for the pro-plaintiff bias expressed by Brennan, the Supreme Court of Oregon, and Professors Weintraub and Borchers is that considerations of corrective justice typically are on the side of plaintiffs. Of course, where it applies, the argument that categories of plaintiffs whose litigational capacity is significantly inferior to that of the relevant defendant-category supports a pro-plaintiff tilt; moreover, considerations of regulatory policy and efficient administration of justice may in some contexts cause a legal order to provide a forum that is more favorable to plaintiffs than defendants. But these possibilities do not establish the appropriateness, in principle, of a pro-plaintiff bias in jurisdictional matters.[60]

An argument of an entirely different order may provide general support for such a bias where, as in the United States, the legal system's operative jurisdictional rules and principles depend in large measure on the interpretation that courts give to constitutional standards such as due process or natural justice. The argument that for the United States a pro-plaintiff tilt in jurisdictional matters is desirable runs as follows: American state legislation either explicitly or through judicial interpretation today typically claims state-court adjudicatory authority to

---

59   *Idem* 309.

A thoughtful discussion of how "the social perceptions of ... space" have changed in America over the course of the last two centuries and the significance of these changes for American jurisdictional theory and practice is T. Kogan, "Geography and Due Process: The Social Meaning of Adjudicative Jurisdiction", 22 *Rut. L. J.* 627-657 (1991). Kogan makes clear that the change from a society of "Island Communit[ies]" to a "highly interdependent society" made physical location in space – both psychologically and practically considered – far less significant. Like Brennan, however, Kogan fails to point out that these changes affected plaintiffs and defendants, considered collectively, in equal measure. Both assume, without offering any principled justification, that, in light of the changes, the *actum sequitur* principle – or ideal – should be turned on its head.

60   See Buchner, *supra* footnote 9, at 86.

the constitutionally permissible extent.[61] Accordingly, except in the unlikely event of preemption of the field by federal legislation that establishes relatively clear-cut jurisdictional rules and principles,[62] adjudicatory claims will be largely controlled by the Supreme Court's interpretation and application of the due process clause. However, that clause does not authorize the Court to do what is needed, namely, accommodate appropriately the legitimate jurisdictional concerns of plaintiffs, defendants, and politically organized society and – to the extent possible – devise predictable and easily administered rules and principles implementing these accommodations.

In the circumstances, arguably simplicity and clarity can be achieved only by accepting all but the most grossly excessive claims of adjudicatory authority. On this basis, Professor Weintraub would respect a state's claim to adjudicatory authority so long as the state has "some rational basis for wishing to decide the case".[63] Procedural justice is sacrificed to procedural economy and simplicity.[64]

(b)   Preferring plaintiffs in order to equalize litigational capacity

When the litigational capacity of a category of defendants is significantly greater than that of the related plaintiffs' category,[65] considerations of procedural justice may require that one or more additional forums be made available in order to restore jurisdictional balance. For example, individual consumers, who buy from out-of-state firms supplying regional or global markets, characteristically have markedly less multistate litigational capacity than do the legal persons with which they deal.

To take this litigational imbalance into account, Article 16, paragraphs 1 and 2, of the Brussels Regulation provides that

---

61   See Chap. II. D. 1. *(b)* (i), pp. 57-59, *supra.*

62   As a constitutional matter, there is federal authority to regulate the adjudicatory authority of American courts, both state and federal, as well for interstate as international controversies. The very large question remains, of course, whether the political will to address such issues either domestically or internationally can be found now or in the foreseeable future.

63   See Weintraub, *supra* footnote 54, at 545.

64   The power theory, so long as it insists on intellectual rigour, can be rationalized in terms of this trade-off. For example, tag jurisdiction, though on occasion grossly unfair in its operation, is straightforward in its application as were most applications of the type of *quasi in rem* jurisdiction formerly available under *Harris* v. *Balk.* See Chap. III. A. 2. *(a)*, pp. 88-92, *supra.*

65   The analysis focuses on categories – or classes – of parties. Considerations of litigational efficiency bar the argument that a particular plaintiff – for example, one who happens to be a multi-millionaire – has litigational capacity greater than that of a particular defendant – for example, a corporation that is breaking even or losing money.

A consumer[66] may bring proceedings against the other party[67] to a contract either in the courts of the Member State in which that party is domiciled or in the courts for the place where the consumer is domiciled.

Proceedings may be brought against a consumer by the other party to the contract only in the courts of the Member State in which the consumer is domiciled."

Another context in which plaintiffs are provided additional jurisdictional choices in order to equalize litigational ability is that of fire and life insurance. *McGee* v. *International Life Insurance Co.*[68] provides a classic example of a jurisdictional basis justified on the ground that defendant insurance companies have significantly greater ability, as compared with those they insure, to bear the burdens of litigating abroad. A resident of California purchased a life insurance policy from an Arizona corporation in 1944. In 1948, International Life assumed the original insurer's obligation. Thereafter, premiums were paid by mail to the defendant's Texas office. When the insured died in 1950, the company refused to pay the beneficiary on the ground that the death was due to suicide. Neither the original insurer nor the defendant had ever had an office or agent in California, and, so far as the record showed, the defendant had "never solicited or done any insurance business in California apart from the policy involved here".[69] California "based its jurisdiction on a state statute which subjects foreign corporations to suit in California on insurance contracts with residents of that State ...".[70]

The beneficiary, who was unable to collect the judgment in California since the company had no assets there, sought to enforce it in Texas. Enforcement was refused by the Texas courts on the ground that California lacked jurisdiction over the defendant company. The matter was brought to the Supreme Court of the United States, which held that Texas had improperly denied full faith and credit to the California judgment because, in the circumstances of the case, there was no constitutional bar to California's exercise of adjudicatory authority over the defendant.

Justice Black wrote for a unanimous Court:

> It is sufficient for purposes of due process that the suit was based on a contract which had substantial connection with [California] .... The contract was delivered in California, the premiums were mailed from there and the insured was a resident of that State when he died. It cannot be denied that California has a manifest interest in providing effective means of redress for its residents when their insurers refuse to pay claims .... When claims were small or moderate individual claimants frequently could

---

66   A "consumer", as defined in Article 15 of the Regulation, normally belongs to a category of local parties.

67   The non-consumer party to a consumer contract will normally not be localized. See especially Article 15 (1) *(c)*.

68   355 US 220 (1957).

69   *Idem* 222.

70   *Idem* 221.

not afford the cost of bringing an action in a foreign forum – thus in effect making the company judgment proof. Often the crucial witnesses – as here on the company's defense of suicide – will be found in the insured's locality. Of course there may be inconvenience to the insurer if it is held amenable to suit in California where it had this contract but certainly nothing which amounts to a denial of due process.[71]

Article 9 of the Brussels I Regulation adopts an approach similar to that of *McGee*.

> An insurer domiciled in a Member State may be sued: … *(b)* in another Member State, in the case of actions brought by the policy-holder, the insured or a beneficiary, in the courts for the place where the plaintiff is domiciled … .

The examples given illustrate, but by no means exhaust,[72] the contexts in which a category of plaintiffs arguably has a legitimate claim to an additional forum or forums in light of the defendant category's greater litigational capacity. In contests between localized plaintiffs and multistate defendants it is difficult to justify breaking a jurisdictional tie in the latter's favor.[73]

---

71   *Idem* 223-224.

72   See, e.g., Article 19 of the Brussels I Regulation:
> An employer domiciled in a Member State may be sued:
> 1.   in the courts of the Member State where he is domiciled; or
> 2.   in another Member State:
>   *(a)*   in the courts for the place where the employee habitually carries out his work or in the courts for the last place where he did so, or
>   *(b)*   if the employee does not or did not habitually carry out his work in one country, in the courts for the place where the business which engaged the employee is or was situated.

73   Theoretically, the approach in terms of equality in litigation ability could be applied to restrict the use of some normally available jurisdictional bases when the *plaintiff's* category enjoys significantly greater litigational capacity than does the relevant defendant's category. This is done, in a sense, by Articles 9 and 16 of the Brussels Regulation, and by the *McGee* case; they do not extend to insurance companies or mail order houses suing insureds or consumers the special jurisdictional basis – namely, the plaintiff's domicile – that is available to plaintiff insureds and consumers. Withholding from plaintiffs in general a jurisdictional basis available to a particular category of plaintiffs is, however, from the perspective of design and administration, far more feasible than withdrawing a generally available basis from a particular category of plaintiffs.

Chapter V Consent and Adjudicatory Authority: Consequences of Splitting Causes of Action, Participating as a Litigant, and Choice of Forum Agreements

A. Introductory

1. General Remarks

This chapter considers two issues: (1) the consequences for the exercise of adjudicatory authority of initiating, or otherwise participating as a party in, an action before a state's courts; (2) the effects of agreements concluded between presently, or potentially, adverse parties that particular forums shall – or shall not – have adjudicatory authority over controversies that have arisen, or may arise, between these parties.

Consent plays a role in discussion of both issues; in the first, the concept of submission is employed as well. The notion of consent is used more precisely and restrictively than in some general discussions of adjudicatory authority. Professor Cappalli argues, for example, that jurisdiction is frequently based on a metaphorical conception of consent "implied through benefits obtained or risks created by the party while inside the political forum in which the court sits".[1]

During the heyday of the power theory, consent as a metaphor played an important role in general jurisdictional theory. In the United States, the first basis on which jurisdiction was exercised over non-local juridical persons was rationalized in terms of "consent". Legislation, passed in the early decades of the nineteenth century, invoked the state's power to exclude foreign corporations from doing business in the state and required that they consent to state-court jurisdiction over causes of action arising from business done locally on their behalf.[2] By the end of the second decade of the twentieth century, this form of "consent" jurisdiction had been displaced by the more capacious and flexible "presence" theory; activities carried on within a state on behalf of a foreign corporation were taken to establish its "presence" there for jurisdictional purposes.

In the late 1920s, the consent metaphor, previously invoked principally where juristic persons were in question, was applied to non-local natural persons

---

1   R. Cappalli, "Locke as the Key: A Unifying and Coherent Theory of in Personam Jurisdiction", 43 *Case W. Res. L. Rev.* 97, at 102 (1992).

2   See Chap. III. A. 2. *(b)* (ii), pp. 93 *et seq., supra.*

involved in local automobile accidents.[3] The metaphor, though sorely strained, served to justify asserting adjudicatory authority that is today seen as resting not on true consent but on the parties' and the controversy's connections with the forum state.

Our concern in Chapter V is not with claims of adjudicatory authority based on metaphorical consent, but with jurisdictional claims grounded on various expressions of arguably true consent. Does such consent, standing alone, justify a legal order's exercising adjudicatory authority over the controversy to which the "consent" was directed? Conversely, to what extent are party agreements not to litigate in some – or all – other forums respected?

2.   *The Two Paradigmatic Situations*

Two paradigmatic situations are considered. The first involves "unilateral consent" to the exercise of adjudicatory authority given through participation in litigation. The second involves agreement by presently or potentially adverse parties that particular public or private forums shall – or shall not – have adjudicatory authority in certain circumstances. In the first instance, "consent" runs to a state and is expressed by participating in litigation in its courts; in the second, "consent" takes the form of a bilateral exercise of private autonomy by which the parties seek to control *ex ante* the choice of forum in controversies to which they are or may become parties.

Stipulations regarding the availability *vel non* of particular forums are contracts, albeit of a special type. As such, they raise issues not only respecting the extent to which parties may control the exercise of a state's adjudicatory authority but also issues common to contracts generally: are the exercises of party autonomy in question acceptable in principle? If so, are they governed by the general law of contract or by a special contractual regime?

A party's participation in litigation, without more, establishes a relationship with the forum state from which, depending on that state's law, various consequences flow. To the extent permitted by the relevant norms of international or constitutional law, a state is free to treat even a party's casual or unwilling participation as a unilateral "consent" or submission to its adjudicatory authority. Extreme positions respecting the significance of party participation, in particular, refusing to allow defendants to appear specially to contest the forum's adjudicatory authority, clearly rest on a Hobson's choice that does not constitute "consent" in any ordinary sense of the term.

---

3   See *Hess* v. *Pawloski*, 274 US 352 (1927), discussed Chap. III. A. 3., pp. 95 *et seq., supra.*

B.   The Extent of Party Control over the Preclusive Effects of Litigating: Herein of "Splitting"

1.   *Introductory*

The basic themes of Chapter V are the consequences, on the one hand, of party participation in litigation and, on the other, of party agreements respecting the exercise – or non-exercise – of a state's adjudicatory authority. A distinct, but related, theme – considered below – is the extent to which the parties can control the dimensions of the controversy that the court seized is to decide. This matter is, of course, of great importance for the recognition and enforcement of non-local judgments.[4] A judgment's dimensions also determine the consequences that seizing the local courts has for subsequent litigation in those courts – and potentially courts of other states as well – of factually or legally related controversies.

The "splitting" problem arises, of course, regardless of the ground of adjudicatory authority invoked. Accordingly, "splitting" could be considered in a general discussion of the grounds upon which adjudicatory authority is exercised. The rationale for discussing the subject here is that splitting's problematic is the converse of that presented by party control over the availability *vel non* of particular forums. The latter raises issues respecting the extent to which parties can control a forum's exercise of adjudicatory authority; the former, of the extent to which parties control the consequences of the resulting adjudication for subsequent litigation in the same court system of factually or legally related controversies. The scope of adjudicatory authority based on participation in court proceedings as a litigant is intertwined not only with a legal order's position on the dimensions of "cause of action" and functionally equivalent conceptions but raises as well the issue of the balance to be struck between the planning principle and private autonomy. Even when in many respects legal systems espouse similar values where economic planning or market control are in question, their positions on discrete procedural issues can differ greatly as the American and German positions on "splitting" illustrate. The permissive position taken by the German system contrasts sharply with the American system's search for economy and efficiency above all else. On the other hand, in prorogation and derogation matters, the German system, which originally allowed parties great freedom, has become more restrictive over time in order to protect, *inter alia*, consumers while American law, which until relatively recently disfavored derogation clauses, has, since World War II, increasingly recognized party autonomy in these matters.

History, and the accidents of history, general cultural, economic and political considerations, legal theory, institutions, and practices, all play roles – of varying importance – in the shaping of law, including the law of procedure. The weight

---

4   For a discussion of recognition and enforcement, see A. von Mehren, "Recognition and Enforcement of Foreign Judgments – General Theory and the Role of Jurisdictional Requirements", 167 *Recueil des cours* 9-112 (1980).

that legal orders give to plan and private economy are discussed in general terms later in this Chapter.[5]

2.   The Maximum Preclusive Effect of an Adjudication

A party's failure to seek the fullest measure of relief arguably due him under the relevant facts and law should not constitute a vice that precludes further local litigation unless, at the time that the contours of the proceedings were definitively set, the party was aware that he could have sought the relief. Procedural economy and efficiency can, absent exceptional circumstances, hardly justify penalizing a party for not requesting relief based on factual materials of which he could not have known until after his pleadings were final. Accordingly, in every legal system, the *outer* limits of "cause of action" and functionally comparable concepts are closely connected with the system's procedural rules governing pleadings and discovery.

(a)   American law
(i)   At common law and under Field's Code[6]

The interaction between procedural arrangements and practices, on the one hand, and the concept of "cause of action" and rules respecting "splitting", on the other, are clearly seen in American theory and practice. Before the merger of "law" and "equity", in common-law systems a party proceeding at "law" did not "split" a cause of action by not seeking "equitable relief" (e.g., specific performance) or by failing to raise an "equitable" defense (e.g., fraud, illegality, mistake). Furthermore, the concentrated nature of trials at "law" and the lack of pretrial discovery meant that causes of action could hardly be shaped – as they are in contemporary American theory and practice[7] – by the "transaction" or circumstances out of which the claims arose. The pretrial pleading process was definitive; it required plaintiffs and defendants to state, in turn, unequivocally and responsively the legal theory or theories on which each relied. Exchange of pleadings continued until, with respect to every point raised, agreement or disagreement between the parties had been established. Only the controversy as thus defined could be considered at the trial stage; moreover, under "the common law forms of action, ... a plaintiff ordinarily was not permitted to join in one action claims formulated under different forms of action".[8]

---

5   See D. 1., pp. 207 *et seq.*, *infra.*

6   For general background, see R. Millar, *Civil Procedure of the Trial Court in Historical Perspective* (New York, NY, The Law Center of New York University, 1952). A brief discussion of Field's Code is found in A. von Mehren, *Law in the United States: A General and Comparative View* 19-21 (Deventer & Boston, MA, Kluwer, 1988).

7   See (ii), pp. 179 *et seq.*, *infra.*

8   Restatement Second of Judgments, Introduction, at 7 (St. Paul, Minn., American Law Institute Publishers, 1982).

At common law and, to a somewhat lesser degree, under Field's Code of Civil Procedure,[9] a claimant had "to state his claims with fairly definite particulars as to time, place, cause, and consequences".[10] These particulars could not be materially changed at the trial stage by amendment of the pleadings or by the introduction of evidence. Furthermore,

> within the narrow framework of pleaded issues the parties were dependent on their own resources for proof. Discovery was almost non-existent at common law and very cumbersome in equity .... [Consequently,] it was often said that the issue in two actions was the same only if the evidence was the same ....[11]

(ii)   Under the Federal Rules of Civil Procedure and comparable State systems

The relatively narrow concepts of "cause of action", appropriate under both common-law and Field-Code procedural practices, were rendered disfunctional by the pleading and discovery procedures provided by the Federal Rules of Civil Procedure (1938), as amended, and by numerous state laws that took their cue from the Rules.

> [T]he premise of the Federal Rules ... [by the twentieth century's close was] that a party should be able to state his claim on any and every permissible foundation available under the substantive law .... [I]f a pleader describes generally the transaction by which he is aggrieved, the action may not be dismissed under the Federal Rules unless it is evident that no substantive theory can support his action .... Similar latitude is allowed in affirmative defenses, counterclaims, and claims against third parties. 'Claim' for purposes of *res judicata* under the Federal Rules thus ordinarily refers to the transaction involved rather than legal formulations about the transaction ....[12]

As the scope of the concept of "claim" increased as a function of the more and more robust discovery available to the parties, so did litigation costs and delays. Over several decades the complaint was voiced by the bar and the public that discovery was too costly.[13] In 2000, the Rules were amended to require judicial

---

9   See *idem* 8.

10   *Ibid.*

11   *Idem* 8-9.

12   *Idem* 9.

13   For several decades the broad scope of discovery had been vigorously criticized as a source of needless expense and delay due to overuse of Rule 26. See C. Wright and M. Kane, *Federal Practice and Procedure: Federal Practice Deskbook* §86, at 782 (St. Paul, MN, West Group, 2002).
The 2000 amendments to Rule 26 *(b)* 1 essentially adopt the "earlier ABA [American Bar Association] proposals". *Idem* at 794. "The right of attorneys to make discovery requests without court authorization now is limited to matters 'relevant to the claim or defense of any party'." *Ibid.* The amendment does not make any change in the scope of potential discovery; it conditions discovery, however, upon court authorization

authorization for discovery that is not "relevant to the claim or defense of any party". The hope is to retain the dispute-resolution efficiency of adjudication – the concept of "claim" and "cause of action" have remained unchanged – while reducing the likelihood of overuse and possible misuse of discovery.

Contemporary American civil procedure thus ordinarily provides the plaintiff a "full and fair" opportunity to make every claim and defense that can arise from a given transaction's or situation's factual elements and the substantive rules arguably implicated by those facts. Accordingly, the American conception of "claim" for purposes of the general rule concerning "splitting" is broad and inclusive; it encompasses "all rights of the plaintiff to remedies against the defendant with respect to all or any part of the transaction, or series of connected transactions, out of which the action arose".[14]

The limits of the concept of "cause of action" and the rules respecting "splitting" that have successively flowed from procedural arrangements and practices under the traditional common law, the Field procedural codes, and the Federal Rules of Civil Procedure correspond rather closely to the notional upper limit set in each period to "cause of action". Relaxations that allow a degree of "splitting" have resulted from fine-tuning of the system's rules to ensure procedural justice in light of particular situations that occur only rarely or in rather special circumstances.[15]

Contemporary American theory and practice respecting the limits of the "cause of action" concept and the rules respecting "splitting" rest on a philosophy of procedural economy and efficiency, reinforced by a strong belief that finality and repose are fundamental social values that law must serve. The rules reinforce "the authoritativeness of the law itself …. [A]t some point arguable questions of right and wrong for practical purposes simply cannot be argued anymore".[16] Finality and repose are, of course, served directly by the law respecting the recognition and enforcement of judgments. But, reinforced by policies of judicial economy and efficiency, the values of finality and repose have come in contemporary American theory and practices to affect profoundly as well practice and theory respecting the dimensions of what must, at least for purposes of local litigation, be claimed to avoid loss of one's rights through "splitting".

(b) German law

The debate about the extent to which a party must, at the risk of forfeiture, litigate in one action all claims that constitute a single cause of action – a major theme in contemporary American theory and practice – has no true counterpart in contemporary German law. With the promulgation of the ZPO in 1877 the proce-

---

where the matter to be discovered is not relevant to a claim or defense that a party has already made. See *ibid.*

14   *Idem* §24, Dimensions of "Claim" for Purposes of Merger or Bar – General Rule Concerning "Splitting", para. (1).

15   For further particulars and examples, see 3 *(a)*, pp. 182 *et seq., infra.*

16   Restatement Second of Judgments, *supra* footnote 8, Introduction, at 11.

dural system of the Reich was, so far as institutional arrangements are concerned, free to adopt an approach to "splitting" in line with American procedure either as it then was or as it would become with the advent of the Federal Rules of Civil Procedure (1938). The German solution differs fundamentally, however, from American practice both past and present. Here, as in other respects, the German law was shaped by two fundamental principles: party disposition *(Dispositions-maxime)* and party presentation *(Verhandlungsmaxime)*. The first accords the parties the responsibility to determine the subject matter and the scope of their litigation. The second calls on the parties to present factual proof for each contested factual allegation and requires the court to base its decision solely on the material submitted by the parties.[17] The German system's primary concern since 1877 has thus not been with the functionally appropriate concept of claim in light of German procedural arrangements and considerations of procedural efficiency and economy but with whether, in fairness to the adversary, some limits should not be set to party control over the dimensions of the litigation. For German law, "splitting" is problematic only if it results in a situation that is egregiously unfair to the other party.

In this context the German concept of the "object in controversy" *(Streitge-genstand)* – a concept that can be likened in some respects to the American "cause of action" – becomes relevant: the scope of the object in controversy, initially determined by the dimensions of the relief sought by the plaintiff in his complaint *(Klageantrag)*, is crucial for such issues as joining of actions *(Klagehäufung)*,[18] amendment of pleadings *(Klageänderung)*[19] and *lis alibi pendens (Rechtshängig-keit)*.[20] More importantly, it also determines the scope of the *res judicata* effect of judgments *(Rechtskraft)*,[21] which is functionally equivalent to the American doctrine of claim preclusion.[22] Unlike its American counterpart, however, *Rechtskraft* is not primarily concerned with procedural economy and efficiency. It rather aims at protecting the reasonable expectations of the parties by strictly limiting the binding effect of a court's judgment to the object in controversy. In order to avoid unfair surprise with regard to the claim preclusion effects of judgments, their *Rechtskraft* is limited to the object in controversy and includes neither prelimi-

---

17   See for a detailed account of the two principles see P. Murray and R. Stürner, *German Civil Justice*, at 156-160 (Durham, N.C., Carolina Academic Press, 2004); *Münchener Kommentar zur Zivilprozeßordnung* (-Lüke), Vol. 1 (Munich, C. H. Beck, 2nd ed. 2000), Einleitung No. 167-210, Zöller (-Greger), *Kommentar zur ZPO* (Cologne, Dr. Otto Schmidt, 25th ed., 2005), Vor §128, No. 9.

18   See ZPO §260.

19   See ZPO §263 and §264.

20   See ZPO §261.

21   See ZPO §322.

22   For a comparative analysis of American, German, and Japanese concepts of claim and issue preclusion see K. Koshiyama, *Rechtskraftwirkungen und Urteilsanerkennung nach amerikanischem, deutschem und japanischem Recht* (Tübingen, Mohr Siebeck, 1996).

nary questions (for instance, the validity of the contract in an action for payment) nor any factual determinations regardless whether the court's reasoning rests on them.[23]

Prior to the adoption of the ZPO a broader concept of *Rechtskraft* had been advocated by, among others, Friedrich Carl von Savigny.[24] The drafters of the ZPO explicitly rejected the idea;[25] provision was made in ZPO §256 (2) for the filing of interlocutory declaratory actions regarding certain preliminary questions *(Zwischenfeststellungsklage)* but this provision, in effect, reiterated the principles of dispositive election and party presentation.

The narrow German concept of *Rechtskraft* has the advantage of producing relatively few controversies about preclusive effects of judgments but the disadvantage of permitting essentially duplicative litigation about closely connected, or even identical, factual and legal issues. To avoid such litigation, some German scholars now favor adoption of a broader concept of *Rechtskraft*, that would give greater preclusive effects to prior litigation where disputes are connected.[26] The German courts and most German scholars have, in principle, rejected these proposals. For certain types of situations, however, the courts have cautiously given a broader meaning to the concept of *Rechtskraft*.[27] In this context, the issue of splitting of actions is currently discussed in Germany; the debate is reflected below.[28]

3.   Contemporary Practice

(a)   American law

American civil procedure holds a broad conception of cause of action, one that rests on the underlying transaction rather than the juridical theory on which the claim is based; a claim is split to the extent that "remedies against the defendant with respect to all or any part of the transaction, or series of connected transactions, out of which the action arose", are not sought.[29] A valid and final judgment,

---

23   See Murray and Stürner, *supra* footnote 17, at 357-362; *Münchener Kommentar zur Zivilprozeßordnung* (-Gottwald), *supra* footnote 17, §322, No. 78-126, Zöller (-Greger), *supra* footnote 17, Vor §322, No. 30-51. See also A. Zeuner, "Objektive Grenzen der Rechtskraft", in H. Bernstein, U. Drobnig and H. Kötz (eds.), *Festschrift für Konrad Zweigert* 603, at 612-617 (Tübingen, Mohr Siebeck, 1981).

24   *System des heutigen römischen Rechts*, Vol. VI, at 350, 429, 451 (Berlin, Veit, 1847).

25   See *Münchener Kommentar zur Zivilprozeßordnung* (-Gottwald), *supra* footnote 17, §322, No. 78; F. Stein and M. Jonas (-Leipold), *Kommentar zur Zivilprozeßordnung*, Vol. 4/1 (Tübingen, Mohr Siebeck, 21st ed., 1998), §322, No. 77.

26   See, most notably, Zeuner's concept of "rechtlicher Sinnzusammenhang": Zeuner, *supra* footnote 23.

27   See Stein and Jonas (-Leipold), *supra* footnote 25, §322, Nos. 212-220.

28   See 3. *(b)*, pp. 185 *et seq., infra*.

29   Restatement Second of Judgments, para. (1) of §24. Dimensions of "Claim" for Purposes of Merger or Bar – General Rule Concerning "Splitting".

in favor of the plaintiff, merges his rights; he "cannot thereafter maintain an action on the original claim or any part thereof ...".[30] Merger occurs

> even though the plaintiff is prepared in the second action
> (1)   To present evidence or grounds or theories of the case not presented in the first action, or
> (2)   To seek remedies or forms of relief not demanded in the first action.[31]

On occasion, the court does, however, exercise a degree of discretion in establishing the dimensions of "claim" for purposes of merger:

> (2)   What factual grouping constitutes a 'transaction', and what groupings constitute a 'series', are to be determined pragmatically, giving weight to such considerations as whether the facts are related in time, space, origin, or motivation, whether they form a convenient trial unit, and whether their treatment as a unit conforms to the parties' expectations or business understanding or usage.[32]

It is recognized that these criteria are "not capable of a mathematically precise definition"; they are to be applied "with attention to the facts of the cases".[33] Furthermore, "a delicate balance" is to be struck "between, on the one hand, the interests of the defendant and of the courts in bringing litigation to a close and, on the other, the interest of the plaintiff in vindication of a just claim".[34] In particular,

> "[f]or reasons of substantive policy in a case involving a continuing or recurrent wrong", a plaintiff, at his option, is allowed "to sue once for the total harm, both past and prospective, or to sue from time to time for the damages incurred to the date of suit."[35]

Splitting is also permitted when "[t]he parties have agreed in terms or in effect that the plaintiff may split his claim, or the defendant has acquiesced therein".[36] The latter type of splitting has a counterpart in the principle that a defendant loses the right to object to the court's adjudicatory authority if he participates in the action on the merits unless he has raised the jurisdictional issue within the time specified by the court's rules.[37]

---

30   *Idem*, para. (1) of §18. Judgment for Plaintiff – The General Rule of Merger.
31   *Idem* §25. Exemplifications of General Rule Concerning Splitting.
32   *Idem* §24.
33   *Idem*, Comment *b*, Transaction: application of a pragmatic standard, 198, at 199.
34   *Ibid.*
35   *Idem* §26. Exceptions to the General Rule Concerning Splitting, para. 1 *(e)*.
36   *Idem*, para. (1) *(a)*.
37   See C. 2., pp. 188 *et seq., infra.*

Express reservations by a court of "the plaintiff's right to maintain ... [a] second action" are also respected[38] and exceptions are made on grounds of fairness where

> [t]he plaintiff was unable to rely on a certain theory of the case or to seek a certain remedy or form of relief in the first action because of the limitations on the subject matter jurisdiction of the courts or restrictions on their authority to entertain multiple theories or demands for multiple remedies or forms of relief in a single action, and the plaintiff desires in the second action to rely on that theory or to seek that remedy or form of relief .... [39]

The policy of judicial efficiency and economy served by rules against splitting is also relaxed, albeit infrequently, on grounds of fairness and reliance where

> [t]he judgment in the first action was plainly inconsistent with the fair and equitable implementation of a statutory or constitutional scheme, or it is in the sense of the scheme that the plaintiff should be permitted to split his claim ...".[40]

Finally, what can be seen as a public-policy exception is available in rare cases where

> [i]t ... [can be] clearly and convincingly shown that the policies favoring preclusion of a second action are overcome for an extraordinary reason, such as the apparent invalidity of a continuing restraint or condition having a vital relation to personal liberty or the failure of prior litigation to yield a coherent disposition of the controversy.[41]

Present purposes do not require further discussion of the contemporary American approach to the "splitting" problem; it suffices to reiterate that, overall, great weight is given to considerations of procedural economy and efficiency and little to party wishes. A clear agreement between the parties to "split" the cause of ac-

---

38   *Idem*, para. (1) *(b)*.

39   *Idem*, para. (1) *(c)*.

40   *Idem*, para. (1) *(d)*.

41   *Idem*, para. (1) *(f)*.
For a discussion of this "small category of cases", see *idem*, Comment *i*. *Extraordinary situations where merger or bar is inapposite (Subsection (1)* (f)), at 242-244. For example, a spouse, who sues for separate maintenance on ground of desertion and prevails, should not be barred from later instituting an action for divorce on grounds that existed at the time the maintenance suit was brought. Neither social policy nor procedural justice countenances depriving a spouse of a more drastic remedy because a less drastic one was first asserted. See *idem* 243, Illustration 8.
In practice, exceptions based on the prior litigation having failed to yield a coherent remedy are "extremely rare". Such a situation could "occur ... when the disposition of a claim and counterclaim in a prior action has left the parties with inconsistent interests in the disputed property". *Idem* 243, Comment *i*.

tion is recognized, however. A residual discretion rests with the court where the prohibition of "splitting" offends procedural justice.

(b) German law

The considerations of procedural economy and efficiency that American jurists advance to support a system that disfavors "splitting" play a minor role in German procedural thinking respecting the practice. So long as the subject matter of the claim is such as to make it feasible, the German system allows a "splitting of action" *(Teilklage)*. This result flows quite naturally from the principle of party disposition *(Dispositionsmaxime)*.[42] Moreover, certain aspects of German civil procedure encourage the practice. In Germany, counsel fees and court costs – payable by the losing party – are calculated on the basis of the value actually placed in controversy *(Streitwert)*.[43] For instance, a plaintiff, seeking damages for breach of contract but fearing to lose the case because he may be unable to establish the existence of a valid contract, is likely to bring an action for a relatively small amount in order to "test" the opinion of the court and reduce substantially the cost of litigation in case he loses. If the plaintiff succeeds with his limited action, the defendant will often be prepared to comply with the judgment with respect to the remaining damage claims unless the total amount of damages suffered by the plaintiff is disputed. Should the defendant refuse to pay more than the judgment rendered orders, the plaintiff, unlike under the American doctrine of claim preclusion (merger), can file a second action for the remaining amount without the German concept of *Rechtskraft* standing in the way of further litigation.[44] This holds true even if the plaintiff in the first proceedings did not disclose that the claim was limited *(verdeckte Teilklage)*.[45] However, in subsequent proceedings the court is, under the prevailing view among German courts[46] and scholars,[47] in no way bound by the first decision; the court can, for instance, dismiss the action on the ground that the parties had not concluded a valid contract. If the defendant wishes to ensure through the first proceedings a final resolution

---

42   See *supra* p. 181.

43   See for court costs, the §11 (2) of the Court Cost Law *(Gerichtskostengesetz – GKG)*. See for counsels' fees §2 (1) of the Law on the Compensation of Attorneys *(Gesetz über die Vergütung der Rechtsanwältinnen und Rechtsanwälte – RVG)*, which has replaced the Law on the Fees for Attorneys *(Bundesgebührenordnung für Rechtsanwälte – BRAGO)* as of 1 July 2004.

44   See *supra* p. 181. See also Murray and Stürner, *supra* footnote 17, at 357-358; *Münchener Kommentar zur Zivilprozeßordnung* (-Gottwald), *supra* footnote 17, §322, No. 118-119; Zöller (-Greger), *supra* footnote 17, Vor §322, Nos. 47-48.

45   See BGH, 9 April 1997, 135 *BGHZ* 178, 181; Murray and Stürner, *supra* footnote 17, at 357-358; *Münchener Kommentar zur Zivilprozeßordnung* (-Gottwald), *supra* footnote 17, §322, No. 119; Zöller (-Greger), *supra* footnote 17, Vor §322, Nos. 47-48.

46   See BGH, 9 April 1997, 135 *BGHZ* 178, 181.

47   See *Münchener Kommentar zur Zivilprozeßordnung* (-Gottwald), *supra* footnote 17, §322, No. 119; Zöller (-Greger), *supra* footnote 17, Vor §322, Nos. 47-48.

of all controversial issues between the parties, he must seek a negative declaratory judgment with regard to those issues that are not within the *Streitgegenstand* upon which the plaintiff has asked the court to decide.

The narrow scope of *Rechtskraft*, according to the majority position in Germany, is dramatically exemplified when the plaintiff loses the first case. Here, even if the court dismissed the action on the ground that there was no contract at all that could have been broken, its judgment does not preclude the plaintiff bringing a second action for the damages not claimed in the first action.[48] In these subsequent proceedings the plaintiff is free to argue that there was a valid and binding contract between the parties. This situation has provoked a growing number of German scholars to argue that, at least in such cases, the *Rechtskraft* of the first judgment should extend to the invalidity of the contract because the court, in order to dismiss a limited action, must always scrutinize the whole alleged contractual relationship between the parties; the action is not dismissed unless the court is convinced that the claim is not justified. Enlarging in these situations the *Rechtskraft* of the first judgment was first proposed by Fitting in the nineteenth century;[49] in recent decades prominent scholars have joined the minority camp.[50] No German scholar, however, has so far argued for a solution comparable to the American doctrine of merger. Indeed, the German system of calculating courts costs and counsel fees on the basis of the value placed in controversy[51] is seen by some as excluding the American approach regarding "splitting".[52]

The German law's traditional approach to the "splitting" issue gives great weight to party control over the preclusive effects of law suits at the expense of procedural economy and efficiency. This approach has the advantage of avoiding the complications that can arise under the complex American effort to maximize the efficiency of law suits without compromising fair treatment of the parties so far as the suit's preclusive effects are concerned. On the other hand, it gives little weight to the efficient use of litigation as a dispute-resolution process and to society's interest in coherence and repose.

---

48   See, e.g., *ibid.*

49   Fitting, Bemerkungen zur Reichs-Civilprocessordnung, 2 *ZZP* 266, at 270-271 (1880); see also Zitelmann, "Rechtskraft bei Theilforderungen", 8 *ZZP* 254-282 (1885).

50   See D. Leipold, "Teilklagen und Rechtskraft", in K. Bettermann, M. Löwisch, H. Otto and K. Schmidt (eds.), *Festschrift für Albrecht Zeuner* 431-449 (Tübingen, Mohr (Siebeck), 1994).

51   See p. 185, *supra*.

52   See, e.g., *Münchener Kommentar zur Zivilprozeßordnung* (-Gottwald), *supra* footnote 17, §322, No. 120.

C. Adjudicatory Authority Grounded on Participation in Court Proceedings as a Litigant

1. In General

It stands to reason that, when one initiates litigation he accepts, in principle, the court's adjudicatory authority with respect to his claims regardless whether the adjudication's result ultimately favors him. A disappointed plaintiff can hardly assert that the court he seized lacked jurisdiction over him.[53] The defendant's position is different; it must be established that there existed as to him a free-standing basis of general, category-specific, or specific jurisdiction.

But how far does the adjudicatory authority that the forum acquires over parties before it in the role of plaintiffs extend? Is general jurisdiction established comparable in scope to the adjudicatory authority based on a natural person's domicile or habitual residence or a legal person's place of incorporation? Or is the authority specific in nature so that it covers only claims arising out of the same controversy as the claims made by the plaintiff? Furthermore, what are the jurisdictional consequences for a defendant or a third party who assumes the role of plaintiff by raising claims against the initial plaintiff?

These difficult and vexing issues are intertwined with a legal order's position on, and its policies respecting, the dimensions of "cause of action" and functionally equivalent conceptions, and its attitude towards "splitting". The considerations of procedural economy and efficiency that support the broad conception of "cause of action" held by American theory and practice and the strongly held American policy against splitting are compatible with treating participation in the role of a plaintiff as a free standing ground of general jurisdiction.[54] Conversely, the relatively narrow concept of *Streitgegenstand*, held in German procedural theory and practice, as well as the party's right under German procedural law to split, when feasible, the object in controversy, support the German view that participation as a plaintiff establishes only a basis of specific jurisdiction; the adjudicatory authority established reaches only claims "arising out of" or "closely connected with" the controversy that generates the claims brought by the initial plaintiff.[55]

Before considering the jurisdictional consequences of participating in litigation as a plaintiff, the much less complex problem of the jurisdictional consequences of participation in litigation as a defendant is discussed.

---

53   See E. Riezler, *Internationales Zivilprozeßrecht und prozessuales Fremdenrecht* 313 (Berlin, de Gruyter & Tübingen, Mohr (Siebeck), 1949).

In class actions, often many members of the plaintiff class are unidentified and, accordingly, arguably cannot be taken to consent or submit to the forum's authority. Such plaintiffs are assimilated to identified plaintiffs by assuming their consent unless the class member, once notified of the proceedings, opts out of the action.

54   See 3. *(a)*, pp. 194 *et seq., infra.*

55   See 3. *(b)*, pp. 199 *et seq., infra.*

2. Participation without Objection as a Defendant

(a) Introductory

A defendant that chooses to participate in court proceedings without objection is universally taken to accept the appropriateness of the forum exercising adjudicatory authority over the pending action.[56] What constitutes an appearance and when a challenge to jurisdiction must be lodged in order to be effective vary from one forum to another. In international litigation, where defendants (and their lawyers) may well be unfamiliar with local procedural practice, defendants may inadvertently lose their right to challenge the court's jurisdiction. Article 5 of the Draft Hague Convention on International Jurisdiction and Foreign Judgments in Civil and Commercial Matters of 30 October 1999[57] seeked to provide a convention rule as to when unraised jurisdictional objections are lost:

> 1.   Subject to Article 12 [Exclusive jurisdiction] a court has jurisdiction if the defendant proceeds on the merits without contesting jurisdiction.
> 2.   The defendant has the right to contest jurisdiction no later than at the time of the first defense on the merits.[58]

Rules respecting appearance balance, on the one hand, the forum's and the parties' interests in litigational efficiency and economy against, on the other hand, the forum's and the defendant's interests in ensuring that the defendant's procedural as well as his substantive rights are protected. Basically three solutions are possible: (1) the defendant must choose between proceeding on the merits and defaulting; (2) the defendant must proceed first on the issue of adjudicatory authority; only after it is resolved can he proceed on substantive issues; (3) the defendant can challenge the forum's jurisdiction and proceed on the merits at the same time; the court will determine whether jurisdictional issues shall be litigated before the merits or concurrently with them.

(b) American theory and practice

The Common Law traditionally treated a "general appearance" by the defendant as "consent" for jurisdictional purposes. Such an appearance was made when the defendant appeared for any purpose, including that of objecting to jurisdiction.

---

56   The forum may, of course, decline to exercise its authority. For example, it may consider that another forum has exclusive adjudicatory authority over the matter.

57   The Draft Convention of October 1999 was followed by an Interim Text in June 2001. However, as of 2005 chances are very low that the Convention will ever be enacted. See for a detailed discussion of the Hague project Chapter VII B. 3. and C., pp. 358, *infra*.

58   The Interim Text of June 2001 accepted the overall approach of the 1999 Draft with suggested refinements: "[The defendant shall have the right to contest jurisdiction under Articles [white list] [at least until] [no later than at] the time of the first defense on the merits.]"

Most common-law legal orders allowed, however, defendants to make a special appearance – that is to say, a challenge limited to the forum's jurisdiction – without appearing generally. Indeed, many common-law legal orders went further and allowed defendants to plead both to the jurisdiction and to the merits without waiving the right to litigate the issue of adjudicatory authority.[59]

A few American states took the view, however, that a defendant who "asks for relief which the court may grant only if it has jurisdiction over him", enters "a general appearance even though the defendant protests at the same time that he does not submit himself to the jurisdiction of the court".[60]

In *York* v. *Texas*,[61] the Supreme Court of the United States held that a Texas statute which so provided was constitutional. By the end of the 1960s, the two states – Texas and Mississippi – that had long refused to permit special appearances had changed their positions.[62] The Restatement Second of Conflict of Laws, promulgated in 1969, provides in §81, Special Appearances, that "[a] state will not exercise judicial jurisdiction over an individual who appears in an action for the sole purpose of objecting that there is no jurisdiction over him". As Comment *a* Rationale to §81 explains, failure to recognize such special appearances

> would ... work serious hardship on a defendant who has a defense to the merits of the case as well as a defense to the jurisdiction. It would force him to run the risk of surrendering one or the other of these defenses.

The US Supreme Court would today doubtless hold unconstitutional a state's refusal to allow special appearances.[63] In all events, it is highly unlikely that any state will return to the rule in *York* v. *Texas*.

It is worth noting that the issue raised by *York* v. *Texas* can arise as well in arbitration where the tribunal's adjudicatory authority derives from party consent. Does an appearance that is not a voluntary expression of consent but rather to contest the tribunal's adjudicatory authority, alone or in combination with a

---

59   See Restatement Second of Conflict of Laws §33. Appearance as Defendant, Comment *d*, *What constitutes a general appearance*, at 137 (St. Paul, Minn., American Law Institute Publishers, 1971). Statutes that require defendants to set up all their defenses in the answer are usually "construed to allow a defendant to plead to the jurisdiction and to the merits without waiving the jurisdictional defense". *Ibid*.

60   *Ibid*.

61   137 US 15 (1890).

62   See R. Weintraub, *Commentary on the Conflict of Laws*, §4.37, at 284 (New York, NY, Foundation Press, 4th ed., 2001).

63   In *Burnham* v. *Superior Court of California*, 495 US 604 (1990) (see Chap. III. A. 6., pp. 107 *et seq.*) the court unanimously accepted the view that "[f]or new procedures, hitherto unknown, the due process clause requires an analysis to determine whether 'traditional notions of fair play and substantial justice' have been offended". *Idem* 622. The rule in *York* v. *Texas* never satisfied the "generally observed" standard and would presumably be held unconstitutional under *International Shoe*.

defense on the merits, establish the arbitral tribunal's adjudicatory authority? In *First Options of Chicago, Inc.* v. *Kaplan*[64] the Supreme Court of the United States set aside the arbitrators' holding that it did. Justice Breyer explained that

> merely arguing the arbitrability issue to an arbitrator does not indicate a clear willingness to arbitrate that issue, i.e., a willingness to be effectively bound by the arbitrator's decision on that point.[65]

The same result is reached as well in civil-law jurisdictions. In setting aside an award against the Arab Republic of Egypt,[66] the Cour d'appel de Paris remarked, *inter alia*, that

> the fact of defending a case on the merits before ... an adjudicatory body *[jurisdiction]*, after having raised its lack of jurisdiction cannot imply waiver of the jurisdictional defense[.] [T]he Egyptian State had legitimate reasons for defending the case on the merits, even before arbitrators whom it deemed to lack jurisdiction, in order to attempt to mitigate the prejudice which might result from an award against it[.] It is also important to note that since the arbitral tribunal is the judge of its own jurisdiction [subject to ultimate court review], in fact the A.R.E. had to appear before it to manifest its opposition to its opponents' claims *(thèse)*. This again underlines the difference between terms of reference [the notice *(acte de mission)* of 3 May 1980,] signed by a pleader anxious to avoid defaulting and an arbitration agreement [a *compromis*]... characterized by the freely expressed will of the parties to grant the arbitrators jurisdiction [i.e., adjudicatory authority] *(compétence)*[.][67]

(c)   German theory and practice

From its inception in 1877, the German ZPO has included a jurisdictional provision – ZPO §39 – dealing with the issue of appearance as a defendant. The original version of ZPO §39 made explicit its reliance on the normative concept of consent by providing that "tacit agreement [on jurisdiction] shall be assumed"

---

64   514 US 938 (1995).

65   *Idem* 946. Justice Breyer here uses "arbitrability" in the sense of adjudicatory authority.

66   *Arab Republic of Egypt* v. *Southern Pacific Properties, Ltd. & Southern Pacific Properties (Middle East), Ltd.*, 112 *Journal du droit international* 129 (1985) (Cour d'appel de Paris, 12 July 1984) (note B. Goldman 142-158). An English translation of the opinion is found in 23 *Int'l Legal Materials* 1049-1060 (1984). For discussion of the decision, see Fouchard, Gaillard and Goldman, *On International Commercial Arbitration* (ed. E. Gaillard and J. Savage), No. 508, at 292-294 (The Hague, Boston, MA and London, Kluwer Law Int'l., 1999).

67   English translation of *idem* 135-136, 23 *Int'l Legal Materials* at 1054. The material contained in brackets has been added by the author and does not appear in the French text or the English translation.

when in an oral hearing *(mündliche Verhandlung)*[68] the defendant presents its substantive demands to the court. The original provision was, and its successor still is, found in the Code under the Title "Agreement respecting the Jurisdiction of the Courts".[69] As amended in 1974, ZPO §39 Sentence 1 provides as follows:

> The jurisdiction of a court of first instance shall ... be established by the fact that the defendant, without asserting the lack of jurisdiction, presents to the court in an oral hearing demands respecting the principal matter *[Hauptsache]* ....

Although in terms ZPO §39 covers only subject-matter jurisdiction and venue *(örtliche Zuständigkeit)*, its applicability to jurisdiction to adjudicate in the international sense is universally recognized.[70]

ZPO §39 applies in the first-instance courts provided by the German system for civil and commercial matters: the Local Courts *(Amtsgerichte)* and the District Courts *(Landgerichte)*.[71] The *Amtsgerichte*, where proceedings are handled by single judges are largely charged with relatively small claims and has no appellate function.[72] The *Landgerichte*, which are far less numerous than the *Amtsgerichte*, handle the more important claims and serve both well as courts of first instance and as appellate courts.[73] Proceedings take place, depending upon a variety of considerations, before one or three judges.[74]

---

68   For a discussion of German civil procedure in first instance, and comparison with American first-instance procedure, see B. Kaplan, A. von Mehren, and R. Schaefer, "Phases of German Civil Procedure, Parts I & II", 71 *Harv. Law Rev.* 1193-1268, 1443-1473 (1958). The concept of *mündliche Verhandlung* is discussed in Part I at 1221-1232.

69   This Title also contains §38, which regulates party stipulations regarding jurisdiction. See D. 2. *(c)* (ii), pp. 220 *et seq., infra.*

70   See, e.g., H. Schack, *Internationales Zivilverfahrensrecht*, at 173, No. 485 (Munich, C. H. Beck, 4th ed., 2006). For a discussion of the ZPO's failure here and elsewhere to address the differences between venue and jurisdiction to adjudicate in the international sense, see Chap. II. D. 2. *(b)*, pp. 65 *et seq., supra.*

71   See for a detailed account of the German judicial system Murray and Stürner, *supra* footnote 17, at 47-65.

72   See §23 of the Law on the Organization of Courts *(Gerichtsverfassungsgesetz – GVG)*.

73   GVG §§71, 72.

74   Prior to 2002, most of the cases pending at the *Landgerichte* were handled by a panel of three judges *(Zivilkammer)*. However, with the coming into force of the reform law of 2001 this has been changed. Now, ZPO §348 (1) Sentence1 provides that cases pending at the *Landgerichte* will always be decided by a single judge *(Originärer Einzelrichter)*. According to ZPO §348 (1) Sentence 2 Nos. 1 and 2 a panel of three judges will hear the case only (1) if the single judge is a probationary judge *(Richter auf Probe)* who does not have at least one year of experience in civil cases and (2) if the case belongs to one of the categories enumerated in ZPO §348 (1) Sentence 2 No. 2 a) to k). However, even in these two cases ZPO §348a (1) allows for decision

Reflecting the informal quality of the *Amtsgericht* procedure and the right of parties to represent themselves §39 Sentence 2 provides that failure to assert the lack of jurisdiction will not establish jurisdiction if the court has not given the notice required under ZPO §504. ZPO §504 provides that

> [i]n the event that the *Amtsgericht* lacks subject-matter jurisdiction or venue [or by extension, adjudicatory jurisdiction in the international sense], it shall so advise the defendant before hearing the principal matter and point out the consequences of pleading to the principal matter without objection.

Since the court must point out the consequences of proceeding on the merits without objection, a defendant can hardly fail through inadvertence to challenge the court's adjudicatory authority.

The notification requirement of ZPO §504 does *not* extend to *Landgericht* proceedings. There, parties must be represented by an attorney[75] and it is assumed that counsels know the law. This may be an appropriate assumption for issues of subject-matter jurisdiction and venue, which arise in many cases, but not for jurisdiction to adjudicate in the international sense, which arises relatively infrequently and can be *terra incognita* even for seasoned attorneys.[76]

To obtain the benefit of ZPO §39, the defendant need not limit itself to a challenge of the court's adjudicatory authority without raising objections on the merits. Accordingly, the defendant may plead subsidiarily on the merits *(hilfsweises Vorbringen)* so long as the lack, in principle, of jurisdiction is also asserted.[77]

(d)   The Brussels Convention and Regulation

Since all the legal orders party to the Brussels instruments are familiar with the concept and practice of basing adjudicatory authority on a party's participation in litigation as a defendant,[78] it is no surprise that the Convention addresses the issue. Article 18 of the Convention provides:

---

by a single judge (*Obligatorischer Einzelrichter*) provided that the case neither raises factual nor legal difficulties nor an issue of fundamental significance. As a result, the reform law has led to more first instance decisions by single judges. See for a detailed discussion of the latest reform of civil procedure G. Rühl, Preparing Germany for the 21st century: The Reform of the Code of Civil Procedure, 6 *German Law Journal* 909-912 (2005).

75   ZPO §78 (1) Sentence 1.

76   See Schack, *supra* footnote 70, at 173, No. 485.

77   See, e.g., *Münchener Kommentar zur Zivilprozeßordnung* (-Patzina), *supra* footnote 17, §39, No. 6; S. Schulte-Beckhausen, *Internationale Zuständigkeit durch rügelose Einlassung im europäischen Zivilprozeßrecht*, at 208, footnote 225 (Bielefeld, Gieseking, 1994); Zöller (-Vollkommer), *supra* footnote 17, Vor §39, No. 5.

78   *Idem* 41-64.

Apart from jurisdiction derived from other provisions of this Convention, a court of a Contracting State before which a defendant enters an appearance shall have jurisdiction. This rule shall not apply where appearance was entered solely to contest the jurisdiction, or where another court has exclusive jurisdiction by virtue of Article 16.

The word "solely" in the English text and the corresponding words *"nur"*, *"solo"*, and *"uitsluitend"* in the German, Italian and Dutch texts in conjunction with the French text which omitted "solely" created uncertainty as to whether defendants could challenge the court's jurisdiction while concurrently defending on the merits.[79] The European Court of Justice in *Elefanten Schuh GmbH* v. *Jacqmain* held that the French text best expressed the *telos* of the Convention.[80] According to the Court, a defendant meets the requirements of Article 18 even where he does not "solely" contest jurisdiction but defends as well on the merits of the claim, provided that the challenge to jurisdiction is made no later than is the first defense on substance. The Brussels Regulation of 2002 has resolved the issue by omitting the word "solely" in Article 24, which differs only in technical details from Article 18 of the Convention.

For purposes of Article 18 of the Brussels Convention and Article 24 of the Brussels Regulation, nothing turns on whether professional legal representation was required for the proceedings. Some German scholars have argued that ZPO §39 Sentence 2 and §504 apply to proceedings before German courts in which jurisdiction turns on Article 18 or Article 24.[81] The majority – and presumably correct – view is that the application of national provisions relating to jurisdictional issues is excluded.[82] Thus, defendants in *Amtsgericht* or comparable proceedings are in a less favorable position, jurisdictionally speaking, under the Brussels system than they would be were national law taken into account.

---

79   For further details and references regarding the debate see O. Sandrock, "Die Prorogation der internationalen Zuständigkeit eines Gerichts durch hilfsweise Sacheinlassung des Beklagten", 78 *ZVglRWiss* 177-220 (1979); Schulte-Beckhausen, *supra* footnote 77, at 206-219.

80   Case C-150/80 – [1981] ECR 1671.

81   See, e.g., *Münchener Kommentar zur Zivilprozeßordnung* (-Patzina), *supra* footnote 17, §39, No. 15.

82   See J. Kropholler, *Europäisches Zivilprozeßrecht*, Art. 24, No. 5 (Frankfurt am Main, Verlag Recht und Wirtschaft, 8th ed., 2005); Schulte-Beckhausen, *supra* footnote 77, at 227-229; Peter F. Schlosser, *EU-Zivilprozessrecht*, Art. 18, No. 1 (Munich, C. H. Beck, 2nd ed., 2003).

3.   *Participation in the Role of Plaintiff*

(a)   American theory and practice

(i)   *The traditional position*

Long before the changes in procedural theory and practice that underpin contemporary American views on "splitting" and on the dimensions of "cause of action" had taken place,[83] an American view respecting the jurisdictional consequences of assuming the role of plaintiff was well established. Under common-law and Field-Code pleading alike, such participation established an independent ground of general jurisdiction over plaintiffs. In 1938, in retrospect a watershed year for American procedural theory and practice, Justice Stone wrote in *Adam v. Saenger*[84] that

> [t]he plaintiff having, by his voluntary act of demanding justice from the defendant, submitted himself to the jurisdiction of the court, there is nothing arbitrary or unreasonable in treating him as being there for all purposes for which justice to the defendant requires his presence. It is the price which the state may exact as the condition of opening its courts to the plaintiff ....[85]

The claim made in *Adam* by the defendant against the plaintiff arose from the same controversy as the claim brought by the plaintiff. Nothing in the opinion's analysis turned on this circumstance, however. The holding relies on the normative principle of doing "justice to the defendant". The Restatement First of Conflicts of Laws,[86] promulgated some five years after the *Adam* decision, reaches the same result; however, its Section 83, Jurisdiction over Plaintiff, reasons essentially in power-theory terms:

> A plaintiff by bringing an action in a state subjects himself to the jurisdiction of the state as to the claims sued upon, and, if the law of the state so provides at the time the plaintiff brings his action, as to any set-off, counter-claim or cross-action brought against him by the defendant during the pendency of the first action.

The rule of *Adam v. Saenger* was appropriate so long as American procedural theory and practice were shaped by the common law and the Field Code:

> [U]nder older concepts of territorial jurisdiction, a state court's territorial jurisdiction generally extended only to persons physically within its boundaries ... . Accordingly, non-residents could be subjected to jurisdiction only if they happened to come within the state. Even then, non-residents were generally accorded immunity from

---

83   See pp. 178 *et seq., supra.*

84   303 US 59 (1938), *reh. denied*, 303 US 666 (1938).

85   *Idem* 67-68.

86   St. Paul, Minn., American Law Institute Publishers, 1943.

service of process while coming, going, and being in attendance at court,[87] an immunity extended precisely for the purposes of inducing the attendance that the state could not compel.

The rule of immunity was qualified, however, by the rule that a non-resident plaintiff could be subjected to a counter-action in litigation he had begun. As originally formulated, the proposition was that the plaintiff, by bringing the action, submitted himself to the jurisdiction of the court for 'all purposes for which justice to the defendant requires his presence'. Adam v. Saenger …. This formulation … can best be understood by reference to its original procedural context. When the rule evolved in the 19th century, the scope of permissible counterclaims was very narrow and the rules of permissive joinder of parties similarly narrow. As a result, the plaintiff's submission to the court subjected him only to claims by the defendant and, of those, only ones that arose out of the transaction sued on or which were assertable as set-offs, those being prevalent procedural limitations on counterclaim.[88]

(ii)   The present standing of the rule in Adam v. Saenger
a.   The Restatements Second of Conflict of Laws and of Judgments

Despite the general acceptance of the functional or instrumental approach to conflict of laws that had, by the late 1960s, brought about a "revolution" in American thinking and practice in the field of private international law, the Restatement Second of Conflict of Laws accepted the traditional formula and solution regarding the jurisdictional consequences of appearing as a plaintiff. The Restaters did not discuss the appropriateness of the rule of *Adam* v. *Saenger* for procedural regimes whose practices are shaped not by the common law or the Field Code but by the Federal Rules of Civil Pro-cedure. Section 34, Appearance as a Plaintiff, of the Restatement Second of Conflict of Laws (1969) flatly states that:

> A state has power to exercise judicial jurisdiction [in any of its courts] over an individual who brings an action in the state in that action and, to the extent that local law of the state so provides at the time of the bringing of the action, in any action which the defendant may bring against him by way of counterclaim or independent cross-action.

The "rationale" offered is simply that

> [t]he plaintiff brings the action and determines the locale of the suit. It is not unreasonable that the plaintiff should be subject to a wider range of jurisdiction than a defendant who makes a general appearance.[89]

---

87   Differing views are held of the appropriate scope of the immunity from service of process while present in the state in connection with on-going litigation. See *Northern Light Technology, Inc.* v. *Northern Lights Club*, 236 F. 3d 57 (1st Cir. 2001).

88   Restatement Second of Judgments §9. Jurisdiction over Litigants concerning Other Claims, Comment *a, Rationale*, at 92.

89   Restatement Second of Conflict of Laws, Comment *a, Rationale*, §34, at 139.

The Restatement Second of Judgments, promulgated in 1980, explores the issue whether, given the changes in procedural rules and practices that the Federal Rules of Civil Procedure initiated in 1938, the *Adam* rule was still appropriate. The Judgments Restaters took the position that Section 34 of the Restatement of Conflict of Laws is "both too broad and too narrow".[90] On the one hand, Section 34 now operated in too permissive a fashion; a defendant is allowed to

> assert any claim he has against a plaintiff, whether related to the original transaction or not. He may join additional parties in such a counter-claim, thus adding persons potentially having still more remote claims against the plaintiff. A defendant may implead third parties, and third parties may in many instances intervene; these additional parties in turn have opportunity to assert new claims and counterclaims. Thus, given modern joinder rules, the theory of submission to jurisdiction would subject the plaintiff to claims quite unrelated to the transaction upon which he had brought suit.[91]

On the other hand, §34 is too restrictive in certain circumstances:

> In origin the rule applied only to the specific court in which the party appeared and did not authorize exercise of jurisdiction by another court. Hence, it did not encompass the situation where the counter-action could not be maintained as a counterclaim but had to be brought in another tribunal within the state. For example, where law and equity were separated, a defendant with an equitable cross-action arising from the transaction could not counterclaim in a common law action by a plaintiff; he had to bring an independent suit. The concept of submission to the jurisdiction of the court by its very terms did not include such a situation, but the rule was expanded to hold that a party to litigation in one 'side' of the court was subject to jurisdiction in its other side ...[92]

The Restatement Second of Judgments abandons the approach of Section 34 and addresses "the problem of jurisdiction over a litigant through the principle of pro-

---

90   Restatement Second of Judgments §9, Comment *a*, *Rationale*, at 93.
91   *Ibid.*
92   *Ibid.*
      Restatement Second of Judgments faults Section 34 on yet another ground. The section "does not refer to claims against defendants"; accordingly, the jurisdictional effects of a defendant's claim against the initial plaintiff do not extend beyond the cause of action initiated by the defendant to include other causes of action arising out of the same transaction or controversy. Restatement Second of Judgments, §9, Comment *a*, *Rationale*, at 94. Thus, a defendant that assumes the role of plaintiff enjoys a greater degree of jurisdictional protection than does an initial plaintiff.

cedural fairness and convenience that finds expression in the 'minimum contacts' rule":[93]

> [T]he relevant question is not simply whether a party has submitted to the jurisdiction of the court. It is whether the additional claim being interjected into the controversy is so related to the original controversy that it ought to be entertained at the same time. When applicable procedure permits the additional claim to be asserted in the original action, for example by counterclaim or through a third party's intervention, the pending action is enlarged. When procedural limitations or limitations on the competency of the court foreclose that possibility, the additional claim may be asserted in whatever is the appropriate coordinate tribunal. In either event, the premise is that the original action is properly located under the rules of territorial jurisdiction. The problem then is essentially whether the additional claim is sufficiently related to the original action that it has a 'reasonable relationship' to the forum state ... . If the claim lacks such a connection, then it ought to be maintained only when an independent basis of territorial jurisdiction exists with respect to it.[94]
>
> [The aforesaid] ... applies to all parties, plaintiff, defendant, and parties who intervene or are brought in as third parties. It deals with the effect of being a party on becoming amenable to jurisdiction regarding another claim. It does not exclude the possibility that a party might be independently subject to jurisdiction regarding such a claim.[95]

Restatement Second of Judgments thus limits the jurisdictional consequences of participating in the role of the plaintiff to a form of specific jurisdiction. Its Section 9, Jurisdiction over Litigants concerning Other Claims, provides that:

> A court may exercise jurisdiction over a person who is a party to a pending action in that or another court of the state in which the court is located when the claim involved arose out of the transaction that is the subject of the pending action or is one that may in fairness be determined concurrently with that action.

Under Section 9,

> [i]f the newly inserted claim is neither related to the transaction that was the subject of the original suit nor one that ought to be heard as an offset, the court may not properly exercise jurisdiction over the new claim simply because the person against whom it is asserted is a party to the action.[96]

When the additional claim does not arise out of the same transaction as the original claim but is "only secondarily related" to that transaction, it is "a question of

---

93   *Idem*, 94.

94   *Ibid.*

95   *Idem*, Comment *b*, *Scope*, 94-95.

96   *Idem*, Comment *c*, *Relationship between claims*, to §9, 96.

degree and circumstance" whether the connection is sufficient to ground jurisdiction under the standard of the Restatement's Section 24 (2):

> [Are] the facts ... related in time, space, origin, or motivation, ... [do] they form a convenient trial unit, and ... [does] their treatment as a unit conform[] to the parties' expectations or business understanding or usage?

When the claims are for money, and accordingly may be offset, it may well be appropriate to allow the parties to settle accounts between them. Taking into account the "purposes of justice", a court may, however, "decline to entertain ... offsetting claims .... [For example, the defendant would be denied permission to claim an offset that would give him] an unwarranted preference among creditors of the plaintiff."[97]

From the promulgation in 1980 of the Restatement Second of Judgments until the revision of 1988 of the Restatement Second of Conflict of Laws, the positions of these Restatements were in tension on the jurisdictional consequences of appearing before a court as a plaintiff. The Judgment Restatement's analysis was more consistent with the interest-based teleological approach that characterized American conflict-of-laws thinking in the second half of the twentieth century. On the other hand, the Restatement of Conflict of Laws, itself profoundly influenced by interest analysis, accepted the rule of *Adam v. Saenger*.

The 1988 Revision of the Restatement Second of Conflict of Laws adopted the approach of the Judgments Restatement. Section 34, Appearance as a Plaintiff, was revised "to conform with Section 9 of the Restatement Second of Judgments":[98]

> A state has power to exercise judicial jurisdiction over an individual who brings an action in the state with respect to a claim that arises out of the transaction which is the subject of the action or is one that may in fairness be determined concurrently with that action.

b.   Is the rule in *Adam v. Saenger* still constitutional?

The Restatement Second of Conflict of Laws, as originally promulgated, viewed the rule in *Adam v. Saenger* as clearly constitutional. The Revision of 1988 and the Restatement Second of Judgments leave the issue open. The Restaters of Judgments remark that

> [i]t may be that the Constitutional limitations on a state's territorial jurisdiction do not prevent a state from exercising so broad an authority, although the leading case, Adam v. Saenger ... does not on its facts or in its language so suggest ... .[99]

---

97   *Idem*, 96.

98   Restatement Second of Conflict of Laws (1988 Revision), Reporter's Note, at 44.

99   Restatement Second of Judgments, Comment *a, Rationale*, at 93.

The 1988 Revision of the Restatement Second of Conflict of Laws is somewhat less reserved:

> The Constitution may afford a State of the United States an even wider scope of jurisdiction ... [and permit a State to] exercise judicial jurisdiction over a plaintiff with respect to any claim that can be asserted against him by the defendant or by a third party regardless of its relation to the original action ... .[100]

International Shoe clearly supports a "reasonableness" limitation that allows for taking specific, but not general, jurisdiction over plaintiffs. On the other hand, if accepted by the Supreme Court, the long-standing practice criterion of *Burnham* – which postdates the Restatements – might support the claim of general jurisdiction[101] as does the strong policy against "splitting" and the broad dimensions of "cause of action" that have flowed from the philosophy and pleading practices that inform the Federal Rules of Civil Procedure. Despite fundamental changes that have occurred in neighbouring areas of American law, *Adam* v. *Saenger*'s claim of general jurisdiction over plaintiffs is perhaps a constitutional, though not the preferable, rule; the jurisdiction claimed may be seen as resting on a powerful normative proposition: if you ask for justice from an adjudicator, you must accept that he is also appropriate to render justice to those who seek justice from you.[102]

Practical constraints and litigation considerations may well render these speculations idle; in practice only rarely is a counterclaim made that is entirely unrelated to the transaction or occurrence with respect to which the plaintiff is suing. The worst-case scenario that the Restaters of Judgments feared[103] apparently happens only infrequently, if at all. Were there a practical reason for resolving these theoretical issues, presumably they would have long since been addressed by both theory and practice.

(b)   German theory and practice
(i)   Introductory

As will appear, contemporary German law regarding the measure of adjudicatory authority to which the initiator of litigation is subject developed in the course of a long history during which positions were taken comparable to those today advanced, respectively, by the Restatement Second of Conflicts and the Restatement Second of Judgments.

Here, as in many other areas, contemporary German theory and practice has been shaped by Germanic law, on the one hand, and Roman law, on the other. In 476 Odovakar deposed Romulus Augustulus; the disintegration of the Roman

---

100   Restatement Second of Conflict of Laws (1988 Revision), Comment *a*, *Rationale and scope of jurisdiction*, at 42-43.

101   See Chap. III. A. 6., pp. 107 *et seq.*, *supra*.

102   See the discussion of similar concepts in German law, pp. 201-202, *infra*.

103   See the quotation from Restatement Second of Judgments, p. 197, *supra*.

Empire in the West was complete. With the disappearance of the political and cultural force that had created and maintained legal and political unity, the Roman courts and administrators vanished and Roman law was, in large measure, replaced by various less developed forms of Germanic law.

The Roman law that so largely disappeared in the West, continued in the Eastern Empire with its capital at Constantinople. It was there, more than a half century after the fall of the Western Empire, that the Emperor Justinian ordered in 528 the preparation of a compilation, systematization, and consolidation of Roman law that came to be known as the *Corpus juris civilis*.[104]

Justinian's *Corpus juris* came to western Europe in 544 when the Eastern Empire reconquered Italy. But it was not to become important for the development of law in the West until five centuries later. The elements of Roman law that survived during this period were those that persisted in memory or as custom and habit. The Church preserved in its law and culture much of Roman civilization. The system of personal laws that prevailed in the Germanic kingdoms subjected the Roman element of the population to Roman law, but that law was obscure and corrupted.

In the late eleventh century, the West's rediscovery of the *Corpus juris* started with Irnerius's lectures at Bologna. Thus began for Western Europe the study of the *Corpus juris* as a coherent, systematic body of law. On the continent of Europe, the universities soon became the growing point of law. The scholar's concern for structure and coherence led to the *Corpus juris* being viewed as a source of legal principles. Four centuries later, the Roman law, developed in the universities, was received by the Germanic courts *in complexu*, in its totality, by a *Reichskammergerichtsordnung* of 1495.

Although prior to the reign of Justinian (527-565), the plaintiff's bringing an action had no jurisdictional consequence for claims against him,[105] Justinian took the view that all claims related to the original controversy should be considered together in order to achieve a comprehensive resolution of the dispute. Accordingly, the defendant could seize the court of counterclaims arising out of the controversy that was the subject of the pending action:[106] on the other hand,

---

104   Officially promulgated between 533 and 534, the *Corpus juris* comprises the Institutes (a systematic treatise intended for the use of law students), the Digest (a compilation, systematization, and consolidation of the writings of the great Roman jurists, revised to reflect the current law), the Code (a collection of imperial enactments up to 534), and the Novels (an unofficial collection of post-534 imperial enactments that was later included in the *Corpus juris*).

105   See J. von Planck, *Die Mehrheit der Rechtsstreitigkeiten im Prozessrecht* 80 (Göttingen, Dieterich, 1844).

106   See Cod. Book 7, Title 45, No. 14:

As that distinguished man, Papinian, very properly stated in his book of Questions, that a judge could not only discharge the defendant from liability, but could [also] render a decision against the plaintiff himself, if, ... he should find that ... [the plaintiff] was indebted to the defendant. We also order this rule to be extended so that the judge may be permitted to render a decision against the plaintiff, and require him to either pay or

counterclaims entirely unrelated to the transaction sued upon by the plaintiff could only be brought if the defendant established an independent basis of adjudicatory jurisdiction.[107] The jurisdictional consequences of participating in the role of plaintiff were thus limited to a form of specific jurisdiction. Later in his long reign, Justinian gave greater weight to comprehensive dispute-resolution. He made all counterclaims compulsory, regardless of connexity, while the plaintiff's action was pending.[108]

Under medieval Germanic law, one who participated in litigation subjected himself to the court's general jurisdiction.[109] According to the Mirror of Saxon Law *(Sachsenspiegel)*, a systematic collection of legal rules and principles compiled by Eike von Repgau (1180-1235) in the thirteenth century,[110] the defendant could bring even entirely unrelated counterclaims without having to show an independent basis of jurisdiction.[111] In contrast with Roman law, the rules of Germanic law respecting jurisdiction for counterclaims were not primarily intended to achieve comprehensive dispute resolution. General jurisdiction over the plaintiff rested, instead, on a notion of procedural fairness: where you seek justice you must also be prepared to render justice.[112] Moreover, providing general jurisdiction over plaintiffs would deter, it was thought, the bringing of unfounded actions designed to harass the defendant.[113] In addition to serving procedural fairness,

---

do something without allowing any exception to be pleaded against ... [the judge] on the ground that he is not a competent judge of the plaintiff, for ... [the plaintiff] should not object to have the same judge whom he had accepted in the beginning of the case decide against him at the end.

Translation: S. Scott, *The Civil Law*, Vol. XIV, at 189 (Cincinnati, Ohio, The Central Trust Company, 1932).

107   Justinian's rationale – "[that one cannot object if] the ... judge whom he had accepted ... decide against him" – is arguably broad enough to cover unrelated counter-claims. The edict was not so interpreted, however. See Planck, *supra* footnote 105, at 83-85.

108   See Nov. 96, Chap. 2:

We decree that if anyone should think that another who has sued him is indebted to him, he shall not, in his turn, bring an action against ... [that person] before another judge, but must bring it before the same one who already has cognizance of the case, who shall dispose of both actions .... [A defendant who wishes to bring his action before another judge may] wait until the first action against himself has been decided, and then he can institute proceedings before a different magistrate.

Translation: Scott, *supra* footnote 106, Volume XVI, at 352.

109   See J. Schröder, *Internationale Zuständigkeit* 584 (Opladen, Westdeutscher Verlag, 1971).

110   For a general discussion of the *Sachsenspiegel* see F. Wieacker, *A History of Private Law in Europe* 78-79 (Oxford, University Press, 1995); H. Berman, *Law and Revolution: The Formation of the Western Legal Tradition* 503-505 (Cambridge, MA, Harvard University Press, 1983).

111   Sachsenspiegel, *Landrecht* I 60, 3.

112   See Schröder, *supra* footnote 109, at 583-584.

113   See *Idem* 584.

the Germanic rule took into account the practical difficulties that, at the time, were encountered in conducting cross-border litigation; in light of the difficulty of litigating abroad, parties should at least be able to bring unconnected counter-claims against a foreign party that had seized local courts.[114] This jurisdiction was, however, not always available to foreign defendants.[115]

With the reception *in complexu* of Roman law in Germany during the six-teenth and seventeenth centuries, German jurists came to rely increasingly on a policy of comprehensive dispute-resolution which appeared to have shaped the received rules respecting jurisdiction over counterclaims. In the period imme-diately preceding the drafting of the Code of Civil Procedure (ZPO) of 1877, the practices of the German states differed as to whether jurisdiction over unrelated counterclaims was established by the plaintiff's seizing the court. The majority of the states probably favored recognizing in such cases general jurisdiction over the plaintiff[116].

(ii)   The German Code of Civil Procedure (ZPO)

The ZPO of 1877, rejecting what was perhaps the majority practice at the time, did not recognize the plaintiff's initiation of an action as a ground for exercising general jurisdiction over him. ZPO §33 of the Code provides instead a ground of specific jurisdiction:

> A counterclaim *(Widerklage)* can be filed in the court where the claim *(Klage)* is brought, when the counterclaim is connected with the claim asserted in the com-plaint or with the means of defense produced *(vorgebrachten Verteidigungsmitteln).*
> The foregoing does not apply when, with regard to an action for the counterclaim, a party agreement respecting the jurisdiction of the court is not permitted by §40 (2).[117]

In the view of the drafters of the ZPO,[118] the recognition of general jurisdiction over the plaintiff might well have been justified under the conditions that pre-vailed before the formation of the German Reich. Under the new federal rules of civil procedure, however, it would be much easier than before to seek justice from someone domiciled in another part of Germany; accordingly, such broad

---

114   See Planck, *supra* footnote 105, at 353.

115   See *Idem* 353-354.

116 See Schröder, *supra* footnote 109, at 584.

117   ZPO §40 (2) is discussed on p. 224. Paragraph 2 denies effect to party agreements respecting jurisdiction when an exclusive jurisdiction is provided for the counter-claim.

118   See C. Hahn (continued by B. Mugdan), *Die gesammten Materialien zu den Reichs-Justizgesetzen*, Vol. II/1, 158 (Berlin, R. v. Decker's Verlag, 2nd ed., 1881).

adjudicatory authority[119] over the plaintiff would not be needed.[120] The drafters of the ZPO further argued that the oral character of the trial under the federalized procedural rules that the ZPO introduced, supported specific, but not general, jurisdiction. As distinguished from written proceedings used in the past by some States, allowing the defendant in oral trial proceedings to make claims entirely unrelated to the pending action could easily lead to a troubling confusion in the proceedings *(bedenkliche Verwirrung des Verfahrens)*.[121] This argument seems, in light of what orality came to mean in practice, little more than an unconvincing make-weight.

The application of ZPO §33 has not given rise to problems in practice so far as jurisdiction to adjudicate is concerned. It is almost universally accepted that the provision only applies to counterclaims brought by the initial defendant.[122] Third parties wishing to make a counterclaim against the plaintiff have to establish an independent basis of jurisdiction. The most controversial jurisdictional issue is whether the section applies to offset *(Aufrechnung)*, a problem considered below in the context of the Brussels Regulation.[123] Considerable disagreement also exists as to whether ZPO §33, apart from providing a basis of specific jurisdiction, establishes a general requirement for counterclaims to be connected with the original claim. Although some older cases appear to require some connection in all case,[124] the currently prevailing view of the commentators is that no such connection is required if the counterclaim does not rely on ZPO §33.[125] As a result, the defendant is not precluded to bring an unrelated counterclaim if an independent basis of jurisdiction exists. For present purposes, discussion of this problem is unnecessary.

---

119 In discussing adjudicatory authority for purposes of §33 and related provisions, the drafters of the ZPO did not distinguish between venue and adjudicatory authority in the international sense. See Chap. II. D. 2. *(b)* (i), pp. 65 *et seq., supra* see also BGH, 20 May 1981, 34 *NJW* 2642 (1981).

120 See K. Otte, *Umfassende Streitentscheidung durch Beachtung von Sachzusammenhängen* 593 (Tübingen, Mohr Siebeck, 1998).

121 See Hahn, *supra* footnote 118, at 158.

122 See, e.g., BGH, *supra* footnote 119.

123 See pp. 204-207, *infra*.

124 See, e.g., BGH, 12 February 1981, 34 *NJW* 1217 (1981); W. Eickhoff, *Inländische Gerichtsbarkeit und internationale Zuständigkeit für Aufrechnung und Widerklage* 33-34 (Berlin, Duncker & Humblot, 1985).

125 Baumbach, Lauterbach, Albers and Hartmann, *Kommentar zur Zivilprozeßordnung* (Munich, C. H. Beck, 64th ed., 2006), §33, No. 1; *Münchener Kommentar zur Zivilprozeßordnung* (-Patzina), *supra* footnote 17, §33, No. 2; Thomas and Putzo (-Putzo), *Zivilprozessordnung* (Munich, C. H. Beck, 27th ed., 2005), §33, No. 1; Zöller (-Vollkommer), *supra* footnote 17, Vor §33, No. 1. See also Murray and Stürner, *supra* footnote 17, at 234.

(c)   The Brussels Convention and Regulation

The Brussels Convention contains a provision dealing with counterclaims that has survived essentially unchanged the conversion of the Convention into a Regulation. Article 6 No. 3 of both the Convention and the Regulation provides a ground of specific jurisdiction:

> A person domiciled in a Member State may also be sued:
>
> ...
>
> 3.   on a counter-claim arising from the same contract or facts on which the original claim was based, in the court in which the original claim is pending[]."

The difference between this provision and ZPO §33, discussed above, is clear: the ZPO draws on a general – and broader – concept of connection between the original claim and the counterclaim;[126] Article 6 No. 3 of Brussels requires that the counterclaim arises "from the same contract or facts on which the original claim was based". The Jenard Report on the Brussels Convention explains the considerations that led to the more restrictive formulation of Article 6 No. 3:

> It has been made clear that in order to establish this jurisdiction the counterclaim must be related to the original claim. Since the concept of related actions is not recognized in all the legal systems, the provision in question, following the draft Belgian Judicial Code, states that the counterclaim must arise from the contract or from the facts on which the original claim was based.[127]

The language used by the Brussels Convention did not provide in all cases a clear answer as to when a counterclaim is related to the original claim: when do a claim and a counterclaim arise from the same facts for the purposes of Article 6 No. 3?[128] Answering this question has been further complicated by the fact that the concept of related actions, rejected by the drafters, plays an important role in other provisions contained in the Brussels instruments. The Section dealing with "*lis pendens* – related actions" defines the term "related actions". Article 28 (3) of the Regulation, Article 22 (3) of the Convention, provides that:

> For the purposes of this Article, actions are deemed to be related where they are so closely connected that it is expedient to hear and determine them together to avoid the risk of irreconcilable judgments resulting from separate proceedings.

---

126   S. Leible, in T. Rauscher (ed.), *Europäisches Zivilprozeßrecht*, Vol. 1 (Munich, Sellier, 2nd ed. 2006), Art. 6 Brüssel I-VO, No. 26; Thomas and Putzo (-Hüßtege), *supra* footnote 125, Art. 6, No.5.

127   Report by Mr. P. Jenard on the Convention of 27 September 1968 on jurisdiction and the enforcement of judgments in civil and commercial matters, [1979] OJ C 59, 1, at 28.

128   For a discussion of this issue, see Otte, *supra* footnote 120, at 643-648.

In light of this definition, some are tempted to interpret Article 6 No. 3 in the same way. In 1993, a Danish appeal court, facing the issue, referred to the European Court of Justice the question whether the language in the Convention's Article 6 No. 3 was more restrictive than the expression "related actions" in the third paragraph of its Article 22.[129]

The Court found it unnecessary to answer the question in view of its reply to another question referred to it by the Danish court at the same time;[130] however, Advocate General Léger discussed the issue briefly. He expressed the view that Article 6 No. 3 and Article 22 (3) address two distinct procedural situations and, accordingly, should not to be construed in the same way. Article 22 (3), is not contained in Section 2 on "Special jurisdiction" but in Section 9 "Lis pendens – related actions". Moreover, the definition in Article 22 of "related actions" was "[f]or the purposes of this Article" – which suggests it is irrelevant for the interpretation of other provisions. The Advocate General also noted that Article 22, unlike Article 6 No. 3, did not confer jurisdiction, but simply stated what was to be done in the event of related actions pending before different courts.

The Advocate General's inclination to apply Article 6 No. 3 more restrictively than Article 22 (3), accords with the predominant view among legal scholars.[131] Some of his arguments, however, seem less powerful under the Regulation of 2002. Its revised provision respecting joint defendants, Article 6 No. 1, and its Article 28 (3), replacing Article 22 (3), now use the same concept of related actions. Since Article 6 (1) confers jurisdiction and is, moreover, systemically very close to Article 6 No. 3, the argument that the definition of related actions provided by the Regulation in Article 28 (3) should be used in interpreting Article 6 No. 3 is plausible, though perhaps not conclusive.

The other question raised by the Danish appeal court in the *Danvaern* case related to the interpretation of the term "counterclaim". The Danish court had asked whether the Convention's Article 6 No. 3 only applied to counterclaims proper or also to offsets. The German *Bundesgerichtshof* had dealt with the issue in the same year. It interpreted the Convention as requiring that an offset be treated as a counterclaim for the purposes of Article 6 No. 3 and held that a connection in the meaning of this provision had to be established between the claim and the claim that was to be used in the offset.[132] For the Danish court, the issue was complicated by the fact that the Danish text of Article 6 No. 3 used a term (*mod-fordringer*), which, under Danish law, covered not only typical counterclaims but also some situations that in other legal systems would be denominated offsets.

The issue is of practical importance primarily in situations where the defendant wants to offset a claim that *(a)* cannot be brought before the court seized on

---

129   *Danvaern Production A/S v. Schuhfabriken Otterbeck GmbH & Co.*, Case C-341/93 [1995] ECR I-2053.

130   This question is discussed on pp. 205 *et seq., infra.*

131   See, e.g., Kropholler, *supra* footnote 82, Art. 6, No. 38. But see Otte, *supra* footnote 120, at 644-646.

132   BGH, 12 May 1993, 44 *NJW* 2753 (1993).

an independent ground of jurisdiction, *(b)* lacks the necessary connection with the original claim pursuant to Article 6 No. 3, and *(c)* whose basis is controversial under the applicable substantive law.[133]

In answering the question asked by the Danish court, the European Court of Justice disagreed with the German *Bundesgerichtshof*. Emphasizing the structural differences between counterclaims, on the one hand, and offsets, on the other, it ruled that Article 6 No. 3

> applies only to claims by defendants which seek the pronouncement of a separate judgment or decree. It does not apply to the situation where a defendant raises, as a pure defense, a claim, which he allegedly has against the plaintiff. The defenses which may be raised and the conditions under which they may be raised are governed by national law.[134]

Accordingly, the Brussels Convention sets no jurisdictional barriers to using a claim as an offset; when so used, a claim is regarded as a mere defense which – under the Convention – does neither require the kind of connection envisioned in Article 6 No. 3 nor any other independent ground of jurisdiction. However, by leaving the conditions for raising a defense to the national laws of civil procedure the European Court of Justice sparked a new controversy, especially in Germany, that has revolved around the following question: May national laws of civil procedure require an independent basis for jurisdiction for a claim that is to be used as an offset? More specifically, may national laws require a connection such as in Article 6 No. 3? Some German scholars have answered this question in the affirmative and argued that the ruling of the *Bundesgerichtshof* is, in its essence, still consistent with the decision of the European Court of Justice because the German law of civil procedure requires an independent basis of jurisdiction for any claim that is to be used as an offset.[135] And although such basis of jurisdiction – in light of the ruling by the European Court of Justice – could not be found in the provisions of the Convention, recourse could be made to ZPO §33 and its connectedness principle.[136] However, the prevailing view among German commentators is that the national laws may not provide for any such requirement within the scope of application of the Convention.[137] The *Bundesgerichtshof* itself has not ruled on

---

133   See Kropholler, *supra* footnote 82, Art. 6, No. 42; Leible, in Rauscher, *supra* footnote 126, Art. 6 Brüssel I-VO, No. 30.

134   *Danværn Production A/S, supra* footnote 129, at 2077.

135   On this debate see M. Kannengießer, *Die Aufrechnung im internationalen Privat- und Verfahrensrecht* (Tübingen, Mohr Siebeck, 1998), at 144-184; Kropholler, *supra* footnote 82, Art. 6, Nos. 42-45; Leible, in Rauscher, *supra* footnote 126, Art. 6 Brüssel I-VO, Nos. 30-32; Thomas and Putzo (-Hüßtege), *supra* footnote 125, Art. 6, No. 7.

136   See for a detailed account of ZPO §33 *supra* pp. 22 *et seq.*

137   Kropholler, *supra* footnote 82, Art. 6, No. 45; Leible, in Rauscher, *supra* footnote 126, Art. 6 Brüssel I-VO, No. 32; Thomas and Putzo (-Hüßtege), *supra* footnote 125, Art. 6, No. 7.

the question so far. In a 2002 decision the court rather refused to decide the issue because it was not relevant for the case at hand.[138]

D. Party Agreement Respecting the Exercise of Adjudicatory Authority: Prorogation and Derogation

1. *Introductory*

(a) Plan and private autonomy: in general

No polity is so localized or so cosmopolitan – so homogeneous or so heterogeneous – that it can dispense with ordering principles and procedures through which social, political, and economic choices are made and implemented. These principles and procedures vary from epoch to epoch and society to society. Since the industrial revolution, especially in technologically advanced economies, blends or mixtures of central planning and private autonomy have dominated the theory and practice of social and economic ordering. Each principle has its advantages and defects; at least in relatively complex societies, exclusive reliance on either is not encountered.

To the extent that a society accepts private autonomy, decisions are, in principle, to be made by the parties. The premise is that, so long as the integrity of the contracting – or obligation assuming – process is assured, in the overwhelming majority of cases results will be beneficial and socially acceptable. Adherents of the planning principle, on the other hand, entrust decisions to those in charge of the larger group or community whose members are affected. The experience, independence, integrity, and objectivity of the planners ensure that their decisions will be principled and wise. The decisions thus made may directly determine rights and create duties, or, alternatively, concern the procedure or framework within which others are to make decisions respecting these matters.

Ordering occurs as well without direct recourse to either plan or agreement. It may result from planning processes or private agreements to which legal sanction does not attach. "Ethical" or "religious" principles that did not originate from, and cannot be changed by, either authoritative planning or private agreement, may cause parties to fulfill commitments they have made.

Indeed, forms of social ordering lacking governmental sanctions may maintain themselves and operate effectively even when inconsistent with the legalities of a situation. A merchant may refrain from challenging a legally defective arbitral award because to do so would be "incompatible with honour and with the need for trust among businessmen".[139] The very nature of certain areas of life, e.g. family

---

138   BGH, 7 November 2001, 52 *NJW* 2182 (2002). However, in the decision the *Bundesgerichtshof* held that in light of *Danværn Production A/S v. Schuhfabriken Otterbeck GmbH & Co.* it had to accept that Article 6 (3) did not apply to an offset.

139   U. Kornblum, "Grenzfragen des ordre public in der privaten Schiedsgerichtsbarkeit", 29 *KTS* 143, at 145 (1968).

relations, is, moreover, such as to make ordering through contract or plan largely unfeasible.

The fundamental advantage of the planning process is that it can advance social purposes even where these do not coincide with the particular interests of private persons, and can do so in the most direct and efficient manner. The fundamental advantage of private autonomy is that it serves to stimulate the initiative and prudence of those making decisions; it is they who will largely reap the benefits and suffer the harms that result. Moreover, particularly in a complex society, decisions made by those affected may be more likely to meet their needs than are decisions made by planning officials.

As ordering principles, plan and private autonomy have offsetting advantages and disadvantages; no society dispenses entirely with either. Ideological considerations may well, however, prevent a society from striking the optimum balance, in efficiency and instrumental terms, between the two principles.

> [N]o legal technique is an end in itself and none is ideologically neutral. The impact of ideology upon civil procedure [and law in general] depends on the ideological view of the relationship between the individual and society.[140]

All legal orders set limits to the respective ordering roles of plan and of party autonomy. To some extent, these reflect the particular legal order's degree of commitment to each principle. Where the substantive results reached through the operations of one ordering process are poor or the process itself is seen as seriously defective, it may be displaced, in whole or in part, by the competing ordering principle.

Objections on grounds of illegality or immorality to ordering rest not on the quality of the ordering process but on either the inappropriateness of the ordering's purpose (e.g., contracts for sexual relations) or on the improper effects that the ordering has on the interests of third parties (e.g., a contract to transport stolen goods). In the latter part of the twentieth century, policies designed to protect economically weaker parties (e.g., consumers and employees) – together with the increasing importance widely given to the planning principle (e.g., economic regulations to ensure competition) – have in many societies altered the balance that was struck earlier in the century between plan and private autonomy.

(b) Plan, private autonomy, and dispute resolution

Contemporary legal orders have through plan developed official dispute-resolution mechanisms. To what extent can private autonomy control the working of this machinery? Can the parties regulate by agreement the identity of, and procedures used by, the adjudicators that are to decide the controversy between them?

---

140 M. Cappelletti and B. Garth, "Introduction – Policies, Trends and Ideas in Civil Procedure", Chap. 1, No. 11 (1987) (ed. M. Cappelletti), XVI *Int. Enc. Comp. L., Civil Procedure* (Tübingen, Mohr Siebeck, and The Hague, Boston, MA, and London, Martinus Nijhoff).

The spectrum of possibilities runs from *(a)* party agreements that substitute a private dispute-resolution process – arbitration in particular – for official courts, through *(b)* party stipulations for exclusive jurisdiction of the courts of one legal order to *(c)* agreements that allow for party choice among the courts of several States and exclude the courts of other States from exercising adjudicatory authority.

In general, societies strongly committed to the planning principle accord less importance to private autonomy than do "liberal" societies. Although civil- and common-law legal systems, along with socialist systems,

> have recognized the interest of the state in certain types of private disputes, such as those involving personal status and domestic relations questions, labor disputes, antitrust actions, and proceedings for the defense of civil liberties[][, t]he tradition in the WEST ... has been to regard civil procedure as part of the private domain outside of the concern of the state. Criminal law, in contrast, is entrusted to the state and public enforcement machinery. In the SOCIALIST countries the concept of 'public interest and welfare' requires courts regularly to consider of paramount importance the effects of proceedings on third parties, the community, and the state. While the difference may increasingly be only one of degree, the procedural systems of the WESTERN countries have retained certain common characteristics which contrast [as of 1986] dramatically with the principles shared by the EAST EUROPEAN countries.[141]

Private autonomy's role in the ordering of civil procedure in legal systems that follow the western European model rests on the principle of party disposition, the *Dispositionsmaxime*.[142] This principle contains several subsidiary propositions: *(a)* generally speaking, a court cannot institute a proceeding *ex officio*; *(b)* claims, defenses, and counterclaims are to be asserted by the parties; *(c)* the court's judgment does not address issues that the parties have not raised nor accord relief that they have not requested; *(d)* in principle, only the parties can settle a case; and *(e)* only a party can challenge a judgment.[143]

In polities where plan rather than private autonomy is the preferred method of ordering the economy and society, these propositions are not accepted; the parties have, as well, relatively little control over the identity of, and the procedures used by, the adjudicating authority. Before the collapse of the Soviet Union, the socialist systems of Eastern Europe gave, for example, the State Attorney ex-

---

141   *Idem* 12 (citations omitted).

142   See *ibid.* and the literature there cited.

143   See *idem* 13 and the literature there cited.
       Various aspects of the principle of party disposition are discussed in connection with the problem of party control over the preclusive efforts of litigation. See B. 2. (b), pp. 180 *et seq.*, *supra*. In this area of law, the parties' right of disposition is significantly greater in many civil law systems than in common law systems, especially those in the United States.

tensive power to initiate, and to intervene in, civil litigation.[144] "[B]oth the court and the state attorney generally ... [had, moreover,] an affirmative duty to seek out any counterclaims which ... [might] exist between the parties."[145]

Under the procedural codes in force in the Soviet Union prior to its disintegration, plaintiffs were not free to withdraw suits, defendants could not concede, and the parties could not settle if to do so would, in the court's opinion, "violate the law or the rights or legally protected interest of any person".[146] In the Western world, private parties remain largely free to dispose by agreement of contested substantive rights; they are, however, less "free to control the *manner* in which the proceeding will unfold".[147] In continental European countries until well into the nineteenth century "civil procedure was considered ... something which interested only the parties, or, in the German phrase, [was the] *'Sache der Parteien'*".[148] In the latter part of the nineteenth century judicial control over the unfolding of proceedings began to expand. The speed of change varied from legal system to legal system, as did the institutional reasons that were in considerable measure the driving force of change. By the end of the twentieth century, court proceedings had come to be seen as "a matter of public concern ... governed by the requisites of orderly and expeditious judicial administration".[149]

2.   *Prorogation and Derogation*[150]

In the course of the last century, civil- and common-law systems alike have witnessed a decline in party control over the unfolding of the proceedings. In other respects, however, the parties have retained a large measure of control over the working of the dispute-resolution process. They present the case and can withdraw or settle it.

Except where the efficiency and expeditiousness of the unfolding of the case would be prejudiced, or special considerations apply, exercises of private autonomy that affect the operations of official dispute-resolution processes are controlled in considerable measure by the rules and principles that apply to consensual ar-

---

144   See *ibid.*

145   *Idem* 14.

146   *Idem* 17.

147   *Idem* 18.

148   *Idem* 19.

149   *Idem* 18. For an excellent comparative discussion of this development, see *Idem* 18-28.

150   A thoughtful and comparative comparative discussion of the advantages offered – and the difficulties presented – by choice of court agreements, is A. Haines, *Choice of Court Agreements in International Litigation: Their Use and Legal Problems to Which They Give Rise in the Context of the Interim Text [of 2001]*, Permanent Bureau of the Hague Conference, General Affairs, Prel. Doc., No. 18 (February 2002) (English and French texts), Nos 1-26, at 4-17.

rangements generally.[151] These limitations on private autonomy flow *not* from the agreement's procedural consequences but from mandatory rules, applicable to all exercises of party autonomy, designed to prevent, *inter alia*, fraud, overreaching, and parties' failure to understand the commitments they are assuming. Such limitations result from the *telos* not of procedure or dispute resolution but of party autonomy itself. The point is well and clearly expressed by the United States Federal Arbitration Act of 1925, in §2:

> [A] contract to settle by arbitration a controversy thereafter arising ... shall be valid, irrevocable, and enforceable, save upon such grounds as exist at law or in equity for the revocation of any contract.[152]

Some legal orders, including the German, had already taken in the nineteenth century the position that, subject to the general law of contract, exclusive forum-selection agreements were enforceable in principle.[153] Many other legal orders, especially common-law systems, including the federal and state systems in the United States, took the position that was to obtain in the United States until the 1920s:[154] exclusive forum-selection agreements sought to "oust" the courts from their jurisdiction and, as such, were in principle unenforceable.

(a)   Principal issues
(i)   *The significance of the general law of contract for forum-selection clauses*
As already remarked, party agreements respecting adjudicatory authority raise many issues common to contracts generally: Are the mandatory rules, applicable in principle to exercises of party autonomy, satisfied? Were the parties' respective bargaining power so disproportionate that their "agreement" respecting adjudicatory authority is not to be enforced? Is the relevant clause unenforceable because it is in small type and tucked away in a standard-form contract? Is the contract one of adhesion and its forum-selection clauses accordingly unenforceable?

In the course of the nineteenth and twentieth centuries, in every legal order the general law of contract has struggled with these issues. In light of considerations of administrability, efficiency, and relevant economic considerations, on the one hand, and the concern to protect less sophisticated or economically weaker parties, on the other, rules and principles have been proposed that would strike an appropriate balance between party autonomy and mandatory protective rules. Accommodations have evolved over time and have varied from legal order to legal order. They respond as well to political and social changes as to new forms of organization, distribution, and production. The rise of mass markets and

---

151   See *(a) (i)*, pp. 211 *et seq.*, *infra*.
152   9 USC Chap. 1, §2.
153   See *(c)* (ii), pp. 220 *et seq.*, *infra*.
154   See *(c)* (i), pp. 214 *et seq.*, *infra*.

the wide-spread use of standard-form and adhesion contracts that such markets require resulted in new rules and principles of contract law.

As standard-form contracts typically came to incorporate forum-selection clauses, two types of reactions occurred. Many legal orders developed new principles and practices of contract law in an attempt to ensure that party agreement would continue to be a socially acceptable, as well as an economically efficient, ordering principle. Alternatively, the planning principle largely replaced private autonomy and promised both efficiency and social justice.

These developments in general contract law affect how a legal order views – and regulates – forum-selection clauses. We do not here, however, delve deeply into the general law of contract.[155] Our discussion focuses rather on the treatment that the legal order accords forum-selection clauses without giving particular attention to whether similar results are reached under general contract law when other issues, non-procedural in their nature, are regulated by adhesion contracts.

(ii) Can parties by agreement displace or modify official dispute-resolution processes?

We now turn to the particular problems that this sub-chapter addresses. Do party agreements that pass muster under the mandatory rules applicable to contracts in general face an additional hurdle when they seek to displace or modify the official dispute-resolution processes that are in principle available for adjudication of the controversy in question? For example, is an agreement enforceable that provides for arbitration of all disputes that may arise out of, or in connection with, a supply contract between two corporations? Is a forum-selection clause, contained in a sales contract, enforceable even if the transaction and the parties have no connection with the chosen forum? If the parties stipulate that their forum of choice is to have exclusive jurisdiction, will forums that would be competent but for the stipulation decline jurisdiction?

(b) Stipulations for non-exclusive jurisdiction: prorogation clauses

We first consider a basic, but relatively uncontroversial, issue: is a non-exclusive forum-selection clause, by which the parties agree that a matter may be litigated in a forum that would otherwise not have adjudicatory authority but does not preclude proceedings in other forums, enforceable if the agreement satisfies the mandatory rules of the general law of obligation or contract? Since traditionally plaintiffs are taken to submit to jurisdiction by seizing the court and the court's adjudicatory authority over defendants is established by their general appearance, most legal orders had little difficulty in accepting non-exclusive forum-selection clauses including those concluded by the parties *prior* to the arising of the con-

---

155   For a full discussion on a comparative basis of relevant aspects of the general law of contracts see K. Neumeyer, "Contracting Subject to Standard Terms and Conditions", Chap. 12 (1999), VII *Int. Enc. Comp. L.: Contracts in General* (ed. A. von Mehren) (Tübingen, Mohr Siebeck, and Dordrecht, Boston, MA, Lancaster, Martinus Nijhoff).

troversy. Such clauses do not prevent either party, once a controversy arises, from seizing another forum. Moreover, until late in the twentieth century, most procedural laws did not apply *lis pendens* rules internationally;[156] accordingly, prorogation clauses were not formidable weapons except where, as in a *cognovit* note, a party had concurrently both waived notice and the opportunity to be heard and empowered his adversary's attorney to confess judgment in the adversary's favor.[157]

(c)   Stipulations for exclusive jurisdiction: derogation clauses

Exclusive forum-selection clauses are problematic where future disputes are in question.[158] On the one hand, here the arguments of efficiency and commercial utility that support the use of forum-selection clauses are strongest. Enforceable derogation clauses often enable individuals both to plan their economic activities more effectively and to assess more accurately the litigational risks that arise from those activities. At the same time, by displacing official dispute-resolution processes, such clauses deprive economically weaker or less experienced parties of procedural and substantive protection that would otherwise be available to them. They can allow more sophisticated or less scrupulous parties to manipulate the dispute-resolution process to their advantage.

When stipulations for exclusive jurisdictions are enforceable, in practice the issue arises with some frequency as to whether the parties intended that the stipulated forum be exclusive. The parties' failure to make clear their intentions is not always due to inadvertence. They may either fear that interjection of this issue into the negotiations will threaten their deal or not appreciate the significance of the distinction. Where the parties come from legal orders that provide, in the absence of specific agreement on the point, a presumption for or against exclusivity,

---

156   See Chap. VI. D. 1. *(b)*, pp. 292 *et seq.*, *infra*.

157   The Supreme Court of the United States gave effect to a *cognovit* note in an interstate case in *National Equipment Rental, Ltd.* v. *Szukhent*, 375 US 311 (1964). The Court opined that "it is settled ... that parties to a contract may agree in advance to submit to the jurisdiction of a given court, to permit notice to be served by the opposing party, or even to waive notice altogether". *Idem* 315-316.

At least in consumer transactions, today most states of the United States consider use of *cognovit* notes an unfair practice. For a brief survey of the present standing of these notes in the United States, see Weintraub, *supra* footnote 62, at 136-138, §4.5.

158   Stipulations for exclusive jurisdiction over controversies that have already arisen are far less problematic, but relatively rare in practice. When parties conclude a derogation agreement after the controversy has arisen, each is in a position to evaluate the situation and their stipulation can be seen as akin to a settlement agreement. Agreements to arbitrate, entered into after the controversy has arisen, provide the most usual and important example of such stipulations. Long before arbitration agreements concluded *before* a controversy had arisen were enforced, agreements to arbitrate a pending controversy were given effect. See Judge Frank in *Kulukundis Shipping Co., S.A.* v. *Amtorg Trading Corp.*, 126 F. 2d 978, at 982 (2d Cir. 1942).

each may assume that the presumption to which he is accustomed will apply and, therefore, see no need to resolve the issue explicitly.

Article 17 of the Brussels Convention of 1968 addressed the situation by providing that where parties,

> one or more of whom is domiciled in a Contracting State, have agreed that a court or the courts of a Contracting State are to have jurisdiction to settle any disputes which have arisen or which may arise in connection with a particular legal relationship, that court or those courts shall have exclusive jurisdiction .... .

This language was susceptible of the interpretation that every forum-selection clause, even if explicitly qualified, was exclusive. Indeed, the chief draftsman of the Brussels Convention explained in his report that "[t]his solution was required if one wanted to avoid different courts being seized and then rendering contradictory or even entirely different decisions".[159] In 1999, Article 17 was revised by deleting "exclusive" in the first sentence of the first paragraph and adding a new sentence: "Such jurisdiction shall be exclusive unless the parties have agreed otherwise." Article 23, the Brussels Regulation's counterpart to the Convention's Article 17, contains identical language. The Draft Hague Convention on International Jurisdiction and Foreign Judgments in Civil and Commercial Matters, adopted by a Special Commission of the Hague Conference on Private International Law on 30 October 1999, likewise provides that a valid forum-selection clause establishes "exclusive" jurisdiction "unless the parties have agreed otherwise".[160]

Many legal orders in the closing decades of the twentieth century adopted a presumption in favor of exclusivity by statute or case law. At the same time, groups whose claim to protection against exclusivity provisions is strong – in particular, consumers and lower-level employees – were protected by denying effect to such clauses when invoked against them.

(i)   American law

In the early decades of the twentieth century, forum selection – except in the form of arbitration clauses – was little discussed in the United States. The First Restatement of Conflict of Laws (1934) approached the subject in a cautious and ambiguous fashion. The topic was addressed only in comments attached to §617, State Creating Right Cannot Prevent Its Enforcement in Other States, which deals with the entirely different problem of a State's power to require that rights created by its law be enforced only in its courts. Comment a, When access to courts limited by contract between the parties remarks that:

> Parties to a contract may provide that all actions for breach of the contract shall be brought only in a certain court and the courts of other states will usually give effect

---

159 Jenard Report, *supra* footnote 127, at 37.

160 Article 4 of the Interim Text of June 2001 contains the same language. For a careful and comprehensive analysis of Article 4, see Haines, *supra* footnote 150, *passim*.

to such a provision; but the requirement can be imposed only by consent of the parties and as a term of a contract. If the parties agree, it is not like the case of one state prescribing by its statute what the courts of another state may do.

The Restatement Second of Conflict of Laws (1969) faces the problem of forum-selection directly in §80 and endorses, in principle and without distinguishing between prorogation and derogation clauses, the proposition that such clauses should be recognized and enforced unless they are "unfair or unreasonable". Control remains with the courts, however. Section 80, Limitations [on judicial jurisdiction] imposed by contract of parties, states unequivocally that "[t]he parties' agreement as to the place of action cannot oust a state of judicial jurisdiction, but such an agreement will be given effect unless it is unfair or unreasonable".

The *Rationale* provided by the Restaters for §80 is a mixture of *forum non conveniens* law ("the fact that the action is brought in a State other than that designated in the contract affords ground for holding that the forum is an inappropriate one and ... the court in its discretion should refuse to entertain th[e] action"), general contract law ("a provision ... will be disregarded if it is the result of overreaching or the unfair use of general bargaining power"), and procedural considerations (the selection will be disregarded "if the forum chosen by the parties would be a seriously inconvenient one for the trial of a particular action"). The Reporter's Note to §80 indicates that, in the 1950s and 1960s, courts were "reluctant to dismiss an action on the ground that it was brought in a state other than the one selected by the parties in their contract".

In 1972, *The Bremen* v. *Zapata Off-Shore Co.*,[161] a case in admiralty, was decided by the Supreme Court of the United States: relying on *Carbon Black Export, Inc.* v. *The Monrosa*,[162] the District Court and the Court of Appeals had refused enforcement to a forum-selection clause providing that "[a]ny dispute arising [under the towing contract between Zapata, an American corporation, and Unterweser, a German corporation,] must be treated before the London Court of Justice".[163]

Setting aside the judgment below, Chief Justice Burger wrote for the Court as follows:

> The expansion of American business and industry will hardly be encouraged if, notwithstanding solemn contracts, we insist on a parochial concept that all disputes must be resolved under our laws and in our courts. Absent a contract forum, the considerations relied on by the Court of Appeals would be persuasive reasons for holding an American forum convenient in the traditional sense, but in an era of expanding

---

161   407 US 1 (1972).

162   254 F. 2d 297 (5th Cir. 1958), *writ of cert. dismissed as improvidently granted*, 359 US 180 (1959). Justice Harlan, joined by Justices Frankfurter, Whittaker and Stewart dissented. *Idem* 184-186: "Avoidance of decision now on a question bound to recur ... [is] both unsatisfactory and unsound judicial administration." *Idem* 186.

163   407 US at 2.

world trade and commerce, the absolute aspect of the *Carbon Black* case has little place and would be a heavy hand indeed on the future development of international commercial dealings by Americans. We cannot have trade and commerce in world markets and international waters exclusively on our terms, governed by our laws, and resolved in our courts.[164]

The Chief Justice recognized that forum-selection clauses had historically not been favored by American courts. "Although this view ... still has considerable acceptance, other courts are tending to adopt a more hospitable attitude towards forum-selection clauses";[165] "It is the view ... adopted by the Restatement of the Conflict of Laws",[166] "It accords with ancient concepts of freedom of contract ..."[167]

> [T]he courts of England meet the standards of neutrality and long experience in admiralty litigation. The choice of forum was made in an arms-length negotiation by experienced and sophisticated businessmen, and absent some compelling countervailing reason, it should be honored by the parties and enforced by the courts.[168]

The Court vacated the judgment of the Court of Appeals and remanded the case for further proceedings consistent with its opinion.

The *Bremen* decision spurred the acceptance of exclusive-forum clauses not only in federal courts but in the state courts as well.[169] The 1986 revision of §80

---

164   *Idem* 9.

165   *Idem* 9-10.

166   *Idem* 11. In footnote 13, the Opinion cites §80 of the Second Restatement of Conflict of Laws.

167   *Idem* 11.

168   *Idem* 12.

169   An *Erie* issue (see pp. 249 *et seq., infra*) arises with respect to the *Bremen* rule when federal-court jurisdiction rests on the diverse citizenship of the parties. The problem is often by-passed in practice on the premise that the relevant state and federal laws respecting the validity of forum-selection clauses are essentially the same. Cf. *Excell, Inc.* v. *Sterling Boiler and Mechanical, Inc.,* 106 F. 3d 318, at 320 (10th Cir. 1997); *Lambert* v. *Kysar,* 983 F. 2d 1110, at 1116 (1st Cir. 1993) ("[A]s we discern no material discrepancy between Washington state law and federal law, we need [not] confront ... the daunting question whether forum selection clauses are to be treated as substantive or procedural for *Erie* purposes").
The issue whether the *Bremen* rule applies where litigation is before a federal court on the basis of diversity jurisdiction is but one of the several complex problems that arise under *Erie*. For a thoughtful and thorough discussion of the broad problem see A. Stein, "*Erie* and Court Access", 100 *Yale LJ* 1935-2006 (1991). The *Erie* issue that arises when parties stipulate for a particular *official* dispute-resolution process has a counterpart in party stipulations for arbitration, a *private* dispute-resolution process. See E. 3. *(b)* (ii), pp. 249 *et seq., infra.*
Dispute resolution by arbitrators rather than by judges is clearly outcome-determinative. If this characteristic is decisive for *Erie* purposes, where the putatively applicable

of the Second Restatement of Conflict of Laws reflects the increasingly benign attitude of American theory and practice towards such clauses in the wake of the *Bremen* decision. As revised, §80 accepts forum-selection clauses: "The parties' agreement as to the place of the action will be given effect unless it is unfair or unreasonable." The Reporter's Note in principle asserts that "[t]he original black-letter rule is entirely correct. It seems, however, unnecessary to state the obvious fact that the parties cannot by their agreement oust a state of judicial jurisdiction."

The comments to revised §80 do not differ fundamentally from the "blunderbuss" analysis provided by the 1969 comments on the original version of the section. The Restaters' attitude towards the use of forum-selection clauses is, however, now much more supportive than in 1969. Indeed, under *Comment c, Other situations*, to §80

> [t]he burden of persuading the court that[, despite the forum-selection clause,] stay or dismissal of the action would be unfair or unreasonable is upon the party who brought the action.[170]

---

state law differs from the federal law, the former should apply in diversity cases. Of course, to the extent that American arbitration law is federalized – as it now largely is in light of the New York Convention and the *Southland* decision (see E. 3. *(b)* (ii) *d* and E. 4., pp. 254 *et seq.*, *infra*), *Erie* issues vanish.

Where the stipulation is for a judicial forum, the *Erie* problem is more difficult to resolve. As remarked above, in such cases courts usually are content to by-pass the issue where, as is frequently the case, the state and the federal common-law are, for practical purposes, the same.

The federal courts that have faced this *Erie* issue are divided; "[a] clear majority of the circuits has concluded that forum selection clauses are a procedural venue matter to be governed by federal common law". *K & V Scientific Co., Inc. v. Bayerische Motoren Werke Aktiengesellschaft ("BMW")*, 164 F. Supp. 2d 1260, at 1266 (D. New Mexico 2001). "Only the Fourth and the Eighth Circuits currently appear committed to the proposition that the enforceability of forum selection clauses is a substantive matter for purposes of *Erie* to be determined under state law." *Idem* 1267. The District Court chose to follow the majority's lead and to "find[] that federal common law governs the interpretation and enforcement of forum selection clauses in diversity cases". *Idem* 1268.

The judicial analysis to date of the *Erie* problem posed by forum-selection clauses lacks clarity and analytical rigour. Where the applicable law considers exclusive forum-selection clauses unenforceable, the rule is outcome determinative – and hence "substantive" – for *Erie* purposes. To speak – as federal courts do – of the rule being a "procedural venue matter" – *Idem* 1266 – is to resolve the *Erie* issue by using obfuscating jargon. The formula – "procedural venue matter[s]" – neither identifies relevant state and federal interests nor compares and evaluates them. When the Supreme Court eventually faces, as it must, the *Erie* dimensions of the *Bremen* rule, one can hope for a deeper, fuller, and more convincing analysis.

170   The Reporter's Note cites the *Bremen* in support of this allocation of the burden of persuasion.

The 1986 comments discuss various situations in which forum-selection clauses are arguably unfair or unreasonable. These include situations in which mandatory rules of the general law of contract respecting "fraud, duress, the abuse of economic power or other unconscionable means"[171] are violated. Forum-selection clauses are also to be disregarded on some grounds that are not found in general contract law. For example, a clause will be disregarded if "the courts of the chosen state would be closed to the suit or would not handle it effectively or fairly".[172] Here the Restaters have in mind not only cases of what can be seen as adjudicatory authority by necessity ("jurisdiction would be lacking in the chosen state or ... no court in that state would be competent to hear the suit") but also cases where assuming jurisdiction would be clearly inappropriate because there was "good reason to believe that the plaintiff would be dealt with unfairly in the chosen state".[173]

Stipulations are appropriately disregarded as well if they are "so seriously ... inconvenient that to require the plaintiff to bring suit there would be unjust".[174] In applying this test, the Restaters distinguish between cases in which the controversy to be litigated arose *before* the parties had agreed upon the forum and cases in which the forum was selected thereafter. In the latter case, courts generally assume that the parties were aware of the "claimed inconvenience" and selected the forum nonetheless. Even where the forum was stipulated *before* the controversy arose, the agreement should be respected except "in the rare situation where the chosen state would be a seriously inconvenient place for the trial [and proceeding] in the state of the forum would be far more convenient".[175]

The foregoing comments subject forum-selection clauses to standards that do not derive from the general law of contract. The Restaters of 1986 also moved in the opposite direction by relaxing the general contract-law respecting contracts of adhesion where prorogation or derogation clauses are in question.

> Relevant ..., *but not of itself controlling*, would be the fact that the provision was contained in an adhesion, or take-it-or-leave-it, contract whose provisions the party bringing the action was compelled to accept without agreement or discussion.[176]

The general trend in American theory and practice favoring forum selection seen in the evolution of §80 of the Second Restatement of Conflicts is evident as well in

---

171   Comment *c* to §80.

172   *Ibid.*

173   *Ibid.*

174   *Ibid.*

175   *Ibid.* The comment further remarks that the argument for respecting a forum stipulation is strengthened when the parties have also stipulated for the application of that state's law.

176   Comment *c* to §80 (emphasis added).

the Uniform Foreign Money-Judgments Recognition Act.[177] Its §4 *(b)* (5) provides that:

> A foreign judgment need not be recognized if the proceeding in the foreign court was contrary to an agreement between the parties under which the dispute in question was to be settled otherwise than by proceeding in court.

As originally promulgated in 1969 and as revised in 1986, Restatement Second envisages situations in which a derogation clause will be denied effect for reasons other than violations of mandatory rules of general-contract law. Here considerations specific to the legal order's dispute-resolution system and its notions of procedural justice impose limitations on private autonomy stricter than those required by the law of contractual obligation in general.

Beginning in 1991, the converse development is seen. For a considerable period, in the United States the view had prevailed "that an effective consent to jurisdiction must involve parties of relatively equal bargaining strength and [result from] actual bargaining".[178] In *Carnival Cruise Lines, Inc.* v. *Shute*[179] the Supreme Court rejected the proposition that "a nonnegotiated forum-selection clause in a form ticket contract is never enforceable because it is not the subject of bargaining".[180]

Justice Blackmun sets out various considerations that support "reasonable" exclusive forum-selection clauses in adhesion contracts for transportation:

> First, a cruise line has a general interest in limiting the fora in which it potentially could be subject to suit ... Additionally, a clause establishing *ex ante* the forum for dispute resolution has the salutary effect of dispelling any confusion about where suits arising from the contract must be brought and defended, sparing litigants the time and expense of pretrial motions to determine the correct forum and conserving judicial resources that would otherwise be devoted to handling these motions. Finally, it stands to reason that passengers who purchase tickets containing a forum clause like that at issue in this case benefit in the form of reduced fares reflecting the savings that the cruise line enjoys by limiting the fora in which it may be sued.[181]

The differences between the *Bremen* and the *Carnival Cruise Lines* situations are dramatic. The former is "virtually the best-case scenario for the enforcement of

---

177   13 Pt. II ULA 39 (2002).

178   E. Scoles, P. Hay, P. Borchers and S. Symeonides, *Conflict of Laws*, § 6.3, at 342 (St. Paul, Minn., West Group, 4th ed., 2004).

179   499 US 585 (1991).

180   *Idem* 593.

181   *Idem* 593-594 (citations omitted).

... a [forum-selection] clause"; the latter represents perhaps "the worst case with which to defend ... [such a] clause".[182]

Both cases may well be correctly decided, however.[183] In all events, the recent emergence of electronic commerce raises in a new – perhaps fundamentally different – and intractable context the issue of forum selection.[184]

Merchants embrace *Carnival Cruise Lines* while consumer advocates insist that consumers must have the right to seek relief in their home courts.

(ii) German law
a.   Introductory

In common-law systems, as a general matter, party stipulations respecting venue and subject-matter jurisdiction are not permitted in principle but are acceptable only to the extent that the legal order expressly provides for party choice. Requirements allocating cases on a geographical basis among courts of a single legal order (venue provisions) and provisions allocating particular types of controversies – for example, civil and commercial matters, criminal matters, administrative matters, or employment and labour matters – to particular judicial hierarchies (subject-matter jurisdiction) are seen as intended to ensure the efficient operation of the dispute-resolution hierarchies that each legal system provides. In view of these purposes, party stipulations addressing these issues could be seen as conceptually more problematic than stipulations respecting jurisdiction to adjudicate. So far as parties are concerned, however, stipulations of the latter type typically impose the greater burden. Accordingly, where parties thought to deserve special protection are concerned, forum-selection clauses may well be more problematic than are venue or subject-matter jurisdiction selection clauses. In all events, common-law jurists are surprised by the great freedom that the German Code of Civil Procedure of 1877 (ZPO) gave the parties to stipulate not only on adjudicatory authority, but also on venue[185] and subject-matter jurisdiction. ZPO §38, as promulgated in 1879, provided that "a court of first instance that lacks jurisdiction acquires it if the parties expressly or implicitly so agree".

The broad power given to parties to stipulate on these matters was subject to only three limitations set out in ZPO §40. The stipulation had to be directed to a

---

182   M. Solimine, "Forum-Selection Clauses and the Privatization of Procedure", 25 *Cornell Int'l. LJ* 51, at 101 (1992).

183   Solimine concludes that both decisions were correct. See *ibid*.

184   See A. Haines, *The Impact of the Internet on the Judgments Project: Thoughts for the Future*, Permanent Bureau of the [Hague] Conference, General Affairs, Prel. Doc., No. 17 (February 2002) (English and French texts), No. 1-18, at 4-21.

185   The inclusion of venue provisions can be explained by the failure of German jurists at the time to distinguish between venue and adjudicatory jurisdiction. See Chap. II. D. 2. *(b)* (i), p. 66, *supra*. According the same treatment to subject-matter jurisdiction is more difficult to explain but was never seriously contested. See Stein and Jonas (-Bork), *Kommentar zur Zivilprozeßordnung*, Vol. 1 (Tübingen, Mohr Siebeck, 22d ed., 2003), §38, No. 1.

specific legal relationship and controversies arising from it, the claim had not to be one for which an exclusive jurisdiction was provided, and the claim had to be pecuniary in nature *(vermögensrechtliche Streitigkeit)*.[186] Special requirements of form were not imposed on forum-selection agreements.

The drafters of the 1877 Code remarked on the broad freedom *(weiten Spielraum)* given to the parties.[187] They believed that forum-selection agreements would be just and balanced because they were negotiated between parties of roughly equal bargaining power and skill.[188] The only concern expressed, that the broad freedom to select the forum would lead to an unbalanced allocation among the courts of judicial business, was dismissed as purely theoretical.[189]

In the course of the early decades of the twentieth century the practice of using standard-form contracts *(Allgemeine Geschäftsbedingungen)* for all kinds of purposes, including choice of forum, became more and more common. Increasingly, provisions in standard-form contracts respecting jurisdiction were not negotiated but imposed, typically upon the "weaker" party in terms of economic power and social standing. In light of these abuses, prominent scholars began to suggest prohibition of party stipulations on jurisdiction.[190] Distinguishing between stipulations on subject-matter jurisdiction and venue, on the one hand, and jurisdiction to adjudicate in the international sense, on the other, many asserted that, *in international settings*, choice of the legal order that was to exercise jurisdiction was usually motivated by justified interests of the parties.[191] A Draft Reform Act of 1931 proposed the modest step of requiring that party stipulations on jurisdiction be made in writing; the draft was not adopted.[192]

b.   Circumstances that led to the 1974 Reform Act

By the early 1970s, the practice of using standard-form contracts had become commonplace in virtually all legal relationships, including those between large businesses and consumers. Insurance companies included clauses in their standard-form contracts providing for exclusive jurisdiction of the courts at their seat. Consumers concluding such contracts were often not aware of the practical consequences of these provisions, namely, that in case of a dispute arising out of the contract they would have to defend themselves, or bring their claims, before courts located in another part of Germany or even abroad, often hundreds of miles away from their home.

---

186   For the concept of "pecuniary claims", see *supra* footnote 88.

187   See Hahn, *supra* footnote 118, at 160.

188   *Ibid.*

189   *Ibid.*

190   See, e.g., Stein and Jonas (-Bork), *Kommentar zur Zivilprozeßordnung*, Vol. 1 (Tübingen, Mohr Siebeck, 21st ed., 1993), vor §38, No. 1.

191   See, e.g., G. Schiedermair, *Vereinbarungen im Zivilprozeß* 88-90 (Bonn, Ludwig Röhrscheidt Verlag, 1935).

192   See W. Löwe, "Das neue Recht der Gerichtsstandsvereinbarung", 27 *NJW* 473, at 473 (1974).

Another common, and for consumers even more dangerous, tactic used by companies to avoid litigating at the consumer's domicile involved contractual agreements on the place of performance. ZPO §29 provides a *forum contractus* at the place where the obligation in dispute is to be performed. The original version of the provision did not limit the parties' freedom to agree on the place of performance, even if the agreement was made for purely jurisdictional purposes.[193] Accordingly, a prorogation was achieved by providing in standard-form contracts that "the place of performance is Hamburg [the seat of the company]".

Such practices became very widespread and were increasingly considered an abuse of private autonomy. In some courts, roughly a third of the suits filed were based on prorogation clauses.[194] The *actor sequitur* principle, intended to require the plaintiff to sue the defendant at his domicile,[195] was superseded in practice by forum-selection clauses favoring the stronger party. Because consumer contracts were still typically local in nature, these clauses applied primarily to venue requirements and, accordingly, did not impose as great a burden on consumers as would have agreements respecting jurisdiction to adjudicate in the international sense.

A serious problem respecting prorogation clauses arose in the early 1970s in default proceedings *(Versäumnisverfahren)*. ZPO §331 provided that, in principle, when a defendant fails to appear at an oral hearing the court must accept all factual allegations made by the plaintiff. Before the 1974 Reform Act, this rule applied to allegations respecting jurisdiction and venue.[196] Companies suing customers in the courts of the company's seat needed in default cases only to allege the existence of a prorogation clause.[197] By virtue of ZPO §331, in light of the defendant's failure to appear for the oral hearing, the court had, in rendering a judgment by default, to disregard written objections filed by the defendant. Since the oral hearing often took place before courts quite distant from the defendant's home, in practice a high percentage of judgments against consumers was rendered by default.

c.   The 1974 Reform Act

Prior to the 1974 Act, abuses of the ZPO's liberal regime respecting jurisdictional agreements could be addressed only under general contract law. But that body of

---

193   In 1974, ZPO §29 was amended to provide that agreements respecting the place of performance of a contract did not establish the jurisdiction *(Zuständigkeit)* of the local courts if the parties were not merchants *(Kaufleute)* in the sense of §1 of the Commercial Code.

194   See Löwe, *supra* footnote 192, at 473, footnote 6.

195   See Chap. VI., pp. 262 *et seq., supra*.

196   In 1974, ZPO §331 was amended to provide that the rule did "[n]ot apply to allegations *(Vorbringen)* respecting the court's jurisdiction *(Zuständigkeit)* under §29, para. 2 and §39". The court must now establish *ex officio* whether it has jurisdiction.

197   See A. Baumbach and W. Lauterbach, *Zivilprozeßordnung* (Munich, C. H. Beck, 27th ed., 1963), §331, No. 2.

law did not offer much protection.[198] To set an agreement aside, defendants had to establish that the plaintiff had behaved fraudulently *(arglistige Täuschung)* or had violated morality *(Sittenwidrigkeit)*.[199] The courts were also prepared to invalidate a derogation of German jurisdiction that amounted to a denial of justice.[200] The threshold for such relief was, however, very high. Moreover, as remarked above, in default proceedings written objections on these grounds filed by the defendant could not be taken into account by virtue of ZPO §331.

The debate on the revision of ZPO §§38-40 began in 1973 when the Free State of Bavaria submitted to the *Bundesrat* a Draft Reform Act prohibiting jurisdictional agreements where one or more of the parties were non-merchants.[201] At the outset, the Federal Government – composed, at the time, of Social Democrats and Liberals – was reluctant to adopt so far-reaching a reform. A commission of experts, set up by the Federal Ministry of Justice, had already suggested the less radical steps of requiring that party agreements on jurisdiction and venue be made in writing in a separate legal document and that courts check whether these formalities were satisfied even in default proceedings. Ultimately, the proposal of the experts was found insufficient; the Federal Government changed its position and the 1974 Reform Act was unanimously adopted in the *Bundestag*.

Under the new legislation, the parties' freedom to select the forum is severely limited.[202] More specifically, under the ZPO parties may select the forum only in certain circumstances and only under certain – substantive and formal – conditions: first, according to ZPO §38 (1) and (3) parties are allowed to select the forum before a controversy has arisen, where all parties qualify as merchants under §1 of the Commercial Code *(Kaufleute)*, as legal entities under public law *(juristische Personen des öffentlichen Rechts)* or as special funds under public law *(öffentlich-rechtliche Sondervermögen)* or where at least one of the parties is not subject to general jurisdiction in Germany, Second, according to ZPO §38 (3) No. 2 parties may agree on the forum if they do so just for the case that one of the parties transfers its domicile *(Wohnsitz)* or habitual residence *(gewöhnlicher Aufenthalt)* to a location where the ZPO does not apply or for the case that one of the party' domicile or habitual residence is unknown when the claim is brought. Third, according to ZPO §38 (3) No. 1 parties may arrange for the forum after a dispute has arisen.

---

198 Had the 1976 Act on Standard Form Contracts *(Gesetz zur Regelung des Rechts der Allgemeinen Geschäftsbedingungen)* already been adopted, the situation would have been quite different. See *infra* footnote 206.

199 Baumbach and Lauterbach, *supra* footnote 197, §29, No. 1B; §40, No. 2.

200 See Stein and Jonas (-Bork), *supra* footnote 185, §38, No. 32.

201 For a brief account of the history of the 1974 Draft Reform Act and the political background, see Löwe, *supra* footnote 192, at 473.

202 In a 1982 decision the *Bundesgerichtshof* even spoke of a contractual provision "violating the prohibition, in principle, of forum-selection agreements". BGH, 6 October 1982, 36 *NJW* 159, at 162 (1983).

However, for any such stipulation to be valid further requirements must be met: first, according to ZPO §40 (1) the stipulation must relate to a specific legal relationship. Second, according to ZPO §40 (2) No. 1 it must be pecuniary in nature or, if it is non-pecuniary in nature, it must not fall within the subject-matter jurisdiction of the *Amtsgerichte*. Third, ZPO §40 (2) No. 2 requires jurisdiction or venue not to be exclusive. Fourth, ZPO §38 (3) provides any forum selection agreement to be explicit and in writing. If the stipulation is made because at least one of the parties is not subject to general jurisdiction in Germany, ZPO §38 (2) allows the stipulation to be made orally and confirmed in writing.[203] Only if the parties qualify as merchants, legal entities under public law or special funds under public law, the formal requirements set out in ZPO §38 (2) and (3) need not to be met, regardless whether the forum selected is German or foreign.[204]

All in all, compared to the situation prior to 1974, the ZPO's approach to forum-selection clauses has become quite complicated.[205] However, despite the detailed provisions of ZPO §38 and §40 German law does not offer complete protection against abuses of private autonomy. A foreign company, using its standard-form contract for a transaction with a German consumer, can still stipulate for the jurisdiction of the courts at its seat. Such stipulation will be effective unless the law applicable under the forum's choice-of-law rules provides otherwise.[206]

---

203   If one of the parties is subject to general jurisdiction in Germany, ZPO §38 (2) requires the parties to choose the court at the place where that party is subject to either general or special jurisdiction. This limitation does not operate, however, where the parties select a foreign court.

204   This is clearly the majority position among German courts and scholars. See, e.g., Stein and Jonas (-Bork), *supra* footnote 185, §38, No. 13. Some jurists take the view that merchants are required to comply with the formal requirements of ZPO §38, para. 2, when they stipulate in an international setting. The language of ZPO §38 (*"ferner"* and *"im übrigen"*) indicates that the minority view is incorrect.

205   Where international litigation is in question, additional complexity results from the fact that the Brussels Convention and Regulation trump national-law provisions on party stipulations. See (iii), pp. 225 *et seq., infra*.

206   Until very recently, the 1976 *Gesetz zur Regelung des Rechts der Allgemeinen Geschäftsbedingungen* (AGBG) addressed the concerns raised by standard-form contracts in general. With effect from 1 January 2002, the AGBG has been incorporated into §§305-310 of the German Civil Code *(Bürgerliches Gesetzbuch)* without altering the substance of the provisions of interest for the present discussion. Where German law applies pursuant to the relevant choice-of-law rules, the AGBG provisions, as incorporated in §§305-310 of the BGB, now regulate party stipulations on jurisdiction. In the late 1970s some jurists regarded ZPO §§38-40 as determining exhaustively all limitations on parties' right to stipulate. See K. Schiller, "Gerichtsstandsklauseln in AGB zwischen Vollkaufleuten und das AGBG", 32 *NJW* 636-637 (1979). Under the AGBG, prorogations of foreign courts contracts with non-merchants could, depending on the circumstances of the individual case, be challenged on the grounds that they were not properly agreed to by the customer (AGBG §2), constituted an unfair surprise *(überraschende Klausel)*, or violated the principles of good faith *(unangemes-*

(iii) The Brussels Convention and Regulation
a.   The original Convention

In his official report on the drafting of the Brussels Convention of 1968, the *rapporteur* – Paul Jenard of Belgium – remarked that "although agreement was readily reached on the basic principle of including ... [prorogation of] jurisdiction [by consent] in the Convention, the Committee spent considerable time in drafting Article 17" of Section 6, "Prorogation of Jurisdiction".[207] Article 17 provided that

> If the Parties, one or more of whom is domiciled in a Contracting State, have, by agreement in writing or by an oral agreement evidenced in writing, agreed that a court or the courts of a Contracting State are to have jurisdiction to settle any disputes which have arisen or which may arise in connection with a particular legal relationship, that court or those courts shall have exclusive jurisdiction.
>
> Agreements conferring jurisdiction shall have no legal force if they are contrary to the provisions of Article 12 or 15, or if the courts whose jurisdiction they purport to exclude have exclusive jurisdiction by virtue of Article 16.[208]
>
> If the agreement conferring jurisdiction was concluded for the benefit of only one of the parties, that party shall retain the right to bring proceedings in any other court which has jurisdiction by virtue of this Convention.

The drafters sought to strike a balance between "not impeding commercial practice while, at the same time, denying effect to contract clauses that might go unread".[209] Once prorogation of jurisdiction through agreement is permitted, on occasion difficult choices must be made between, on the one hand, protecting inexperienced or economically and socially weaker parties from overreaching by more experienced or stronger parties and, on the other, recognizing established commercial practices. Widely differing views have been – and will continue to be – held in different times and in different societies on the proper balance between consumer and employee protection and promoting economically efficient and predictable commercial activity. The history of Article 17 from 1968 onwards can

---

sene *Benachteiligung nach den Geboten von Treu und Glauben). The incorporation of the AGBG into the BGB did not change the decisional law developed prior to 2002.

207 Jenard Report, *supra* footnote 127, at 37.

208 Article 12 limits prorogation clauses in insurance contracts in order to protect policyholders; Article 15 has comparable provisions protecting the "buyer or borrower" in instalment sales or loan contracts; Article 16 establishes exclusive jurisdiction over various matters including "proceedings which have as their object rights *in rem*, or tenancies of, immovable property", "the validity of the constitution, the nullity or the dissolution of companies or other legal persons, or the decisions of their organs", and "registration and validity of patents, trade marks, designs, or other similar rights required to be deposited or registered".

209 Jenard Report, *supra* footnote 127, at 17.

be understood as a constant struggle to achieve an appropriate balance between these objectives.[210]

b.   The 1978 amendments

On the occasion of the accession in 1978 to the Brussels Convention of the United Kingdom and Ireland, both common-law jurisdictions, and Denmark, various amendments were made. Some of those took into account common-law institutions, for example the trust, not found in the civil-law systems of the Convention's original signatory States.[211] In addition, changes were made to take into account important legal developments that had occurred since 1968 in the legal systems of the six original member States. In particular, greater attention was given to consumer protection.[212] Section 4 was titled: jurisdiction over consumer contracts. Article 13 was enlarged to cover, in addition to contracts "for the sale of goods on instalment credit terms" and contracts "for a loan repayable by instalments, or for any other form of credit, made to finance the sale of goods", "any other contract for the supply of goods or a contract for the supply of services", if:

(a)   in the State of the consumer's domicile the conclusion of the contract was preceded by a specific invitation addressed to him or by advertising, and

(b)   the consumer took in that State the steps necessary for the conclusion of the contract.

The 1978 amendments introduced limitations on party autonomy not contained in the 1968 version of Article 17. On the other hand, an amendment to the provisions respecting the formal requirements applicable to prorogation agreements, supported party autonomy. The 1968 Convention required "a written agreement or ... an oral agreement confirmed in writing". In 1976, the European Court of Justice had interpreted this language narrowly as it applied to jurisdiction clauses incorporated in standard-form contracts.

---

210   See Schlosser, *supra* footnote 82, Art. 23, No. 1.

211   New third and fourth paragraphs were added to Article 17:

   (3)   The court or courts of a Contracting State on which a trust instrument has conferred jurisdiction shall have exclusive jurisdiction in any proceedings brought against a settlor, trustee or beneficiary, if relations between these persons or their rights or obligations under the trust are involved.

   (4)   Agreements or provisions of a trust instrument conferring jurisdiction shall have no legal force if they are contrary to the provisions of Articles 12 or 15, or if the courts whose jurisdictions they purport to exclude have exclusive jurisdiction by virtue of Article 16.

212   See generally Report by Peter Schlosser on the Convention of 9 October 1978 on the Association *[sic]* of the Kingdom of Denmark, Ireland and the United Kingdom of Great Britain and Northern Ireland to the Convention on jurisdiction and the enforcement of judgments in civil and commercial matters and to the Protocol on its interpretation by the Court of Justice, [1979] OJ C 59, 71, at 80.

Segoura v. *Bonakdarian*[213] held that, in the case of a contract concluded orally, the requirements of the first paragraph of Article 17 were not satisfied unless the vendor's confirmation in writing, accompanied by notification of the general conditions of sale, had been accepted in writing by the purchaser. The purchaser's failure to raise objections against a confirmation issued unilaterally by the other party did not amount to his acceptance of the jurisdiction-conferring clause.[214] The Court did not distinguish between merchants and private individuals. Thus, the decision threatened to end the widespread German trade practice that relied on so-called merchants letters of confirmation *(kaufmännisches Bestätigungssch-reiben*[215]*)*.

The drafters of the 1978 amendment considered excessive the formal requirements imposed by the 1968 Convention as interpreted by the European Court of Justice. The Schlosser Report on the 1978 Convention explains that the Court's interpretation

> does not cater adequately for the customs and requirements of international trade. In particular, the requirement that the other party to a contract with anyone employing general conditions of trade has to give written confirmation of their inclusion in the contract before any jurisdiction clause in those conditions can be effective is unacceptable in international trade. International trade is heavily dependent on standard conditions, which incorporate jurisdiction clauses. Nor are those conditions in many cases unilaterally dictated by one set of interests in the market ... These are the factors behind the relaxation of the formal provisions for international trade in the amended version of Article 17.[216]

The 1978 amendments sought to resolve the difficulty by adding an additional formal requirement to Article 17: a prorogation clause is valid as a matter of form "in international trade or commerce, [if it is] in a form which accords with practices in that trade or commerce of which the parties are or ought to be aware".

c.   The 1989 amendments

With the accession of Spain and Portugal, the text of Article 17 (1) was again amended to clarify its formal requirements. The new language was taken directly from the Lugano Convention.[217] Unchanged after the accession of Austria, Swe-

---

213   *Segoura* v. *Bonakdarian*, Case C-25/76, [1976] ECR 1851; see also *Estasis Salotti* v. *Rüwa*, Case C-24/76, [1976] ECR 1831.

214   *Ibid.*

215   Under this doctrine of German law, the failure to reply to a letter of confirmation in commercial relationships following an allegedly reached oral agreement is deemed an approval of the latter's content. Much of German commercial practice relies on this doctrine.

216   Schlosser Report, *supra* footnote 212, at 124-125.

217   See Report by M. de Almeida Cruz, M. Desantes Real and P. Jenard on the accession of the Kingdom of Spain and the Portuguese Republic to the Convention on jurisdic-

den and Finland to the Brussels Convention in 1996, the 1989 text provides as
follows:

> If the parties, one or more of whom is domiciled in a Contracting State, have agreed
> that a court or the courts of a Contracting State are to have jurisdiction to settle any
> disputes which have arisen or which may arise in connection with a particular legal
> relationship, that court or those courts shall have jurisdiction. Such an agreement
> conferring jurisdiction shall be either:
> *(a)*   in writing or evidenced in writing; or
> *(b)*   in a form which accords with practices which the parties have established be-
>   tween themselves; or
> *(c)*   in international trade or commerce, in a form which accords with a usage of
>   which the parties are or ought to have been aware and which in such trade or
>   commerce is widely known to, and regularly observed by, parties to contracts of
>   the type involved in the particular trade or commerce concerned.
> Where such an agreement is concluded by parties, none of whom is domiciled in a
> Contracting State, the courts of other Contracting States shall have no jurisdiction
> over their disputes unless the court or courts chosen have declined jurisdiction.

The 1989 Convention also added a new paragraph 5 to Article 17. It deals with jurisdiction in matters relating to contracts of employment. The new provision was
designed to protect employees who, from the socio-economic point of view, are
regarded as the weaker party in the employment relationship. The amendment
was inspired by the Lugano Convention; however, Lugano's Article 17 (5) was not
adopted.[218] The Lugano solution was considered needlessly restrictive in that it
denied the employee the right to invoke an agreement on jurisdiction concluded
prior to the dispute even if the agreement is favorable for him. Article 17 (5) of
Brussels, as amended in 1989, provides as follows:

> In matters relating to individual contracts of employment an agreement conferring
> jurisdiction shall have legal force only if entered into after the dispute has arisen or if
> the employee invokes it to seize courts other than those for the defendant's domicile
> or those specified in Article 5 (1).

d.   The Brussels Regulation

In the Brussels Regulation,[219] which entered into force on 1 March 2002, Article
23 addresses "prorogation of jurisdiction". In only two respects does the Article
differ significantly from Article 17 of the Brussels Convention: firstly, a new paragraph 2 provides that "[a]ny communication by electronic means which provides
a durable record of the agreement shall be equivalent to 'writing'". Secondly, Arti-

---

tion and the enforcement of judgments in civil and commercial matters, [1990] OJ C
189, 35, at 47.

218   This is one of the few textual differences between the two conventions.

219   See for a detailed discussion Chapter II. D. 3. *(b)* (ii), pp. 72 *et seq., supra.*.

cles 18-21, which comprise Section 5, extend to employees protection given under the Brussels Convention only to consumers and insureds. The Regulation thus continues the Brussels system's tendency to restrict private autonomy in order to protect socially or economically weaker parties.[220]

E.   Party Stipulations for a Private Dispute-Resolution Process of Their Own Design: Arbitration Agreements

Private autonomy as a principle of ordering – tempered by planning – remains in most societies of central importance to economic life. International commercial arbitration involves the constitution through an exercise of private autonomy of a private tribunal with its own procedural and even substantive rules of law. Acceptance of the principle of private autonomy does not logically require that a legal order also accept privately created and sustained dispute-resolution mechanisms; private ordering that occurs within the legal context of a politically and socially organized society differs in significant respects from private ordering that aspires to create its own legal order. Unlike the former, the latter displaces procedural and institutional arrangements designed to ensure the integrity of private ordering as a process. Moreover, this expression of private autonomy significantly reduces – or even removes – society's control over the development and adaptation of substantive rules and principles that regulate significant areas of economic intercourse.[221]

Today most legal systems accept and support, though in different measure and especially for international transactions, commercial arbitration. Until the latter decades of the twentieth century, however, such was not the case.

1.   France

The French Revolution (1789) wrote *finis* to a legal order burdened not only with a variety of competing judicial hierarchies, each with its own intricate, slow, and costly procedures, but also by obscure and complex substantive-law regimes that were, in many respects, out of touch with contemporary needs and realities. This state of affairs and the epoch's optimistic rationalism serve to explain the euphoria with which, as the 18th century came to its close, French thinking accepted arbitration.

In 1790, the Constituent Assembly characterized arbitration as the most reasonable method "for terminating disputes between citizens".[222] Although enthusiasm for arbitration declined somewhat in the next decade,[223] Article 3 of the Loi

---

220 See pp. 225-229, *supra*.

221 See A. von Mehren, "International Commercial Arbitration: The Contribution of the French Jurisprudence", 46 *La. L. Rev.* 1045, at 1045 (1986).

222 Quoted by Hello in his conclusions in *Compagnie l'Alliance* v. *Prunier*, Cass. civ., 10 July 1843, S. 1843.I.564, at 566.

223 See von Mehren, *supra* footnote 221, at 1046.

sur l'organisation des tribuneaux of 1800[224] proclaimed that "the right of citizens to have their controversies judged by arbitrators of their choice is in no way restricted; the decision of these arbitrators will not be subject to any review unless the contrary is expressly provided".

In light of this background, it is perhaps surprising that the Code of Civil Procedure (1806) addressed explicitly only a limited form of arbitration: the *compromis* (an agreement to arbitrate a dispute that had already arisen between the parties). Book III, *Des Arbitrages* contains 26 articles. The first of these, Article 1003, allows parties to "compromise *(compromettre)* rights that they may dispose of freely". "To be valid, the agreement to arbitrate must designate the objects in dispute and name the arbitrators."[225] This requirement is easily satisfied when a *compromis* – an agreement to arbitrate a dispute that has already arisen – is in question. On the other hand, in a *clause compromissoire* – an agreement to arbitrate disputes that may arise in the future with respect to an existing legal relationship – the requirement can rarely, if ever, be satisfied. Other articles deal with arbitral procedure as well as judicial review and enforcement of awards. None specifically addresses, however, the issue of the *clause compromissoire*'s validity.

> For nearly four decades, French jurists disagreed as to the validity of these agreements. A grave question, on which judicial practice *(the jurisprudence)* was long unsettled, was whether … the *clause compromissoire* was valid. For a long time the *jurisprudence* was inclined to uphold the validity of the *clause compromissoire* … . [Such] a clause is not a *compromis* but rather a *promesse de compromettre*.[226]

The 1843 decision of the Cour de cassation in *Comp. l'Alliance* v. *Prunier,*[227] which held the *clause compromissoire* unenforceable under Article 1006, was entirely unexpected; it caused "a great sensation from both the doctrinal and practical points of view".[228] The high Court's decision rested in part on technical grounds and, in part, on policy considerations. The Court's discomfort with arbitration clauses contained in standard-form adhesion contracts was prophetic:

> [I]n effect, the company l'Alliance, whose principal office is in Paris, and which does business throughout France, wants, by Article 15 of the policy, to force the insureds, regardless of how large or small may be the loss, to constitute at Paris – where most of the insureds do not have any business connection, and even do not know anybody

---

224 Bulletin de Lois de la République, No. 103, at 15 (27 ventôse an VIII (1800)).

225 Art. 1006.

226 A. Tissier, A. Darras and H. Louiche-Desfontaines, *Code de Procédure Civile Annoté,* Vol. II, Art. 1006, No. 50, at 1116 (Paris, Librairie de la Société de Recueil Général des Lois et des Arrêts, 1904).

227 Cass. civ., 10 July 1843, D. 1843.1.343, S. 1843.1.561.

228 Devill, Note to Cass. civ., 10 July 1843, S. 1843.1.561, at 562.

–, far from the place where the fire occurred and where the losses cannot be verified and evaluated, an arbitral tribunal that would judge finally.[229]

In 1843 the French general law of contract had not yet developed rules to protect economically weaker or unsophisticated parties to adhesion contracts. Accordingly, the Cour de cassation, to protect the policy holders in *Prunier*, felt compelled to sacrifice the *promesse de compromettre* across the board.

After the 1843 reversal of arbitration's fortune in *Prunier*, almost a century and half of effort by the French courts, legislature, and executive was required to create a modern and effective arbitration law.[230] In 1981, Titles 5 and 6 of Book IV, *L'arbitrage*, of the New Code of Civil Procedure were promulgated.[231] They provide comprehensive and effective regimes for both non-domestic and domestic arbitration.

2.   *Prussia and the German Reich*

For present purposes, the history of arbitration in modern Germany can be taken to begin in 1793, the year in which the *Allgemeine Gerichtsordnung für die Preußischen Staaten* entered into force. The *Ordnung's* Second Title, *Vom Gerichtsstande* (§§167-176) regulated arbitration and contained the ambiguity found in Book III of the French *Code of Civil Procedure*. Section 167 of the *Gerichtsordnung* provides that: "when the parties have full and unlimited power to dispose of a dispute, there may be a compromise *(Kompromiß)* to submit the existing dispute to arbitration".

In discussing §167 in 1825, a leading contemporary commentary does not raise the question whether a *clause compromissoire* – as distinguished from a *compromis (Kompromiß)* – is enforceable in Prussian law.[232] Prior to the establishment of the German Reich in 1871 and the entrance into force in 1879 of the *Zivilprozeßordnung* of 1877,[233] whether a *clause compromissoire* was – or should be – enforceable was disputed in Prussia and other Germanic states. The drafters of the ZPO remarked that "German practice *(deutsche Praxis)*" had come to treat

---

229   *Compagnie l'Alliance* v. *Prunier, supra* footnote 222, at 568.

230   See generally von Mehren, *supra* footnote 221.

231   Book IV was enacted by executive decree under Article 37 of the French Constitution of 1958. Large areas of civil procedure that "fall within the domain of law" but are of "a regulatory character" have been since 1958 constitutionally within the executive's rather than the legislature's authority.

232   See M. Grävell, *Praktischer Kommentar zur allgemeinen Gerichtsordnung für die preußischen Staaten*, Vol. I, at 377 (Comment to §§167-170) (Erfurt, Keysersche Buchhandlung 1825).

233   See Hahn, *supra* footnote 118, at 490.

"a contract to submit a future dispute to arbitration as legally valid if the legal relationship is indicated from which the contract arises".[234]

(a) Book X of the *Zivilprozeßordnung* (1877)
(i) *In general*

In the course of the nineteenth century the absolute State conception that dominated Europe in the previous century was challenged by the conception of the constitutional State. The latter left considerable room for private autonomy to operate within the legal order. The legal regime provided by Book X of the *Zivilprozeßordnung* rested on the proposition that economic and social forces should be allowed a large measure of free play.

The ZPO of 1877 addressed arbitration in its *Zehntes Buch: Schiedsrichterliches Verfahren* (§§851-872). In 1900, the ZPO was revised to take into account the entrance into force on 1 January 1900 of the Reich's unifying and innovating codification of substantive law – the *Bürgerliche Gesetzbuch*. §§851-872 of the ZPO became §§1025-1048. Few changes in, or additions to, Book X were made until 1996,[235] however.

Book X did much more than resolve clearly, and favorably for arbitration's users, the issue whether agreements to arbitrate future disputes were binding and enforceable. §863 (§1037) provided an approach to the *Kompetenz-Kompetenz* problem that facilitated arbitration and was later followed by other legal systems. Arbitration was, moreover, released from strict observation of national substantive and procedural law; within limits of fairness and reasonableness, the parties were free to innovate by agreement.[236] The grounds for setting aside awards recognized by §867 do not include failure to observe rules of national substantive or

---

234 *Ibid*. The drafters refer to "the willingness of local *Landesherren* to approve statutes of corporations and societies" that contain such clauses. *Ibid*.

235 The most significant change perhaps was the adding, in 1930, of §1044, which specifically applies to foreign arbitral awards. The section's first paragraph provided that, absent conflicting treaty provisions, a foreign award that has, under the law applicable to it, become binding can be declared enforceable under the procedure provided for domestic awards.
     A second paragraph provided that the request for a declaration of enforceability of a foreign award is to be refused when (1) the award is not legally effective which, in the absence of an applicable treaty obligation, is to be determined under the law applicable to the arbitral proceeding; (2) recognition would lead to a result clearly incompatible with a significant *(wesentlichen)* fundamental principle of German law; (3) the party was not appropriately *(ordnungsmäßig)* represented, unless the conduct of the process was expressly or impliedly approved; or (4) the party was not heard in the proceedings. The award is not set aside; instead the court declares it unenforceable domestically. ZPO §1044 (3). Should an award declared enforceable subsequently be set aside, lifting of the declaration of enforcement can be requested. ZPO §1044 (4).

236 Cf. H. Krause, *Die geschichtliche Entwicklung des Schiedsgerichtswesens in Deutschland* 106 (Berlin, Carl Heymanns Verlag, 1930).

procedural law that would be applicable in the local courts.[237] Indeed, the parties are specifically authorized to exclude local requirements as to legal representation and party presentation of their case, and the arbitrators can be excused from providing reasons for their decision.

The drafters of Book X had reason to – and did – praise their own work:

> In all the reforms and proposals for reform [so far] the effort has been to put aside the limitations that were set by the law previously in force to the flowering of arbitration. This draft shares these ambitions: in light of the idea and the goal of arbitration it has provided procedures that are so simple and so practical that all justified demands are satisfied and, if the arbitrators are well chosen, good results are assured.[238]

(ii) The arbitration law of Book X

Book X, as originally enacted in 1877 and as revised in 1900, provided the first arbitration law that is modern in conception. Its provisions are briefly analysed below.

The Book's first section, §851 (§1025), describes the area of legal rights and duties that are considered suitable for arbitration: Arbitration may decide, with "legal effect *(rechtliche Wirkung)* [controversies,] insofar as the parties have the right to compromise the controversy *(über den Gegenstand des Streits einen Vergleich zu schließen)*".[239] §852 clearly regulates the long debated and previously unresolved issue whether agreements to arbitrate future disputes are enforceable in principle: such agreements are enforceable so long as the agreement is "in respect of a definite legal relationship *(Rechtsverhältnis)* and the legal controversy ... [arose] out of that relationship".[240] The Book goes on to provide a legal regime that enables arbitrators to proceed effectively and to enlist the assistance of courts where needed.

General standards for the conduct of the arbitral proceedings were established: §860 (§1034) provides that the arbitrators must, before rendering their award, hear the parties and determine, to the extent they consider necessary, the facts from which the controversy arose. The arbitrators can otherwise proceed in their free discretion unless the parties have agreed upon the procedure to be followed. Arbitrators can hear witnesses and experts who voluntarily appear before

---

237 Germany has maintained the restrictive approach to the grounds on which arbitration awards can be set aside, which is expressed in §867, ever since, cf. ZPO §1041 of 1900 and the present ZPO §1059.

238 Hahn, *supra* footnote 118, at 489.

239 Here the draft follows earlier legislation of German states. The drafters explain that the capacity under substantive law to compromise claims, includes *(begreift)* the capacity to enter into an arbitration agreement. *Idem* 490.

240 The section reads as follows:

> An arbitration agreement with respect to a future legal controversy does not have any legal effect when the agreement is not in respect of a definite legal relationship and the legal controversies arising out of this relationship.

them. They may not, however, require witnesses or experts to swear an oath nor can they take a party oath.[241]

Book X, perhaps for the first time in the modern history of arbitration, addressed in §863 the problem of *Kompetenz-Kompetenz*. Since an arbitral tribunal's adjudicatory authority, unlike that of a court, is not institutional but consensual in nature, deriving, at least initially, from the parties' agreement to arbitrate, a logical dilemma is presented when a party challenges the tribunal's authority on the ground that the agreement is void or does not cover some or all of the issues that a party has asked the tribunal to decide. As a practical matter, the arbitral process would pay a heavy price in reduced efficiency and expedition if such challenges to the tribunal's adjudicatory authority had to be resolved by a court before the arbitration could proceed. §863 provided a reasonable and effective solution: the arbitral proceedings can continue and an award can be rendered. A court will not, however, enforce the award if it concludes that the arbitral tribunal lacked jurisdiction.

(b) The Reform Act of 1998

Judged by twenty-first century standards, Book X was the most modern arbitration law of its day. It was to survive essentially unchanged until 1998. In the course of more than a century, however, Book X aged and became less and less user-friendly. On a few occasions, the legislature sought to take economic and social changes into account but no attempt was made to overhaul the Act as a whole. A 1930 Reform Act[242] added §§1042a-1042d that provided for a declaration of enforceability of awards *(Vollstreckbarerklärung des Schiedsspruchs)* and regulated as well recognition and enforcement of foreign awards (§1044), a matter that was left open in 1877. In 1933, the legislator addressed concerns raised by the widespread recourse to arbitration in situations where one of the parties was socially or economically significantly "weaker" than the other. In an effort to ensure deliberation and reflection by parties before they agree to arbitrate, formal requirements were imposed on arbitration agreements between non-merchants (§1027). More importantly, a second paragraph was added to §1025 providing that arbitration agreements resulting from an abuse of economic and social superiority were invalid. These amendments were inconsistent with the liberal philosophy of Book X and contributed to its decline.

In connection with a revision of choice-of-law rules in 1986, the legislature eased requirements for an award's validity; in particular, §1039 was amended to dispense with the requirement that all the arbitrators sign the award and a less restrictive public policy *(ordre public)* exception was introduced by §1041 (1), No. 2, and §1044 (2).[243]

---

241 §861. For the handling under German law of oaths in court proceedings, see Kaplan, von Mehren and Schaefer, *supra* footnote 68, at 1244.

242 RGBl. I 361 (1930).

243 The new text paralleled the revised public-policy exception for choice-of-law contained in Article 6 EGBGB.

The 1986 reforms were too few and came too late. The UNCITRAL working group charged with preparing a Model Arbitration Law wrote in 1985 that

> the model law will doubtless be of use [not only to developing countries but also] to a considerable number of industrialized countries whose legislation is antiquated in this area and has been made obsolete by the practice of modern international commercial arbitration ([e.g.] Federal Republic of Germany).²⁴⁴

The government report in support of the 1998 Reform Act described the shortcomings of the amended 1879 Act as follows:

> The provisions of the Tenth Book of the Code of Civil Procedure ... are out-dated. For the most part, they still stem from the year in which the ZPO came into force (1879) .... Until the adoption [in 1930] of the provisions respecting the recognition and enforcement of foreign awards, the law in force did not contain special regulations for international arbitration proceedings although they were of primary importance and had in recent decades become of even greater importance. Moreover, the statutory provisions in part no longer reflected legal reality *(Rechtswirklichkeit)* and were, in consequence, regularly set aside by party agreement. (For example, a three-member tribunal was typically substituted for the two-member tribunal provided by §1028 ZPO.) Under the ZPO, arbitral proceedings were left almost entirely to the discretion of the arbitrators unless party agreement provided otherwise. Compare §1034 (2) ZPO. Modern procedural statutes limit significantly, however, the arbitrators' discretion in light of the goal of legal security *(Rechtssicherheit)*. The complicated proceedings required to obtain a declaration of an award's enforceability and the extensive review available against judicial decisions were incompatible with the objective of conducting expeditiously and concluding promptly arbitral proceedings; foreign parties were especially intimidated by these aspects [of arbitration in Germany] .... It is true that, insofar as the statute contained gaps that could be filled, the lacuna were, for the most part, taken care of by judicial decision *(Rechtsprechung)* and scholarly writing .... The fact that the German law of arbitration procedure had thereby been thoroughly modernized, was understood only by experts who knew the fine points of German law. Typically, foreign parties and their lawyers, who chose the place of arbitration especially because of the law there in force, relied entirely on the statutory texts. From this perspective, many parts of the German law must be seen as outmoded.²⁴⁵

Despite Book X's shortcomings, distinguished scholars recognized that many of its provisions were "per se very liberal".²⁴⁶ The Book's difficulties were, for the

---

244   UN doc. *A/CN.9/263* of 19 March 1985, para. A.1.9 *(b)*.

245   BT-Drs. 13/5274 (12 July 1996).

246   K. Berger, *Wirtschaftsschiedsgerichtsbarkeit* 38 (Cologne, de Gruyter, 1992).

most part, not due to its substantive rules but to its lack of transparency and of "user friendliness". As Berger points out:

> Arbitration laws are geared not so much to the domestic lawyer who is familiar with his or her legal system but to the foreign party that expects an easy-to-read and easy-to-work-with arbitration law for its arbitration in a third, 'neutral' country .... The foreign practitioner 'has to feel at home' immediately when reading the law.[247]

The new arbitration law of 1998, based on the UNCITRAL Model Law, has been praised as "one of the most modern and up to date arbitral legislations in Europe".[248] The most important changes are in the law's structure and style. In forty-one detailed provisions, it provides a comprehensive regulatory framework that is understandable by, and accessible to, foreign lawyers. The fact that the German legislation follows quite closely the UNCITRAL Model Law is important in this connection.

In some significant respects the statute departs from the UNCITRAL Model Law. The former applies to international and domestic arbitrations alike and is not limited to commercial arbitrations. When the parties have failed to designate the applicable law for the arbitration, in view of the 1980 Rome Convention on the Law Applicable to Contractual Obligations, §1051 adopts the closest-connection test rather than allowing, as does Article 28 of the Model Law, the arbitral tribunal to "apply the law determined by the conflict of laws rules which it considers applicable". The new law distinguishes for purposes of enforcement between domestic and foreign awards. So far as foreign awards are concerned, §1061, adopting the approach of Article 142 of the Swiss Code of Private International Law, incorporates the relevant provisions of the New York Convention; for domestic awards, §1060 follows the approach of the old law by providing for a declaration of enforceability.

---

247   K. Berger, *Das neue Recht der Schiedsgerichtsbarkeit / The New German Arbitration Law* 44 (Cologne, RWS Verlag, 1998).

248   See *Idem* 39.
   For example, the 1998 Act gives the German courts authority to set aside only awards rendered in Germany (the territorial principle); they can only refuse recognition and enforcement, pursuant to the applicable rules of law, to awards made *under* German law (rejection of the jurisdictional principle). See ZPO §1025 (1). Traditionally, continental European legal systems invoked the jurisdictional principle. The New York Convention of 1958 in Article V 1 *(e)* permits setting aside by the courts of States party to the Convention under either or both principles: an award can be "set aside ... by a competent authority of the country in which, or under the law of which, that award was made".

3.   *Common-Law Jurisdictions*

(a)   England

Unlike France and the Germanic States, England had struggled early and successfully to establish centralized political authority with a monopoly of the administration of justice. England's success shaped the common law in many ways, the most profound of which was to locate the growing point of private law not in codes or other forms of legislation, nor in the executive's sphere, but in the courts of justice. Understandably, these courts were not enamored of private tribunals.

As the nineteenth century began, the courts of England and the United States had little, if any, sympathy for arbitration. Some rejected the *clause compromissoire* – just as French and German courts – out of concern to protect weak or ill-informed parties or doubts respecting the quality of private justice. The large majority justified their hostile position on the ground that executory arbitration agreements were, in their very nature, "against public policy, because they 'oust the jurisdiction' of the courts".[249]

Not until the century's end did modern England give effect to agreements to arbitrate.[250] The 1889 Arbitration Act[251] accepted arbitration as a dispute-resolution process but provided for significant judicial control over the work of the arbitrators. The "special" or "case-stated" procedure that the Act's Section 19 established remained the hallmark of English arbitration until the enactment of the Arbitration Act of 1979.

Section 21 of the Arbitration Act of 1950 provided, for example, that

(1)   An arbitrator or umpire may, and shall if so directed by the High Court, state –
    (a)   any question of law arising in the course of the reference; or

---

249   Judge Jerome Frank, writing for the court, in *Kulukundis Shipping Co., S.A. v. Amtorg Trading Corp.*, 126 F. 2d 978, at 983 (2d Cir. 1942).
      At least a few scholars challenge the generally held "ouster" explanation of the non-binding quality of arbitration clauses for yet non-existing disputes: "It was ... perceived by at least some courts that the existence of genuine mutual assent was suspect when parties agreed to arbitrate a future dispute, and that a dispute resolution clause could be a trap for the unwary." P. Carrington and P. Haagen, [1996] Sup. Ct. Rev. 331, at 340. There is general agreement that *executed* agreements to arbitrate were "as enforceable in federal and most state courts as were judicial judgments". *Idem* at 339; cf. also Judge Frank, 126 F. 2d 978, at 983.

250   Prior to 1687, agreements to arbitrate were effectively sanctioned by requiring the parties to give a penal bond, obligating them to accept the arbitrators' award. Cf. *Vynor's Case* (1609), 8 Coke Repr. 81 b. The Statute of Fines and Penalties, enacted in 1687 (8 & 9 Will. III c. 11, sec. 81), made penal bonds useless. The statute limited recovery on a bond to the loss suffered and proved, an amount which, in the case of a refusal to arbitrate, it was impossible to quantify.

251   52 & 53 Vict. c. 49.

(b)   an award or any part of an award, in the form of a special case for the decision of the High Court.[252]

The Arbitration Act of 1979 went a considerable distance in the direction of allowing arbitration proceedings to function on their own with judicial controls, to the extent they were permitted, operating in principle only after the arbitral phase was concluded. In its first section, the Act repealed Section 21 and abrogated as well the common-law jurisdiction of the High Court to set aside or remit an award on the ground of errors of fact or law appearing on the award's face. The High Court retained power to grant leave to appeal where the determination of the issue of fact in question could substantially affect the rights of a party. The Act also introduced an important innovation; parties, subject to some exceptions, could exclude such review in "non-domestic arbitration agreements".[253]

The Arbitration Act of 1996[254] was the culmination of an effort that began in the 1980s to make England a more attractive seat for international commercial arbitration. The case-stated procedure and other forms of judicial monitoring of English arbitral proceedings and of the resulting awards, permitted under the 1950 and 1979 Acts, had made arbitration in England increasingly unattractive to potential users as other countries relaxed judicial supervision over international arbitrations. To restore the competitiveness of English arbitration, the 1996 Act repealed Part I of the 1950 Act and all of the 1979 Act. The 1996 Act is far more detailed than its predecessors; it resolves important issues and clarifies many matters.

For present purposes, the Act's most important provisions are Sections 45 (1) and 69 (1); they address the extent to which the parties can control the extent and manner of judicial supervision of the arbitral process and the resulting award. Section 45 (1) provides that "the court may on the application of a party to arbitral proceedings (upon notice to the other parties) determine any question of law arising in the course of the proceedings which the court is satisfied substantially affects the rights of one or more of the parties". Section 69 (1) states that "a party to arbitral proceedings may (upon notice to the other parties and to the tribunal) appeal to the court on a question of law arising out of an award made in the proceedings". In each section this language is preceded and followed by identical language: "Unless otherwise agreed by the parties"; "An agreement to dispense with reasons for the award shall be considered an agreement to exclude the courts' jurisdiction under this section."

---

252   Arbitration Act of 1950, 14 & 15 Geo. 6, s. 27. See also Section 22 (court order remitting an award in whole or in part to the arbitrator for reconsideration) and Section 23 (court order setting aside an arbitral award where an arbitrator has "misconducted himself or the proceedings"). In addition, under Section 4, for "sufficient reason" the court could in effect break an arbitration clause.

253   See Section 3 (1). In "domestic arbitration agreements", exclusion was also permissible but only if agreed to *after* the arbitration had been commenced. See *idem* (6).

254   The Act entered into force on 31 January 1997. S.I. 1996, No. 3146.

The 1979 Act distinguished between domestic and non-domestic agreements for various purposes, the most important of which was the extent to which the parties could by agreement exclude judicial supervision of the arbitral proceedings and the tribunal's holdings. The 1996 Act, as drafted, did not abolish that distinction. There was agreement that the parties in non-domestic arbitrations could exclude Sections 45 (1) and 69 (1); however, whether to permit exclusion was still under discussion for domestic arbitrations. In order to avoid delaying the legislation, the decision was made to leave the issue open. Accordingly, a separate section – 87 – continued the existing rule for domestic arbitrations. Section 87 was placed in a separate part of the Act and made subject to repeal, if and when desired, by a positive joint resolution of each House of Parliament.

Shortly before the 1996 Act received the Royal Assent on 17 June 1996, a court of first instance held that the distinction between domestic and non-domestic arbitrations as made in the Consumer Arbitration Agreements Act of 1988 was incompatible with European Community law on either, or both, of two scores:[255] As a restriction on the freedom to provide services, the distinction was contrary to Article 59 (now Article 49) of the Treaty of Rome or, alternatively, was an unlawful discrimination under Article 6 (now Article 12) of the Treaty. The possibility of removing the element of discrimination by widening the definition of "domestic" in the 1996 Act was considered but found to be unworkable. The decision was taken, therefore, to abolish the distinction; accordingly, §87 was not brought into force.[256] "As a result, a mandatory stay is in principle available in any case where proceedings are brought in breach of an agreement to refer a dispute to arbitration."[257] The domestic- non-domestic distinction having disappeared, the parties can exclude by agreement judicial review that Sections 45 and 69 otherwise provide.

The user-friendliness that the 1996 Act displays has, of course, its price. Inexperienced, economically weaker parties are accorded less protection than in the past. Moreover, as controversies in fields such as insurance and maritime matters are lost to arbitration, the English courts are deprived of a part of the raw material they need if they are in the future to develop and refine these and other branches of the law of international commerce.

---

255 The thirteenth edition of Dicey and Morris mistakenly assumes that the Court of Appeal's decision in *Philip Alexander Securities and Futures Ltd.* v. *Bamberger*, [1997] I. L. Pr. 73 (CA 1996) predates the giving of the Royal Assent of 17 June. See A. Dicey and J. Morris, *The Conflict of Laws*, at 609-610, No. 16-038 (London, Sweet & Maxwell, 13th ed., 2000). The decision on appeal was handed down on 12 July.

256 See S.I. 1996, No. 3146.

257 Dicey and Morris, *supra* footnote 255, at 610, No. 16-038.

(b) United States
(i) A general view

Beginning in the latter part of the nineteenth century, the approaches of English and American law to arbitration began to diverge. As described immediately above, the English accepted arbitration but provided considerable – and intrusive – judicial control over on-going arbitrations and applied demanding standards in reviewing the arbitrators' findings of fact and conclusions of law. Into the early decades of the twentieth century, American courts continued to treat arbitration agreements as unenforceable in principle. An agreement that a court action would not be permitted until arbitrators had adjudicated a limited, clearly specified, issue was, however, generally given effect.[258]

The American Law Institute's first Restatement of Contracts, promulgated in 1932, stated in §550 that

> a bargain to arbitrate either an existing or a possible future dispute is not illegal, unless the agreed terms of arbitration are unfair, but will not be specifically enforced, and only nominal damages are recoverable for its breach.[259] Nor is any bargain to arbitrate a bar to an action on the claim to which the bargain relates.

It was considered "an elementary proposition of the common law ... , and ... [was] almost universally accepted by the American courts, that future dispute clauses and provisions for arbitration are revocable".[260]

By 1979, the picture had changed completely. The Second Restatement of Contracts, promulgated in that year, observed in an Introductory Note to Topic 1, Unenforceability in General, of its Chapter 8, Unenforceability on Grounds of Public Policy, that the Chapter does not provide "detailed rules ... on fields in which legislation has become preeminent".[261]

It was noted, however, that

> A particularly important change has been effected by statutes relating to arbitration, which have now been enacted in so many jurisdictions that it seems likely that even in the remaining states, there has been a change in the former judicial attitude of hostility toward agreements to arbitrate future disputes (see Restatement Second, Conflict of Law, Introductory Note to Topic 5, Chapter 8). Such agreements are now widely used and serve the public interest by saving court time ...[262]

---

258 See A. Corbin, *Contracts*, Vol. VIA, §1431 (St. Paul, Minn., West Publishing, 1962).

259 Restatement Second of Conflict of Laws explains that "it was deemed that ... [the aggrieved party] could not have suffered injury by being required to litigate his case before the court ...". See Introductory Note to Commercial Arbitration, *Idem* 716.

260 W. Sturges, *A Treatise on Commercial Arbitrations and Awards*, §15, at 45 (Kansas City, Mo., Vernon, 1930).

261 Restatement of Contracts 2d, Vol. II, at 3 (St. Paul, Minn., American Law Institute Publisher, 1981).

262 *Idem* 4.

The distinction of being the first American jurisdiction to establish a "modern" arbitration regime belongs to New York which, by the Arbitration Act of 1920,[263] made agreements to arbitrate disputes arising in the future enforceable and irrevocable.

The Congress of the United States followed New York's lead in 1925 by enacting the United States Arbitration Act.[264] The Act's key provision is §2. Validity, irrevocability and enforcement of agreements to arbitrate:

> A written provision in any maritime transaction or a contract evidencing a transaction involving commerce to settle by arbitration a controversy thereafter arising out of such contract or transaction, or the refusal to perform the whole or any part thereof, or an agreement in writing to submit to arbitration an existing controversy arising out of such a contract, transaction, or refusal, shall be valid, irrevocable, and enforceable, save upon such grounds as exist at law or in equity for the revocation of any contract.

In 1955 the National Conference on Uniform State Laws approved a Uniform Arbitration Act. The Act,[265] which provides a model for legislative action by individual States,[266] is far more detailed than the FAA. In nineteen sections, it addresses validity of the arbitration agreement; proceedings to compel or stay arbitration; appointment of arbitrators by courts; majority action by arbitrators; the right to

---

263 New York Laws of 1920, Chap. 275, effective 19 April 1920.
For a discussion of the Act and its early history, see L. Popkin, "Judicial Construction of the New York Arbitration Law of 1920", 11 *Cornell LQ* 329-352 (1926). New York's arbitration law is now contained in Article 75 – Arbitration of the New York Civil Practice Law, §§7501-7514.

264 Act of 12 February 1925, Chap. 213, 43 Stat. 883; codified as amended at 9 USC §§1-14 (1982). The Act is today commonly referred to as the Federal Arbitration Act.

265 See I. Macneil, R. Speidel and T. Stipanovich, *Federal Arbitration Law*, Vol. I, §5.4.2, at 5:9-5:11 (Boston, MA, New York, NY, Toronto and London, Little, Brown and Co., 1994).

266 The 1955 Act had been preceded by the 1924 Uniform Arbitration Act. The latter challenged the approach of the 1920 New York Act and the FAA. Under that Act, arbitral agreements respecting future disputes were revocable. This non-modern act was adopted in Nevada in 1925, and in Utah, Wyoming, and North Carolina in 1927. No further adoptions took place. See I. Macneil, *American Arbitration Law: Reformation – Nationalization – Internationalization* 54 (New York, NY, and Oxford, Oxford University Press, 1992). The intrigue and bitterness of the struggle between the conservative Commissioners on Uniform State Laws and the reformers that backed the New York Act and the Federal Arbitration Act are described *idem* 48-55.
The 1955 Act "proved to be a powerful weapon in the final push of the reformers in the states". *Idem* 56. In this respect, it can be compared with the UNCITRAL Model Law of 1985. A few states of the United States have adopted the Model Law for reasons analogous to those that prompted Germany to follow it quite closely. See pp. 234-236, *supra*.

representation by an attorney; witnesses, subpoenas, depositions; form and timing of the award; change of the award by the arbitrators; fees and expenses of the arbitrators; court confirmation of the award; vacating an award; modification or correction of the award; granting a judgment or decree based on an award; jurisdiction of courts of the state to enforce arbitral agreements under the Act and to enter judgment on an award; and venue.[267]

The Act's §1 provides that

> a provision in a written contract to submit to arbitration any controversy thereafter arising between the parties is valid, enforceable and irrevocable, save upon such grounds as exist at law or in equity for the revocation of any contract.

An award can be vacated by court order under §12 where (1) it "was procured by corruption, fraud or other undue means"; (2) "[t]here was evident partiality by an arbitrator appointed as a neutral or corruption in any of the arbitrators or misconduct prejudicing the rights of any party"; (3) "[t]he arbitrators exceeded their powers"; (4) "[t]he arbitrators refused to postpone the hearing upon sufficient cause being shown therefor or refused to hear evidence material to the controversy or otherwise so conducted the hearing, contrary to the provisions of Section 5 , as to prejudice substantially the rights of any party"; or (5) "[t]here was no arbitration agreement and the issue was not adversely determined in proceedings under Section 2 and the party did not participate in the arbitration hearing without raising the objection".

An award can be modified or corrected under §13 where:

(1)   There was an evident miscalculation of figures or an evident mistake in the description of any person, thing or property referred to in the award;

(2)   The arbitrators have awarded upon a matter not submitted to them and the award may be corrected without affecting the merits of the decision upon the issues submitted; or

(3)   The award is imperfect in a matter of form, not affecting the merits of the controversy.

In 1985, the United Nations Commission on International Trade Law adopted a Model Law on International Arbitration. The Law seeks to provide a comprehen-

---

267   See 7 Pt. I ULA 6 (1997). The Act "has been one of the most successful acts of the National Conference of Commissioners on Uniform State Laws ...". T. Heinsz, "The Revised Uniform Arbitration Act: Modernizing, Revising, and Clarifying Arbitration Law" [2001] *J. Dispute Res.* 1. "Of the forty-nine jurisdictions with arbitration statutes, thirty-five of these have adopted the UAA and fourteen have based their statutes in some form upon the UAA." *Ibid.* See also S. Hayford, "Federal Preemption and Vacatur: The Bookend Issues under the Revised Uniform Arbitration Act", [2001] *J. Dispute Res.* 67-88.

sive, modern arbitration statute that will be acceptable worldwide and, over time, adopted by many national legislatures.[268]

The Model Law can be seen as a global counterpart to federal-system unification efforts such as the 1955 Uniform Arbitration Act. The Model Law is more complete and up-to-date than the 1955 Act. It has been adopted by eight states of the United States: California, Connecticut, Florida, Georgia, North Carolina, Ohio, Oregon, and Texas. The adoption in Connecticut has been the most complete; the law was enacted in its full text, without changes, except for the addition of a 37th article which states: "This Act may be cited as the UNCITRAL Model Law on International Commercial Arbitration."[269]

The Model Law has been adopted by a significant number of countries and has influenced arbitration legislation enacted in other countries.[270]

The first countries which adopted ML-based legislation were Canada (1986), Cyprus (1987), Bulgaria and Nigeria (1988), Australia and Hong Kong (1989), Scotland (1990), Peru, Bermuda, the Russian Federation, Mexico, and Tunisia (1993).[271]

More recently, the Model Law has influenced the 1996 Act applicable in England, Northern Ireland, and Wales,[272] and the German Act of 1998.[273]

In 1995, the National Conference of Commissioners on Uniform State Laws undertook a study that led to the Conference adopting, in August 2000, the Revised Uniform Arbitration Act of 2000.[274] By the end of 2005, twelve states – Alaska, Colorado, Hawaii, Nevada, New Jersey, New Mexico, North Carolina, North Dakota, Oklahoma, Oregon, Utah and Washington – had adopted the new act.[275]

The Act's drafters worked under a constraint to which their 1955 predecessors had not been subjected: the federalization of American arbitration law resulting from the Supreme Court's 1985 decision in the *Southland* case. The 1955 Act did not face a preemptive FAA; the 2000 Act does. Accordingly, it seeks to "provide the states [with] a template for updating their arbitration acts that mini-

---

268 According to an UNCITRAL update in August 2006, 51 jurisdictions have adopted the Model Law. See UNCITRAL Status of Conventions and Model Laws of 6 August 2006.

269 Publ. Act No. 89-179, 1989, Conn. Legis. Serv. (West) approved January 1989 Regular Session in force since 1 October 1991.

270 See T. Várady, J. Barceló, and A. von Mehren, International Commercial Arbitration 62 (St. Paul, Minn., West Group, 3d. ed. 2006).

271 See *idem* 62, footnote 13.

272 See pp. 237-239 *passim, supra*.

273 See pp. 234-236, *supra*.

274 See Heinsz, *supra* footnote 267, at 2. The complete text of the act is set forth in 7 Pt. I ULA 10 (2005).

275 See 7 Pt. I ULA (2005), 2006 Cumulative Annual Pocket Part, at 1.

mizes concerns that ... [their] legislative efforts might eventually be mooted by the FAA".[276] For doctrinal reasons as well as

> [t]he general absence of definitive federal law regarding ... 'procedural' issues[,] the Drafting Committee ... [concluded that] there is no palpable threat of federal preemption in ... [the procedural] sphere, especially when state law addressing these matters is intended to further, not hinder, the commercial arbitration ... process ...[277]

The drafters assumed that amendment of the FAA, in the foreseeable future, to address such matters as "notice, consolidation, arbitrator immunity, pre-hearing procedure and discovery, [and] court enforcement of pre-award arbitral rulings ..." was unlikely.[278] The Uniform Act thus provided, in their view, an opportunity to create a nation-wide, well-designed, modern, and harmonized procedural regime for commercial arbitration.[279] The Act contains, *inter alia*, provisions designed to accommodate transactions by electronic means, including electronic arbitration,[280] and tackles the inherently difficult task of disclosure by arbitrators,[281] as well as provisional[282] (Section 8) and final[283] (Section 21) remedies.

The complex and controversial issue of consolidating arbitrations is also addressed: unless the parties to an arbitration have specifically provided otherwise in the arbitration agreement, courts *may*

> order consolidation if (1) there is a multiparty situation where all involved have arbitration agreements, (2) the claims arise out of essentially the same or related transactions, (3) common issues of law or fact create the possibility of conflicting decisions if the cases were arbitrated in separate proceedings, and (4) the prejudice from failure to consolidate is not outweighed by delay or prejudice to parties opposing consolidation. Moreover, the court may decide to consolidate some of the claims and allow others to be resolved in separate arbitration proceedings if that would be a more appropriate result. However, a court is precluded from ordering consolidation of arbitral proceedings where the parties' arbitration agreement prohibits consolidation.[284]

---

276   Hayford, *supra* footnote 267, at 80.

277   *Ibid.*

278   *Ibid.*

279   See *ibid.*

280   See Heinsz, *supra* footnote 267, at 9-10.

281   *Idem* 17-20.

282   *Idem* 21-22.

283   *Idem* 22-26.

284   *Idem* 13-14 (footnotes omitted). It will be interesting to see how widely the opt-out clause will be used. The Uniform Act "does not address the much debated issue of class-action arbitrations". *Idem* 15.

The perplexing problem of discovery in arbitration is taken up in Section 17. The drafters did not accede to the demands of some that Federal Rules discovery, largely conducted by parties and potentially very extensive in character, be allowed in arbitration. The resulting expense and delay would, in their view, deprive arbitration of its comparative advantage over court litigation in speed, informality, and expense. On the other hand, fairness frequently requires that at least some discovery be allowed.

> The RUAA resolves the difficult arbitral discovery issues by allowing parties to adopt their own discovery rules, including the full panoply of procedures allowed in the judicial process. If the parties do not provide for discovery rules in their arbitration agreement, then Section 17, as a default mechanism, authorizes arbitrators to decide whether to allow discovery, and, if so, to what extent. Normally arbitrators will allow only limited discovery under the standards of Section 17 *(c)*. Although arbitrators have authority to involve third parties in discovery and the arbitral process, the statute recognizes that, as nonparties, these persons are entitled to greater protections from unwarranted interference. Section 17 *(g)* makes the means to compel out-of-state witnesses to attend arbitral discovery proceedings or hearings more efficient. Section 17 not only adapts discovery to evolving arbitration practice, but also maintains arbitration's identity separate and apart from litigation.[285]

The likely compatibility of the provisions discussed above with the FAA supports their inclusion in the Revised Uniform Arbitration Act; conversely, fears that provisions respecting other matters might ultimately prove to be incompatible with the FAA, contributed to the Act's failure to address them. For example, the question was debated at length whether parties should be allowed to provide in their arbitration agreement for judicial review of the resulting award.[286] Many opposed allowing "opting-in" to judicial review on the ground that permitting this practice would destroy the effectiveness and integrity of arbitration as a dispute-resolution process. At the end of the day, these critics foresaw a hybrid process emerging that was less efficient and more costly than either stand-alone arbitration or court litigation. The more compelling argument, however, against allowing "opting-in" was perhaps

> the present uncertainty in federal and state law concerning the propriety of additional grounds for judicial review of arbitral decisions, such as contractual agreements to reverse for errors of law or fact …. In particular, neither the Drafting Committee nor NCCUSL wanted to risk preemption of the important section on vacatur because an opt-in provision would run contrary to future federal law.[287]

---

285 *Idem* 50-51.
286 See *Idem* 27-28. The few federal and state courts that have addressed the issue are split. See *idem* 28-30.
287 *Idem* 29-30.

Pre-emption concerns likewise caused the drafters to omit from Section 23 *(a)* of the Revised Act manifest disregard of the law and public policy as grounds for vacating awards. Since these bases for vacatur have traditionally been non-statutory, their absence in the Revised Act will not interfere with current practices by the courts.[288] Not only would it have been difficult to draft the requisite statutory language but "[p]reemptive issues would ... arise ... [should] the Supreme Court define[] the law of vacatur for ... [the ground in question] differently from that developed by a RUAA provision".[289]

(ii)   The "federalization" of American arbitration law

The rise of modern arbitration in the United States began not with reforming federal legislation but with the New York Act of 1920. Today almost all states have state arbitration acts, the majority based on the Uniform Act of 1955.[290] The Federal Arbitration Act of 1925, which originally had a single chapter, now has three.[291] The new chapters implement international obligations, assumed by the United States after World War II, under the New York Convention of 10 June 1958 on the Recognition and Enforcement of Foreign Arbitral Awards and the Inter-American Convention of 30 January 1975 on International Commercial Arbitration.

The federalism issues that arise for American arbitration law distinguish it – like so many other areas of American law – from French, German, and English law. In the United States, the federal and the state governments have each developed – through legislation and judicial decisions – their respective arbitration laws. As a result, American practice faced – and still faces – problems of great importance and considerable complexity whose resolution has changed over time. These problems, for the most part, do not arise in French, German, and English law;[292] they include such questions as: does adjudicatory authority in arbitration

---

288   See *idem* 35.

289   *Idem* 33.

290   The states were at first slow to adopt modern arbitration acts; only thirteen had done so by 1931; and by 1958 only three more had acted. See Macneil, *et al., supra* footnote 265, §10.3.1, at 10:8, footnote 7. After 1958, the Uniform Act of 1955 took over the field.

291   Chapter 2 was added in 1970 (see 84 Stat. 692); two new sections were passed by Congress in October of 1988 and renumbered in December of 1990 (see PL 669 and PL 702). Chapter 3 was added in August 1990 (see PL 101-369).

292   The United States, aside from the problems discussed above resulting from the federal structure of its polity, faces – as do many other States, unitary and federal alike – difficult issues respecting the relationship between, on the one hand, the State's obligations under international instruments such as the New York Convention of 1958, and, on the other hand, under the State's national arbitration law.
United States jurists hold, for example, differing views on how the FAA of 1925, as amended, meshes and interrelates with the New York Convention. Section 208, Chapter II, of the FAA, which implements the Convention, provides that Chapter I of the 1925 Act, as amended, "applies to actions and proceedings brought under ...

matters rest in federal or in state court, or in both? Where federal and state arbitration laws clash, which law prevails? Is the relevant law – generally contract law – but, when in issue, as well property, agency, or corporation law – to be derived (1) from generally accepted principles of law, (2) from the law of the legal order whose law would, were the controversy before a court, govern as a matter of choice of substantive law, or (3) from yet another source?[293]

The many intricacies of the relationship between federal and state law where arbitration is involved are not considered here. The discussion is limited to explaining how the Federal Arbitration Act, arguably conceived in strictly proce-

---

chapter [II] to the extent that chapter [I] is not in conflict with ... chapter [II] or the Convention as ratified by the United States". Some contend that §208 incorporates into Chapter II only §2, which provides that written arbitration agreements are enforceable subject only to "such grounds as exist at law or in equity for the revocation of any contract". Others would incorporate as well §§10-11, which address the confirmation and modification of awards.

The argument against incorporation of these sections is that they address vacatur (setting aside) while Articles III-V of the New York Convention address recognition and enforcement. The grounds for setting-aside and for denying recognition and enforcement may, or may not, rest on comparable policies. The failure of the FAA of 1925 to address enforcement resulted, however, not from policy considerations but from the fact that the Act did not address foreign awards and, accordingly, dealt only with setting-aside.

Had the drafters of Chapter II of the FAA been arbitration technicians, they would have been aware of the different thrusts of Chapters I and II. To the extent that the interaction of these chapters is to turn not on drafting technicalities but on policy considerations, a strong argument can be made that "[s]ection 208 should be read to exclude from incorporation into Chapter II only those Chapter I provisions less favorable to enforcement than their counterparts in the Convention". K. Davis, "Unconventional Wisdom: A New Look at Articles V and VII of the Convention on the Recognition and Enforcement of Foreign Arbitral Awards", 37 *Texas Int'l. Law J.* 43, at 74 (2002).

Article VII of the New York Convention also raises the issue of the interaction between a State's international obligations and its national law of arbitration. Article VII (1) of the New York Convention provides that

[t]he provisions of the present Convention shall not ... deprive any interested party of any right he may have to avail himself of an arbitral award in the manner and to the extent allowed by the law or the treaties of the country where such award is sought to be relied upon.

The Article V-Article VII issue has arisen in several countries, is much debated, and typically unresolved, as is the case in the United States. Professor Kenneth Davis in an excellent paper discusses the drafting history of these articles, the jurisprudence of various countries regarding the issues they raise, and the arguments of policy urged to support the various positions taken. See *idem* 43-87.

293 The prevailing view is that, in arbitrations within the scope of the Federal Arbitration Act, the general law of the state whose substantive law would govern, were the controversy to be adjudicated by a court, is to be applied. See Macneil, *et al., supra* footnote 265, §10.7.1, at 10:49-10:50.

dural terms, came to supersede state arbitration laws in litigation before state courts and the consequential changes that followed for the interaction between federal and state law respecting arbitration.[294]

a.   The original understanding

In 1925, the generally accepted learning was that "[a]ll matters of procedure are governed by the law of the forum".[295] According to Comment *a* to §585 of the Restatement First of Conflict of Laws, procedural matters included "access to courts, the conditions of maintaining or barring actions, the method of dealing with foreign law, and proceedings after judgments".

Under the broad and abstract concept of procedure that §585 exemplifies, the parties' ousting of court adjudication in favor of arbitration raises a procedural issue. Enacted as a "procedural statute", the FAA originally applied – and, as a "procedural" law, could only apply – to proceedings in federal courts.[296] The contemporary "commentators … [were] unanimous in their treatment of the FAA as an act governing only in the federal courts".[297] By the same token, federal courts considered state arbitration law – whether based on state common law or on state statutory law – inapplicable in federal courts.[298]

Although unrealistic in the political climate of the 1920s, Congress could have provided that the FAA would apply as well to the arbitration of controversies within the federal interstate and foreign-commerce powers. The enactors of the FAA relied, however, solely on Congress's power to prescribe procedures for federal courts. Accordingly, the expansion of Congress's commerce-clause powers after 1925 was not seen at the time as affecting in any way the FAA's scope.

Section 2, which addresses scope, provides that the Act does not apply to contracts in purely *intrastate* commerce. The limitation is stated indirectly: only "contract[s] evidencing a transaction involving commerce" – which §1 defines as "commerce among several States or with foreign nations …" – are covered by the Act. When read not in the light of the understandings and juristic assumptions of the 1920s but in light of changes in thinking and practice that were to come, perhaps this language can be understood as invoking substantive commerce powers. It was not so read at the time, however, but solely as an exercise by Congress of its

---

294   The profound changes that have occurred in the course of the latter half of the twentieth century in the interactions of federal and state arbitration law are epitomized by the attention the drafters of the Uniform Arbitration Act of 1955 gave to the issue of federal preemption – none – and that given by the drafters of the Revised Uniform Arbitration Act of 2000 – a great deal. See pp. 243-244, *supra*.

295   Restatement of Conflict of Laws §585 (St. Paul, Minn., American Law Institute, 1934).

296   See Macneil *et al.*, *supra* footnote 265, §10.1, at 10:4. For a full discussion of the Act's intellectual history, see Macneil, *supra* footnote 266, at 83-133.

297   See Macneil *et al.*, *supra* footnote 265, §10.3.3, at 10:11.

298   *Idem* §10.2, at 10:6.

power over procedure in the federal courts; the language respecting commerce served simply to limit the scope of that exercise.[299]

b.   The erosion of the conceptual structure on which the original understanding
      rested: the significance of *Erie R.R. v. Tompkins*

Understood as a procedural statute, the FAA does not apply in state courts; by the same token comparable state legislation is inapplicable in federal courts. The overruling of *Swift v. Tyson*[300] by *Erie R.R. v. Tompkins*[301] set in motion forces that, in time, were to transform the "FAA from the procedural statute that congress had enacted 13 years before [*Erie R.R.* was decided] into a substantive statute greatly reducing the powers of the states".[302]

In *Swift*, the Supreme Court held that Section 34 of the Judiciary Act of 1789, Chapter 20, which provided that

> [t]he laws of the several states, except where the constitution, treaties or statutes of the United States shall otherwise require or provide, shall be regarded as rules of decision, in trials at common law, in cases where they apply,

did not direct federal courts to follow state laws except those

> strictly local, that is to say, ... the positive statutes of the state, and the construction thereof adopted by the local tribunals, and ... rights and titles to things having a permanent locality, such as the rights and titles to real estate, and other matters immovable and intraterritorial in their nature and character.[303]

It had never been the high Court's view

> that the section did apply, or was designed to apply, to questions of a more general nature, not at all dependent upon local statutes or local usages of a fixed and permanent operation, as, for example, to the construction of ordinary contracts or other written instruments, and especially to questions of general commercial law, where the state tribunals are called upon to perform the like functions as ourselves, that is, to ascertain, upon general reasoning and legal analogies, what is the true exposition of the contract or instrument, or what is the just rule furnished by the principles of commercial law to govern the case. And we have not now the slightest difficulty in holding, that ... section [34], upon its true intendment and construction, is strictly limited to local statutes and local usages of the character before stated, and does not extend

---

299 It was apparently feared that, were *entirely intrastate* arbitrations covered, the Act could be held unconstitutional as a violation of states' rights. See *idem* §10.5.3, at 10:25.

300 41 US (16 Pet.) 1 (1842).

301 304 US 64 (1938).

302 Macneil *et al.*, *supra* footnote 265, §10.4.1, at 10:12.

303 41 US (16 Pet.) at 18.

to contracts and other instruments of a commercial nature, the true interpretation and effect whereof are to be sought, not in the decisions of the local tribunals, but in the general principles and doctrines of commercial jurisprudence. Undoubtedly, the decisions of the local tribunals upon such subjects are entitled to, and will receive, the most deliberate attention and respect of this Court; but they cannot furnish positive rules, or conclusive authority, by which our own judgments are to be bound up and governed. The law respecting negotiable instruments may be truly declared in the language of Cicero, adopted by Lord Mansfield in Luke v. Lyde, 2 Burr. 883, 887, to be in a great measure, not the law of a single country only, but of the commercial world. *Non erit alia lex Romae, alia Athenis; alia nunc, alia posthac, sed et apud omnes gentes, et omni tempore, una eademque lex obtinebit.*[304]

In 1938, *Erie R.R.* v. *Tompkins* overruled *Swift* v. *Tyson*. Story's decision had been severely criticized on various grounds. Justice Holmes saw the decision as resting on the "fallacy" that "a transcendental body of law [existed] outside of any particular State but obligatory within it unless and until changed by statute".[305] In his opinion for the Court in *Erie R.R.*, Justice Brandeis remarked that the doctrine of *Swift* had produced not the hoped-for benefits but "mischievous results":[306]

Persistence of state courts in their own opinions on questions of common law prevented uniformity; and the impossibility of discovering a satisfactory line of demarcation between the province of general law and that of local law developed a new well of uncertainties.

On the other hand, the mischievous results of the doctrine had become apparent. Diversity of citizenship jurisdiction was conferred in order to prevent apprehended discrimination in state courts against those not citizens of the state. Swift v. Tyson introduced grave discrimination by non-citizens against citizens. It made rights enjoyed under the unwritten 'general law' vary according to whether enforcement was sought in the state or in the federal court; and the privilege of selecting the court in which the right should be determined was conferred upon the non-citizen. Thus, the doctrine rendered impossible equal protection of the law. In attempting to promote uniformity of law throughout the United States, the doctrine had prevented uniformity in the administration of the law of the state.[307]

---

304 *Idem* 18-19.

Section 34 became the Rules of Decision Act. 26 USC §1692. The Act provides that

The laws of the several states, except where the Constitution or treaties of the United States or Acts of Congress otherwise require or provide, shall be regarded as rules of decision in civil actions in the courts of the United States, in cases where they apply.

305 *Black & White Taxicab and Transfer Co.* v. *Brown & Yellow Taxicab and Transfer Co.*, 276 US 518, 532, at 533.

306 304 US at 74.

307 *Idem* 74-75 (footnotes omitted).

The Copernican revolution that *Erie* wrought had no immediate consequences for the FAA. The black-letter proposition that forum law governed procedural matters was not touched by *Erie*. The philosophy that animated *Erie*, that "rights ... [should not] vary according to whether [their] enforcement was sought in the state or in the federal court",[308] was, however, ultimately to affect profoundly the understanding of what was "procedural" and what "substantive".

The policies that inform *Erie* and its progeny require that those rules of decision which have more than trivial consequences for the giving and denial of relief, should not turn on whether the matter is brought before a state or a federal court unless it is not practical to vary the rule from case to case. The implications of this position for the substance-procedure dichotnomy were pointed out in *Guaranty Trust Co. of N.Y. v. York*:[309]

> In essence, the intent of ... [*Erie*] was to insure that, in all cases where a federal court is exercising jurisdiction solely because of the diversity of citizenship of the parties, the outcome of the litigation in the federal court should be substantially the same, so far as legal rules determine the outcome of a litigation, as it would be if tried in a State court.[310]

Variations on the "outcome test" propounded in *Guaranty Trust* are encountered; for present purposes they do not require discussion. It is enough to note that the results of court litigation and of arbitration are likely to be different. Those who arbitrate "must content themselves with looser [or at least different] approximations to the enforcement of their rights than those that the law accords them, when they resort to its machinery".[311] Since courts are quite capable of applying non-local arbitration laws, for *Erie* purposes the FAA was to be characterized as "substantive" rather than "procedural" in nature.[312]

c.   The post-Erie change in the understanding of the FAA

Erie thus put at risk the doctrinal proposition on which the FAA's applicability in diversity cases rested. Under an outcome test, arbitration *vel non* is clearly a matter of "substance". It would follow that the FAA applied in federal courts only if the Act exercised substantive federal power under the commerce clause or some other grant of authority to the federal government. If such a power is exercised, the Act applies as well in state courts, except where purely intrastate arbitrations are concerned. The approach to characterization of "substance" and "procedure"

---

308   *Ibid.*

309   326 US 99 (1945).

310   *Idem* 109.

311   Judge Learned Hand, in *American Almond Products Co. v. Consolidated Pecan Sales Co.*, 144 F. 2d 448, at 450 (2d Cir. 1944).

312   For a discussion of the significance of *Erie* for the handling by federal courts of forum-selection clauses, see *supra* footnote 169.

that flows from *Erie* thus destroyed the basis for the 1925 allocation of authority between the FAA and state arbitration acts.

Almost two decades passed before the Supreme Court addressed the changed situation. *Bernhardt* v. *Polygraphic Co. of America*[313] involved a suit, originally brought in a Vermont state court, and then remanded to the federal court on grounds of diversity of citizenship. The dispute concerned an employment contract that contained an arbitration clause. The US district court denied the employer's request that the state court proceedings be stayed; for *Erie* purposes, arbitration is to be characterized as substantive and accordingly governed by Vermont law, under which agreements to arbitrate were revocable until an award had been made. The Court of Appeals, treating arbitration as procedural, held that the FAA applied and reversed. The Supreme Court granted certiorari. In an opinion by Justice Douglas, the Court reversed the Court of Appeals but on a ground that did not implicate the substance-procedural dichotomy. The matter was outside the scope of the FAA because the contract of employment did not evidence, as §2 required, "a transaction involving commerce".[314]

In *Robert Lawrence Company* v. *Devonshire Fabrics, Inc.*,[315] the Second Circuit drew the logical conclusion from Justice Douglas's dictum that, under *Erie*, arbitration was substantive.[316] At issue was whether fraud in the inducement of a contract containing an agreement to arbitrate tainted not only the container contract but also the arbitration clause. At the time, New York arbitration law did not recognize the separability doctrine; consequently, unless the parties had expressly provided otherwise, the arbitration clause shared the fate of the container contract. If the latter never came into existence, neither did the former. As interpreted by the Second Circuit, however, the FAA accepted the doctrine of separability.

In his opinion for the Court, Judge Medina opined that

> [i]t is reasonably clear that the Congress intended by the Arbitration Act to create a new body of federal substantive law affecting the validity and interpretation of arbi-

---

313   350 US 198 (1956).

314   *Idem* 202.

   In a dictum, the Court indicated that, in its view, "arbitration touched on substantive rights, which Erie ... held were governed by local law ...". *Ibid.* The Court recognized that the *Shanferoke Coal* decision (293 US 449 (1935)) "applied the Federal Act in a diversity case. But that decision antedated Erie ... and did not consider the larger question presented here ...". *Ibid.*

315   271 F. 2d 402 (2d Cir. 1959), *cert. granted*, 362 US 909, *cert. dismissed* under Rule 60, 364 US 801 (1960). Ironically, the *Lawrence* case involved the first modern arbitration statute enacted in the United States, that of New York, whose position on the separability issue had, however, remained pre-modern.

316   See *supra* footnote 169.

tration agreements .... This is a declaration of national law equally applicable in state and federal courts.[317]

In *Prima Paint Corp.* v. *Flood & Conklin Mfg. Co.*,[318] the arbitration clause in question – unlike the clause in *Bernhardt* – was contained in "a transaction involving commerce" among the several States; consequently, the arbitral proceedings were within the FAA's scope. Justice Fortas saw the issue as

> whether [in diversity cases] Congress may prescribe how federal courts are to conduct themselves with respect to subject matter over which Congress plainly has power to legislate. The answer to that can only be in the affirmative. And it is clear beyond dispute that the federal arbitration statute is based upon and confined to the incontestable federal foundations of 'control over interstate commerce and over admiralty.'[319]

Justice Fortas concluded by observing that "[f]ederal courts are bound to apply rules enacted by Congress with respect to matters – here, a contract involving commerce – over which it has legislative power".[320]

Justice Black's long – and, on occasion, sharply worded[321] – dissenting opinion challenges the majority's views on many scores. Near its close, the dissent opines that

> [t]he Court ... does not hold today, as did Judge Medina, that the body of federal substantive law created by federal judges under the Arbitration Act is required to be applied by state courts. A holding to that effect – which the Court seems to leave up in the air – would flout the intention of the framers of the Act. Yet under this Court's opinion today – that the Act supplies not only the remedy of enforcement but a body of federal doctrines to determine the validity of an arbitration agreement – failure to make the Act applicable in state courts would give rise to 'forum shopping' and an unconstitutional discrimination that both Erie and Bernhardt were designed to eliminate. These problems are greatly reduced if the Act is limited, as it should be, to

---

317   *Idem* 406-407.

318   388 US 395 (1967). Justice Harlan joined in the Court's opinion and noted that he "would also affirm the judgment below on the basis of Robert Lawrence Co... ". *Idem* 407. Justice Black, joined by Justice Douglas and Justice Stewart, dissented. *Idem* 407-425.

319   *Idem* 405.

320   *Idem* 406.

321   The opinion begins by characterizing as "fantastic" the holding of the Court "that the legal issue of a contract's voidness because of fraud is to be decided by persons designated to arbitrate factual controversies arising out of a valid contract between the parties. And the arbitrators who the Court holds are to adjudicate the legal validity of the contract need not even be lawyers ... and even if qualified to apply the law, not bound to do so ...". *Idem* 407.

its proper scope: the mere enforcement in federal courts of valid arbitration agreements.[322]

The FAA's applicability in state courts was to remain unclear for another 17 years. Indeed, "[f]or a long time countless arbitrations were conducted and litigated on the undiscussed and unstated assumption that state law governed ...".[323] Meanwhile, the federal courts continued to develop substantive principles. *Prima Paint* had accepted the important proposition that the arbitration contract was separable – or autonomous – from the underlying contract that contained it. *Moses H. Cone Memorial Hospital* v. *Mercury Construction Corp.*[324] held that

> any doubts concerning the scope of arbitrable issues as a matter of federal law should be resolved in favor of arbitration, whether the problem at hand is the construction of the contract language itself or an allegation of waiver, delay, or a like defense to arbitrability.[325]

In 1984 the Supreme Court finally made clear in *Southland Corp.* v. *Keating*[326] "that Prima Paint had indeed nationalized American arbitration law".[327] Three years later, *Perry* v. *Thomas*[328] reiterated the *Southland* principle and clarified the relation between state law and the FAA by adopting "the principle that the law of the particular state supplies the contract law infrastructure for the FAA".[329]

d.   The Southland decision (1984): concepts, history, and policy in tension

In *Southland* the Supreme Court for the first time had to face squarely the issue whether the FAA creates substantive rights that must be enforced by state courts. Justice O'Connor, joined in dissent by Justice Rehnquist, concluded, on the basis of the legislative history, that "Congress did not intend the FAA to govern state-court proceedings".[330] Justice Stevens, concurring in part and dissenting in part, agreed with the majority that "an arbitration clause that is enforceable if the action is brought in a federal court is equally enforceable if the action is brought in a state court".[331] Stevens rested his position not on the legislative history of the

---

322   *Idem* 424-425 (footnotes omitted).

323   Macneil *et al.*, *supra* footnote 265, §10.5.1, at 10:17.

324   460 US 1 (1983).

325   *Idem* 24-25.

326   465 US 1 (1984), recently confirmed in *Buckeye Check Cashing, Inc.* v. *Cardegna*, 126 S.Ct. 1204, 1208 et seq. (2006).

327   Macneil *et al.*, *supra* footnote 265, §10.5.1, at 10:18.

328   482 US 483 (1987).

329   Macneil *et al.*, *supra* footnote 265, §10.6.2.3, at 10:32.

330   465 US 3, 21, at 27.

331   *Idem* 17, at 17.

Federal Arbitration Act, but on the changes in policies and doctrinal positions that had occurred since its enactment:

> Justice O'Connor's review of the legislative history ... demonstrates [for him] that the 1925 Congress ... viewed the statute as essentially procedural in nature, ... [He is, however,] persuaded that the intervening developments in the law compel the conclusion that the Court ... reached ..."[332]

Chief Justice Burger's opinion for the Court opines that: "Although the legislative history is not without ambiguities, there are strong indications that Congress had in mind something more than making arbitration agreements enforceable only in the federal courts."[333] To support this proposition, the Chief Justice quotes from the 1924 House Report accompanying the bill:

> The purpose of this bill is to make valid and enforcible [sic] agreements for arbitration contained *in contracts involving interstate commerce ..., or* which may be the subject of litigation in the Federal courts.[334]

The majority opinion's discussion of the Act's legislative history, which does not address Justice O'Connors's analysis has, with good reason, been characterized as "shoddy".[335]

In the decades since 1925, arbitration's role in commercial matters had become far more important and increasingly international. By 1984 arbitrations with significant non-domestic elements were, in practice, in many aspects largely governed by the New York Convention rather than by national or state arbitration law. In the commercial and political climate of the closing decades of the twentieth century, the reluctance of legislators and judges to displace state law that had delayed the accession of the United States to the New York Convention until 1970 had been replaced by strong support for arbitration, especially in the federal courts and the courts of commercially important states.

The question remains whether it would have been more appropriate in judicial-process terms for the Court to have undertaken a principled analysis that considered the role of arbitration, the policies that supported, as the century neared its close, federalization of American arbitration law, and the consequences of transferring from state to federal law control over the protection, if any, to be accorded such especially vulnerable groups as consumers, "blue-collar" workers, and franchisees, rather that adopting – as the Court did – a cruder approach that

---

332 *Ibid.*

333 *Idem* 3, at 12.

334 *Idem* 12-13 (emphasis and *"[sic]"* supplied by the court).
    It is likely that the "or" in the quoted passage is a clerical or typographical error for "and". See Macneil, *supra* footnote 265, at 118 ("The intention of the writers of the Report was one of addition, not of alternative *[sic]*").

335 Macneil *et al., supra* footnote 265, §10.5.3, at 10:25.

may avoid complexities and ambiguities that might have resulted had another path been taken.

By 1984, political and social dynamics in the United States were such that many state governments were much more likely than the federal government to provide protection against overreaching arbitration agreements in order to protect socially or economically vulnerable groups. Conversely, the federal government is today more concerned than are many states with predictability and efficiency in general.

State law can no longer provide grounds for the revocation of certain types of arbitration agreements – for example agreements between employers and employees or manufacturers and consumers – that are not recognized "at law or in equity for the revocation of any contract". So far as state law respecting arbitration is concerned, what goes for manufacturer-consumer or employer-employee agreements must go for all other types of arbitration agreements. It is all or nothing at all. Had the majority in *Southland* read history as creatively where state protection of vulnerable groups was concerned as they did on the issue whether, generally speaking, arbitration in state courts was subject to the FAA, the Justices could have dealt with the problem that many believe now requires a revamping of the FAA.

In all events, *Southland* marked a point of no return for arbitration law in the United States. A decade after *Southland* was decided, the Commissioners on Uniform State Laws began to work on the Revised Uniform Arbitration Act of 2000. Unlike their predecessors in the 1920s and 1950s, they laboured in the shadow of federal law, treaty, statutory and decisional.

> [T]he strong policy of federal preemption under the FAA acted as a backdrop to all the discussions of the Drafting Committee while it deliberated the ... [Revised Uniform Arbitration Act of 2000]. To avoid federal preemption problems for the RUAA, the Drafting Committee worked diligently to write provisions consistent with the FAA's pro-arbitration policy and not to treat law regarding state arbitration statutes different *[sic]* from the general state law of contracts.[336]

4.   Supranational Arbitration Law: The New York Convention of 1958

The position that arbitration has come to occupy as the third millennium begins does not rest on national arbitration laws alone. Of great significance have been theories respecting the source and nature of arbitral authority, the needs of international trade and commerce, the work of international organizations both private – e.g., the American Arbitration Association, the International Chamber of Commerce, and the London Court of International Arbitration – and public

---

336   Heinsz, *supra* footnote 267, at 5. The issue of federal preemption and the RUAA is taken up in considerable detail in Hayford, *supra* footnote 267, *passim*. For a full and thoughtful discussion of the preemption problem see also P. Carrington and P. Haagen, *supra* footnote 249, at 370-391.

– e.g., the United Nations and the UN Commission on International Trade Law (UNCITRAL).

The United Nations (New York) Convention on the Recognition and Enforcement of Foreign Arbitral Awards[337] provides the foundation on which the presently existing international system of private dispute resolution largely rests. The Convention applies as well

> to the recognition and enforcement of arbitral awards made in the territory of a State other than the State where the recognition and enforcement of such awards are sought, and arising out of differences between persons, whether physical or legal [][as] ... to arbitral awards not considered as domestic awards in the State where their recognition and enforcement are sought.[338]

Directly or through their chosen arbitrators, the parties can control virtually every aspect of the adjudication process; moreover, by and large, effective enforcement of the resulting awards is assured.

The Convention confers on parties to a valid arbitration agreement the power to oust courts of their adjudicatory authority. Article II of the Convention provides in part as follows:

1. Each Contracting State shall recognize an agreement in writing under which the parties undertake to submit to arbitration all or any differences which have arisen or which may arise between them in respect of a defined legal relationship, whether contractual or not, concerning a subject matter capable of settlement by arbitration.
2. The court of a Contracting State, when seized of an action in a matter in respect of which the parties have made an agreement within the meaning of this article, shall, at the request of one of the parties, refer the parties to arbitration, unless it finds that the said agreement is null and void, inoperative or incapable of being performed.

Once an award is rendered, Article III obliges each Contracting State to recognize it "as binding" and enforce it "in accordance with the rules of procedure of the territory where the award is relied upon, under the conditions laid down in ... articles ... [IV[339]-V]". Under Article V (1), the court addressed may refuse "[r]ecognition and enforcement ... [only if] ... the party against whom it is invoked" establishes that

---

337   Opened for signature 10 June 1958, entered into force 7 June 1959, 21 *UST* 2517, *TIAS*, No. 6997, 330 *UNTS* 38.

338   Article I (1); see also Article V (1): "Recognition and enforcement of an award may be refused ... if ... *(e)* The award has ... been set aside or suspended by a competent authority of the country in which, or under the law of which, that award was made."

339   Article IV requires documentation of the award and of the agreement to arbitrate.

[t]he parties ... are under some incapacity, ... the [arbitration] agreement is not valid ...; or ... proper notice of the appointment of the arbitrator or of the arbitration proceedings [was not given, or the party] ... was otherwise unable to present his case; or ... [t]he award deals with a difference not ... falling within the terms of the submission to arbitration or decides matters beyond the scope of the submission to arbitration ...; or ... [t]he composition of the arbitral authority or the arbitral procedure was [improper]; or ... [t]he award has not yet become binding ..., or has been set aside or suspended by a competent authority of the country in which, or under the law of which, that award was made.

Under Article 5 (2),

[r]ecognition and enforcement of an arbitral award may also be refused if ... : ... [t]he subject matter of the difference is not capable of settlement by arbitration under the law of ... [the] country [addressed]; or ... ; ... [t]he recognition or enforcement of the award would be contrary to the public policy of that country".

The New York Convention thus obliges Contracting States to respect party agreements to arbitrate[340] and to recognize and enforce the resulting awards[341] except where the arbitration was, in product or process, seriously defective, a party lacked capacity to arbitrate, the subject matter was not appropriate for arbitration, or recognition or enforcement was contrary to the public policy of the State addressed. For recognition and enforcement purposes, the Convention does not admit *révision au fond*. Where the local law so provides,[342] "a competent authority of the country in which, or under the law of which, ... [they were] made" can review awards on their merits and set aside or suspend them. Nothing in the Convention prevents, moreover, the State of the arbitration's seat from providing, as English law did in the Arbitration Act of 1889, a "special case procedure" that permits significant judicial intervention in on-going arbitration proceedings with respect both to legal and factual issues that arise.

In the contemporary world, arbitration has become a "moveable feast", largely free from unwanted interventions. Absent process defects – but despite deficiencies respecting the merits – recognition and enforcement of awards are assured in States where the award is non-domestic and has not been suspended or set-aside by a court of a State entitled to do so. By siting their arbitration in a State that sets awards aside only when natural justice or due process norms are clearly violated, parties are usually able to ensure the enforceability of awards. The parties' freedom of choice respecting the site of arbitration has caused legal orders to mod-

---

340 Art. II.

341 Arts. III-V.

342 Article 5 (1) *(e)* recognizes that awards can be "set aside or suspended by a competent authority of the country in which, or under the law of which, ... [they were] made." The Conventions does not regulate the grounds on which such setting-asides or suspensions can be ordered.

ify their national laws governing arbitration to meet the requirements of those who prefer private-dispute resolution to national-court litigation. The successive changes in English arbitration law in the last decades of the twentieth century and the enactment of the German Arbitration Act of 1998 were due in no small measure to pressures from the English[343] and German[344] legal professions for an arbitration regime under which international commercial arbitrations could be conducted on their territory without unwanted judicial intrusion and control.

Arbitral awards have become more free-standing for another reason as well. The jurisdictional theory, which saw the arbitral tribunal as exercising adjudicatory authority delegated by a sovereign State, has been undermined by theories that reason from contract and function. Increasingly, awards are seen as anational.[345] Once a contractual and instrumental view of arbitral authority is accepted, no theoretical basis remains that supports setting aside awards. With free-standing arbitral awards, the only issue is whether to recognize and enforce the arbitral process's product. Arbitral tribunals no longer form part of an official governmental hierarchy. Just as is the case when an official hierarchy charged with dispute resolution provides a definite adjudication, the sole issue to be addressed is becoming that of recognition and enforcement *vel non*.

---

343 See pp. 237-239, *supra*.

344 See pp. 234-236, *supra*.

345 For discussion of anational awards and the nature of the adjudicatory authority exercised by arbitrators, see Davis, *supra* footnote 296, at 43-88.

Chapter VI Forum Shopping and Fine-tuning: Herein of *Forum Non Conveniens*, Antisuit Injunctions, and *Lis Pendens*

In Chapter IV, the question was explored whether, in contemporary legal systems, defendants are – and should be – preferred by rules and principles respecting the adjudicatory authority exercised by courts. In light of the multiplicity of forums that are, in contemporary practice, typically available to the moving party, it was concluded that the *actor sequitur* principle did not reflect today's realities. Chapter VI considers a related topic: the extent to – and the manner in – which a party's forum-choice can be modified against the parties' wish to achieve a higher level of procedural justice or to protect governmental concerns. Broadly speaking, may – and should – courts "fine tune" their exercises of adjudicatory authority in the international sense?

As will appear, there is great variety in the positions taken by contemporary legal orders on this issue. Tradition, legal culture, accidents of history, differing practical and economic circumstances, and much more have shaped the practices and positions held by States respecting jurisdictional fine-tuning. Our discussion seeks to explain the forces that have shaped each system's views.

Here, as in many areas of procedural law and of law generally, history explains different practices and philosophies of civil-law and common-law systems. The civil law, whose intellectual tradition arose from scholarly reflection in university halls shaping a powerful codification movement in the aftermath of the French Revolution, has been far less hospitable to "fine-tuning" than have common law systems. In civil-law systems, jurisdictional rules and principles are *designed* by legislatures and *applied* by judges. Judicial "fine-tuning" compromises, in the civilian's eyes, the predictability and administrability that all law – substantive and procedural alike – should display. The common law's approach to these matters is closer to that of practicing lawyers and judges drawn from the practicing bar.

The growing point of law in common-law systems still remains much more in courts than did – and does – the growing point in civil-law systems. In every area of the common law, judges do more than apply the law; they also *provide* it in their decisions. Accordingly, two propositions on which fine-tuning rests remain more congenial to common-law thinking and practice: judges shape and refine legal rules and principles; in applying these rules and principles, judges further may take into account, in varying measure, the specific facts of the controversy to be decided.

The appropriateness of principles and rules respecting a legal order's adjudicatory authority in the international sense can be tested either by "group-norm" or "case-specific" standards.[1] Common law systems recognize general jurisdiction, category-specific jurisdiction, and specific jurisdiction;[2] civil-law systems recognize only the first two jurisdictional types – both of which can be validated only in group-norm terms. Specific jurisdiction, which must be validated in "controversy-specific" terms, is rejected as neither practical nor administrable and as conferring a power on judges that is inappropriate for them to exercise. The objections that cause civil-law systems to eschew specific jurisdiction apply, of course, as well to fine-tuning.

The fine-tuning techniques discussed in this chapter have roots that go back to the nineteenth century or earlier, but fine-tuning has come in the last half of the twentieth century to be used in ever increasing measure due to legal, economic, and cultural changes. The emergence of class actions, developments in national laws respecting product liability, the increasingly litigious character of economic relations, and the "globalization" of many aspects of economic and legal activity have led to more aggressive tactics by lawyers and increasingly higher stakes for parties and Governments.

The United Kingdom's and Ireland's entry to the European Union inevitably led to clashes of the civil- and common-law legal cultures and drew the attention to the issue of "fine-tuning" thus setting the stage for a distinctive blend of legal cultures. Only after a long period of evolution can the results be fully understood.

A.   Forum Choice by the Moving Party and the Level Playing-Field Principle

The ideal of a level playing field is an important component of procedural justice. Only to the extent that one can justify giving decisive weight to countervailing considerations such as policies favoring local parties, vindicating strong regulatory concerns or effectuating a philosophy of jurisdiction based on power, a legal system should, in principle, not claim adjudicatory authority where to do so would result in an egregiously unleveled field for the parties.

Violations of the level-field principle can result not only from application of a legal order's general rules and principles establishing adjudicatory authority. The rule may also be violated because multiple forums, based either on the same or on different jurisdictional grounds, are available in other legal systems that afford the moving party a wider range of choice. Inconsistency can also result from

---

1   Compare the discussion in Chap. III. A. 5., pp. 105 *et seq.*, *supra*, of the United States and Germany in assessing the appropriateness of adjudicatory authority.

2   See Chap. I. C. 3., pp. 24 *et seq.*, *supra*.

the excessive range of choice among forums enjoyed in the particular case by the moving party.[3]

1.   *The Significance for Procedural Justice of Differences between Legal Systems*

Since every forum's administration of justice differs in some respects from that of every other forum, if more than one forum is available, the party that seizes the court almost always enjoys an advantage. Just how great it is depends on the extent to which the procedural, conflictual, and substantive rules and principles differ in the available forums. The differences may be of trivial importance; often they are very significant, indeed crucial. A manufacturer may be liable in one state without regard to fault for harm caused by its product but responsible in another only where the harm suffered was brought about by a defect resulting from negligence in the course of the product's manufacture. Cultural, economic, and sociological aspects of the society whose courts are seized of a matter can affect profoundly the adjudicators' holdings. For example, is compensation to be given for pain and suffering and in what measure; what is the proper role of fault in determining tortious or delictual liability? Choice-of-law rules frequently differ between systems;[4] even when they are facially similar, they may well yield different results if only because every legal order has a more or less strong tendency to apply its own domestic-law norms (especially with respect to rules arguably procedural in nature).[5]

---

3   The problem of excessive choice can be addressed by legal systems in their general law of jurisdiction not only by limiting the number of different bases among which the moving party can choose, but also by eschewing the use of jurisdictional bases that typically make multiple forums available. Among the objections to the rule in the American case of *Harris* v. *Balk*, no longer constitutional (see *Schaffer* v. *Heitner*, discussed at length in Chap. III. A. 4. *(b)*, pp. 102 *et seq.*, *supra*), was that it opened many forums – all having the same characteristics, jurisdictionally speaking – and thus provided the moving party with a range of choice among forums that made a mockery of the level-field principle.

4   On the (limited) effectiveness that unification of choice of law rules can have, see 3. (b), pp. 266 *et seq.*, *infra*.

5   This tendency is encouraged by the problematic *lex fori* principle of international procedural law held by many legal systems. See H. Schack, *Internationales Zivilver-fahrensrecht*, at 13-14, Nos. 39-45 (Munich, C. H. Beck, 4th ed., 2006). Perhaps more fundamental, however, is the tendency – sometimes pejoratively called the "homeward trend" – of judges and lawyers to apply the court's local law to substantive issues because it is accessible and they approve of it. Some choice-of-law theories explicitly favor on these grounds, among others, a strong role for the *lex fori*. See J. Kropholler, *Internationales Privatrecht*, at 42-49 (Tübingen, Mohr Siebeck, 6th ed., 2006); A. Ehrenzweig, *Private International Law (Second Part)*, at 89-90, 107-110 (Leyden, Sijthoff & Dobbs Ferry, NY, Oceana Publications, 1967); L. McDougal, R. Felix and R. Whitten, *American Conflicts Law §98. Application of the Better Rule of Law*, at 366-369 (Ardsley, NY, Transnational Publishers, 5th ed., 2001).

Furthermore, differences in rules and arrangements respecting the gathering, presentation, and evaluation of evidence can be extremely important. The availability of wide-ranging discovery may offer great advantages to one party and cause great disadvantages to the other. Whether findings of fact are made by laymen alone, by laymen and judges sitting together, or by judges alone can be outcome-determinative.

Other matters that vary with the forum selected are significant even though they cannot be said to determine outcomes directly. Litigation expenses – including transportation, court and lawyers' fees – often vary considerably as do the rules respecting whether, and to what extent, the losing party must reimburse the successful party for expenses incurred. Finally, the institutions, attitudes, and values of a forum may be markedly more familiar and congenial for one party than for the other. In all legal systems, considerations of simplicity and convenience entitle the moving party to seize – at least initially – the court that he prefers from among those that are, under their respective laws of adjudicatory jurisdiction, authorized to entertain the matter.

In single-system or single-state controversies or situations, one available forum can also be more advantageous for the moving party than another.[6] For example, a claim arising out of an accident can at times be litigated either in the locality where the accident occurred or in the community where the defendant lives. Especially where juries are available, in an action to recover damages for injuries suffered in an automobile accident, the plaintiff may prefer an urban venue on the theory that city-folk tend to favor plaintiffs and hold more expansive views as to what constitutes appropriate compensation than do country-folk. The justice administered by different courts of the same legal order is, however, far less likely to vary fundamentally in character or quality than is the justice rendered in courts of separate legal orders. In multisystem or multistate cases, plaintiffs often have grounds for preferring litigation in one system's courts while defendants would prefer the courts of another system. The probability of differences between the plaintiff's and the defendant's forum preferences grows as the range of choice open to the party that controls selection – normally the plaintiff – increases.

2.   *Forum Shopping*

The moving party's search for the forum that is most advantageous for him is seen by some as an "unethical and inefficient" act that "abus[es] the adversary system and squander[s] judicial resources".[7] Unless the assumption is plausible that par-

---

6   See generally "Note: Forum Shopping Reconsidered", 103 *Harv. L. Rev.* 1677, at 1678-1680 (1990).

7   *Idem* 1677. See also J. Kropholler, "Das Unbehagen am forum shopping", in D. Henrich and B. von Hoffmann (eds.), *Festschrift für Karl Firsching* 165-173 (Munich, C. H. Beck, 1985).

ties seeking redress are typically in the right[8] or – at least – typically litigationally disadvantaged when compared with their opponents, it is difficult to consider the advantage that initiative thus confers justified except as a matter of administrative convenience: it permits one party to determine in significant measure the rules and principles under which a dispute with the other party is to be decided. Where several forums are available the moving party will usually choose the one he considers most likely to favor his cause.[9]

As a matter of convenience and administrability, choice of forum must be usually left, in the first instance, to the moving party. It neither follows, however, that every choice made by that party is "perfectly legitimate",[10] nor that such choice as the party enjoys among different forums is illegitimate. Indeed, choice reduces the possibility that the selecting party will be required to pursue his cause on a playing field whose tilt egregiously favors the other party; from this perspective the cause of convenience and administrability as well as procedural justice in a larger sense are served.[11]

Forum shopping in the pejorative sense occurs as connecting factors with different characteristics proliferate and – or – connecting factors that can generate multiple forums become widely available. The need for fine-tuning to channel litigation to appropriate forums increases as a function of the variety and number of forums in which controversies can be litigated.

3. The Role of Public International Law and International Conventions

(a) Public international law

Global control of forum shopping would be advanced by the creation of an international order that ensured the propriety and limited the variety of bases of adjudicatory authority.[12] Nothing along these lines has appeared – or is likely to appear – in the theory or practice of international law. Some authors consider

---

8   See *idem* 1689 (arguing that forum shopping furthers the "goal of providing a remedy for every injury").

9   See *The Atlantic Star*, [1974] AC 436, at 471 (HL 1973); see generally F. Juenger, "Judicial Control of Improper Forum Selection: Some Random Remarks and a Comment on How Not to Do It", in J. Goldsmith (ed.), *International Dispute Resolution: The Regulation of Forum Selection* 311-323 (Irvington, NY, Transnational Publ., 1997).

10   H. Schack, "Die Versagung der deutschen internationalen Zuständigkeit wegen forum non conveniens und lis alibi pendens", 58 *RabelsZ* 40, at 47 (1994). An English version of this article forms part of an excellent collection of papers: J. Fawcett (ed.), *Declining Jurisdiction in Private International Law* (Oxford, Clarendon Press, 1995). Schack's article appears as "Chapter 9 – Germany" on at 189-205; the passage quoted is at p. 196, *supra*.

11   See *ibid.*

12   Since only exceptionally will a unique forum be assigned for given classes of controversies, global efforts to provide for uniform application of uniform choice-of-law rules may be desirable as well.

public international law irrelevant.[13] Others disagree, arguing that international law requires a genuine link between the forum and either the parties or the subject-matter before adjudicatory authority can be exercised.[14] Even if this requirement were widely accepted, it would have limited consequences; in all likelihood only minimal restrictions, already required by some states' constitutional law, would result. Rarely have states invoked international-law norms by entering diplomatic protests against other states' claims of adjudicatory jurisdiction.[15] Moreover, public international law can hardly provide fine-tuning; at best, it only yields abstract principles in need of concretisation for individual cases.

(b) "Decisional harmony" and forum shopping

Universal conventions regulating choice of law have had only limited impact in reducing the potential for forum shopping; "decisional harmony", which traditionally private international law theory, especially in Continental Europe, thought would end the practice by ensuring uniformity in the applicable substantive rules, has proved to be a mirage. If all forums actually applied the same choice-of-law rules, the advantage enjoyed by the party that selects the forum would be reduced, though by no means entirely eliminated.[16] In all events, as a new century dawns, achieving decisional harmony through universal international conventions regulating choice of law seems even more elusive than when the twentieth century began.

   Some regional conventions regulating choice of law for discrete areas of law have enjoyed a measure of success. One purpose – only partially achieved – of the European Union's Rome Convention on the Law Applicable to Contractual Obligations of 1980 was to inhibit "forum shopping" by unifying conflicts rules.[17]

---

13   See M. Akehurst, "Jurisdiction in International Law", [1972-1973] *BYIL* 145, at 170-177; J. Kropholler, "Internationale Zuständigkeit", in *Handbuch des Internationalen Zivilverfahrensrechts*, Vol. I, Chap. III, at 213-216, Nos. 39-48 (Tübingen, Mohr (Siebeck), 1982). In the absence of truly international rules regulating adjudicatory authority, each State has to determine in a sovereign manner when to assume jurisdiction. BGH, 18 March 1959, 30 *BGHZ* 1, at 3-4.

14   See, e.g., J. Bertele, *Souveränität und Verfahrensrecht*, at 181-194, 220-327 (Tübingen, Mohr (Siebeck), 1998).

15   See Akehurst, *supra* footnote 13, at 176-177.

16   See Schack, *supra* footnote 10, 58 *RabelsZ* at 47; see generally 1., pp. 263 *et seq.*, *supra.*

17   See the Giuliano and Lagarde Report, [1980] OJ C 282, 1, at 4-5; *G.I.E. Groupe Concorde and Others* v. *The Master of the Vessel Suhadiwarno Panjan and Others* – Case C-440/97, [1999] ECR I-6307, No. 30 ("there is[, the court perhaps optimistically wrote,] no risk that the law applicable to the determination of the place of performance will vary depending on the court seized, since the conflict rules enabling the law applicable to the contract to be determined have been standardised in the Contracting States by the Convention of 19 June 1980 on the Law applicable to Contractual Obligations"). This view is echoed in the European Commission's Green Paper on the conversion of the Rome Convention into a Community instrument, COM (2002) 654 final, of 14 January 2003, at 9, in which the Commission states: "By unifying the Member States' rules on conflict of laws, the Rome Convention ensures that the same

Of course, a convention's potential for moderating the advantages of forum selection is diminished if it provides for alternative reference or, more importantly, uses open-ended choice-of-law standards such as "the most significant connection".[18] Nor can conventions harmonize important aspects of the administration of justice set out above. Removing many of these differences would require international harmonization of procedural rules,[19] a Herculean task. Nor can conventions do much to overcome a party's lack of familiarity with the court's language and culture or equalize travel and other costs that depend on the forum selected.

4.   The Instruments of Judicial Fine-tuning

(a)   *Forum non conveniens* stays

The least problematic form of judicial fine-tuning occurs where a court, seized of a matter, entertains the argument that procedural justice would be better served if the litigation were to proceed in another state. When certain requirements are satisfied, the doctrine of *forum non conveniens* allows courts to direct the plaintiff to seek adjudication of the controversy elsewhere. By invoking the *forum non conveniens* doctrine, a court offers to forgo – if the alternative forum is willing to entertain the matter – the exercise of adjudicatory authority in order to secure what is, in its view, a more co-operative, economical, and harmonious administration of justice internationally. Wisely used, such abstention can contribute to the creation and maintenance of a just and efficient international legal order.

---

solution will be applied as to the substance irrespective of the court hearing the case and thus reduces the risk of forum-shopping in the European Union." Meanwhile the Commission has published a proposal for a Regulation of the European Parliament and the Council on the law applicable to contractual obligations ("Rome I"), COM (2005) 650 final.

18   See, generally, P. Lagarde, "Le principe de proximité dans le droit international privé contemporain – Cours général de droit international privé", 196 *Recueil des cours* 9-238 (1986).

19   In 1987 the European Commission set up a Working Group for the Approximation of the Civil Procedure Law, the so-called Storme-Commission, to draw up a "European Judicial Code". However, the Commission concluded that the differences between European legal systems made harmonisation practically impossible and submitted only a fragmented draft. See M. Storme (ed.), *Rapprochement du Droit Judiciaire de l'Union Européenne – Approximation of Judiciary Law in the European Union* (Dordrecht, Boston, MA and London, Kluwer, 1994); A. Stadler, "Das Europäische Zivilprozessrecht – Wie viel Beschleunigung verträgt Europa?", 24 *IPRax* 2, at 3-4 (2004). See for attempts to harmonize civil procedural on a worldwide level G. Hazard, M. Taruffo, R. Stürner and H. Gidi, "Introduction to the Principles and Rules of Transnational Civil Procedure", 33 *NYU J. Int'l Law & Politics* 769-784 (2001); G. Hazard *et al.*, "Fundamental Principles of Transcontinental Civil Procedure", *Idem* 785-792; G. Hazard *et al.*, "Rules of Transnational Civil Procedure", *Idem* 793-859; R. Stürner, "The Principles of Transnational Civil Procedure", 69 *RabelsZ* 201_(2005); ALI/Unidroit, *Principles of Transnational Civil Procedure* (Cambridge, Cambridge University Press 2006).

(b)   Antisuit injunctions

Although possible in theory, in practice, a court of one state never orders the court of another to refuse – or cease – to entertain the matter. Antisuit injunctions are not

> adressed to and intended to bind another court .... [T]he jurisdiction of the foreign court is [not] in question and the injunction is [not] an order that the foreign court desist from exercising the jurisdiction given to it by its own domestic law.... When an English court makes a restraining order, it is making an order which is addressed only to a party which is before it.[20]

Nonetheless, such injunctions – even if well intended – are seen as an intrusive act, designed to safeguard the enjoining legal system's adjudicatory authority and substantive policies. Antisuit injunctions granted by the English Court of Appeal in the *Laker* litigation[21] were characterized by American courts as "a direct interference"[22] and as "intrusive".[23]

(c)   Overlapping and conflicting proceedings: *Lis pendens*

Where a matter can be litigated in the courts of more than one legal order, parties may initiate overlapping and conflicting proceedings. In some systems, such situations can be addressed through *forum non conveniens* stays or antisuit injunctions. A court may stay proceedings when it considers that another state's courts – whether or not already seized – can deal more appropriately with the matter. Contrariwise, an antisuit injunction may be issued if the court considers *itself* to be the more appropriate forum.[24] Fine-tuning can thus occur as well when a court declines to exercise adjudicatory authority that, in principle, it enjoys, as when it orders a party *not* to litigate a matter in a foreign court that would exercise adjudicatory authority in the matter.

Legal systems that do not utilize these instruments of fine-tuning can – unless the resulting judgment comes before their courts for enforcement – either do nothing or invoke the objective standard of first in time to eliminate overlapping or potentially conflicting litigation. The *lis pendens* doctrine requires that the

---

20   Lord Hobhouse of Woodborough, in *Turner* v. *Grovit and Others*, [2002] 1 WLR 107, No. 23 (HL 2001).

21   *British Airways Board* v. *Laker Airways Ltd.*, [1984] QB 142 (CA 1983). See p. 291, *infra*.

22   *Laker Airways Ltd.* v. *Pan American World Airways*, 559 F. Supp. 1124, at 1128, footnote 14 (DDC 1983), affd. sub nom. *Laker Airways Ltd.* v. *Sabena, Belgian World Airways*, 731 F. 2d 909 (DC Cir. 1984).

23   *Laker Airways Ltd.* v. *Pan American World Airways*, 577 F. Supp. 348, at 352 (DDC 1983).

24   Antisuit injunctions will not be granted to protect proceedings in the courts of a third State. See *Airbus Industrie G.I.E.* v. *Patel*, [1999] 1 AC 119, at 134-140 (HL 1998). See C. I. 2. *(a)* (ii), pp. 283 *et seq., infra.*

court dismiss – or stay – an action if the same matter is already pending before another court. The difference in approach from *forum non conveniens* is fundamental; the appropriate forum is identified on the objective basis of temporal priority without regard to general considerations of procedural justice.

B.   *Forum non conveniens*: Contemporary Theory and Practice

1.   Civil-Law Jurisdictions

Although Scottish law – in various respects a civil-law system – was the first to develop a *forum non conveniens* doctrine[25] and Quebec has recently introduced a moderate form of the doctrine,[26] most civil-law jurisdictions deny their courts general discretionary power to decline jurisdiction.[27] French jurists explain that "the law determines whether a judge has jurisdiction; if he is competent, he must decide without power to 'refuse to exercise his jurisdictional authority *(compétence juridictionnelle)*'.'[28] German jurists insist that

> legal security *(Rechtssicherheit)* requires jurisdictional rules *(Zuständigkeitsregeln)* that are comprehensible *(überschaubar)* and, above all, clear and precise. Introducing the doctrine of *forum non conveniens* into the German system of jurisdiction, which rests on legislatively standardized jurisdictional policies *(gesetzlich typisierten Zuständigkeitsinteressen)*, would render the system incoherent ....[29]

Civil-law jurisdictions do recognize certain very limited surrogates for *forum non conveniens*; these vary in scope and importance from one legal order to another.[30]

---

25   See 2., pp. 270 *et seq., infra.*

26   Article 3135 Civil Code of Québec (C.c.Q.), introduced in 1991, provides that:

> Even though a Quebec authority has jurisdiction to hear a dispute, it may exceptionally and on an application by a party, decline jurisdiction if it considers that the authorities of another country are in a better position to decide.

See Statutes of Québec (L.Q., 1991, c. 64, a. 3135). See G. Saumier, *"Forum non Conveniens*: Where are we now?", 12 *SCLR* (2d) 121, at 129-133 (2000).

27   See Fawcett, *supra* footnote 10, at 8.

28   H. Gaudemet-Tallon, "Les régimes relatifs au refus d'exercer la compétence juridictionnelle en matière civile et commerciale: Forum non conveniens, lis pendens", 46 *Rev. int. dr. comp.* 423-435 (1994). An English version of this article appears in Fawcett, *supra* footnote 10, at 175-187. French law relies on the concept of *forum conveniens* to explain the assertion by French courts of jurisdiction by necessity. See *idem* 423-424; 176 in Fawcett, *supra* footnote 10.

29   Schack, *supra* footnote 10, 58 *RabelsZ* at 45-46 (the translation above departs in certain respects from the English version of Schack's German text in Fawcett); see also Ch. Dorsel, *Forum non conveniens*, at 132-191 (Berlin, Duncker & Humblot, 1996); K. Siehr, *Internationales Privatrecht*, at 512 (C. F. Müller, Heidelberg, 2001).

30   See Fawcett, *supra* footnote 10, at 24-27.

Thus, the German *Bundesgerichtshof*'s interpretation of ZPO §23,[31] requiring a sufficient connection to the forum (*hinreichender Inlandsbezug*) takes into account some considerations relevant for *forum non conveniens* purposes.[32] Moreover, German courts have, on occasion, employed considerations akin to *forum non conveniens* in the context of the granting of legal aid to foreign plaintiffs bringing an action against a German defendant.[33] Under Dutch law, Article 3 (c) of the Code of Civil Procedure requires a sufficient connection with the Netherlands for proceedings initiated by a petition to the court.[34] For the most part, however, such substitutes "operate[] only in very limited circumstances, such as certain family law matters".[35] Civil-law jurisdictions generally align themselves with the French and German position: As a matter of principle, jurisdictional fine-tuning through *forum non conveniens* or related doctrines is not proper.

2.   Common-Law Jurisdictions

The doctrine of *forum non conveniens* allows, where an appropriate alternative forum is available, a court to stay – and ultimately refuse to hear – a case within its adjudicatory authority on the basis that it is, in the circumstances, not an appropriate forum. Similar techniques had long been known and applied in maritime law; the general doctrine, however, originated in Scotland in the course of the nineteenth century.[36] In 1925, it was set out by Lord Summer in *Société du Gaz de Paris* v. *La Société Anonyme de Navigation "Les Armateurs Français"*:

---

31   See Chap. III. B. 5. *(a)* (ii), pp. 142 *et seq., supra.*

32   See, e.g., O. Hartwieg, "Forum Shopping zwischen Forum Non Conveniens und 'hinreichendem Inlandsbezug'", 51 *JZ* 109-118 (1996).

33   See P. Mankowski, "Fiscus non conveniens – oder: Einzug der Lehre vom forum non conveniens in das deutsche Recht der Prozeßkostenhilfe?", 19 *IPRax* 155-158 (1999).

34   Article 3 (c) provides that "[a] court has jurisdiction if the petition has a sufficient connection with the legal sphere of The Netherlands". The Dutch Code of Civil Procedure has recently been reformed. Prior to the reform that became effective as of 1 January 2002, Article 3 (c) was to be found in Article 429c (15) albeit with slightly different wording. See for a detailed account of the reform of the Dutch Code of Civil Procedure G. R. Rutgers, "Die Reform des niederländischen Zivilprozessrechts", 7 *ZZPInt* 193 (2002).

35   Fawcett, *supra* footnote 10, at 27.

36   For an excellent discussion of the emergence of the *non conveniens* doctrine in Scottish, English, and American Law, see A. Nuyts, *L'exception de forum non conveniens*, Nos. 51-90 (Brussels, Bruylant, 2003).
       The first comprehensive modern discussion of the Scotish plea of *forum non conveniens* is A. Anton, *Private International Law* 148-154 (Edinburgh, W. Green & Son, 1967). For an authoritative, recent discussion of the doctrines in Scottish law and in English law, see P. Beaumont, "Great Britain", in Fawcett, *supra* footnote 10, at 207-220.

The object in the words *'non conveniens'* ... is to find that *forum* which is the more suitable for the ends of justice and which is preferable because pursuit of litigation in that forum is [on the facts before the court, so far as can be measured in advance,] more likely to secure those ends.[37]

At one time rejected in both England and the United States,[38] the doctrine was taken up after World War II by American federal courts and by the courts of many American states.[39] More recently, the English courts have followed suit.[40]

The degree of inappropriateness that local adjudication must exhibit before a plaintiff will be referred to another forum varies from one common-law system to another; some courts are much less willing than others to disturb plaintiffs' choices.[41] Moreover, some legal systems' application of the doctrine takes into account not only considerations of justice as between the parties but also public concerns respecting the burden on the local administration of justice[42] and the forum's regulatory policies.[43] The principal difference between the general approach of courts in the United Kingdom and the United States is that public concerns can

---

37   (1925) 23 *Ll. L. Rep.* 209, at 212 (HL 1925).

38   See J. Fawcett, "General Report", in Fawcett, *supra* footnote 10, at 21-24; *St. Pierre* v. *South American Stores (Garth and Chaves) Ltd.*, [1936] 1 KB 382, at 398 (CA 1935); *Cohens* v. *Virginia*, 19 US (6 Wheat.) 264 (1821).

39   See L. Del Duca and A. Zaphiriou, "Rules for Declining to Exercise Jurisdiction in Civil and Commercial Matters: Forum Non Conveniens, Lis Pendens", 42 (Supplement) *Am. J. Comp. L.* 245, at 249-251 (1994), with some adaptations, in Fawcett, *supra* footnote 10, at 403-407; E. Scoles, P. Hay, P. Borchers and S. Symeonides, *Conflict of Laws* 492-508 (St. Paul, Minn., West Group, 4rd ed., 2004). Scoles *et al.* remark that the doctrine "is designed to avoid the hardship on the defendant and on the court that can result from undue forum shopping possible under accepted concepts of jurisdiction". *Idem* 492 et seq.

40   See *The Atlantic Star*, [1974] AC 436 (HL 1973); *MacShannon* v. *Rockware Glass Ltd.*, [1978] AC 795 (HL 1978).

41   The High Court of Australia, for example, applies the relatively strict standard that a stay should be granted only if to proceed would work a serious injustice by being oppressive and vexatious to the defendant. Cf. *Voth* v. *Manildra Flour Mills Pty. Ltd.*, (1990) 97 ALR 124 ("clearly inappropriate forum" test contrasted with "appropriate forum" test); confirmed recently in *Regie National des Usines Renault SA* v. *Zhang*, [2002] HCA 10; P. Prince, "Bhopal, Bougainville and Ok Tedi: Why Australia's *forum non conveniens* Approach Is Better", 47 *Int. & Comp. LQ* 573-598 (1998); R. Garnett, "Stay of Proceedings in Australia: A 'Clearly Inappropriate' Test?", 23 *Melb. U. L. Rev.* 30-64 (1999); see generally J. Epstein, "Australia", in Fawcett, *supra* footnote 10, at 82-89.

42   The English view is said to be that the plea of *forum non conveniens* "cannot be sustained ... on grounds of public interest or public policy that the litigation should be conducted elsewhere ...". Lord Hope of Craighead in *Lubbe and others* v. *Cape Plc*, [2000] 4 All ER 268, at 287 (HL 2000).

43   In the English view, "if the interests of all parties and the ends of justice require that the action in this country should be stayed, a stay ought to be granted however desir-

play a decisive role in the United States while in the United Kingdom they play no role unless they can be seen as private concerns. In all events, to the extent that the doctrine is recognized, a trial court enjoys a significant control over the exercise of the adjudicatory authority that it has in principle.

(a)   The United States

Prior to Justice Stone's 1945 decision in *International Shoe Co.* v. *State of Washington*[44] American jurisdictional theory and practice evaluated claims of adjudicatory authority *ex ante* and pursuant to group-norm standards. The dominant theory saw adjudicatory authority as an expression of territoriality based power. In this scheme of things, neither theory nor practice supported the proposition that courts could, in light of the circumstances of the particular controversy, fine tune their exercise of adjudicatory authority. The jurisdictional philosophy that *International Shoe* espoused supported an *ex post*, controversy-specific, approach to jurisdiction to adjudicate. At the same time, the decision relaxed the jurisdictional restraints that flowed from *Pennoyer* v. *Neff.*[45] In 1947, the Supreme Court accepted the *forum non conveniens* doctrine for domestic litigation in *Gulf Oil Corp.* v. *Gilbert*;[46] *International Shoe* can claim responsibility for both the intellectual climate and the practical consideration – the need to rein in jurisdictional claims that would no longer be constrained by *Pennoyer* v. *Neff* – that led to the *Gilbert* decision. In 1981, responding to the same general considerations, in *Piper Aircraft Corp.* v. *Reyno*,[47] the Court approved the use of the doctrine by federal courts in international cases.[48] State law, generally speaking, followed the federal law after 1947 and again after 1981.

Speaking in broad-brush terms, a *forum non conveniens* stay may be granted – and ultimately a dismissal ordered – if two requirements are met: interests (public and private) must be considered, and an adequate alternative forum must be

---

able it may be on grounds of public interest or public policy that the action should be tried" in England. *Ibid.*

44   See Chap. III. A. 4., pp. 97 *et seq., supra.*

45   See Chap. III. A. 1., *(b)* (ii), pp. 85 *et seq., supra.*

46   330 US 501 (1947).
In 1948, a statutory transfer mechanism was adopted – Act of 25 June 1948, Chap. 646, 62 Stat. 869, 937 (codified at 28 USC §1404 *(a)* (2006) – for federal litigation that could properly be litigated in a another federal court. See S. Burbank, "Jurisdictional Equilibration, the Proposed Hague Convention and Progress in National Law", 49 *Am. J. Comp. L.* 203, at 211-212 (2001). Since then "[t]he doctrine of forum non conveniens survives in federal courts only where the alternative forum is in a foreign country". *Ravelo Monegro* v. *Rosa*, 211 F. 3d 509, at 513 (9th Cir. 2000). "[F]ederal decisional law has proved[, nonetheless,] a substantial continuing influence on the tenor of many states' law whose reach includes cases that could, as well as those that could not, be lodged in another American court." Burbank, *supra*, at 211-212.

47   454 US 235 (1981).

48   See Burbank, *supra* footnote 46, at 211-215.

shown to be available. Adequacy may be found even if the parties' respective prospects for success will be significantly affected by the change of venue. A matter can be stayed or dismissed on *non conveniens* grounds even though the substantive law applicable in the alternative forum is less favorable to the plaintiff. Indeed,

> [i]n holding that the possibility of a change in law unfavorable to the plaintiff should not be given substantial weight, we also necessarily hold that the possibility of a change in law favorable to the defendant should not be considered.[49]

Nor do such considerations as the absence in the alternative forum of juries, the prohibition of contingent-fee arrangements, or different community standards respecting compensation in themselves preclude a *non conveniens* stay or dismissal.[50]

In determining whether the plaintiff has selected an appropriate forum, US federal courts take into account the connections of the real parties-in-interest and of potential witnesses with the selected and the alternative forums, relative litigation costs, availability of witnesses and defendants,[51] and the burden on each forum's judicial system. A court can make a *non conveniens* dismissal or stay subject to conditions, such as the defendant's submission to the jurisdiction of the alternative forum and his waiver of prescription as a defense.[52] Defendants have been required to admit liability and to proceed to trial in the foreign court only on the issue of damages.[53] State and federal courts today generally hold similar – though by no means identical – positions respecting *forum non conveniens* stays

---

49   454 US at 252, note 19.

50   See *In re Union Carbide Corp. Gas Plant Disaster at Bhopal, India in Dec. 1984*, 809 F. 2d 195, at 202 (2d Cir. 1987), cert. denied sub nom. *Executive Comm. Members* v. *Union of India*, 484 US 871 (1987).

51   For example, whether potential third-party defendants can be impleaded. See *Piper Aircraft* v. *Reyno*, 454 US at 259.

52   In the *Bhopal* case, the federal district court, in addition to these conditions, required that the defendant agree to submit to discovery under the Federal Rules of Civil Procedure and, subject to due-process defenses, to satisfy any judgment against it. See *In re Union Carbide Corporation Gas Plant Disaster at Bhopal, India in December, 1984*, 634 F. Supp. 842, at 867 (SDNY 1986). Upon appeal, the Circuit Court deleted the additional conditions. *In re Union Carbide Corp.*, 809 F. 2d at 204.

53   See, *e.g.*, *Pain* v. *United Technologies Corp.*, 637 F. 2d 775 (2d. Cir. 1980), cert. denied, 454 US 1128 (1981).

   Pain and like cases in which courts condition *forum non conveniens* stays or dismissals on the defendant's willingness to stipulate to liability with damages to be determined by an alternative forum raise the question whether such bifurcation is permissible. The Supreme Court of the State of Washington, sitting *en banc*, addressed the issue in *Myers et al* v. *Boeing Co.*, 794 P. 2d 1272, at 1282-1283 (Wash. 1990). The Court was prepared to accept the practice when "the liability issue was resolved without trial and dismissal [or stay] was granted to resolve the only remaining issue, damages". *Idem* 1283. Doubts were expressed, however, respecting the propriety of one state's

and dismissals.[54] The states are free, however, to take quite different positions and some do. The Supreme Court of Texas held, for example, in *Dow Chemical Co. v. Castro Alfaro*[55] that to apply the doctrine in personal injury or wrongful death actions was precluded by Texas's "open courts" statute.

(b) England

The doctrine of *forum non conveniens* was in general use in the United States before it was adopted in England. Its "role there ... is slightly different and the American authorities have not directly contributed to the development of the English doctrine".[56]

The adjudicatory authority exercised by the English courts under Order 11, Rule 1, of the Rules of the Supreme Court[57] is discretionary in nature; accordingly, what amounts to a *forum conveniens* test is built into all Order 11 assertions of jurisdiction. For national law the only context in which the doctrine of *forum non conveniens* as such comes into question – aside from certain matrimonial causes – is where jurisdiction has been established by serving the defendant with a writ during his presence in England. Although jurisdiction based on service can be highly inappropriate, the traditional view was that the jurisdictional claim was of right and the action could not be stayed on *forum non conveniens* grounds. By the late 1980s, however, the House of Lords had decided that in these cases a stay is to

> be granted on the ground of *forum non conveniens* where the court is satisfied that there is some other available forum, having competent jurisdiction, which is the ap-

---

courts trying the liability, and another state's courts the damages, issue. See *idem* 1282-1283.

54   See Scoles *et al., supra* footnote 39, at 502.

55   786 SW 2d 674 (Tex. 1990). The *Alfaro* rule was set aside in 1993 by Texas Civ. Pra. Rem. Code §71.051 (applicable only to cases filed after 1 September 1993). See generally C. Scherz, "Section 71.051 of the Texas Civil Practices and Remedies Code – The Texas Legislature's Response to *Alfaro*: *Forum non conveniens* in Personal Injury and Wrongful Death Litigation", 46 *Baylor L. Rev.* 99-139 (1994).

56   A. Dicey and J. Morris, *The Conflict of Laws*, at 390, No. 12-011 (London, Sweet & Maxwell, 13th ed., 2000).

57   The Rules of the Supreme Court (RSC) were reenacted as Schedule 1 to the Civil Procedure Rules (1999). At the English common law, a so-called action *in personam* (see Chap. I. B. 1., p. 22, *supra*) does not, except in matrimonial causes, lie against a defendant unless he has been served with a writ while present in England. To relieve the resulting plight of plaintiffs, the Common Law Procedure Act of 1852 gave the courts a discretionary power to summon absent defendants, English or foreign, when England was the *forum conveniens*. Under RSC Order 11, which now governs the exercise of this adjudicatory authority, a court *may*, in certain circumstances, permit service of a writ of summons – ordinarily by giving the defendant due notice – upon an absent defendant.

propriate forum for the trial of the action, i.e. in which the case may be tried more suitably for the interests of all the parties and the ends of justice.[58]

A stay is not

refused simply because the plaintiff will thereby be deprived of 'a legitimate personal or juridical advantage', provided that the court is satisfied that substantial justice will be done in the available appropriate forum.[59]

Nor is it

normally appropriate for the court to compare the quality of justice obtainable in a foreign forum which adopts a different procedural system (such as that of the civil law) with that obtainable in a similar case conducted in an English court.[60]

A stay will only be granted if a two-step test is satisfied: first, the defendant must establish that there is another court with competent jurisdiction which is clearly and distinctly more appropriate; second, it must not be unjust to deprive the claimant of his right to trial before the court seized.[61] A stay can be conditioned on the defendant agreeing to the plaintiff's retention of security and the defendant's waiver of any time bar applicable to proceeding in the alternative jurisdiction.[62]

Plaintiffs will have great difficulty in establishing that "substantial justice" will *not* be done by the forum in which "the case may be tried more suitably for the interests of all the parties and the ends of justice".[63] For example, "the absence of established procedures ... for handling group actions" in the more appropriate forum when the forum seized has a well developed law for the trial of "groups" or "class" actions does not suffice.[64] Lord Bingham of Cornhill remarked in the *Lubbe* case that

---

58   Lord Goff of Chieveley (himself of Scottish ancestry) in *Spiliada Maritime Corp.* v. *Cansulex Ltd.*, [1987] AC 460, at 476 (HL 1986) and quoted by him in *Connelly* v. *R.T.Z. Corporation plc.*, [1998] AC 854, at 871 (HL 1997).

59   Dicey and Morris, *supra* footnote 56, at 398, No. 12-025.

60   *Ibid*. It is further remarked (*idem* 398-399, No. 12-025) that

      [t]here may be cases in which there is a risk that justice will not be obtained in a foreign court for ideological or political reasons, or because of the inexperience or inefficiency of the judiciary or excessive delay in the conduct of business of the courts, or the unavailability of appropriate remedies. But a would-be plaintiff in the English court who wishes to resist a stay of English proceedings on such a ground must assert it candidly and support the allegation with positive and cogent evidence.

61   *Spiliada Maritime Corp.* v. *Cansulex Ltd.*, [1987] AC at 475-478; *Connelly* v. *R.T.Z. Corp. plc*, [1998] AC at 871-873.

62   See Dicey and Morris, *supra* footnote 56, at 399, No. 12-026.

63   Lord Goff in *Spiliada Maritime Corp.*, *supra* footnote 61, at 474.

64   Lord Bingham of Cornhill in the *Lubbe* case, [2000] 4 All ER 268, at 280.

this objection, standing alone, ... [is not] compelling. It involves the kind of procedural comparison which the English Court should be careful to eschew, and the evidence is clear that South African Courts have inherent jurisdiction to adopt procedures appropriate to the cases they are called upon to handle .... In England, there has been a vast amount of litigation by victims of asbestos dust without resort to group actions. Whether by a form of group action or otherwise, I have no doubt that the High Court of South Africa will be able to devise and adopt suitable procedures for the efficient despatch of business such as this. None of the evidence or submissions on behalf of the plaintiffs suggests any significant obstacle to that efficient despatch by the Court of cases before it."[65]

Accordingly, although litigation in South Africa would clearly be far more difficult – and, very likely, far less rewarding – for the plaintiffs, the English proceedings in the *Lubbe* case would no doubt have been stayed had there been any realistic way for the plaintiffs to finance the litigation in South Africa, however, legal aid was no longer provided there for claims sounding in money, including personal injury claims. As a partial surrogate for legal aid, legislation had recently been enacted authorizing contingent-fee arrangements. Had financing the litigation through such arrangements been a realistic possibility, *forum non conveniens* stay would, in all probability, have been granted.

Lord Bingham of Cornhill concluded, however, that contingent-fee funding was most unlikely. For him,

the absence, as yet, of developed procedures for handling group actions in South Africa reinforces the submissions made by the plaintiffs on the funding issue. It is one thing to embark on and fund a heavy group action where the procedures governing the conduct of the proceedings are known to and understood by experienced judges and practitioners. It may be quite another where the exercise is novel and untried. There must then be an increased likelihood of interlocutory decisions, which are contentious, with the likelihood of appeals and delay. It cannot be assumed that all judges will respond to this new procedural challenge in the same innovative spirit. The exercise of jurisdiction by the South African High Court through separate territorial divisions, while not a potent obstacle in itself, could contribute to delay, uncertainty and cost. The procedural novelty of these proceedings, if pursued in South Africa, must in my view act as a further disincentive to any person or body considering whether or not to finance the proceedings.[66]

Accordingly, the Court refused to stay the English proceedings.

---

65   *Idem* 280 (footnote omitted), quoting, in part, from the decision of the Court of Appeal (per Pill LJ) granting a *forum non conveniens* stay.

66   *Ibid.*

(c)   Contemporary evaluations of the doctrine

Evaluations of the doctrine of *forum non conveniens* vary considerably. The doctrine has been highly praised: "since it is founded upon the exercises of self restraint by independent jurisdictions, it can be regarded as one of the most civilised of legal principles".[67] Its propriety and overall usefulness are, however, challenged on various grounds: judges should not be entrusted with such a broad discretionary power; the doctrine compromises legal security and predictability and breeds litigation; plaintiffs have a right – in some systems constitutional in nature – to proceed in a forum determined by rules of law rather than judicial discretion.[68]

Both the United Kingdom and the United States initially took relatively restrictive views on when invocation of the doctrine was appropriate; a court could not refuse to hear a case within its jurisdiction unless convinced that doing so "would work an injustice because it would be oppressive or vexatious to [the defendant] or would be an abuse of the process of the court in some other way ...".[69] In recent decades, the abuse of process approach has steadily lost ground, first in the United States and then in England.[70] Today, in a number of common-law jurisdictions considerations of convenience or unsuitability suffice to justify a *forum non conveniens* stay.[71] This development permits public-law concerns to play a larger role than before. One senses in the evolution from an "abuse" towards an "appropriateness" standard the influence, in some degree, of the *actor sequitur forum rei* principle[72] and of the predicament faced by certain legal systems that attract plaintiffs "as a moth is drawn to the light".[73] Systems that offer such ameni-

---

67   *Airbus Industrie G.I.E.* v. *Patel*, [1999] 1 AC at 141. See also *Baltimore & Ohio R.R.* v. *Kepner*, 314 US 44, at 55-56 (1941) (J. Frankfurter, dissenting) ("a manifestation of a civilized system"); *Rogers* v. *Guaranty Trust Co.*, 288 US 123, at 151 (1933) (J. Cardozo, dissenting) ("an instrument of justice").

68   See Fawcett, *supra* footnote 10, at 21-24. For an English jurist's unfavorable critique of the law of *forum non conveniens* in the United States and England, see D. Robertson, "*Forum Non Conveniens* in America and England: 'A Rather Fantastic Fiction'", 103 *LQ Rev.* 398, at 414-421 (1987).

69   Robertson, *supra* footnote 68, at 399 (quoting *St. Pierre* v. *South American Stores (Garth & Chaves) Ltd.*, [1936] KB 382, at 398 (CA 1936)).

70   *Idem* at 399.

71   See Fawcett, *supra* footnote 10, at 10-21.

72   For a discussion of this principle, see Chap. IV, pp. 153 *et seq.*, *supra*.

73   Paraphrasing Lord Denning in *Smith Kline & French Laboratories Ltd. and Others* v. *Bloch*, [1983] 2 All ER 72, at 74 (CA 1982):

As a moth is drawn to the light, so is a litigant drawn to the United States. If he can only get his case into their courts, he stands to win a fortune. At no cost to himself; and at no risk of having to pay anything to the other side. The lawyers there will conduct the case 'on spec' as we say, or on a 'contingency fee' as they say. The lawyers will charge the litigant nothing for their services but instead they will take 40 per cent. of the damages, if they win the case in court, or out of court on a settlement. If they lose, the litigant will have nothing to pay to the other side. The courts in the United States have no such costs deterrent as we have. There is also in the United States a right to trial by jury. These are

ties as wide-ranging discovery, contingent-fee arrangements, jury trial, and generous quantification of damages may well need *forum non conveniens* to protect not only defendants but also courts against litigation that, but for the aforesaid advantages, would have been brought elsewhere. Of course, when defendants invoke the doctrine they seek to select the forum; accordingly "trial judges applying the doctrine of *forum non conveniens* must walk a delicate line to avoid implicitly sanctioning forum-shopping by either litigant at the expense of the other".[74]

An important normative objection to the *forum non conveniens* doctrine rests on the concern that it may be utilized to make litigational and procedural advantages available to domestic – while denying them to foreign – parties. According different treatment to parties simply because they are local is inconsistent with the level playing-field principle. Yet, though less markedly than in the past,[75] courts are typically reluctant to dismiss actions brought by local parties:

> In any situation, the balance must be very strongly in favor of the defendant, before the plaintiff's choice of forum should be disturbed ... and the balance must be even stronger when the plaintiff is an American citizen and the alternative forum is a foreign one.[76]

To the extent that the convenience-suitability approach to *forum non conveniens* displaces the abuse-of-process approach, preferring a local plaintiff, largely without regard to the procedural and litigational significance of the controversy's overall relationship to the forum, becomes increasingly inappropriate. Rule 327 *(a)* of the New York Civil Practice Law and Rules provides a standard that courts increasingly apply: "The domicile or residence in this state of any party to the action shall not preclude the court from staying or dismissing the action." US federal courts

> have recently begun to acknowledge that judicial unwillingness to dismiss actions to competent courts abroad on grounds of citizenship alone may merely reflect an unthinking orientation overly protective of American plaintiffs – even those that live abroad – and insufficiently sensitive to the ability of foreign courts to perform their adjudicatory functions as well as do the courts of the United States ....[77]

---

prone to award fabulous damages. They are notoriously sympathetic and know that the lawyers will take their 40 per cent. before the plaintiff gets anything. All this means that the defendant can be readily forced into a settlement. The plaintiff holds all the cards.

74   *Pain* v. *United Technologies Corp.*, 637 F. 2d at 784.

75   Applying the *forum non conveniens* doctrine in *Wiwa* v. *Royal Dutch Petroleum Co.*, 226 F. 3d 88 (2d Cir. 2000), the Second Circuit remarked, citing, *inter alia, Piper,* that "[w]hile any plaintiff's selection of a forum is entitled to deference, the deference increases as the plaintiff's ties to the forum increase".

76   *Olympic Corp.* v. *Société Générale*, 462 F. 2d 376, at 378 (2d Cir. 1972).

77   *Pain* v. *United Technologies Corp.*, 637 F. 2d at 796-797 (footnotes and internal quotations omitted). Similar concerns as to US courts favoring American over foreign

The normative standard of equal treatment is espoused by some – but by no means all – contemporary jurists.[78]

C.   Antisuit Injunctions

Just as *forum non conveniens*, the antisuit injunction is an instrument of fine-tuning that can serve to channel litigation to a more – or the most – appropriate forum; from this perspective *forum non conveniens* and antisuit injunctions are the two sides of one coin. But there is a crucial difference: by invoking *forum non conveniens*, a court forgoes the exercise of adjudicatory authority in order to improve the quality of justice rendered in matters that can be brought before the courts of more than one legal order. An antisuit injunction, on the other hand, can – no matter how well intended – be seen as an intrusive act even though it does not operate directly on the foreign court[79]. Foreign courts – even those that themselves use on occasion antisuit injunctions – may well regard such injunctions as serious interferences with their process; indeed, American courts characterized the antisuit injunctions granted by the English Court of Appeal in the *Laker* litigation[80] as "a direct interference" and as "intrusive".

1.   *Civil-Law Jurisdictions*

Consistent with their attitude towards *forum non conveniens*, but more categorically, most civil-law jurisdictions reject the use of antisuit injunctions.[81] "[S]uch a possibility is inconceivable in French law which would consider it an intolerable

---

plaintiffs are held by European scholars. See, e.g., Schack, *supra* footnote 5, at 177, No. 496.

78   See J. Duval-Major, "One-Way Ticket Home: The Federal Doctrine of forum non conveniens and the International Plaintiff", 77 *Cornell L. Rev.* 650, at 681 (1992) ("A foreign plaintiff should receive the same deference a United States plaintiff would receive."); Juenger, *supra* footnote 9, at 315; F. Juenger, "Forum non Conveniens – Who needs it?", in Reinhold Geimer (ed.), *Wege zur Globalisierung des Rechts – Festschrift für Rolf A. Schütze zum 65. Geburtstag* 317, at 330-331 (Munich, C. H. Beck, 1999); Schack, *supra* footnote 5, at 176, No. 496.

79   See Dicey and Morris, *supra* footnote 56, at 414, No. 12-057; *Turner* v. *Grovit and Others*, [2000] 1 QB 345, at 364 (CA 1999) ("[T]he reinstatement of injunctive relief in favor of the plaintiff entails not the slightest disrespect to the Spanish court. It is of course elementary that there is no question of our requiring that court to do or refrain from anything.").

80   See p. 268, *supra*; see also *British Airways Board* v. *Laker Airways Ltd.*, [1984] QB 142 (CA 1983); *Laker Airways Ltd.* v. *Pan American World Airways*, 559 F. Supp. 1124, at 1128, footnote 14 (DDC 1983), affd. sub nom. *Laker Airways Ltd.* v. *Sabena, Belgian World Airways*, 731 F. 2d 909 (DC Cir. 1984); *Laker Airways Ltd.* v. *Pan American World Airways*, 577 F. Supp. 348, at 352 (DDC 1983).

81   See Gaudemet-Tallon, *supra* footnote 28, at 434-435; Schack, *supra* footnote 10, 58 *RabelsZ* at 56-57 (at 203-205 in Fawcett).

intrusion into the functioning of a foreign system of justice."[82] Just as French law,[83] German law "counters forum shopping abroad ... not with antisuit injunctions but first at the stage of recognition of judgments".[84] In the wake of the *Laker* litigation,[85] the availability of antisuit injunctions was discussed at some length on the European continent; so far, however, no change has occurred in legislation or court practices.[86] Nor are foreign antisuit injunctions – including those based on forum-selection or arbitration clauses – recognized.[87]

The position and analysis of the Oberlandesgericht Düsseldorf in a 1996 decision exemplifies the views of civil-law systems generally. In refusing to recognize an antisuit injunction given by an English court,[88] the Oberlandesgericht em-

---

82   Gaudemet-Tallon, *supra* footnote 28, at 434. *In Banque Worms* v. *Epoux Brachot*, J.C.P. 2002.II, 10 201, however, the French *Cour de cassation* approved, in principle, of an injunction issued by the *Cour d'appel* of Versailles in the course of insolvency proceedings pending in France against a French debtor bank in order to refrain it from seizing certain assets located in Spain. The *Cour de cassation* held that such an order did not violate jurisdictional limits of the French courts since it was addressed to the defendant personally and was awarded by the court with legitimate jurisdiction over the merits of the proceedings. The order has been described as "an intriguing hybrid" since it comprises elements of both a freezing- and an antisuit injunction; H. Muir-Watt, "Injunctive Relief in the French Courts: A Case of Legal Borrowing", 62 C. L.J. (2003) 573, at 575. Muir-Watt, *ibid.*, further notes that "the ease with which an antisuit injunction seems to have found its way into French law can be explained by the fact that it was introduced here under cover of a freezing order, no doubt perceived as less intrusive."

83   "It is thus only ... [by applying a jurisdictional test when recognition is sought in France] that the French law offers" a protection against abusive claims of adjudicatory authority by foreign courts. *Idem* 435.

84   Schack, *supra* footnote 10, 58 *RabelsZ* at 56.

85   See p. 291, *infra*.

86   See J. Kurth, *Inländischer Rechtsschutz gegen Verfahren vor ausländischen Gerichten*, 115-117 (Berlin, Duncker & Humblot, 1989); W. Hau, *Positive Kompetenzkonflikte im Internationalen Zivilprozeßrecht*, 201-210 (Frankfurt am Main, Peter Lang, 1996); R. Geimer, *Internationales Zivilprozessrecht*, 379-381, No. 1116-1121 (Cologne, Dr. Otto Schmidt, 5th ed., 2005). But see the decision of the French *Cour de cassation* referred to *supra*, footnote 82.
      It is worth noting that German courts did give antisuit injunctions under the old and restrictive German law of divorce. The Reichsgericht would occasionally enjoin divorce proceedings on the ground that a delict is committed by a party who initiates proceedings in a foreign court whose law of divorce is less strict than the German law. See, e.g., *RG*, 30 March 1938, 157 *RGZ* 136; see also E. Riezler, *Internationales Zivilprozessrecht und prozessuales Fremdenrecht* 338-340 (Berlin, de Gruyter & Tübingen, Mohr (Siebeck), 1949).

87   See Geimer, *supra* footnote 86, at 346, No. 1014, at 607, No. 1945b and at 873, No. 2792.

88   The injunction was given in *Phillip Alexander Securities and Futures Ltd.* v. *Bamberger and Others*, [1997] I. L. Pr. 73 (CA 1997).

phasized that the courts of each State decide for themselves, under the relevant domestic procedural legislation and international treaties, as well their adjudicatory authority as their obligation to respect the procedural claims of other courts, domestic or foreign. That the antisuit injunction is directed to parties rather than courts does not sufficiently protect a State's sovereignty. The plaintiff's coerced failure to proceed prevents a forum from exercising its adjudicatory authority; injunctions directed to local plaintiffs and to local courts thus produce equivalent effects.[89]

2. Common-Law Jurisdictions

(a) England and Scotland[90]

(i) Introductory

Just as with *forum non conveniens*, English and Scottish law regarding antisuit injunctions are quite similar.[91] At least since the early nineteenth century, "English courts have ... exercised a jurisdiction to restrain a party from instituting or prosecuting proceedings in a foreign court."[92] The ready English acceptance of antisuit injunctions in litigations with international dimensions can be explained, at least in part, by the long use in England of injunctions to control the exercise of adjudicatory authority by competing domestic-court hierarchies.[93]

At first, English courts applied essentially the same standards for antisuit injunctions as for *forum non conveniens*.[94] The antisuit injunction's intrusive quality led, in time, to a stiffening of the requirements for its granting. As Lord Goff put it,

---

89   See OLG Düsseldorf, 10 January 1996, 109 *ZZP* 221, at 222-223 (English translation in [1997] I. L. Pr. 320) (arbitration clause); see also H.-P. Mansel, "Grenzüberschreitende Prozeßführungsverbote (antisuit injunctions) und Zustellungsverweigerung", 7 *EuZW* 335-340 (1996) (approving refusal to recognize); M. Lenenbach, "Antisuit Injunctions in England, Germany and the United States: Their Treatment under European Civil Procedure and the Hague Convention", 20 *Loy. LA Int'l & Comp. LJ* 257, at 317-321 (1998) (criticizing refusal of recognition).

90   Scottish law has an important civil-law tradition. For present purposes, however, Scottish and English law are closely related.

91   See *Société Nationale Industrielle Aérospatiale* v. *Lee Kui Jak*, [1987] AC 871, at 896 (PC 1987).

92   Dicey and Morris, *supra* footnote 56, at 414, No. 12-057.

93   Antisuit injunctions first appeared in England as writs of prohibition from the common-law courts to the ecclesiastical courts to curb the latters' claims of adjudicatory authority. See G. Bermann, "The Use of Antisuit Injunctions in International Litigation", 28 *Colum. J. Trans. L.* 589, at 593 (1990); see generally E. Dumbauld, "Judicial Interference with Litigation in Other Courts", 74 *Dick. L. Rev.* 369, at 375-378 (1969); T. Hartley, "Comity and the Use of Antisuit Injunctions in International Litigation", 35 *Am. J. Comp. L.* 487, at 489-490 (1987). Later, the Court of Chancery used the same technique against the common-law courts.

94   *Castanho* v. *Brown and Root (UK) Ltd.*, [1981] AC 557 (HL 1980).

where there is simply a difference of view between the English court and the foreign court as to which is the natural forum, [the proposition that] the English court can arrogate to itself by the grant of an injunction, the power to resolve that dispute[] [would] be inconsistent with comity, and indeed ... disregard the fundamental requirement that an injunction will only be granted where the ends of justice so require.[95]

It follows that

where a remedy for a particular wrong is available both in the English ... court and in a foreign court, the English ... court will, generally speaking, only restrain the plaintiff from pursuing proceedings in the foreign court if such a suit would be vexatious or oppressive. This presupposes that, as a general rule, the English ... court must conclude that it provides the natural forum for the trial of the action; and further, since the court is concerned with the ends of justice, that account must be taken not only of injustice to the defendant if the plaintiff is allowed to pursue the foreign proceedings, but also of injustice to the plaintiff if he is not allowed to do so. So the court will not grant an injunction if, by doing so, it will deprive the plaintiff of advantages in the foreign forum of which it would be unjust to deprive him. Fortunately, however, ... that problem can often be overcome by appropriate undertakings given by the defendant, or by the granting of an injunction upon appropriate terms; just as, in cases of stay of proceedings [i.e. *forum non conveniens* stays], the parallel problem of advantages to the plaintiff in the domestic forum which is, prima facie, inappropriate, can likewise often be solved by granting a stay upon terms.[96]

The standard articulated by Lord Goff obtains in England and, with only minor differences, in Canada.[97] Australia, on the other hand, takes a more restricted stance; antisuit injunctions are given only "if there is nothing which can be gained by [the foreign proceedings] over and above what may be gained in local proceedings".[98]

---

95   *Société Aérospatiale, supra* footnote 91, at 895.
96   *Idem* 896-897.
      The complex and numerous undertakings agreed to by the Société nationale industrielle aerospatiale are set out in an appendix to their Lordships' judgment, see *idem* 903-905.
97   See *Amchem Products Ltd. v. British Columbia (Workers' Compensation Board)* [1993] 1 Can. SCR 897; see also J.-G. Castel & J. Walker, *Canadian Conflict of Laws*, Vol. 1, §13.4, 13-16 (Canada, LexisNexis Butterworths, 6th ed., 2005 [loose leaf ed.]).
98   See *CSR Ltd. v. Cigna Insurance Australia Ltd.*, 189 CLR 345, at 393 (HCA 1997).

(ii)   A landmark decision: Airbus Industries G.I.E. v. Patel and Others
a.   The litigation

Airbus Industrie[99] explicates the contemporary approach of United Kingdom courts to antisuit injunctions in the absence of treaty obligations. The case arose from the crash of an Airbus A-320 aircraft in India. Members of two families of Indian origin, British citizens living in London, were aboard; four family members died in the crash; four were injured. Actions on their behalf were brought in India against Indian Airlines Corporation, the employer of the pilots of the aircraft, and against HAL, the authority in charge of the airport where the crash occurred. A settlement was reached with IAC, but the proceedings against HAL continued.

In 1992, the plaintiffs brought actions in Texas against various parties that had connections either with the design and production of the aircraft or with its operations. Among them was Airbus Industrie GIE, the French company, which had designed and assembled the aircraft at Toulouse in France.

Texas took jurisdiction on the ground that Airbus Industries "had at some time in the past done business with a Texas based corporation ... which had its corporate head office in Texas".[100] At the time, Texas law did not allow *forum non conveniens* challenges.[101]

> [N]either Airbus Industries nor any of the claimants had any actual connection with Texas ... nor was it relevant that the subject-matter had no connection [with] and ... no relevant witness or evidence was to be found in the state of Texas.[102]

The principle of strict liability in Texas law only requires claimants "to establish that some part of the aircraft was in a defective condition and that the condition of that part was a cause of the claimant's injury".[103] In addition, Texas provides for punitive damages and allows contingent-fee arrangements.[104]

Airbus responded by bringing proceedings in India to enjoin the Indian claimants from pursuing their claim in Texas. In connection with its action, Airbus gave various undertakings to the Indian courts, including waiving any claim to State immunity and certain statute of limitation defenses, providing in India the relevant documents and employee witnesses regardless of their location, and to satisfy any final judgment entered against it by the Indian courts.[105]

---

99   [1999] 1 AC 119. The decision is praised as a potential model for American jurisprudence by K. Anderson, "Comment: What Can the United States Learn from English Antisuit Injunctions? An American Perspective on *Airbus Industrie G.I.E. v. Patel*", 25 *Yale J. Int'l L.* 195-232 (2000).

100   [1997] 2 Lloyd's Rep. 8, at 11 (CA 1996).

101   *Ibid.* By statute, the *Alfaro* rule was set aside in 1993. See *supra* footnote 55.

102   *Ibid.*

103   *Ibid.*

104   See *Ibid.*

105   *Idem* at 12.

Airbus Industries won a Pyrrhic victory in the Indian courts. They enjoined further prosecution of the Texas litigation but, lacking adjudicatory authority over the Indian claimants and their assets, this decision created no rights or obligations in England. The court of first instance in England "rightly rejected the arguments of Airbus Industries that it was entitled to enforce, or at least have recognized, the Indian judgment against the English claimants in ... [England]".[106]

Airbus then sought in England, residence of the Indian plaintiffs in the Texas action, an antisuit injunction against their pursuing the Texas action on the ground that proceeding there "would be contrary to justice and/or vexatious or oppressive".[107] The judge of first instance refused to grant an injunction;[108] he was reversed in the Court of Appeal,[109] which was, in turn, reversed by the House of Lords.[110]

b.   The comity requirement

Traditionally, English courts have granted antisuit injunctions

> to restrain the pursuit of proceedings overseas which is unconscionable. The focus is, therefore, on the character of the defendant's conduct, as befits an equitable remedy such as an injunction. In particular, ... no requirement has been imposed specifically to prevent the grant of an antisuit injunction in circumstances which amount to a breach of comity. The present case raises for the first time, and in a stark form, the question whether such a requirement should be recognised and, if so, what form it should take.[111]

Lord Goff concluded that comity does not permit a court to enjoin proceedings abroad that concern a controversy without connections to the State from whose courts relief is requested. In his view,

> [i]n effect, the English court ... [was] being asked to grant an injunction ... where, unusually, the English jurisdiction has no interest in, or connection with, the matter in question .... [S]uch a course is not open to the English Courts because, for the reasons ... given, it would be inconsistent with comity. In a world which consists of

---

106   *Ibid.* Airbus had asked the judge in the first instance to recognize and enforce the Indian injunction. Colman J. refused, pointing out that neither the Common Law, nor the Foreign Judgments (Reciprocal Enforcement) Act of 1933 allows for enforcing foreign judgments other than money judgments; foreign court orders can be used as an estoppel, but not enforced affirmatively. See *Airbus Industrie G.I.E.* v. *Jaisukh Arjun Bhai Patel and Others*, [1996] I. L. Pr. 465, at 473-474 (QB 1996).

107   [1999] 1 AC 119 (HL 1998).

108   *Airbus Industrie G.I.E.* v. *Jaisukh Arjun Bhai Patel and Others*, [1996] I. L. Pr. 465 (QBD 1996).

109   *Airbus Industrie G.I.E.* v. *Patel and Others*, [1997] 2 Lloyd's Rep. 8 (CA 1996).

110   *Airbus Industrie G.I.E.* v. *Patel*, [1999] 1 AC 119 (HL 1998).

111   *Airbus Industries G.I.E.*, [1999] 1 AC at 134.

independent jurisdictions, interference, even indirect interference, by the Courts of one jurisdiction with the exercise of the jurisdiction of a foreign Court cannot … be justified by the fact that a third jurisdiction is affected but is powerless to intervene. The basic principle is that only the Courts of an interested jurisdiction can act in the matter; and if they are powerless to do so, that will not of itself be enough to justify the Courts of another jurisdiction to act in their place. Such are the limits of a system which is dependent on the remedy of an antisuit injunction to curtail the excesses of a jurisdiction which does not adopt the principle, widely accepted throughout the common law world, of *forum non conveniens*.[112]

At the end of the day, when a disinterested forum grants an antisuit injunction it acts as an officious intermeddler. Comity would, of course, allow the French courts to enjoin further proceedings in Texas. But, as a civil-law jurisdiction, France rejects in principle enjoining actions before the courts of another legal order.[113]

c.   Comity in alternative forum cases

Lord Goff went on to analyse the interconnections between the issues posed by a *forum non conveniens* stay and a request for an antisuit injunction in the same matter:

> [T]he court [considering a *forum non conveniens* stay] must determine whether there is another forum that is clearly more appropriate…. [W]here there is no one forum that is the most appropriate, the domestic forum wins out by default and refuses a stay, provided it is an appropriate forum. In this step of the analysis, the domestic court as a matter of comity must take cognizance of the fact that the foreign court has assumed jurisdiction. If, applying the principles relating to *forum non conveniens* outlined above, the foreign court could reasonably have concluded that there was no alternative forum that was clearly more appropriate, the domestic court should respect that decision and the application should be dismissed. When there is a genuine disagreement between the courts of our country and another, the courts of this country should not arrogate to themselves the decision for both jurisdictions. In most cases it will appear from the decision of the foreign court whether it acted on principles similar to those that obtain here, but, if not, then the domestic court must consider whether the result is consistent with those principles. In a case in which the domestic court concludes that the foreign court assumed jurisdiction on a basis that is inconsistent with principles relating to forum non conveniens and that the foreign court's conclusion could not reasonably have been reached had it applied those principles, it

---

112   *Idem* 140-141.
  An English court that gave an antisuit injunction in these circumstances could be seen as asserting a form of universal jurisdiction in order to remedy a wrong that would otherwise go unpunished. In this sense, *Airbus Industries* raises a problem that is central in human rights cases.

113   But see now the case mentioned *supra* footnote 82.

must go then to the second step of the *[Aérospatiale]* test – i.e., whether to grant an injunction on the ground that the ends of justice require it.[114]

If, in the circumstances, granting an antisuit injunction comes into question, must the foreign proceedings be "vexatious and harassing", or is it sufficient that they be "inconvenient"? In limiting antisuit injunctions to extreme cases of vexation,[115] a system takes primarily into account the behaviour of the litigating parties. The focus is not, as in *forum non conveniens*, on whether the other court is the "natural forum" when all relevant factors are taken into account. Contrariwise, courts applying the "inconvenience" test approach to antisuit injunctions as well as to *forum non conveniens* stays ask which court is more appropriately seized of the matter.

(b) The United States

In view of the Full Faith and Credit requirement contained in the Constitution of 1789, one might assume that in American practice antisuit injunctions would be available, if at all, only with respect to proceedings that were foreign in the international sense. Perhaps both because antisuit injunctions had been used traditionally in English law to control the exercise of adjudicatory authority by different domestic courts and because, after the Constitution replaced the Articles of Confederation, the several states continued to exercise considerable sovereign powers in matters pertaining to the administration of justice, injunctions against a party participating in sister-state proceedings survived challenge on full-faith-and-credit as well as equal-protection grounds.[116]

---

114   *Airbus Industrie G.I.E.*, [1999] 1 AC at 139.

115   Lord Goff remarked in *Airbus Industrie G.I.E.* that

> the traditional way in which the principles applicable in cases of antisuit injunctions have been formulated in … [England] corresponds to the 'laxer' approach applied in the Fifth, Seventh and Ninth Circuits [in the United States], in that the latter refers to vexation, oppression and inequitable hardship.

Idem 139-140.

The "general principle" outlined in *Airbus Industrie* is, however, in his view, "close to the stricter approach adopted by the Second Circuit, the Sixth Circuit and the District of Columbia Circuit in the United States." *Idem* 139. The several approaches of the Federal Courts of Appeal are discussed pp. 287-291, *infra*.

116   *Cole* v. *Cunningham*, 133 US 107 (1890) (5-3 decision). Chief Justice Fuller remarked in his majority opinion that

> [t]he jurisdiction of the English Court of Chancery to restrain persons within its territorial limits and under its jurisdiction from doing anything abroad, whether the thing forbidden be a conveyance or other act *in pais*, or the institution or the prosecution of an action in a foreign court, is well settled.

Idem 116-117.

In his dissenting opinion, Justice Miller argued that Section 1 (full faith and credit) and Section 2 (privileges and immunities) of Article 4 of the Constitution of the United States were intended

Antisuit injunctions have been granted in interstate practice where the action brought in the sister state sought to evade local exemption laws in insolvency cases, would vex or harass the defendant, or would result in additional expense and inconvenience to him that would be avoided by the suit being brought locally.[117]

In view of the wide acceptance of the antisuit injunction in sister-state practice and the non-applicability of the full-faith-and-credit command internationally, it would be most surprising if the American courts refrained from the use of these injunctions in international practice. Constitutional arguments – not available where sister-state practice is in question – can be made, however, against enjoining participation in pending or future proceedings in an internationally foreign court. Such injunctions may have foreign-policy implications, constitute state intrusion into an area of federal authority,[118] and raise, in federal cases, issues respecting the allocation of authority among the branches of the federal government. These considerations are doubtless taken into account by courts in deciding whether to enjoin litigation abroad; however, constitutionally based standards controlling the use of antisuit injunctions against proceedings in foreign courts have not emerged.

Granting – whether by a state or a federal court[119] – of antisuit injunctions in international practice is thus for the United States law a matter of judicial discretion. Federal courts hold diverging views as to whether a "strict" or a "lax" standard should be used when they assess the requirements of international comity in these cases.[120] After stating that, as a general rule, "a federal court has a duty to

---

to prevent conflicts between courts of the different States, over the same matters, by establishing the rule that whatever is done or decided in one State shall be respected in every other State, when properly proved before it. It is one feature of the general idea which is found all through the Constitution.

Idem 134, at 136.

117　See "Comment: Full Faith and Credit to Foreign Injunctions", 26 *U. Chi. L. Rev.* 633, at 633-634 (1959).

118　See Bermann, *supra* footnote 93, at 604-605.

119　The ability of federal courts to constrain litigation in state courts is limited by the federal Anti-Injunction Act – 28 USC §2283 (2006). See Burbank, *supra* footnote 46, at 213. It provides that

[a] court of the United States may not grant an injunction to stay proceedings in a State court except as expressly authorized by Act of Congress, or where necessary in aid of its jurisdiction, or to protect or effectuate its judgments.

120　For a comprehensive survey of federal court decisions between 1980 and 1998, see M. Trevino de Coale, "Stay, Dismiss, Enjoin, or Abstain?: A Survey of Foreign Parallel Litigation in the Federal Courts of the United States", 17 *BU Int'l LJ* 79-114 (1999). See also L. Teitz, "Taking Multiple Bites of the Apple: A Proposal to Resolve Conflicts of Jurisdiction and Multiple Proceedings", 26 *Int'l Law.* 21, at 36-38 (1992) (discussing both approaches).

exercise the jurisdiction Congress has given it",[121] Chief Judge Posner expressed a preference for the "'laxer standard', which allows an injunction against litigating in a foreign forum upon a finding that letting the two suits proceed would be gratuitously duplicative".[122] The

> courts that follow the stricter standard believe that considerations of international comity require that the domestic and foreign cases be distinguished and that a greater showing of need be required for an injunction in the latter type of case.[123]

That is not to say that the "laxer standard" assigns no weight to comity but, unlike the stricter standard, it does not

> presume a threat to international comity whenever an injunction is sought against litigating in a foreign court .... [T]he opponent [must supply] ... some indication that the issuance of an injunction really would throw a monkey wrench, however small, into the foreign relations of the United States.[124]

(i)   Recognition of sister-state injunctions

In domestic US situations, the question arises whether a sister-state's antisuit injunction must be given effect. The Full Faith and Credit Clause contains no language distinguishing injunctions from other kinds of "judicial Proceedings" entitled to such credit; nevertheless, "the obligation came to be tied to the existence of a judgment".[125] The Supreme Court has never held that antisuit injunctions are so entitled[126] and state-court decisions giving effect to them have invoked "a spirit

---

121   *Allendale Mutual Ins. Co. et al* v. *Bull Data Systems, Inc.*, 10 F. 3d 425, at 430 (7th Cir. 1993); for a later episode, that has no direct bearing on the issue here discussed, see 32 F. 3d 1175 (7th Cir. 1994).

122   *Allendale*, 10 F. 3d at 431. See also M. Redish, "Intersystemic Redundancy and Federal Court Power: Proposing a Zero Tolerance Solution to the Duplicative Litigation Problem", 75 *Notre Dame L. Rev.* 1347-1376 (2000) (arguing that, in the case of parallel litigation, a court must either stay its proceedings on the ground of *forum non conveniens* or enjoin the proceedings abroad).

123   *Allendale*, 10 F. 3d at 431 (citing *Laker Airways Ltd.* v. *Sabena*, 731 F. 2d 909 (DC Cir. 1984)). See also S. Swanson, "The Vexatiousness of a Vexation Rule: International Comity and Antisuit Injunctions", 30 *Geo. Wash. J. Int'l L. & Econ.* 1-37 (1996) (discussing why comity supports the stricter test).

124   *Allendale, supra* footnote 123, at 431.

125   Burbank, *supra* footnote 46, at 209. In *Baker* v. *General Motors*, 522 US 222 (1998), the Supreme Court affirmed this position.

126   Four arguments are advanced for denying full faith and credit to antisuit injunctions: (1) one state would be able to control another's exercise of adjudicatory authority; (2) in some contexts, recognition would violate the Privileges and Immunities Clause of the Constitution; (3) a legislative attempt to localize by statute litigation respecting a given cause of action is not entitled to full faith and credit and greater effect should not be accorded to a court's localization effort; (4) "judicial Proceedings" for the pur-

of just interstate comity"[127] rather than the Constitution.[128] State "courts regularly disregard such decrees"[129] and, from time to time, react by giving a counter-injunction.[130]

An interesting and subtle issue remains open: what happens if the enjoined party pursues the sister-state action and prevails? Is the resulting judgment entitled to full faith and credit in the enjoining state? Presumably, the judgment is so entitled and must be enforced. But may the enjoining state still punish for contempt the party who defied its injunction? "Is it an acceptable accommodation of the competing interests to require enforcement of the judgment but allow an offsetting contempt toll by the enjoining state?"[131] Justice Ginsburg has argued that

> the national full faith and credit policy should override the local interest of the enjoining state,[] [thus leaving] to the injunction ... [only the] limited office [of notifying] the state in which litigation has been instituted of the enjoining state's appraisal of forum conveniens.[132]

(ii) Retaliatory antisuit injunctions

An antisuit injunction can lead in common-law jurisdictions to a counter-injunction. The enjoined party, instead of obeying the injunction, proceeds abroad and

---

pose of the Full Faith and Credit Clause are limited to adjudication of the merits of the ultimate controversy. See Comment, *supra* footnote 117, at 637-642. The Comment concludes that these arguments are not persuasive (*Idem* 638-642) and suggests (*Idem* 635) that the full faith and credit command requires that an antisuit injunction be recognized "by dismissing the action whose prosecution has been enjoined". See also Bermann, *supra* footnote 93, at 603-604.

127   *Gilman* v. *Ketcham*, 84 Wis. 60, at 66, 54 NW 395, at 396 (1893).

128   Comment *b* (Rationale) to §103 (Limitations on Full Faith and Credit), Restatement (Second) of Conflict of Laws – revised in 1988 by deleting a brief, and for present purposes irrelevant, discussion on the full faith and credit owed to sister-state custody decrees, see Restatement (Second) of Conflicts of Laws (1988 Revisions), Reporter's Note to §103, at 111 – explains:

> There will be extremely rare occasions ... when recognition of a sister State judgment would require too large a sacrifice by a State of its interests in a matter in which it is primarily concerned. On these extremely rare occasions, the policy embodied in full faith and credit will give way before the national policy that requires protection of the dignity and of the fundamental interests of each individual State. So, full faith and credit does not require a State to recognize a sister State injunction against suit in its courts on the ground that it is an inconvenient forum. This is because a State, subject to [constitutionally required] jurisdictional limitations, should be permitted to decide for itself, and without dictation from another State, what cases its courts will hear ....

129   Bermann, *supra* footnote 93, at 602.

130   See, e.g., the *James* litigation, discussed *infra*.

131   R. Ginsburg, "Judgments in Search of Full Faith and Credit: The Last-in-Time Rule for Conflicting Judgments", 82 *Harv. L. Rev.* 798, at 830 (1969).

132   *Ibid*.

asks the court there to enjoin, in turn, the other party from proceeding further in the court that gave the first injunction.

This tactic's potential for disruption is illustrated by *James* v. *Grand Trunk Western R.R. Co.*[133] A resident of Michigan was killed in a railroad accident in Michigan. His widow, although seeking recovery under the Michigan Wrongful Death Act, brought the action in Illinois. At the railroad's behest, a Michigan court enjoined the Illinois proceedings. The plaintiff thereupon sought, and obtained, in Illinois an injunction against the railroad's observation of the Michigan injunction. The Supreme Court of Illinois indicated that, had the point been urged, it might well have ordered dismissal of the Illinois action on *forum non conveniens* grounds.[134] The court considered unacceptable, however, Michigan's interference with a suit already begun in Illinois:

> [T]his court need not, and will not, countenance having its right to try cases, of which it has proper jurisdiction, determined by the courts of other States, through their injunctive process.[135]

Justice Schaefer, in dissent, questioned the propriety of Michigan's injunction, though he recognized that the Illinois concern for the plaintiff and for the underlying situation was minimal.[136] On the facts of the case, however, he – unlike the majority – was not prepared to add to "this unseemly kind of judicial disorder" by a retaliatory injunction.[137]

In light of the "unseemly ... judicial disorder" that can result from an antisuit injunction followed by a counter-injunction, antisuit injunctions should – absent special justifying circumstances – be granted in private-law matters only where the enjoining forum acts on the basis of legitimate procedural concerns that rest on a party's failure to respect mutually agreed or statutorily imposed limitations on forum choice,[138] on a party's effort to gain unwarranted preferential treatment by, for example, litigating claims outside pending bankruptcy proceedings, or on steps taken by a party "acting in bad faith with the intent and purpose of frustrating or obstructing proceedings properly before the ... [enjoining court]".[139]

Antisuit injunctions on these grounds do not asperse the quality of justice provided by the court in which the enjoined party wished to proceed. That court may nevertheless object on sovereignty grounds and determine, without attaching any weight to the motives of the enjoining court, whether to issue a counter-

---

133   14 Ill. 2d 356, 152 NE 2d 858 (1958), *cert. denied*, 358 US 915 (1958).

134   *Idem* at 362, 152 NE 2d at 862.

135   *Idem* at 372, 152 NE 2d at 867.

136   *Idem* 372, at 375, 152 NW 2d 867, at 868.

137   *Ibid.*

138   Common examples are binding arbitration agreements and exclusive forum-selection clauses.

139   *Turner* v. *Grovit and Others*, [2001] UKHL 65 No. 21 (HL 2001).

injunction. The court should, however, take into account whether the enjoining court had a legitimate procedural concern in light of the party conduct that led to the antisuit injunction. For legal orders that invest their courts with contempt power, an injunction is, in such circumstances, an appropriate sanction for egregious party behaviour and, as such, should not provoke a counter-injunction.

International litigation in which important and conflicting *governmental* economic and regulatory policies of two nations clash can well lead to a battle of injunctions. In the *Laker* litigation, injunctions were sought and obtained from the English courts ordering English parties to drop antitrust and other regulatory proceedings in the United States against British Airways and other airlines. The enjoined parties responded by requesting the United States court to enjoin the other airlines from further participating in the English action. Ultimately, the House of Lords vacated the injunctions granted by the lower court.[140] The British Government was dismayed with this decision because the continuing American proceedings ran afoul of the Government's efforts to privatize British Airways. After the direct involvement of Prime Minister Thatcher and President Reagan, the US Justice Department terminated the grand jury investigation of the alleged conspiracy underlying the American litigation.[141] Where such impasses arise, a solution may ultimately require diplomatic intervention.

One might expect that "injunction wars" would be more frequent than appears to be the case.[142] The apparent dearth of counter-injunctions can perhaps be explained in part on the ground that most courts are reluctant to grant an antisuit injunction in the first place. And those granted may largely be of the types that have a strong claim of legitimacy. A further important reason is, of course, the exclusion in most civil-law jurisdictions of relief in the form of an antisuit injunction. The sovereignty principle is seen as forbidding a State from seeking to control, albeit indirectly, another State's decision whether to exercise its adjudicatory authority. States that hold this view cannot retaliate to an antisuit injunction by issuing a counter-injunction. Diplomatic protests might be lodged with the State whose court issued such an injunction but this step is rarely taken in practice.

---

140   *British Airways Board* v. *Laker Airways*, [1985] AC 58 (HL 1984).

141   The civil action was settled. See *New York Times*, 13 July 1985, at 29, col. 7. See generally N. Hachigian, "Essential Mutual Assistance in International Antitrust Enforcement", 29 *Int'l Law*, 117, 125-126 (1995) and the authorities cited *supra* footnote 93.

142   Cf. Trevino de Coale, *supra* footnote 120, *passim*.

D.   Avoiding Duplicative Litigation: The *Lis Pendens* Doctrine as an Alternative to Judicial Fine-tuning[143]

1.   *In General*

Regardless of the form dispute-resolution takes, it is rarely – if ever – costless. Where judicial proceedings are involved, typically the costs are significant both for society and for the parties. Duplicative litigation should therefore not proceed unless countervailing policies can be advanced that justify the additional costs in time and money. In the absence of such policies, the question remains, which of two or more proceedings should be continued, in particular, should the only relevant criterion be temporal priority.

Litigation can be completely – or only partially – duplicative. The reasons for avoiding duplicative litigation justify considering actions identical even though one seeks coercive relief and the other a declaration of non-liability.[144] On the other hand, actions that have the same object and raise the same legal and factual issues but are between different parties are not considered duplicative although they may be candidates for consolidation. The distinction between identical and "connected" litigation reflects the considerable measure of party control over litigation that most Western legal systems recognize.

Other considerations speak for or against consolidation when the legal or factual issues are significantly different or the actions have significantly different objectives.[145]

(a)   In local litigation

The handling of duplicative local proceedings varies significantly from legal system to legal system. The important point for present purposes is that the *lis pendens* problem is typically addressed when it arises with respect to local litigation.

Speaking in very general terms, priority in time is normally decisive in intramural litigation. Where a matter is pending in one court of the state, later-in-time duplicative proceedings in another court of the state are barred by civil- and com-

---

143   The special situation faced by the *lis pendens* principle where the pending proceedings seek a declaratory judgment of non-liability is discussed, 5., pp. 304 *et seq., infra*.

144   See the discussion of the *Gubisch* and *"Tatry"* cases, D. 5. *(c)* (ii), pp. 312 *et seq., infra*.

145   The Report of the ILA Committee on International Civil and Commercial Litigation (2000) remarks that "the development of rules to deal with related[, as distinguished from competing,] actions serves a distinct policy objective, not so far expressed by any of the techniques ... [under discussion]. Namely, that of consolidation of international litigation." See London/Leuven Principles on Declining and Referring Jurisdiction in Civil and Commercial Matters. Drafted by the International Law Association's Committee on Civil and Commercial Litigation, the Principles were adopted by the Association at its 69th Conference, held in London in July 2000. See ILA, *Report of the Sixty-Ninth Conference* 167-171 (Wales, UK, Cambrian Printers, 2000), No. 9, at 7. The Principles are analysed by the Rapporteur, Dr. C. McLachlan, in his *Report: Declining & Referring Jurisdiction in International Litigation, idem* 137-166.

mon-law systems alike. Allowing plural actions to proceed would be uneconomic, create difficulties should the outcome in the parallel actions be inconsistent, and serve no useful purpose. Article 100 of France's New Code of Civil Procedure requires, for example, dismissal of a later identical litigation if either party so requests. (The second-seized court may also invoke the exception at its discretion.) Where connected proceedings are in question, under Article 101 a request – directed to either the first or the later seized court – can be made by a party to transfer, in "the interest of good justice", the pending litigation to the other court; granting such requests is essentially in the court addressed's discretion.[146]

(b) In multistate and international litigation

In non-local litigation, on the other hand, duplicative proceedings were traditionally not barred in any State by an essentially automatic *lis pendens* rule. In such cases, recourse could be had in some systems to the *forum non conveniens* doctrine or to an antisuit injunction. In most systems, common- and civil-law alike, the situation was not addressed until recognition and enforcement abroad were sought. Once a definitive adjudication had been obtained, some significance was given by most legal orders to the fact that the controversy had already been adjudicated in whole or in part. The policy issues raised and the various views respecting their proper resolution are addressed in the literature on recognition and enforcement of foreign judgments.[147] It is out of place to address them here; one should keep in mind, however, that the policy considerations respecting the relevance of temporal priority before – and after – adjudication of overlapping or related disputes are not entirely dissimilar.

When litigation between the same or related parties involving the same or similar issues is already pending in a foreign forum, the question is posed whether local courts should decline to exercise jurisdiction in the interest of co-operative, economical, and harmonious administration of justice for non-domestic controversies. Applying the *lis pendens* principle to international litigation not only creates administrative difficulties when the courts in question have different rules respecting such matters as when they are seized and what constitutes a duplicative action, but also encourages a party race to the court house and is, as a general matter, far more likely to be outcome determinative than where parallel litigation is handled in two local courts.[148] The arguments for and against seeking to avoid duplicative litigation are, accordingly, more complex and the appropriate conclusions less clear. Should the second forum, in principle, defer to the first? Or do

---

146 Cass. civ. 2nd, 5 July 1978, Gaz. Pal. 1978 2nd sem. J.624 (no discretion, however, to deny motion where the lower court found "*connexité*"; but compare J. Viatte, footnote to *idem*, with Gaudemet-Tallon, *supra* footnote 28, at 428).

147 The author's views respecting these issues are discussed in A. von Mehren, "Recognition and Enforcement of Foreign Judgments – General Theory and the Rôle of Jurisdictional Requirements", 167 *Recueil des cours* 13-112 (1980).

148 The reason for this lies in the differences between litigational systems described A.1., pp. 263 *et seq.*, *supra*.

these situations present for the legal system only a special case of the appropriate-court problem that cannot be appropriately addressed except case-by-case under the *forum non conveniens* doctrine?

In all events, legal systems that reject the *forum non conveniens* doctrine and the use of antisuit injunctions must choose between allowing the local litigation to proceed despite the parallel foreign action or staying or dismissing the domestic litigation if certain conditions – in particular, that the judgment resulting from the foreign proceeding is likely to be entitled to local recognition and enforcement – are satisfied. For legal systems that accept the *forum non conveniens* doctrine, the issue is largely whether significant weight is to be given to temporal priority in determining whether the other forum is so appropriate as to justify a *forum non conveniens* stay or so inappropriate that an antisuit injunction is called for.

2.   Civil-Law Jurisdictions

The German Code of Civil Procedure's provision that applies the *lis pendens* principle to domestic litigation[149] is extended by analogy to international situations; when a "foreign proceeding presumably *(voraussichtlich)* will lead to a judgment entitled to recognition ('recognition prognosis')", a later German proceeding must be stayed.[150] The same position is taken by Swiss law.[151]

The French system was traditionally far less willing than the German to apply *lis pendens* internationally. At the urging of French jurists,[152] the Cour de cassation in 1974 finally made the *lis pendens* exception applicable to international proceedings.[153] Where the foreign and local proceedings are essentially identical, the French judge may – at his discretion – now stay the later-in-time French proceeding if he considers that the foreign proceeding will result in a judgment that satisfies French requirements for recognition.[154] When the foreign and French actions

---

149   ZPO §261 (3), No. 1.

150   Schack, *supra* footnote 10, 58 *RabelsZ* at 51-52 (196-197 in Fawcett).

151   Article 9 of the Swiss Federal Act on Private International Law provides that

When an action having the same subject matter is already pending between the same parties in a foreign country, the Swiss court shall stay the case if it is to be expected that the foreign court will, within a reasonable time, render a decision capable of being recognized in Switzerland.

Compare Article 7 of the Italian Act on Private International Law (Law of 31 May 1995).

152   Notably D. Holleaux; see his "La litispendance internationale", [1971-1973] *Travaux Comité fr. dr. int. priv.* 203-218 (1974).

153   See Cass. civ. 1st, 26 November 1974, 64 *Rev. crit. dr. int. priv.* 491 (1975), (note D. Holleaux, *idem* 495-503); 102 *Jour. dr. int.* 108 (1975) (note A. Ponsard, *idem* 110-119); see H. Gaudemet-Tallon, "La litispendance internationale dans la jurisprudence française", in *Mélanges dédiés à D. Holleaux* 121, at 121-124 (Paris, Litec, 1990).

154   But see M.-L. Niboyet-Hoegy, "Les conflits de procédures", [1995-1996] *Travaux comité fr. dr. int. priv.* 71-86 (1999) (arguing for a strict priority principle).

are not identical but connected, French jurists on the whole take the position that French courts should defer, where a good administration of justice so indicates, to foreign courts. The Cour de cassation recognizes this possibility but leaves the matter to the lower courts' complete discretion.[155] So far, the French courts have shown little inclination to extend Article 101 by analogy to international litigation and stay French proceedings where connexity exists.[156]

3.   *Common-law Jurisdictions*

Legal systems that accept *forum non conveniens* do not embrace the first-in-time principle in dealing with duplicate litigation in the international arena. For them, a *forum non conveniens* problem is presented in which temporal priority is often of little weight.

(a)   Scotland and England

In Scotland, "[t]he plea of *lis alibi pendens* does not apply to proceedings before foreign courts and its place is taken by the plea of *forum non conveniens*".[157] The Scottish courts – perhaps due to their civil-law background – consider, however, "prior initiation of ... proceedings [abroad] ... an element of special importance";[158] yet "the crucial question ... [remains] whether the foreign court is one in which in all the circumstances, 'the case may be tried more suitably for the interest of all the parties and for the ends of justice'".[159] The English position gives less weight to priority in time: "the existence of simultaneous proceedings is simply an additional factor relevant to the determination of the appropriate forum".[160] Indeed,

> the foreign proceedings may be of no relevance at all, for example, if one party has commenced them for the purpose of demonstrating the existence of a competing jurisdiction, or if the proceedings have not passed beyond the stage of initiating process. But if genuine proceedings have been started and have had some impact on the dispute between the parties, especially if it is likely to have a continuing effect, then this may be a relevant (but not necessarily decisive) factor when considering whether the foreign jurisdiction provides the appropriate forum.[161]

---

155   Cf. Cass. civ. 1st, 20 October 1987, *Bull. civ.* I, No. 275, at 198.

156   Gaudemet-Tallon, *supra* footnote 28, at 429.

157   Anton, *supra* footnote 36, at 152.

158   *Ibid.*

159   *Ibid.*

160   Dicey and Morris, *supra* footnote 56, at 400, No. 12-030. See *The Abidin Daver* [1984] AC 398, at 411-412 (HL 1983).

161   *Idem*, at 401, No. 12-030 (notes omitted).

Essentially, an English court thus applies the same *forum non conveniens* test regardless whether other proceedings are already pending in an alternative forum.[162]

(b) The United States

Given the federal nature of the United States legal system, the language of Article IV, Section 1, of the Constitution of the United States,[163] and considerations of orderliness and economy within the federal system, one might expect to find in American law a doctrine of *lis pendens* at least for duplicative sister-state litigation.[164] The *lis pendens* principle is, however, only rarely available even when sister-state proceedings are in question. It may well be that only one state – Illinois – applies the first-in-time principle.[165]

A "state [of the United States] may entertain an action even though an action on the same claim is pending in another state",[166] without regard to "whether the two actions are both instituted in State courts or in federal courts or one in a State court and the other in a federal court".[167] When conflicting judgments result, the difficulty is resolved by requiring enforcement of the *judgment* first-in-time.[168]

Rejection of *lis pendens* for sister-state litigation perhaps need not, as a matter of policy, entail a similar rejection for international litigation. Politically and psychologically, however, it is difficult to argue that the first-in-time principle is more appropriate for internationally foreign than for sister-state proceedings. In all events, few American courts have applied the *lis pendens* doctrine to interna-

---

162   See *de Dampierre* v. *de Dampierre*, [1988] AC 92, at 108 (HL 1987).

163   "Full Faith and Credit shall be given in each State to the public Acts, Records, and judicial Proceedings of every other State."

164   Special considerations may apply to duplicative federal- and state-court litigation. See Redish, *supra* footnote 122; Burbank, *supra* footnote 46.

165   See 735 Ill. Comp. Stat. 5/2-619 *(a)* (3) (West 1993) ("Defendants may ... file a motion for dismissal of the action or other appropriate relief [where] ... (3) ... there is another action pending between the same persons for the same cause").

166   Restatement (Second) of Conflict of Laws §86.

167   *Idem* comment *a*.
       Comment *a* fails to footnote that "[w]hen parallel litigation is pending in two federal courts, something very close to a system of lis pendens operates, with a strong preference in favor of the first filed case". Burbank, *supra* footnote 46, at 213. The federal Transfer Statute of 1948 (see *supra* footnote 46) considers the federal court system a unity for transfer purposes. Accordingly, when one federal court transfers a case to another, the applicable law does not change as it might were a *forum non conveniens* dismissal in question. See Burbank, *supra* footnote 46, at 212.

168   "The rule does not result in imposition of double liability on the defendant, since the judgment first handed down effectively bars further prosecution of the second action. As between States of the United States, this latter result is required by full faith and credit." *Ibid.* For the complications that can result when the second court did not give effect to the first court's judgment, see *Treinies* v. *Sunshine Mining Co.*, 308 US 66 (1939).

tional cases;[169] a dismissal or stay, if granted, will rest on a *forum non conveniens* analysis in which the fact that a parallel foreign proceeding was pending when the local action was initiated is, on occasion, given weight.[170]

Where duplicative proceedings are pending in a *federal* – rather than a state – and a *foreign* court, the federal courts are currently split as to whether they should ordinarily refuse to stay their proceedings or instead apply the *forum non conveniens* doctrine. One group reasons by analogy to the approach adopted where duplicative proceedings are pending in federal and state courts. In such cases, the principle has emerged that, the Congress having given adjudicatory authority, the federal courts are generally obliged to exercise it.[171] Federal courts should, therefore, stay their proceeding in light of foreign proceedings only in "exceptional circumstances". The competing approach draws an analogy with §1404 *(c)* transfers between federal courts of litigation that could properly be litigated in another federal court.[172] In these cases, the "court's ability to stay an action is 'incidental' to its 'inherent power'"; accordingly, each federal court has broad discretion to stay its proceedings.[173] Hardly any consideration is given to whether the analogous application of domestic rules to international litigation makes sense in light of the different contexts.[174]

---

169   Bermann, *supra* footnote 93, at 610.

170   Cf. *ibid*: "[I]t is difficult as a policy matter to conclude that priority in timing should count as anything more than one among many different factors to be considered in the international antisuit injunction setting." See also N. Schulte, Die anderweitige (ausländische) Rechtshängigkeit im U.S.-amerikanischen Zivilprozessrecht, pp. 153-196 (Berlin, Duncker & Humblot, 2001).

171   *Colorado River Water Conservation District* v. *United States*, 424 US 800 (1976); see also *Neuchatel Swiss General Ins. Co.* v. *Lufthansa Airlines*, 925 F. 2d 1193, at 1195 (9th Cir. 1991). (Norris, J.: "Even if the litigants had made somewhat more progress in Geneva than in the district court by the time the stay motion was heard, the mere fact that parallel proceedings may be further along does not make a case 'exceptional' for the purpose of invoking the Colorado River exception to the general rule that federal courts must exercise their jurisdiction concurrently with courts of other jurisdictions …. Finally, the fact that the parallel proceedings are pending in a foreign jurisdiction rather than in a state court is immaterial. We reject the notion that a federal court owes greater deference to foreign courts than to our own state courts".) The rule that the court must, in principle, exercise its jurisdiction bears some resemblance to the civil-law conception of a plaintiff's right to a court; see Chap. III. B. 4. *(a)*, p. 133, *supra*.

172   See *supra* footnote 46.

173   *Landis* v. *North-American Co.*, 299 US 248 (1936); see *Goldhammer and DD UK Ltd.* v. *Dunkin' Donuts, Inc.*, 59 F. Supp. 2d 248, at 253-256 (D. Mass. 1999) (discussing various relevant factors).

174   See Burbank, *supra* footnote 46, at 220-221.

4.   The Brussels Convention and Regulation

(a)   In general

Where fully duplicative proceedings are in question, the approach of the Brussels Convention and Regulation contrasts starkly with American, English, and Scots practice; indeed, Brussels accords even greater effect to the first-in-time principle than was traditionally given by civil-law systems. Article 27 of the Regulation – Article 21 of the Convention – sets out a strict *lis pendens* rule:[175]

1.   Where proceedings involving the same cause of action and between the same parties are brought in the courts of different Member States, any court other than the court first seized shall of its own motion stay its proceedings until such time as the jurisdiction of the court first seized is established.

2.   Where the jurisdiction of the court first seized is established, any court other than the court first seized shall decline jurisdiction in favor of that court.

On the other hand, with regard to proceedings that are not identical but merely related, the Brussels Regulation takes in Article 28 – Article 22 of the Convention – a position not without a certain similarity to that held by common-law jurisdictions:[176]

1.   Where related actions are pending in the courts of different Member States, any court other than the court first seized may stay its proceedings.

2.   Where these actions are pending at first instance, any court other than the court first seized may also, on the application of one of the parties, decline jurisdiction if the court first seized has jurisdiction over the actions in question and its law permits the consolidation thereof."

3.   For the purposes of this Article, actions are deemed to be related where they are so closely connected that it is expedient to hear and determine them together to avoid the risk of irreconcilable judgments resulting from separate proceedings.

The court *second* seized of a related action is thus free, at its discretion, to extend the *lis pendens* effect of the earlier action if the court first seized has, in principle,

---

175   Article 27 tracks Article 21 of the Convention except that the latter speaks of "Contracting States". Equivalent provisions are contained in Article 19 of the Brussels IIa Regulation (Article 11 of the Brussels II Regulation) and in the Lugano Convention. Furthermore, under Article 54B (2) *(b)*, Lugano applies

in relation to lis pendens or to related actions as provided for in Articles 21 and 22 [Articles 27 and 28 of the Brussels Regulation], when proceedings are instituted in a Contracting State which is not a member of the European Communities and in a Contracting State which is a member of the European Communities.

176   Article 28 of the Regulation differs somewhat from Article 22 of the Convention. Like Article 21 of the Regulation, it replaces "Contracting State" with "Member State", speaks of "pending at first instance" in paragraph 2, and omits the language in paragraph 1 while slightly rephrasing the passage; paragraph 3 is unchanged.

jurisdiction over the later-in-time action and its law permits consolidation of the two proceedings. In so doing, the court second seized can be seen as applying a *forum non conveniens* doctrine in order to concentrate the litigation of both actions in the court where the first action was originally brought. The general policy underlying *lis pendens*, judicial economy and avoiding inconsistent judgments, is thus advanced.

The Brussels approach combines the rigid *lis pendens* rule of Article 27 (formerly Article 21) with the more flexible quasi-*forum non conveniens* approach of Article 28 (formerly Article 22). Here determination of what constitutes "the same cause of action and ... the same parties", becomes crucial. When causes of action qualify as "the same" is discussed, notably with regard to the relation between negative declaratory and coercive proceedings[177] on the one hand and the relation between claims and defence submissions on the other hand,[178] but also in more general terms.[179] As to the second criterion (identity of parties), the Court of Justice has suggested that complete identity is not required so long as there is complete identity of interests as, for example, in certain situations between insured and insurer.[180] Thus, Article 27 may be applicable to some multiple-parties cases but not to others.[181]

One further problem arises for Articles 27 and 28 that does not occur when parallel proceedings in the courts of a single legal system are in question: when is an action "brought"? The Court of Justice has originally left this question to national law,[182] thus creating uncertainty and opening the door for manipulation.

---

177   See for a detailed account *infra* pp.304 *et seq.*

178   In a recent judgment the European Court of Justice held that Article 21 of the Convention had to be construed as meaning that, in order to determine whether two claims have the same subject-matter, account should be taken only of the claims of the respective applicants and not of the defense submissions raised by a defendant. See *Gantner Electronic GmbH* v. *Basch Exploitatie Maatschappij BV* – Case C-111/01, [2003] ECR-I 4207; recently confirmed in *Maersk Olie & Gas A/S* v. *Firma M./ de Haan en W. de Boer* – Case C-39/02, [2004] ECR I-9657.

179   See H. Rüßmann, "Die Streitgegenstandslehre und die Rechtsprechung des EuGH – nationales Recht unter gemeineuropäischem Einfluß?", 111 *ZZP* 399-427 (1998); W.-D. Walker, "Die Streitgegenstandslehre und die Rechtsprechung des EuGH – nationales Recht unter gemeineuropäischem Einfluß?", *idem* 429-454; B. Heiderhoff, "Diskussionsbericht zu Streitgegenstandslehre und EuGH", *Idem* 455-462; see also K. Otte, H. Prütting and H. Dedek, "The GROTIUS Program: Proposals for Amending Article 21 and 22 of the Brussels Convention", 8 *Eur. Rev. Pr. L.* 257, at 258-266 (2000) (comparing national laws).

180   *Drouot Assurances SA* v. *Consolidated Metallurgical Industries (CMI Industrial Sites) and Others* – Case C-351/96, [1998] ECR I-3075, at 3097.

181   See J. Kropholler, *Europäisches Zivilprozeßrecht*, Art. 27, No. 5 (Frankfurt am Main, Verlag Recht und Wirtschaft, 8th ed., 2005).

182   *Zelger* v. *Salinitri* – Case C-129/83, [1984] ECR 2397. Proposals for an autonomous definition are made by S. Isenburg-Epple, *Die Berücksichtigung ausländischer Rechtshängigkeit nach dem Europäischen Gerichtsstands- und Vollstreckungsübereinkom-*

For example, in *Molins Plc* v. *G.D. S.P.A.*,[183] Molins had presented a claim form on 13 July to the English court; the form was served on GD in Italy on 30 July 1999. In the meantime, GD had brought an action before an Italian court on 19 July, received permission to fax the writ to Molins, and did so on 20 July. The English Court of Appeal decided that the Italian courts had not been properly seized "in accordance with the Brussels Convention", since transmission of the claim form by fax did not constitute valid service either under Article 15 of the Hague Service Convention or under a bilateral treaty between Italy and the UK; the English court therefore refused to stay its proceedings.

The Brussels Regulation seeks to clarify the priority issue in a new Article 30:[184]

> For the purposes of this Section, a court shall be deemed to be seized
> 1. at the time when the document instituting the proceedings or an equivalent document is lodged with the court, provided that the plaintiff has not subsequently failed to take the steps he was required to take to have service effected on the defendant, or
> 2. if the document has to be served before being lodged with the court, at the time when it is received by the authority responsible for service, provided that the plaintiff has not subsequently failed to take the steps he was required to take to have the document lodged with the court.

The new provision is an important improvement; it establishes a quasi-autonomous concept of the moment when a court is seized. Article 30 does not, however, resolve all the problems; it is likely to be controversial in practice whether the plaintiff has taken "the steps he was required to take". A fully autonomous definition of when a court is seized could avoid many of these difficulties but entail major changes in many national rules of civil procedure in Europe.

---

men vom 27.9.1968 120-130 (Frankfurt/Main Main *et al.*, Peter Lang, 1992); Ch. Dohm, *Die Einrede ausländischer Rechtshängigkeit im deutschen internationalen Zivilprozeßrecht*, 103-142 (Berlin, Duncker & Humblot, 1996); Hau, *supra* footnote 86, at 148-151.

183 [2000] 2 Lloyd's Rep. 234 (CA 2000).

184 The Brussels Regulation's Preamble provides the following comment on the new provision:

> In the interests of the harmonious administration of justice it is necessary to minimise the possibility of concurrent proceedings and to ensure that irreconcilable judgments will not be given in two Member States. There must be a clear and effective mechanism for resolving cases of lis pendens and related actions and for obviating problems flowing from national differences as to the determination of the time when a case is regarded as pending. For the purposes of this Regulation that time should be defined autonomously.

(b) The Gasser case

From the beginning, the Brussels Convention has contained a strong *lis pendens* provision: a court seized of a duplicative action in the sense of Article 21, "shall of its own motion stay its proceedings until such time as the jurisdiction of the court first seized is established". Once that court's jurisdiction "is established, any court other than the court first seized shall decline jurisdiction ...". The strong civilian preference for rigid over flexible rules is clear. It has recently been firmly reinforced by the European Court of Justice in its decision in the *Gasser* case.[185]

The reference by the *Oberlandesgericht Innsbruck* (Austria) for a preliminary ruling to the European Court of Justice in the proceedings between *Erich Gasser Gesellschaft m.b.H* v. *MISAT s.r.l.*[186] raised the issue of *lis pendens* in several contexts.

The first issue, referred to the Court and relevant for the present discussion, is whether the *lis pendens* rule of Article 21 applies where "the second court has exclusive jurisdiction pursuant to an agreement conferring jurisdiction under Article 17 of the Brussels Convention". The Article, in pertinent part, provides that,

> If the parties, one or more of whom is domiciled in a Contracting State, have agreed that a court or the courts of a Contracting State are to have jurisdiction to settle any disputes which have arisen or which may arise in connection with a particular legal relationship, that court or those courts shall have exclusive jurisdiction.

The *lis pendens* issue raised by the *Gasser* reference arises as well when the second court's jurisdictional claim rests on any of the grounds of adjudicatory authority set out in Section 5, Exclusive Jurisdiction.[187] Whether the *lis pendens* provision of Article 21 trumps the exclusive jurisdiction provided by the Convention is a matter of no small concern.

The reasoning advanced by the plaintiff in the Austrian action, *Gasser* – as well as the Government of the United Kingdom in its submission to the Court – that Article 17 should be given preference over Article 21 in a case where the court second seized had jurisdiction over the controversy under an exclusive choice of forum clause, was endorsed by Advocate General Léger in his opinion delivered on 9 September 2003.[188] Reiterating the European Court's decision in the *Overseas Union* case,[189] according to which the obligations of the court second seized under Article 21 were "without prejudice to the case where the court second seized has exclusive jurisdiction under the [Brussels] Convention and in particular under

---

185 Case C-116/02, [2003] ECR I-14693.

186 Case C-116/02, [2002] OJ C 144, at 17-18.

187 Section 6, Exclusive Jurisdiction, of the Regulation contains the same language. The text of Article 16 is summarized *supra* Chap. V. footnote 208.

188 Paras. 57 *et seq.* of the Advocate General's opinion.

189 Case C-351/89, [1991] ECR I-3317.

Article 16 thereof", the Advocate General summarized the arguments in support of extending this reasoning to the present case as follows:

> First, courts designated under an agreement conferring jurisdiction in accordance with Article 17 have jurisdiction which may be described as exclusive. Second, the argument that the court second seized is obliged to comply with the requirements of Article 21 even if it has exclusive jurisdiction under an agreement conferring jurisdiction is such as to undermine the effectiveness of Article 17 and the legal certainty that attaches to it. Third, the risk of irreconcilable decisions can be significantly reduced.[190]

Strictly speaking, there was no case of *lis pendens*, since only the court second seized but not the court first seized actually had jurisdiction and the only decision the court first seized could take was to dismiss the case for lack of jurisdiction. The Advocate-General thus opined that the court second seized, having jurisdiction under an exclusive choice of court clause, can, in derogation from Article 21, decide the case before it without waiting for the decision of the court first seized if the jurisdiction of the court second seized is established beyond doubt.[191]

The Court of Justice, however, did not follow the Advocate-General's recommendations. In the Court's view, a deviation from the strict first-in-time rule enshrined in Article 21 was not warranted. The fact that the court second seized presumably had exclusive jurisdiction over the controversy under Article 17 did not

> call in question the application of the procedural rule contained in Article 21 of the Convention, which is based clearly and solely on the chronological order in which the courts involved are seized.[192]

Neither would the court second seized ever be in a better position to determine whether the court first seized had jurisdiction. Moreover, the Court of Justice views its strict interpretation of Article 21 as affirmed by Article 19 of the Convention (Article 25 of the Regulation), which provides that "[w]here a court of a Contracting State is seized of a claim which is principally concerned with a matter over which the courts of another Contracting State have exclusive jurisdiction by virtue of Article 16, it shall declare of its own motion that it has no jurisdiction", but makes no mention of Article 17. Finally, the risk of a party's making use of the Article 21 mechanism for employing delay tactics, to which the UK Government pointed in its submission to the Court, could not call in question the interpretation of Article 21 as deduced from its wording and purpose.[193]

---

190 Para. 57 of the Advocate-General's Opinion.

191 Para. 83 of the Advocate-General's Opinion.

192 Case C-116/02, [2003] ECR I-14693, at para. 47.

193 *Idem*, para. 53. For critical comments on the ECJ's decision see H. Grothe, "Zwei Einschränkungen des Prioritätsprinzips im europäischen Zuständigkeitsrecht: auss-

The reference in *Gasser* posed, as well, a second issue of importance – one that can arise in any proceeding:

> Can the fact that court proceedings in a Contracting State take an unjustifiably long time (for reasons largely unconnected with the conduct of the parties), so that material detriment may be caused to one party, have the consequence that the court other than the court first seized, within the meaning of Article 21, is not allowed to proceed in accordance with that provision?

The Court, unsurprisingly, perhaps, in light of its answer to the previous question, and on this count in concurrence with the opinion of the Advocate-General, answered this question in the negative.[194] Allowing for an exception to the application of Article 21 of the Convention with respect to unusually protracted proceedings in one Member State would be contrary to the letter, spirit and the aim of the Convention. Neither would the proposition that Article 21 ceases to apply after a certain amount of time find any basis in the provisions of the Convention, nor would such an exception be compatible with the notion of mutual trust which the Contracting States accord to each other's legal systems and judicial institutions, on which the Brussels instruments are based.

The questions dealt with by the Court of Justice in this case illustrate the problems that arise for complex, modern adjudicatory systems that strongly prefer rigid over flexible rules that are reluctant to vest discretion in judges, and whose courts lack power to sanction egregious party behavior. As will be seen,[195] the structural concerns that are revealed by the references to the Court of Justice made in the *Gasser* litigation arise as well with respect to *forum non conveniens* and antisuit injunctions.

---

chließliche Gerichtsstände und Prozessverschleppung, 25 *IPRax* 205-212 (2005); L. Mance, "Exclusive Jurisdiction Agreements and European Ideals", 120 *L.Q.R.* 357-365 (2004); R. Fentiman, "Access to Justice and Parallel Proceedings in Europe" [2004] *C.L.J.* 312-314; R. Fentiman, "Case C-116/02, Erich Gasser GmbH v. MISAT Srl, mudgment of the Full Court of 9 December 2003, nyr", 41 *C.M.L.Rev.* 241-259 (2005) For a sympathetic comment see Ch. Thiele, "Anderweitige Rechtshängigkeit im Europäischen Zivilprozessrecht – Rechtssicherheit vor Einzelfallgerechtigkeit", 50 *RIW* 285-289 (2004). For a recent confirmation of the predominant continental-European view that Article 17 does not take precedence over Article 21 see LG Bonn, 26 June 2003, 50 *RIW* 460 (2004).

194   *Idem* 70-73.
195   See pp. 334-335 and E. 4. *(b)*, pp. 341 *et seq., passim, infra.*

5.   The Significance of Temporal Priority for Negative Declaratory Judgments[196]

A party, knowing that an action for coercive relief is likely to be brought against him, may be able to initiate an action for a negative declaratory judgment to establish that he owes the other party nothing or significantly less than the latter claims. Where such actions are entertained, by appearing in the procedural role of plaintiff, a natural defendant enjoys the advantage of selecting the forum, from among those available, in which to litigate. In multistate or international controversies, the litigation-initiating party's control – through forum selection – over the applicable conflictual, procedural, and substantive law may provide a strong motivation for a party – threatened by a coercive action – to seek declaratory relief. Should then a legal order adopt for such cases *lis pendens* rules or approaches towards declaratory relief different from those applied in general?

(a)   The availability of declaratory relief
(i)   When should declaratory relief be available in principle?

In strictly local litigations, declaratory relief is ordinarily sought in one or the other of two situations:[197]

(1)   The controversy has ripened to a point where one of the parties could invoke a coercive remedy (i.e. a suit for damages or an injunction) but has not done so; and

(2)   Although the controversy is real and immediate, it has not ripened to such a point, and it would be unfair or inefficient to require the parties to wait for a decision.

The two types of controversies differ in a respect that, although often overlooked, is crucial. In cases of the first variety, declaratory relief would not be needed had the party entitled to coercive relief brought an action to enforce his rights. In the second variety, on the other hand, since no coercive action is yet possible, the parties' respective rights and duties can presently only be clarified by one of them bringing an action for a declaratory judgment.

In cases of the second variety, at the time that the decision to seek declaratory relief is made, it is not known whether a case of the first variety will ultimately arise. A classic example is *Willing* v. *Chicago Auditorium Association.*[198] There the long-term lessees of a large auditorium and their landlord disagreed on whether

---

196   An earlier version of this subsection appeared as A. von Mehren, "The Transmogrification of Defendants into Plaintiffs: Herein of Declaratory Judgments, Forum Shopping, and *Lis Pendens*", in J. Basedow, K. Hopt and H. Kötz (eds.), *Festschrift für Ulrich Drobnig* 409-424 (Tübingen, Mohr Siebeck, 1998).

197   See *Tempco Electric Heater Corp.* v. *Omega Engineering, Inc.*, 819 F. 2d 746, at 749 (7th Cir. 1987).

198   277 US 274 (1928).

the lessees, without the landlord's consent, were entitled to demolish the existing building and replace it with a more modern – and presumably more profitable – facility. A "controversy as to legal rights existed ... [and] urgently require[d] settlement".[199] The lessees could have brought matters to a head by starting to demolish the auditorium, but, in doing so, they would have run the risk of incurring substantial liability. Since declaratory relief in such cases is given so that a party can determine where it stands without exposing itself to substantial liability and, moreover, *ex hypothesi* a coercive action could not presently be brought, such declaratory actions should be considered equivalent, for present purposes, to a coercive action brought by an aggrieved party.

In the first group of cases, on the other hand, a coercive action could presently be brought by one party; that party would then be the plaintiff in every sense of the term. Procedurally, he initiates the action; substantively, he seeks coercive relief. When the declaratory action is brought, however, by the party against whom a parallel coercive action could be initiated, that party is not a plaintiff in the sense of one who seeks coercive relief. To signify in these situations the difference between plaintiffs who seek coercive relief and those who do not, the latter are at times referred to as natural defendants.[200]

(ii)   When is such relief available in practice?[201]

Judicial relief usually presupposes a legal injury already inflicted by the defendant on the plaintiff. On occasion, however, a party will seek relief to avert future legal injury.

In the former situation, coercive (or repressive) relief is sought; in the latter the relief requested is preventive in nature.[202] Such "action[s] for declaratory judgment[s] ... [are] a product of recent times; ... [the action] was only developed in the nineteenth century".[203] "English law and practice, down to relatively mod-

---

199   E. Borchard, *Declaratory Judgments* 189 (Cleveland, OH, Banks-Baldwin, 2nd ed., 1941). In *Willing*, the US Supreme Court saw the action, as Justice Stone later observed in *Nashville, Chattanooga & St. Louis Railway Co.* v. *Wallace*, 288 US 249, at 262 (1933), as an effort to obtain a "decision advising what the law would be on an uncertain or hypothetical state of facts" and accordingly refused declaratory relief. Today, in the *Willing* situation declaratory relief is available in the United States.

200   By the same token, plaintiffs in declaratory actions could be called "unnatural" plaintiffs, and defendants, "unnatural" defendants. These inelegant expressions are not encountered, however.

201   For a recent survey of different European legal systems' positions see Otte, Prütting and Dedek, *supra* footnote 179, at 260-266.

202   For a comparative discussion of how these remedies operate in different legal systems, see A. Blomeyer, Chap. 4, "Types of Relief Available (Judicial Remedies), Nos. 51-110 (1982)", Vol. XVI, *Civil Procedure, Int. Enc. Comp. L.* (M. Cappelletti and B. Garth, eds.) (Tübingen, Mohr (Siebeck), and The Hague, Boston, Mass., London, Martinus Nijhoff).

203   *Idem* No. 84.

ern times, regarded the commission of *wrong*, public or private, as practically an essential condition to invoking the judicial arm of the State."[204]

In the United States, the first statute providing for declaratory actions was passed in New Jersey in 1915. In 1922, the Commissioners on Uniform State Laws promulgated the Uniform Declaratory Judgments Act,[205] now widely adopted.[206] Language contained in Article III, Section 2, of the US Constitution – the "judicial power shall extend to ... Cases ... [and] Controversies" – had delayed enactment of a federal declaratory judgment act until the constitutional issue was laid to rest in 1933 by the Supreme Court.[207]

Civil-law systems have also had difficulties with actions for declaratory judgments.[208] Still today, it is said that in French law an actual interest – *"un intérêt né et actuel"* – must have arisen before a declaratory action can be brought.[209] "[A] mere eventual interest does not suffice."[210]

In the eighteenth and nineteenth centuries, Germanic legal systems pioneered by providing in their procedural codes for declaratory judgments. The German Code of Civil Procedure (1877) followed the lead of these codes in §231 – now §256 – which provides that

> An action may be brought for the declaration of the existence or nonexistence of a legal relationship *(Rechtsverhältnis)*, or for the declaration of the genuineness or spuriousness of a document *(Urkunde)*, provided the plaintiff has a legal interest in having promptly *(alsbald)* determined the legal relation or the genuineness or spuriousness of the document.

The German courts normally allow the other party to avoid the *lis pendens* effect of a declaratory action commenced under §256 by bringing a later action for

---

204 Borchard, *supra* footnote 199, at 189. For a comprehensive discussion of United Kingdom law on the subject, see I. Zamir, Lord Woolf and J. Woolf, *The Declaratory Judgment* (London, Sweet and Maxwell, 3rd ed., 2002).

205 12 ULA 313 (1996) (Section 1) and 12A ULA 3 (1996) (Section 2 to 17).

206 As of 2006, the Act has been adopted in 43 states. See 12 ULA (1996), 2006 Cumulative Annual Pocket Part, at 73.

207 *Nashville, Chattanooga & St. Louis Railway Co.* v. *Wallace*, 288 US 249 (1933), held that a "case or controversy" was present "so long as the case retains the essentials of an adversary proceeding, involving a real, not a hypothetical, controversy". *Idem* 264. The Federal Declaratory Judgment Act, enacted in 1934, is contained in 28 USC §§2201-2202.

208 For a brief survey see Blomeyer, *supra* footnote 202, No. 84; see also Borchard, *supra* footnote 199, *passim*.

209 See J. Héron, *Droit judiciaire privé*, at 54, No. 59 (Paris, Montchrestien, 1991); G. Couchez, *Procédure civile*, at 92-93, No. 239 (Paris, Dalloz, 1998).

210 J. Vincent and S. Guinchard, *Procédure civile*, at 144-145, Nos. 105-106 (Paris, Dalloz, 26th ed., 2001); see also P. Herzog, *Civil Procedure in France*, at 241-242 (The Hague, Nijhoff, 1967).

damages or other coercive relief resting on the same cause of action; the "legal interest in having [the legal relation] immediately determined" is usually better and more fully served by adjudicating the coercive rather than the declaratory action.[211] Displacement of the latter avoids the possibility that parallel litigation respecting the same controversy will result in inconsistent judgments.[212] Although challenged by many jurists as inconsistent with the principle of procedural equality and economy,[213] the courts continue to proceed in domestic litigation along the lines described above.

In the contemporary world, the availability for local controversies of relief by way of a declaratory judgment thus varies from one legal system to another. Arguably, less stringent requirements for declaratory relief might be imposed in multistate or international controversies where a forum has serious reservations respecting the quality of justice available in the court that the other party would likely seize. In all events, the criteria that must be satisfied to obtain such relief in local matters presumably apply as well in multistate or international controversies; the issue remains whether, in light of forum-selection concerns, additional requirements should be imposed on declaratory actions in non-local matters.

---

211 BGH, 22 January 1987, 99 *BGHZ* 340; BGH, 7 July 1994, 47 *NJW* 3107, at 3108 (1994). Displacement does not occur, however, if the declaratory action is ripe – or nearly so – for decision and the coercive action is less advanced, see *BGHZ* 99, at 342; or where the coercive action is inadmissible, see *BGHZ* 33, 398, at 399. On the other hand, where a coercive action is pending, an action for a declaratory judgment based on the same cause of action is barred. BGH, 20 January 1989, 42 *NJW* 2064 (1989).

212 BGH, 22 January 1987, 99 *BGHZ* 340.
One feature of German procedural law specific to declaratory actions deserves mention here: in an action seeking a declaration that the plaintiff is not indebted to the defendant, the latter prevails only if he carries the burden of persuading the adjudicator that the plaintiff is indebted to him in a given amount. (When the defendant – the natural plaintiff – prevails on this issue, he can – relying on the judgment in the declaratory action as *res judicata* – establish his claim and obtain an enforceable judgment against the natural defendant.) BGH, 2 March 1993, 46 *NJW* 1716 (1993); BGH, 25 October 1991, 45 *NJW* 1101 (1992); A. Baumbach, W. Lauterbach, J. Albers and P. Hartmann (-Hartmann), *Kommentar zur Zivilprozeßordnung* (Munich, C. H. Beck, 64th ed., 2006), §256, No. 47. On occasion, a German court does not realize that the burden of persuasion with respect to liability in actions for negative declaratory judgments usually rests on the defendant rather than the plaintiff. Placing the burden of persuasion is a responsibility of the court; however, once a judgment is final, any judicial error committed does not affect the judgment's *res judicata* effects. BGH, 10 April 1986, 39 *NJW* 2508 (1986).

213 See E. Stein and M. Jonas (-Schumann), *Kommentar zur Zivilprozeßordnung*, Vol. 3 (Tübingen, Mohr Siebeck, 21st ed., 1994), §256 VI, No. 126; U. P. Gruber, "Das Verhältnis der negativen Feststellungsklage zu den anderen Klagearten im deutschen Zivilprozeß – Plädoyer für eine Neubewertung", 117 *ZZP* 133-162 (2004).

(b) Tactical forum shopping by natural defendants in international situations[214]

The negative declaratory judgment is a "forum shopping" tool in that it enables the natural defendant to choose among the available forums. These forums will, in part, correspond to those available for a coercive action brought by the natural plaintiff. Generally speaking, the range of choice open to the negative-declaratory-judgment plaintiff is likely to be smaller; many legal orders disfavor declaratory actions especially when forum selection is seen as the reason for bringing the action.[215] Should the natural defendant be able to capture the litigational advantage natural plaintiffs enjoy through their ability to select among forums?

The principle of equal treatment, at least at first blush, as well as considerations of simplicity, support allowing natural defendants to enjoy, by initiating declaratory actions, the advantages that control of forum-choice gives.[216] In the long run, however, allowing natural defendants free rein in bringing actions for negative declaratory judgments encourages a race to the court house that will frequently not only require natural plaintiffs – now defendants – to make litigation decisions under great time pressures but impede as well settlement negotiations. In light of these considerations, national legal orders understandably hold differing views as to whether negative declaratory actions should be accorded the same treatment for *lis pendens* purposes as are coercive actions, in particular, should legal orders that accept *lis pendens* apply the first-in-time principle in favor of declaratory proceedings?[217]

(i) French and German practices

In a French or German court, natural defendants have little opportunity to obtain the initiative in international controversies by bringing an action for a negative declaratory judgment. French courts – reluctant to entertain declaratory actions

---

214 An interesting discussion of highly sophisticated forms of forum selecting – including not only negative declaratory judgments but also antisuit injunctions, *lis pendens*, and *forum non conveniens* – that may be available to natural defendants is A. Lowenfeld, "Forum Shopping, Antisuit Injunctions, Negative Declarations, and Related Tools of International Litigation", 91 *Am. J. Int'l Law* 314-324 (1997). The negative declaratory judgment differs from the other techniques named in that ordinarily only natural defendants can benefit from its use.

215 See *(a)* (ii), pp. 305 *et seq., supra.*

216 Haimo Schack argues that one who seeks to defend himself against a claim that he considers unjustified should have the same right to select a forum that is favorable to him as has one who seeks a coercive judgment. See H. Schack, "Gerechtigkeit durch weniger Verfahren", 16 *IPRax* 80, at 82 (1996). This opinion is shared by Hau, *supra* footnote 86, at 137-138; P. Widmer and B. Maurenbrecher, "What's Negative about Negative Declarations?", in N. Vogt *et al.* (eds.), *The International Practice of Law – Liber Amicorum for Thomas Bär and Robert Karrer* 263, at 283-284 (Basle, Frankfurt am Main, Helbing and Lichtenhahn, and The Hague, London, Boston, Kluwer Law International, 1997).

217 See *(c)*, pp. 311 *et seq., infra.*

even in domestic matters "involving disputed clauses in commercial contracts"[218] – can with relative ease refuse to make the remedy available for international controversies.[219] In German law, the problem can be handled by applying to international controversies the rule – developed by the courts for domestic controversies – that allows a natural plaintiff to displace an action for a declaration of non-liability by bringing a coercive action.

The German courts now seem prepared to extend this approach to international litigation where neither the Brussels Regulation nor the Lugano Convention applies. A decision of the Landgericht Hamburg of 1 October 1980 allowed a later-in-time coercive action, brought in Brazil, to displace an action for a negative declaratory judgment pending in Hamburg.

> Had the action for damages been brought in Hamburg as a counterclaim the plaintiff's interest in a negative declaration would have been extinguished …. The situation is no different when the action for damages is brought in Brazil.[220]

The Bundesgerichtshof, although it has yet to face the issue squarely, has indicated that it might well accept the Hamburg approach. In a decision of 11 December 1996 the high court remarked that the interest in legal protection of the party that brings a first-in-time negative declaratory action would not disappear should the courts of another country have to decline, on *lis pendens* – or other – grounds, to decide a parallel, later-in-time coercive action.[221] The court's observation suggests that, *mutatis mutandis*, where the coercive action would be decided on the merits, the earlier declaratory action would be displaced.[222] This inference is particularly plausible because, since Article 21 of the Brussels Convention governed the case, the court's remark was unnecessary, indeed, inappropriate.[223]

(ii)   Common-law practices

English and United States laws are considerably more receptive to declaratory actions than is French law but have no counterpart to the German practice that gives a natural plaintiff the choice between litigating a declaratory action brought by a natural defendant or initiating himself a coercive action. As a result, both legal systems have faced the question whether special rules, designed to limit the

---

218   Herzog, *supra* footnote 210, at 242.

219   In commenting on the *"Tatry"* case (1994) (see *(c)*, pp. 311 *et seq., infra*), Evelyne Tichadou sanguinely remarks that the action for a negative declaration is "unknown to French law and to the national laws also of most of the other Contracting States". 84 *Rev. crit. dr. internat. privé* 600, at 607 (1995). Accordingly, "only a limited amount of forum shopping will be possible". *Ibid.*

220   [1980] IPRspr., No. 23, at 75.

221   See BGH, 11 December 1996, 134 *BGHZ* 201, at 209-210.

222   See P. Huber, Note, 52 *JZ* 799, at 800 (1997) (the court's discussion suggests this result).

223   See *ibid.*

tactical advantages that natural defendants can derive from negative declaratory actions, should be developed.

In England, "a declaration that a person is not liable in an existing or possible action is one that will hardly ever be made".[224] Indeed, a legal system may restrain a defendant "from instituting or continuing proceedings in a foreign court if a proper case of injustice were made out ... [but decline to give the plaintiff] any declaration of right".[225]

> [C]laims for negative declarations are a novel type of pre-emptive forum shopping with novel implications .... [Such c]laims for declarations, and in particular negative declarations, must be viewed with great caution in all situations involving possible conflicts of jurisdiction, since they lend themselves to improper attempts at forum shopping."[226]

Proceedings for a negative injunction in England will accordingly be stayed where a foreign court is the *forum conveniens*[227] and English courts are reluctant "to authorise service out of the jurisdiction under Order 11, r. 1 (1), i.e. Rule 27, in a claim for a negative declaration".[228] Indeed, there appear to be "few cases involving litigation in more than one country where a party is likely to gain an advantage by claiming a negative declaration in England".[229] Nor do English courts give "much weight" to a proceeding "in a foreign court for a negative declaration in determining whether the foreign court is the appropriate forum for the purpose of staying English proceedings ...".[230]

---

224   *Guaranty Trust Co.* v. *Hanny*, [1915] 2 KB 536, at 564-565 (CA 1915); see A. Bell, "The Negative Declaration in Transnational Litigation", 111 *L. Quart. Rev.* 674, at 679-683 (1995).

225   Dicey and Morris, *supra* footnote 56, at 420, No. 12-067.

226   *Saipem S.P.A.* v. *Dredging VO2 B.V. and Geosite Surveys Ltd. (The Volvox Hollandia)*, [1988] 2 Lloyd's Rep. 361, at 371 (CA 1988).

227   See Dicey and Morris, *supra* footnote 56, at 402, No. 12-034; *Camilla Cotton Oil* v. *Granadex S.A.*, [1976] 2 Lloyd's Rep. 10 (HL 1976).

228   Dicey and Morris, *supra* footnote 56, at 402, No. 12-034; see also *The Volvox Hollandia, supra* footnote 226.

229   L. Collins, "The Marc Rich Case and Actions for Negative Declarations", in *Mélanges en l'honneur de Jacques-Michel Grossen* 385, at 390 (Basle, Helbing & Lichtenhahn, 1992), reprinted in L. Collins, *Essays in International Litigation and the Conflict of Laws* 275, at 280 (Oxford, Clarendon Press, and New York, Oxford University Press, 1994).

230   Dicey and Morris, *supra* footnote 56, at 402, No. 12-034; see also *E.I. du Pont de Nemours* v. *Agnew*, [1987] 2 Lloyd's Rep. 585 (CA 1987). Indeed, the foreign proceedings for a negative declaration "may be so artificial as to justify the grant of an injunction by an English court to restrain them". *Ibid.*; see also *Sohio Supply Co.* v. *Gatoil (USA) Inc.*, [1989] 1 Lloyd's Rep. 588 (CA 1988).

American courts are prepared to entertain an action for a negative declaratory judgment where, to the detriment of the natural defendant, the natural plaintiff delays in filing suit.[231]

> [T]he issuance of a declaratory judgment is discretionary [citation omitted; however,] a suit for declaratory judgment aimed solely at wresting the choice of forum from the 'natural' plaintiff will normally be dismissed and the case allowed to proceed in the usual way.[232]

(c)   Should *lis pendens* protection be accorded to actions for negative declaratory judgments?

(i)   *The positions of national legal orders*

Absent international commitments to do otherwise, some legal systems – including the French, English, and American – give their courts a broad discretion whether to stay or dismiss local proceedings where parallel actions, including actions for a negative declaratory judgment, have already been initiated abroad. On the other hand, some – among them the German and Swiss – apply *lis pendens* internationally as a matter of principle; thus, when a "foreign proceeding probably will result in a judgment susceptible of recognition and enforcement in Germany", a later-in-time parallel German proceeding must be stayed.[233] Legal orders that accept the first-to-be-seized rule face the issue whether it applies in the same way to coercive, declaratory, and negative declaratory proceedings.

Certainty and ease of application, as well as the principle of equal treatment, support applying *lis pendens* on the same terms across the board. Giving priority to a first-in-time negative declaratory action initiated abroad by a natural defendant puts pressure, however, on each party to race to its preferred court house in order to enjoy the advantage of forum choice. Once litigation respecting matters that might well have been settled out of court is commenced, expense and delay will increase, and frictions between legal orders grow, as the parties struggle to control the choice of forum. In an effort to discourage practices that have these consequences, a legal order could well refuse to accord *lis pendens* effects to prior-in-time negative declaratory actions that constitute preemptive strikes.

Adopting for international litigation the approach developed by the German courts for local controversies would reduce these undesirable consequences; the natural plaintiff could displace a parallel, first-in-time foreign negative declaratory action by bringing a coercive action in another State unless the declaratory

---

231 *Tempco Electric Heater Corp.* v. *Omega Engineering, Inc.*, 819 F. 2d 746, at 749 (7th Cir. 1987).

232 *Allendale*, 10 F. 3d at 431.

233 See p. 294, *supra*. A similar approach is now followed in Italian law, Art. 7 No. 3 of the law no. 218 of 31 May 1995. Before 1995, Italian law regarded pending foreign proceedings as wholly irrelevant. See M. A. Lupoi, "The New Lis Pendens Provisions in the Brussels I and II Regulations", 7 *ZZPInt* 149, at 150, fn. 6 (2002).

action were already ripe – or nearly so – for decision.[234] Negative declaratory actions would continue to serve in international situations the purpose for which they are designed; they could be pursued where it would be unfair or inefficient to require the natural defendant to wait for the natural plaintiff to initiate a coercive action. On the other hand, by promptly initiating a coercive action, the natural plaintiff could frustrate the natural defendant's effort to control forum-choice. A better balance between the positions of natural plaintiffs and natural defendants could thus be achieved and races to the court house discouraged.

Many German commentators argue, however, that a legal order should treat declaratory and coercive proceedings alike for *lis pendens* purposes.[235] The displacement solution is seen as somewhat complex and inefficient. The principal argument advanced against it is, however, that one who seeks to defend himself against a claim that he considers unjustified should have the same right to select the forum that he favors in which to litigate the issue of liability *vel non* as does one who seeks a coercive judgment. "Here the priority principle is significantly more just than the protection of one who claims a right [i.e., the natural plaintiff]."[236]

(ii)   The European Union's position

Regardless of the view that one takes on the general issue of how the *lis pendens* principle should apply to declaratory proceedings, the arguments for giving such proceedings the benefit of *lis pendens* are strongest where the principle's applicability within a close economic and political association – a federation or confederation, for example – is in question. After all, the choice of forum should be less significant since associated or sister States tend to be more similar in their values and in the quality of justice that each provides than are legal orders whose association is less intimate. Moreover, the associative structure can ensure that the legal orders in question will recognize *lis pendens* and apply the principle consistently, thus eliminating free-loading concerns.[237]

a.   The applicability issue is posed: Gubisch

In 1986, the applicability of Article 21 of the Brussels Convention to a negative declaratory action was considered by the European Court of Justice in *Gubisch Maschinenfabrik KG* v. *Giulio Palumbo*.[238] Palumbo, an Italian, had placed an order for a straightening planer and moulder manufactured by Gubisch, a German company. Palumbo refused to take delivery, whereupon Gubisch initiated an ac-

---

234   See pp. 308-310, *supra*.

235   See *Münchener Kommentar zur Zivilprozeßordnung* (-Lüke), Vol. 1 (Munich, C. H. Beck, 2nd ed. 2000), §256, No. 61-62; Gruber, *supra* footnote 213, at 148-154.

236   Schack, *supra* footnote 216, at 82.

237   The *lis pendens* principle is in the United States, however, only rarely available even for sister-state actions. See 3. *(b)*, pp. 296 *et seq., supra*.

238   Case-C 144/86, [1987] ECR 4861. Judge K. Bahlmann's Report for the Hearing is at *idem* 4862-4866; the Opinion of Advocate General Mancini is at *idem* 4867-4870.

tion in Germany for the price of the machine, presumably under Article 5 (1). Thereafter, Palumbo brought proceedings against Gubisch in the Italian courts

> for a declaration that the contract was inoperative on the ground that his order had been revoked before it reached Gubisch for acceptance. In the alternative, ... discharge [of the contract is requested] on the ground that Gubisch had not complied with the time-limit for delivering.[239]

Gubisch objected that the Italian courts lacked jurisdiction under Article 21 of the Brussels Convention. The court of first instance dismissed the *lis pendens* objection.[240] Gubisch brought the jurisdictional issue to the Court of Cassation; it referred to the European Court of Justice the following question:

> Does a case where, in relation to the same contract, one party applies to a court in a Contracting State for a declaration that the contract is inoperative (or in any event for its discharge) whilst the other institutes proceedings before the courts of another Contracting State for its enforcement fall within the scope of the concept of *lis pendens* pursuant to Article 21 of the Brussels Convention of 27 September 1968?[241]

The Court considered written observations presented by each party, by the German and Italian Governments, and by the European Commission[242] as well as the views of the Advocate General[243]. The Italian Government and the Advocate General took the position that Article 21 should be interpreted restrictively. The German Government and the Commission argued that it should be applied in order "to avoid conflicts of jurisdiction and incompatible judgments"[244]. Only the analysis of Advocate General Mancini suggested that, in determining the article's applicability, the fact that one of the actions in question sought a negative declaratory judgment should be taken into account[245].

The Court of Justice held that Article 21 applied

---

239   *Idem* 4872.

240   *Idem* 4867.

241   *Idem* 4873.

242   See *idem* 4863-4866.

243   *Idem* 4867-4870.

244   *Idem* 4864.

245   Mancini pointed out that application of Article 21 would

> not provide all the advantages which are claimed for it by its exponents. With regard to obligations, for instance, it would be sufficient to challenge the validity of a contract in order to paralyse, by raising an objection of lis pendens, any subsequent action brought on the basis of that contract before the courts of another State ... .

Idem 4869.

in the interests of the proper administration of justice within the Community, to prevent parallel proceedings before the courts of different Contracting States and to avoid conflicts between decisions which might result therefrom.[246]

In her commentary on the decision, Professor Hélène Gaudemet-Tallon points out that the first-in-time rule gives "the most aggressive party a formidable weapon" in the form of an action to declare non-liability; an action that may be in "bad faith and [initiated] to obtain a jurisdictional advantage ...".[247]

b.   The Court of Justice treats coercive and negative declaratory actions alike: "Tatry"

In 1994, the Court of Justice again considered the applicability of Article 21 to a *lis pendens* situation involving an action for a negative declaratory judgment. In this case, unlike in *Gubisch*, the action for a negative declaratory judgment was the first to be initiated.[248] *"Tatry"* is a much more complex case than *Gubisch*; multiple actions had been brought at different times and involved several unrelated parties. Five questions were referred by the English Court of Appeal to the Court of Justice. One presented the issue raised in *Gubisch*; the Court again applied the first-in-time rule:

On a proper construction of Article 21 of the Convention, an action seeking to have the defendant held liable for causing loss and ordered to pay damages has the same cause of action and the same object as earlier proceedings brought by that defendant seeking a declaration that he is not liable for that loss.[249]

The *"Tatry"* decision raises the question whether the policy con-siderations on which *Gubisch* and *"Tatry"* primarily rest – prevention of parallel proceedings and avoidance of conflicting decisions – can be accomplished without opening the way to pre-emptive strikes by natural defendants and creating an environment that encourages races to the court house. Where the coercive proceeding is first-in-time, as in *Gubisch*, *lis pendens* does not prevent the race but does preserve the natural plaintiff's forum-selection advantage. Where the sequence of the proceedings is reversed, as in *"Tatry"*, the race occurs and the preemptive strike succeeds as well. Much can be said for the view, expressed by an American federal court, that applying the first-to-file rule to a declaratory judgment action has "the virtue of certainty and ease of application ... [but] the cost – a rule which

---

246 *Idem* 4874.

247 Comment on Gubisch, 77 *Rev. crit. dr. internat. privé* 374, at 376 (1988).

248 *The Owners of the Cargo Lately Laden on Board the Ship "Tatry"* v. *The Owners of the Ship "Maciej Rataj"* – Case C-406/92, [1994] ECR I-5439, at 5463.

249 *Idem* 5481.

will encourage an unseemly race to the court house, and quite likely, numerous suits – is simply too high".[250]

c.   Critique of the "Tatry" solution

Given the language of Article 21 of the Brussels Convention (Article 27 of the Regulation), the Court of Justice probably had little choice but to apply the *lis pendens* rule in the same manner in the two cases. The issue remains whether a better solution for the *"Tatry"* situation would be to adopt for international litigation the approach developed by the German courts for local litigation.

Under the German approach, where the declaratory action is first-in-time, the natural plaintiff can displace it by bringing a parallel coercive action unless the earlier action is already ripe – or nearly so – for decision. Declaratory actions continue to serve the purposes for which they are intended; they give the natural defendant a means to clarify the legal situation where the natural plaintiff delays unduly in invoking a coercive remedy or where, although a real and immediate controversy exists, it has not yet ripened to the point at which a party can maintain a coercive action.[251] This result is accomplished, however, without incurring the costs that the *"Tatry"* solution entails.[252]

---

250 *Tempco, supra* footnote 231, at 750.

251 See *(a)* (i), pp. 304 *et seq., supra.*

252 Schack has suggested that for international litigation involving parallel negative declaratory and coercive actions, German courts should exercise discretionary powers based on the need of the party bringing the German action for legal protection *(Rechtsschutzbedürfnis).* In some circumstances, the court could allow the German action to proceed; in others, the court could suspend – rather than dismiss – the later-in-time German action so that the party bringing it might ultimately enjoy, if appropriate, advantages such as the right to claim interest while the controversy was pending and the tolling of prescription periods. See Schack, *supra* footnote 5, at 267-268, No. 764.

  If this approach, arguably an application of ZPO §148 by analogy, were applied to first-in-time actions initiated abroad, whether declaratory or coercive in nature, German courts would exercise a discretionary power in *lis pendens* cases akin to – though far less extensive than – the general *forum non conveniens* power exercised by common-law courts. The proposal is interesting but would do little to avoid competitive races to the court house between natural defendants and natural plaintiffs.

  A recent dissertation – Dohm, *supra* footnote 182, at 283-286 – rejects Schack's approach on grounds of equal treatment. A somewhat similar solution from a different starting point is offered by K. Otte, *Umfassende Streitentscheidung durch Beachtung von Sachzusammenhängen* (Tübingen, Mohr (Siebeck), 1998). Otte's starting point and main interest is the avoidance of conflicting litigation respecting the same controversy. See *idem* 1-11. He assumes – which may not be correct – that the broadest possible resolution of the underlying controversy will always result from deciding the natural plaintiff's action. See *idem* 226-235. Consequently, absent special considerations, the natural plaintiff should, in Otte's view, be allowed a certain time period within which he can bring a coercive action.

Where the German approach applies, the natural plaintiff need not fear a pre-emptive strike by the natural defendant. If the latter does initiate a declaratory action, the former has a reasonable period of time in which to decide whether to allow the proceedings to continue or to begin a coercive action. Accordingly, parties are not put under severe pressure to engage in desperate races to a court house and the natural defendant is unable to deprive the natural plaintiff of the right that the latter normally has of selecting the forum for litigation.[253]

The principal score on which the pure first-to-file approach can be preferred to the displacement solution rests on the proposition that natural defendants should enjoy, where feasible, forum-selecting opportunities analogous to those enjoyed by natural plaintiffs. In the larger scheme of things this appeal to the principle of equality is hardly persuasive. Until relatively recent times, only coercive actions were entertained and the *"Tatry"* problem could not arise. Jurisdictional equations have been largely framed in the light of considerations respecting where it is typically appropriate for a person to seek relief; when declaratory relief is sought, it may well be that different considerations should control the allocation of adjudicatory authority. Today many more legal orders entertain declaratory judgments and do so more readily than in the past; except for the equality argument, the justifications for this change in attitude do not support giving natural defendants a fully equal opportunity to control forum-selection.

The basic objection to the *"Tatry"* solution is not that it allows natural defendants to control forum-selection but rather its consequences for litigation practice. Where a controversy can be litigated in either a coercive or a declaratory action, technically speaking there is no reason why the party that initiates the proceeding should not – ultimately as well as initially – control the choice of forum. The difficulty is that, when party control turns on a strict first-to-file rule, forces are set in motion that will often disrupt the normal pace and progress of litigation. Parties are invited, as it were, to compete for the right to select the forum by racing to their respective court houses.

> The natural defendant *(Anspruchsgegner)* has, by quickly bringing a negative declaratory action, the same opportunity to select the court that will decide as does the natural plaintiff *(Leistungskläger)*.[254]

The adverse consequences that encouraging such races can have include premature litigation decisions and a climate less favorable for settlement negotiations. The situation could be greatly improved by setting aside the natural defendant's selection of a forum for a declaratory action when the natural plaintiff initiates, within a reasonable period of time, a parallel coercive action.

---

253 Compare Collins, *supra* footnote 229, at 283-287; *The Maciej Rataj*, [1991] 2 Lloyd's Rep. 458 (QBD (Adm. Ct.) 1991).

254 Kropholler, *supra* footnote 181, Art. 27, No. 10.

6.   Comparative Remarks

The Common Law and the Brussels approaches to *lis pendens* problems are entirely different in the case of proceedings that both consider fully identical. Where the controversies are not identical, both systems provide, on the other hand, flexible solutions that take into account more than just the moment when the two courts were seized. (An important difference is, of course, that under Brussels only the court second seized has discretion to stay proceedings.) Brussels here differs markedly from many national civil-law systems, in particular the German, whose courts exercise almost no discretion in these matters.[255] The strong civilian preference for rigid over flexible rules, seen in national approaches to these problems, may explain why the Brussels provisions respecting related actions have, until recently, hardly been considered by either the doctrine or the courts.[256] The divergence in views respecting what constitutes identity of actions and of parties sharply reduces the predictability and administrability of Article 27 – Article 21 of the Convention; as a consequence, the flexible approach of Article 28 – Article 22 of the Convention – becomes more appealing.

Where identical actions are in question, today the issue whether temporal priority should be the *only* decisive factor for the purposes of staying actions with regard to possible or actual proceedings in other courts, or *only one among many* factors to be considered, sharply divides the civil-law systems and Brussels from the common-law world. Here again, the positions taken depend heavily on the relative weights the legal systems give to predictability and flexibility. Some systems believe that parallel proceedings are to be avoided at all costs; others are ready to allow them to go forward on occasion but disagree as to when.

Articles 27 and 28 are of considerable interest in another perspective as well: the continental European rejection of the *forum non conveniens* doctrine rests in part on the proposition that it is improper and, in legal systems such as that of Germany, even unconstitutional for the court to refuse to exercise the adjudicatory authority conferred on it by law. The *gesetzliche Richter* is not free to refuse to adjudicate on such grounds as the relative inconvenience of the forum seized in comparison with an alternative forum that was not seized. Under Article 28 (2) of the Regulation, however, where a related – but not identical – action is pending at first instance in the court of a different Member State, the court *second* seized may, on its own motion or that of a party, "decline jurisdiction if the court first seized has jurisdiction over the action in question and its law permits the consolidation thereof". A comparable discretionary authority is not given to the court seized of the related action first-in-time.

---

255   But see the general provision in ZPO §148 (court has discretion to suspend proceedings if the resolution of the case depends on the existence of a legal relationship constituting the subject of another pending action).

256   See S. Baumgartner, "Related Actions", 3 *ZZPInt* 203, at 204 (1998); see also J. Lüpfert, *Konnexität im EuGVÜ* (Berlin, Duncker & Humblot, 1997), reviewed by P. Huber in 64 *RabelsZ* 429-437 (2000).

Article 28 disregards propositions that continental European jurists have insisted are fundamental to the Brussels system. In the first place, the article is inconsistent with the *gesetzlicher Richter* principle in the same sense that the doctrine of *forum non conveniens* is: judges are given a far-reaching discretionary power. They are not only free to decline jurisdiction when the conditions of Article 28 (2) are satisfied but to decide under Article 28 (3) whether actions "are so closely connected that it is expedient to hear and determine them together to avoid the risk of irreconcilable judgments resulting from separate proceedings".

Where consolidation of related actions is in question, except in one respect, Article 28 is comparable to a robust doctrine of *forum non conveniens*: under Article 28, only one court – that second seized – exercises discretionary authority while, in *forum non conveniens* cases, the court seized of a matter has discretion in deciding whether to stay its proceedings in favor of another court which, in turn, exercises its discretion in deciding whether to accept the reference. This difference hardly avoids the theoretical and practical objections that have been raised with respect to *forum non conveniens* by the continental European jurists.

Yet Article 28 (2) differs from *forum non conveniens* in a further respect: the former invites either party to invoke the court's discretionary power; at least in practice, only defendants invoke *forum non conveniens*. The adoption of Article 28 calls in question the argument of principle that judges should not exercise a discretion as to whether they will exercise the adjudicatory authority that the legislature has granted. In due course, perhaps Article 28 will lead the European Union to a recognition that a modest and restrained doctrine of *forum non conveniens* can serve the international order well.

Arguably, Article 28 is less consistent with the spirit of Brussels than is *forum non conveniens*. If the court of reference has no power to reject the referral, the discretionary power exercised by the referring judge under Article 28 would clearly be broader than that exercised by the judge in *forum non conveniens* cases. (Indeed, Article 28 would recognize a direct interference with the jurisdiction of the court first seized and violate the equality principle in a more egregious fashion than an antisuit injunction.) However, while some European jurists indeed argue that the referral under Article 28 should be binding *de lege ferenda*, they seem to agree that it is not *de lege lata*.[257]

E.   Fine-tuning in an Evolving European Union

1.   In General

The emergence of the European Union has complicated the analysis and understanding of fine-tuning theory and judicature in Western Europe. Three bodies of law can, depending on the circumstances, influence one's jurisprudential views and one's interpretation and application of the relevant instruments: EU law, na-

---

257   See, e.g., Kropholler, *supra* footnote 181, Art. 28, No. 9; Schack, *supra* footnote 5, at 269, No. 768.

tional law, or a cumulation thereof. The issues raised are by no means fully understood or resolved. They are deeply influenced by the beholder's legal and cultural background. Before the emergence of the European Union, legal culture and background shaped, of course, both national and international practices. Absent international instruments, however, each nation ultimately controlled the law that governed in its courts. The contemporary structure is far more complicated, and the problems raised are not infrequently of exquisite complexity and difficulty.

(a) The Union's evolution

The institutional roots of what is now known as the European Union date back to the early 1950s. In 1952, Belgium, France, West Germany, Italy, Luxembourg and the Netherlands formed the European Coal and Steel Community (ECSC)[258] in post-war Europe thereby establishing, perhaps for the first time, independent – "supra-national" – institutions for the administration of economic sectors whose decisions were binding on the Member States.[259] The success of the ECSC led the same six States to join five years later the treaties on the European Atomic Energy Community (Euratom) and the European Economic Community (EEC) to the ECSC structure. While the former provided for common policies in the nuclear sector, the EEC Treaty – also known as the Treaty of Rome – aimed at creating a common market and promoting economic expansion, growth and co-operation by, *inter alia,* assuring the free movement of goods, persons, services, and capital. The institutional structure of the EEC, modeled after the ECSC, consisted of a Commission, a Council, an Assembly, and a Court of Justice.

The next two decades were characterized by significant enlargements of the Communities' powers and membership. In 1973, Denmark, Ireland, and the United Kingdom joined, Greece (in 1981), Portugal, and Spain (in 1986) followed suit during the 1980s, and the 1995 accession of Austria, Finland, and Sweden brought the number of Member States to fifteen. In the single largest – and, in many respects, most ambitious – expansion to date, ten more states joined the Union in 2004, comprising a number of Central and Eastern European countries that were, to varying degrees, formerly part of the Soviet bloc – the three Baltic states of Estonia, Latvia and Lithuania, Poland, Hungary, Slovenia, the Czech Republic and Slovakia – as well as Cyprus and Malta.

The Single European Act of 1986 conferred new powers on the EEC, for example, over social policy, research and technical development, as well as the environment; however, for the time being, the general – primarily economic – objectives of the EEC remained unchanged.

The Treaty on the European Union – signed in Maastricht in 1992 – introduced for the first time new general aims by extending the Community's objec-

---

258   See M. Anderson, "A Tougher Row to Hoe: The European Union's Ascension as a Global Superpower Analyzed through the American Federal Experience", 29 *Syracuse J. Int'l L. & Com.*, 83, at 88 (2001).

259   See K. Lenaerts and P. van Nuffel, R. Bray (ed.), *Constitutional Law of the European Union*, at 3-4, No. 1-002 (London, Sweet & Maxwell, 2nd ed., 2005).

tives to encompass non-economic subjects and, *inter alia*, to create a monetary union by 1999. Indeed, the Treaty "extended the sphere of action of the ... [EEC] to such an extent that the title 'European Economic Community' was replaced by 'European Community' [EC]".[260] Under the Maastricht Treaty, the European Union now is built on three "pillars".[261] The first pillar comprises the original Community treaties; the second and third – which are not subject to the democratic and judicial control mechanisms of the first pillar – introduced a new form of governmental co-operation in the areas of foreign and security policy as well as home affairs and judicial co-operation. In May 1999, the first pillar was significantly strengthened by the entering into force of the Treaty of Amsterdam signed by the Member States almost two years earlier. The Treaty, *inter alia*, transferred most of the third-pillar powers to the EC, thereby opening the way for considerably more extensive integration and harmonization in the area of judicial affairs, one example of which is the Brussels Regulation of 2002.

As the brief foregoing account of the constitutional history of the EU makes clear, the current European Union is now far more than the purely economic community that began in the middle of the previous century. Economic regulations have been supplemented by, *inter alia*, a common currency, a European citizenship, a vast power of the EU institutions to legislate, and the introduction of powers respecting foreign and security policy. Transferring these powers to the Union, the Member States have agreed to limit their own sovereignty.[262] In this

---

260   *Idem* 9, No. 1-010.

261   For some time it seemed as if the Pillar structure would soon be a relict of the past: The Treaty Establishing a Constitution for Europe, [2004] OJ C 310, 1, that was agreed upon in June 2004, endows the Union with a single institutional structure. However, after the French and the Dutch did not approve of the Constitution its chances of becoming effective are very low. See *infra* p. 322.

262   There are, despite profound historical differences, interesting and suggestive parallels between the problems that will face the European Union respecting the allocation of authority to administer justice and establish substantive rules and principles and the task that in the late eighteenth century, on the Atlantic coast of the North American Continent, 13 former British colonies, having proclaimed their independence from the British Crown, undertook.
    With the Declaration of Independence in 1776, each of the former colonies claimed full control over the allocation of authority to create, adopt, and apply its own laws. The Continental Congress, called by the former colonies, approved the Articles of Confederation on 15 November 1777. On 1 March 1781, after the last state had ratified the Articles, "Congress declared the Confederation of the United States 'completed and perpetual'". J. Kaminski, "The Articles of Confederation", *Oxford Companion to United States History*, at 51 (P. S. Boyd, ed. in chief) (Oxford, Oxford University Press, 2001).
    The association of sovereign states that the Articles created was weak. Each state had one vote; Congress "could act only on the states, not on individuals". *Ibid.* The vote of nine states was required to pass legislation in those areas in which Congress had legislative powers. See *ibid.*

sense, Union law has become autonomous from the national law of the member States and enjoys supremacy.[263] Its

> [a]utonomy is protected by the power of the [European Court of Justice] to 'ensure that in the interpretation and application of the Treaty the law is observed', as well as by the authority given the ECJ to interpret the 'federal' basic law of the EU and the validity of the acts of the EU institutions when raised in the courts of a member state.[264]

The European Union must be seen, therefore, as something more than a classic confederation of independent States. On the other hand, the Union still lacks the features that would turn it into a full-fledged political federation.[265] The EU Treaty, for example, did not endow the Union with legal personality; commentators thus see the Union as existing through the co-ordinated, unified appearance of the original communities as well as its Member States in joint leverage of their respective powers.[266] A significant change in appearance, as well as in substance, of the legal foundations of the European Union, is marked by the politically charged process that led to the approval of a European Constitution by the EU heads of state and government in June 2004.[267] The Constitution, among

---

> [P]ower to regulate foreign or domestic commerce, to levy and collect taxes and to raise an army [was not given to Congress]. It could only request the states to pay their share of federal expense and supply soldiers for the Continental Congress.

Ibid.
Several attempts to amend – which required unanimity – the Articles to strengthen Congress' hand failed. In 1787, a Constitutional Convention was called to revise them. As one of its first steps, the Convention – acting without the unanimous consent of the states and, accordingly, unconstitutionally – "voted to abandon the Articles altogether and draft a new constitution". *Ibid.* A radically different document was produced in Philadelphia, adopted by the Convention and, after ratification by the requisite number of states (nine), entered into force in 1789 and the process of establishing the federal system and working out the constitutional allocations of power between the several states and the nation began.
The European Union may well stand, as the third millennium begins, on the verge of facing tasks that are comparable in scope and difficulty to those the United States faced in 1789.

263   See L. Catá Backer, "The Extra-National State: American Confederate Federalism and the European Union", 7 *Colum. J. Eur. L.* 173, at 195 (2001).

264   *Idem* 195-196 (footnotes omitted).

265   See G. Hirsch, "EG: Kein Staat, aber eine Verfassung?" 53 *NJW* 46, at 47 (2000); D. Shine, "The European Union's Lack of Internal Borders in the Practice of Law, A Model for the United States?", 29 *Syracuse J. Int'l L. & Com.* 207, at 260 (2001).

266   See M. Pechstein and Ch. Koenig, "Rechtspersönlichkeit für die Europäische Union?", 8 *EuZWR* 225 (1997).

267   Treaty Establishing a Constitution for Europe, [2004] OJ C 310, 1. See Editorial Comments, "A Consittution for Europe", 41 *C. M. L. Rev.* 899-907 (2004); M. Ruffert,

other things, grants legal personality to the European Union[268] and incorporates the European Charter of Fundamental Rights.[269] However, after the French and the Dutch did not approve of the new framework for the European Union in the referendums of 29 May 2005 and 1 June 2005 the chances of the Constitution to become effective are very low. Whether it would have had the desired effects – the turning of the European Union into a true "European Federation" – was an open question anyway.[270]

(b) The relationship between the two Union courts and the national courts of Union Members

The European court system comprises two courts, namely the European Court of Justice (ECJ) and the European Court of First Instance (ECFI).[271] Both courts have 25 judges (one from each Member State);[272] the ECJ judges are assisted by eight Advocate-Generals.[273] These courts are to ensure that the Treaties establishing the European Communities and the rules and directives issued by the competent Community institutions are correctly interpreted and applied; they do not function as appellate bodies on matters of purely national law.[274] Nor do they automatically hear all disputes that involve the application and interpretation of Community law. Indeed, the institutional framework of the European court system leaves such application and interpretation to the national courts; they are "the courts with general jurisdiction for Community law".[275] The ECJ and the ECFI, on

---

"Schlüsselfragen der Europäischen Verfassung der Zukunft, Grundrechte – Institutionen – Kompetenzen – Ratifizierung", 39 *Europarecht* 165-201 (2004).

268 Article I-7 of the Constitution.

269 Part II, Articles II-61 to II-114 of the Constitution,

270 See M. Brewer, "The European Union and Legitimacy: Time for a European Constitution", 34 *Cornell Int'l LJ* 555, at 582-584 (2001); U. Di Fabio, "A European Charter: Towards a Constitution for the Union", 7 *Colum. J. Eur. L.* 159, at 159-160 (2001).

271 Under the European Constitution, the name of the ECFI would be changed to "General Court". See Article I-29 (1) para.1 of the Constitution.

272 See EC Treaty, Art. 222 para. 1 (*ex* Art. 166 para. 1) and Art. 225 (2) (*ex* Art. 168 a (2)). See also Articles I-29 (2) and III-356 of the Constitution. The number of judges at the ECJ is based strictly on the 'one judge per member state' principle, whereas the Court of First Instance consists of *at least* one judge per member state, the exact number to be fixed in the Statute of the Court of Justice.

273 See EC Treaty, Art. 222 para. 1 (*ex* Art. 166 para. 1). See also Article III-354 para. 1 of the Constitution.

274 See EC Treaty, Art. 220 (*ex* Art. 164). Article I-29 (1) of the Constitution provides that the Court of Justice "shall ensure respect for the law in the interpretation and application of the Constitution".

275 See Report of the Court of Justice on Certain Aspects of the Application of the Treaty on European Union – Contribution of the Court of First Instance for the Purposes of the 1996 Intergovernmental Conference P15 (May 1995). This division of labor between the European and the national courts would remain under the European Con-

the other hand, have adjudicatory authority only where expressly provided for in the Treaties. There are essentially four such areas.[276] Firstly, the Commission can bring an action to determine whether a Member State has fulfilled its obligations under Community law.[277] If the Court finds that these obligations have not been fulfilled, the Member State concerned must comply without delay.[278] Secondly, another Member State may make an application of the same nature,[279] although this is rarely done.[280] Thirdly, the European courts decide disputes between the Community's institutions. A Member State, the Council, the Commission or, in certain circumstances, the Parliament, may apply for the annulment of all or part of an item of Community legislation or bring an action against a Community institution for its failure to act.[281] Lastly, the European courts afford legal protection to natural and legal persons in a variety of cases.[282] They hear, for example, actions brought by individuals seeking the annulment of a legal measure, which is of direct and individual concern to them[283] or damage claims brought against the Community.[284]

The type of adjudicatory authority most relevant for the present discussion falls within the last category. Under EC Treaty Article 234 (1) (ex Article 177 (1)) the ECJ has jurisdiction if a national court or tribunal makes a reference for a preliminary ruling on, *inter alia*, the interpretation of the EC Treaty or on the validity or interpretation of Community acts. Only courts or tribunals against whose decision there is no judicial remedy under national law *may* make such a reference; a court or tribunal *must* refer the matter "if it considers that a decision on the question is necessary to enable it to give judgment".[285] Although a literal understanding of Article 234 (1) appears to confine the ECJ to merely *interpreting* – i.e. not *applying* – Community law, the line between the two tasks is not always easy to draw. Indeed, the Court has held that to secure the uniform application of the law,

---

stitution. See Barents, "The Court of Justice in the Draft Constitution", 11 *Maastricht Journal of European and Comparative Law* 212 (2004).

276 See Lenaerts and van Nuffel, *supra* footnote 259, at 443-446, No. 10-074. For many of these disputes – including the reference for a preliminary ruling (see *infra*) – the ECJ has exclusive adjudicatory authority; others may be decided by the ECFI, subject to a right of appeal to the ECJ on points of law only. See *idem* 333-334, No. 7-065.

277 See EC Treaty, Art. 226 para. 2 (*ex* Art. 169 para. 2). See also Article III-360 para. 2 of the Constitution.

278 See EC Treaty, Art. 228 (*ex* Art. 171). See also Article III-362 (1) of the Constitution.

279 See EC Treaty, Art. 227 (*ex* Art. 170). See also Article III-361 of the Constitution.

280 See Lenaerts and van Nuffel, *supra* footnote 259, at 445, No. 10-074.

281 See EC Treaty, Arts. 230-233 (*ex* Arts. 173-176).

282 See Lenaerts and van Nuffel, *supra* footnote 259, at 445, No. 10-074.

283 See EC Treaty, Art. 230 para. 4 (*ex* Art. 173 para. 4). See also Article III-365 (4) of the Constitution.

284 See EC Treaty, Art. 235 (*ex* Art. 178). See also Article III-370 of the Constitution.

285 See EC Treaty, Art. 235 (*ex* Art. 178). See also Article III-370 of the Constitution.

the special field of judicial cooperation under ... [Art. 234] ... requires the national court and the Court of Justice, both keeping with[in] their respective jurisdiction ... to make direct and complementary contributions to the working out of a decision.[286]

No matter to what extent the Court's decision eventually determines the outcome of the main proceedings, however, it is always "preliminary" in that it falls to the national court to dispose of the case.[287] A judgment given by the ECJ under Article 234 binds the national court that referred the case as well as all other courts that deal with the case at a later stage of the proceedings.[288] Moreover, the binding effect of the ECJ's judgment is not limited to the specific case in which it was given, but extends to all national courts and tribunals, subject to those courts' right to make a further reference to the ECJ.[289]

2.   The 1968 Convention's raison d'être: Ensuring "a True Internal Market"

The Brussels Convention of 1968 sought to ensure "a true [single,] internal market between the [Member States] ... [in which] legal protection and ... legal certainty" were assured.[290] In the name of efficiency, predictability, and simplicity, only limited opportunities were provided for fine-tuning and exercises of adjudicatory authority by one State's courts could be challenged in the courts of other Member States only at the stage of recognition and enforcement and only on relatively limited grounds.[291]

---

286   Schwarze v. Einfuhr- und Vorratsstelle für Getreide und Futtermittel – Case C-16/65, [1965] ECR 877, 889.

287   See K. Lenaerts, D. Arts and I. Maselis, in R. Bray (ed.), *Procedural Law of the European Union*, at 193, No. 6-027 (London, Sweet & Maxwell, 2nd ed. 2006).

288   See *idem* 130, No. 6-031.

289   See *idem* 132, No. 6-035.

290   Report by Mr. P. Jenard on the Convention of 27 September 1968 on jurisdiction and the enforcement of judgments in civil and commercial matters (Jenard Report), [1979] OJ C 59, 1, at 4.

291   The permitted grounds of challenge at the recognition stage, set out in Article 27, as amended, of the Convention and Article 34 of the Regulation are: (1) public policy (the Regulation inserts "manifestly" before "public policy"); (2) in the case of judgment by default, failure to "duly" serve the defendant "in sufficient time to enable him to arrange for his defense" (the Regulation deletes "duly" and adds after "defense" "unless the defendant failed to commence proceedings to challenge the judgment when it was possible for him to do so"); (3) irreconcilability "with a judgment given in a dispute between the same parties in the State where recognition is sought" (the Regulation inserts "Member" before "State" and substitutes "in which" for "where"); (4) decisions respecting preliminary questions "concerning the status or legal capacity of natural persons, rights in property arising out of a matrimonial relationship, wills or succession ... unless the same result would have been reached by the application of the rules of private international law of ... [the] State [addressed]" (this ground does not appear in the Regulation); (5) irreconcilability "with an earlier judgment

The intensity of the effort to ensure, legally speaking, efficiency, predictability, and simplicity in the operation of that market is seen in the principle that recognition *cannot* be denied to judgments rendered under the Convention on the ground that the court of origin lacked adjudicatory authority. Article 28 allows such challenges only in matters relating to insurance (Section 3), consumer contracts (Section 4), and exclusive jurisdiction (Section 5 – rights *in rem* in immovable property or tenancies of immovable property,[292] internal affairs of legal persons and of associations of natural persons, validity of entries in public registers, and proceedings concerned with the enforcement of judgments). Claims of exclusive jurisdiction based on forum-selection clauses (Section 6 – Prorogation of jurisdiction) does *not* ground refusing recognition to judgments rendered by a non-agreed forum.[293] Furthermore, in deciding upon the jurisdictional issues that can be raised, the court addressed is "bound by the findings of fact on which the court of the State of origin based its jurisdiction ... [and] the test of public policy referred to in ... Article 27 may not be applied to rules relating to jurisdiction".[294]

3.   The Brussels Instruments' Approach to Judicial "Fine-tuning"

The principal techniques of jurisdictional fine-tuning – *forum non conveniens* and antisuit injunctions – available to national legal systems in international litigation were known, of course, to the drafters of the Brussels Convention of 1968 and the Regulation of 2001. The Convention was originally drafted by civil-law jurists. Not until the negotiations in the 1970s that led to the accession in 1975 of the United Kingdom and the Republic of Ireland, did common-law jurists have a say in shaping the Convention. Unsurprisingly, the Brussels approach to fine-tun-

---

given in a non-contracting State involving the same cause of action and between the same parties, provided that this latter judgment fulfils the conditions necessary for its recognition in the state addressed" (the Regulation substitutes for "a non-contracting" "another Member State or in a third State" and adds "Member" before "State" which is capitalized).

Recognition can also be denied on the basis of Article 59 of the Convention (obligations assumed under other Conventions, subject to certain qualifications). The Regulation, which does not contain a comparable provision, provides in Article 72 that it

shall not affect agreements by which Member States undertook, prior to the entry into force of this Regulation pursuant to Article 59 of the Brussels Convention, not to recognise judgments given, in particular in other Contracting States to that Convention, against defendants domiciled or habitually resident in a third country where, in cases provided for by Article 4 of that Convention, the judgment could only be founded on a ground of jurisdiction specified in the second paragraph of Article 3 of that Convention.

292   A special rule applies to proceedings respecting immovable property for temporary private use. See Article 16 (1) *(b)*.

293   See Kropholler, *supra* footnote 181, Art. 35, No. 14.

294   Article 28.

ing still today strongly reflects civilian theory and practice. It provides neither for *forum non conveniens* stays nor for antisuit injunctions.

The presence of common-law jurists at the negotiating table and the involvement of common-law systems in applying and interpreting the Brussels instruments have come, however, to influence the European Union's thinking and practice respecting fine-tuning in various ways. In the first place, the question now arises of the extent to which there is room for common-law courts to use techniques of fine-tuning to which they are accustomed but for which neither the Convention nor Regulation provides. Secondly, the possibility is presented of creating over time a legal tradition that will blend elements of the civil- and the common-law traditions. These basic questions, along with a myriad of specific and technical issues, are posed by the problems that have arisen – and will continue to arise – respecting judicial fine-tuning in litigation that trenches on a Brussels instrument.

The original Convention of 1968 contained a group of provisions that in a measure draw both on the common- and civil-law approaches to fine-tuning. Article 4 from the beginning provided that, with respect to defendants not domiciled in what is now the European Union, "the jurisdiction of the courts of each Contracting ['Member'] State shall", subject to certain exceptions,[295] "be determined [*not* by the Brussels rules but] by the [local] law of [the forum] ... State". Arguably, this provision recognizes the right of each State to apply its own procedural law where the Convention does not, explicitly or by necessary implication, require otherwise.

The Convention also broke new ground in international practice by providing for a form of fine-tuning where "related" actions, defined in Article 22 – Article 28 of the Regulation – as actions "so closely connected that it is expedient to hear and determine them together to avoid the risk of irreconcilable proceedings", are pending in the courts of different European Union States. Although technically quite different from, and far more limited in scope than, the common-law doctrine of *forum non conveniens*, the two provisions are, in terms of technique and purpose, somewhat akin.

---

295   The exceptions made by the Convention in Article 16, Exclusive jurisdiction, are (1) "proceedings which have as their object rights *in rem* in immovable property or tenancies of immovable property[, subject to an exception intended to cover short-term vacation rentals,] ... ; (2) "proceedings ... [respecting] ... the validity of the constitution, the nullity or the dissolution of companies or other legal persons or associations ..., or the decisions of their organs ..."; (3) "proceedings which have as their object the validity of entries in public registers ..."; (4) "proceedings concerned with the registration or validity of patents, trade marks, designs, or other similar rights required to be deposited or registered ...". The exceptions contained in Article 22 of the Regulation are essentially the same as those provided by Article 16 of the Convention. Article 23 of the Regulation further provides for enforceable prorogation agreements when certain formal and other requirements are satisfied.

During the early decades of the Convention's existence, apparently little use was made of the consolidation technique provided by Article 22.[296] Still today, in many respects the provisions on related actions remain *terra incognita*.[297] This lack of interest is perhaps due to the reluctance of the Union's civil-law jurisdictions to indulge in fine-tuning by judges even in the interest of judicial economy and the avoidance of inconsistent judgments.

Recently, however, civil-law countries seem to have given up part of their resistance towards judicial fine-tuning. The Brussels IIa Regulation of 27 November 2003,[298] which has replaced the Brussels II Regulation as of 1 March 2005, at first blush appears to endorse the *forum non conveniens* doctrine.[299] Under the heading "Transfer to a court better placed to hear the case", Article 15 – placed at the end of Section 2, Parental Responsibility – provides that

1.   By way of exception, the courts of a Member State having jurisdiction as to the substance of the matter may, if they consider that a court of another Member State, with which the child has a particular connection, would be better placed to hear the case, or a specific part thereof, and where this is in the best interest of the child:

 (a)   stay the case or the part thereof in question and invite the parties to introduce a request before the court of that other Member State in accordance with paragraph 4; or

 (b)   request a court of another Member State to assume jurisdiction in accordance with paragraph 5.

This provision certainly injects an element of discretion into the otherwise rigid jurisdiction framework of the Brussels instruments. The transfer mechanism established by Article 15 does, however, upon closer inspection, differ significantly from the notion(s) of *forum non conveniens* espoused by common-law jurisdictions. First, its application is linked to the very specific requirement of the best interests of the child. Second, the child must have a "particular connection" with the alternative forum, which is defined further in para. 3. Form a literal reading of para. 3, the connecting factors enumerated therein, constituting such "particular

---

296   Case law on the provision is sparse and predominately dates back only to the late 1980s, see, e.g., the references given by Kropholler, *supra* footnote 181, Art. 27, Nos. 1-25 and Art. 28, Nos. 1-10.

297   See p. 298, *supra*.

298   See *supra* Chap. II. D. 3. *(c).*, p. 76.

299   See E. Jayme and Ch. Kohler, "Europäisches Kollisionsrecht 2003: Der Verfassungskonvent und das Internationale Privat- und Verfahrensrecht", 23 *IPRax* 485, at 492 (2003); A. Schulz, "Die Verordnung (EG) Nr. 2201/2003 (Brüssel IIa) – Eine Einführung", 57 *NJW Supplement Vol 6,* 2 (2004); J. von Staudinger (-Spellenberg), *Kommentar zum Bürgerlichen Gesetzbuch: EGBGB/Internationales Verfahrensrecht in Ehesachen,* (Berlin & New York, NY, Sellier & de Gruyter, Neubearbeitung, 2005), Art. 15 EheGVO.

connection" appear to be meant exhaustive. The range of factors that the court initially seized must take into account is thus much more limited than under a full-fledged *forum non conveniens* analysis. Moreover, the Brussels IIa Regulation – like the other Brussels instruments – operates within a system with a high degree of cooperation, supervised by the European Court of Justice, whereas the interplay of the court in various legal orders of the common law is much more loosely regulated by the notion of comity. Therefore, under Brussels IIa, if the party or the parties fail to seize the alternative, more appropriate forum, or if that forum fails to accept jurisdiction over the case at hand within a certain period of time, the court initially seized is compelled to retain jurisdiction over the case. See Article 15, paras. 4 and 5. Under a proper *forum non conveniens* analysis, on the other hand, the question whether the foreign forum will actually become seized of the matter is only relevant as one of many factors in the equation. Finally and also unlike as under the common law approach, a request for the transfer of the case can be made by the court of the appropriate forum itself, para. 2 (c). Overall, therefore, the Article 15 mechanism only bears a vague resemblance to the doctrine of *forum non conveniens* as developed and currently employed by the courts in common law jurisdictions.

4.   Fine-tuning under the Forum's Local Law in Matters that Trench on a Brussels Instrument

Currently there are only two EU courts, the European Court of Justice and the Court of First Instance. They are charged with maintaining the unity of Union law by providing binding interpretation of that law in responding to referrals by national courts and by ruling on challenges to applications of Union law by national courts. The nature and scope of the adjudicatory authority of the Union courts are thus such that the fine-tuning issue never arises. In the longer run, it may well prove impossible for the Union to operate efficiently and effectively without providing for Union courts charged with adjudicating controversies on their merits. The designers of the procedural law for such a court system would, of course, have to face the issue whether fine-tuning should be permitted at all and, if so, in what circumstances and to what degree.

Today, fine-tuning issues can arise only in national courts. For the courts of civil-law systems, the issue is easily resolved. As a matter of tradition and practice, they, almost without exception, consider fine-tuning, whether through *forum non conveniens* stays or antisuit injunctions, improper. Their traditional position is only strengthened when the litigation in question touches on matters or controversies that involve the European Union. There is, accordingly, no tension between the national laws of these legal orders and EU law. For them the result is the same regardless of whether national or EU law applies.

The fine-tuning issue presents itself differently to national-court systems that consider *forum non conveniens* stays and antisuit injunctions appropriate tools to achieve, in certain circumstances, a higher degree of procedural justice. The United Kingdom courts, long accustomed to these techniques, have been reluctant to forego their use completely. Unlike the great majority of continental European jurists, many English jurists do not consider every use of these techniques incompatible, in principle, with the spirit and letter of Brussels.

The compatibility issue can arise in many, varied – and still largely unexplored – situations. A full discussion here of the problem is not feasible. A few situations involving *forum non conveniens* stays and antisuit injunctions are discussed to illustrate the issues that arise and the arguments that are advanced.

Were procedural law for *European Union* courts in question, uniform rules would presumably be called for.[300] Union courts of general jurisdiction may eventually be established; today, the Brussels instruments are, however, interpreted and applied by national courts. Accordingly, *except* as constrained by Union instruments or regulations, each national court is free to follow its own procedural rules and practices.

Two principal issues have arisen: firstly, to what extent does Union law apply to international litigation in which only one of the courts involved is a Union Member State, secondly, where litigation involves two Union Member States, are there circumstances in which the relevant Brussels instrument can properly be interpreted as allowing – though not requiring – national courts to grant *forum non conveniens* stays or issue antisuit injunctions directed against litigants or their assets?

(a)   *Forum non conveniens*

(i)   *Introductory*

What grounds of policy can, from a European perspective, be advanced against fine-tuning through the *forum non conveniens* doctrine? One may think the doctrine unwise and inconsistent with a judge's role, but is it appropriate to impose one's view on legal orders that see the matter differently? Should perhaps each State be free to decide if and how its courts fine tune their exercise of adjudicatory authority where to do so does not affect adversely the administration of justice in other Member States? Any State can, of course, by categorically refusing to entertain requests for *non conveniens* referrals protect its courts from the inconvenience of handling referral requests. In effect, the Member States in the civil-law tradition have done precisely this. The English courts have not taken the

---

300 For a century and a half, uniformity was not called for in the US federal system, however. Section 5 of the Conformity Act of 1 June 1872, had provided

> That the practice, pleadings, and forms and modes of proceedings in other than equity and admirality causes in the circuit and district courts of the United States shall conform, as near as may be, to the practice, pleadings, and forms and modes of proceeding existing at the time in like causes in the courts of record of the State within which such circuit or district courts are held, any rule of court to the contrary notwithstanding: *Provided, however*, that nothing herein contained shall alter the rules of evidence under the laws of the United States, and as practiced in the courts thereof.

Variations of this conformity approach had been in effect since 1789. On 16 September 1938, the Federal Rules of Civil Procedure came into effect and, for the first time, the rules of civil procedure in all federal courts were, in principle, the same.

same course; they have accepted the view that *forum non conveniens* stays are not permitted where the litigation involves two or more Member States. In other situations, where the Union's interest is not as great, they have continued to follow their traditional procedures. The arguments advanced are addressed in *In re Harrods* and *Owusu v. Jackson*.

(ii)   The English view

a.   In re Harrods

In 1913, Harrods (Buenos Aires) Ltd. was incorporated in England; its status as an English corporation with its registered office in London had not changed since. The company's business was, however, always carried out exclusively in Argentina and its central management and control had been concentrated there as well.

> [T]he English incorporation of the company may fairly be regarded as an anomalous historical survival …. In parallel with its somewhat ghostly legal existence in England the company has a legal, in addition to a robust corporeal, existence in Argentina ….[301]

In July 1989, Harrods' minority shareholder (49 per cent), a company incorporated in Switzerland, brought an action alleging that the majority shareholder (51 per cent), likewise a Swiss corporation, was conducting the company's affairs in a fashion "unduly prejudicial" to the minority shareholder. The relief sought was either an order, directing the majority shareholder to purchase the minority's stock in the company, or its winding-up under the Insolvency Act of 1986. The majority shareholder sought a stay on *forum non conveniens* grounds. The Court of Appeal agreed that Argentina was the appropriate forum but one judge[302] opposed granting a stay in light of uncertainty respecting remedies available to the minority shareholder in Argentina.

On interlocutory appeal from the decision of the Queen's Bench,[303] the majority shareholder argued, *inter alia*, that the Brussels Convention did not preclude the court from staying, under the English *forum non conveniens* doctrine, its proceedings in favor of the Argentine courts. The Convention provided, so the argument went, "a complete code for determining which courts are appropriate for deciding disputes as between member states of the EEC but does not deal with questions of jurisdiction affecting other states".[304] In these circumstances, a stay "is of no interest to the other EEC member states and does not impair the principles of the Convention …".[305]

---

301   *In Re Harrods (Buenos Aires) Ltd.*, [1992] Ch. 72, at 125 (CA 1991) (Lord Justice Bingham).

302   Dillon, L.J., *idem* 107-109.

303   *In Re Harrods*, [1992] Ch. at 86 (CA 1991).

304   *Ibid.*

305   *Idem* 87. In support of his argument, counsel cited, *inter alia*, L. Collins, "Forum non conveniens and the Brussels Convention", 106 *LQ Rev.* 535, at 538-539 (1990). The pas-

Counsel for Ladenimor, the minority shareholder, took the view that his opponent sought to impose a limitation on the Convention's scope that ran counter to its letter and spirit:

> The Convention is designed to provide a simple, certain and uniform set of rules which confer on member states their jurisdiction in international matters, and enable a litigant to know immediately, by looking at the Convention, whether and where he can sue a person domiciled in a member state. By contrast, the practical effect of [the majority shareholder] Intercomfinanz's submissions is that the courts of the member states continue to apply their own rules of private international law unless and until there is a conflict between the member states. The international nature of the scope of the Convention emerges particularly clearly from the use in the French and Italian versions of the Preamble of the literal translation of the words 'in the international order'.....
> Intercomfinanz's approach, however, is that the Convention may or may not apply, depending on whether or not there is an inter-member State dispute. That effectively means that a plaintiff deciding where to sue cannot simply look at the Convention but must investigate the private international law rules of several States. It is not appropriate to resort to a convention which provides for jurisdiction for a set of rules for resolving conflicts.[306]

Dillon, L.J., saw

> [t]he crucial question in the ... case ... [as] whether the English court can stay, strike out or dismiss proceedings on the ground of forum non conveniens, where the defendant in the English proceedings is domiciled in England, but the conflict of jurisdiction is between the jurisdiction of the English court and the jurisdiction of the courts of a state which is not a contracting state, no other contracting state being involved.[307]

---

sage is quoted by Bingham, L.J., at the end of his opinion, *idem* 98-103, at 103:
> When the European Court comes to consider the application of the Convention to non-contracting states, it should seek the answer in treaty interpretation, and ultimately in public international law. The Convention was intended to regulate jurisdiction *as between* the contracting states. Thus the Convention provides that in principle domiciliaries of a contracting state should be sued in that state, subject to important and far-reaching exceptions, and not in other contracting states. Once a court in a contracting state has jurisdiction it is entitled, vis-à-vis other states, to exercise that jurisdiction and other courts cannot. But the states which were parties to the Convention had no interest in requiring a contracting state to exercise a jurisdiction where the competing jurisdiction was in a non-contracting state. The contracting states were setting up an intra-Convention mandatory system of jurisdiction. They were not regulating relations with non-contracting states. (Emphasis in original.)

306   *Idem* 88-89.
307   *Idem* 90, at 93.

In answering that question, Dillon L.J., remarked that he found

> it difficult to give much weight to the [Jenard and Schlosser Reports[308]] ... because ... [they] are general statements ... which can be used as pointers either way, without themselves solving the question in issue ... .[309]

The Convention was in Dillon's view "an agreement between the contracting states among themselves"; he rejects the proposition

> that the framework of the Convention would be destroyed if there were available to the English court a discretion to refuse jurisdiction, on the ground that the courts of a non-contracting state were the appropriate forum, in a case with which no other contracting state is in any way concerned. [He can] not accept that article 2 has the very wide mandatory effect which ... [some] would ascribe to it where the only conflict is between the courts of a single contracting state and the courts of a non-contracting state.[310]

Bingham, L.J., reached the same conclusion as Dillon L.J. He placed greater reliance on the proposition that the contracting States in 1968 were "setting up an intra-Convention mandatory system of jurisdiction" rather than "regulating relations with non-contracting states", however.[311] The third judge, Stocker, L.J. gave no reasons, remarking only that he had "read the judgments of Dillon and Bingham L.J., which ... [he] agree[d] with and ha[d] nothing to add."[312]

An appeal was brought to the House of Lords; it stayed the proceedings and referred the following questions to the European Court of Justice to obtain definitive interpretations of the Convention:

> ii.   Does the 1968 Convention apply to govern the jurisdiction of the courts of a Contracting State in circumstances where there is no conflict of jurisdiction with the courts of any other Contracting State?
>
> ii.(a) Is it inconsistent with the 1968 Convention where jurisdiction is founded on Article 2 [domicile of defendant] for a court of a Contracting State to exercise a discretionary power available under its national law to decline to hear proceedings brought against a person domiciled in that State in fa-

---

308 See *supra* footnote 290 and in Chap. V. footnote 212 respectively.

309 *In Re Harrods*, [1992] Ch. at 96 (CA 1991).
Bingham, L.J., discussed the Report's significance for the *Harrods* problem in similar terms; indeed, he thought there was "an obvious danger in seizing on occasional passages here and there in these long and closely-reasoned reports to support one view or the other when it is acknowledged that the present question was never squarely addressed". *Idem* 98-103, at 101.

310 *Idem* 97-98.

311 The quoted language is from Bingham, L.J.'s opinion, at *idem* 101.

312 *Idem* 98.

vor of the courts of a non-Contracting State, if the jurisdiction of no other
Contracting State under the 1968 Convention is in question?

ii.*(b)* If so, is it inconsistent in all circumstances or only in some and, if so, in
which?³¹³

Before the Court of Justice had addressed these issues, the case was settled and
removed from that Court's docket.³¹⁴

b.   *Owusu* v. *Jackson*

Issues that *In re Harrods* raised but left unanswered arose some years later in
Andrew Owusu v. *Nugent B Jackson, Mammee Bay Resorts Limited et al.*³¹⁵ The
claimant, Owusu, and one of the defendants, Jackson, were English domiciliaries.
The other five defendants were Jamaican limited liability companies.

The action arose out of an accident that the plaintiff suffered while vacation-
ing in 1997 in Jamaica. He walked into the sea until the water was at waist level,
dived, and "struck his head against a submerged sand bank", fracturing his spine.
He was left paralysed below the neck. The claim against the first defendant was in
contract. Jackson had rented Owusu a holiday villa with access to a private beach.
The latter maintained that an implied term of the contract was that the beach
would be reasonably free of hidden dangers. Owusu's claims against the Jamaican
defendants all sounded in tort.

The trial judge stated that "but for the fact that he was precluded [, in his
view,] by the Brussels Convention from staying the action against D1, he would
have no hesitation in holding that Jamaica was a more appropriate forum than
England".³¹⁶ He felt himself

> driven, however, to the conclusion that England and not Jamaica was the appropri-
> ate forum. He could not stay the action against D1 here, and he said that in these
> circumstances if he granted the other defendants a stay the likelihood was that courts
> in the two jurisdictions would end up trying the same factual issues upon the same or
> similar evidence, with the possibility that they might reach different conclusions. He
> therefore refused the applications of D3, D4 and D6.³¹⁷

Lord Justice Brooke's opinion for the Court of Appeal, after discussing various
issues raised by the controversy, considered in some detail the issue of Commu-

---

313   [1992] OJ C 219, at 4, of 26 August 1992.

314   See [1994] OJ C 103, at 9, of 11 April 1994.

315   [2002] EWCA Civ 877 (CA 2002).

316   *Idem*, No. 20.

317   *Idem*, No. 21.

nity law presented by the case[318]. He began by distinguishing *UGIC* v. *Group Josi Reinsurance Co.*[319] In *Josi*, the European Court of Justice

> was concerned with a case in which the plaintiffs, a Canadian company, were domiciled in a non-member state, and there was a dispute whether the Belgian defendants should be sued in France (where the claimants' brokers were domiciled) or in Belgium (the place of the defendants' domicile) ....[320]

In the Lord Justice's view:

> The situation which confronts ... [this court] is a different one. It has not been suggested that the courts of any other member state might be involved. The competing jurisdictions are England (a member state) and Jamaica (a non-member state). If, as the claimant submits, the language of Article 2 is mandatory even in this context, D1 would have to be sued in England, in the courts of his domicile, and it would not be open to the claimant to sue him in Jamaica, where the harmful event occurred, because Jamaica is not another contracting state (see Article 5 (3)), and it is not permissible to create an exception to the rule in Article 2 unless express provision is made to that effect in the Convention.[321]

To resolve the controversy respecting Community law, the Court of Appeal referred two questions to the European Court of Justice:

> 1.   Is it inconsistent with the Brussels Convention on Jurisdiction and the Enforcement of Judgments 1968, where a claimant contends that jurisdiction is founded on Article 2, for a court of a Contracting State to exercise a discretionary power, available under its national law, to decline to hear proceedings brought against a person domiciled in that State in favor of the courts of a non-Contracting State: *(a)* if the jurisdiction of no other Contracting State under the 1968 Convention is in issue; *(b)* if the proceedings have no connecting factors to any other Contracting State?
> 2.   If the answer to question 1 *(a)* or *(b)* is yes, is it inconsistent in all circumstances or only in some and if so which?[322]

The Court of Appeal had expressed its views respecting how these questions should be answered. It pointed out that the issue to be resolved arose as well with respect to procedural practices other than the doctrine of *forum non conveniens*:

---

318   *Idem*, Nos 27-58.
319   Case C-412/98, [2000] ECR I-5925.
320   [2002] EWCA Civ 877, No. 40.
321   *Idem*, No. 41.
322   *Idem*, No. 60, Order.

The present case is concerned with the doctrine of *forum non conveniens*, when applied as between a member state and a non-member state. But it might just as easily have been concerned with the doctrine of *lis alibi pendens*, or 'prorogation of jurisdiction', or the rule that disputes concerned with rights *in rem* over immovable property should be heard in the state where the property is situated, or any of the other situations for which the Brussels Convention provides discretionary or mandatory exceptions (in Sections 2 to 6 of Title 2 of the Convention). If Article 2 is mandatory, then a defendant domiciled in England must be sued in England in all such cases even if the Convention would allow or require the action to be brought in the courts of another member state if a domiciliary of another member state was involved.[323]

The referring court pointed out the complications and practical difficulties, as well as the disruption of harmonious relations with non-Brussels States that subjecting these controversies to the strict Brussels regime would entail:

We mention this ... so that the European Court of Justice may understand some of the practical difficulties which the courts of a member state which applies *forum conveniens* principles may encounter in their normally harmonious relationships with the courts of non-member states in cases where no other member state is involved if the claimant's strict interpretation of Article 2 (i) of the Brussels Convention is correct. In particular, it may possibly lead to a situation in which the courts of a member state and the courts of a non-member state may try the same *lis* on the same or similar evidence and reach conflicting conclusions.[324]

(iii) The View of the European Court of Justice

The European Court of Justice delivered its judgment in *Owusu* v. *Jackson* on 1 March 2005.[325] It answered the first question submitted by the Court of Appeal by holding that the Brussels Convention

precludes a court of a Contracting State from declining the jurisdiction conferred on it by Article 2 ... on the ground that a court of a non-Contracting State would be a more appropriate forum for the trial of the action even if the jurisdiction of no other Contracting State is in issue or the proceedings have no connecting factors to any other Contracting State.[326]

In its reasoning the Court first pointed out that Article 2 of the Brussels Convention did not only applied to cases involving the courts of a number of Contracting States but also covered cases involving the courts of a single Contracting State and those of a non-Contracting State:

---

323   *Idem*, No. 45.

324   *Idem*, No. 35.

325   Case C-281/02, [2005] ECR I-1383.

326   [2005] ECR I-1383, para. 46.

Nothing in the wording of Article 2 of the Brussels Convention suggests that the application of the general rule of jurisdiction laid down by that article solely on the basis of the defendant's domicile in a Contracting State is subject to the condition that there should be a legal relationship involving a number of Contracting States .... Of course, as is clear from the Jenard report on the Convention ..., for the jurisdiction rules of the Brussels Convention to apply at all the existence of an international element is required. However, the international nature of the legal relationship at issue need not necessarily derive, for the purposes of the application of Article 2 of the Brussels Convention, from the involvement, either because of the subject-matter of the proceedings or the respective domiciles of the parties, of a number of Contracting States.[327]

The Court went on:

The purpose of the fourth indent of Article 220 of the EC Treaty ... on the basis of which the Member States concluded the Brussels Conventions, is to facilitate the working of the common market through the adoption of rules of jurisdiction for disputes relation thereto and through the elimination, as far as is possible, of difficulties concerning the recognition and enforcement of judgments in the territory of the Contracts States .... However, the uniform rules of jurisdiction contained in the Brussels Convention are not intended to apply only to situations in which there is a real and sufficient link with the working of the internal market, by definition involving a number of Member States. Suffice it to observe in that regard that the consolidation as such of the rules on conflict of jurisdiction and on the recognition and enforcement of judgments, effected by the Brussels Convention in respect of cases with an international element, is without doubt intended to eliminate obstacles to the functioning of the internal market which may derive from disparities between national legislations on the subject.[328]

The Court then explained that the Brussels Convention precluded a court of a Contracting State from applying the doctrine of *forum non conveniens* and declining to exercise the jurisdiction conferred on it by Article 2 of the Convention. It held, that

Article 2 of the Brussels Convention is mandatory in nature and that, according to its terms, there can be no derogation from the principle it lays down except in the cases expressly provided for by the Convention .... It is common ground that no exception on the basis of the *forum non conveniens* doctrine was provided for by the authors of the Convention ....[329]

---

327 *Idem*, paras. 24-26.
328 *Idem*, paras. 33-34.
329 *Idem*, para. 37.

The Court continued:

> Respect for the principle of legal certainty, which is one of the objectives of the Brussels Convention, would not be fully guaranteed if the court having jurisdiction under the Convention had to be allowed to apply the *forum non conveniens* doctrine. According to its preamble, the Brussels Convention is intended to strengthen in the Community the legal protection of persons established therein, by laying down common rules on jurisdiction to guarantee certainty as to the allocation of jurisdiction among the various national courts before which proceedings in a particular case may be brought....[330]

The Court added that

> ... allowing *forum non conveniens* in the context of the Brussels Convention would be likely to affect the uniform application of the rules of jurisdiction contained therein in so far as that doctrine is recognized only in a limited number of Contracting States, whereas the objective of the Brussels Convention is precisely to lay down common rules to the exclusion of derogating national rules.[331]

In view of the second question relating to the precise scope of preclusion of *forum non conveniens* the Court refused to give an answer. It held that the procedure provided for in Article 234 EC was an instrument of cooperation between the Court and national courts by means of which the former provides the latter with interpretation of such Community law as is necessary for them to give judgment in cases upon which they are called to adjudicate. It was not meant to produce advisory opinions on general or hypothetical questions.

As a result of the Courts refusal to rule on the second question it remains unclear whether the *forum non conveniens* is precluded in other cases involving the courts of a Contracting State and a non-Contracting State. An open question, for example, is whether English courts may refuse to decide a case if jurisdiction under the Convention is not based on Article 2. However, considering the Court's reasoning in view of legal certainty and predictability it seems likely that it disapproves of the doctrine of *forum non conveniens* all together.[332]

---

330   *Idem*, para. 39.

331   *Idem*, para. 43.

332   See F. Blobel, "Unzulässigkeit der forum-non-conveniens-Doktrin im Europäischen Zivilprozessrecht – EuGH, Urteil vom 1. März 2005, Rs C-281/02 - Owusu", *GPR* 2005, 140, at 141; Ch. Heinze and A. Dutta, "Ungeschriebene Grenzen für europäische Zuständigkeiten bei Streitigkeiten mit Drittstaatenbezug", 25 *IPRax* 224, 226-227 (2005); P. Mankowski, "Entwicklungen im Internationalen Privat- und Prozessrecht 2004/2005 (Teil 2)", 51 *RIW* 561, at 564-565 (2005). See for a critical account of the decision R. Fentiman, "National Law and the European Jurisdiction Regime", in A. Nuyts & N. Watté (eds.), *International Civil Litigation in Europe and Relations with Thirds States*, 83-128 (Brussels, Bruylant, 2005).

(iv) Do the Brussels instruments forbid in all or some situations the courts of Member States granting forum non conveniens stays?

The drafters of the 1968 Convention, of its subsequent revisions, and of the Brussels Regulation of 2002 have not addressed the issue of *forum non conveniens* stays. None of the original Member States permitted such stays; the issue apparently did not arise during the negotiations that led to the accession of the United Kingdom and the Republic of Ireland whose courts were empowered by their national law to grant *non conveniens* stays in certain situations. Nor has the issue been ventilated in connection with subsequent negotiations, including those on the Lugano Convention.

Accordingly, a number of complex issues remain unresolved respecting both the scope of application of the Brussels instruments and, where they apply, whether and when national courts can fine tune their implementation of adjudicatory authority through such instruments as *forum non conveniens* stays and antisuit injunctions. It is clear, of course, that the Brussels instruments, where applicable, do not confer those powers on national courts;[333] they must derive, if at all, from the State's national law. Much debated on the other hand, is the extent to which, in certain cases, Brussels has, firstly, the power to forbid such practices and, secondly, has exercised that power.[334]

The Brussels instruments are generally understood to apply when at least two Member States are significantly connected with the dispute (*intra* Union disputes). Whether international disputes with connections to only one Brussels member also fall within the instruments' scope is disputed. Some argue that they apply when the defendant is, as in *Harrods*,[335] a domiciliary of a Member State.[336] In all events in *Harrods*, other than the United Kingdom, the only States significantly connected with the case were Argentina and Switzerland.[337] The English Court of Appeal, in those circumstances, reached the conclusion that the case did not fall within the Convention's scope.[338]

---

333   See, e.g. R. Brand, "Comparative Forum non Conveniens and the Hague Convention on Jurisdiction and Judgments", 37 *Tex. Int'l L.J.* 467, at 489 (2002).

334   See, e.g., Ch. Erwand, *Forum non conveniens und EuGVÜ*, 214-222 (Frankfurt/Main, Peter Lang, 1995); P. Huber, *Die englische forum non conveniens-Doktrin und ihre Anwendung im Rahmen des Europäischen Gerichtsstands- und Vollstreckungsübereinkommens* (Berlin, Duncker & Humblot, 1994); Ch. Thiele, "Forum non conveniens im Lichte europäischen Gemeinschaftsrechts", 48 *RIW* 696-700 (2002).

335   Harrods was, however, not a defendant in the sense that the plaintiff was demanding substantive relief from the company; the minority shareholder was seeking a winding up of the company more favorable for it than that urged by the majority shareholder.

336   See, e.g., Kropholler, *supra* footnote 181, before Art. 2, No. 8; Huber, *supra* footnote 334, at 197; Thiele, *supra* footnote 334, at 698.

337   Had the Lugano Convention been in force at the time, its linkage with the Brussels Convention might have been relevant on the scope issue.

338   See *In Re Harrods*, [1992] Ch. at 97-98 (CA 1991).

The situation in *Owusu* differs in important respects from that in *Harrods*. In the first place, the plaintiff and one of the six defendants were domiciled in England; the other five defendants were Jamaicans. The controversy was, as in *Harrods*, connected with only *one* Member State and the plaintiff and one defendant were *both* domiciled in that State. These facts ground for some commentators an argument that did not arise in *Harrods*: the Convention must apply in light of an alleged Brussels policy to ensure all Union plaintiffs the availability of the most appropriate forum of all – the defendant's domicile.[339]

This line of argument to ground Convention jurisdiction over the English defendant is problematic on two scores. The *Owusu* litigation can be seen, so far as the English plaintiff and defendant are concerned, as either international or domestic but not intra-Union in nature so that arguably[340] the Convention does not apply.[341] Secondly, the involvement of non-Union defendants and the non-Union forum could well support a consolidation of the litigation in Jamaica. If so, arguably, the policy of assuring the English plaintiff of a predictable forum that can not fine tune its exercise of adjudicatory authority should, in the circumstances, perhaps yield to the desirability of consolidating the litigation to avoid possibly conflicting judgments.[342]

To the extent that the Brussels instruments apply to the litigation in issue, what answers have been – or should be – given to the question whether a measure of fine-tuning through the giving of *forum non conveniens* stays is permissible? In discussing the question, one should bear in mind that the Brussels instruments, if they speak to the issue at all, do so by their silence. The problem never occurred to the drafters of the Convention; as already remarked, in none of the original Member States did courts grant such stays.

Analysis is further complicated because the Brussels instruments use the term "jurisdiction" which is ambiguous as applied to *forum non conveniens* stays. A common-law jurist does not see granting a *forum non conveniens* stay as a court's refusal to exercise its adjudicatory authority but as an effort to elicit an-

---

339   The Brussels instruments consider the basic and preferable ground of adjudicatory authority to be the defendant's domicile; other jurisdictional grounds provided by the instruments are characterized as "special" and are, *unlike* domicile, not to be given an expansive interpretation. See Chap. IV., pp. 157-158, *supra*.

340   Some jurists take the view that the Convention applies to purely domestic cases but normally is not invoked because there is no need to determine whether the local court is exercising adjudicatory authority under the Convention, under domestic rules, or under both. See Peter F. Schlosser, EU-Zivilprozessrecht, Art. 2 EuGVVO, No. 5 (Munich, C. H. Beck, 2nd ed., 2003); Thiele, *supra* footnote 334, at 698.

341   See, e.g. Schack, *supra* footnote 5, at 88, No. 239.

342   Consolidation is permitted by Article 6 (1) of the Brussels instruments when the defendant is domiciled in a Member State "where he is one of a number of defendants, in the courts for the place where any one of them is domiciled". Since the only defendant domiciled in a Member State is English, there seems no Union policy applicable to the Jamaican defendants that requires an extreme bootstrapping effort. But see Thiele, *supra* footnote 334, at 700.

other legal system's collaboration in the carrying out of that task. This effort may fail, in which event the court will exercise its full adjudicatory authority. Where the effort succeeds, in many cases the referring court will resolve certain aspects of the controversy either by decision or by requiring that stipulations be given on various issues. The court making a *forum non conveniens* referral thus typically decides a significant part of the controversy with which it was seized.

The Brussels instruments, quite understandably, have no terminology that covers the jurisdictional situation created when a *forum non conveniens* stay is granted. The referring court clearly exercises adjudicatory authority, albeit in a perhaps more complex and less predictable fashion than would its civil-law counterpart. What takes place is not well captured by the term "jurisdiction" alone; elements that can, for lack of a better term, be characterized as "procedure" are also present.

In these circumstances, it is difficult to say the silence of the Brussels instruments either permits or prohibits fine-tuning through *forum non conveniens* stays. Perhaps the only question that should be put at this stage in the Union's development is whether, at least for the relatively limited class of controversies discussed, each national legal system should not be able to order *forum non conveniens* stays in accordance with that legal system's practices. Do not the proportionality[343] and subsidiarity[344] principles support the proposition that continuation of a nation's traditional practices in such matters is desirable? Furthermore, are the UK courts not right that aspects of their administration of justice will be adversely affected[345] if this important fine-tuning instrument is no longer available?

Generally speaking, does not *forum non conveniens* provide a control over national-court litigation that is needed by legal systems which provide wide-ranging discovery, contingent-fee arrangements, jury trial, and generous damages quantification? The courts of these systems need protection from forum-shopping where, but for these advantages, the action would have been brought elsewhere.[346] It is telling that the *forum non conveniens* doctrine has been adopted principally by common-law jurisdictions – which provide the aforesaid attractions – and only rarely by civil-law jurisdictions. Discretionary control over litigation is far more pressing concern in common-law countries than in their civil-law counterparts. Do not these fundamental differences in the administration of justice in common- and civil-law courts give the former, at least where the action does not trench on clearly applicable Brussels' policies, a raison d'être for *forum non conveniens* stays that the latter lack.

---

343   See Lenaerts and van Nuffel, *supra* footnote 259, at 109-114, Nos. 5-036-5-044.

344   See EC Treaty Art. 5 para. 2 (*ex* Art. 3b) and *idem* 99-106, Nos. 4-042-4-049. See also Article III-11 (3) of the European Constitution.

345   See pp. 330 *et seq., supra.*

346   See pp. 277-278, *supra.*

(b)   Antisuit injunctions
(i)   *Introductory*

The Brussels instruments could, had their drafters so desired, have provided for either full fledged antisuit injunctions directed against national courts of Union States or for antisuit injunctions aimed at parties. Absent agreement between sovereign parties, the doctrine of sovereignty forbids direct interference in the administration of justice in a State or nation. Indirect interference through orders addressing parties are tolerated in considerable measure.

The Brussels instruments do not, of course, authorize common-law style antisuit injunctions against the courts of other Union States nor against parties to litigations – present of future – in those courts. The civil-law nations that drafted the Convention of 1968 were wedded to the principle of sovereignty; their courts lacked, in addition, the technical instrument – contempt powers – which deflects the sovereignty objection. Indeed, the traditions and practices of all except the Union's common-law jurisdictions strongly oppose the issuance of antisuit injunctions.

The evolution of the European Union has been such that the sovereignty doctrine has by now lost much of its force with respect to intra-Union matters. The Union, if it were so inclined, could authorize the courts of a Member State to enjoin, in certain situations, the claiming and exercising of adjudicatory authority by the courts of another Member State. In the absence of a fully developed system of Union courts, granting such authority to national courts could fill gaps – and thus reinforce – the Brussels system in ways that would arguably benefit the system as a whole. Any such effort is probably doomed to fail because, in the long run, it would require utilization by all national courts of such injunctions to ensure that the appropriate national court would adjudicate the controversy in question. The *Turner* case illustrates one situation in which a general power of national courts to issue antisuit injunctions could be justified.

(ii)   **Turner v. Grovit and Others**[347]

The *Turner* case presents the issue whether it is permissible to use antisuit injunctions to fine tune in litigation involving the same or closely connected actions before the courts of two – or more – Member States.[348] On 2 March 1998, Turner had commenced proceedings in the industrial (later the employment) tribunal in London asserting claims for unfair and wrongful dismissal.[349] Three days thereafter, his employer formally notified him that his contract had been terminated.

---

347   [2001] UKHL 65 (HL 2001) referring question of interpretation to the European Court of Justice; [2000] QB 345 (CA 1999).

348   The Spanish court could have stayed its proceedings or declined jurisdiction under Article 22 of the Convention (see pp. 298-300, *supra*) to consolidate the proceedings in the English court. The English court seeks, through the antisuit injunction, to reach the same result.

349   See (2000) QB 245 (CA 1999), at 353.

Some seven months later, the employer brought an action against Turner for breach of contract in the courts of Madrid, Spain.

> Neither ... [the] contents [of the statement of the claim], nor any of the documents annexed to it, gave the Spanish court the least indication of the terms of the ruling on jurisdiction which had been made by the [London] employment tribunal the previous month.[350]

Had the Spanish court known of the pending English proceedings, it would have been required to stay the proceedings under Article 21 of the Convention.[351]

Turner did not appear in the Spanish proceedings but sought from the English court in December

> an injunction to restrain Mr. Grovit and Harada [Turner's employer] from procuring C.S.A. [a related company] to continue, and to restrain C.S.A. itself from continuing, the action in the Madrid court.[352]

Turner argued

> that the Spanish claim ... [was] effectively an abuse of process designed to place him under financial pressure by making him defend himself in Spain in proceedings in which he is obliged to employ a local lawyer, [and] that in fact the proceedings are baseless ....[353]

The Court of Appeal took the position that, where

> proceedings had been launched in another Brussels Convention jurisdiction for no purpose other than to harass and oppress a party who is already a litigant here, the English court possesses the power to prohibit by injunction the plaintiff in the other jurisdiction from continuing the foreign process.[354]

Laws L.J. further remarked:

> The court's power to protect its own process by the grant of an antisuit injunction is not in my judgment confined, in the Brussels Convention context, to a case where the

---

350   *Ibid.*

351   For a discussion of the *lis pendens* rule in Article 21 of the Convention – Article 27 of the Regulation – see pp. 298, *supra*. The official French version of Article 21 uses more explicit language than the English version (see p. 298, *supra*): "Lorsque des demandes ayant le même objet et la même cause" replaces "cause of action".

352   *Idem* 351.

353   *Idem* 353.

354   *Idem* 357.

English court or tribunal has established jurisdiction under article 21[355], or plainly possesses exclusive jurisdiction as for instance under article 17[356]. If it were so confined, it would not be a general power to prevent abuse of process at all: it would be a restricted power exercisable only to protect or vindicate the Brussels Convention rules as to jurisdiction. But the English court's right and duty to prevent abuse is inherent and at large. It could only be restricted by statute. In my judgment there is nothing in the Brussels Convention (which, of course, by virtue of the executive provisions of the Act of 1982, as amended, constitutes domestic statute law), which imposes any such restriction. Mr. Hickey for the plaintiff suggested that article 24, which I have set out, assists his case for an injunction. I entertain some doubt as to that; I consider that the primary focus of article 24 is to allow the courts of one state to take interim measures, such as the grant of a freezing injunction, so as to protect the integrity and efficacy of proceedings even though another state has jurisdiction in relation to them. I would rest my view of the power to prevent abuse by an antisuit injunction on the inherent jurisdiction of the English court[357] ....

[Moreover,] C.S.A. failed – and it can only have been done deliberately – to inform the Spanish court of the [London] tribunal's ruling, or of the fact that any jurisdictional issue had arisen in the tribunal. If the proceedings in Madrid were brought in good faith, it seems to me simply obvious that C.S.A. would have made clear to the court at the outset that there was an extant ruling to the effect that an English tribunal had jurisdiction to decide whether the plaintiff had been wrongly or unfairly dismissed in the very same factual context as it, C.S.A., was deploying in the Spanish proceedings. In fact, although as I have said it annexed to the statement of claim Form IT1 and the plaintiff's witness statement made for his application to the tribunal (but *not* Harada's Form IT3), the text of its pleading where that application was described was in my judgment seriously misleading .... [358]

The Court concluded that

[t]he documents [presented to it] lead to the ineluctable conclusion that ... the Spanish proceedings were intended and intended only to oppress the plaintiff and as such fall to be condemned as abusive as a matter of elementary principle.[359]

---

355 See p. 298, *supra*.

356 See also Article 23 – Article 29 of the Regulation – which provides that "[w]here actions come within the exclusive jurisdiction of several courts, any court other than the court first seized shall decline jurisdiction in favor of that court".

357 [2000] QB at 358.

358 *Idem* 358-359.
    The court characterized as well other portions of the defendant's presentation to the Spanish court in highly uncomplimentary terms: "a plain lie in paragraph 33 of ... [Grovit's] affidavit; "[n]o less mendacious"; "whose vice is compounded by its evasiveness"; "[i]t is inconceivable that this was unknown to Mr. Grovit when he swore his affidavit [for the Spanish court]". *Idem* 361-362.

359 *Idem* 362.

Laws L.J. concluded his opinion by assuring the Spanish court that granting

> injunctive relief in favor of the plaintiff entails not the slightest disrespect to the Span-
> ish court. It is of course elementary that there is no question of our requiring that
> court to do or refrain from anything. I consider that the grant of relief would under-
> pin and support the proper application of the Brussels Convention, to which, it goes
> without saying, the Spanish courts are as loyal as are those of this jurisdiction.[360]

The Appeals Committee of the House of Lords granted, on terms, the defendants'
petition for leave to appeal.[361] On 13 December 2001 the House of Lords referred
the following question, respecting *Turner* v. *Grovit and Others*,[362] to the European
Court of Justice:

> Is it inconsistent with the Convention on Jurisdiction and the Enforcement of Judg-
> ments in Civil and Commercial Matters signed at Brussels on 27 September 1968
> (subsequently acceded to by the United Kingdom) for the courts of the United King-
> dom to grant restraining orders against defendants who are threatening to commence
> or continue legal proceedings in another Convention country when those defendants
> are acting in bad faith with the intent and purpose of frustrating or obstructing pro-
> ceedings properly before the English court?[363]

The reference contained as well a statement of facts,[364] an explanation of reasons
that led to the reference being cast in the terms quoted above,[365] and a discussion
of the legal nature of "antisuit" injunctions:[366]

> When an English court makes a restraining order, it is making an order which is ad-
> dressed only to a party which is before it. The order is not directed against the foreign
> court ... .[367]

The Court of Justice delivered its judgment on 27 April 2004.[368] Following the
recommendations of the Advocate General it held that an antisuit injunction, enjoining a litigant not to initiate or further pursue proceedings in another Member State was incompatible with the Brussels Convention even when the party to
which the injunction was addressed was acting in bad faith with a view to frus-

---

360 *Idem* 364.
361 *Ibid.*
362 [2001] UKHL 65 (HL 2001).
363 *Idem*, No. 21.
364 *Idem*, Nos. 4-19.
365 *Idem*, No. 20.
366 See *idem*, Nos. 22-23.
367 *Idem*, No. 23.
368 Case C-159/02, [2004] ECR I-3565.

trating the existing proceedings. In its reasoning the Court availed itself of the arguments usually put forward against the use of antisuit injunctions in an EU-context:

> ... the Convention is necessarily based on the trust which the Contracting States accord to one another's legal systems and judicial institutions. It is that mutual trust which has enabled a compulsory system of jurisdiction to be established, which all the courts within the purview of the Convention are required to respect, and as a corollary the waiver by those States of the right to apply their internal rules on recognition and enforcement of foreign judgments in favour of a simplified mechanism for the recognition and enforcement of judgments."[369]

The Court continued:

> It is inherent in that principle of mutual trust that, within the scope of the Convention, the rules on jurisdiction that it lays down, which are common to all the courts of the Contracting States, may be interpreted and applied with the same authority by each of them .... Similarly, otherwise than in a small number of exceptional cases listed in the first paragraph of Article 28 of the Convention ... the Convention does not permit the jurisdiction of a court to be reviewed by a court in another Contracting State .... However, a prohibition imposed by a court, backed by a penalty, restraining a party from commencing or continuing proceedings before a foreign court undermines the latter court's jurisdiction to determine the dispute. Any injunction prohibiting a claimant from bringing such an action must be seen as constituting interference with the jurisdiction of the foreign court which, as such, is incompatible with the system of the Convention.[370]

The Court rejected the proposition that the interference would only be indirect, since the granting of the injunction still implied an assessment of the appropriateness of bringing proceedings in a foreign court, which was only for that court to make. Even if the injunction would be regarded as a mere procedural measure, the Court pointed out, it had to be borne in mind that, according to the decision in *Hagen*, national procedural rules could not be applied in such a way as to impair the effectiveness of the Convention. Finally, the Court rejected the view that antisuit injunctions would minimize the risk of conflicting decisions and avoid multiplicity of proceedings as this would undermine the special provisions on *lis pendens* and related proceedings.[371]

---

369 *Idem*, para. 24.

370 *Idem*, paras. 25-28.

371 See for a detailed account of the *Turner* v. *Grovit* see A. Briggs, "Anit-Suit Injunctions and Utopian Ideals", 120 *L.Q.R.* 529-533 (2004); A. Dutta and Ch. Heinze, "Prozessführungsverbote im englischen und europäischen Zivilverfahrensrecht", *ZEuP* 2005, 428-458; J. Krause, "Turner/Grovit – Der EuGH erklärt Prozessführungsverbote für unvereinbar mit dem EuGVÜ", 50 *RIW* 533-541 (2004); Th. Kruger, "The Anti-Suit

All in all, the Court disapproved of the use of antisuit injunctions under the Brussels Convention. And although the question referred to by the House of Lords was framed rather narrowly, pertaining only to so-called abuse-of-process cases and not those cases, more frequent in practice, where an antisuit injunction is issued to enforce or safeguard an English forum selection or arbitration clause, the comprehensive language of the answer makes it evident that the Court disapproved of antisuit injunctions generally, thus, in effect, eliminating this remedy in intra-EU cases.[372]

(iii) Are antisuit injunctions compatible with the Brussels instruments?

By their very nature, antisuit injunctions are more problematic than are *forum non conveniens* stays or dismissals. The latter involve a measure of co-operation between legal orders; the former can be seen as gratuitous interference by one legal order with the workings of another.[373] In the Brussels context, there are structural considerations that should preclude in certain situations the use of such injunctions. For example, a court second seized of a matter has little, if any, basis under Brussels for asserting a right to enjoin on-going proceedings in the court first seized. Injunctions find some structural support, however, where a Brussels-State court does not respect an exclusive jurisdiction provided by a Brussels instrument,[374] an arbitration

---

Injunction in the European Judicial Space: Turner v. Grovit", 53 *Int'l. & Comp. L. Q.* 1030-1040 (2004); Th. Rauscher, "Unzulässigkeit einer anti-suit injunction unter Brüssel I", 24 *IPRax* 405-405 (2004).

372   To this effect also A. Briggs, *supra* footnote 371, at 529; Dutta and Heinze, *supra* footnote 371, at 458; Krause, *supra* footnote 371, at 539-541; Rauscher, *supra* footnote 371, at 408-409.

373   See p. 279, *supra*.

374   See *Bank* v. *Aeakos Compania Naviera*, [1994] 1 I. L. Pr. 413 (CA 1993); see also Dicey and Morris, *supra* footnote 56, at 447, No. 12-127. The exclusive jurisdictions in question are set out above. See *supra* Chap. V. footnote 208.

agreement,[375] a forum-selection clause,[376] or *lis pendens* rules.[377] In these contexts, the Brussels instruments are defective in the sense that they do not provide robust procedures to protect the rules and principles that the instruments establish. The response to the question referred by the House of Lords to the Court of Justice in *Turner* v. *Grovit and Others* should at least begin to make clear whether, in its approach to the fine-tuning issue discussed above, the European Union is capable of appreciating and tolerating different values and approaches that are, instrumentally speaking, compatible with the structure of, and the overall goals pursued by, the Brussels instruments.

The contention that the English courts took actions in violation of the spirit of Brussels is considerably stronger in *Turner* v. *Grovit* than in *Harrods*. The former invokes an antisuit injunction, in its nature more aggressive and intrusive than an invocation of the *forum non conveniens* doctrine. Nevertheless, it is arguable that, in certain circumstances, it is proper for a court of a European Union State to enjoin a party from prosecuting an action in the courts of another Union State. The disquiet that antisuit injunctions arise in civil-law courts derives from the relative lack of control that courts in the civil-law tradition have over the conduct of litigants before them. The procedural law of contemporary civil-law systems does not provide effective sanctions for abuses of process by conduct such as

---

375 Article 1 (4) of the Brussels instruments excludes arbitration from the scope of the Convention and the Regulation.

In *Marc Rich* v. *Società Italiana Impianti* – Case C-190/89, [1991] ECR I-3855, responding to questions respecting Article 1 (4)'s interpretation put by the British Court of Appeal, the Court of Justice replied in part that where

> by virtue of its subject-matter, such as the appointment of an arbitrator, a dispute falls outside the scope of the convention, the existence of a preliminary issue which the court must resolve in order to determine the dispute cannot, whatever that issue may be, justify application of the convention.

Idem 3902.

The Court of Justice later qualified its 1991 response; the arbitration exclusion does not extend to assumptions of jurisdiction challenged on *jurisdictional* grounds. See Kropholler, *supra* footnote 181, Art. 1, No. 44; *Van Uden Maritime BV, trading as Van Uden Africa Line* v. *Kommanditgesellschaft in Firma Deco-Line and Another* – Case C-391/95, [1998] ECR I-7091, at 7131 ("Where the parties have *validly* excluded the jurisdiction of the courts in a dispute arising under a contract and have referred that dispute to arbitration, there are no courts of any State that have jurisdiction as to the *substance* of the case for the purposes of the Convention") (emphasis added).

The issue whether the Brussels Convention applied and rendered impermissible the issuance of an antisuit injunction in support of an agreement to arbitrate was referred to the Court of Justice in 1997. The parties settled the case before the Court rendered a decision. See *Toepfer International GmbH* v. *Société Cargill, France*, [1998] 1 Lloyd's Rep. 379 (CA 1997).

376 See Schlosser, *supra* footnote 340, Art. 34-36 EuGVVO, No. 5. But see Ch. Thiele, "Antisuit injunctions im Lichte europäischen Gemeinschaftsrechts", 48 *RIW* 383, at 386 (2002).

377 See Lenenbach, *supra* footnote 89, at 311-312.

occurred in *Turner* v. *Grovit*. But should the absence of a procedural counterpart in itself be a sufficient reason to prohibit the practice of another Union State that is in significant respects compatible with – indeed supportive of – the Brussels system?

Systematically speaking, enjoining *Grovit* and company from further proceeding in Spain is consistent with the policies pursued by the Brussels instruments through *lis pendens*. The civil-law tradition does not countenance the use by its courts of contempt powers. But this inhibition should not require courts with other traditions to follow suit where their tradition allows action supportive of the basic rules and principles contained in the Brussels instruments. It is appropriate to "regard [as Brussels does,] the political goal of institutional harmony as paramount" but, when institutional harmony is not threatened, room should be found to recognize "the justice of the case ...".[378]

F.   Judicial Fine-tuning: Comparative Reflections

The approaches of (purely) civil-law jurisdictions, on the one hand, and common-law and mixed jurisdictions, on the other, to *forum non conveniens* and antisuit injunctions are markedly different. The former, by and large, use neither; both are, with varying frequency, utilized by the latter.

To some extent, the differences in practices can be explained on the ground that common-law jurisdictions, as exemplified by the English and American, have traditionally tended to claim adjudicatory authority in the international sense more aggressively and broadly than have those civil-law jurisdictions that approach adjudicatory authority over non-local controversies along the general lines of the German system.[379] With the rise of *specific* jurisdiction[380] in the United States after the Supreme Court's 1945 decision in *State of Washington* v. *International Shoe*,[381] which launched an instrumental approach to adjudicatory authority in the international sense, American jurisdictional theory became even more embracive and, in the view of some, more aggressive. Neither *forum non conveniens* nor antisuit injunctions are exclusively twentieth-century institutions and practices;[382] their practical significance and importance increased dramatically, however, during the century's second half, in England as well as the United States.

---

378   Cf. T. Hartley, "Antisuit Injunctions and the Brussels Jurisdiction and Judgment Convention", 49 *Int'l. & Comp. LQ* 166, at 170 (2000). But see Thiele, *supra* footnote 376, at 385-386.

379   Traditionally, Germany has been significantly less aggressive in its claims of adjudicatory authority than have civil-law systems in the French tradition; the latter claim, for example, general jurisdiction over non-local controversies where either the plaintiff or the defendant is a national. See Chap. III., pp. 158-161, *supra*.

380   See Chap. III. A. 4., pp. 97 *et seq.*, *supra*.

381   328 US 310 (1945).

382   See pp. 270 and 281 respectively, *supra*.

As English and American theory and practice respecting the assertion of adjudicatory authority opened new vistas, the need increased to "fine tune" jurisdictional practices. Comparably dramatic and pervasive changes in jurisdictional theory and practice have not occurred in continental Europe. Arguably, the French system – in light of its very aggressive claims of adjudicatory authority based on the French nationality of either party – had a real need at least for *forum non conveniens*. That need had, however, arisen long before the doctrine or antisuit injunctions were employed by either English or American courts. On the other hand, the emergence in the second half of the twentieth century of what is now the European Union reduced the need for jurisdictional fine-tuning in continental Europe. Moreover, as Lord Goff of Chieveley remarked in his opinion in *Airbus Industrie G.I.E.* v. *Patel*[383]

> [o]n the continent of Europe, in the early days of the European Community, the essential need was seen to be to avoid ... clash[es] between member states of the same community. [This need led to the Brussels Convention which] allocated [jurisdiction] on the basis of well-defined rules.[384]

Common-law jurists, except in relationships to which a Brussels instrument applies, face, as Lord Goff put it, "a jungle of separate, broadly based, jurisdictions all over the world",[385] whose "potential excesses ... are generally curtailed by the adoption of the principle of *forum non conveniens* – a self-denying ordinance ..."[386] The approaches of the civil- and common-law worlds to fine-tuning are indeed "the fruit of a distinctive legal history, and also reflect to some extent cultural differences ..."[387]

A simplistic explanation for current practices respecting *forum non conveniens* and antisuit injunctions may suffice to explain the position taken by civil-law jurisdictions generally. Fine-tuning is undertaken at the expense of administrability and predictability; its use by common-law and rejection by civil-law jurisdictions is but one expression of the relative weight that each assigns to these values when they conflict with other procedural values. As Trevor Hartley puts it with respect to antisuit injunctions:[388]

> The question is ... whether the institutional value of harmony between courts should prevail over the more personal value of justice in the individual case. Most lawyers in the common-law world would say that individual justice should prevail; civilian lawyers, on the other hand, might see things differently.

---

383 [1999] 1 AC 119 (HL 1998).

384 *Idem* 131-132.

385 *Idem* 132.

386 *Ibid.*

387 *Idem* 131.

388 Hartley, *supra* footnote 378, at 171.

No single approach to fine-tuning is optimal. Courts face two dangers: the Scylla of imposing their own standards of litigational justice on the world, and the Charybdis of being blind not only to the problematic of applying their standards to a particular case but also to the legitimate concerns of other systems with an interest in the case. A middle way should be found.[389] If *forum non conveniens* is confined to cases where the other forum is clearly more appropriate, over the long run relatively little predictability is lost as plaintiffs have, from the start, the opportunity to bring their actions in the more appropriate forum. The increased predictability that results from acceptance of the "clearly more appropriate" standard could well channel litigation to that forum without the need to invoke *forum non conveniens*.

Turning to antisuit injunctions, clearly more restrictive standards than those utilized for *forum non conveniens* should, in principle, be employed; clashes between different courts are possible and the court that initially enjoins can in many – but not all – cases[390] be seen as arrogation of supremacy. The party's behaviour in bringing an action elsewhere should be highly and improperly vexatious to the adversary before enjoining proceedings abroad is considered.

---

389   A thoughtful and innovative effort to find a "middle way" for determining the priority of competing actions within an international system is the London/Leuven Principles, *supra* footnote 145.

390   See the discussion pp. 281-282, *supra*.

Part 3

Epilogue

Chapter VII Convergence and Compromise in Private International Law: The Role of International Instruments

A. Introductory

1. Legal Cultures and Their Interpenetration

Comparative study of any, or all, of private international law's branches – jurisdiction, choice of law, and recognition and enforcement of foreign judgments – requires consideration of the cultural, moral, economic, political, and social contexts that, as they change over time, shape – and reshape – a society and its legal order. Change may occur rapidly or slowly; it may reinforce a society's elements of uniqueness or cause diverse societies to converge. Seen in a broad perspective, the civil-law and common-law traditions have each maintained their integrity for a period roughly corresponding to the second millennium of the Christian era. In the course of the third millennium, however, these two traditions may well interpenetrate and create one – or several – new legal traditions.

During the second millennium, system interpenetration has, of course, occurred on many occasions and in many respects. The rise of a *lex mercatoria*, resting not on local laws, but on shared practices and usages of merchants, was an early form of interpenetration. Anational international commercial arbitration, based on the United Nations Convention on the Recognition and Enforcement of Foreign Arbitral Awards of 1958, provides a late twentieth-century example of a not altogether different phenomenon.

Greater interpenetration clearly must result from the enormous increase in cross-border and inter-system activity that has occurred in the last half century as well as the related willingness of most legal systems to give increasing recognition to private autonomy by both tempering mandatory rules of law and allowing parties greater freedom to choose the forum in which to litigate and the law to be applied. New technology in the form of the Internet has created strong incentives for harmonization to promote economic efficiency. Indeed, convergence in many areas of law will come about through the working of the market place if the philosophy of a free, unregulated market prospers globally.

Convergence between case-law and codified systems could take place as well because of the tension between the claims of system and structure, on the one hand, and of just, fact-specific solutions, on the other. Each perspective has a contribution to make to a wise and humane system of justice. As the values in tension are incommensurate, no permanent balance is likely to be struck; accordingly an element of instability exists on both sides of the equation that can cause one system to move closer to – or retreat from – another system's position.

The experience of the twentieth century strongly suggests that, as societies and economies become increasingly complex and inter-related, legal orders will draw more than in the past on both the civil-law and the common-law traditions in thinking about law and its administration. At the level of method and style, the number of legal orders no longer squarely in either the codification- or the case-law tradition has increased; at the same time, these systems have become more complex. The twenty-first century may well witness a continuation of these developments. The European Union has brought about a confrontation of the civil law, the common law, and the mixed Scottish and Scandinavian systems. Will this combination result in a new system that blends in an original fashion these disparate legal traditions?

2.   The Twentieth Century and Globalization

In the course of the twentieth century, cross-border activity in most, if not all, areas of social, intellectual, and commercial activity increased significantly in both volume and intensity. Our lives as individuals, as members of groups and associations economic, political, and social in nature, as citizens of nations, and as members of the human race have become increasingly "delocalized". In many respects, we lead far more globalized lives than our forefathers did when the nineteenth century ended.

These changes in our world's infrastructure and conditions of living have profoundly affected almost every aspect of our existence. The problems created and the forces released have many consequences, some profound – others trivial, some conflicting – others harmonious or convergent. These developments have led to international efforts to regulate various aspects of the rules and practices of private international law including those that address jurisdiction to adjudicate and recognition and enforcement of foreign judgments.

In its nature, private international law is concerned with contexts in which two or more legal orders have a significant stake. Efforts to provide mechanisms for handling controversies respecting such matters began in ancient times and have continued ever since. Interest in establishing, through multilateral international instruments, various rules and practices of private international law grew in the last half of the nineteenth century. One consequence was the creation in 1893 of the Hague Conference on Private International Law. Efforts to "conventionalize" areas of private international law have continued throughout the twentieth century; its closing decades saw the entrance into force of the United Nations Convention on the Recognition and Enforcement of Foreign Arbitral Awards of 1958, the European Union's Brussels Convention on jurisdiction and the enforcement of judgments in civil and commercial matters of 1968, and the Lugano Convention of 1988. In the century's last decade, the Hague Conference began work on a worldwide convention on jurisdiction and the recognition and enforcement of foreign judgments.

B.   The Task of Achieving Convergence and Harmonization

1.   *The Design of International Instruments: Single, Mixed, and Double Conventions*

Traditionally, treaties dealing with jurisdiction and enforcement matters were single; they regulated recognition and enforcement – indirect jurisdiction – but not direct jurisdiction.[1] Not until the second half of the twentieth century, do double conventions – treaties that address both jurisdiction to adjudicate and recognition and enforcement of foreign judgments – appear. The pioneering multilateral double convention was the United Nations Convention on the Recognition and Enforcement of Foreign Arbitral Awards of 1958.[2] Despite its title, the New York Convention regulates not only recognition, but also jurisdiction to adjudicate.

---

1   A single convention regulates, as its name indicates, only one subject, either that of the rendering court's adjudicatory authority or the court addressed's obligation to enforce. Conceptually, a single convention could be drafted dealing solely with either term in the equation. Single conventions, subject possibly to rare exceptions, address the second term, enforcement. A single convention that addresses the first term could reduce for its adherents the "free loader" problem that arises when some legal orders assert claims of adjudicatory authority while others exercise greater self-restraint by forbidding the use of dubious bases. But, when one must choose between this approach and regulating enforcement, modest prevention of "free loading" by others is less attractive than ensuring recognition abroad of certain categories of judgments rendered by one's courts. This is especially so if little agreement exists as to what constitutes exorbitant bases.

A convention that regulates one term in the binary jurisdictional equation strongly and the other weakly, qualifies conceptually as a double convention where both terms are directly regulated to a non-trivial degree. The Hague Convention on Choice of Court of 25 November 1965 is highly unusual in that it can be seen as either a single convention, regulating only the consequences of forum selection clauses for the court of origin's adjudicatory authority, or as a double convention that also requires Contracting States to recognize foreign judgments, based on choice-of-forum clauses that meet the Convention's standards, on terms no less favorable than those applied to comparable judgments grounded on other bases of adjudicatory authority that satisfy the State's jurisdictional test for enforcement. The Hague Conference's Permanent Bureau sees the 1965 Convention as "only provid[ing] for jurisdiction". Hague Conference on Private International Law, General Affairs, Prel. Doc., No. 16 (February 2002) (English and French texts), at 8, footnote 8. This characterization leaves out of account the Convention's Article 8 which provides that the decision of "a chosen court ... shall be recognized and enforced in other contracting States in accordance with the rules for the recognition and enforcement of foreign judgments in force in those States".

2   See Chap. V. E. 4., pp. 256 *et seq., supra.*

In 1968, the first convention to deal broadly with both jurisdiction and recognition appeared, the Brussels Convention on jurisdiction and the enforcement of judgments in civil and commercial matters[3]. As a full-fledged double convention must, Brussels requires that certain bases of jurisdiction be made available, prohibits the use of all other jurisdictional bases, and mandates that all judgments rendered on convention-required bases be, subject to certain prescribed defenses, recognized and enforced in all States party to the convention.

Single and double conventions lie at the two extremes of a spectrum. The former are appropriate where the States party do not have strong political and economic commitments *inter se* and their views and practices respecting recognition and enforcement of foreign adjudications diverge in significant respects. The latter are feasible where the legal orders concerned share comparable legal traditions and cultures *or* where economic and political considerations that favor participation are strong enough to overcome relevant objections, based on divergences between, on the one hand, the particular State's legal tradition and culture and, on the other, the tradition and values that infuse the package of rules and principles which must be accepted by those who wish to become parties to the double convention in question.

Between single and double conventions fall mixed conventions. The flexibility and adaptability that such a convention can provide results from the division of adjudicatory authority, like Caesar's Gaul, into three parts: required, prohibited, and unregulated (permitted).

The mixed-convention design is appropriate where States have become to a significant extent economically and politically inter-dependent but do not aspire to political or economic union. Such instruments can combine elements of single and double conventions in various mixes depending on the degree of convergence that the States in question have reached with respect to the issues that the convention addresses.

Mixed conventions have an affinity with both single and double conventions. Like double conventions, they (1) proscribe the use of certain "exorbitant" jurisdictional bases and (2) prescribe that certain "required" bases be provided, which, when invoked, will entitle the resulting judgment to recognition and enforcement in States party to the convention. On the other hand, mixed – like single – conventions, recognize a third jurisdictional category whose use results in judgments that may, or may not, be recognized and enforced by the foreign court addressed.

---

3   Some federal systems, in particular the United States, have long provided functional approximations of double conventions. Technically, the American system specifies prohibited, but not required, bases; states may, but are not constitutionally required to, invoke jurisdiction if the claim of adjudicatory authority is constitutionally permissible. In American practice, constitutionally permitted bases can be seen as equivalent to required bases in the sense that, generally speaking, every state takes jurisdiction where the Constitution permits. States are, of course, required by the full faith and credit clause of the federal constitution to recognize and enforce sister-state judgments rendered on a constitutionally acceptable basis of adjudicatory authority.

A mixed convention cannot give as much definitive information as does a double convention. To the extent that it prescribes and proscribes principles and rules respecting direct and indirect jurisdiction, however, it clarifies and stabilizes international practice and assists plaintiffs and defendants alike in understanding the risks and opportunities faced in litigating international controversies.

2.   Regional Harmonization: The Brussels Convention

The Brussels Convention of 1968 initiated a new epoch in the effort to achieve convergence in matters of jurisdiction and enforcement. Unlike most previous harmonization efforts, Brussels is not a universal but a regional convention. It achieved a degree of harmonization and convergence respecting these matters far greater than any previous international instrument had obtained. In this the drafters were greatly assisted by the circumstance that the legal cultures of the six original Member States – Belgium, France, the Federal Republic of Germany, Italy, Luxembourg, and the Netherlands – had, in many respects, already been harmonized by historical forces.

The high degree of harmonization that the drafters of Brussels sought to – and did – achieve, would have been far more elusive had the United Kingdom, representing the common-law tradition, been at the negotiating table in Brussels.

Due ultimately to the gathering economic and political momentum of the movement towards a European federation, the Brussels mould, set in 1968, has proved to be unbreakable. States that had crafted a regional convention to advance an emerging economic and political union, had little need or incentive to strike meaningful compromises with States that, after 1973, aspired to join that union. The club offered admission only on a take-it-or-leave-it basis.

It should be noted, moreover, that regional conventions can provide an institutional advantage that universal conventions cannot offer. Because of their political cohesion, the former can establish tribunals to ensure the uniform application and interpretation of regional instruments. The European Economic Union, as it then was called, took advantage of this possibility by giving such authority in 1971 to the European Court of Justice by a Protocol to the Brussels Convention. In the course of the Hague Conference's work on various conventions, including the jurisdiction and recognition and enforcement convention, the institutional problems entailed in providing tribunals to ensure the uniform interpretation and application of a universal convention have been discussed at length. The practical and political difficulties that would have to be overcome to provide a tribunal to oversee the interpretation and application of Hague conventions seem, however, well nigh insurmountable.

3.   *Worldwide Harmonization: The Proposed Hague Convention on International Jurisdiction and Foreign Judgments*[4]

The story the Hague negotiations tell respecting harmonization and meaningful compromise is not yet complete. Work on a jurisdiction and enforcement convention began in October 1996, when the States represented at the Conference's Eighteenth Session decided "to include in the Agenda of the Nineteenth Session the question of jurisdiction, and recognition and enforcement of foreign judgements in civil and commercial matters".[5] What transpired between that October and the century's end is summarized in the Interim Text of June 2001 which compiles the results of Commission II's deliberation in June 2001 during the first stage of the Conference's Nineteenth Session. The text, prepared by the Permanent Bureau and the Co-reporters, is 35 pages in length, contains 192 footnotes, numerous bracketed provisions, and provisions with internal brackets, as well as many alternative provisions. A fair proportion of these signifiers of disagreement goes to drafting points rather than basic disagreement. Others represent, however, views that diverge significantly respecting the provision's basic approach or philosophy. Here the draft reveals deep seated divergence on basic issues. Instead of achieving harmony and striking, where harmonization proved to be an illusive goal, meaningful compromises, the drafters came to an impasse.

(a)   The project's initial stage
(i)   *The United States proposal for a mixed convention*

In the early 1990s, before proposing that the Hague Conference work on a mixed convention, the United States reached two conclusions: firstly, the proposed convention should not be limited, as was traditionally the case, to recognition and enforcement but should address as well jurisdiction to adjudicate; secondly, the convention should provide certain jurisdictional bases that could be invoked as of right and prohibit the use of certain other bases. In addition, permitted bases – that is bases neither required nor prohibited – should be recognized. The enforceability of judgments rendered on these bases would depend not upon the Convention but on the law of the State addressed. A number of publications

---

4   The author has been a member of the United States delegation from the beginning of the negotiations on the proposed Convention. The views expressed here are his own; they represent US policy, if at all, only coincidentally.

5   Final Act of the Eighteenth Session, Part B, No. 1, 35 *ILM* 1391, at 1405 (1996). For an account of another member of the US Delegation of the negotiations, see R. Brand, "Jurisdictional Common Ground: In Search of a Global Convention", in J. Nafziger and S. Symeonides (eds.), *Law and Justice in a Multi-State World: Essays in Honor of Arthur Taylor von Mehren* 11-32 (Ardsley, NY, Transnational Publishers, 2002). The story of The Hague effort's genesis and the negotiations that produced the interim text of June 2001 is told by the Co-Reporter, the late Peter Nygh, in "Arthur's Baby: The Hague Negotiations for a World-wide Judgments Convention". In *idem* 151-172.

sought to familiarize jurists in Europe, the United States, and elsewhere with the mixed-convention concept and the advantages it could offer.[6]

The United State's advocacy of the mixed-convention format rested on two considerations. Firstly, such a convention would provide, for plaintiffs and defendants alike, useful guidance and appropriate protection at the litigation, as well as the enforcement, stage. Secondly, a significant degree of divergence exists worldwide – and is likely to persist for the foreseeable future – with respect to a variety of issues regarding jurisdiction to adjudicate and recognition and enforcement of foreign judgments. Accordingly, a broadly acceptable convention would require compromises and have to accept divergences that a double convention could not accommodate. The binary conception on which the Brussels Convention rests – that only two jurisdictional categories are to be recognized, required and prohibited – was, in the United States' view, unworkable where the legal systems concerned disagreed on such basic issues as whether rules of adjudicatory authority should favor plaintiffs or defendants and judges have considerable or little discretion in exercising adjudicatory authority and recognizing foreign judgments.

(ii)   The Special Commission's preference for a double convention

Had the Hague's Special Commission both fully understood and accepted the concept of a mixed convention and sought to design one that could be widely acceptable, the negotiations at The Hague and their product might have been very different. From the beginning, however, most of the negotiators aspired to produce a double convention. Indeed, the 1996 recommendation that the Hague Conference take up the project "favored the preparation of a double Convention limiting itself, as do the Conventions of Brussels and Lugano, to bases for assuming jurisdiction which are accepted and those which are rejected".[7]

Not until 14 June 1999 – four days before the close of its fourth session – and then only in a half-hearted and technical sense did the Special Commission accept the mixed-convention format. At the Sixty-fifth Plenary Meeting of the

---

6   The author first discussed the mixed-convention approach in 1993: A. von Mehren, "Recognition of United States Judgments Abroad and Foreign Judgments in the United States", 57 *RabelsZ* 449, at 456-459 (1993), and further developed the proposal in "Recognition and Enforcement of Foreign Judgments: A New Approach for the Hague Conference?", 57 *Law & Contemp. Probs.* 271 (1994); "The Case for a Convention-mixte Approach to Jurisdiction to Adjudicate and Recognition and Enforcement of Foreign Judgments", 61 *RabelsZ* 86-92 (1997); "Remarks by Arthur T. von Mehren upon Receiving the 1997 Leonard J. Theberge Award for Private International Law", 31 *Int'l Lawyer* 722-727 (1997); and "Enforcing Judgments Abroad: Reflections on the Design of Recognition Conventions", 24 *Brooklyn J. Int'l L.* 17-29 (1998).

7   *Proceedings of the Eighteenth Session 30 September to 19 October 1996*, Vol I, *Miscellaneous Matters* 63, col. 2 (The Hague, SDU Publishers, 1999).

Special Commission, during the discussion that preceded the vote on Article 17 which addressed this fundamental issue,[8]

> [s]everal experts noted that the very fact of providing for jurisdictions based on national law indicated that the present negotiations were moving towards the conclusion of a mixed rather than a double convention. Several experts affirmed that they still aspired to a double convention: others noted, however, that it was merely being realistic to recognize that in a global context only a mixed convention could be achieved.[9]

From its start, the Special Commission worked in the shadow of two double conventions – Brussels and Lugano. In spirit and inspiration, the Commission's product was not a mixed convention but a close-knit double convention with none of the flexibility and room for development that a mixed convention could have provided.

The strong attraction that the double convention model had for so many of the negotiators at The Hague is explainable on many grounds. In the first place, well over half of the countries represented were parties to either the Brussels or the Lugano Convention or aspired to become members of the European Union. Secondly, Brussels and Lugano countries had a stake in enlarging the scope and influence of their instruments. Finally, Brussels and Lugano were both in force and appeared to be – and in many ways were – functioning very well. These circumstances seem to have mesmerized many delegations into assuming that the Brussels regional model was appropriate for a worldwide convention.

The circumstances that stood in the way of most delegations from Brussels and Lugano countries accepting the proposition that what was good for a regional convention was not necessarily good for a worldwide convention were reinforced by the limited role that creative compromises had played in the evolution of those Conventions. The Six had struck only a few compromises to accommodate the original member States. For example, domicile (Art. 2) and place of performance (Art. 5 (1)) were not defined in the convention but left to national law. Furthermore, when the United Kingdom acceded to the Convention in 1978, its special needs were accommodated in several instances; for example, although trusts are unknown to most civil-law systems, Article 17 allowed stipulations for exclusive jurisdiction over certain issues respecting a trust's administration. No place was found, however, for the Scottish doctrine of *forum non conveniens* nor was Brussels' strict *lis pendens* rule relaxed.

---

8   Article 17 provides:

> Subject to Articles 4, 5, 7, 8, 12 and 13, the Convention does not prevent the application by Contracting States of rules of jurisdiction under national law, provided that this is not prohibited under Article 18.

9   Report of Meeting, No. 65, at 1.

(b) Matters for which the Special Commission achieved a measure of harmonization or struck a meaningful compromise

From the beginning of its deliberations in 1996 the Special Commission devoted considerable time and energy to efforts to achieve convergence and harmonization in certain matters and to strike meaningful compromises in others. The areas addressed included: the provision of a modest *forum non conveniens* doctrine; qualification of the *lis pendens* principle where an action for a negative declaratory judgment is first-in-time; and enforceability of damage awards.

(i) Forum non conveniens

By the closing decades of the twentieth century, common-law jurisdictions had, for the most part, come to accept at least a moderate version of the doctrine of *forum non conveniens.* On the other hand, with few exceptions, civil-law jurisdictions still maintained their traditional hostility to courts exercising discretion with respect to the exercise of adjudicatory authority. The civil-law view prevailed in the Brussels Convention; the United Kingdom had come to the bargaining table too late to obtain a place for *forum non conveniens.*

The *forum non conveniens* doctrine raises a broad and fundamental issue: to what extent should a court seized have discretion to decline to exercise its adjudicatory authority in whole or in part in light of circumstances particular to the case before it? By the closing decades of the twentieth century, in many common-law jurisdictions judges were of the view that they had some discretion in exercising their adjudicatory authority. The degree of discretion varied significantly, however, from legal system to legal system. On the other hand, the civil-law tradition firmly opposed allowing judges to exercise any discretion. *Forum non conveniens* thus presented for the negotiators at The Hague an issue on which widely divergent views were held. Efforts to harmonize those views or to strike a true compromise did not succeed.

One solution considered in the effort to strike a compromise was to leave the issue of *forum non conveniens* to national law. Another was to include a harmonizing provision in the convention upon which all involved could agree. The latter approach prevailed but the compromise struck gives such modest scope for *forum non conveniens* that one must doubt its efficacy.

The Interim Text's Article 22, Exceptional circumstances, provides that

1. In exceptional circumstance, when the jurisdiction of the court seized is not founded on an exclusive choice of court agreement valid under Article 4, or on Article 7, 8 or 12, the court may, on application by a party, suspend the proceedings if in that case it is clearly inappropriate for that court to exercise jurisdiction and if a court of another State has jurisdiction and is clearly more appropriate to resolve the dispute. Such application must be made no later than at the time of the first defense on the merits.

2. The court shall take into account, in particular —
    (1) any inconvenience to the parties in view of their habitual residence;

    (2)   the nature and location of the evidence, including documents and witnesses, and the procedures for obtaining such evidence;

    (3)   applicable limitation or prescription periods;

    (4)   the possibility of obtaining recognition and enforcement of any decision on the merits.

3.   In deciding whether to suspend the proceeding, a court shall not discriminate on the basis of the nationality or habitual residence of the parties.

Article 22 imposes standards for exercising *forum non conveniens* powers that are, by and large, both normatively and functionally, appropriate: the court seized initially may only suspend its proceedings; dismissal is not permitted until – and to the extent that – the court of the other State takes jurisdiction.[10] Also acceptable is the prohibition of suspension where the court's jurisdiction rests on a valid exclusive choice–of-forum agreement or upon an Article 12 basis of exclusive jurisdiction. Likewise, the prohibition of discrimination for *forum non conveniens* purposes "on the basis of the nationality or habitual residence of the parties" is appropriate.[11] More problematic is the exclusion of discretionary suspension where the court's jurisdiction rests on Article 7 or 8. These articles establish, in certain cases, a special jurisdiction for consumers and employees at their habitual residence. The protective concerns that these forums have for their consumers and employees should remove any likelihood that their courts will suspend – and ultimately dismiss, in whole or in part – proceedings unless suspension and dismissal are fully justified by exceptional circumstances.

    An important issue remains unclear under Article 22 as presently drafted: does it or the forum's national law respecting *forum non conveniens* suspensions and dismissals apply when the court's jurisdiction rests not on a ground provided by the Convention but upon one permitted by national law? Article 22, as presently drafted, can be read as supporting either view.[12] The philosophy that underlies the mixed-convention design supports the position that, when national law grounds the courts' jurisdiction, it should govern *forum non conveniens* suspensions and dismissals as well. An effort to achieve a meaningful compromise respecting the *forum non conveniens* doctrine should clearly allow the forum's views to prevail where neither a required nor a prohibited jurisdictional basis is invoked.

---

10   Article 22 (5) *(a)* of the Interim Text.

    In many instances, a court may require party stipulations as a condition for ordering a stay or dismissal. A court may also decide some subjects of controversy and refer other aspects to the courts of another legal order.

11   Article 22 (3) of the Interim Text.

12   If the *forum non conveniens* doctrine is a rule of jurisdiction, the national law applies. Article 17 provides that "the Convention does not prevent application by Contracting States of rules of jurisdiction under national law" if the rule "is not prohibited under Article 18". See P. Nygh and F. Pocar, *Report of the Special Commission* (Prel. Doc., No. 11) 89.

Article 22, as it appears in the Interim Draft of 2001, establishes two requirements for *forum non conveniens* stays and dismissals: The moving party must establish (1) that it would be "clearly inappropriate for ... [the] court [initially seized] to exercise jurisdiction" and (2) that "a court of another State has jurisdiction and is clearly more appropriate to resolve the dispute". For normative as well as efficiency considerations, only the second requirement seems appropriate for *forum non conveniens* purposes.

The doctrine of *forum non conveniens* as developed in common-law jurisdictions does not address, as the first requirement of Article 22 does, the appropriateness, in principle, of the forum exercising adjudicatory power. The doctrine seeks rather to fine tune the application of jurisdictional rules and principles.[13] The issue is whether, in light of the concrete situation, procedural justice, broadly defined, is better served by litigation in the courts of another legal order. Answering that question depends not on an *abstract* assessment of the quality of the court initially seized's jurisdictional claim but on a *concrete-comparative* determination whether it is clearly more appropriate for the litigation to proceed not in the State whose courts are seized but in the courts of another – specified – State. Besides being inapposite, the "clearly inappropriate" standard is needlessly costly in terms of time and money. A meaningful compromise would allow suspensions and dismissals when the court seized determines that it is clearly less appropriate for it rather than the alternative court to adjudicate the matter.

To turn Article 22 into a meaningful compromise, revision to give greater scope to the *forum non conveniens* doctrine may be required. A first step in the direction of such a compromise would be to make clear that, when the action's jurisdictional basis is provided by national law, that law also regulates *forum non conveniens* suspensions and dismissals. A second step would be to allow *forum non conveniens* suspensions and dismissals where the court seized determines that it is clearly less appropriate for it than for the alternative court to exercise jurisdiction.

(ii) Lis pendens

Until the twentieth century was well begun, in common- and civil-law systems alike the position was taken that the *lis pendens* principle applied only to intramural litigation. The arguments supporting the *lis pendens* principle in extramural litigation became stronger, as such litigation became more frequent. Common-law jurisdictions began to take temporal priority into account but only as one, relatively insignificant, factor in their *forum non conveniens* calculus. In light of the civil law's rejection of the *forum non conveniens* doctrine, civil-law systems had to choose between rejecting or accepting in principle the *lis pendens* doctrine. In the drive to create a European Common Market, legal and economic considerations supported acceptance. From the beginning, the Brussels Convention recognized the first-in-time principle.[14]

---

13   See the discussion in Chap. VI. B., pp. 269 *et seq., supra.*

14   See Chap. VI. D. 4. *(a)*, pp. 298 *et seq., supra.*

In the Hague negotiations, the Special Commission sought to achieve convergence by allowing courts some discretion in deciding whether to exercise their adjudicatory authority. Article 23 of the October 1999 Preliminary Draft accepts, in principle, *lis pendens*:

> 1.   When the same parties are engaged in proceedings in courts of different Contracting States and when such proceedings are based on the same causes of action, irrespective of the relief sought, the court second seized shall suspend the proceedings if the court first seized has jurisdiction and is expected to render a judgment capable of being recognized under the convention in the State of the court second seized, unless the latter has exclusive jurisdiction under Article 4 or 13.

Having done so, the drafters took two steps that limit the *lis pendens* principle. The first recognizes an exception to the rule. Where the first-in-time action "seeks a determination that ... [the plaintiff] has no obligation to the defendant" and the second action seeks "substantive relief", Article 21 (1) does not apply.[15] In such cases "the court first seized shall suspend the proceedings at the request of the party if the court second seized is expected to render a decision capable of being recognized under the Convention".[16] The provision rests on considerations that apply only to the particular case of a first-in-time proceeding for a negative declaratory judgment that is followed by an action elsewhere seeking substantive relief in the same matter.

Paragraph 7 of Article 21 further qualifies the *lis pendens* rule by allowing the court first seized to grant a *forum non conveniens* stay in favor of the court second seized:

> 7.   This Article shall not apply if the court first seized, on application by a party, determines that the court second seized is clearly more appropriate to resolve the dispute, under the conditions specified in Article 22 *[forum non conveniens]*.

(iii) Damage awards

Among the national legal systems represented at The Hague considerable disagreement in theory and practice exists respecting the types of damages that can be awarded and the standards applicable to their quantification. The economic and sociological circumstances that significantly affect damage assessment vary considerably from one society to another. Many legal systems refuse, as a matter of principle, to enforce awards of punitive and multiple damages. On occasion, awards of ordinary damages also present difficulties. Some legal systems do not enforce damages awarded for "pain and suffering"; furthermore, for institutional,

---

15   Article 21 (6) of the Interim Text.

16   Article 21 (6) *(b)* of the Interim Text. For a full discussion of the *lis pendens* problem posed by negative declaratory judgments, see Chap. VI. D. 5., pp. 304 *et seq., supra*.

economic, and sociological reasons, quantification of many types of damages can vary greatly from one legal order to another.

Traditionally, the measure of enforcement to be accorded to money judgments was not considered in functional terms. Questions such as the following were neither put nor analysed: is the claimed loss one for which the relevant legal system or systems provide relief? If so, does that relief take the form of damages awarded by courts, of social security benefits, or of relief of another kind? To the extent that relief takes the form of money-damages, to what extent should economic and sociological differences affect quantification? Rather than making a functionally based comparative analysis, the "principle" was accepted that the law applicable to a judgment is the law under which it was rendered, that is to say the law of the State of origin. Accordingly, a foreign judgment was enforceable as rendered unless the public policy of the State addressed could be interposed to deny enforcement.

Recognizing that views differed sharply not only as to whether certain forms of damages, in particular, multiple and punitive damages, should be enforced but also as to the standards and assumptions on which damages in general were to be calculated, Article 32, Damages, of the Special Commission's Draft Convention of October 1999 provided in certain circumstances for partial rather than full enforcement of damage awards. The Article envisages comparative analysis to determine whether a common denominator can be found in the State of origin's and the State addressed's law of damages. The Interim Text of June 2001, in Article 33, Damages, departs in some details – but not fundamentally – from the October 1999 text.

The approach of the Hague draft to the problems presented by awards of money-damage rests on a functional comparative analysis[17] coupled with the proposition that the common-denominator principle provides, for the controversy in question, a better solution than the all-or nothing principle. The approach identifies the area of convergence in the handling of the controversy at hand and thus provides case-specific justice. Of course, it does so at the cost of imposing a greater burden on the court addressed than does the competing all-or-nothing principle.

C.   The Teachings of the Hague Experience

As the new century began, efforts to draft a Hague jurisdiction and enforcement convention that would be widely acceptable had reached an impasse. The degree of convergence and compromise required to make the projected convention broadly attractive had not been achieved; difficulties of many sorts had arisen.

---

17   Compare Article 33 (2) and (3) of the Interim Text.

1.   The Changing Scene

In the closing decades of the twentieth century, an unprecedented cascade of technological, sociological, political, and commercial changes began. Of these, the most profound and perplexing resulted from the new technology of the internet and the rise of internet commerce. Technical and economic assumptions on which rested many aspects of the theory and practice of adjudicatory authority in international controversies were not valid for this new sector of the economy; novel issues and new dilemmas were posed. Ever more protean, e-communications and e-commerce now pose intractable problems for all branches of private international law. The Hague Conference, endeavouring to draft a jurisdiction and judgments convention, finds itself adrift between the Scylla of "undermin[ing] the goal of encouraging the nascent e-commerce industry"[18] and the Charybdis of "exclud[ing] e-commerce from the scope of the [Hague] project as a way of moving forward".[19] For the next several decades, it seems likely that at least broad agreement will be possible on only two propositions: consensus on how the Convention should deal with e-commerce cannot be achieved; the Convention *must* address e-commerce.[20]

The political scene has also seen changes – in particular, the emergence of the European Union – that emphasize *regional* harmonization of the law respecting the assumption of adjudicatory authority and the recognition of non-local judgments. Once such harmonization is well under way, the national Governments involved have a large stake in the new *status quo*; the region's interest in negotiating a world-wide convention on different terms and with other solutions inevitably declines.

The increased complexity and specialization of modern technology, of commercial and corporate structures and procedures, and of government regulation have also contributed to making the task undertaken in the late 1990s by the Hague Conference far more difficult than it would otherwise have been. For many areas of private international law, one now must be a specialist in the structure and economy of each area of activity that will be significantly affected in order to understand the considerations to be taken into account in drafting a jurisdiction and recognition convention.

Driven in part by the negotiators' need to understand an increasingly complex world, interest groups have been consulted far more than in the past. Where these groups disagree, as is often the case, on the positions to be taken, national delegations must seek to harmonize the views of their own constituencies or, at least, to strike acceptable compromises. To a degree, delegations thus face internally the perplexing and intractable problems of harmonization and compromise that the Hague Conference has collectively encountered.

---

18   A. Haines, *The Impact of the Internet on the Judgments Project: Thoughts for the Future*, Permanent Bureau of the Conference, General Affairs, Prel. Doc., No. 17 (Feb. 2002) (English and French texts) No. 5, at 6.

19   *Ibid.*

20   See *idem* No. 5, at 6.

2.   Efforts to Achieve Convergence and to Strike Compromises: The First Stage (June 2001) of the Nineteenth Diplomatic Session

In an effort to achieve broader consensus than that reached by the Special Commission, it was agreed to suspend, at least for the first stage of the diplomatic session, the Conference's Rules of Procedure for Plenary Meetings, which limits debate and provides for voting under a strict majority principle. Instead, the Session would seek to reach *consensus* on the issues thought to be crucial if the resulting convention was to be acceptable on a world-wide basis. To prepare the ground for the June 2001 deliberations, informal discussions, open to all delegations, began in the fall of 2000. Using various formats, a considerable number of well-attended meetings were held. These gave opportunity for collaborative work and wide consultation that deepened the delegates' understanding of the problems that stood in the way of agreement and provided a time-frame that allowed for rather full exploration of various proposals. It was hoped that this innovation, coupled with an increased willingness to take advantage of the mixed-convention format, would both bring about convergence and pave the way for compromises where basic disagreements persisted.

In "at least six major areas" the June 2001 Session failed, however, to reach consensus:

A   the Internet and e-commerce;

B   activity based jurisidiction;

C   consumer contracts (in particular Article 7) and employment contracts (in particular Article 8);

D   patents, trademarks, copyrights and other intellectual property rights (Article 12 and 10, among others);

E   the relationship with other instruments on jurisdiction and recognition and enforcement of judgments, in particular regional instruments, more particularly the Brussels and Lugano Conventions and the Brussels Regulation (see Annex I to the interim Text);

F   bilateralisation (Article 42).[21]

The significance of failure for the Conference's future work on the Convention project turns, of course, on the area of disagreement in question:

[S]ome affect the structure of the Convention as a whole (E, F); on others there has been a debate (but no agreement) that they might be treated in a special way (C, D). The difficulty in resolving the issues surrounding activity-based jurisdiction (B) is matched only by its critical importance in negotiating a mixed convention. Finally, the Internet and e-commerce (A) deserve special attention because of their two-fold impact on the Judgments Project. On the one hand, the Internet environment adds to the complexity of the issues to be resolved in specific provisions; on the other hand, it

---

21   Prel. Doc., No. 16, *supra* footnote 1, No. 5, at 5.

reinforces the common need for a global framework on jurisdiction and enforcement in civil and commercial matters.[22]

(a)   A scaled-down or a comprehensive convention?

In their efforts to draft a jurisdiction and enforcement convention that could be accepted world-wide, the Hague negotiators considered various techniques through which convergence and harmonization might be achieved. Some argued for covering only those matters on which consensus could be attained. The subject matters that have been mentioned for possible inclusion in such a convention include forum-selection clauses agreed between businesses, general jurisdiction based on the defendant's habitual residence, and – or – the defendant's appearance in court on the merits without challenging jurisdiction. The ways in which a comprehensive jurisdiction and judgment convention could be scaled-back are, of course, manifold.

Many believe that, to be successful, a jurisdiction and judgments convention would have to be relatively comprehensive. Among the techniques that could assist efforts to achieve a broadly acceptable comprehensive convention is the use of carve-outs. General jurisdiction based on doing of substantial business without requiring that the claim arise from that business might, for example, be acceptable if product liability, intellectual-property claims, and electronic commerce were not covered.

Article 1, Substantive Scope, of the Interim Text contains proposals, some agreed and others still under discussion, that would exclude various matters, covered by Article 1 of the Brussels Regulation,[23] from the Hague Convention's scope. One such is "admiralty or maritime matters", an area in which the laws of the negotiating Hague States differ in significant respects.

The Interim Text of 2001's scope has been further reduced by deleting provisions, contained in the Hague Special Commission's Draft of October 1999, that were inspired by what is now Article 6 (1) and (2) of the Brussels Regulation. Article 6 (1) provides for suing multiple defendants "in the courts for the place where any one of them is domiciled, provided the claims are so closely connected that

---

22   *Ibid.*

23   The first two paragraphs of Article 1 of the Brussels Regulation are identical with Article 1 of the Brussels Convention, which was never amended:

This Convention shall apply in civil and commercial matters whatever the nature of the court or tribunal. It shall not extend, in particular, to revenue, customs or administrative matters.

The Convention shall not apply to:

1.   the status or legal capacity of natural persons, rights in property arising out of a matrimonial relationship, wills and succession;

2.   bankruptcy, proceedings relating to the winding-up of insolvent companies or other legal persons, judicial arrangements, compositions and analogous proceedings;

3.   social security;

4.   arbitration.

it is expedient to hear and determine them together to avoid the risk of irrecon-cilable judgments resulting from separate proceedings"; Article 6 (2) establishes jurisdiction over "a third party in an action on a warranty or guarantee or in any other third-party proceeding, in the court seized of the original proceedings ...". The Hague Special Commission's Draft of 1999 contained in Article 15, Multiple Defendants,[24] and Article 17, Third Party Claims,[25] improved versions of Article 6 (1) and (2). Nevertheless, for some delegations, including that of the United States, these provisions raised serious issues of procedural justice. To achieve consensus, the Interim Draft of 2001 omitted them.

(b)   The difficulty of agreeing on the bases of jurisdiction to be prohibited

In June 2001 it proved extremely difficult to strike meaningful compromises. Un-surprisingly, the most significant disagreements – those respecting which juris-dictional bases should be required, and which prohibited – concerned the reach of each State's adjudicatory authority. The wide diversity in the views held re-specting this subject is seen in the debate over Article 18, Prohibited Grounds of Jurisdiction. The article, as it appears in the Interim Draft, is replete with brackets within brackets and explanatory and qualifying notes.

Several variants of the first paragraph of Article 18 were considered. The most restrictive prohibits "the application of a rule of jurisdiction provided for under the national law of a Contracting State ... if there is no substantial connec-tion between that State and the dispute". The United States opposed this language. Not only was it seen as too restrictive; in the absence of an international tribunal to ensure its uniform interpretation and application, it would also give too great weight to the views of the court addressed.

The United States objected on the same grounds to language in the first sen-tence of paragraph 2 of Article 18. In its view, Article 18 should be written, as note 108 of the Interim Text explains,

---

24   Article 15 provided

> A plaintiff bringing an action against a defendant in a court of the State in which that defendant is habitually resident may also proceed in that court against other defendants not habitually resident in that State if
> *(a)*   the claims against the defendant habitually resident in that State and the other defendants are so closely connected that they should be adjudicated together to avoid a serious risk of inconsistent judgments, and
> *(b)*   as to each defendant not habitually resident in that State, there is a substantial connection between that State and the dispute involving that defendant.

25   Article 17 provided that

> A court which has jurisdiction to determine a claim under the provisions of the Con-vention shall also have jurisdiction to determine a claim by a defendant against a third party for indemnity or contribution in respect of the claim against the defendant to the extent that such an action is permitted by national law, provided that there is a substan-tial connection between that State and the dispute involving that third party.

to emphasize the basic concept of the Convention that there be a limited number of required bases of jurisdictions [sic] that are generally accepted, a limited number of jurisdictional bases so universally disapproved as exorbitant that they should be listed as prohibited jurisdictions and that any other jurisdiction not listed in either category should remain open for the exercise of jurisdiction under national law. (The 'grey' zone) ... .

The note concludes with a laconic observation: "There was no consensus on the deletion of paragraph 1."

(c)   A Step Back: The Hague Convention on Choice of Court Agreements

At the end of the Nineteenth Session, held in June 2001, a decision on whether further work should be undertaken on the proposed Hague Convention could not be reached. In order to find a way forward, the Commission on General Affairs and Policy of the Hague Conference, meeting in April 2002, decided that the Permanent Bureau, assisted by an Informal Working Group, should prepare a text for a less inclusive convention not addressing some of the controversial areas involving consumer, electronic commerce, and intellectual property cases. It was agreed upon that the starting point for this Working Group would be such core areas as jurisdiction based on choice of court agreements in business-to-business cases, submission, defendant's forum, counterclaims, trusts, physical torts and certain other possible grounds. However, after three meetings, the Informal Working Group proposed to scale down the project to a convention on choice of court agreements in business-to-business cases and submitted a Draft Convention on Exclusive Choice of Courts Agreements. After positive reactions from the Member States were received, meetings of the Special Commission in December 2003, March 2003 and April 2004 produced another draft. At the Twentieth Diplomatic Session in June 2005, a slightly revised version was finally adopted.[26]

---

26   Convention on Choice of Court Agreements. The text is available at the website of the Hague conference at http://www.hcch.net. See for a first detailed overview of the new convention G. Rühl, "Das Haager Übereinkommen über die Vereinbarung gerichtlicher Zuständigkeiten: Rückschritt oder Fortschritt?", 25 *IPRax* 410-415 (2005); T. Kruger, "The 20th Session of The Hague Conference: A New Choice of Court Convention and the Issue of EC Membership", 55 *Int. & Comp. LQ* 447-455 (2006); "Note: Private International Law – Civil Procedure – Hague Conference Approves Uniform Rules of Enforcement for International Forum Selection Clauses – Convention on Choice of Court Agreements, concluded June 30, 2005", 119 *Harv. L. Rev.* 931-938 (2006); L. Teitz, "The Hague Choice of Court Convention: Validating Party Autonomy and Providing an Alternative to Arbitration", 53 *Am. J. Comp. L.* 543-558 (2006). See also the report on the only slightly different 2004 draft M. Dogauchi and T. C. Hartley, *Draft Report on the Preliminary Draft Convention on Exclusive Choice of Court Agreements* (2004) available at http://hcch.net and H. Buxbaum, "Forum Selection in International Contract Litigation: The Role of Judicial Discretion", 12 *Willamette J. Int'l. L. & Disp. Resol.* 185 (2004).

The new Convention on Choice of Court Agreements is more limited in its scope and effect than the previously submitted drafts for a full-fledge jurisdiction and enforcement convention. Instead of providing a comprehensive set of provisions jurisdictional provisions it concentrates on exclusive choice of forum clauses. Instead of regulating the recognition and enforcement of all foreign judgments civil and commercial matters it focuses on the recognition and enforcement of judgments that are based on exclusive choice of court agreements. However, despite – or maybe because of – this limitation it offers the possibility of both realistic success and a foundation from which to consider possible future work on multilateral harmonization.

(i)   One ground of jurisdiction

In contrast to the originally proposed comprehensive Hague Convention on Jurisdiction and Recognition and Enforcement of Foreign Judgments the Convention on Choice of Courts Agreements provides only for one ground of "required" jurisdiction: an exclusive choice of court agreement.[27] A court of a Contracting State selected in such an agreement must exercise jurisdiction unless the agreement is "null and void" under the law of the chosen court.[28] A non-chosen, or derogated court, is required to suspend or dismiss its proceedings.[29] It may only refuse to do so if

(a)   the choice of court agreement is null and void under the law of the chosen court;

(b)   a party lacked the capacity to conclude the agreement under the law of the State of the court seized;

(c)   giving effect to the agreement would lead to a manifest injustice or would be manifestly contrary to the public policy of the State of the court seized;

(d)   for exceptional reasons beyond the control of the parties, the agreement cannot reasonably be performed; or

(e)   the chosen court has decided not to hear the case.[30]

(ii)   Unregulated bases of jurisdiction and excluded matters

As there is only one ground of "required" jurisdiction and no set of "prohibited" or "permitted" bases as under the originally envisaged mixed convention the unregulated area is very wide. It consists of all cases not covered by an exclusive choice of court agreement as well as all cases that touch on matters excluded from the scope of the Convention. In all these cases, Contracting States are free to exercise, or not to exercise, jurisdiction. The courts of other Contracting States are free to recognize, or not to recognize such judgments.

---

27   Article 1 (1).

28   Article 5 (1).

29   Article 6.

30   Article 6.

The list of excluded matters is vast and mirrors the difficult and tenacious negotiations in The Hague: according to Article 2 (1) the Convention does not apply to consumer contracts and employment contracts.[31] Article 2 (2) further exempts the following matters from the scope of application:

(a)   the status and legal capacity of natural person;
(b)   maintenance obligations;
(c)   other family law matters, including matrimonial property regimes and other rights or obligations arising out of marriage or similar relationships;
(d)   wills and succession;
(e)   insolvency, composition and analogous matters
(f)   the carriage of passengers and goods;
(g)   marine pollution, limitation of liability for maritime claims, general average and emergency towage and salvage;
(h)   anti-trust (competition) matters;
(i)   liability for nuclear damage;
(j)   claims for personal injury brought by or on behalf of natural persons;
(k)   tort or delict claims for damage to tangible property that do not arise from a contractual relationship;
(l)   rights *in rem* in immovable property, and tenancies of immovable property;
(m)   the validity, nullity, or dissolution of legal persons, and the validity of decisions of their organs;
(n)   the validity of intellectual property rights other than copyright or related rights;
(o)   infringements of intellectual property rights other than copyright or related rights, except where infringement proceedings are brought for breach of a contract between the parties relating to such rights, or could have been brought for breach of that contract;
(p)   the validity of entries in public registers.[32]

The fact that the Convention excludes many important matters from its scope of application can be deplored. Certainly, it will reduce the impact of the Convention and its role in international civil litigation. However, it seems that no more meaningful compromise was possible.

(iii) Forum non conveniens *and* lis pendens

The doctrines of *forum non conveniens* and *lis pendens* were two of the few matters on which the negotiators reached consensus at the Nineteenth Diplomatic Conference in 2001. Articles 22 and 23 of the Interim Text allowed limited recourse to both doctrines under certain circumstances. However, it banned their application if jurisdiction of the court seized was founded on an exclusive choice

---

31   Article 2 (1) (a) and (b).

32   Article 2 (2) (a) to (p). Article 21 of the Convention additionally allows Contracting States to declare that it will not apply the Convention to other specific matters.

of court agreement.[33] The new Convention –being limited to exclusive choice of court agreements – follows this latter approach: it provides in Article 5 (2) that a court having jurisdiction under the Convention shall not decline to exercise jurisdiction on the ground that the dispute should be decided in a court of another State The Convention, therefore, precludes – in principle – resort to both the doctrine of *forum non conveniens* and the doctrine of *lis pendens*.[34]

However, at least *forum non conveniens* considerations are not completely banned from the Convention: Article 19 of the Convention allows Contracting States to declare that its courts may refuse to determine disputes to which an exclusive choice of court agreement applies, if except for the location of the chosen court, there is no connection between that State and the parties or the dispute. The Convention, therefore, allows Contracting States to decline adjudication in wholly foreign cases and, thus, leaves the door ajar for some considerations typically made under the doctrine of *forum non conveniens*.[35]

(iv) Recognition and enforcement

Recognition and enforcement of foreign judgments is covered by the new Convention only insofar as a judgment is based on an exclusive choice of court agreement as defined by the Convention.[36] According to Article 8 (1) a judgment given by a court of a Contracting State designated in an exclusive choice of court agreement shall be recognized and enforced in other Contracting States. However, recognition and enforcement may be refused if the Convention provides for specific grounds of refusal.[37] Additionally, recognition and enforcement of damage awards

---

33   See Articles 22 and 23 of the Interim Text of 2001. For a detailed discussion see *supra* pp. 361 *et seq.*

34   See Buxbaum, *supra* footnote 26, at 209; Dogauchi and Hartley, *supra* footnote 26, Art. 5, para. 98-100; Rühl, *supra* footnote 26, at 412.

35   See Buxbaum, *supra* footnote 26, at 209; Rühl, *supra* footnote 26, at 412.

36   According to Article 3 (a) an "exclusive choice of court agreement" means an agreement concluded by two or more parties that meets the requirements of paragraph c) and designates for the purpose of deciding disputes which have arisen or may arise in connection with a particular legal relationship, the courts of one contracting State or one or more specific courts in one Contrating State to the exclusion of the jurisdiction of any other courts. According to Article 3 (c) an exclusive choice of courts agreement must be concluded or documented (i) in writing; or (ii) by any other means of communication, which renders information accessible so as to be usable for subsequent reference.

37   According to Article 9 (a) to (g) a court may refuse recognition and enforcement if
   (a)   the agreement was null and void under the law of the State of the chosen court, unless the chosen court has determined that the agreement is valid;
   (b)   a party lacked the capacity to conclude the agreement under the law of the requested State;
   (c)   the document which instituted the proceedings or an equivalent document, including the essential elements of the claim, was not notified to the defendant in sufficient time or in the appropriate manner;

may be limited to a certain amount if, and to the extent that, the judgment awards damages, including exemplary or punitive damages that do not compensate a party for actual loss or harm suffered.[38] However, in contrast to Article 33 of the Interim Text 2001[39] and an earlier version of 2004[40] Article 11 does not explicitly require application of a functional comparative analysis and the common-denominator principle. Instead, it allows courts to refuse recognition and enforcement of non-compensatory damage awards regardless of whether such damages are recoverable in the forum. Whether this approach will prove to be successful in practice remains to be seen. However, it is to be welcomed that Article 11 – just like Article 33 of the Interim Text of 2001 – declines to apply the all-or-nothing principle and strives for justice on a case-by-base basis.

3. Universal Conventions in Matters of Private International Law: Twenty-first Century Prospects

In the first half of the twentieth century, international instruments dealing with private international law, including jurisdiction and recognition and enforcement of judgments, were either bilateral or universal in character. Harmonization on a bilateral basis was, by and large, compatible with efforts to achieve harmonization on a worldwide basis. The former prepared the ground for – and supplemented – the latter.

The second half of the century witnessed the rise of a third type of international instrument, one multilateral in nature but regional rather than universal in scope. In 1968, the Brussels Convention changed fundamentally the role of international instruments in the area of jurisdiction and enforcement of foreign judgments by harmonizing the law respecting these matters on a regional basis. To the bilateral and the universal approaches to harmonization, a regional approach was thus added. The regional and universal approaches have, at least so far, proved to be incompatible where harmonization of the general law of jurisdiction to adjudicate and recognition and enforcement of foreign judgments is concerned. Put

---

(d)   the judgment was obtained by fraud in connection with a matter of procedure;

(e)   recognition and enforcement would be manifestly incompatible with the public policy of the requested State, including situations where the specific proceedings leading to the judgment were incompatible with fundamental principles of procedural fairness of that State.

(f)   the judgment is inconsistent with a judgment given in the requested State in a dispute between the same parties; or

(g)   the judgment is inconsistent with an earlier judgment given in another State between the same parties and involving the same cause of action, provided that the earlier judgment fulfils the conditions necessary for its recognition in the requested State.

38   See Article 33 of the Interim Text of 2001.

39   See *supra* pp. 364 *et seq.*

40   See Article 15 of the Draft Convention on Exclusive Choice of Courts Agreement available at http://www.hcch.net.

another way, once a regional harmonization of these matters is in place, the parties to the regional instrument have a greatly reduced incentive to harmonize the same area of law on a universal basis.[41]

If this analysis is correct, universal instruments cannot hope to harmonize effectively the general areas of private international law once effective regional harmonizations, dealing broadly with the subject matter, are in place. The most that can then be accomplished is to provide a general convention to fill the space not yet occupied by existing regional harmonizations. Such a general harmonization will, however, find it difficult to attract support.

Universal instruments harmonizing broad areas of the law of jurisdiction and enforcement of judgments do not have a bright future. Efforts to harmonize the law respecting topics for which a consensus is attainable can well be fruitful, however. This approach would seek universal harmonizations compatible with the regional harmonizations in force. The required degree of compatibility may exist with respect to jurisdiction and enforcement in several areas of considerable importance. These include exclusive choice-of-forum clauses in business-to-business contracts,[42] place-of-injury jurisdiction for *physical* injury in products liability cases, and jurisdiction in the defendant's home-forum for most claims.

More problematic specific provisions that deserve consideration include, for litigation between businesses or professionals, jurisdiction based on the place of performance of a contract or on activity respecting its conclusion and performance. To the extent that consensus was reached on discrete solutions, a universal international instrument could displace regional harmonizations for controversies that were not entirely intraregional.

---

41   The existence of regional instruments, alongside bilateral and universal conventions, also complicates markedly the problem of which instrument governs relationships that are potentially regulated by more than one instrument. Difficulties are encountered in reaching agreement on the weight to be given to various policy considerations and in drafting implementing texts. The annotated Interim Text, prepared by the Permanent Bureau of the Hague Conference and the Co-reporters on the basis of the discussions of the jurisdiction and judgments project in June 2001 sets out four proposals in Annex 1. See *idem* 31-33. These are briefly discussed by the Co-reporters, Peter Nygh and Fausto Pocar, in their Report on the General Commission's work. See *idem* 117-118. The proposals are both highly complex and various. The Co-reporters close their analysis by observing that "the provision or provisions adopted must regulate the relationship between the Convention and other international instruments from the viewpoint both of direct international jurisdiction and of the recognition and enforcement of judgments". *Idem* 118.

42   It is thought that, were such a jurisdictional basis available, in many situations parties would prefer litigation in a pre-determined judicial forum to arbitration under the New York Convention.
For a general discussion of the choice-of-forum proposal and related matters, see R. Brand, "Forum Selection and Forum Rejection in US Courts: One Rationale for a Global Choice of Court Convention", in J. Fawcett, *Reform and Development of Private International Law – Essays in Honour of Sir Peter North* 51-87 (Oxford, Oxford University Press, 2002).

There are also areas of the law for which world-wide regulation is preferable to regional regulation because the controversies that arise are widely and randomly dispersed. For such matters, a universal convention has advantages that regional conventions lack. The most striking example of such a convention is the New York Convention on the Recognition and Enforcement of Foreign Arbitral Awards of 1958. Because under the New York Convention arbitration has become a "movable feast", the universal convention has largely displaced regional conventions addressing the same subject matters.

Two recent Hague Conventions, the Convention of October 1980 on the Civil Aspects of International Child Abduction and that of 22 May 1993 on Protection of Children and Co-Operation in Respect of Intercountry Adoption, illustrate another context in which a universal convention offers advantages that regional conventions cannot. In the nature of things, abductors will seek out safe havens; regional conventions will, in practice, be evaded. Most abductions from a member State of the European Union would, were the Union to have only a Brussels abduction convention, be to States not party to the regional convention. Furthermore, in areas such as child abduction and adoption, where national agencies are charged with supervising responsibilities, the attraction of a universal convention is clear.

D.   The Future

As of 2005, the myriad of forces – *inter alia*, historical, economic, political, intellectual, and cultural – that have affected the Hague experiment have become more complex and less stable. What was thought to be the playing field when the project was undertaken has changed dramatically. The vast river of history is now swifter and more turbulent than it was when the work began. In particular, the struggle of uniformity versus diversity has become more intense. Will efficiency and administrability concerns result in legal orders generally according less weight to concerns for justice in specific cases? Striking a proper balance between proportionality and subsidiarity, on the one hand, and efficiency and administrability, on the other, become ever more difficult and contentious.

These issues will be played out on many stages and over many years. What the Hague Conference can accomplish in the future will depend on broader developments. What transpires will tell us much about how thinking and practice are likely to develop in the twenty-first century respecting adjudicatory authority and recognition and enforcement of foreign judgments.

Index

THE HAGUE ACADEMY OF INTERNATIONAL LAW MONOGRAPHS

1. Ian Brownlie, *The Rule of Law in International Affairs: International Law at the Fiftieth Anniversary of the United Nations*, 1998   ISBN 90 411 1068 2

2. Shabtai Rosenne, *The Perplexities of Modern International Law*, 2004
                                                    ISBN 90 04 13692 4

3. Theodor Meron, *The Humanization of International Law*, 2006
                                                    ISBN 90 04 15060 9

4. Symeon C. Symeonides, *The American Choice-of-Law Revolution: Present and Future*, 2006   ISBN 90 04 15219 9

5. Arthur T. von Mehren, *Adjudicatory Authority in Private International Law: A Comparative Study*, 2007   ISBN 978 9004 15881 8